Forward

Our purpose for publishing the documents issued by the National Institu... ......andards and Technology (NIST) is twofold. First of all, each NIST title in and of itself is very informative, however I am of the opinion that they should be looked at from the standpoint that each title is an integral part of a holistic cybersecurity strategy. Rather than look at each title just by itself, we need to look at them in groups based on how they are interrelated and designed to work together to improve cybersecurity.

For example, this particular group on PRIVACY SECURITY includes the following titles:

NIST SP 800-53 R **5**   Security and Privacy Controls for Federal Information Systems and Organizations

NIST SP 800-53A R 4   Assessing Security and Privacy Controls

NIST SP 800-122   Guide to Protecting the Confidentiality of Personally Identifiable Information (PII)

NIST SP 800-188   De-Identifying Government Datasets - (2nd DRAFT)

NISTIR 8053   De-Identification of Personal Information

NISTIR 8062   Introduction to Privacy Engineering and Risk Management in Federal Systems

In order to assemble the entire picture of privacy security – from what it is, how it works, what the vulnerabilities are, and how to mitigate them, one must assemble all of these documents. Only by going through all of them can a person understand the complete picture. Leave one of them out and you would be missing a valuable piece of the privacy security puzzle.

Why buy a book you can download for free?

That brings me to the second reason to publish the NIST standards and that is the logistics of it all. These 7 publications are over 770 pages. That's enough paper to fill two large three-ring binders. Nobody has an assistant anymore, so an engineer that is paid $75 an hour has to do this. The amount of time it would take an engineer to print all 7 publications (using a network printer shared with 100 other people – and it's out of paper, and the toner is low), punch holes in 770 pages and assemble the binders would take hours.

Our ability to deliver any NIST document quickly and efficiently is unmatched because we are printing books on demand and we are backed up by Amazon, so the titles are easy to find and simple to order. Just search Amazon.com by NIST number and you can have a copy shipped to you in a matter of days. We print all books a full 8 ½ inches by 11 inches, with large text. If there are color images in the publication, the book is probably in color, unless the color is merely decorative, in which case we print in black and white to keep the cost to you as low as possible. The ePub is also available for Kindle, iPad, and Android tablet.

Luis Ayala,
My email is cybah@webplus.net   Our website is: cybah.webplus.net
4th Watch Books is a Service Disabled Veteran Owned Small Business (SDVOSB).

CyberSecurity Standards Library™

Get a Complete Library of Over 300 Cybersecurity Standards on 1 Convenient DVD!

The **4th Watch CyberSecurity Standards Library** is a DVD disc that puts over 300 current and archived cybersecurity standards from NIST, DOD, DHS, CNSS and NERC at your fingertips! Many of these cybersecurity standards are hard to find and we included the current version and a previous version for many of them. The DVD includes four books written by Luis Ayala: **The Cyber Dictionary, Cybersecurity Standards, Cyber-Security Glossary of Building Hacks and Cyber-Attacks**, and **Cyber-Physical Attack Defenses: Preventing Damage to Buildings and Utilities**.

- ✓ DVD includes many Hard-to-find Cybersecurity Standards - some still in Draft.
- ✓ Docs are organized by source and listed numerically so each standard is easy to locate.
- ✓ The listing of standards on the DVD includes an abstract of the subject, and date issued.
- ✓ PDF format for use on PC, Mac, eReaders, or tablets.
- ✓ No need for WiFi / Internet.
- ✓ Save countless hours of searching and downloading.
- ✓ Carry in a briefcase - terrific for travel.

4th Watch Publishing is releasing the CyberSecurity Standards Library DVD to make it easier for you to access the tools you need to ensure the security of your computer networks and SCADA systems. We also publish many of these standards on demand so you don't need to waste valuable time searching for the latest version of a standard, printing hundreds of pages and punching holes so they can go in a three-ring binder. **Order on Amazon.com**

The DVD works on PC and Mac with the standards in PDF format. To view the CyberSecurity Standards Library on the DVD, a computer with a DVD drive is required. The most current version of your internet browser, at least 2GB of RAM, and current version of Adobe Reader is recommended. (Compatible browsers include Internet Explorer 8+, Mozilla Firefox 4+, Apple Safari 5+, Google Chrome 15+)

Security and Privacy Controls for Information Systems and Organizations

JOINT TASK FORCE

INITIAL PUBLIC DRAFT

This publication contains a comprehensive catalog of technical and nontechnical **security** and **privacy** controls. The controls can support a variety of specialty applications including the *Risk Management Framework*, *Cybersecurity Framework*, and *Systems Engineering Processes* used for developing systems, products, components, and services and for protecting organizations, systems, and individuals.

NIST

**National Institute of
Standards and Technology**
U.S. Department of Commerce

Draft NIST Special Publication 800-53
Revision 5

Security and Privacy Controls for Information Systems and Organizations

August 2017

U.S. Department of Commerce
Wilbur L. Ross, Jr., Secretary

National Institute of Standards and Technology
Kent Rochford, Acting NIST Director and Under Secretary of Commerce for Standards and Technology

Authority

This publication has been developed by NIST to further its statutory responsibilities under the Federal Information Security Modernization Act (FISMA) of 2014, 44 U.S.C. § 3551 *et seq.*, Public Law (P.L.) 113-283. NIST is responsible for developing information security standards and guidelines, including minimum requirements for federal information systems, but such standards and guidelines shall not apply to national security systems without the express approval of appropriate federal officials exercising policy authority over such systems. This guideline is consistent with the requirements of the Office of Management and Budget (OMB) Circular A-130.

Nothing in this publication should be taken to contradict the standards and guidelines made mandatory and binding on federal agencies by the Secretary of Commerce under statutory authority. Nor should these guidelines be interpreted as altering or superseding the existing authorities of the Secretary of Commerce, Director of OMB, or any other federal official. This publication may be used by nongovernmental organizations on a voluntary basis and is not subject to copyright in the United States. Attribution would, however, be appreciated by NIST.

National Institute of Standards and Technology Special Publication 800-53, Revision 5
Natl. Inst. Stand. Technol. Spec. Publ. 800-53, Rev. 5, **494 pages** (August 2017)
CODEN: NSPUE2

Public comment period: August 15 through September 12, 2017

National Institute of Standards and Technology
Attn: Computer Security Division, Information Technology Laboratory
100 Bureau Drive (Mail Stop 8930) Gaithersburg, MD 20899-8930
Email: **sec-cert@nist.gov**

All comments are subject to release under the Freedom of Information Act (FOIA).

Reports on Computer Systems Technology

The Information Technology Laboratory (ITL) at the National Institute of Standards and Technology (NIST) promotes the U.S. economy and public welfare by providing technical leadership for the Nation's measurement and standards infrastructure. ITL develops tests, test methods, reference data, proof of concept implementations, and technical analyses to advance the development and productive use of information technology (IT). ITL's responsibilities include the development of management, administrative, technical, and physical standards and guidelines for the cost-effective security of other than national security-related information and protection of individuals' privacy in federal information systems. The Special Publication 800-series reports on ITL's research, guidelines, and outreach efforts in information systems security and its collaborative activities with industry, government, and academic organizations.

Abstract

This publication provides a catalog of security and privacy controls for federal information systems and organizations to protect organizational operations and assets, individuals, other organizations, and the Nation from a diverse set of threats including hostile attacks, natural disasters, structural failures, human errors, and privacy risks. The controls are flexible and customizable and implemented as part of an organization-wide process to manage risk. The controls address diverse requirements derived from mission and business needs, laws, Executive Orders, directives, regulations, policies, standards, and guidelines. The publication describes how to develop specialized sets of controls, or overlays, tailored for specific types of missions and business functions, technologies, environments of operation, and sector-specific applications. Finally, the consolidated catalog of controls addresses security and privacy from a functionality perspective (i.e., the strength of functions and mechanisms) and an assurance perspective (i.e., the measure of confidence in the security or privacy capability). Addressing both functionality and assurance ensures that information technology products and the information systems that rely on those products are sufficiently trustworthy.

Keywords

Assurance; availability; computer security; confidentiality; FISMA; information security; integrity; personally identifiable information; Privacy Act; privacy controls; privacy functions; privacy requirements; Risk Management Framework; security controls; security functions; security requirements; system; system security.

Acknowledgements

This publication was developed by the *Joint Task Force Transformation Initiative* Interagency Working Group with representatives from the Civil, Defense, and Intelligence Communities in an ongoing effort to produce a unified information security framework for the federal government. The National Institute of Standards and Technology wishes to acknowledge and thank the senior leaders from the Departments of Commerce and Defense, the Office of the Director of National Intelligence, the Committee on National Security Systems, and the members of the interagency technical working group whose dedicated efforts contributed significantly to the publication. The senior leaders, interagency working group members, and their organizational affiliations include:

Department of Defense

John A. Zangardi
Acting DoD Chief Information Officer

Thomas P. Michelli
Acting Principal Deputy and DoD Chief Information Officer

Essye B. Miller
*Deputy Chief Information Officer for Cybersecurity
and DoD Senior Information Security Officer*

John R. Mills
Director, Cybersecurity Policy, Strategy, and International

National Institute of Standards and Technology

Charles H. Romine
Director, Information Technology Laboratory

Donna Dodson
Cybersecurity Advisor, Information Technology Laboratory

Matt Scholl
Chief, Computer Security Division

Kevin Stine
Chief, Applied Cybersecurity Division

Ron Ross
FISMA Implementation Project Leader

Office of the Director of National Intelligence

Raymond Cook
Assistant DNI and Chief Information Officer

Jennifer Kron
Deputy Chief Information Officer

Sue Dorr
*Director, Information Assurance Division
and Chief Information Security Officer*

Wallace Coggins
Director, Security Coordination Center

Committee on National Security Systems

Essye B. Miller
Chair

Cheryl Peace
Co-Chair

Kevin Dulany
Tri-Chair—Defense Community

Peter H. Duspiva
Tri-Chair—Intelligence Community

Daniel Dister
Tri-Chair—Civil Agencies

Joint Task Force Transformation Initiative Interagency Working Group

Ron Ross *NIST, JTF Leader*	Kevin Dulany *Department of Defense*	Dorian Pappas *Intelligence Community*	Kelley Dempsey *NIST*
Jody Jacobs *NIST*	Victoria Pillitteri *NIST*	Taylor Roberts *OMB*	Naomi Lefkovitz *NIST*
Ellen Nadeau *NIST*	Charles Cutshall *OMB*	Esten Porter *The MITRE Corporation*	Ned Goren *NIST*
David Black *The MITRE Corporation*	Rich Graubart *The MITRE Corporation*	Daniel Faigin *Aerospace Corporation*	Christian Enloe *NIST*

In addition to the above acknowledgments, a special note of thanks goes to Peggy Himes, Jim Foti, and Elizabeth Lennon of NIST for their superb technical editing and administrative support. The authors also wish to recognize Kristen Baldwin, Carol Bales, John Bazile, Jon Boyens, Sean Brooks, Ruth Cannatti, Kathleen Coupe, Keesha Crosby, Dominic Cussatt, Ja'Nelle DeVore, Jennifer Fabius, Jim Fenton, Matthew Halstead, Hildy Ferraiolo, Ryan Galluzzo, Robin Gandhi, Mike Garcia, Paul Grassi, Marc Groman, Matthew Halstead, Kevin Herms, Scott Hill, Ralph

Jones, Martin Kihiko, Raquel Leone, Michael McEvilley, Kirsten Moncada, Elaine Newton, Michael Nieles, Michael Nussdorfer, Celia Paulsen, Andrew Regenscheid, Joe Stuntz, members of the Federal Privacy Council's Risk Management Subcommittee, and the technical staff from the NIST Computer Security Division and Applied Cybersecurity Division for their exceptional contributions in helping to improve the content of the publication. And finally, the authors also gratefully acknowledge the significant contributions from individuals and organizations in the public and private sectors, both nationally and internationally, whose insightful and constructive comments improved the overall quality, thoroughness, and usefulness of this publication.

Historical Contributions to NIST Special Publication 800-53

The authors wanted to acknowledge the many individuals who contributed to previous versions of Special Publication 800-53 since its inception in 2005. They include Marshall Abrams, Dennis Bailey, Lee Badger, Curt Barker, Matt Barrett, Nadya Bartol, Frank Belz, Paul Bicknell, Deb Bodeau, Paul Brusil, Brett Burley, Bill Burr, Dawn Cappelli, Roger Caslow, Corinne Castanza, Mike Cooper, Matt Coose, Dom Cussatt, George Dinolt, Randy Easter, Kurt Eleam, Denise Farrar, Dave Ferraiolo, Cita Furlani, Harriett Goldman, Peter Gouldmann, Tim Grance, Jennifer Guild, Gary Guissanie, Sarbari Gupta, Priscilla Guthrie, Richard Hale, Bennett Hodge, William Hunteman, Cynthia Irvine, Arnold Johnson, Roger Johnson, Don Jones, Lisa Kaiser, Stu Katke, Sharon Keller, Tom Kellerman, Cass Kelly, Eustace King, Steve LaFountain, Annabelle Lee, Robert Lentz, Steve Lipner, Bill MacGregor, Tom Macklin, Tom Madden, Robert Martin, Erika McCallister, Tim McChesney, Michael McEvilley, Rosalie McQuaid, Peter Mell, John Mildner, Pam Miller, Sandra Miravalle, Joji Montelibano, Doug Montgomery, George Moore, Mark Morrison, Sherrill Nicely, Robert Niemeyer, LouAnna Notargiacomo, Pat O'Reilly, Tim Polk, Karen Quigg, Steve Quinn, Mark Riddle, Ed Roback, Cheryl Roby, George Rogers, Scott Rose, Mike Rubin, Karen Scarfone, Roger Schell, Jackie Snouffer, Ray Snouffer, Murugiah Souppaya, Gary Stoneburner, Keith Stouffer, Marianne Swanson, Pat Toth, Glenda Turner, Pat Viscuso, Joe Weiss, Richard Wilsher, Mark Wilson, John Woodward, and Carol Woody.

Notes to Reviewers

As we push computers to "the edge" building an increasingly complex world of interconnected information systems and devices, security and privacy continue to dominate the national dialog. The Defense Science Board in its 2017 report, Task Force on Cyber Defense, provides a sobering assessment of the current vulnerabilities in the U.S. critical infrastructure and the information systems that support the mission essential operations and assets in the public and private sectors.

> "...The Task Force notes that the cyber threat to U.S. critical infrastructure is outpacing efforts to reduce pervasive vulnerabilities, so that for the next decade at least the United States must lean significantly on deterrence to address the cyber threat posed by the most capable U.S. adversaries. It is clear that a more proactive and systematic approach to U.S. cyber deterrence is urgently needed..."

There is an urgent need to further strengthen the underlying information systems, component products, and services that we depend on in every sector of the critical infrastructure—ensuring those systems, components, and services are sufficiently trustworthy and provide the necessary resilience to support the economic and national security interests of the United States. This update to NIST Special Publication 800-53 (Revision 5) responds to the call by the Defense Science Board by embarking on a proactive and systemic approach to develop and make available to a broad base of public and private sector organizations, a comprehensive set of safeguarding measures for all types of computing platforms, including general purpose computing systems, cyber-physical systems, cloud and mobile systems, industrial/process control systems, and Internet of Things (IoT) devices. Those safeguarding measures include security and privacy controls to protect the critical and essential operations and assets of organizations and the personal privacy of individuals. The ultimate objective is to make the information systems we depend on more penetration resistant to attacks; limit the damage from attacks when they occur; and make the systems resilient and survivable.

Revision 5 of this foundational NIST publication represents a one year effort to develop the next generation security and privacy controls that will be needed to accomplish the above objectives. It includes changes to make the controls more consumable by diverse consumer groups including, for example, enterprises conducting mission and business operations; engineering organizations developing information systems and systems-of-systems; and industry partners building system components, products, and services. The major changes to the publication include:

- Making the security and privacy controls more *outcome-based* by changing the structure of the controls;

- Fully *integrating* the privacy controls into the security control catalog creating a consolidated and unified set of controls for information systems and organizations, while providing summary and mapping tables for privacy-related controls;

- Separating the control selection *process* from the actual *controls*, thus allowing the controls to be used by different communities of interest including systems engineers, software developers, enterprise architects; and mission/business owners;

- Promoting integration with different risk management and cybersecurity approaches and lexicons, including the Cybersecurity Framework;

- Clarifying the relationship between security and privacy to improve the selection of controls necessary to address the full scope of security and privacy risks; and

- Incorporating new, state-of-the-practice controls based on threat intelligence and empirical attack data, including controls to strengthen cybersecurity and privacy governance and accountability.

In separating the process of control selection from the security and privacy controls, a significant amount of tailoring guidance and other informative material previously contained in Special Publication 800-53 was eliminated from the publication. That content will be moved to other publications such as NIST Special Publication 800-37 (Risk Management Framework) during the next update cycle for that document. The context will also remain active in Special Publication 800-53 Revision 4, until the subsequent publication becomes final. NIST continues to work with the privacy community to better integrate privacy and security controls, and is particularly interested in how best to achieve such integration in this publication.

Your feedback on this draft publication is important to us. We appreciate each contribution from our reviewers. The very insightful comments from both the public and private sectors, nationally and internationally, continue to help shape the final publication to ensure that it meets the needs and expectations of our customers. NIST anticipates producing the final draft of this publication in October 2017 and publishing the final version not later than **December 29, 2017**.

- **RON ROSS**
  NATIONAL INSTITUTE OF STANDARDS AND TECHNOLOGY

COMMON SECURITY AND PRIVACY FOUNDATIONS

In developing standards and guidelines required by FISMA, NIST consults with federal agencies, state, local, and tribal governments, and private sector organizations to improve information security and privacy; avoid unnecessary and costly duplication of effort; and ensure that its publications are complementary with the standards and guidelines used for the protection of national security systems. In addition to a comprehensive and transparent public review and vetting process, NIST is engaged in a collaborative partnership with the Office of Management and Budget, Office of the Director of National Intelligence, Department of Defense, Committee on National Security Systems, and the Federal Privacy Council—and has established a risk management framework applicable to both information security and privacy for the federal government. This common foundation for security and privacy provides the Civil, Defense, and Intelligence Communities of the federal government and their contractors, more cost-effective, flexible, and consistent ways to manage security and privacy risks to organizational operations and assets, individuals, other organizations, and the Nation. The unified framework also provides a strong basis for reciprocal acceptance of authorization decisions and facilitate information sharing and collaboration. NIST continues to work with public and private sector entities to establish mappings and relationships between the information security and privacy standards and guidelines developed by NIST and those developed by external organizations.

DEVELOPMENT OF INFORMATION SYSTEMS, COMPONENTS, AND SERVICES

With a renewed nation-wide emphasis on the use of trustworthy information systems and supply chain security, it is essential that organizations can express their security and privacy requirements with clarity and specificity in order to engage the information technology industry and obtain the systems, components, and services necessary for mission and business success. Accordingly, this publication provides controls in the System and Services Acquisition (SA) family that address requirements for the development of information systems, system components, and system services. To that end, many of the controls in the SA family are directed at developers of those systems, components, and services. It is important for organizations to recognize that the scope of the controls in that family includes information system, component, and service development and the developers associated with such development whether the development is conducted internally or externally by industry partners (manufacturers, vendors, integrators) through the contracting and acquisition processes. The affected controls in the control catalog include SA-8, SA-10, SA-11, SA-15, SA-16, SA-17, SA-20, and SA-21.

SECURITY AS A DESIGN PROBLEM

"Providing satisfactory security controls in a computer system is in itself a system design problem. A combination of hardware, software, communications, physical, personnel and administrative-procedural safeguards is required for comprehensive security. In particular, software safeguards alone are not sufficient."

-- *The Ware Report*
Defense Science Board Task Force on Computer Security, 1970.

INFORMATION SYSEMS — A BROAD-BASED PERSPECTIVE

As we push computers to "the edge" building an increasingly complex world of interconnected information systems and devices, security and privacy continue to dominate the national dialog. There is an urgent need to further strengthen the underlying information systems, component products, and services that we depend on in every sector of the critical infrastructure—ensuring those systems, components, and services are sufficiently trustworthy and provide the necessary resilience to support the economic and national security interests of the United States. NIST Special Publication 800-53 (Revision 5) responds to this need by embarking on a proactive and systemic approach to develop and make available to a broad base of public and private sector organizations, a comprehensive set of security and privacy safeguarding measures for all types of computing platforms, including general purpose computing systems; cyber-physical systems; cloud and mobile systems; industrial and process control systems; and Internet of Things (IoT) devices. Those safeguarding measures include both security and privacy controls to protect the critical and essential operations and assets of organizations and personal privacy of individuals. The ultimate objective is to make the information systems we depend on more penetration resistant to attacks; limit the damage from attacks when they occur; and make the systems resilient and survivable.

Table of Contents

Prologue

"...Through the process of risk management, leaders must consider risk to US interests from adversaries using cyberspace to their advantage and from our own efforts to employ the global nature of cyberspace to achieve objectives in military, intelligence, and business operations... "

"...For operational plans development, the combination of threats, vulnerabilities, and impacts must be evaluated in order to identify important trends and decide where effort should be applied to eliminate or reduce threat capabilities; eliminate or reduce vulnerabilities; and assess, coordinate, and deconflict all cyberspace operations..."

"...Leaders at all levels are accountable for ensuring readiness and security to the same degree as in any other domain..."

THE NATIONAL STRATEGY FOR CYBERSPACE OPERATIONS
OFFICE OF THE CHAIRMAN, JOINT CHIEFS OF STAFF, U.S. DEPARTMENT OF DEFENSE

"Networking and information technology is transforming life in the 21st century, changing the way people, businesses, and government interact. Vast improvements in computing, storage, and communications are creating new opportunities for enhancing our social wellbeing; improving health and health care; eliminating barriers to education and employment; and increasing efficiencies in many sectors such as manufacturing, transportation, and agriculture.

The promise of these new applications often stems from their ability to create, collect, transmit, process, and archive information on a massive scale. However, the vast increase in the quantity of personal information that is being collected and retained, combined with the increased ability to analyze it and combine it with other information, is creating valid concerns about privacy and about the ability of entities to manage these unprecedented volumes of data responsibly.... A key challenge of this era is to assure that growing capabilities to create, capture, store, and process vast quantities of information will not damage the core values of the country...."

"...When systems process personal information, whether by collecting, analyzing, generating, disclosing, retaining, or otherwise using the information, they can impact privacy of individuals. System designers need to account for individuals as stakeholders in the overall development of the solution. ...Designing for privacy must connect individuals' privacy desires with system requirements and controls in a way that effectively bridges the aspirations with development...."

THE NATIONAL PRIVACY RESEARCH STRATEGY
NATIONAL SCIENCE AND TECHNOLOGY COUNCIL, NETWORKING AND INFORMATION TECHNOLOGY RESEARCH AND DEVELOPMENT PROGRAM

INTRODUCTION

THE NEED TO PROTECT INFORMATION, SYSTEMS, ORGANIZATIONS, AND INDIVIDUALS

Modern information systems[1] can include a wide variety of computing platforms, including, for example, industrial and process control systems; general purpose computing systems; cyber-physical systems; weapons systems; super computers; communications systems; environmental control systems; embedded devices and sensors; and small form factor devices such as smart phones and tablets. The commonality in these computing platforms is that they contain computers with complex software and firmware and provide a capability that supports the essential missions and business functions of organizations.

Security controls are the safeguards or countermeasures prescribed for an information system or an organization to protect the confidentiality, integrity, and availability of the system and its information. Privacy controls are the administrative, technical, and physical safeguards employed within an agency to ensure compliance with applicable privacy requirements and to manage privacy risks. Security and privacy controls are selected and implemented to satisfy a set of defined security and privacy requirements and to manage risk.[2] The selection and effective implementation of security and privacy controls are important tasks that can have significant implications on the operations and assets of organizations as well as the welfare of individuals and the Nation.[3]

There are several key questions that should be answered by organizations when addressing their security and privacy concerns:

- What security and privacy controls are needed to satisfy the organization's security and privacy requirements and to adequately manage risk?

- Have the security and privacy controls been implemented or is there an implementation plan in place?

- What is the desired or required level of assurance (i.e., confidence) that the selected security and privacy controls, as implemented, are effective in their application?[4]

The answers to these questions are not given in isolation, but rather in the context of an effective risk management process for the organization that identifies, assesses, responds to, and monitors on an ongoing basis, security and privacy risks arising from its information and systems. The security and privacy controls in this publication are recommended for use by organizations to satisfy their information security and privacy requirements. The controls are employed as part of a well-defined and effective risk management process that supports organizational information security and privacy programs. In turn, organizational information security and privacy programs support the missions and business functions of the organization.

---

[1] An *information system* is a discrete set of information resources organized for the collection, processing, maintenance, use sharing, dissemination, or disposition of information.

[2] Security and privacy requirements are typically derived from applicable laws, Executive Orders, directives, policies, and regulations.

[3] Organizational operations include mission, functions, image, and reputation.

[4] Security and privacy control effectiveness addresses the extent to which the controls are implemented correctly, operating as intended, and producing the desired outcome with respect to meeting the designated security and privacy requirements for the system.

It is of paramount importance that responsible officials understand the security and privacy risks and other factors that could adversely affect organizational operations and assets, individuals, other organizations, and the Nation.[5] These officials must also understand the current status of organizational security and privacy programs and the security and privacy controls planned or in place to protect information, information systems, and organizations in order to make informed judgments and investments that respond to identified risks in an acceptable manner. The ultimate objective is to manage the risks through the selection and implementation of security and privacy controls.

1.1 PURPOSE AND APPLICABILITY

This publication establishes controls for federal information systems[6] and organizations. The use of these controls is mandatory, in accordance with the provisions of the Federal Information Security Modernization Act[7] (FISMA), which require the development and maintenance of minimum controls to protect federal information and information systems. The controls can be implemented within any organization or information system that processes, stores, or transmits information. This publication is intended to help organizations manage risk and to satisfy the security and privacy requirements in FISMA, the Privacy Act of 1974, OMB policies (e.g., OMB Circular A-130), and designated Federal Information Processing Standards, among others, by:

- Providing a comprehensive and flexible catalog of security and privacy controls to meet current protection needs and the demands of future needs based on changing threats, requirements, and technologies;

- Creating a foundation for the development of assessment methods and procedures for determining the effectiveness of the controls; and

- Improving communication among organizations by providing a common lexicon that supports discussion of security, privacy, and risk management concepts.

While the controls established in this publication are for federal information systems and organizations, state, local, and tribal governments, as well as private sector organizations are encouraged to consider using these guidelines, as appropriate.

Finally, the controls in the catalog are independent of the specific process employed to select those controls. Such selection processes can be part of an organization-wide risk management process, a life cycle-based systems engineering process, or a risk management or cybersecurity framework.[8] The control selection criteria can be guided and informed by many factors, for example, stakeholder protection needs and concerns; mission and business needs; standards and best practices; and requirements to comply with laws, Executive Orders, directives, policies, and regulations. The comprehensive nature of the security and privacy controls coupled with a flexible, risk-based control selection process, can help organizations comply with applicable security and privacy requirements and achieve adequate security for their information systems.

---

[5] This includes risk to critical infrastructure and key resources described in Homeland Security Presidential Directive 7.

[6] A *federal information system* is an information system used or operated by an agency, by a contractor of an agency, or by another organization on behalf of an agency.

[7] Information systems that have been designated as national security systems, as defined in 44 U.S.C., Section 3542, are not subject to the requirements in FISMA, however, the controls established in this publication may be selected for national security systems as otherwise required (e.g., the Privacy Act of 1974) or with the approval of federal officials exercising policy authority over such systems. CNSS Instruction 1253 provides guidance for *national security systems*.

[8] OMB Circular A-130 requires federal agencies to use the NIST Risk Management Framework for the selection of controls for federal information systems.

1.2 TARGET AUDIENCE

This publication is intended to serve a diverse audience including.

- Individuals with system, information security, privacy, or risk management and oversight responsibilities including, for example, authorizing officials, Chief Information Officers, Senior Agency Information Security Officers, and Senior Agency Officials for Privacy;

- Individuals with system development responsibilities including, for example, mission or business owners, program managers, systems engineers, systems security engineers, privacy engineers, software developers, systems integrators, and acquisition or procurement officials;

- Individuals with security and privacy implementation and operations responsibilities including, for example, mission or business owners, system owners, information owners or stewards, system administrators, system security or privacy officers;

- Individuals with security and privacy assessment and monitoring responsibilities including, for example, auditors, Inspectors General, system evaluators, control assessors, independent verifiers and validators, and analysts; and

- Commercial entities including industry partners, producing component products and systems, creating security and privacy technologies, or providing services or capabilities that support information security or privacy.

1.3 ORGANIZATIONAL RESPONSIBILITIES

Achieving adequate security and privacy throughout an organization is a complex, multifaceted undertaking that requires:

- Well-defined and clearly articulated security and privacy requirements for systems and organizations;

- Rigorous security and privacy planning and system life cycle management;

- The use of trustworthy information system components based on state-of-the-practice hardware, firmware, and software development processes;

- The application of system security and privacy engineering principles and practices to effectively integrate system components into information systems;

- The employment of security and privacy practices that are well documented and integrated into and supportive of the institutional and operational processes of organizations; and

- Continuous monitoring of information systems and organizations to determine the ongoing effectiveness of security and privacy controls, changes in information systems and environments of operation, and the state of security and privacy organization-wide.[9]

Organizations must realistically assess risks to organizational operations and assets, individuals, other organizations, and the Nation that arise from the execution of their missions and business functions and by placing information systems into operation or continuing operations. Realistic assessments of risk require a thorough understanding of the susceptibility to threats based on the vulnerabilities within information systems and organizations and the likelihood and potential adverse impacts of successful exploitations of such vulnerabilities by those threats.[10] These risk

---

[9] NIST Special Publication 800-137 provides guidance on continuous monitoring of systems and organizations.
[10] NIST Special Publication 800-30 provides guidance on the risk assessment process.

assessments also require an understanding of privacy risks.[11] To address these concerns, security and privacy requirements must be satisfied with the full knowledge and understanding of the risk management strategy of the organization considering the cost, schedule, and performance issues associated with the design, development, acquisition, deployment, operation, and sustainment of organizational information systems.

The catalog of security and privacy controls can be effectively used to protect organizations, individuals, and information systems from traditional and advanced persistent threats in varied operational, environmental, and technical scenarios. The controls can also be used to demonstrate compliance with a variety of governmental, organizational, or institutional security and privacy requirements. Organizations have the responsibility to select the appropriate security and privacy controls, to implement the controls correctly, and to demonstrate the effectiveness of the controls in satisfying security and privacy requirements.[12]

Organizational risk assessments can inform the security and privacy control selection process. The selection process results in an agreed-upon set of security and privacy controls addressing specific mission or business needs consistent with organizational risk tolerance.[13] The process preserves, to the greatest extent possible, the agility and flexibility that organizations need to address an increasingly sophisticated and hostile threat space, mission and business requirements, rapidly changing technologies, and many of environments of operation. Security and privacy controls can also be used in developing *overlays* or for unique or specialized missions or business applications, information systems, operational environments, technologies, and/or communities of interest.[14]

1.4 RELATIONSHIP TO OTHER PUBLICATIONS

This publication establishes a set of controls with the breadth and depth to satisfy a diverse set of requirements, including security and privacy requirements,[15] that have been levied on information systems and organizations—and that are consistent with and complementary to other established national and international security and privacy standards. To develop a broadly applicable and technically sound set of controls for information systems and organizations, many sources were considered during the development of this publication. These sources included requirements and controls from the defense, financial, healthcare, intelligence, manufacturing, industrial control, and audit communities as well as national and international standards organizations. The security and privacy controls in this publication have been mapped to international security and privacy standards to help ensure maximum usability and applicability. In addition, the controls in this publication have been mapped to the requirements for federal information systems included in OMB Circular A-130, *Managing Information as a Strategic Resource*.[16]

---

[11] NIST Internal Report 8062 introduces privacy risk concepts.

[12] NIST Special Publication 800-53A provides guidance on assessing the effectiveness of controls.

[13] Authorizing officials or their designated representatives, by accepting the security and privacy plans, agree to the set of security and privacy controls proposed to meet the security and privacy requirements for organizations and systems.

[14] Appendix G provides guidance for tailoring security and privacy control baselines and for developing overlays to support the specific protection needs and requirements of stakeholders and their organizations.

[15] Security and privacy requirements are those requirements levied on a system or organization that are derived from applicable laws, Executive Orders, directives, regulations, policies, standards, and mission/business needs to ensure the confidentiality, integrity, and availability of information processed, stored, or transmitted and individual privacy.

[16] OMB Circular A-130 establishes general policy for the planning, budgeting, governance, acquisition, and management of federal information, personnel, equipment, funds, IT resources and supporting infrastructure and services.

1.5 REVISIONS AND EXTENSIONS

The security and privacy controls described in this publication represent the state-of-the-practice protection measures for individuals, information systems, and organizations. The controls are reviewed and revised periodically to reflect the experience gained from using the controls; new or revised laws, Executive Orders, directives, regulations, policies, and standards; changing security and privacy requirements; emerging threats, vulnerabilities, attack and information processing methods; and the availability of new technologies. The security and privacy controls in the control catalog are also expected to change over time as controls are withdrawn, revised, and added. In addition to the need for change, the need for stability is addressed by requiring that proposed modifications to security and privacy controls go through a rigorous and transparent public review process to obtain public and private sector feedback and to build a consensus for such change. This provides a stable, flexible, and technically sound set of security and privacy controls for the organizations that use the control catalog.

1.6 PUBLICATION ORGANIZATION

The remainder of this special publication is organized as follows:

- **Chapter Two** describes the fundamental concepts associated with security and privacy controls including the relationship between requirements and controls; the basic structure of controls and how the controls are organized in the consolidated catalog; the different types of controls; the grouping of controls into baselines; the use of common controls and inheritance of security and privacy capabilities; and assurance and trustworthiness.

- **Chapter Three** provides a consolidated catalog of security and privacy controls and control enhancements[17] including supplemental guidance to explain the purpose and meaning of the controls and to provide useful information regarding control implementation and assessment; a list of related controls to show useful relationships dependencies among controls; and a list of references to supporting publications that may be helpful to organizations.

- **Supporting appendices** provide additional information on the use of security and privacy controls including: general references;[18] definitions and terms; acronyms; exemplar control baselines for organizations and information systems; summary tables for security and privacy controls by families; summary and mapping tables for privacy-related controls; tailoring guidance for controls and baselines; keywords; and control mappings to international standards.

---

[17] The security and privacy controls in Special Publication 800-53 are available online and can be obtained in various formats from the NIST web site.

[18] Unless otherwise stated, all references to NIST publications in this document are to the most recent version of those publications.

CHAPTER TWO

THE FUNDAMENTALS
STRUCTURE, TYPE, AND ORGANIZATION OF SECURITY AND PRIVACY CONTROLS

This chapter presents the fundamental concepts associated with security and privacy controls including: the relationship between requirements and controls; the structure of controls and how the controls are organized in the consolidated control catalog; the different types of controls for information systems and organizations; the purpose of control baselines and how tailoring is used to customize controls and baselines; and the importance of control assurance for both security and privacy and its effect on achieving trustworthy systems.

2.1 REQUIREMENTS AND CONTROLS

Before embarking on the process of selecting security and privacy controls, it is important to understand the relationship between controls and requirements.[19] A requirement is a statement that translates or expresses a specific need including associated constraints and conditions.[20] A requirement levied on an information system or an organization can be derived from different sources, including for example, laws, Executive Orders, directives, policies, regulations, and mission/business needs. Requirements address the capability the information system is designed to provide, for example, processing payroll transactions, simulating weather patterns, controlling industrial processes, or performing genome sequencing for advanced medical research.

Security and privacy requirements are a subset of the requirements that can be levied on an information system or organization. Security requirements ensure the confidentiality, integrity, and availability of information being processed, stored, or transmitted by the information system. Privacy requirements advance individual privacy associated with an organizations's creation, collection, use, processing, storage, maintenance, dissemination, disclosure, or disposal of personally identifiable information. Such requirements can be used in a variety of contexts from policy- and oversight-related activities to life cycle-related activities that involve information systems development and engineering disciplines.

Security and privacy controls for information systems and organizations help satisfy security and privacy requirements. Controls can be used in a variety of contexts and can serve many purposes. When used in the security and privacy context, controls[21] are designed to address the protection needs of organizations, information systems, and individuals. Such needs are specified by a set of security and privacy requirements. Security and privacy controls help an organization satisfy security and privacy requirements and defined security and privacy policies. It is important to understand the complementary nature of requirements and controls and how they work together to protect organizations, information systems, and individuals.

---

[19] There is no single, prescribed, or mandatory relationship between requirements and controls. The relationship is completely dependent on the organization's use of controls, which may be dynamic and evolving.

[20] See ISO/IEC/IEEE 29148.

[21] In accordance with OMB Circular A-130, security controls are the safeguards or countermeasures prescribed for an information system or an organization to protect the confidentiality, integrity, and availability of the system and its information. Privacy controls are the administrative, technical, and physical safeguards employed within an agency to ensure compliance with applicable privacy requirements and manage privacy risks.

Finally, information systems represent a complex human-human environment, and as such, the functions of the systems can be realized by technological and human elements. Accordingly, the mechanisms implementing security and privacy controls in information systems can include both technical and non-technical (i.e., administrative) controls. These controls are represented in the broad array of families in the consolidated control catalog in Chapter Three. In addition, security and privacy controls can be employed in a variety of contexts supported by different types of risk-based decision processes. For example, the controls may be used as part of the Risk Management Framework[22] or a comprehensive, life cycle-based systems engineering process.[23] Controls can be viewed as generalized statements that express the security and privacy functions or capabilities necessary to ensure compliance with applicable requirements and to manage risk.

Irrespective of how organizations define the terms *requirement* and *control*, it is important for organizations to clearly establish the relationship so that expectations for security and privacy can be achieved given stakeholder protection needs and concerns for individual privacy; assumptions; constraints placed upon organizations; trade-space decisions; cost, schedule, and performance considerations; and risk management decisions.

2.2 CONTROL STRUCTURE AND ORGANIZATION

Security and privacy controls described in this publication have a well-defined organization and structure. For ease of use in the security and privacy control selection and specification process, controls are organized into twenty *families*.[24] Each family contains security and privacy controls related to the specific topic of the family. A two-character identifier uniquely identifies each control family, for example, PS (Personnel Security). Security and privacy controls may involve aspects of policy, oversight, supervision, manual processes, and automated mechanisms that are implemented by systems or actions by individuals. Table 1 lists the security and privacy control families and their associated family identifiers.

TABLE 1: SECURITY AND PRIVACY CONTROL FAMILIES

ID	FAMILY	ID	FAMILY
AC	Access Control	MP	Media Protection
AT	Awareness and Training	PA	Privacy Authorization
AU	Audit and Accountability	PE	Physical and Environmental Protection
CA	Assessment, Authorization, and Monitoring	PL	Planning
CM	Configuration Management	PM	Program Management
CP	Contingency Planning	PS	Personnel Security
IA	Identification and Authentication	RA	Risk Assessment
IP	Individual Participation	SA	System and Services Acquisition
IR	Incident Response	SC	System and Communications Protection
MA	Maintenance	SI	System and Information Integrity

---

[22] See NIST Special Publication 800-37.

[23] See NIST Special Publication 800-160.

[24] Of the twenty control families in NIST Special Publication 800-53, seventeen families are aligned with the security requirements in FIPS Publication 200. In addition to those families, three other families address privacy and program management considerations.

Security and privacy controls have the following structure: a base *control* section; a *supplemental guidance* section; a *control enhancements* section; a *related controls* section; and a *references* section. The *control* section prescribes a security or privacy capability to be implemented. Such capability is achieved by the activities or actions, automated or nonautomated, carried out by information systems, organizations, and individuals. Organizations designate the responsibility for control design, implementation, management, and monitoring. Organizations have flexibility to implement the controls selected in whatever manner that satisfies the organizational mission or business needs, consistent with law, regulation, and policy.

For some security and privacy controls in the control catalog, a degree of flexibility is provided by allowing organizations to define specific values for designated parameters associated with the controls. This flexibility is achieved as part of a tailoring process using *assignment* and *selection* statements embedded within the controls and enclosed by brackets. These parameter statements give organizations the capability to customize controls based on stakeholder security and privacy requirements. The requirements can evolve from a variety of sources including, for example, mission and business needs, laws, Executive Orders, directives, policies, regulations, standards, guidelines, or industry best practices. Risk assessments and organizational risk tolerance are also important factors in defining the values for control parameters.[25] While the parameter statements provide flexibility, organizations are responsible for choosing and assigning the parameters for each selected control. Once specified, the values for the assignment and selection statements become a permanent part of the control. The implementation of the control is assessed against the completed control statement. In contrast to assignment statements, selection statements narrow the range of potential input values by providing a specific list of items from which organizations must choose.

The *supplemental guidance* section provides non-prescriptive, additional information for a security or privacy control. Organizations can apply the guidance as needed, when defining, developing, implementing, or assessing controls. The supplemental guidance provides important considerations for implementing controls in the context of mission or business requirements, operational environments, or assessments of risk. Supplemental guidance can also explain the purpose or meaning of controls and often includes examples. Control enhancements may also contain supplemental guidance. This occurs when the guidance is not applicable to the entire control but instead is focused on the control enhancement.

The *related controls* section provides a list of security or privacy controls that directly impact or support the implementation of a control or control enhancement. Security and privacy control enhancements are related to their base control. Related controls that are referenced in the base control are not repeated in the control enhancements. There may, however, be related controls identified for control enhancements that are not referenced in the base control (i.e., the related control is only associated with that specific control enhancement).

The *control enhancements* section provides statements of security and privacy capability to add functionality or specificity to a base control or to increase the strength of a base control. In both cases, the control enhancements are used in information systems and environments of operation that require greater protection than provided by the base control due to the potential adverse organizational or individual impacts or when organizations require additions to the base control functionality or assurance based on organizational assessments of risk. Control enhancements are

---

[25] In general, organization-defined *parameters* used in assignment and selection statements in the base security and privacy controls apply also to the control enhancements associated with those controls.

numbered sequentially within each control section that the enhancements can be easily identified when
selected to supplement the base control.

Each control enhancement has a short subtitle to indicate the intended function or capability
provided by the enhancement. In the AU-4 example, if the control enhancement is selected, the
control designation becomes AU-4(1). The numerical designation of a control enhancement is
used only to identify that enhancement within the control. The designation is not indicative of the
strength of the control enhancement, level or degree of protection, or any hierarchical relationship
among the enhancements. Control enhancements are not intended to be selected independently.
That is, if a control enhancement is selected, then the corresponding base control must also be
selected and implemented. This intent is reflected in the control baselines in Appendix D.

The *references* section includes a list of applicable standards, guidelines and other useful
references that are relevant to a control or control enhancement.[26] The references section also
contains hyperlinks to specific publications for obtaining additional information for control
development, implementation, assessment, and monitoring.

The following example illustrates the structure of a typical control:

Control
Parameter

AU-4   AUDIT STORAGE CAPACITY

Base
Control

Control: Allocate audit record storage capacity to accommodate [*Assignment: organization-defined
audit record retention requirements*].

Supplemental Guidance: Organizations consider the types of auditing to be performed and the audit
processing requirements when allocating audit storage capacity. Allocating sufficient audit storage
capacity reduces the likelihood of such capacity being exceeded and resulting in the potential loss
or reduction of auditing capability.

Related Controls: AU-2, AU-5, AU-6, AU-7, AU-9, AU-11, AU-12, AU-14, SI-4.

Control Enhancements:

(1)   AUDIT STORAGE CAPACITY | TRANSFER TO ALTERNATE STORAGE

Control
Enhancement

**Off-load audit records [*Assignment: organization-defined frequency*] onto a different system or
media than the system being audited.**

Supplemental Guidance: Off-loading is a process designed to preserve the confidentiality and
integrity of audit records by moving the records from the primary system to a secondary or
alternate system. It is a common process in systems with limited audit storage capacity; the
audit storage is used only in a transitory fashion until the system can communicate with the
secondary or alternate system designated for storing the audit records, at which point the
information is transferred.

Related Controls: None.

References: None.

2.3 TYPES OF CONTROLS

There are three distinct types of security and privacy controls in Chapter Three. These include:
common controls, *system-specific* controls, and *hybrid* controls. The control types define the
scope of applicability for the control; the shared nature or inheritability of the control; and the
responsibility for control development, implementation, assessment, and authorization. Each type

---

[26] Publications listed in the *references section* refer to the most recent versions of those publications. References are
provided to assist organizations in applying the security and privacy controls and are not intended to be inclusive or
complete.

of control has a specific focus and objective which helps organizations implement the controls effectively and obtain the expected protection benefits. Deploying certain types of controls may also achieve cost benefits by leveraging security and privacy capabilities across many information systems and environments of operation.

Common controls are security or privacy controls whose implementation results in a capability that is *inheritable* by multiple information systems or programs. Controls are deemed inheritable when the information system or program receives protection from the implemented control but the control is developed, implemented, assessed, authorized, and monitored by entities other than those responsible for the system or program. The security and privacy capabilities provided by common controls can be inherited from many sources including, for example, mission/business lines, organizations, enclaves, sites, environments of operation, or other information systems or programs. Many of the controls needed to protect information systems including, for example, physical and environmental protection controls, personal security controls, and many privacy controls, are candidates for common control status. Common controls can include technology-based controls, for example, boundary protection controls, access controls, identification and authentication controls, and controls that are part of cross-domain solutions. The development, implementation, assessment, authorization, and monitoring cost of common controls can be amortized across multiple information systems, programs, and organizational elements.

COMMON CONTROL IMPLEMENTATION

The selection of common controls is most effectively accomplished on an organization-wide basis with the involvement of the senior leadership who understand organizational priorities, the importance of organizational operations and assets, and the importance of the information systems that support those operations and assets. These senior leaders are in the best position to assign responsibilities for developing, implementing, assessing, authorizing, and monitoring common controls.

Organizations assign responsibility for common controls to appropriate officials. These officials, designated as *common control providers*, develop, implement, assess, authorize, and monitor the organization-defined common controls.[27] The identification and selection of common controls is most effectively accomplished as an organization-wide exercise with the active involvement of executive-level personnel including, for example, mission and business owners, risk executives, authorizing officials, Chief Information Officers, Senior Agency Information Security Officers, Senior Agency Officials for Privacy, information owners or information stewards, system owners, and other key stakeholders. The organization-wide common control selection process considers the security and privacy controls necessary to adequately respond to the risks arising from the use of the systems or program inheriting the controls.[28] Common controls that affect multiple, but not all systems and programs within the organization, could benefit from taking a similar approach.

---

[27] Organizational officials at the senior leadership level assign responsibility for the development, implementation, assessment, authorization, and monitoring of common controls to appropriate entities. Such entities can be internal or external to the organization.

[28] Each potential common control is reviewed for applicability to each organizational system or program.

Common controls are documented in organization-wide security and privacy program plans. The controls may also be documented in the security and privacy plans for information systems that inherit those controls or in situations where the common controls are implemented within specific systems.[29] Organizations can describe common controls in a single document or in multiple documents with references to other documents, as appropriate. If program plans contain multiple documents, organizations specify in each document the officials responsible for development, implementation, assessment, authorization, and monitoring of the respective common controls. When common controls are included in a separate security or privacy plan for an information system, the security or privacy program plans indicate which separate security or privacy plans contain a description of the common controls.

Security and privacy controls not designated as common controls are considered *system-specific* or *hybrid* controls. System-specific controls are the primary responsibility of information system owners and the authorizing officials for those systems. Organizations can designate a security or privacy control as *hybrid* if one part of the control is common and another part of the control is system-specific. For example, an organization may implement the Contingency Planning control using a predefined template for the master contingency plan for all organizational information systems with individual information system owners tailoring the plan for system-specific uses, where appropriate. The division of hybrid controls into common and system-specific parts may vary by organization, depending on the types of information technologies employed, assignment of responsibilities, and the methods used by the organization to manage its controls.

INHERITED RISK

Organizations consider the inherited risk from the use of common controls. Security and privacy plans, security and privacy assessment reports, and plans of action and milestones for common controls (or a summary of such information) are made available to information system owners (for information systems inheriting the controls) after the information is reviewed and approved by the senior official or executive responsible and accountable for the common controls. It is therefore important that both internal and external common control providers keep common control status information current.

The determination as to whether a security or privacy control is a common, hybrid, or system-specific control is context-dependent. Security and privacy controls cannot be determined to be common, hybrid, or system-specific simply based on reviewing the language of the control. For example, a control may be designated as a system-specific control for one information system, and at the same time be designated as a common control for another information system (i.e., inheriting the control from the first system). One method to determine if a system-specific control may also be designated as a common control for other information systems is to consider who or what depends on the functionality of that control. If a certain part of an information system or solution external to the system depends on the control, then that control may be a candidate for common control status.

---

[29] Organizations ensure that any security or privacy capabilities provided by common controls (i.e., security or privacy capabilities inheritable by other organizational entities) are described in sufficient detail to facilitate understanding of the control implementation by inheriting entities.

Partitioning security and privacy controls into common, hybrid, and system-specific controls can result in significant savings to organizations in implementation and assessment costs as well as a more consistent application of controls organization-wide. While the partitioning of controls into common, hybrid, and system-specific controls is straightforward and intuitive conceptually, the actual application takes planning and coordination. It is necessary to first determine what security and privacy capabilities are needed before organizations assign specific responsibility for how the security and privacy controls are implemented, operated, and maintained.

2.4 SECURITY AND PRIVACY CONTROL RELATIONSHIP

While security and privacy requirements are authoritatively sourced to different laws, regulations, or policies, there is also a strong relationship between the security and privacy domains. One of the *Fair Information Practice Principles* (FIPPs) is security—a key principle to help ensure the protection of personally identifiable information and individual privacy. Therefore, controls used to manage the confidentiality, integrity, and availability of information and information systems when selected and implemented for information systems that create, collect, use, process, store, maintain, disseminate, disclose, or dispose of personally identifiable information, address security and privacy concerns. Nonetheless, individual privacy cannot be achieved solely through securing personally identifiable information. Consequently, this publication contains controls designed to meet privacy requirements and to manage the privacy risks associated with an organizations's creation, collection, use, processing, storage, maintenance, dissemination, disclosure, or disposal of personally identifiable information separate from security concerns. Figure 1 illustrates the totality of security and privacy concerns, reflecting common areas of concern and those areas of concern that are unique.

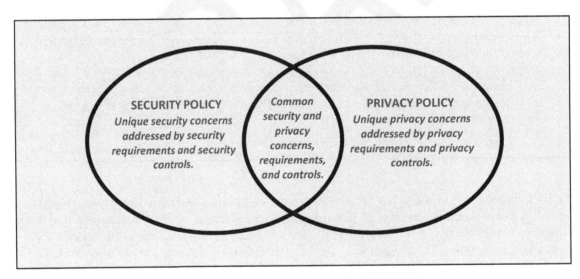

FIGURE 1: SECURITY AND PRIVACY RELATIONSHIP

The security and privacy controls in this publication are incorporated into a consolidated control catalog in Chapter Three. Appendix F provides a summary of the privacy controls and control enhancements predominantly for addressing unique privacy concerns. Appendix F is intended to help organizations identify the controls and control enhancements for which privacy programs have primary responsibility. For some controls and enhancements, the selection authority and oversight is shared with the security programs. These controls and controls enhancements are designated as *joint* controls—that is, the controls and control enhancements can address security and privacy requirements. In those situations, organizations may opt to do a joint implementation or alternatively the privacy program and security program may implement the respective privacy and security aspects of the control or enhancement separately.

For example, in joint control AT-2, the privacy program may develop and conduct separate privacy-focused training or it could choose to develop coordinated privacy and security training with the security program. For controls and control enhancements that are not considered joint, privacy programs have the sole authority to select and oversee the controls and enhancements. In addition to Appendix F, the security and privacy tables in Appendix E indicate which privacy controls are considered joint controls. However, organizations have the flexibility to identify other controls as privacy or joint controls, as appropriate.

Throughout the control catalog, there may be references to privacy controls or considerations in various security controls because in some contexts, these security controls could provide privacy protections or could create privacy risks depending on the implementation. Although security programs may be responsible for these controls, organizations may have privacy programs and security progams collaborate on how to manage the nexus with privacy. To maintain awareness and support collaboration between privacy and security programs, organizations may use the keywords in Appendix H to locate privacy references in security controls that are not designated as joint controls.

2.5 CONTROL BASELINES

A significant challenge for organizations is selecting a set of security and privacy controls which, if correctly implemented and determined to be effective, adequately responds to mission and business risk while complying with security and privacy requirements defined by applicable laws, Executive Orders, regulations, policies, and directives. There is no single set of controls that addresses all security and privacy concerns in every situation. However, choosing the most appropriate controls for a specific situation or system to adequately respond to risk requires a fundamental understanding of the organization's missions and business priorities; the mission and business functions the systems will support, and the environments where the systems will operate. It also requires close collaboration with key organizational stakeholders. With that understanding, organizations can demonstrate how to effectively and cost-effectively assure the confidentiality, integrity, and availability of organizational information and systems as well as the privacy of individuals in the context of supporting the organization's mission and business functions.

To assist organizations in selecting the set of controls for their systems that is commensurate with risk, the concept of a control *baseline* is introduced. A control baseline is a collection of controls from Chapter Three specifically assembled or brought together to address the protection needs of a group, organization, or community of interest.[30] The control baseline provides a generalized set of controls that represents an initial starting point for the subsequent tailoring activities that can be applied to the baseline to produce a more targeted or customized security and privacy solution for the entity it is intended to serve. The selection of controls for control baselines can be based on a variety of factors including, for example, sector-specific requirements, threat information, organizational assumptions and constraints, mission or business requirements, types of systems, operating environments, specific technologies, or laws, Executive Orders, regulations, policies, directives, standards, or industry best practices. The control baselines are tailored or customized

---

[30] The U.S. Government, in accordance with the requirements set forth in FISMA, OMB Circular A-130, and Federal Information Processing Standards, has established federally-mandated security control baselines. The baselines for non-national security systems are listed in Appendix D. These control baselines can be used to address the confidentiality, integrity and availability of personally identifiable information. Criteria that support federal agency selection of privacy controls are listed in Appendix F.

for each organization, sector, or individual company based on specific operating conditions and other factors. Tailoring activities are described in greater detail in Appendix G.

2.6 ASSURANCE AND TRUSTWORTHINESS

The trustworthiness of systems, system components, and system services is an important part of the risk management strategies developed by organizations. Whether systems are deployed to support the national air traffic control system, a major financial institution, a nuclear power plant, or the military services and warfighters, the systems must be reliable, trustworthy, and resilient in the face of increasingly sophisticated and pervasive threats—and also support the privacy of individuals. To understand how to achieve trustworthy systems and the role assurance plays, it is important to first define the term *trustworthiness*. Trustworthiness, in this context, means simply worthy of being trusted to fulfill whatever critical requirements may be needed for a particular component, subsystem, system, network, application, mission, business function, enterprise, or other entity.[31] Trustworthiness requirements can include, for example, attributes of reliability, dependability, performance, resilience, safety, security, privacy, and survivability under a range of potential adversity in the form of disruptions, hazards, threats, and privacy risks. Effective measures of trustworthiness are meaningful only to the extent the requirements are sufficiently complete and well-defined, and can be accurately assessed.[32]

Two fundamental components affecting the trustworthiness of systems are *functionality* and *assurance*. Functionality is defined in terms of the security and privacy features, functions, mechanisms, services, procedures, and architectures implemented within organizational systems and programs and the environments in which those systems and programs operate. Assurance is the measure of confidence that the system functionality is implemented correctly, operating as intended, and producing the desired outcome with respect to meeting the security and privacy requirements for the system—thus possessing the capability to accurately mediate and enforce established security and privacy policies. Security and privacy controls address both functionality and assurance. Some controls focus primarily on functionality. Other controls focus primarily on assurance. Finally, certain controls can support functionality and assurance. Assurance-related controls are identified in the security and privacy control summary tables in Appendix E.

THE COMPELLING ARGUMENT FOR ASSURANCE

Organizations specify assurance-related controls to define activities performed to generate relevant and credible evidence about the functionality and behavior of organizational systems and to trace the evidence to the elements that provide such functionality and behavior. This evidence is used to obtain a degree of confidence that the information systems satisfy stated security and privacy requirements—and do so while effectively supporting the organizational missions and business functions while being subjected to threats in the intended environments of operation.

---

[31] P. Neumann, *Principled Assuredly Trustworthy Composable Architectures*, CDRL A001 Final Report, SRI International, Menlo Park, CA, December 28, 2004.

[32] NIST Special Publication 800-160 provides guidance on systems security engineering and the application of security design principles to achieve trustworthy systems.

THE CONTROLS

SECURITY AND PRIVACY CONTROLS, ENHANCEMENTS, AND SUPPLEMENTAL GUIDANCE

This catalog of security and privacy controls provides a range of protection measures for systems, organizations, and individuals.[33] The controls have been designed to facilitate compliance with applicable laws, Executive Orders, directives, policies, regulations, and standards. The security and privacy controls in the catalog with few exceptions, have been designed to be policy, technology, and sector neutral. This means that the controls focus on the fundamental measures necessary to protect information and the privacy of individuals during processing, while in storage, and during transmission. It should also be noted that while the security and privacy controls are largely policy, technology, and sector neutral, that does not imply that the controls are policy, technology, and sector unaware. Understanding policies, technologies, and sectors is necessary so that the controls are meaningful and relevant when implemented. Employing a policy, technology, and sector neutral control catalog has the following benefits:

- It encourages organizations to focus on the security and privacy functions and capabilities required for mission and business success and the protection of information and the privacy of individuals, irrespective of the technologies that are employed in their systems;

- It encourages organizations to analyze each security and privacy control for its applicability to specific technologies, environments of operation, missions and business functions, and communities of interest; and

- It encourages organizations to specify security and privacy policies as part of the tailoring process for controls that have variable parameters.

In the few cases where specific technologies are referenced in controls, organizations are cautioned that the need to provide adequate security and privacy may well go beyond the requirements in a single control associated with a technology. Many of the needed protection measures are obtained from the other controls in the catalog allocated to the initial control baselines and the privacy selection criteria as the starting point for the development of security and privacy plans using the tailoring process. NIST Federal Information Processing Standards, Special Publications, and Interagency Reports provide guidance on security and privacy controls for specific technologies and sector-specific applications including, for example, smart grid, healthcare, cloud, mobile, industrial and process control systems, and Internet of Things (IoT) devices.

Security and privacy controls in the catalog are expected to change over time, as controls are withdrawn, revised, and added. To maintain stability in security and privacy plans, security and privacy controls will not be renumbered each time a control is withdrawn. Rather, notations of controls that have been withdrawn are maintained in the catalog for historical purposes. Controls may be withdrawn for a variety of reasons including, for example, the function or capability provided by the control has been incorporated into another control or is redundant to an existing control; or the control is deemed to be no longer necessary or effective.

---

[33] A catalog of security and privacy controls is also available online in different formats.

New security and privacy controls will be developed on a regular basis using information from national-level threat and vulnerability databases; information on the latest tactics, techniques, procedures, and tools used by adversaries; and an improved understanding of how to mitigate the risks to the privacy of individuals arising from information processing. Proposed modifications to the security and privacy controls and control baselines will be carefully considered during each revision cycle, considering the need for stability of the control catalog and the need to respond to changing threats, vulnerabilities, technologies, attack methods, and processing methods. The objective is to raise the level of information security and privacy over time.

COMPLIANCE AND DUE DILIGENCE

Compliance necessitates organizations exercising *due diligence* regarding information security, privacy, and risk management. Security and privacy due diligence requires organizations to establish a risk management program that uses the inherent flexibility in NIST publications to select and implement security and privacy controls that meet their mission and business needs. Using risk management frameworks and processes is essential in developing, implementing, and maintaining the protection measures that are necessary to address stakeholder needs and the current threats to organizational operations and assets, individuals, other organizations, and the Nation. Employing effective risk-based processes, procedures, methods, and technologies helps to ensure that information systems and organizations have the necessary trustworthiness and resiliency to support essential missions and business functions, the U.S. critical infrastructure, and continuity of government.

3.1 ACCESS CONTROL

Quick link to Access Control summary table

AC-1 ACCESS CONTROL POLICY AND PROCEDURES

Control:

a. Develop, document, and disseminate to [*Assignment: organization-defined personnel or roles*]:

    1. An access control policy that:

        (a) Addresses purpose, scope, roles, responsibilities, management commitment, coordination among organizational entities, and compliance; and

        (b) Is consistent with applicable laws, Executive Orders, directives, regulations, policies, standards, and guidelines; and

    2. Procedures to facilitate the implementation of the access control policy and the associated access controls;

b. Designate an [*Assignment: organization-defined senior management official*] to manage the access control policy and procedures;

c. Review and update the current access control:

    1. Policy [*Assignment: organization-defined frequency*]; and

    2. Procedures [*Assignment: organization-defined frequency*];

d. Ensure that the access control procedures implement the access control policy and controls; and

e. Develop, document, and implement remediation actions for violations of the access control policy.

Supplemental Guidance: This control addresses the establishment of policy and procedures for the effective implementation of the controls and control enhancements in the AC family. The risk management strategy is an important factor in establishing policy and procedures. Comprehensive policy and procedures help provide security and privacy assurance. Security and privacy program policies and procedures at the organization level may make the need for system-specific policies and procedures unnecessary. The policy can be included as part of the general security and privacy policy or can be represented by multiple policies reflecting the complex nature of organizations. The procedures can be established for security and privacy programs and for systems, if needed. Procedures describe how policies or controls are implemented and can be directed at the personnel or role that is the object of the procedure. Procedures can be documented in system security and privacy plans or in one or more separate documents. It is important to recognize that restating controls does not constitute an organizational policy or procedure.

Related Controls: IA-1, PM-9, PM-25, PS-8, SI-12.

Control Enhancements: None.

References: NIST Special Publications 800-12, 800-30, 800-39, 800-100; NIST Interagency Report 7874.

AC-2 ACCOUNT MANAGEMENT

Control:

a. Define and document the types of system accounts allowed for use within the system in support of organizational missions and business functions;

b. Assign account managers for system accounts;

c. Establish conditions for group and role membership;

d. Specify authorized users of the system, group and role membership, and access authorizations (i.e., privileges) and other attributes (as required) for each account;

e. Require approvals by [*Assignment: organization-defined personnel or roles*] for requests to create system accounts;

f. Create, enable, modify, disable, and remove system accounts in accordance with [*Assignment: organization-defined policy, procedures, and conditions*];

g. Monitor the use of system accounts;

h. Notify account managers within [*Assignment: organization-defined time-period for each situation*]:

    1. When accounts are no longer required;

    2. When users are terminated or transferred; and

    3. When individual system usage or need-to-know changes for an individual;

i. Authorize access to the system based on:

    1. A valid access authorization;

    2. Intended system usage; and

    3. Other attributes as required by the organization or associated missions and business functions;

j. Review accounts for compliance with account management requirements [*Assignment: organization-defined frequency*];

k. Establish a process for reissuing shared/group account credentials (if deployed) when individuals are removed from the group; and

l. Align account management processes with personnel termination and transfer processes.

Supplemental Guidance: System account types include, for example, individual, shared, group, system, guest, anonymous, emergency, developer/manufacturer/vendor, temporary, and service. The identification of authorized users of the system and the specification of access privileges reflects the requirements in other controls in the security plan. Users requiring administrative privileges on system accounts receive additional scrutiny by appropriate organizational personnel responsible for approving such accounts and privileged access, including, for example, system owner, mission/business owner, or chief information security officer. Organizations may choose to define access privileges or other attributes by account, by type of account, or a combination of both. Other attributes required for authorizing access include, for example, restrictions on time-of-day, day-of-week, and point-of-origin. In defining other account attributes, organizations consider system-related requirements and mission/business requirements. Failure to consider these factors could affect system availability.

Temporary and emergency accounts are intended for short-term use. Organizations establish temporary accounts as a part of normal account activation procedures when there is a need for short-term accounts without the demand for immediacy in account activation. Organizations establish emergency accounts in response to crisis situations and with the need for rapid account activation. Therefore, emergency account activation may bypass normal account authorization processes. Emergency and temporary accounts are not to be confused with infrequently used accounts including, for example, local logon accounts used for special tasks or when network resources are unavailable. Such accounts remain available and are not subject to automatic disabling or removal dates. Conditions for disabling or deactivating accounts include, for example,

When shared/group accounts or temporary accounts are no longer required, or when individuals are transferred or terminated. Some types of system accounts may require specialized training.

Related Controls: AC-3, AC-5, AC-6, AC-17, AC-18, AC-20, AC-24, AU-9, CM-5, IA-2, IA-8, MA-3, MA-5, PE-2, PL-4, PS-2, PS-4, PS-5, PS-7, SC-7, SC-13, SC-37.

Control Enhancements:

(1) ACCOUNT MANAGEMENT | AUTOMATED SYSTEM ACCOUNT MANAGEMENT

Employ automated mechanisms to support the management of system accounts.

Supplemental Guidance: The use of automated mechanisms can include, for example, using email or text messaging to automatically notify account managers when users are terminated or transferred; using the system to monitor account usage; and using telephonic notification to report atypical system account usage.

Related Controls: None.

(2) ACCOUNT MANAGEMENT | REMOVAL OF TEMPORARY AND EMERGENCY ACCOUNTS

Automatically [*Selection: remove; disable*] temporary and emergency accounts after [*Assignment: organization-defined time-period for each type of account*].

Supplemental Guidance: This control enhancement requires the removal or disabling of both temporary and emergency accounts automatically after a predefined time-period has elapsed, rather than at the convenience of the systems administrator. Automatic removal or disabling of accounts provides a more consistent implementation.

Related Controls: None.

(3) ACCOUNT MANAGEMENT | DISABLE ACCOUNTS

Automatically disable accounts when the accounts:

(a) **Have expired;**

(b) **Are no longer associated to a user;**

(c) **Are in violation of organizational policy;**

(d) **Are no longer used by applications, services, or the system; and**

(e) **Have been inactive for [*Assignment: organization-defined time-period*].**

Supplemental Guidance: None.

Related Controls: None.

(4) ACCOUNT MANAGEMENT | AUTOMATED AUDIT ACTIONS

Automatically audit account creation, modification, enabling, disabling, and removal actions, and notify [*Assignment: organization-defined personnel or roles*].

Supplemental Guidance: None.

Related Controls: AU-2, AU-12.

(5) ACCOUNT MANAGEMENT | INACTIVITY LOGOUT

Require that users log out when [*Assignment: organization-defined time-period of expected inactivity or description of when to log out*].

Supplemental Guidance: This control enhancement is behavior/policy-based and requires users to take physical action to log out when they are expecting inactivity longer than the defined period.

Related Controls: AC-11.

(6) ACCOUNT MANAGEMENT | DYNAMIC PRIVILEGE MANAGEMENT

Implement the following dynamic privilege management capabilities: [*Assignment: organization-defined list of dynamic privilege management capabilities*].

Supplemental Guidance: In contrast to conventional access control approaches which employ static system accounts and predefined user privileges, dynamic access control approaches rely on run time access control decisions facilitated by dynamic privilege management such as attribute based access control (ABAC). While user identities remain relatively constant over time, user privileges typically change more frequently based on ongoing mission or business requirements and operational needs of organizations. Dynamic privilege management can include, for example, immediate revocation of privileges from users, as opposed to requiring that users terminate and restart their sessions to reflect any changes in privileges. Dynamic privilege management can also include those mechanisms that change user privileges based on dynamic rules as opposed to editing specific user profiles. Examples include automatic adjustments of user privileges if they are operating out of their normal work times, their job function or assignment changes, or if systems are under duress or in emergency situations. This control enhancement also includes the effects of privilege changes, for example, the changes to encryption keys used for communications.

Related Controls: AC-16.

(7) ACCOUNT MANAGEMENT | ROLE-BASED SCHEMES

    (a) **Establish and administer privileged user accounts in accordance with a role-based access scheme that organizes allowed system access and privileges into roles;**

    (b) **Monitor privileged role assignments; and**

    (c) **Revoke access when privileged role assignments are no longer appropriate.**

Supplemental Guidance: Privileged roles are organization-defined roles assigned to individuals that allow those individuals to perform certain security-relevant functions that ordinary users are not authorized to perform. These privileged roles include, for example, key management, account management, network and system administration, database administration, and web administration.

Related Controls: None.

(8) ACCOUNT MANAGEMENT | DYNAMIC ACCOUNT MANAGEMENT

Create, activate, manage, and deactivate [*Assignment: organization-defined system accounts*] dynamically.

Supplemental Guidance: Approaches for dynamically creating, activating, managing, and deactivating system or service/application accounts rely on automatically provisioning the accounts at run time for entities that were previously unknown. Organizations plan for the dynamic creation, activation, management, and deactivation of these accounts by establishing trust relationships, business rules, and mechanisms with appropriate authorities to validate related authorizations and privileges.

Related Controls: AC-16.

(9) ACCOUNT MANAGEMENT | RESTRICTIONS ON USE OF SHARED AND GROUP ACCOUNTS

Only permit the use of shared and group accounts that meet [*Assignment: organization-defined conditions for establishing shared and group accounts*].

Supplemental Guidance: Before permitting the use of shared or group accounts, organizations consider the increased risk due to the lack of accountability with such accounts.

Related Controls: None.

(10) ACCOUNT MANAGEMENT | SHARED AND GROUP ACCOUNT CREDENTIAL CHANGE

Change shared and group account credentials when members leave the group.

Supplemental Guidance: This control enhancement is intended to ensure that former group members do not retain access to the shared/group account.

Related Controls: None.

(11) ACCOUNT MANAGEMENT | USAGE CONDITIONS

Enforce [*Assignment: organization-defined circumstances and/or usage conditions*] for [*Assignment: organization-defined system accounts*].

Supplemental Guidance: This control enhancement helps to enforce the principle of least privilege, increase user accountability, and enable more effective account monitoring. Such monitoring includes, for example, alerts generated if the account is used outside of specified parameters. Organizations can describe the specific conditions or circumstances under which system accounts can be used, for example, by restricting usage to certain days of the week, time of day, or specific durations of time.

Related Controls: None.

(12) ACCOUNT MANAGEMENT | ACCOUNT MONITORING FOR ATYPICAL USAGE

    (a) Monitor system accounts for [*Assignment: organization-defined atypical usage*]; and

    (b) Report atypical usage of system accounts to [*Assignment: organization-defined personnel or roles*].

Supplemental Guidance: Atypical usage includes, for example, accessing systems at certain times of the day and from locations that are not consistent with the normal usage patterns of individuals working in organizations. Account monitoring may inadvertently create privacy risks. Data collected to identify atypical usage may reveal previously unknown information about the behavior of individuals. Organizations assess and document these risks in their privacy impact assessment and make determinations that are in alignment with their privacy program plan.

Related Controls: AU-6, AU-7, CA-7, IR-8, SI-4.

(13) ACCOUNT MANAGEMENT | DISABLE ACCOUNTS FOR HIGH-RISK INDIVIDUALS

Disable accounts of users posing a significant risk within [*Assignment: organization-defined time-period*] of discovery of the risk.

Supplemental Guidance: Users posing a significant risk to organizations include individuals for whom reliable evidence or intelligence indicates either the intention to use authorized access to systems to cause harm or through whom adversaries will cause harm. Such harm includes the potential adverse impacts to organizational operations and assets, individuals, other organizations, or the Nation. Close coordination and cooperation among authorizing officials, system administrators, and human resource managers is essential for timely execution of this control enhancement.

Related Controls: AU-6, SI-4.

(14) ACCOUNT MANAGEMENT | PROHIBIT SPECIFIC ACCOUNT TYPES

Prohibit the creation and use of [*Selection (one or more): shared; guest; anonymous; temporary; emergency*] accounts for access to [*Assignment: organization-defined information types*].

Supplemental Guidance: NIST Special Publications 800-162, 800-178.

Related Controls: PS-4.

(15) ACCOUNT MANAGEMENT | ATTRIBUTE-BASED SCHEMES

    (a) Establish and administer privileged user accounts in accordance with an attribute-based access scheme that specifies allowed system access and privileges based on attributes;

    (b) Monitor privileged attribute-based assignments;

    (c) Monitor changes to attributes; and

    (d) Revoke access when privileged attribute-based assignments are no longer appropriate.

Supplemental Guidance: Privileged roles are organization-defined roles assigned to individuals that allow those individuals to perform certain security-relevant functions that ordinary users are not authorized to perform. These privileged roles include, for example, key management, account management, network and system administration, database administration, and web administration.

Related Controls: None.

References: NIST Special Publications 800-162, 800-178.

AC-3   ACCESS ENFORCEMENT

Control: Enforce approved authorizations for logical access to information and system resources in accordance with applicable access control policies.

Supplemental Guidance: Access control policies control access between active entities or subjects (i.e., users or processes acting on behalf of users) and passive entities or objects (i.e., devices, files, records, domains) in organizational systems. In addition to enforcing authorized access at the system level and recognizing that systems can host many applications and services in support of organizational missions and business operations, access enforcement mechanisms can also be employed at the application and service level to provide increased information security.

Related Controls: AC-2, AC-4, AC-5, AC-6, AC-16, AC-17, AC-18, AC-19, AC-20, AC-21, AC-22, AC-24, AC-25, AU-9, CA-9, CM-5, CM-11, IA-2, IA-5, IA-6, IA-7, IA-11, MA-3, MA-4, MA-5 MP-4, PM-25, PS-3, SC-2, SC-3, SC-4, SC-13, SC-28, SC-31, SC-34, SI-4.

Control Enhancements:

(1) ACCESS ENFORCEMENT | RESTRICTED ACCESS TO PRIVILEGED FUNCTIONS
[Withdrawn: Incorporated into AC-6].

(2) ACCESS ENFORCEMENT | DUAL AUTHORIZATION
Enforce dual authorization for [*Assignment: organization-defined privileged commands and/or other organization-defined actions*].

Supplemental Guidance: Dual authorization may also be known as two-person control. Dual authorization mechanisms require the approval of two authorized individuals to execute. Organizations do not require dual authorization mechanisms when immediate responses are necessary to ensure public and environmental safety.

Related Controls: CP-9, MP-6.

(3) ACCESS ENFORCEMENT | MANDATORY ACCESS CONTROL
Enforce [*Assignment: organization-defined mandatory access control policy*] over all subjects and objects where the policy:

(a) Is uniformly enforced across all subjects and objects within the boundary of the system;

(b) Specifies that a subject that has been granted access to information is constrained from doing any of the following;

  (1) Passing the information to unauthorized subjects or objects;

  (2) Granting its privileges to other subjects;

  (3) Changing one or more security attributes on subjects, objects, the system, or system components;

  (4) Choosing the security attributes and attribute values to be associated with newly created or modified objects; or

  (5) Changing the rules governing access control; and

(c) Specifies that [*Assignment: organization-defined subjects*] may explicitly be granted [*Assignment: organization-defined privileges*] such that they are not limited by any of the above constraints.

Supplemental Guidance: Mandatory access control is a type of nondiscretionary access control. The above class of mandatory access control policies constrains what actions subjects can take with information obtained from data objects for which they have already been granted access. This prevents the subjects from passing the information to unauthorized subjects and objects. This class of mandatory access control policies also constrains what actions subjects can take with respect to the propagation of access control privileges; that is, a subject with a privilege cannot pass that privilege to other subjects. The policy is uniformly enforced over all subjects and objects to which the system has control. Otherwise, the access control policy can be circumvented. This enforcement is provided by an implementation that meets the reference monitor concept as described in AC-25. The policy is bounded by the system boundary (i.e., once the information is passed outside of the control of the system, additional means may be required to ensure that the constraints on the information remain in effect).

The trusted subjects described above are granted privileges consistent with the concept of least privilege (see AC-6). Trusted subjects are only given the minimum privileges relative to the above policy necessary for satisfying organizational mission/business needs. The control is most applicable when there is a policy mandate that establishes a policy regarding access to controlled unclassified information or classified information and some users of the system are not authorized access to all such information resident in the system. This control can operate in conjunction with AC-3(4). A subject constrained in its operation by policies governed by this control is still able to operate under the less rigorous constraints of AC-3(4), but policies governed by this control take precedence over the less rigorous constraints of AC-3(4). For example, while a mandatory access control policy imposes a constraint preventing a subject from passing information to another subject operating at a different sensitivity label, AC-3(4)

permit the subject to pass the information to any subject with the same sensitivity label as the
subject.

Related Controls: SC-7.

(4) ACCESS ENFORCEMENT | DISCRETIONARY ACCESS CONTROL

Enforce [*Assignment: organization-defined discretionary access control policy*] over defined
subjects and objects where the policy specifies that a subject that has been granted access to
information can do one or more of the following:

(a) Pass the information to any other subjects or objects;

(b) Grant its privileges to other subjects;

(c) Change security attributes on subjects, objects, the system, or the system's components;

(d) Choose the security attributes to be associated with newly created or revised objects; or

(e) Change the rules governing access control.

Supplemental Guidance: When discretionary access control policies are implemented, subjects
are not constrained regarding what actions they can take with information for which they have
already been granted access. Thus, subjects that have been granted access to information are
not prevented from passing (i.e., the subjects have the discretion to pass) the information to
other subjects or objects. This control enhancement can operate in conjunction with AC-3(3).
A subject that is constrained in its operation by policies governed by AC-3(3) is still able to
operate under the less rigorous constraints of this control enhancement. Therefore, while AC-
3(3) imposes constraints preventing a subject from passing information to another subject
operating at a different sensitivity level, AC-3(4) permits the subject to pass the information
to any subject at the same sensitivity level. The policy is bounded by the system boundary.
Once the information is passed outside of the control of the system, additional means may be
required to help ensure that the constraints remain in effect. While the older, more traditional
definitions of discretionary access control require identity-based access control, that limitation
is not required for this use of discretionary access control.

Related Controls: None.

(5) ACCESS ENFORCEMENT | SECURITY-RELEVANT INFORMATION

Prevent access to [*Assignment: organization-defined security-relevant information*] except during
secure, non-operable system states.

Supplemental Guidance: Security-relevant information is any information within systems that
can potentially impact the operation of security functions or the provision of security services
in a manner that could result in failure to enforce system security policies or maintain the
isolation of code and data. Security-relevant information includes, for example, filtering rules
for routers/firewalls, cryptographic key management information, configuration parameters
for security services, and access control lists. Secure, non-operable system states include the
times in which systems are not performing mission/business-related processing, for example,
the system is off-line for maintenance, troubleshooting, boot-up, or shut down.

Related Controls: CM-6, SC-39.

(6) ACCESS ENFORCEMENT | PROTECTION OF USER AND SYSTEM INFORMATION

[Withdrawn: Incorporated into MP-4 and SC-28].

(7) ACCESS ENFORCEMENT | ROLE-BASED ACCESS CONTROL

Enforce a role-based access control policy over defined subjects and objects and control access
based upon [*Assignment: organization-defined roles and users authorized to assume such roles*].

Supplemental Guidance: Role-based access control (RBAC) is an access control policy that
restricts system access to authorized users. Organizations can create specific roles based on
job functions and the authorizations (i.e., privileges) to perform needed operations on the
systems associated with the organization-defined roles. When users are assigned to the
organizational roles, they inherit the authorizations or privileges defined for those roles.
RBAC simplifies privilege administration for organizations because privileges are not
assigned directly to every user (which can be a significant number of individuals for mid- to
large-size organizations) but are instead acquired through role assignments. RBAC can be
implemented either as a mandatory or discretionary form of access control. For organizations

implementing RBAC with mandatory access controls, the requirements in AC-3(3) define the scope of the subjects and objects covered by the policy.

Related Controls: PE-2.

(8) ACCESS ENFORCEMENT | REVOCATION OF ACCESS AUTHORIZATIONS

Enforce the revocation of access authorizations resulting from changes to the security attributes of subjects and objects based on [*Assignment: organization-defined rules governing the timing of revocations of access authorizations*].

Supplemental Guidance: Revocation of access rules may differ based on the types of access revoked. For example, if a subject (i.e., user or process) is removed from a group, access may not be revoked until the next time the object is opened or the next time the subject attempts a new access to the object. Revocation based on changes to security labels may take effect immediately. Organizations provide alternative approaches on how to make revocations immediate if systems cannot provide such capability and immediate revocation is necessary.

Related Controls: None.

(9) ACCESS ENFORCEMENT | CONTROLLED RELEASE

Release information outside of the established system boundary only if:

(a) **The receiving [*Assignment: organization-defined system or system component*] provides [*Assignment: organization-defined security safeguards*]; and**

(b) **[*Assignment: organization-defined security safeguards*] are used to validate the appropriateness of the information designated for release.**

Supplemental Guidance: Systems can only protect organizational information within the confines of established system boundaries. Additional security controls may be needed to ensure that such information is adequately protected once it is passed beyond the established system boundaries. In situations where the system is unable to determine the adequacy of the protections provided by entities outside its boundary, as a mitigating control, organizations determine procedurally whether the external systems are providing adequate security. The means used to determine the adequacy of security provided by external systems include, for example, conducting inspections or periodic testing and assessments; establishing agreements between the organization and its counterpart organizations; or some other process. The means used by external entities to protect the information received need not be the same as those used by the organization, but the means employed are sufficient to provide consistent adjudication of the security policy to protect the information.

This control enhancement requires systems to employ technical or procedural means to validate the information prior to releasing it to external systems. For example, if the system passes information to another system controlled by another organization, technical means are employed to validate that the security attributes associated with the exported information are appropriate for the receiving system. Alternatively, if the system passes information to a printer in organization-controlled space, procedural means can be employed to ensure that only appropriately authorized individuals gain access to the printer. This control enhancement is most applicable when there is some policy mandate that establishes policy regarding access to the information, and that policy applies beyond the realm of a particular system or organization.

Related Controls: SC-16.

(10) ACCESS ENFORCEMENT | AUDITED OVERRIDE OF ACCESS CONTROL MECHANISMS

Employ an audited override of automated access control mechanisms under [*Assignment: organization-defined conditions*] by [*Assignment: organization-defined roles*].

Supplemental Guidance: In certain situations, for example, where there is a threat to human life or an event that threatens the organization's ability carry out critical missions or business functions, an override capability for access control mechanisms may be needed. Such override conditions are defined by organizations and are used only in those limited circumstances.

Related Controls: AU-2, AU-6, AU-10, AU-12, AU-14.

(11) ACCESS ENFORCEMENT | RESTRICT ACCESS TO SPECIFIC INFORMATION

Restrict direct access to data repositories containing [*Assignment: organization-defined information types*].

Supplemental Guidance: This control enhancement is intended to provide flexibility regarding access control of specific pieces of information within a system. For example, role-based access could be employed to allow access to only a specific type of personally identifiable information within a database rather than allowing access to the database in its entirety.

Related Controls: None.

(12) ACCESS ENFORCEMENT | ASSERT AND ENFORCE APPLICATION ACCESS

(a) Require applications to assert, as part of the installation process, the access needed to the following system applications and functions: [*Assignment: organization-defined system applications and functions*]; and

(b) Provide an enforcement mechanism to prevent other-than-asserted access.

Supplemental Guidance: This control enhancement is intended to address applications that need to access existing system applications and functions including, for example, user contacts; global positioning system; camera; keyboard; microphone; network; or phones or other files.

Related Controls: CM-7.

(13) ACCESS ENFORCEMENT | ATTRIBUTE-BASED ACCESS CONTROL

Enforce attribute-based access control policy over defined subjects and objects and control access based upon [*Assignment: organization-defined attributes to assume access permissions*].

Supplemental Guidance: Attribute-based access control (ABAC) is an access control policy that restricts system access to authorized users based on their organizational attributes, such as job function; environmental attributes, such as time of day; and resource attributes, such as the classification of a document. Organizations can create specific rules based on attributes and the authorizations (i.e., privileges) to perform needed operations on the systems associated with the organization-defined attributes and rules. When users are assigned to attributes defined in ABAC policies or rules, they can be provisioned to a system with appropriate privileges or dynamically granted access to a protected resource upon access. ABAC can be implemented either as a mandatory or discretionary form of access control. For organizations implementing ABAC with mandatory access controls, the requirements in AC-3(3) define the scope of the subjects and objects covered by the policy.

Related Controls: PE-2.

References: NIST Special Publications 800-57-1, 800-57-2, 800-57-3, 800-162; NIST Interagency Report 7874.

AC-4 INFORMATION FLOW ENFORCEMENT

Control: Enforce approved authorizations for controlling the flow of information within the system and between interconnected systems based on [*Assignment: organization-defined information flow control policies*].

Supplemental Guidance: Information flow control regulates where information can travel within a system and between systems (as opposed to who is allowed to access the information) and without explicit regard to subsequent accesses to that information. Flow control restrictions include, for example, keeping export-controlled information from being transmitted in the clear to the Internet, blocking outside traffic that claims to be from within the organization, restricting web requests to the Internet that are not from the internal web proxy server, and limiting information transfers between organizations based on data structures and content. Transferring information between systems in different security domains with different security policies introduces risk that such transfers violate one or more domain security policies. In such situations, information owners or stewards provide guidance at designated policy enforcement points between interconnected systems. Organizations consider mandating specific architectural solutions when required to enforce specific security policies. Enforcement includes, for example, prohibiting information transfers between interconnected systems (i.e., allowing access only); employing hardware mechanisms to enforce one-way information flows; and implementing trustworthy regrading mechanisms to reassign security attributes and security labels.

Organizations commonly employ information flow control policies and enforcement mechanisms to control the flow of information between designated sources and destinations within systems and between interconnected systems. Flow control is based on the characteristics of the information and/or the information path. Enforcement occurs, for example, in boundary protection devices that employ rule sets or establish configuration settings that restrict system services, provide a packet-filtering capability based on header information, or message-filtering capability based on message content. Organizations also consider the trustworthiness of filtering/inspection mechanisms (i.e., hardware, firmware, and software components) that are critical to information flow enforcement. Control enhancements 3 through 22 primarily address cross-domain solution needs which focus on more advanced filtering techniques, in-depth analysis, and stronger flow enforcement mechanisms implemented in cross-domain products, for example, high-assurance guards. Such capabilities are generally not available in commercial off-the-shelf information technology products.

Related Controls: AC-3, AC-6, AC-16, AC-17, AC-19, AC-21, AU-10, CA-9, CM-7, PM-25, SC-4, SC-7, SC-16, SC-31.

Control Enhancements:

(1) INFORMATION FLOW ENFORCEMENT | OBJECT SECURITY ATTRIBUTES

Use [*Assignment: organization-defined security attributes*] associated with [*Assignment: organization-defined information, source, and destination objects*] to enforce [*Assignment: organization-defined information flow control policies*] as a basis for flow control decisions.

Supplemental Guidance: Information flow enforcement mechanisms compare security attributes associated with information (data content and data structure) and source/destination objects, and respond appropriately when the mechanisms encounter information flows not explicitly allowed by information flow policies. For example, an information object labeled *Secret* would be allowed to flow to a destination object labeled *Secret*, but an information object labeled *Top Secret* would not be allowed to flow to a destination object labeled *Secret*. Security attributes can also include, for example, source and destination addresses employed in traffic filter firewalls. Flow enforcement using explicit security attributes can be used, for example, to control the release of certain types of information.

Related Controls: None.

(2) INFORMATION FLOW ENFORCEMENT | PROCESSING DOMAINS

Use protected processing domains to enforce [*Assignment: organization-defined information flow control policies*] as a basis for flow control decisions.

Supplemental Guidance: Within systems, protected processing domains are processing spaces that have controlled interactions with other processing spaces, enabling control of information flows between these spaces and to/from data/information objects. A protected processing domain can be provided, for example, by implementing domain and type enforcement. In domain and type enforcement, system processes are assigned to domains; information is identified by types; and information flows are controlled based on allowed information accesses (determined by domain and type), allowed signaling among domains, and allowed process transitions to other domains.

Related Controls: SC-39.

(3) INFORMATION FLOW ENFORCEMENT | DYNAMIC INFORMATION FLOW CONTROL

Enforce dynamic information flow control based on [*Assignment: organization-defined policies*].

Supplemental Guidance: Organizational policies regarding dynamic information flow control include, for example, allowing or disallowing information flows based on changing conditions or mission/operational considerations. Changing conditions include, for example, changes in organizational risk tolerance due to changes in the immediacy of mission/business needs, changes in the threat environment, and detection of potentially harmful or adverse events.

Related Controls: SI-4.

(4) INFORMATION FLOW ENFORCEMENT | FLOW CONTROL OF ENCRYPTED INFORMATION

Prevent encrypted information from bypassing [*Assignment: organization-defined flow control mechanisms*] by [*Selection (one or more): decrypting the information; blocking the flow of the encrypted information; terminating communications sessions attempting to pass encrypted information*; [*Assignment: organization-defined procedure or method*]].

Supplemental Guidance: Content checking, security policy filters, and data type identifiers are examples of flow control mechanisms.

Related Controls: SI-4.

(5) INFORMATION FLOW ENFORCEMENT | EMBEDDED DATA TYPES

Enforce [*Assignment: organization-defined limitations*] on embedding data types within other data types.

Supplemental Guidance: Embedding data types within other data types may result in reduced flow control effectiveness. Data type embedding includes, for example, inserting executable files as objects within word processing files, inserting references or descriptive information into a media file, and compressed or archived data types that may include multiple embedded data types. Limitations on data type embedding consider the levels of embedding and prohibit levels of data type embedding that are beyond the capability of the inspection tools.

Related Controls: None.

(6) INFORMATION FLOW ENFORCEMENT | METADATA

Enforce information flow control based on [*Assignment: organization-defined metadata*].

Supplemental Guidance: Metadata is information used to describe the characteristics of data. Metadata can include structural metadata describing data structures or descriptive metadata describing data contents. Enforcing allowed information flows based on metadata enables simpler and more effective flow control. Organizations consider the trustworthiness of metadata regarding data accuracy (i.e., knowledge that the metadata values are correct with respect to the data), data integrity (i.e., protecting against unauthorized changes to metadata tags), and the binding of metadata to the data payload (i.e., ensuring sufficiently strong binding techniques with appropriate levels of assurance).

Related Controls: AC-16, SI-7.

(7) INFORMATION FLOW ENFORCEMENT | ONE-WAY FLOW MECHANISMS

Enforce [*Assignment: organization-defined one-way information flows*] using hardware mechanisms.

Supplemental Guidance: None.

Related Controls: None.

(8) INFORMATION FLOW ENFORCEMENT | SECURITY POLICY FILTERS

Enforce information flow control using [*Assignment: organization-defined security policy filters*] as a basis for flow control decisions for [*Assignment: organization-defined information flows*].

Supplemental Guidance: Organization-defined security policy filters can address data structures and content. For example, security policy filters for data structures can check for maximum file lengths, maximum field sizes, and data/file types (for structured and unstructured data). Security policy filters for data content can check for specific words enumerated values or data value ranges, and hidden content. Structured data permits the interpretation of data content by applications. Unstructured data refers to digital information without a data structure or with a data structure that does not facilitate the development of rule sets to address the sensitivity of the information conveyed by the data or the flow enforcement decisions. Unstructured data consists of bitmap objects that are inherently non-language-based (i.e., image, video, or audio files); and textual objects that are based on written or printed languages. Organizations can implement more than one security policy filter to meet information flow control objectives.

Related Controls: None.

(9) INFORMATION FLOW ENFORCEMENT | HUMAN REVIEWS

Enforce the use of human reviews for [*Assignment: organization-defined information flows*] under the following conditions: [*Assignment: organization-defined conditions*].

Supplemental Guidance: Organizations define security policy filters for all situations where automated flow control decisions are possible. When a fully automated flow control decision is not possible, then a human review may be employed in lieu of, or as a complement to, automated security policy filtering. Human reviews may also be employed as deemed necessary by organizations.

Related Controls: None.

(10) INFORMATION FLOW ENFORCEMENT | ENABLE AND DISABLE SECURITY POLICY FILTERS

Provide the capability for privileged administrators to enable and disable [*Assignment: organization-defined security policy filters*] under the following conditions: [*Assignment: organization-defined conditions*].

Supplemental Guidance: For example, as allowed by the system authorization, administrators can enable security policy filters to accommodate approved data types.

Related Controls: None.

(11) INFORMATION FLOW ENFORCEMENT | CONFIGURATION OF SECURITY POLICY FILTERS

Provide the capability for privileged administrators to configure [*Assignment: organization-defined security policy filters*] to support different security policies.

Supplemental Guidance: For example, to reflect changes in security policies, administrators can change the list of "dirty words" that security policy mechanisms check in accordance with the definitions provided by organizations.

Related Controls: None.

(12) INFORMATION FLOW ENFORCEMENT | DATA TYPE IDENTIFIERS

When transferring information between different security domains, use [*Assignment: organization-defined data type identifiers*] to validate data essential for information flow decisions.

Supplemental Guidance: Data type identifiers include, for example, filenames, file types, file signatures/tokens, and multiple internal file signatures/tokens. Systems may allow transfer of data only if compliant with data type format specifications.

Related Controls: None.

(13) INFORMATION FLOW ENFORCEMENT | DECOMPOSITION INTO POLICY-RELEVANT SUBCOMPONENTS

When transferring information between different security domains, decompose information into [*Assignment: organization-defined policy-relevant subcomponents*] for submission to policy enforcement mechanisms.

Supplemental Guidance: Policy enforcement mechanisms apply filtering, inspection, and/or sanitization rules to the policy-relevant subcomponents of information to facilitate flow enforcement prior to transferring such information to different security domains. Parsing transfer files facilitates policy decisions on source, destination, certificates, classification, attachments, and other security-related component differentiators.

Related Controls: None.

(14) INFORMATION FLOW ENFORCEMENT | SECURITY POLICY FILTER CONSTRAINTS

When transferring information between different security domains, implement [*Assignment: organization-defined security policy filters*] requiring fully enumerated formats that restrict data structure and content.

Supplemental Guidance: Data structure and content restrictions reduce the range of potential malicious or unsanctioned content in cross-domain transactions. Security policy filters that restrict data structures include, for example, restricting file sizes and field lengths. Data content policy filters include, for example, encoding formats for character sets; restricting character data fields to only contain alpha-numeric characters; prohibiting special characters; and validating schema structures.

Related Controls: None.

(15) INFORMATION FLOW ENFORCEMENT | DETECTION OF UNSANCTIONED INFORMATION

When transferring information between different security domains, examine the information for the presence of [*Assignment: organized-defined unsanctioned information*] and prohibit the transfer of such information in accordance with the [*Assignment: organization-defined security policy*].

Supplemental Guidance: Detection of unsanctioned Information includes, for example, checking all information to be transferred for malicious code and dirty words.

Related Controls: SI-3.

(16) INFORMATION FLOW ENFORCEMENT | INFORMATION TRANSFERS ON INTERCONNECTED SYSTEMS

[Withdrawn: Incorporated into AC-4].

(17) INFORMATION FLOW ENFORCEMENT | DOMAIN AUTHENTICATION

Uniquely identify and authenticate source and destination points by [*Selection (one or more): organization, system, application, service, individual*] for information transfer.

Supplemental Guidance: Attribution is a critical component of a security concept of operations. The ability to identify source and destination points for information flowing in systems, allows the forensic reconstruction of events when required, and encourages policy compliance by attributing policy violations to specific organizations/individuals. Successful domain authentication requires that system labels distinguish among systems, organizations, and individuals involved in preparing, sending, receiving, or disseminating information.

Related Controls: IA-2, IA-3, IA-9.

(18) INFORMATION FLOW ENFORCEMENT | SECURITY ATTRIBUTE BINDING

[Withdrawn: Incorporated into AC-16].

(19) INFORMATION FLOW ENFORCEMENT | VALIDATION OF METADATA

When transferring information between different security domains, apply the same security policy filtering to metadata as it applies to data payloads.

Supplemental Guidance: This control enhancement requires the validation of metadata and the data to which the metadata applies. Some organizations distinguish between metadata and data payloads (i.e., only the data to which the metadata is bound). Other organizations do not make such distinctions, considering metadata and the data to which the metadata applies as part of the payload. All information (including metadata and the data to which the metadata applies) is subject to filtering and inspection.

Related Controls: None.

(20) INFORMATION FLOW ENFORCEMENT | APPROVED SOLUTIONS

Employ [*Assignment: organization-defined solutions in approved configurations*] to control the flow of [*Assignment: organization-defined information*] across security domains.

Supplemental Guidance: Organizations define approved solutions and configurations in cross-domain policies and guidance in accordance with the types of information flows across classification boundaries. The Unified Cross Domain Management Office provides a baseline listing of approved cross-domain solutions.

Related Controls: None.

(21) INFORMATION FLOW ENFORCEMENT | PHYSICAL AND LOGICAL SEPARATION OF INFORMATION FLOWS

Separate information flows logically or physically using [*Assignment: organization-defined mechanisms and/or techniques*] to accomplish [*Assignment: organization-defined required separations by types of information*].

Supplemental Guidance: Enforcing the separation of information flows by type can enhance protection by ensuring that information is not commingled while in transit and by enabling flow control by transmission paths perhaps not otherwise achievable. Types of separable information include, for example, inbound and outbound communications traffic, service requests and responses, and information of differing security categories.

Related Controls: SC-32.

(22) INFORMATION FLOW ENFORCEMENT | ACCESS ONLY

Provide access from a single device to computing platforms, applications, or data residing on multiple different security domains, while preventing any information flow between the different security domains.

Supplemental Guidance: The system, for example, provides a desktop for users to access each connected security domain without providing any mechanisms to allow transfer of information between the different security domains.

Related Controls: None.

References: NIST Special Publications 800-162, 800-178.

AC-5 SEPARATION OF DUTIES

Control:

a. Separate [*Assignment: organization-defined duties of individuals*];

b. Document separation of duties of individuals; and

c. Define system access authorizations to support separation of duties.

Supplemental Guidance: Separation of duties addresses the potential for abuse of authorized privileges and helps to reduce the risk of malevolent activity without collusion. Separation of duties includes, for example, dividing mission functions and system support functions among different individuals and/or roles; conducting system support functions with different individuals; and ensuring security personnel administering access control functions do not also administer audit functions. Because separation of duty violations can span systems and application domains, organizations consider the entirety of organizational systems and system components when developing policy on separation of duties.

Related Controls: AC-2, AC-3, AC-6, AU-9, CM-5, CM-11, CP-9, IA-2, IA-5, MA-3, MA-5, PS-2, SA-17.

Control Enhancements: None.

References: None.

AC-6 LEAST PRIVILEGE

Control: Employ the principle of least privilege, allowing only authorized accesses for users (or processes acting on behalf of users) which are necessary to accomplish assigned tasks in accordance with organizational missions and business functions.

Supplemental Guidance: Organizations employ least privilege for specific duties and systems. The principle of least privilege is also applied to system processes, ensuring that the processes operate at privilege levels no higher than necessary to accomplish required organizational missions or business functions. Organizations consider the creation of additional processes, roles, and system accounts as necessary, to achieve least privilege. Organizations also apply least privilege to the development, implementation, and operation of organizational systems.

Related Controls: AC-2, AC-3, AC-5, AC-16, CM-5, CM-11, PL-2, PM-12, SA-15, SA-17, SC-38.

Control Enhancements:

(1) LEAST PRIVILEGE | AUTHORIZE ACCESS TO SECURITY FUNCTIONS
   Explicitly authorize access to [*Assignment: organization-defined security functions (deployed in hardware, software, and firmware) and security-relevant information*].

   Supplemental Guidance: Security functions include, for example, establishing system accounts, configuring access authorizations (i.e., permissions, privileges), setting events to be audited, and establishing intrusion detection parameters. Security-relevant information includes, for example, filtering rules for routers/firewalls, cryptographic key management information, configuration parameters for security services, and access control lists. Explicitly authorized personnel include, for example, security administrators, system and network administrators, system security officers, system maintenance personnel, system programmers, and other privileged users.

   Related Controls: AC-17, AC-18, AC-19, AU-9, PE-2.

(2) LEAST PRIVILEGE | NON-PRIVILEGED ACCESS FOR NONSECURITY FUNCTIONS

Require that users of system accounts, or roles, with access to [*Assignment: organization-defined security functions or security-relevant information*], use non-privileged accounts or roles, when accessing nonsecurity functions.

Supplemental Guidance: This control enhancement limits exposure when operating from within privileged accounts or roles. The inclusion of roles addresses situations where organizations implement access control policies such as role-based access control and where a change of role provides the same degree of assurance in the change of access authorizations for both the user and all processes acting on behalf of the user as would be provided by a change between a privileged and non-privileged account.

Related Controls: AC-17, AC-18, AC-19, PL-4.

(3) LEAST PRIVILEGE | NETWORK ACCESS TO PRIVILEGED COMMANDS

Authorize network access to [*Assignment: organization-defined privileged commands*] only for [*Assignment: organization-defined compelling operational needs*] and document the rationale for such access in the security plan for the system.

Supplemental Guidance: Network access is any access across a network connection in lieu of local access (i.e., user being physically present at the device).

Related Controls: AC-17, AC-18, AC-19.

(4) LEAST PRIVILEGE | SEPARATE PROCESSING DOMAINS

Provide separate processing domains to enable finer-grained allocation of user privileges.

Supplemental Guidance: Providing separate processing domains for finer-grained allocation of user privileges includes, for example, using virtualization techniques to allow additional user privileges within a virtual machine while restricting privileges to other virtual machines or to the underlying actual machine; employing hardware/software domain separation mechanisms; and implementing separate physical domains.

Related Controls: AC-4, SC-2, SC-3, SC-30, SC-32, SC-39.

(5) LEAST PRIVILEGE | PRIVILEGED ACCOUNTS

Restrict privileged accounts on the system to [*Assignment: organization-defined personnel or roles*].

Supplemental Guidance: Privileged accounts, including super user accounts, are typically described as system administrator for various types of commercial off-the-shelf operating systems. Restricting privileged accounts to specific personnel or roles prevents day-to-day users from having access to privileged information/functions. Organizations may differentiate in the application of this control enhancement between allowed privileges for local accounts and for domain accounts provided they retain the ability to control system configurations for key security parameters and as otherwise necessary to sufficiently mitigate risk.

Related Controls: IA-2, MA-3, MA-4.

(6) LEAST PRIVILEGE | PRIVILEGED ACCESS BY NON-ORGANIZATIONAL USERS

Prohibit privileged access to the system by non-organizational users.

Supplemental Guidance: None.

Related Controls: AC-18, AC-19, IA-2, IA-8.

(7) LEAST PRIVILEGE | REVIEW OF USER PRIVILEGES

(a) **Review [*Assignment: organization-defined frequency*] the privileges assigned to [*Assignment: organization-defined roles or classes of users*] to validate the need for such privileges; and**

(b) **Reassign or remove privileges, if necessary, to correctly reflect organizational mission and business needs.**

Supplemental Guidance: The need for certain assigned user privileges may change over time reflecting changes in organizational missions and business functions, environments of operation, technologies, or threat. Periodic review of assigned user privileges is necessary to determine if the rationale for assigning such privileges remains valid. If the need cannot be revalidated, organizations take appropriate corrective actions.

Related Controls: CA-7.

(8) LEAST PRIVILEGE | PRIVILEGE LEVELS FOR CODE EXECUTION

**Prevent the following software from executing at higher privilege levels than users executing the
software: [*Assignment: organization-defined software*].**

Supplemental Guidance: In certain situations, software applications/programs need to execute
with elevated privileges to perform required functions. However, if the privileges required for
execution are at a higher level than the privileges assigned to organizational users invoking
such applications/programs, those users are indirectly provided with greater privileges than
assigned by organizations.

Related Controls: None.

(9) LEAST PRIVILEGE | AUDITING USE OF PRIVILEGED FUNCTIONS

Audit the execution of privileged functions.

Supplemental Guidance: Misuse of privileged functions, either intentionally or unintentionally
by authorized users, or by unauthorized external entities that have compromised system
accounts, is a serious and ongoing concern and can have significant adverse impacts on
organizations. Auditing the use of privileged functions is one way to detect such misuse, and
in doing so, help mitigate the risk from insider threats and the advanced persistent threat.

Related Controls: AU-2, AU-12.

(10) LEAST PRIVILEGE | PROHIBIT NON-PRIVILEGED USERS FROM EXECUTING PRIVILEGED FUNCTIONS

Prevent non-privileged users from executing privileged functions.

Supplemental Guidance: Privileged functions include, for example, disabling, circumventing, or
altering implemented security or privacy controls, establishing system accounts, performing
system integrity checks, or administering cryptographic key management activities. Non-
privileged users are individuals that do not possess appropriate authorizations. Circumventing
intrusion detection and prevention mechanisms or malicious code protection mechanisms are
examples of privileged functions that require protection from non-privileged users.

Related Controls: None.

References: None.

AC-7   UNSUCCESSFUL LOGON ATTEMPTS

Control:

a. Enforce a limit of [*Assignment: organization-defined number*] consecutive invalid logon
attempts by a user during a [*Assignment: organization-defined time-period*]; and

b. Automatically [*Selection (one or more): lock the account/node for an* [*Assignment:
organization-defined time-period*]; *lock the account/node until released by an administrator;
delay next logon prompt per* [*Assignment: organization-defined delay algorithm*]; *take*
[*Assignment: organization-defined action*]] when the maximum number of unsuccessful
attempts is exceeded.

Supplemental Guidance: This control applies regardless of whether the logon occurs via a local or
network connection. Due to the potential for denial of service, automatic lockouts initiated by
systems are usually temporary and automatically release after a predetermined time established by
organizations. If a delay algorithm is selected, organizations may employ different algorithms for
different components of the system based on the capabilities of those components. Responses to
unsuccessful logon attempts may be implemented at both the operating system and the application
levels.

Related Controls: AC-2, AC-9, AU-2, AU-6, IA-5.

Control Enhancements:

(1) UNSUCCESSFUL LOGON ATTEMPTS | AUTOMATIC ACCOUNT LOCK

[Withdrawn: Incorporated into AC-7].

(2) UNSUCCESSFUL LOGON ATTEMPTS | PURGE OR WIPE MOBILE DEVICE

Purge or wipe information from [*Assignment: organization-defined mobile devices*] based on [*Assignment: organization-defined purging or wiping requirements and techniques*] after [*Assignment: organization-defined number*] consecutive, unsuccessful device logon attempts.

Supplemental Guidance: This control enhancement applies only to mobile devices for which a logon occurs. The logon is to the mobile device, not to any one account on the device. Successful logons to accounts on mobile devices reset the unsuccessful logon count to zero. Purging or wiping may be unnecessary if the information on the device is protected with sufficiently strong encryption mechanisms.

Related Controls: AC-19, MP-5, MP-6.

(3) UNSUCCESSFUL LOGON ATTEMPTS | BIOMETRIC ATTEMPT LIMITING

Limit the number of unsuccessful biometric logon attempts to [*Assignment: organization-defined number*].

Supplemental Guidance: Biometrics are probabilistic in nature. The ability to successfully authenticate can be impacted by many factors, including matching performance and presentation attack detection mechanisms. Organizations select the appropriate number of attempts and fall back mechanisms for users based on these, and other organizationally defined factors.

Related Controls: IA-3.

(4) UNSUCCESSFUL LOGON ATTEMPTS | USE OF ALTERNATE FACTOR

Allow the use of one or more additional authentication factors after the number of organization-defined consecutive invalid logon attempts have been exceeded.

Supplemental Guidance: This control enhancement supports the objective of availability and allows a user that has inadvertently been locked out to use additional authentication factors to bypass the lockout.

Related Controls: IA-3.

References: NIST Special Publications 800-63, 800-124.

AC-8   SYSTEM USE NOTIFICATION

Control:

a. Display [*Assignment: organization-defined system use notification message or banner*] to users before granting access to the system that provides privacy and security notices consistent with applicable laws, Executive Orders, directives, policies, regulations, standards, and guidelines and state that:

1. Users are accessing a U.S. Government system;

2. System usage may be monitored, recorded, and subject to audit;

3. Unauthorized use of the system is prohibited and subject to criminal and civil penalties; and

4. Use of the system indicates consent to monitoring and recording;

b. Retain the notification message or banner on the screen until users acknowledge the usage conditions and take explicit actions to log on to or further access the system; and

c. For publicly accessible systems:

1. Display system use information [*Assignment: organization-defined conditions*], before granting further access to the publicly accessible system;

2. Display references, if any, to monitoring, recording, or auditing that are consistent with privacy accommodations for such systems that generally prohibit those activities; and

3. Include a description of the authorized uses of the system.

Supplemental Guidance: System use notifications can be implemented using messages or warning banners displayed before individuals log in to systems. System use notifications are used only for access via logon interfaces with human users. Such notifications are not required when human interfaces do not exist. Based on an assessment of risk, organizations consider whether or not a secondary system use notification is needed to access applications or other system resources after the initial network logon. Organizations consider system use notification messages or banners displayed in multiple languages based on organizational needs and the demographics of system users. Organizations also consult with the Office of the General Counsel for legal review and approval of warning banner content.

Related Controls: AC-14, PL-4, SI-4.

Control Enhancements: None.

References: None.

AC-9 PREVIOUS LOGON (ACCESS) NOTIFICATION

Control: Notify the user, upon successful logon (access) to the system, of the date and time of the last logon (access).

Supplemental Guidance: This control is applicable to logons to systems via human user interfaces and logons to systems that occur in other types of architectures.

Related Controls: AC-7, PL-4.

Control Enhancements:

(1) PREVIOUS LOGON NOTIFICATION | UNSUCCESSFUL LOGONS

Notify the user, upon successful logon/access, of the number of unsuccessful logon/access attempts since the last successful logon/access.

Supplemental Guidance: None.

Related Controls: None.

(2) PREVIOUS LOGON NOTIFICATION | SUCCESSFUL AND UNSUCCESSFUL LOGONS

Notify the user, upon successful logon/access, of the number of [Selection: successful logons/accesses; unsuccessful logon/access attempts; both] during [Assignment: organization-defined time-period].

Supplemental Guidance: None.

Related Controls: None.

(3) PREVIOUS LOGON NOTIFICATION | NOTIFICATION OF ACCOUNT CHANGES

Notify the user, upon successful logon/access, of changes to [Assignment: organization-defined security-related characteristics/parameters of the user's account] during [Assignment: organization-defined time-period].

Supplemental Guidance: None.

Related Controls: None.

(4) PREVIOUS LOGON NOTIFICATION | ADDITIONAL LOGON INFORMATION

Notify the user, upon successful logon/access, of the following additional information: [Assignment: organization-defined information to be included in addition to the date and time of the last logon/access].

Supplemental Guidance: This control enhancement permits organizations to specify additional information to be provided to users upon logon including, for example, the location of last logon. User location is defined as that information which can be determined by systems, for example, Internet Protocol (IP) addresses from which network logons occurred, notifications of local logons, or device identifiers.

Related Controls: None.

References: None.

AC-10   CONCURRENT SESSION CONTROL

Control: Limit the number of concurrent sessions for each [*Assignment: organization-defined account and/or account type*] to [*Assignment: organization-defined number*].

Supplemental Guidance: Organizations may define the maximum number of concurrent sessions for system accounts globally, by account type, by account, or a combination thereof. For example, organizations may limit the number of concurrent sessions for system administrators or other individuals working in particularly sensitive domains or mission-critical applications. This control addresses concurrent sessions for system accounts and does not address concurrent sessions by single users via multiple system accounts.

Related Controls: SC-23.

Control Enhancements: None.

References: None.

AC-11   DEVICE LOCK

Control:

a.   Prevent further access to the system by initiating a device lock after [*Assignment: organization-defined time-period*] of inactivity or upon receiving a request from a user; and

b.   Retain the device lock until the user reestablishes access using established identification and authentication procedures.

Supplemental Guidance: Device locks are temporary actions taken to prevent logical access to organizational systems when users stop work and move away from the immediate vicinity of those systems but do not want to log out because of the temporary nature of their absences. Device locks are implemented where session activities can be determined. This is typically at the operating system level, but can also be at the application level. Device locks are not an acceptable substitute for logging out of systems, for example, if organizations require users to log out at the end of workdays.

Related Controls: AC-2, AC-7, IA-11.

Control Enhancements:

(1)   DEVICE LOCK | PATTERN-HIDING DISPLAYS

Conceal, via the device lock, information previously visible on the display with a publicly viewable image.

Supplemental Guidance: The pattern-hiding display can include static or dynamic images, for example, patterns used with screen savers, photographic images, solid colors, clock, battery life indicator, or a blank screen, with the caveat that controlled unclassified information is not displayed.

Related Controls: None.

(2)   DEVICE LOCK | REQUIRE USER-INITIATED LOCK

Require the user to initiate a device lock before leaving the system unattended.

Supplemental Guidance: This control enhancement is behavior/policy-based and as such, requires users to take physical action to initiate the device lock.

Related Controls: PL-4.

References: None.

AC-12   SESSION TERMINATION

Control: Automatically terminate a user session after [*Assignment: organization-defined conditions or trigger events requiring session disconnect*].

<u>Supplemental Guidance</u>: This control addresses the termination of user-initiated logical sessions in contrast to SC-10 which addresses the termination of network connections that are associated with communications sessions (i.e., network disconnect). A logical session (for local, network, and remote access) is initiated whenever a user (or process acting on behalf of a user) accesses an organizational system. Such user sessions can be terminated without terminating network sessions. Session termination terminates all processes associated with a user's logical session except those processes that are specifically created by the user (i.e., session owner) to continue after the session is terminated. Conditions or trigger events requiring automatic session termination can include, for example, organization-defined periods of user inactivity, targeted responses to certain types of incidents, time-of-day restrictions on system use.

<u>Related Controls</u>: MA-4, SC-10, SC-23.

<u>Control Enhancements</u>:

(1) SESSION TERMINATION | USER-INITIATED LOGOUTS

Provide a logout capability for user-initiated communications sessions whenever authentication is used to gain access to [*Assignment: organization-defined information resources*].

<u>Supplemental Guidance</u>: Information resources to which users gain access via authentication include, for example, local workstations, databases, and password-protected websites/web-based services.

<u>Related Controls</u>: None.

(2) SESSION TERMINATION | TERMINATION MESSAGE

Display an explicit logout message to users indicating the reliable termination of authenticated communications sessions.

<u>Supplemental Guidance</u>: Logout messages for web page access, for example, can be displayed after authenticated sessions have been terminated. However, for some types of interactive sessions including, for example, file transfer protocol (FTP) sessions, systems typically send logout messages as final messages prior to terminating sessions.

<u>Related Controls</u>: None.

(3) SESSION TERMINATION | TIMEOUT WARNING MESSAGE

Display an explicit message to users indicating that the session is about to end.

<u>Supplemental Guidance</u>: To increase usability, notify users of pending session termination and prompt for activity if users desire to continue the session.

<u>Related Controls</u>: None.

<u>References</u>: None.

AC-13 SUPERVISION AND REVIEW — ACCESS CONTROL

[Withdrawn: Incorporated into AC-2 and AU-6].

AC-14 PERMITTED ACTIONS WITHOUT IDENTIFICATION OR AUTHENTICATION

<u>Control</u>:

a. Identify [*Assignment: organization-defined user actions*] that can be performed on the system without identification or authentication consistent with organizational missions and business functions; and

b. Document and provide supporting rationale in the security plan for the system, user actions not requiring identification or authentication.

<u>Supplemental Guidance</u>: This control addresses situations in which organizations determine that no identification or authentication is required in organizational systems. Organizations may allow a limited number of user actions without identification or authentication including, for example, when individuals access public websites or other publicly accessible federal systems, when individuals use mobile phones to receive calls, or when facsimiles are received. Organizations also

identify actions that normally require identification or authentication but may under certain circumstances, allow identification or authentication mechanisms to be bypassed. Such bypasses may occur, for example, via a software-readable physical switch that commands bypass of the logon functionality and is protected from accidental or unmonitored use. This control does not apply to situations where identification and authentication have already occurred and are not repeated, but rather to situations where identification and authentication have not yet occurred. Organizations may decide that there are no user actions that can be performed on organizational systems without identification and authentication and therefore, the values for assignment statements can be *none*.

Related Controls: AC-8, IA-2, PL-2.

Control Enhancements: None.

(1) PERMITTED ACTIONS WITHOUT IDENTIFICATION OR AUTHENTICATION | NECESSARY USES
[Withdrawn: Incorporated into AC-14].

References: None.

AC-15 AUTOMATED MARKING

[Withdrawn: Incorporated into MP-3].

AC-16 SECURITY AND PRIVACY ATTRIBUTES

Control:

a. Provide the means to associate [*Assignment: organization-defined types of security and privacy attributes*] having [*Assignment: organization-defined security and privacy attribute values*] with information in storage, in process, and/or in transmission;

b. Ensure that the security and privacy attribute associations are made and retained with the information;

c. Establish the permitted [*Assignment: organization-defined security attributes*] for [*Assignment: organization-defined systems*]; and

d. Determine the permitted [*Assignment: organization-defined values or ranges*] for each of the established security and privacy attributes.

Supplemental Guidance: Information is represented internally within systems using abstractions known as data structures. Internal data structures can represent different types of entities, both active and passive. Active entities, also known as *subjects*, are typically associated with individuals, devices, or processes acting on behalf of individuals. Passive entities, also known as *objects*, are typically associated with data structures such as records, buffers, tables, files, inter-process pipes, and communications ports. Security attributes, a form of metadata, are abstractions representing the basic properties or characteristics of active and passive entities with respect to safeguarding information. Privacy attributes, which may be used independently, or in conjunction with security attributes, represent the basic properties or characteristics of an entity with respect to the management of personally identifiable information. Such attributes are used to enable the implementation of the need for the record in the performance of duties, the identification of personal information within data objects, and the identification of permitted uses of personal information. Attributes can be explicitly or implicitly associated with the information contained in organizational systems or system components.

Security and privacy attributes may be associated with active entities (i.e., subjects) that have the potential to send or receive information, to cause information to flow among objects, or to change the system state. These attributes may also be associated with passive entities (i.e., objects) that contain or receive information. The association of security and privacy attributes to subjects and objects is referred to as binding and is inclusive of setting the attribute value and the attribute type. Security and privacy attributes when bound to data or information, enable the enforcement of security policies for access control and information flow control and privacy policies including, for example, for data retention limits and permitted uses of personally identifiable information. Such enforcement occurs through organizational processes or system functions or mechanisms. Binding techniques implemented by systems affect the strength of attribute binding to information. Binding strength and the assurance associated with binding techniques play an important part in the trust organizations have in the information flow enforcement process. The binding techniques affect the number and degree of additional reviews required by organizations. The content or assigned values of the security and privacy attributes can directly affect the ability of individuals to access organizational information.

Organizations can define the types of attributes needed for selected systems to support missions or business functions. There is potentially a wide range of values that can be assigned to any given security attribute. Release markings can include, for example, US only, NATO, or NOFORN (not releasable to foreign nationals). By specifying permitted attribute ranges and values, organizations ensure that the security and privacy attribute values are meaningful and relevant. Labeling refers to the association of security and privacy attributes with subjects and objects represented by the internal data structures within organizational systems. This facilitates system-based enforcement of information security and privacy policies. Labels include, for example, access authorizations, nationality, data life cycle protection (i.e., encryption and data expiration), data subject consents, permissible data uses, affiliation as contractor, and classification of information in accordance with legal and compliance requirements. Conversely, marking refers to the association of security and privacy attributes with objects in a human-readable form. This enables manual, procedural, or process-based enforcement of information security and privacy policies. Examples of attribute types include classification level for objects and clearance (access authorization) level for subjects. An attribute value for both attribute types is *Top Secret*.

Related Controls: AC-3, AC-4, AC-6, AC-21, AC-25, AU-2, AU-10, IP-2, MP-3, PE-22, SC-11, SC-16, SI-12.

Control Enhancements:

(1) SECURITY AND PRIVACY ATTRIBUTES | DYNAMIC ATTRIBUTE ASSOCIATION

Dynamically associate security and privacy attributes with [*Assignment: organization-defined subjects and objects*] in accordance with [*Assignment: organization-defined security and privacy policies*] as information is created and combined.

Supplemental Guidance: Dynamic association of security and privacy attributes is appropriate whenever the security or privacy characteristics of information changes over time. Attributes may change, for example, due to information aggregation issues (i.e., the security and privacy characteristics of individual information elements are different from the combined elements), changes in individual access authorizations (i.e., privileges), changes in the security category of information, and changes in security or privacy policies.

Related Controls: None.

(2) SECURITY AND PRIVACY ATTRIBUTES | ATTRIBUTE VALUE CHANGES BY AUTHORIZED INDIVIDUALS

Provide authorized individuals (or processes acting on behalf of individuals) the capability to define or change the value of associated security and privacy attributes.

Supplemental Guidance: The content or assigned values of security and privacy attributes can directly affect the ability of individuals to access organizational information. Therefore, it is important for systems to be able to limit the ability to create or modify attributes to authorized individuals.

Related Controls: None.

(3) SECURITY AND PRIVACY ATTRIBUTES | MAINTENANCE OF ATTRIBUTE ASSOCIATIONS BY SYSTEM

Maintain the association and integrity of [*Assignment: organization-defined security and privacy attributes*] to [*Assignment: organization-defined subjects and objects*].

Supplemental Guidance: Maintaining the association and integrity of security and privacy attributes to subjects and objects with sufficient assurance helps to ensure that the attribute associations can be used as the basis of automated policy actions. Automated policy actions include, for example, retention date expirations, access control decisions, and information flow control decisions.

Related Controls None.

(4) SECURITY AND PRIVACY ATTRIBUTES | ASSOCIATION OF ATTRIBUTES BY AUTHORIZED INDIVIDUALS

Provide the capability to associate [*Assignment: organization-defined security and privacy attributes*] with [*Assignment: organization-defined subjects and objects*] by authorized individuals (or processes acting on behalf of individuals).

Supplemental Guidance: The support provided by systems can include, for example, prompting users to select specific security or privacy attributes to be associated with specific information objects; employing automated mechanisms to categorize information with appropriate security or privacy attributes based on defined policies; or ensuring that the combination of selected security or privacy attributes selected is valid. Organizations consider the creation, deletion, or modification of security and privacy attributes when defining auditable events.

Related Controls: None.

(5) SECURITY AND PRIVACY ATTRIBUTES | ATTRIBUTE DISPLAYS FOR OUTPUT DEVICES

Display security and privacy attributes in human-readable form on each object that the system transmits to output devices to identify [*Assignment: organization-identified special dissemination, handling, or distribution instructions*] using [*Assignment: organization-identified human-readable, standard naming conventions*].

Supplemental Guidance: System outputs include, for example, pages, screens, or equivalent. System output devices include, for example, printers, notebook computers, video displays on workstations, and personal digital assistants. To mitigate the risk of unauthorized exposure of selected information, for example, shoulder surfing, the outputs display full attribute values when unmasked by the subscriber.

Related Controls: None.

(6) SECURITY AND PRIVACY ATTRIBUTES | MAINTENANCE OF ATTRIBUTE ASSOCIATION BY ORGANIZATION

Require personnel to associate, and maintain the association of [*Assignment: organization-defined security and privacy attributes*] with [*Assignment: organization-defined subjects and objects*] in accordance with [*Assignment: organization-defined security and privacy policies*].

Supplemental Guidance: This control enhancement requires individual users (as opposed to the system) to maintain associations of security and privacy attributes with subjects and objects.

Related Controls: None.

(7) SECURITY AND PRIVACY ATTRIBUTES | CONSISTENT ATTRIBUTE INTERPRETATION

Provide a consistent interpretation of security and privacy attributes transmitted between distributed system components.

Supplemental Guidance: To enforce security and privacy policies across multiple components in distributed systems, organizations provide a consistent interpretation of the attributes used in access enforcement and flow enforcement decisions. Organizations establish agreements and processes to ensure that all distributed system components implement security and privacy attributes with consistent interpretations in automated access and flow enforcement actions.

Related Controls: None.

(8) SECURITY AND PRIVACY ATTRIBUTES | ASSOCIATION TECHNIQUES AND TECHNOLOGIES

Implement [*Assignment: organization-defined techniques and technologies*] with [*Assignment: organization-defined level of assurance*] in associating security and privacy attributes to information.

Supplemental Guidance: The association (i.e., binding) of security and privacy attributes to information within systems is important for conducting automated access enforcement and flow enforcement actions. The association of such attributes can be accomplished with technologies and techniques providing different levels of assurance. For example, systems can cryptographically bind attributes to information using digital signatures with the supporting cryptographic keys protected by hardware devices (sometimes known as hardware roots of trust).

Related Controls: None.

(9) SECURITY AND PRIVACY ATTRIBUTES | ATTRIBUTE REASSIGNMENT

Reassign security and privacy attributes associated with information only via re-grading mechanisms validated using [*Assignment: organization-defined techniques or procedures*].

Supplemental Guidance: Validated re-grading mechanisms are employed by organizations to provide the requisite levels of assurance for security and privacy attribute reassignment activities. The validation is facilitated by ensuring that re-grading mechanisms are single purpose and of limited function. Since attribute reassignments can directly affect security and privacy policy enforcement actions, using trustworthy re-grading mechanisms is necessary to ensure that such mechanisms perform in a consistent and correct mode of operation.

Related Controls: None.

(10) SECURITY AND PRIVACY ATTRIBUTES | ATTRIBUTE CONFIGURATION BY AUTHORIZED INDIVIDUALS

Provide authorized individuals the capability to define or change the type and value of security and privacy attributes available for association with subjects and objects.

Supplemental Guidance: The content or assigned values of security and privacy attributes can directly affect the ability of individuals to access organizational information. Therefore, it is important for systems to be able to limit the ability to create or modify attributes to authorized individuals only.

Related Controls: None.

(11) SECURITY AND PRIVACY ATTRIBUTES | AUDIT CHANGES

Audit changes to security and privacy attributes.

Supplemental Guidance: None.

Related Controls: None.

References: FIPS Publications 140-2, 186-4; NIST Special Publications 800-162, 800-178.

AC-17 REMOTE ACCESS

Control:

a. Establish and document usage restrictions, configuration/connection requirements, and implementation guidance for each type of remote access allowed; and

b. Authorize remote access to the system prior to allowing such connections.

Supplemental Guidance: Remote access is access to organizational systems (or processes acting on behalf of users) communicating through external networks such as the Internet. Remote access methods include, for example, dial-up, broadband, and wireless. Organizations often employ encrypted virtual private networks (VPNs) to enhance confidentiality and integrity over remote connections. The use of encrypted VPNs provides sufficient assurance to the organization that it can effectively treat such connections as internal networks if the cryptographic mechanisms used are implemented in accordance with applicable laws, Executive Orders, directives, regulations, policies, standards, and guidelines. Still, VPN connections traverse external networks, and the encrypted VPN does not enhance the availability of remote connections. VPNs with encrypted tunnels can also affect the capability to adequately monitor network communications traffic for malicious code. Remote access controls apply to systems other than public web servers or systems designed for public access. This control addresses authorization prior to allowing remote access without specifying the specific formats for such authorization. While organizations may use interconnection security agreements to authorize remote access connections, such agreements are not required by this control. Enforcing access restrictions for remote connections is addressed in AC-3.

Related Controls: AC-2, AC-3, AC-4, AC-18, AC-19, AC-20, CM-10, IA-2, IA-3, IA-8, MA-4, PE-17, PL-2, PL-4, SC-10, SI-4.

Control Enhancements:

(1) REMOTE ACCESS | AUTOMATED MONITORING AND CONTROL

Monitor and control remote access methods.

Supplemental Guidance: Automated monitoring and control of remote access methods allows organizations to detect attacks and ensure compliance with remote access policies by auditing connection activities of remote users on a variety of system components including, for example, servers, workstations, notebook computers, smart phones, and tablets.

Related Controls: AU-2, AU-6, AU-12, AU-14.

(2) REMOTE ACCESS | PROTECTION OF CONFIDENTIALITY AND INTEGRITY USING ENCRYPTION

Implement cryptographic mechanisms to protect the confidentiality and integrity of remote access sessions.

Supplemental Guidance: The encryption strength of mechanism is selected based on the security categorization of the information.

Related Controls: SC-8, SC-12, SC-13.

(3) REMOTE ACCESS | MANAGED ACCESS CONTROL POINTS

Route all remote accesses through [Assignment: organization-defined number] managed network access control points.

Supplemental Guidance: Limiting the number of access control points for remote accesses reduces the attack surface for organizations. Organizations consider the Trusted Internet Connections initiative requirements for external network connections.

Related Controls: SC-7.

(4) REMOTE ACCESS | PRIVILEGED COMMANDS AND ACCESS

(a) Authorize the execution of privileged commands and access to security-relevant information via remote access only for [Assignment: organization-defined needs]; and

(b) Document the rationale for such access in the security plan for the system.

Supplemental Guidance: None.

Related Controls: AC-6.

(5) REMOTE ACCESS | MONITORING FOR UNAUTHORIZED CONNECTIONS

[Withdrawn: Incorporated into SI-4].

(6) REMOTE ACCESS | PROTECTION OF INFORMATION

Protect information about remote access mechanisms from unauthorized use and disclosure.

Supplemental Guidance: None.

Related Controls: AT-2, AT-3, PS-6.

(7) REMOTE ACCESS | ADDITIONAL PROTECTION FOR SECURITY FUNCTION ACCESS

[Withdrawn: Incorporated into AC-3(10)].

(8) REMOTE ACCESS | DISABLE NONSECURE NETWORK PROTOCOLS

[Withdrawn: Incorporated into CM-7].

(9) REMOTE ACCESS | DISCONNECT OR DISABLE ACCESS

Provide the capability to expeditiously disconnect or disable remote access to the system within [Assignment: organization-defined time-period].

Supplemental Guidance: This control enhancement requires organizations to have the capability to rapidly disconnect current users remotely accessing the system or disable further remote access. The speed of disconnect or disablement varies based on the criticality of missions or business functions and the need to eliminate immediate or future remote access to systems.

Related Controls: None.

References: NIST Special Publications 800-46, 800-77, 800-113, 800-114, 800-121; NIST Interagency Report 7966.

AC-18 WIRELESS ACCESS

Control:

a. Establish usage restrictions, configuration/connection requirements, and implementation guidance for wireless access; and

b.   Authorize wireless access to the system prior to allowing such connections.

Supplemental Guidance: Wireless technologies include, for example, microwave, packet radio (ultra-high frequency/very high frequency), 802.11x, and Bluetooth. Wireless networks use authentication protocols which provide credential protection and mutual authentication.

Related Controls: AC-2, AC-3, AC-17, AC-19, CA-9, CM-7, IA-2, IA-3, IA-8, PL-4, SC-40, SC-43, SI-4.

Control Enhancements:

(1)   WIRELESS ACCESS | AUTHENTICATION AND ENCRYPTION

Protect wireless access to the system using authentication of [*Selection (one or more): users; devices*] and encryption.

Supplemental Guidance: None.

Related Controls: SC-8, SC-13.

(2)   WIRELESS ACCESS | MONITORING UNAUTHORIZED CONNECTIONS

[Withdrawn: Incorporated into SI-4].

(3)   WIRELESS ACCESS | DISABLE WIRELESS NETWORKING

Disable, when not intended for use, wireless networking capabilities internally embedded within system components prior to issuance and deployment.

Supplemental Guidance: None.

Related Controls: None.

(4)   WIRELESS ACCESS | RESTRICT CONFIGURATIONS BY USERS

Identify and explicitly authorize users allowed to independently configure wireless networking capabilities.

Supplemental Guidance: Organizational authorizations to allow selected users to configure wireless networking capability are enforced in part, by the access enforcement mechanisms employed within organizational systems.

Related Controls: SC-7, SC-15.

(5)   WIRELESS ACCESS | ANTENNAS AND TRANSMISSION POWER LEVELS

Select radio antennas and calibrate transmission power levels to reduce the probability that signals from wireless access points can be received outside of organization-controlled boundaries.

Supplemental Guidance: Actions that may be taken by organizations to limit the unauthorized use of wireless communications outside of organization-controlled boundaries include, for example, reducing the power of wireless transmissions so that the transmissions are less likely to emit a signal that can be captured outside of the physical perimeters of the organization; employing measures such as emissions security to control wireless emanations; and using directional or beam forming antennas that reduce the likelihood that unintended receivers will be able to intercept signals. Prior to taking such mitigating actions, organizations can conduct periodic wireless surveys to understand the radio frequency profile of organizational systems as well as other systems that may be operating in the area.

Related Controls: PE-19.

References: NIST Special Publications 800-48, 800-94, 800-97.

AC-19   ACCESS CONTROL FOR MOBILE DEVICES

Control:

a.   Establish usage restrictions, configuration requirements, connection requirements, and implementation guidance for organization-controlled mobile devices;

b.   Authorize the connection of mobile devices to organizational systems; and

c.   Protect and control mobile devices when outside of controlled areas.

Supplemental Guidance: A mobile device is a computing device that has a small form factor such that it can easily be carried by a single individual; is designed to operate without a physical connection; possesses local, non-removable or removable data storage; and includes a self-contained power source. Mobile device functionality may also include voice communication capabilities, on-board sensors that allow the device to capture information, and/or built-in features for synchronizing local data with remote locations. Examples include smart phones, E-readers, and tablets. Mobile devices are typically associated with a single individual and the device is usually near the individual; however, the degree of proximity can vary depending upon on the form factor and size of the device. The processing, storage, and transmission capability of the mobile device may be comparable to or merely a subset of notebook/desktop systems, depending upon the nature and intended purpose of the device. Controlled areas are areas or spaces for which organizations provide sufficient physical or procedural safeguards to meet the requirements established for protecting information and systems.

Due to the large variety of mobile devices with different characteristics and capabilities, organizational restrictions may vary for the different classes/types of such devices. Usage restrictions and specific implementation guidance for mobile devices include, for example, configuration management, device identification and authentication, implementation of mandatory protective software, scanning devices for malicious code, updating virus protection software, scanning for critical software updates and patches, conducting primary operating system (and possibly other resident software) integrity checks, and disabling unnecessary hardware.

Usage restrictions and authorization to connect may vary among organizational systems. For example, the organization may authorize the connection of mobile devices to the organizational network and impose a set of usage restrictions while a system owner may withhold authorization for mobile device connection to specific applications or may impose additional usage restrictions before allowing mobile device connections to a system. The need to provide adequate security for mobile devices goes beyond the requirements in this control. Many safeguards for mobile devices are reflected in other security controls allocated to the initial control baselines as starting points for the development of security plans and overlays using the tailoring process. There may also be some overlap by the security controls within the different families of controls. AC-20 addresses mobile devices that are not organization-controlled.

Related Controls: AC-3, AC-4, AC-7, AC-17, AC-18, AC-20, CA-9, CM-2, CM-6, IA-3, MP-2, MP-4, MP-5, MP-7, PL-4, SC-7, SC-34, SC-43, SI-3, SI-4.

Control Enhancements:

(1) ACCESS CONTROL FOR MOBILE DEVICES | USE OF WRITABLE AND PORTABLE STORAGE DEVICES
    [Withdrawn: Incorporated into MP-7].

(2) ACCESS CONTROL FOR MOBILE DEVICES | USE OF PERSONALLY OWNED PORTABLE STORAGE DEVICES
    [Withdrawn: Incorporated into MP-7].

(3) ACCESS CONTROL FOR MOBILE DEVICES | USE OF PORTABLE STORAGE DEVICES WITH NO IDENTIFIABLE OWNER
    [Withdrawn: Incorporated into MP-7].

(4) ACCESS CONTROL FOR MOBILE DEVICES | RESTRICTIONS FOR CLASSIFIED INFORMATION
    (a) Prohibit the use of unclassified mobile devices in facilities containing systems processing, storing, or transmitting classified information unless specifically permitted by the authorizing official; and
    (b) Enforce the following restrictions on individuals permitted by the authorizing official to use unclassified mobile devices in facilities containing systems processing, storing, or transmitting classified information:
        (1) Connection of unclassified mobile devices to classified systems is prohibited;
        (2) Connection of unclassified mobile devices to unclassified systems requires approval from the authorizing official;
        (3) Use of internal or external modems or wireless interfaces within the unclassified mobile devices is prohibited; and

(4) Unclassified mobile devices and the information stored on those devices are subject to random reviews and inspections by [*Assignment: organization-defined security officials*], and if classified information is found, the incident handling policy is followed.

(c) Restrict the connection of classified mobile devices to classified systems in accordance with [*Assignment: organization-defined security policies*].

Supplemental Guidance: None.

Related Controls: CM-8, IR-4.

(5) ACCESS CONTROL FOR MOBILE DEVICES | FULL DEVICE AND CONTAINER-BASED ENCRYPTION

Employ [*Selection: full-device encryption; container encryption*] to protect the confidentiality and integrity of information on [*Assignment: organization-defined mobile devices*].

Supplemental Guidance: Container-based encryption provides a more fine-grained approach to the encryption of data/information on mobile devices, including, for example, encrypting selected data structures such as files, records, or fields.

Related Controls: SC-13, SC-28.

References: NIST Special Publications 800-114, 800-124, 800-164.

AC-20 USE OF EXTERNAL SYSTEMS

Control: Establish terms and conditions, consistent with any trust relationships established with other organizations owning, operating, and/or maintaining external systems, allowing authorized individuals to:

a. Access the system from external systems; and

b. Process, store, or transmit organization-controlled information using external systems.

Supplemental Guidance: External systems are systems or components of systems that are outside of the authorization boundary established by organizations and for which organizations typically have no direct supervision and authority over the application of required security controls or the assessment of control effectiveness. External systems include, for example, personally owned systems, components, or devices; privately owned computing and communications devices in commercial or public facilities; systems owned or controlled by nonfederal organizations; and federal systems that are not owned by, operated by, or under the direct supervision and authority of the organization. This includes systems managed by contractors, systems owned by other federal agencies, and systems owned by other organizations within the same agency. This control addresses the use of external systems for the processing, storage, or transmission of organizational information, including, for example, accessing cloud services from organizational systems.

For some external systems (i.e., systems operated by other federal agencies and organizations subordinate to those agencies), the trust relationships that have been established between those organizations and the originating organization may be such, that no explicit terms and conditions are required. Systems within these organizations may not be considered external. These situations occur when, for example, there are pre-existing sharing and trust agreements (either implicit or explicit) established between federal agencies or organizations subordinate to those agencies, or when such trust agreements are specified by applicable laws, Executive Orders, directives, regulations, or policies. Authorized individuals include, for example, organizational personnel, contractors, or other individuals with authorized access to organizational systems and over which organizations have the authority to impose specific rules of behavior with regard to system access. Restrictions that organizations impose on authorized individuals need not be uniform, as those restrictions may vary depending on the trust relationships between organizations. Therefore, organizations may choose to impose different security restrictions on contractors than on state, local, or tribal governments.

This control does not apply to external systems used to access public interfaces to organizational systems. Organizations establish specific terms and conditions for the use of external systems in accordance with organizational security policies and procedures. Terms and conditions address as a minimum: the specific types of applications that can be accessed on organizational systems from external systems, and the highest security category of information that can be processed, stored or transmitted on external systems. If the terms and conditions with the owners of external systems cannot be established, organizations may impose restrictions on organizational personnel using those external systems.

Related Controls: AC-2, AC-3, AC-17, AC-19, CA-3, PL-2, PL-4, SA-9, SC-7.

Control Enhancements:

(1) USE OF EXTERNAL SYSTEMS | LIMITS ON AUTHORIZED USE

Permit authorized individuals to use an external system to access the system or to process, store, or transmit organization-controlled information only after:

(a) Verification of the implementation of required security and privacy controls on the external system as specified in the organization's security and privacy policies and security and privacy plans; or

(b) Retention of approved system connection or processing agreements with the organizational entity hosting the external system.

Supplemental Guidance: This control enhancement recognizes that there are circumstances where individuals using external systems need to access organizational systems. In those situations, organizations need confidence that the external systems contain the necessary security controls so as not to compromise, damage, or otherwise harm organizational systems. Verification that the required security controls have been implemented can be achieved, for example, by external, independent assessments, attestations, or other means, depending on the confidence level required by organizations.

Related Controls: CA-2.

(2) USE OF EXTERNAL SYSTEMS | PORTABLE STORAGE DEVICES

[Selection: Restrict the use of organization-controlled portable storage devices by authorized individuals on external systems using the following [Assignment: organization-defined restrictions]; Prohibit the use of organization-controlled portable storage devices by authorized individuals on external systems].

Supplemental Guidance: Limits on the use of organization-controlled portable storage devices in external systems include, for example, complete prohibition of the use of such devices or restrictions on how the devices may be used and under what conditions the devices may be used.

Related Controls: MP-7, SC-41.

(3) USE OF EXTERNAL SYSTEMS | NON-ORGANIZATIONALLY OWNED SYSTEMS AND COMPONENTS

[Selection: Restrict the use of non-organizationally owned systems or system components to process, store, or transmit organizational information using the following [Assignment: organization-defined restrictions]; Prohibit the use of non-organizationally owned systems or system components to process, store, or transmit organizational information].

Supplemental Guidance: Non-organizationally owned systems or system components include systems or system components owned by other organizations and personally owned devices. There are potential risks to using non-organizationally owned systems or system components. In some cases, the risk is sufficiently high as to prohibit such use. In other cases, the use of such systems or system components may be allowed but restricted in some way. Restrictions include, for example, requiring the implementation of approved security and privacy controls prior to authorizing the connection of non-organizationally owned systems and components; limiting access to certain types of information, services, or applications; using virtualization techniques to limit processing and storage activities to servers or other system components provisioned by the organization; and agreeing to the specified terms and conditions for usage. Organizations consult with the Office of the General Counsel regarding any legal issues associated with using personally owned devices, including, for example, requirements for conducting forensic analyses during investigations after an incident.

Related Controls: None.

(4) USE OF EXTERNAL SYSTEMS | NETWORK ACCESSIBLE STORAGE DEVICES

Prohibit the use of [Assignment: organization-defined network accessible storage devices] in external systems.

Supplemental Guidance: Network accessible storage devices in external systems include, for example, online storage devices in public, hybrid, or community cloud-based systems.

Related Controls: None.

References: FIPS Publication 199.

AC-21 INFORMATION SHARING

Control:

a. Facilitate information sharing by enabling authorized users to determine whether access authorizations assigned to the sharing partner match the access restrictions and privacy authorizations on the information for [*Assignment: organization-defined information sharing circumstances where user discretion is required*]; and

b. Employ [*Assignment: organization-defined automated mechanisms or manual processes*] to assist users in making information sharing and collaboration decisions.

Supplemental Guidance: This control applies to information that may be restricted in some manner based on some formal or administrative determination. Examples of such information include, contract-sensitive information, proprietary information, classified information related to special access programs or compartments, privileged medical information, and personally identifiable information. Risk analyses and privacy impact analyses can provide useful inputs to these determinations. Depending on the information-sharing circumstances, sharing partners may be defined at the individual, group, or organizational level. Information may be defined by content, type, security category, or special access program/compartment.

Related Controls: AC-3, AC-4, AC-16, SC-15.

Control Enhancements:

(1) INFORMATION SHARING | AUTOMATED DECISION SUPPORT

Enforce information-sharing decisions by authorized users based on access authorizations of sharing partners and access restrictions on information to be shared.

Supplemental Guidance: None.

Related Controls: None.

(2) INFORMATION SHARING | INFORMATION SEARCH AND RETRIEVAL

Implement information search and retrieval services that enforce [*Assignment: organization-defined information sharing restrictions*].

Supplemental Guidance: None.

Related Controls: None.

References: NIST Special Publication 800-150; NIST Interagency Report 8062.

AC-22 PUBLICLY ACCESSIBLE CONTENT

Control:

a. Designate individuals authorized to post information onto a publicly accessible system;

b. Train authorized individuals to ensure that publicly accessible information does not contain nonpublic information;

c. Review the proposed content of information prior to posting onto the publicly accessible system to ensure that nonpublic information is not included; and

d. Review the content on the publicly accessible system for nonpublic information [*Assignment: organization-defined frequency*] and remove such information, if discovered.

Supplemental Guidance: In accordance with applicable laws, Executive Orders, directives, policies, regulations, standards, and guidelines, the public is not authorized access to nonpublic information including, for example, information protected under the Privacy Act and proprietary information.

This control addresses systems that are controlled by the organization and accessible to the public, typically without identification or authentication. The posting of information on non-organization systems is covered by organizational policy.

Related Controls: AC-3, AT-2, AT-3, AU-13.

Control Enhancements: None.

References: None.

AC-23 DATA MINING PROTECTION

Control: Employ [*Assignment: organization-defined data mining prevention and detection techniques*] for [*Assignment: organization-defined data storage objects*] to detect and protect against unauthorized data mining.

Supplemental Guidance: Data storage objects include, for example, databases, database records, and database fields. Data mining prevention and detection techniques include, for example, limiting the types of responses provided to database queries; limiting the number and the frequency of database queries to increase the work factor needed to determine the contents of such databases; and notifying organizational personnel when atypical database queries or accesses occur. This control focuses on the protection of organizational information from data mining while such information resides in organizational data stores. In contrast, AU-13 focuses on monitoring for organizational information that may have been mined or otherwise obtained from data stores and is now available as open source information residing on external sites, for example, through social networking or social media websites.

Related Controls: None.

Control Enhancements: None.

References: None.

AC-24 ACCESS CONTROL DECISIONS

Control: Establish procedures to ensure [*Assignment: organization-defined access control decisions*] are applied to each access request prior to access enforcement.

Supplemental Guidance: Access control decisions (also known as authorization decisions) occur when authorization information is applied to specific accesses. In contrast, access enforcement occurs when systems enforce access control decisions. While it is very common to have access control decisions and access enforcement implemented by the same entity, it is not required and it is not always an optimal implementation choice. For some architectures and distributed systems, different entities may perform access control decisions and access enforcement.

Related Controls: AC-2, AC-3.

Control Enhancements:

(1) ACCESS CONTROL DECISIONS | TRANSMIT ACCESS AUTHORIZATION INFORMATION

Transmit [*Assignment: organization-defined access authorization information*] using [*Assignment: organization-defined security safeguards*] to [*Assignment: organization-defined systems*] that enforce access control decisions.

Supplemental Guidance: In distributed systems, authorization processes and access control decisions may occur in separate parts of the systems. In such instances, authorization information is transmitted securely so timely access control decisions can be enforced at the appropriate locations. To support the access control decisions, it may be necessary to transmit as part of the access authorization information, supporting security attributes. This is because in distributed systems, there are various access control decisions that need to be made and different entities make these decisions in a serial fashion, each requiring security attributes to make the decisions. Protecting access authorization information ensures that such information cannot be altered, spoofed, or compromised during transmission.

Related Controls: None.

(2) ACCESS CONTROL DECISIONS | NO USER OR PROCESS IDENTITY

Enforce access control decisions based on [*Assignment: organization-defined security attributes*] that do not include the identity of the user or process acting on behalf of the user.

Supplemental Guidance: In certain situations, it is important that access control decisions can be made without information regarding the identity of the users issuing the requests. These are generally instances where preserving individual privacy is of paramount importance. In other situations, user identification information is simply not needed for access control decisions and, especially in the case of distributed systems, transmitting such information with the needed degree of assurance may be very expensive or difficult to accomplish.

Related Controls: None.

References: NIST Special Publications 800-162, 800-178.

AC-25 REFERENCE MONITOR

Control: Implement a reference monitor for [*Assignment: organization-defined access control policies*] that is tamperproof, always invoked, and small enough to be subject to analysis and testing, the completeness of which can be assured.

Supplemental Guidance: Information is represented internally within systems using abstractions known as data structures. Internal data structures can represent different types of entities, both active and passive. Active entities, also known as subjects, are associated with individuals, devices, or processes acting on behalf of individuals. Passive entities, also known as objects, are typically associated with data structures such as records, buffers, tables, files, inter-process pipes, and communications ports. Reference monitors enforce mandatory access control policies, a type of access control that restricts access to objects based on the identity of subjects or groups to which the subjects belong. The access controls are mandatory because subjects with certain privileges (i.e., access permissions) are restricted from passing those privileges on to any other subjects, either directly or indirectly—that is, the system strictly enforces the access control policy based on the rule set established by the policy. The tamperproof property of the reference monitor prevents adversaries from compromising the functioning of the mechanism. The always invoked property prevents adversaries from bypassing the mechanism and hence violating the security policy. The smallness property helps to ensure the completeness in the analysis and testing of the mechanism to detect weaknesses or deficiencies (i.e., latent flaws) that would prevent the enforcement of the security policy.

Related Controls: AC-3, AC-16, SC-3, SC-11, SC-39, SI-13.

Control Enhancements: None.

References: None.

3.2 AWARENESS AND TRAINING

Quick link to Awareness and Training summary table

AT-1 AWARENESS AND TRAINING POLICY AND PROCEDURES

Control:

a. Develop, document, and disseminate to [*Assignment: organization-defined personnel or roles*]:

 1. A security and privacy awareness and training policy that:

 (a) Addresses purpose, scope, roles, responsibilities, management commitment, coordination among organizational entities, and compliance; and

 (b) Is consistent with applicable laws, Executive Orders, directives, regulations, policies, standards, and guidelines; and

 2. Procedures to facilitate the implementation of the security and privacy awareness and training policy and the associated security and privacy awareness and training controls;

b. Designate an [*Assignment: organization-defined senior management official*] to manage the security and privacy awareness and training policy and procedures;

c. Review and update the current security and privacy awareness and training:

 1. Policy [*Assignment: organization-defined frequency*]; and

 2. Procedures [*Assignment: organization-defined frequency*];

d. Ensure that the security and privacy awareness and training procedures implement the security and privacy awareness and training policy and controls; and

e. Develop, document, and implement remediation actions for violations of the awareness and training policy.

Supplemental Guidance: This control addresses the establishment of policy and procedures for the effective implementation of the controls and control enhancements in the AT family. The risk management strategy is an important factor in establishing policy and procedures. Comprehensive policy and procedures help provide security and privacy assurance. Security and privacy program policies and procedures at the organization level may make the need for system-specific policies and procedures unnecessary. The policy can be included as part of the general security and privacy policy or can be represented by multiple policies reflecting the complex nature of organizations. The procedures can be established for security and privacy programs and for systems, if needed. Procedures describe how policies or controls are implemented and can be directed at the personnel or role that is the object of the procedure. Procedures can be documented in system security and privacy plans or in one or more separate documents. It is important to recognize that restating controls does not constitute an organizational policy or procedure.

Related Controls: PM-9, PS-8, SI-12.

Control Enhancements: None.

References: NIST Special Publications 800-12, 800-30, 800-39, 800-50, 800-100.

AT-2 AWARENESS TRAINING

Control: Provide basic security and privacy awareness training to system users (including managers, senior executives, and contractors):

a. As part of initial training for new users;

b. When required by system changes; and

c. [*Assignment: organization-defined frequency*] thereafter.

<u>Supplemental Guidance</u>: Organizations determine the content of security and privacy awareness training and security and privacy awareness techniques based on the specific organizational requirements and the systems to which personnel have authorized access. The content includes an understanding of the need for information security and privacy and actions by users to maintain security and privacy and to respond to suspected security and privacy incidents. The content also addresses an awareness of the need for operations security. Security and privacy awareness techniques can include, for example, displaying posters, offering supplies inscribed with security and privacy reminders, generating email advisories/notices from senior organizational officials, displaying logon screen messages, and conducting information security and privacy awareness events. Awareness training after the initial training (i.e., described AT-2c) is conducted at a minimum frequency consistent with applicable laws, directives, regulations, and policies. Such training may be satisfied by one or more short ad hoc sessions and include topical information on recent attack schemes, changes to organizational security and privacy policies, revised security and privacy expectations, and/or a subset of topics from the initial training.

<u>Related Controls</u>: AC-17, AC-22, AT-3, AT-4, CP-3, IA-4, IR-2, IR-7, IR-9, PA-2, PL-4, PM-13, PM-22, PS-7, SA-16.

<u>Control Enhancements</u>:

(1) AWARENESS TRAINING | PRACTICAL EXERCISES

Include practical exercises in awareness training that simulate security and privacy incidents.

<u>Supplemental Guidance</u>: Practical exercises may include, for example, no-notice social engineering attempts to collect information, gain unauthorized access, or simulate the adverse impact of opening malicious email attachments or invoking, via spear phishing attacks, malicious web links. Privacy-related practical exercises may include, for example, practice modules with quizzes on handling personally identifiable information and affected individuals in various scenarios.

<u>Related Controls</u>: CA-2, CA-7, CP-4, IR-3.

(2) AWARENESS TRAINING | INSIDER THREAT

Include awareness training on recognizing and reporting potential indicators of insider threat.

<u>Supplemental Guidance</u>: Potential indicators and possible precursors of insider threat can include behaviors such as inordinate, long-term job dissatisfaction, attempts to gain access to information not required for job performance, unexplained access to financial resources, bullying or sexual harassment of fellow employees, workplace violence, and other serious violations of organizational policies, procedures, directives, rules, or practices. Security and privacy awareness training includes how to communicate the concerns of employees and management regarding potential indicators of insider threat through organizational channels in accordance with established policies and procedures.

<u>Related Controls</u>: PM-12.

(3) AWARENESS TRAINING | SOCIAL ENGINEERING AND MINING

Include awareness training on recognizing and reporting potential and actual instances of social engineering and social mining.

<u>Supplemental Guidance</u>: Social engineering is an attempt to trick someone into revealing information or taking an action that can be used to attack or compromise systems. Examples of social engineering include phishing, pretexting, baiting, quid pro quo, and tailgaiting. Social mining is an attempt, in a social setting, to gather information about the organization that may support future attacks. Security and privacy awareness training includes information on how to communicate concerns of employees and management regarding potential and actual instances of social engineering and mining through organizational channels based on established policies and procedures.

<u>Related Controls</u>: None.

<u>References</u>: NIST Special Publication 800-50.

AT-3   ROLE-BASED TRAINING

Control: Provide role-based security and privacy training to personnel with the following roles and responsibilities: [*Assignment: organization-defined roles and responsibilities*]:

a. Before authorizing access to the system or performing assigned duties;

b. When required by system changes; and

c. [*Assignment: organization-defined frequency*] thereafter.

Supplemental Guidance: Organizations determine the appropriate content of security and privacy training based on the assigned roles and responsibilities of individuals and the specific security and privacy requirements of organizations and the systems to which personnel have authorized access, including security-related technical training specifically tailored for assigned duties. Roles that may require role-based security and privacy training include, for example, system owners; authorizing officials; system security officers; privacy officers; enterprise architects; acquisition and procurement officials; systems engineers; system and software developers; system, network, and database administrators; personnel conducting configuration management activities; personnel performing verification and validation activities; auditors; personnel having access to system-level software; security and privacy control assessors; personnel with contingency planning and incident response duties; personnel with privacy management responsibilities; and personnel having access to personally identifiable information. Comprehensive role-based training addresses management, operational, and technical roles and responsibilities covering physical, personnel, and technical safeguards and countermeasures. Such training can include, for example, policies, procedures, tools, methods, and artifacts for the security and privacy roles defined. Organizations provide the training necessary for individuals to fulfill their responsibilities related to operations and supply chain security within the context of organizational information security and privacy programs. Role-based security and privacy training also applies to contractors providing services to federal agencies.

Related Controls: AC-17, AC-22, AT-2, AT-4, CP-3, IR-2, IR-7, IR-9, IR-10, PL-4, PM-13, PM-24, PS-7, SA-3, SA-11, SA-12, SA-16, SA-19.

Control Enhancements:

(1) ROLE-BASED TRAINING | ENVIRONMENTAL CONTROLS
    Provide [*Assignment: organization-defined personnel or roles*] with initial and [*Assignment: organization-defined frequency*] training in the employment and operation of environmental controls.

    Supplemental Guidance: Environmental controls include, for example, fire suppression and detection devices/systems, sprinkler systems, handheld fire extinguishers, fixed fire hoses, smoke detectors, temperature/humidity, heating, ventilation, and air conditioning, and power within the facility. Organizations identify personnel with specific roles and responsibilities associated with environmental controls requiring specialized training.

    Related Controls: PE-1, PE-11, PE-13, PE-14, PE-15.

(2) ROLE-BASED TRAINING | PHYSICAL SECURITY CONTROLS
    Provide [*Assignment: organization-defined personnel or roles*] with initial and [*Assignment: organization-defined frequency*] training in the employment and operation of physical security controls.

    Supplemental Guidance: Physical security controls include, for example, physical access control devices, physical intrusion alarms, monitoring/surveillance equipment, and security guards (deployment and operating procedures). Organizations identify personnel with specific roles and responsibilities associated with physical security controls requiring specialized training.

    Related Controls: PE-2, PE-3, PE-4.

(3) ROLE-BASED TRAINING | PRACTICAL EXERCISES
    Include practical exercises in security and privacy training that reinforce training objectives.

Supplemental Guidance: Practical exercises for security may include, for example, security training for software developers that includes simulated cyber-attacks exploiting common software vulnerabilities, or spear/whale phishing attacks targeted at senior leaders/executives. Practical exercises for privacy may include, for example, practice modules with quizzes on handling personally identifiable information in various scenarios, and model scenarios on conducting privacy impact assessments.

Related Controls: None.

(4) ROLE-BASED TRAINING | SUSPICIOUS COMMUNICATIONS AND ANOMALOUS SYSTEM BEHAVIOR

Provide training to personnel on [*Assignment: organization-defined indicators of malicious code*] to recognize suspicious communications and anomalous behavior in organizational systems.

Supplemental Guidance: A well-trained workforce provides another organizational safeguard that can be employed as part of a defense-in-depth strategy to protect organizations against malicious code coming in to organizations via email or the web applications. Personnel are trained to look for indications of potentially suspicious email for example, receiving an unexpected email, receiving an email containing strange or poor grammar, or receiving an email from an unfamiliar sender but who appears to be from a known sponsor or contractor. Personnel are also trained on how to respond to suspicious email or web communications. For this process to work effectively, organizational personnel are trained and made aware of what constitutes suspicious communications. Training personnel on how to recognize anomalous behaviors in organizational systems can potentially provide early warning for the presence of malicious code. Recognition of such anomalous behavior by organizational personnel can supplement automated malicious code detection and protection tools and systems employed by organizations.

Related Controls: None.

(5) ROLE-BASED TRAINING | PERSONALLY IDENTIFIABLE INFORMATION PROCESSING

Provide personnel who process personally identifiable information with initial and [*Assignment: organization-defined frequency*] training on:

(a) **Organizational authority for collecting personally identifiable information;**

(b) **Authorized uses of personally identifiable information;**

(c) **Content of System of Records Notices;**

(d) **Authorized sharing of personally identifiable information with external parties; and**

(e) **Consequences of unauthorized use or sharing of personally identifiable information.**

Supplemental Guidance: Role-based training on handling personally identifiable information helps prevent unauthorized collections or uses of personally identifiable information.

Related Controls: PA-3, PA-4.

References: NIST Special Publication 800-50.

AT-4   TRAINING RECORDS

Control:

a.   Document and monitor individual system security and privacy training activities including basic security and privacy awareness training and specific role-based system security and privacy training; and

b.   Retain individual training records for [*Assignment: organization-defined time-period*].

Supplemental Guidance: Documentation for specialized training may be maintained by individual supervisors at the option of the organization. The National Archives and Records Administration provides guidance on records retention.

Related Controls: AT-2, AT-3, CP-3, IR-2, PM-14, SI-12.

Control Enhancements: None.

References: None.

AT-5 CONTACTS WITH SECURITY GROUPS AND ASSOCIATIONS

[Withdrawn: Incorporated into PM-15].

3.3 AUDIT AND ACCOUNTABILITY

Quick link to Audit and Accountability summary table

AU-1 AUDIT AND ACCOUNTABILITY POLICY AND PROCEDURES

Control:

a. Develop, document, and disseminate to [*Assignment: organization-defined personnel or roles*]:

   1. An audit and accountability policy that:

      (a) Addresses purpose, scope, roles, responsibilities, management commitment, coordination among organizational entities, and compliance; and

      (b) Is consistent with applicable laws, Executive Orders, directives, regulations, policies, standards, and guidelines; and

   2. Procedures to facilitate the implementation of the audit and accountability policy and the associated audit and accountability controls;

b. Designate an [*Assignment: organization-defined senior management official*] to manage the audit and accountability policy and procedures;

c. Review and update the current audit and accountability:

   1. Policy [*Assignment: organization-defined frequency*]; and

   2. Procedures [*Assignment: organization-defined frequency*];

d. Ensure that the audit and accountability procedures implement the audit and accountability policy and controls; and

e. Develop, document, and implement remediation actions for violations of the audit and accountability policy.

Supplemental Guidance: This control addresses the establishment of policy and procedures for the effective implementation of the controls and control enhancements in the AU family. The risk management strategy is an important factor in establishing policy and procedures. Comprehensive policy and procedures help provide security and privacy assurance. Security and privacy program policies and procedures at the organization level may make the need for system-specific policies and procedures unnecessary. The policy can be included as part of the general security and privacy policy or can be represented by multiple policies reflecting the complex nature of organizations. The procedures can be established for security and privacy programs and for systems, if needed. Procedures describe how policies or controls are implemented and can be directed at the personnel or role that is the object of the procedure. Procedures can be documented in system security and privacy plans or in one or more separate documents. It is important to recognize that restating controls does not constitute an organizational policy or procedure.

Related Controls: PM-9, PS-8, SI-12.

Control Enhancements: None.

References: NIST Special Publications 800-12, 800-30, 800-39, 800-50, 800-100.

AU-2 AUDIT EVENTS

Control:

a. Verify that the system can audit the following event types: [*Assignment: organization-defined auditable event types*];

b. Coordinate the security audit function with other organizational entities requiring audit-related information to enhance mutual support and to help guide the selection of auditable event types;

c. Provide a rationale for why the auditable event types are deemed to be adequate to support after-the-fact investigations of security and privacy incidents; and

d. Specify that the following event types are to be audited within the system: [*Assignment: organization-defined audited events (the subset of the auditable events defined in AU-2 a.) along with the frequency of (or situation requiring) auditing for each identified event*].

Supplemental Guidance: An event is any observable occurrence in an organizational system. Organizations identify audit event types as those events which are significant and relevant to the security of systems and the environments in which those systems operate to meet specific and ongoing audit needs. Audit event types can include, for example, password changes; failed logons or failed accesses related to systems; security attribute changes, administrative privilege usage, PIV credential usage, query parameters, or external credential usage. In determining the set of auditable event types, organizations consider the auditing appropriate for each of the security controls to be implemented. To balance auditing requirements with other system needs, this control also requires identifying that subset of *auditable* event types that are *audited* at a given point in time. For example, organizations may determine that systems must have the capability to log every file access both successful and unsuccessful, but not activate that capability except for specific circumstances due to the potential burden on system performance.

Auditing requirements, including the need for auditable events, may be referenced in other security and privacy controls and control enhancements for example, AC-2(4), AC-3(10), AC-6(9), AC-16(11), AC-17(1), CM-3.f, CM-5(1), IA-3(3.b), MA-4(1), MP-4(2), PA-4.d, PE-3, PM-22, RA-8, SC-7(9), SC-7(15), SI-3(8), SI-4(22), SI-7(8), and SI-10(1). Organizations also include auditable event types that are required by applicable laws, Executive Orders, directives, policies, regulations, standards, and guidelines. Audit records can be generated at various levels, including at the packet level as information traverses the network. Selecting the appropriate level of auditing is an important aspect of an audit capability and can facilitate the identification of root causes to problems. Organizations consider in the definition of auditable event types, the auditing necessary to cover related event types such as the steps in distributed, transaction-based processes and actions that occur in service-oriented architectures.

Related Controls: AC-2, AC-3, AC-6, AC-7, AC-8, AC-16, AC-17, AU-3, AU-4, AU-5, AU-6, AU-7, AU-11, AU-12, CM-3, CM-5, CM-6, IA-3, MA-4, MP-4, PA-4, PE-3, PM-22, RA-8, SC-7, SC-18, SI-3, SI-4, SI-7, SI-10, SI-11.

Control Enhancements:

(1) AUDIT EVENTS | COMPILATION OF AUDIT RECORDS FROM MULTIPLE SOURCES
    [Withdrawn: Incorporated into AU-12].

(2) AUDIT EVENTS | SELECTION OF AUDIT EVENTS BY COMPONENT
    [Withdrawn: Incorporated into AU-12].

(3) AUDIT EVENTS | REVIEWS AND UPDATES
    Review and update the audited events [*Assignment: organization-defined frequency*].
    Supplemental Guidance: Over time, the events that organizations believe should be audited may change. Reviewing and updating the set of audited events periodically is necessary to ensure that the current set is still necessary and sufficient.
    Related Controls: None.

(4) AUDIT EVENTS | PRIVILEGED FUNCTIONS
    [Withdrawn: Incorporated into AC-6(9)].

References: NIST Special Publication 800-92.

AU-3   CONTENT OF AUDIT RECORDS

Control: The system generates audit records containing information that establishes what type of event occurred, when the event occurred, where the event occurred, the source of the event, the outcome of the event, and the identity of any individuals or subjects associated with the event.

Supplemental Guidance: Audit record content that may be necessary to satisfy the requirement of this control, includes, for example, time stamps, source and destination addresses, user or process identifiers, event descriptions, success/fail indications, filenames involved, and access control or flow control rules invoked. Event outcomes can include indicators of event success or failure and event-specific results, for example, the security and privacy state of the system after the event occurred.

Related Controls: AU-2, AU-8, AU-12, AU-14, MA-4, SI-7, SI-11.

Control Enhancements:

(1)   CONTENT OF AUDIT RECORDS | ADDITIONAL AUDIT INFORMATION

   Generate audit records containing the following additional information: [*Assignment: organization-defined additional, more detailed information*].

   Supplemental Guidance: Implementation of this control enhancement is dependent on system functionality to configure audit record content. Detailed information that organizations may consider in audit records includes, for example, full text recording of privileged commands or the individual identities of group account users. Organizations consider limiting the additional audit information to only that information explicitly needed for specific audit requirements. This facilitates the use of audit trails and audit logs by not including information that could potentially be misleading or could make it more difficult to locate information of interest.

   Related Controls: None.

(2)   CONTENT OF AUDIT RECORDS | CENTRALIZED MANAGEMENT OF PLANNED AUDIT RECORD CONTENT

   Provide centralized management and configuration of the content to be captured in audit records generated by [*Assignment: organization-defined system components*].

   Supplemental Guidance: This control enhancement requires that the content to be captured in audit records be configured from a central location (necessitating automation). Organizations coordinate the selection of required audit content to support the centralized management and configuration capability provided by the system.

   Related Controls: AU-6, AU-7.

(3)   CONTENT OF AUDIT RECORDS | LIMIT PERSONALLY IDENTIFIABLE INFORMATION ELEMENTS

   Limit personally identifiable information contained in audit records to the following elements identified in the privacy risk assessment: [*Assignment: organization-defined elements*].

   Supplemental Guidance: Limiting personally identifiable information in audit records when such information is not needed for operational purposes helps reduce the level of privacy risk created by a system.

   Related Controls: None.

   References: NIST Interagency Report 8062.

AU-4   AUDIT STORAGE CAPACITY

Control: Allocate audit record storage capacity to accommodate [*Assignment: organization-defined audit record retention requirements*].

Supplemental Guidance: Organizations consider the types of auditing to be performed and the audit processing requirements when allocating audit storage capacity. Allocating sufficient audit storage capacity reduces the likelihood of such capacity being exceeded and resulting in the potential loss or reduction of auditing capability.

Related Controls: AU-2, AU-5, AU-6, AU-7, AU-9, AU-11, AU-12, AU-14, SI-4.

Control Enhancements:

(1) AUDIT STORAGE CAPACITY | TRANSFER TO ALTERNATE STORAGE

Off-load audit records [*Assignment: organization-defined frequency*] onto a different system or media than the system being audited.

Supplemental Guidance: Off-loading is a process designed to preserve the confidentiality and integrity of audit records by moving the records from the primary system to a secondary or alternate system. It is a common process in systems with limited audit storage capacity; the audit storage is used only in a transitory fashion until the system can communicate with the secondary or alternate system designated for storing the audit records, at which point the information is transferred.

Related Controls: None.

References: None.

AU-5 RESPONSE TO AUDIT PROCESSING FAILURES

Control:

a. Alert [*Assignment: organization-defined personnel or roles*] in the event of an audit processing failure within [*Assignment: organization-defined time-period*]; and

b. Take the following additional actions: [*Assignment: organization-defined actions to be taken*].

Supplemental Guidance: Organization-defined actions include, for example, shutting down the system; overwriting oldest audit records; and stopping the generation of audit records. Examples of audit processing failures include, for example, software and hardware errors; failures in the audit capturing mechanisms; and audit storage capacity being reached or exceeded. Organizations may choose to define additional actions for audit processing failures based on the type of failure, the location of the failure, the severity of the failure, or a combination of such factors. This control applies to each audit data storage repository (i.e., distinct system component where audit records are stored), the total audit storage capacity of organizations (i.e., all audit data storage repositories combined), or both.

Related Controls: AU-2, AU-4, AU-7, AU-9, AU-11, AU-12, AU-14, SI-4, SI-12.

Control Enhancements:

(1) RESPONSE TO AUDIT PROCESSING FAILURES | AUDIT STORAGE CAPACITY

Provide a warning to [*Assignment: organization-defined personnel, roles, and/or locations*] within [*Assignment: organization-defined time-period*] when allocated audit record storage volume reaches [*Assignment: organization-defined percentage*] of repository maximum audit record storage capacity.

Supplemental Guidance: Organizations may have multiple audit data storage repositories distributed across multiple system components, with each repository having different storage volume capacities.

Related Controls: None.

(2) RESPONSE TO AUDIT PROCESSING FAILURES | REAL-TIME ALERTS

Provide an alert in [*Assignment: organization-defined real-time-period*] to [*Assignment: organization-defined personnel, roles, and/or locations*] when the following audit failure events occur: [*Assignment: organization-defined audit failure events requiring real-time alerts*].

Supplemental Guidance: Alerts provide organizations with urgent messages. Real-time alerts provide these messages at information technology speed (i.e., the time from event detection to alert occurs in seconds or less).

Related Controls: None.

(3) RESPONSE TO AUDIT PROCESSING FAILURES | CONFIGURABLE TRAFFIC VOLUME THRESHOLDS

Enforce configurable network communications traffic volume thresholds reflecting limits on auditing capacity and [*Selection: rejects; delays*] network traffic above those thresholds.

Supplemental Guidance: Organizations have the capability to reject or delay the processing of network communications traffic if auditing such traffic is determined to exceed the storage capacity of the system audit function. The rejection or delay response is triggered by the established organizational traffic volume thresholds which can be adjusted based on changes to audit storage capacity.

Related Controls: None.

(4) RESPONSE TO AUDIT PROCESSING FAILURES | SHUTDOWN ON FAILURE

Invoke a [*Selection: full system shutdown; partial system shutdown; degraded operational mode with limited mission/business functionality available*] in the event of [*Assignment: organization-defined audit failures*], unless an alternate audit capability exists.

Supplemental Guidance: Organizations determine the types of audit failures that can trigger automatic system shutdowns or degraded operations. Because of the importance of ensuring mission and business continuity, organizations may determine that the nature of the audit failure is not so severe that it warrants a complete shutdown of the system supporting the core organizational missions and business operations. In those instances, partial system shutdowns or operating in a degraded mode with reduced capability may be viable alternatives.

Related Controls: AU-15.

References: None.

AU-6   AUDIT REVIEW, ANALYSIS, AND REPORTING

Control:

a. Review and analyze system audit records [*Assignment: organization-defined frequency*] for indications of [*Assignment: organization-defined inappropriate or unusual activity*];

b. Report findings to [*Assignment: organization-defined personnel or roles*]; and

c. Adjust the level of audit review, analysis, and reporting within the system when there is a change in risk based on law enforcement information, intelligence information, or other credible sources of information.

Supplemental Guidance: Audit review, analysis, and reporting covers information security-related auditing performed by organizations including, for example, auditing that results from monitoring of account usage, remote access, wireless connectivity, mobile device connection, configuration settings, system component inventory, use of maintenance tools and nonlocal maintenance, physical access, temperature and humidity, equipment delivery and removal, communications at system boundaries, and use of mobile code or VoIP. Findings can be reported to organizational entities that include, for example, the incident response team, help desk, information security group/department. If organizations are prohibited from reviewing and analyzing audit information or unable to conduct such activities, the review/analysis may be carried out by other organizations granted such authority. The frequency, scope, and/or depth of the audit review, analysis, and reporting may be adjusted to meet organizational needs based on new information received.

Related Controls: AC-2, AC-3, AC-6, AC-7, AC-17, AU-7, AU-16, CA-7, CM-2, CM-5, CM-6, CM-10, CM-11, IA-2, IA-3, IA-5, IA-8, IR-5, MA-4, MP-4, PE-3, PE-6, RA-5, SC-7, SI-3, SI-4, SI-7.

Control Enhancements:

(1) AUDIT REVIEW, ANALYSIS, AND REPORTING | AUTOMATED PROCESS INTEGRATION

Employ automated mechanisms to integrate audit review, analysis, and reporting processes to support organizational processes for investigation and response to suspicious activities.

Supplemental Guidance: Organizational processes benefiting from integrated audit review, analysis, and reporting include, for example, incident response, continuous monitoring, contingency planning, and Inspector General audits.

Related Controls: PM-7.

(2) AUDIT REVIEW, ANALYSIS, AND REPORTING | AUTOMATED SECURITY ALERTS

[Withdrawn: Incorporated into SI-4].

(3) AUDIT REVIEW, ANALYSIS, AND REPORTING | CORRELATE AUDIT REPOSITORIES

Analyze and correlate audit records across different repositories to gain organization-wide situational awareness.

Supplemental Guidance: Organization-wide situational awareness includes awareness across all three tiers of risk management (i.e., organizational, mission/business process, and system) and supports cross-organization awareness.

Related Controls: AU-12, IR-4.

(4) AUDIT REVIEW, ANALYSIS, AND REPORTING | CENTRAL REVIEW AND ANALYSIS

Provide and implement the capability to centrally review and analyze audit records from multiple components within the system.

Supplemental Guidance: Automated mechanisms for centralized reviews and analyses include, for example, Security Information Management products.

Related Controls: AU-2, AU-12.

(5) AUDIT REVIEW, ANALYSIS, AND REPORTING | INTEGRATED ANALYSIS OF AUDIT RECORDS

Integrate analysis of audit records with analysis of [*Selection (one or more): vulnerability scanning information; performance data; system monitoring information; [Assignment: organization-defined data/information collected from other sources]]* to further enhance the ability to identify inappropriate or unusual activity.

Supplemental Guidance: This control enhancement does not require vulnerability scanning, the generation of performance data, or system monitoring. Rather, the enhancement requires that the analysis of information being otherwise produced in these areas is integrated with the analysis of audit information. Security Event and Information Management System tools can facilitate audit record aggregation/consolidation from multiple system components as well as audit record correlation and analysis. The use of standardized audit record analysis scripts developed by organizations (with localized script adjustments, as necessary) provides more cost-effective approaches for analyzing audit record information collected. The correlation of audit record information with vulnerability scanning information is important in determining the veracity of vulnerability scans and correlating attack detection events with scanning results. Correlation with performance data can uncover denial of service attacks or other types of attacks resulting in unauthorized use of resources. Correlation with system monitoring information can assist in uncovering attacks and in better relating audit information to operational situations.

Related Controls: AU-12, IR-4.

(6) AUDIT REVIEW, ANALYSIS, AND REPORTING | CORRELATION WITH PHYSICAL MONITORING

Correlate information from audit records with information obtained from monitoring physical access to further enhance the ability to identify suspicious, inappropriate, unusual, or malevolent activity.

Supplemental Guidance: The correlation of physical audit information and audit logs from systems may assist organizations in identifying examples of suspicious behavior or supporting evidence of such behavior. For example, the correlation of an individual's identity for logical access to certain systems with the additional physical security information that the individual was present at the facility when the logical access occurred, may be useful in investigations.

Related Controls: None.

(7) AUDIT REVIEW, ANALYSIS, AND REPORTING | PERMITTED ACTIONS

Specify the permitted actions for each [*Selection (one or more): system process; role; user*] associated with the review, analysis, and reporting of audit information.

Supplemental Guidance: Organizations specify permitted actions for system processes, roles, and/or users associated with the review, analysis, and reporting of audit records through account management techniques. Specifying permitted actions on audit information is a way to enforce the principle of least privilege. Permitted actions are enforced by the system and include, for example, read, write, execute, append, and delete.

Related Controls: None.

(8) AUDIT REVIEW, ANALYSIS, AND REPORTING | FULL TEXT ANALYSIS OF PRIVILEGED COMMANDS

Perform a full text analysis of audited privileged commands in a physically distinct component or subsystem of the system, or other system that is dedicated to that analysis.

Supplemental Guidance: This control enhancement requires a distinct environment for the dedicated analysis of audit information related to privileged users without compromising such information on the system where the users have elevated privileges including the capability to execute privileged commands. Full text analysis refers to analysis that considers the full text of privileged commands (i.e., commands and all parameters) as opposed to analysis that considers only the name of the command. Full text analysis includes, for example, the use of pattern matching and heuristics.

Related Controls: AU-3, AU-9, AU-11, AU-12.

(9) AUDIT REVIEW, ANALYSIS, AND REPORTING | CORRELATION WITH INFORMATION FROM NONTECHNICAL SOURCES

Correlate information from nontechnical sources with audit information to enhance organization-wide situational awareness.

Supplemental Guidance: Nontechnical sources include, for example, human resources records documenting organizational policy violations including, for example, sexual harassment incidents and improper use of organizational information assets. Such information can lead to a more directed analytical effort to detect potential malicious insider activity. Due to the sensitive nature of the information available from nontechnical sources, organizations limit access to such information to minimize the potential for the inadvertent release of privacy-related information to individuals that do not have a need to know. Thus, correlation of information from nontechnical sources with audit information generally occurs only when individuals are suspected of being involved in a security incident. Organizations obtain legal advice prior to initiating such actions.

Related Controls: PM-12.

(10) AUDIT REVIEW, ANALYSIS, AND REPORTING | AUDIT LEVEL ADJUSTMENT
[Withdrawn: Incorporated into AU-6].

References: NIST Special Publications 800-86, 800-101.

AU-7   AUDIT REDUCTION AND REPORT GENERATION

Control: Provide and implement an audit reduction and report generation capability that:

a. Supports on-demand audit review, analysis, and reporting requirements and after-the-fact investigations of security incidents; and

b. Does not alter the original content or time ordering of audit records.

Supplemental Guidance: Audit reduction is a process that manipulates collected audit information and organizes such information in a summary format that is more meaningful to analysts. Audit reduction and report generation capabilities do not always emanate from the same system or from the same organizational entities conducting auditing activities. Audit reduction capability can include, for example, modern data mining techniques with advanced data filters to identify anomalous behavior in audit records. The report generation capability provided by the system can generate customizable reports. Time ordering of audit records can be a significant issue if the granularity of the timestamp in the record is insufficient.

Related Controls: AC-2, AU-2, AU-3, AU-4, AU-5, AU-6, AU-12, AU-16, CM-5, IA-5, IR-4, PM-12, SI-4.

Control Enhancements:

(1) AUDIT REDUCTION AND REPORT GENERATION | AUTOMATIC PROCESSING

Provide and implement the capability to process audit records for events of interest based on [Assignment: organization-defined audit fields within audit records].

Supplemental Guidance: Events of interest can be identified by the content in specific audit record fields, including, for example, identities of individuals, event types, event locations, event times, event dates, system resources involved, Internet Protocol addresses involved, or information objects accessed. Organizations may define audit event criteria to any degree of granularity required, for example, locations selectable by general networking location or selectable by specific system component.

Related Controls: None.

(2) AUDIT REDUCTION AND REPORT GENERATION | AUTOMATIC SORT AND SEARCH

Provide and implement the capability to sort and search audit records for events of interest based on the content of [*Assignment: organization-defined audit fields within audit records*].

Supplemental Guidance: Sorting and searching of audit records may be based upon the contents of audit record fields, for example, date and time of events; user identifiers; Internet Protocol addresses involved in the event; type of event; or event success or failure.

Related Controls: None.

References: None.

AU-8 TIME STAMPS

Control:

a. Use internal system clocks to generate time stamps for audit records; and

b. Record time stamps for audit records that can be mapped to Coordinated Universal Time or Greenwich Mean Time and meets [*Assignment: organization-defined granularity of time measurement*].

Supplemental Guidance: Time stamps generated by the system include date and time. Time is commonly expressed in Coordinated Universal Time (UTC), a modern continuation of Greenwich Mean Time (GMT), or local time with an offset from UTC. Granularity of time measurements refers to the degree of synchronization between system clocks and reference clocks, for example, clocks synchronizing within hundreds of milliseconds or tens of milliseconds. Organizations may define different time granularities for different system components. Time service can also be critical to other security capabilities such as access control and identification and authentication, depending on the nature of the mechanisms used to support those capabilities.

Related Controls: AU-3, AU-12, AU-14.

Control Enhancements:

(1) TIME STAMPS | SYNCHRONIZATION WITH AUTHORITATIVE TIME SOURCE

(a) Compare the internal system clocks [*Assignment: organization-defined frequency*] with [*Assignment: organization-defined authoritative time source*]; and

(b) Synchronize the internal system clocks to the authoritative time source when the time difference is greater than [*Assignment: organization-defined time-period*].

Supplemental Guidance: This control enhancement provides uniformity of time stamps for systems with multiple system clocks and systems connected over a network.

Related Controls: None.

(2) TIME STAMPS | SECONDARY AUTHORITATIVE TIME SOURCE

(a) Identify a secondary authoritative time source that is in a different geographic region than the primary authoritative time source; and

(b) Synchronize the internal system clocks to the secondary authoritative time source if the primary authoritative time source is unavailable.

Supplemental Guidance: It may be necessary to employ geolocation information to determine that the secondary authoritative time source is in a different geographic region.

Related Controls: None.

References: None.

AU-9   PROTECTION OF AUDIT INFORMATION

Control: Protect audit information and audit tools from unauthorized access, modification, and deletion.

Supplemental Guidance: Audit information includes all information, for example, audit records, audit settings, audit reports, and personally identifiable information, needed to successfully audit system activity. This control focuses on technical or automated protection of audit information. Physical protection of audit information is addressed by media protection controls and physical and environmental protection controls.

Related Controls: AC-3, AC-6, AU-6, AU-11, AU-14, AU-15, MP-2, MP-4, PE-2, PE-3, PE-6, SC-8, SI-4.

Control Enhancements:

(1)   PROTECTION OF AUDIT INFORMATION | HARDWARE WRITE-ONCE MEDIA

Write audit trails to hardware-enforced, write-once media.

Supplemental Guidance: This control enhancement applies to the initial generation of audit trails (i.e., the collection of audit records that represents the audit information to be used for detection, analysis, and reporting purposes) and to the backup of those audit trails. The enhancement does not apply to the initial generation of audit records prior to being written to an audit trail. Write-once, read-many (WORM) media includes, for example, Compact Disk-Recordable (CD-R) and Digital Video Disk-Recordable (DVD-R). In contrast, the use of switchable write-protection media such as on tape cartridges or Universal Serial Bus (USB) drives results in write-protected, but not write-once, media.

Related Controls: AU-4, AU-5.

(2)   PROTECTION OF AUDIT INFORMATION | STORE ON SEPARATE PHYSICAL SYSTEMS OR COMPONENTS

Store audit records [*Assignment: organization-defined frequency*] in a repository that is part of a physically different system or system component than the system or component being audited.

Supplemental Guidance: Storing audit information in a repository separate from the audited system or system component helps to ensure that a compromise of the system being audited does not also result in a compromise of the audit records. It may also enable management of audit records as an organization-wide activity. This control enhancement applies to initial generation as well as backup or long-term storage of audit information.

Related Controls: AU-4, AU-5.

(3)   PROTECTION OF AUDIT INFORMATION | CRYPTOGRAPHIC PROTECTION

Implement cryptographic mechanisms to protect the integrity of audit information and audit tools.

Supplemental Guidance: Cryptographic mechanisms used for protecting the integrity of audit information include, for example, signed hash functions using asymmetric cryptography enabling distribution of the public key to verify the hash information while maintaining the confidentiality of the secret key used to generate the hash.

Related Controls: AU-10, SC-12, SC-13.

(4)   PROTECTION OF AUDIT INFORMATION | ACCESS BY SUBSET OF PRIVILEGED USERS

Authorize access to management of audit functionality to only [*Assignment: organization-defined subset of privileged users*].

Supplemental Guidance: Individuals with privileged access to a system and who are also the subject of an audit by that system, may affect the reliability of audit information by inhibiting audit activities or modifying audit records. This control enhancement requires that privileged access be further defined between audit-related privileges and other privileges, thus limiting the users with audit-related privileges.

Related Controls: AC-5.

(5)   PROTECTION OF AUDIT INFORMATION | DUAL AUTHORIZATION

Enforce dual authorization for [*Selection (one or more): movement; deletion*] of [*Assignment: organization-defined audit information*].

Supplemental Guidance: Organizations may choose different solution options for different
types of audit information. Dual authorization mechanisms require the approval of two
authorized individuals to execute. Dual authorization may also be known as two-person
control.

Related Controls: AC-3.

(6) PROTECTION OF AUDIT INFORMATION | READ ONLY ACCESS

Authorize read-only access to audit information to [*Assignment: organization-defined subset of privileged users*].

Supplemental Guidance: Restricting privileged user authorizations to read-only helps to limit
the potential damage to organizations that could be initiated by such users, for example,
deleting audit records to cover up malicious activity.

Related Controls: None.

(7) PROTECTION OF AUDIT INFORMATION | STORE ON COMPONENT WITH DIFFERENT OPERATING SYSTEM

Store audit information on a component running a different operating system than the system or component being audited.

Supplemental Guidance: This control enhancement helps reduce the risk of a vulnerability
specific to an operating system resulting in a compromise of the audit records.

Related controls: AU-4, AU-5, AU-11, SC-29.

References: FIPS Publications 140-2, 180-4, 202.

AU-10 NON-REPUDIATION

Control: Protect against an individual (or process acting on behalf of an individual) falsely denying
having performed [*Assignment: organization-defined actions to be covered by non-repudiation*].

Supplemental Guidance: Types of individual actions covered by non-repudiation include creating
information, sending and receiving messages, and approving information. Non-repudiation
protects individuals against later claims by authors of not having authored certain documents;
senders of not having transmitted messages; receivers of not having received messages; and
individual signatories of not having signed documents. Non-repudiation services can be used to
determine if information originated from a certain individual, or if an individual took specific
actions, for example, sending an email, signing a contract, or approving a procurement request, or
received specific information. Organizations obtain non-repudiation services by employing
various techniques or mechanisms including, for example, digital signatures and digital message
receipts.

Related Controls: AU-9, PM-12, SC-8, SC-12, SC-13, SC-16, SC-17, SC-23.

Control Enhancements:

(1) NON-REPUDIATION | ASSOCIATION OF IDENTITIES

    (a) **Bind the identity of the information producer with the information to [*Assignment: organization-defined strength of binding*]; and**

    (b) **Provide the means for authorized individuals to determine the identity of the producer of the information.**

Supplemental Guidance: This control enhancement supports audit requirements that provide
organizational personnel with the means to identify who produced specific information in the
event of an information transfer. Organizations determine and approve the strength of the
binding between the information producer and the information based on the security category
of the information and relevant risk factors.

Related Controls: AC-4, AC-16.

(2) NON-REPUDIATION | VALIDATE BINDING OF INFORMATION PRODUCER IDENTITY

    (a) **Validate the binding of the information producer identity to the information at [*Assignment: organization-defined frequency*]; and**

    (b) **Perform [*Assignment: organization-defined actions*] in the event of a validation error.**

Supplemental Guidance: This control enhancement prevents the modification of information between production and review. The validation of bindings can be achieved, for example, using cryptographic checksums. Organizations determine if validations are in response to user requests or generated automatically.

Related Controls: AC-3, AC-4, AC-16.

(3) NON-REPUDIATION | CHAIN OF CUSTODY

Maintain reviewer or releaser identity and credentials within the established chain of custody for all information reviewed or released.

Supplemental Guidance: Chain of custody is a process that tracks the movement of evidence through its collection, safeguarding, and analysis life cycle by documenting each person who handled the evidence, the date and time it was collected or transferred, and the purpose for the transfer. If the reviewer is a human or if the review function is automated but separate from the release/transfer function, the system associates the identity of the reviewer of the information to be released with the information and the information label. In the case of human reviews, this control enhancement provides organizational officials the means to identify who reviewed and released the information. In the case of automated reviews, this control enhancement ensures that only approved review functions are employed.

Related Controls: AC-4, AC-16.

(4) NON-REPUDIATION | VALIDATE BINDING OF INFORMATION REVIEWER IDENTITY

(a) **Validate the binding of the information reviewer identity to the information at the transfer or release points prior to release or transfer between [*Assignment: organization-defined security domains*]; and**

(b) **Perform [*Assignment: organization-defined actions*] in the event of a validation error.**

Supplemental Guidance: This control enhancement prevents the modification of information between review and transfer/release. The validation of bindings can be achieved, for example, using cryptographic checksums. Organizations determine validations are in response to user requests or generated automatically.

Related Controls: AC-4, AC-16.

(5) NON-REPUDIATION | DIGITAL SIGNATURES

[Withdrawn: Incorporated into SI-13].

References: FIPS Publications 140-2, 180-4, 186-4, 202; NIST Special Publication 800-177.

AU-11 AUDIT RECORD RETENTION

Control: Retain audit records for [*Assignment: organization-defined time-period consistent with records retention policy*] to provide support for after-the-fact investigations of security and privacy incidents and to meet regulatory and organizational information retention requirements.

Supplemental Guidance: Organizations retain audit records until it is determined that they are no longer needed for administrative, legal, audit, or other operational purposes. This includes, for example, retention and availability of audit records relative to Freedom of Information Act (FOIA) requests, subpoenas, and law enforcement actions. Organizations develop standard categories of audit records relative to such types of actions and standard response processes for each type of action. The National Archives and Records Administration (NARA) General Records Schedules provide federal policy on record retention.

Related Controls: AU-2, AU-4, AU-5, AU-6, AU-9, AU-14, MP-6, RA-5, SI-12.

Control Enhancements:

(1) AUDIT RECORD RETENTION | LONG-TERM RETRIEVAL CAPABILITY

Employ [*Assignment: organization-defined measures*] to ensure that long-term audit records generated by the system can be retrieved.

Supplemental Guidance: This control enhancement helps to ensure that, from a technological perspective, audit records requiring long-term storage (on the order of years) can be accessed

and read when needed. Mechanisms employed by organizations to help facilitate the retrieval of
audit records include, for example, converting records to newer formats, retaining equipment
capable of reading the records, and retaining necessary documentation to help organizational
personnel understand how to interpret the records.

Related Controls: None.

References: None.

AU-12   AUDIT GENERATION

Control:

a.   Provide audit record generation capability for the auditable event types in AU-2 a. at
[*Assignment: organization-defined system components*];

b.   Allow [*Assignment: organization-defined personnel or roles*] to select which auditable event
types are to be audited by specific components of the system; and

c.   Generate audit records for the event types defined in AU-2 d. with the content in AU-3.

Supplemental Guidance: Audit records can be generated from many different system components.
The list of audited event types is the set of event types for which audits are to be generated. These
event types are a subset of all event types for which the system can generate audit records.

Related Controls: AC-6, AC-17, AU-2, AU-3, AU-4, AU-5, AU-6, AU-7, AU-14, CM-5, MA-4,
MP-4, PM-12 SC-18, SI-3, SI-4, SI-7, SI-10.

Control Enhancements:

(1)   AUDIT GENERATION | SYSTEM-WIDE AND TIME-CORRELATED AUDIT TRAIL

Compile audit records from [*Assignment: organization-defined system components*] into a system-
wide (logical or physical) audit trail that is time-correlated to within [*Assignment: organization-
defined level of tolerance for the relationship between time stamps of individual records in the
audit trail*].

Supplemental Guidance: Audit trails are time-correlated if the time stamps in the individual
audit records can be reliably related to the time stamps in other audit records to achieve a time
ordering of the records within organizational tolerances.

Related Controls: AU-8.

(2)   AUDIT GENERATION | STANDARDIZED FORMATS

Produce a system-wide (logical or physical) audit trail composed of audit records in a standardized
format.

Supplemental Guidance: Audit information that is normalized to common standards promotes
interoperability and exchange of such information between dissimilar devices and systems.
This facilitates production of event information that can be more readily analyzed and
correlated. Standard formats for audit records include, for example, system log records and
audit records compliant with Common Event Expressions (CEE). If logging mechanisms
within systems do not conform to standardized formats, systems may convert individual audit
records into standardized formats when compiling system-wide audit trails.

Related Controls: None.

(3)   AUDIT GENERATION | CHANGES BY AUTHORIZED INDIVIDUALS

Provide and implement the capability for [*Assignment: organization-defined individuals or roles*] to
change the auditing to be performed on [*Assignment: organization-defined system components*]
based on [*Assignment: organization-defined selectable event criteria*] within [*Assignment:
organization-defined time thresholds*].

Supplemental Guidance: This control enhancement enables organizations to extend or limit
auditing as necessary to meet organizational requirements. Auditing that is limited to conserve
system resources may be extended to address certain threat situations. In addition, auditing
may be limited to a specific set of event types to facilitate audit reduction, analysis, and

reporting. Organizations can establish time thresholds in which audit actions are changed, for example, near real-time, within minutes, or within hours.

Related Controls: AC-3.

(4) AUDIT GENERATION | QUERY PARAMETER AUDITS OF PERSONALLY IDENTIFIABLE INFORMATION
Provide and implement the capability for auditing the parameters of user query events for data sets containing personally identifiable information.

Supplemental Guidance: Query parameters are explicit criteria that a user or automated system submits to a system to retrieve data. Auditing of query parameters within systems for datasets that contain personally identifiable information augments an organization's ability to track and understand the access, usage, or sharing of personally identifiable information by authorized personnel.

Related Controls: None.

References: None.

AU-13 MONITORING FOR INFORMATION DISCLOSURE

Control: Monitor [*Assignment: organization-defined open source information and/or information sites*] [*Assignment: organization-defined frequency*] for evidence of unauthorized disclosure of organizational information.

Supplemental Guidance: Open source information includes, for example, social networking sites.

Related Controls: AC-22, PE-3, PM-12, RA-5, SC-7.

Control Enhancements:

(1) MONITORING FOR INFORMATION DISCLOSURE | USE OF AUTOMATED TOOLS
Employ automated mechanisms to determine if organizational information has been disclosed in an unauthorized manner.

Supplemental Guidance: Automated mechanisms can include, for example, automated scripts to monitor new posts on selected websites, and commercial services providing notifications and alerts to organizations.

Related Controls: None.

(2) MONITORING FOR INFORMATION DISCLOSURE | REVIEW OF MONITORED SITES
Review the open source information sites being monitored [*Assignment: organization-defined frequency*].

Supplemental Guidance: None.

Related Controls: None.

References: None.

AU-14 SESSION AUDIT

Control: Provide and implement the capability for authorized users to select a user session to capture/record or view/hear.

Supplemental Guidance: Session audits include, for example, monitoring keystrokes, tracking websites visited, and recording information and/or file transfers. Session auditing activities are developed, integrated, and used in consultation with legal counsel in accordance with applicable laws, Executive Orders, directives, policies, regulations, standard, and guidelines.

Related Controls: AC-3, AU-2, AU-3, AU-4, AU-5, AU-8, AU-9, AU-11, AU-12.

Control Enhancements:

(1) SESSION AUDIT | SYSTEM START-UP
Initiate session audits automatically at system start-up.

Supplemental Guidance: None.

Related Controls: None.

(2) SESSION AUDIT | CAPTURE AND RECORD CONTENT

Provide and implement the capability for authorized users to capture, record, and log content related to a user session.

Supplemental Guidance: None.

Related Controls: None.

(3) SESSION AUDIT | REMOTE VIEWING AND LISTENING

Provide and implement the capability for authorized users to remotely view and hear content related to an established user session in real time.

Supplemental Guidance: None.

Related Controls: AC-17.

References: None.

AU-15 ALTERNATE AUDIT CAPABILITY

Control: Provide an alternate audit capability in the event of a failure in primary audit capability that implements [*Assignment: organization-defined alternate audit functionality*].

Supplemental Guidance: Since an alternate audit capability may be a short-term protection employed until the failure in the primary auditing capability is corrected, organizations may determine that the alternate audit capability need only provide a subset of the primary audit functionality that is impacted by the failure.

Related Controls: AU-5, AU-9.

Control Enhancements: None.

References: None.

AU-16 CROSS-ORGANIZATIONAL AUDITING

Control: Employ [*Assignment: organization-defined methods*] for coordinating [*Assignment: organization-defined audit information*] among external organizations when audit information is transmitted across organizational boundaries.

Supplemental Guidance: When organizations use systems and/or services of external organizations, the auditing capability necessitates a coordinated approach across organizations. For example, maintaining the identity of individuals that requested specific services across organizational boundaries may often be very difficult, and doing so may prove to have significant performance and privacy ramifications. Therefore, it is often the case that cross-organizational auditing simply captures the identity of individuals issuing requests at the initial system, and subsequent systems record that the requests emanated from authorized individuals.

Related Controls: AU-6, AU-7.

Control Enhancements:

(1) CROSS-ORGANIZATIONAL AUDITING | IDENTITY PRESERVATION

Require that the identity of individuals is preserved in cross-organizational audit trails.

Supplemental Guidance: This control enhancement applies when there is a need to be able to trace actions that are performed across organizational boundaries to a specific individual.

Related Controls: IA-2, IA-4, IA-5, IA-8.

(2) CROSS-ORGANIZATIONAL AUDITING | SHARING OF AUDIT INFORMATION

Provide cross-organizational audit information to [*Assignment: organization-defined organizations*] based on [*Assignment: organization-defined cross-organizational sharing agreements*].

Supplemental Guidance: Because of the distributed nature of the audit information, cross organization sharing of audit information may be essential for effective analysis of the auditing being performed. For example, the audit records of one organization may not provide sufficient information to determine the appropriate or inappropriate use of organizational information resources by individuals in other organizations. In some instances, only the home organizations of individuals have the appropriate knowledge to make such determinations, thus requiring the sharing of audit information among organizations.

Related Controls: IR-4, SI-4.

References: None.

3.4 ASSESSMENT, AUTHORIZATION, AND MONITORING

Quick link to Assessment, Authorization, and Monitoring summary table

CA-1 ASSESSMENT, AUTHORIZATION, AND MONITORING POLICY AND PROCEDURES

Control:

a. Develop, document, and disseminate to [*Assignment: organization-defined personnel or roles*]:

   1. A security and privacy assessment, authorization, and monitoring policy that:

      (a) Addresses purpose, scope, roles, responsibilities, management commitment, coordination among organizational entities, and compliance; and

      (b) Is consistent with applicable laws, Executive Orders, directives, regulations, policies, standards, and guidelines; and

   2. Procedures to facilitate the implementation of the security and privacy assessment, authorization, and monitoring policy and the associated security and privacy assessment, authorization, and monitoring controls;

b. Designate an [*Assignment: organization-defined senior management official*] to manage the security and privacy assessment, authorization, and monitoring policy and procedures;

c. Review and update the current security and privacy assessment, authorization, and monitoring:

   1. Policy [*Assignment: organization-defined frequency*]; and

   2. Procedures [*Assignment: organization-defined frequency*];

d. Ensure that the security and privacy assessment, authorization, and monitoring procedures implement the security and privacy assessment, authorization, and monitoring policy and controls; and

e. Develop, document, and implement remediation actions for violations of security and privacy assessment, authorization, and monitoring policy.

Supplemental Guidance: This control addresses the establishment of policy and procedures for the effective implementation of the controls and control enhancements in the CA family. The risk management strategy is an important factor in establishing policy and procedures. Comprehensive policy and procedures help provide security and privacy assurance. Security and privacy program policies and procedures at the organization level may make the need for system-specific policies and procedures unnecessary. The policy can be included as part of the general security and privacy policy or can be represented by multiple policies reflecting the complex nature of organizations. The procedures can be established for security and privacy programs and for systems, if needed. Procedures describe how policies or controls are implemented and can be directed at the personnel or role that is the object of the procedure. Procedures can be documented in system security and privacy plans or in one or more separate documents. It is important to recognize that restating controls does not constitute an organizational policy or procedure.

Related Controls: PM-9, PS-8, SI-12.

Control Enhancements: None.

References: NIST Special Publications 800-12, 800-30, 800-39, 800-50, 800-100, 800-122; NIST Interagency Report 8062.

CA-2 ASSESSMENTS

Control:

a. Develop a security and privacy assessment plan that describes the scope of the assessment including:

   1. Security and privacy controls and control enhancements under assessment;

   2. Assessment procedures to be used to determine control effectiveness; and

   3. Assessment environment, assessment team, and assessment roles and responsibilities;

b. Ensure the assessment plan is reviewed and approved by the authorizing official or designated representative prior to conducting the assessment;

c. Assess the security and privacy controls in the system and its environment of operation [*Assignment: organization-defined frequency*] to determine the extent to which the controls are implemented correctly, operating as intended, and producing the desired outcome with respect to meeting established security and privacy requirements;

d. Produce a security and privacy assessment report that document the results of the assessment; and

e. Provide the results of the security and privacy control assessment to [*Assignment: organization-defined individuals or roles*].

Supplemental Guidance: Organizations assess security and privacy controls in organizational systems and the environments in which those systems operate as part of initial and ongoing authorizations; FISMA annual assessments; continuous monitoring; and system development life cycle activities. Assessments ensure that organizations meet information security and privacy requirements; identify weaknesses and deficiencies in the development process; provide essential information needed to make risk-based decisions as part of authorization processes; and ensure compliance to vulnerability mitigation procedures. Organizations conduct assessments on the implemented controls from Chapter Three as documented in security plans and privacy plans. Organizations can use other types of assessment activities such as vulnerability scanning and system monitoring to maintain the security and privacy posture of systems during the entire life cycle. Assessment reports document assessment results in sufficient detail as deemed necessary by organizations, to determine the accuracy and completeness of the reports and whether the controls are implemented correctly, operating as intended, and producing the desired outcome with respect to meeting requirements. Assessment results are provided to the individuals or roles appropriate for the types of assessments being conducted. For example, assessments conducted in support of authorization decisions are provided to authorizing officials, senior agency officials for privacy, and/or authorizing official designated representatives.

To satisfy annual assessment requirements, organizations can use assessment results from the following sources: initial or ongoing system authorizations; continuous monitoring; or system development life cycle activities. Organizations ensure that assessment results are current, relevant to the determination of control effectiveness, and obtained with the appropriate level of assessor independence. Existing control assessment results can be reused to the extent that the results are still valid and can also be supplemented with additional assessments as needed. After the initial authorizations, organizations assess controls during continuous monitoring. Organizations also establish the frequency for ongoing assessments in accordance with organizational continuous monitoring strategies. External audits including, for example, audits by external entities such as regulatory agencies, are outside the scope of this control.

Related Controls: AC-20, CA-5, CA-6, CA-7, PM-9, RA-5, SA-11, SA-12, SC-38, SI-3, SI-12.

Control Enhancements:

(1) ASSESSMENTS | INDEPENDENT ASSESSORS

Employ independent assessors or assessment teams to conduct security and privacy control assessments.

Supplemental Guidance: Independent assessors or assessment teams are individuals or groups conducting impartial assessments of systems. Impartiality implies that assessors are free from any perceived or actual conflicts of interest regarding development, operation, sustainment, or management of the systems under assessment or the determination of control effectiveness. To achieve impartiality, assessors should not create a mutual or conflicting interest with the organizations where the assessments are being conducted; assess their own work; act as management or employees of the organizations they are serving; or place themselves in positions of advocacy for the organizations acquiring their services. Independent assessments can be obtained from elements within organizations or can be contracted to public or private sector entities outside of organizations. Authorizing officials determine the required level of independence based on the security categories of systems and/or the risk to organizational operations, organizational assets, or individuals. Authorizing officials also determine if the level of assessor independence provides sufficient assurance that the results are sound and can be used to make credible, risk-based decisions. This includes determining whether contracted assessment services have sufficient independence, for example, when system owners are not directly involved in contracting processes or cannot influence the impartiality of assessors conducting assessments. When organizations that own the systems are small or organizational structures require that assessments are conducted by individuals that are in the developmental, operational, or management chain of system owners, independence in assessment processes can be achieved by ensuring that assessment results are carefully reviewed and analyzed by independent teams of experts to validate the completeness, accuracy, integrity, and reliability of the results. Organizations recognize that assessments performed for purposes other than direct support to authorization decisions are, when performed by assessors with sufficient independence, more likely to be useable for such decisions, thereby reducing the need to repeat assessments.

Related Controls: None.

(2) ASSESSMENTS | SPECIALIZED ASSESSMENTS

Include as part of security and privacy control assessments, [Assignment: organization-defined frequency], [Selection: announced; unannounced], [Selection (one or more): in-depth monitoring; vulnerability scanning; malicious user testing; insider threat assessment; performance and load testing; [Assignment: organization-defined other forms of assessment]].

Supplemental Guidance: Organizations can conduct specialized assessments including, for example, verification, validation, insider threat assessments, malicious user testing, system monitoring, and other forms of testing. Such assessments can improve readiness by exercising organizational capabilities and indicating current performance levels as a means of focusing actions to improve security and privacy. Organizations conduct these types of specialized assessments in accordance with applicable laws, Executive Orders, directives, policies, regulations, standards, and guidelines. Authorizing officials approve the assessment methods in coordination with the organizational risk executive function. Organizations can incorporate vulnerabilities uncovered during assessments into vulnerability remediation processes.

Related Controls: PE-3, SI-2.

(3) ASSESSMENTS | EXTERNAL ORGANIZATIONS

Accept the results of security and privacy control assessments of [Assignment: organization-defined system] performed by [Assignment: organization-defined external organization] when the assessment meets [Assignment: organization-defined requirements].

Supplemental Guidance: Organizations may rely on security and privacy control assessments of organizational systems by other (external) organizations. Using such assessments and reusing existing assessment evidence can significantly decrease the time and resources required for assessments by limiting the amount of independent assessment activities that organizations need to perform. The factors that organizations consider in determining whether to accept assessment results from external organizations can vary. Such factors include, for example, past assessment experiences the organization has had with the organization conducting the assessment; the reputation that the assessing organization has with regard to assessments; the level of detail of supporting assessment evidence provided; and the mandates imposed by applicable laws, Executive Orders, directives, policies, regulations, standards, and guidelines.

Related Controls: None.

References: FIPS Publication 199; NIST Special Publications 800-37, 800-39, 800-53A, 800-115, 800-122, 800-137; NIST Interagency Report 8062.

CA-3   SYSTEM INTERCONNECTIONS

Control:

a.   Authorize connections from the system to other systems using Interconnection Security Agreements;

b.   Document, for each interconnection, the interface characteristics, security and privacy requirements, and the nature of the information communicated; and

c.   Review and update Interconnection Security Agreements [*Assignment: organization-defined frequency*].

Supplemental Guidance: This control applies to dedicated connections between two or more separate systems and does not apply to transitory, user-controlled connections such as email and website browsing. Organizations consider the risks that may be introduced when systems are connected to other systems with different security and privacy requirements and controls, including systems within the same organization and systems external to the organization. Authorizing officials determine the risk associated with system connections and the appropriate controls employed. If interconnecting systems have the same authorizing official, organizations do not need to develop Interconnection Security Agreements. Instead, those organizations can describe the interface characteristics between the interconnecting systems in their respective security and privacy plans. If interconnecting systems have different authorizing officials within the same organization, the organizations can develop Interconnection Security Agreements or they can describe the interface characteristics between the systems in the security and privacy plans for the respective systems. Organizations may also incorporate Interconnection Security Agreement information into formal contracts, especially for interconnections established between federal agencies and nonfederal organizations. Risk considerations also include systems sharing the same networks. As part of the risk assessment of connecting to external systems, organizations consider the number and types of transitive connections that exist when establishing such connections.

Related Controls: AC-20, AU-16, IA-3, PL-2, RA-3, SA-9, SC-7, SI-12.

Control Enhancements:

(1)   SYSTEM INTERCONNECTIONS | UNCLASSIFIED NATIONAL SECURITY SYSTEM CONNECTIONS

Prohibit the direct connection of an [*Assignment: organization-defined unclassified, national security system*] to an external network without the use of [*Assignment: organization-defined boundary protection device*].

Supplemental Guidance: Organizations typically do not have control over external networks including the Internet. Approved boundary protection devices including, for example, routers and firewalls. mediate communications and information flows between unclassified national security systems and external networks.

Related Controls: None.

(2)   SYSTEM INTERCONNECTIONS | CLASSIFIED NATIONAL SECURITY SYSTEM CONNECTIONS

Prohibit the direct connection of a classified, national security system to an external network without the use of [*Assignment: organization-defined boundary protection device*].

Supplemental Guidance: Organizations typically do not have control over external networks including the Internet. Approved boundary protection devices including, for example, routers and firewalls. mediate communications and information flows between classified national security systems and external networks. In addition, approved boundary protection devices (typically managed interface/cross-domain systems) provide information flow enforcement from systems to external networks.

Related Controls: None.

(3) SYSTEM INTERCONNECTIONS | UNCLASSIFIED NON-NATIONAL SECURITY SYSTEM CONNECTIONS

Prohibit the direct connection of an [Assignment: organization defined unclassified, non-national security system] to an external network without the use of [Assignment; organization-defined boundary protection device].

Supplemental Guidance: Organizations typically do not have control over external networks including the Internet. Approved boundary protection devices including, for example, routers and firewalls mediate communications and information flows between unclassified non-national security systems and external networks.

Related Controls: None.

(4) SYSTEM INTERCONNECTIONS | CONNECTIONS TO PUBLIC NETWORKS

Prohibit the direct connection of an [Assignment: organization-defined system] to a public network.

Supplemental Guidance: A public network is any network accessible to the general public including, for example, the Internet and organizational extranets with public access.

Related Controls: None.

(5) SYSTEM INTERCONNECTIONS | RESTRICTIONS ON EXTERNAL SYSTEM CONNECTIONS

Employ a deny-all, permit-by-exception policy for allowing [Assignment: organization-defined systems] to connect to external systems.

Supplemental Guidance: Organizations can constrain system connectivity to external domains by employing a deny-all, permit-by-exception policy known as *whitelisting*. Organizations determine what exceptions, if any, are acceptable. This control enhancement is applied to a system that is connected to another system. Alternatively, control enhancement SC-7(5) applies to any type of network communications.

Related Controls: SC-7.

(6) SYSTEM INTERCONNECTIONS | SECONDARY AND TERTIARY CONNECTIONS

(a) Identify secondary and tertiary connections to the interconnected systems; and

(b) Take measures to ensure that connections are severed when security and privacy controls on identified secondary and tertiary systems cannot be verified or validated.

Supplemental Guidance: For certain critical systems and applications including, for example, high-value assets, it may be necessary to identify second and third level connections to the interconnected systems. The transparency of the protection measures in place in secondary and tertiary systems connected directly or indirectly to organizational systems is essential in understanding the actual security and privacy risks resulting from those interconnections. Organizational systems can inherit risk from secondary and tertiary systems through those connections and make the organizational systems more susceptible to threats, hazards, and adverse consequences.

Related Controls: None.

References: FIPS Publication 199; NIST Special Publication 800-47.

CA-4 SECURITY CERTIFICATION

[Withdrawn: Incorporated into CA-2].

CA-5 PLAN OF ACTION AND MILESTONES

Control:

a. Develop a plan of action and milestones for the system to document the planned remedial actions of the organization to correct weaknesses or deficiencies noted during the assessment of the controls and to reduce or eliminate known vulnerabilities in the system; and

b. Update existing plan of action and milestones [Assignment: organization-defined frequency] based on the findings from control assessments, impact analyses, and continuous monitoring activities.

Supplemental Guidance: Plans of action and milestones are required documents in authorization packages and are subject to federal reporting requirements established by OMB.

Related Controls: CA-2, CA-7, PM-4, PM-9, RA-7, SI-2, SI-12.

Control Enhancements:

(1) PLAN OF ACTION AND MILESTONES | AUTOMATION SUPPORT FOR ACCURACY AND CURRENCY
Employ automated mechanisms to ensure that the plan of action and milestones for the system is accurate, up to date, and readily available.

Supplemental Guidance: None.

Related Controls: None.

References: NIST Special Publication 800-37.

CA-6 AUTHORIZATION

Control:

a. Assign a senior-level executive or manager as the authorizing official for the system and for any common controls inherited by the system;

b. Ensure that the authorizing official, before commencing operations:

1. Authorizes the system for processing; and

2. Authorizes the common controls inherited by the system; and

c. Update the authorizations [*Assignment: organization-defined frequency*].

Supplemental Guidance: Authorizations are official management decisions by senior officials to authorize operation of systems (including the controls inherited by those systems) and to explicitly accept the risk to organizational operations and assets, individuals, other organizations, and the Nation based on the implementation of agreed-upon security and privacy controls. Authorizing officials provide budgetary oversight for organizational systems or assume responsibility for the mission and business operations supported by those systems. The authorization process is a federal responsibility and therefore, authorizing officials must be federal employees. Authorizing officials are responsible and accountable for security and privacy risks associated with the operation and use of organizational systems. Nonfederal organizations may have similar processes to authorize their systems and senior officials that assume the authorization role and associated responsibilities. Organizations conduct ongoing authorizations of systems by implementing continuous monitoring programs. Robust continuous monitoring programs reduce the need for separate reauthorization processes. Through the employment of comprehensive continuous monitoring processes, critical information contained in authorization packages including the security and privacy plans, security and privacy assessment reports, and plans of action and milestones, is updated on an ongoing basis. This provides authorizing officials, system owners, and common control providers with an up-to-date status of the security and privacy state of their systems, controls, and environments of operation. To reduce the cost of reauthorization, authorizing officials use the results of continuous monitoring processes to the maximum extent possible as the basis for rendering reauthorization decisions.

Related Controls: CA-2, CA-7, PM-9, PM-10, SA-10, SI-12.

Control Enhancements:

(1) AUTHORIZATION | JOINT AUTHORIZATION — SAME ORGANIZATION
Employ a joint authorization process for the system that includes multiple authorizing officials from the same organization conducting the authorization.

Supplemental Guidance: Assigning multiple authorizing officials from the same organization to serve as co-authorizing officials for the system, increases the level of independence in the risk-based decision making process for security and privacy. It also implements the concepts of separation of duties and dual authorization as applied to the system authorization process.

This enhancement is most relevant for interconnected systems, shared systems, and systems with one or more information owners.

Related Controls: AC-6.

(2) AUTHORIZATION | JOINT AUTHORIZATION — DIFFERENT ORGANIZATIONS

Employ a joint authorization process for the system that includes multiple authorizing officials with at least one authorizing official from an organization external to the organization conducting the authorization.

Supplemental Guidance: Assigning multiple authorizing officials, at least one of which comes from an external organization, to serve as co-authorizing officials for the system, increases the level of independence in the risk-based decision making process for security and privacy. It also implements the concepts of separation of duties and dual authorization and as applied to the system authorization process. Employing authorizing officials from external organizations to supplement the authorization official from the organization owning or hosting the system may be necessary when those organizations have a vested interest or equities in the outcome of the authorization decision. This situation may occur with interconnected systems, shared systems, and systems with one or more information owners. Accordingly, the authorizing officials from the external organizations may be considered key stakeholders of the system undergoing authorization.

Related Controls: AC-6.

References: NIST Special Publications 800-37, 800-137; NIST Supplemental Guidance on Ongoing Authorization.

CA-7   CONTINUOUS MONITORING

Control: Develop a security and privacy continuous monitoring strategy and implement security and privacy continuous monitoring programs that include:

a. Establishing the following security and privacy metrics to be monitored: [*Assignment: organization-defined metrics*];

b. Establishing [*Assignment: organization-defined frequencies*] for monitoring and [*Assignment: organization-defined frequencies*] for ongoing assessment of security and privacy control effectiveness;

c. Ongoing security and privacy control assessments in accordance with the organizational continuous monitoring strategy;

d. Ongoing security and privacy status monitoring of organization-defined metrics in accordance with the organizational continuous monitoring strategy;

e. Correlation and analysis of security- and privacy-related information generated by security and privacy control assessments and monitoring;

f. Response actions to address results of the analysis of security- and privacy-related information; and

g. Reporting the security and privacy status of the organization and organizational systems to [*Assignment: organization-defined personnel or roles*] [*Assignment: organization-defined frequency*].

Supplemental Guidance: Continuous monitoring programs facilitate ongoing awareness of threats, vulnerabilities, and information security and privacy to support organizational risk management decisions. The terms continuous and ongoing imply that organizations assess security and privacy controls and associated risks at a frequency sufficient to support risk-based decisions. The results of continuous monitoring generate risk response actions by organizations. When monitoring the effectiveness of controls that have been grouped into capabilities, a root-cause analysis may be needed to determine the specific control that has failed. Continuous monitoring programs also allow organizations to maintain the authorizations of systems and common controls over time in highly dynamic environments of operation with changing mission and business needs, threats, vulnerabilities, and technologies. Having access to security and privacy-related information on a continuing basis through reports and dashboards gives organizational officials the capability to make more effective and timely risk management decisions, including ongoing authorization decisions. Automation supports more frequent updates to hardware, software, and firmware inventories, authorization packages, and other system information. Effectiveness is further enhanced when continuous monitoring outputs are formatted to provide information that is specific, measurable, actionable, relevant, and timely. Continuous monitoring activities are scaled in accordance with the security categories of systems.

Related Controls: AC-2, AC-6, AU-6, CA-2, CA-5, CA-6, CM-3, CM-4, CM-6, CM-11, IA-5, PE-6, PL-2, PM-4, PM-6, PM-9, PM-10, PM-12, PM-14, PM-32, RA-3, RA-5, RA-7, SA-11, SC-5, SC-38, SI-3, SI-4, SI-12.

Control Enhancements:

(1) CONTINUOUS MONITORING | INDEPENDENT ASSESSMENT

Employ independent assessors or assessment teams to monitor the security and privacy controls in the system on an ongoing basis.

Supplemental Guidance: Organizations can maximize the value of control assessments during the continuous monitoring process by requiring that assessments be conducted by assessors with appropriate levels of independence. The level of assessor independence required is based on organizational continuous monitoring strategies. Assessor independence provides a degree of impartiality to the monitoring process. To achieve such impartiality, assessors should not create a mutual or conflicting interest with the organizations where the assessments are being conducted; assess their own work; act as management or employees of the organizations they are serving; or place themselves in advocacy positions for the organizations acquiring their services.

Related Controls: None.

(2) CONTINUOUS MONITORING | TYPES OF ASSESSMENTS

[Withdrawn: Incorporated into CA-2].

(3) CONTINUOUS MONITORING | TREND ANALYSES

Employ trend analyses to determine if security and privacy control implementations, the frequency of continuous monitoring activities, and the types of activities used in the continuous monitoring process need to be modified based on empirical data.

Supplemental Guidance: Trend analyses can include, for example, examining recent threat information regarding the types of threat events that have occurred within the organization or the federal government, success rates of certain types of attacks, emerging vulnerabilities in specific technologies, evolving social engineering techniques, results from multiple control assessments, the effectiveness of configuration settings, and findings from Inspectors General or auditors.

Related Controls: None.

(4) CONTINUOUS MONITORING | RISK MONITORING

Ensure risk monitoring is an integral part of the continuous monitoring strategy that includes the following:

(a) **Effectiveness monitoring;**

(b) **Compliance monitoring; and**

(c) **Change monitoring.**

Supplemental Guidance: Effectiveness monitoring determines the ongoing effectiveness of implemented risk response measures. Compliance monitoring verifies that the required risk response measures are implemented. It also verifies that security and privacy requirements are satisfied. Change monitoring identifies changes to organizational systems and environments of operation that may affect security and privacy risk.

Related Controls: None.

References: NIST Special Publications 800-37, 800-39, 800-53A, 800-115, 800-122, 800-137; NIST Interagency Reports 8011, 8062.

CA-8 PENETRATION TESTING

<u>Control</u>: Conduct penetration testing [*Assignment: organization-defined frequency*] on [*Assignment: organization-defined systems or system components*].

<u>Supplemental Guidance</u>: Penetration testing is a specialized type of assessment conducted on systems or individual system components to identify vulnerabilities that could be exploited by adversaries. Penetration testing goes beyond automated vulnerability scanning and is most effectively conducted by penetration testing agents and teams with demonstrable skills and experience that, depending on the scope of the penetration testing, include technical expertise in network, operating system, and/or application level security. Penetration testing can be used to either validate vulnerabilities or determine the degree of penetration resistance of systems to adversaries within specified constraints. Such constraints include, for example, time, resources, and skills. Penetration testing attempts to duplicate the actions of adversaries in carrying out attacks against organizations and provides a more in-depth analysis of security- and privacy-related weaknesses or deficiencies. Organizations can use the results of vulnerability analyses to support penetration testing activities. Penetration testing can be conducted on the hardware, software, or firmware components of a system and can exercise both physical and technical controls. A standard method for penetration testing includes, for example, pretest analysis based on full knowledge of the target system; pretest identification of potential vulnerabilities based on pretest analysis; and testing designed to determine exploitability of identified vulnerabilities. All parties agree to the rules of engagement before commencement of penetration testing scenarios. Organizations correlate the rules of engagement for the penetration tests with the tools, techniques, and procedures that are anticipated to be employed by adversaries carrying out attacks. Risk assessments guide the decisions on the level of independence required for personnel conducting penetration testing.

<u>Related Controls</u>: SA-11, SA-12.

<u>Control Enhancements</u>:

(1) PENETRATION TESTING | INDEPENDENT PENETRATION AGENT OR TEAM

Employ an independent penetration agent or penetration team to perform penetration testing on the system or system components.

<u>Supplemental Guidance</u>: Independent penetration agents or teams are individuals or groups who conduct impartial penetration testing of organizational systems. Impartiality implies that penetration agents or teams are free from any perceived or actual conflicts of interest with respect to the development, operation, or management of the systems that are the targets of the penetration testing. Supplemental guidance for CA-2(1) provides additional information on independent assessments that can be applied to penetration testing.

<u>Related Controls</u>: CA-2.

(2) PENETRATION TESTING | RED TEAM EXERCISES

Employ [*Assignment: organization-defined red team exercises*] to simulate attempts by adversaries to compromise organizational systems in accordance with applicable rules of engagement.

<u>Supplemental Guidance</u>: Red team exercises extend the objectives of penetration testing by examining the security and privacy posture of organizations and their ability to implement effective cyber defenses. Red team exercises reflect simulated attempts by adversaries to compromise organizational missions and business functions and provide a comprehensive assessment of the security and privacy state of systems and organizations. Simulated attempts by adversaries to compromise missions and business functions and the systems that support those missions and functions may include technology-based attacks and social engineering-based attacks. Technology-based attacks include interactions with hardware, software, or firmware components and/or mission and business processes. Social engineering-based attacks include interactions via email, telephone, shoulder surfing, or personal conversations. Red team exercises are most effectively conducted by penetration testing agents and teams with knowledge of and experience with current adversarial tactics, techniques, procedures, and tools. While penetration testing may be primarily laboratory-based testing, organizations

can use red team exercises to provide more comprehensive assessments that reflect real-world conditions. Red team exercises can be used to improve security and privacy awareness and training and to assess control effectiveness.

Related Controls: None.

(3) PENETRATION TESTING | FACILITY PENETRATION TESTING

Employ a penetration testing process that includes [*Assignment: organization-defined frequency*] [*Selection: announced; unannounced*] attempts to bypass or circumvent controls associated with physical access points to the facility.

Supplemental Guidance: None.

Related Controls: CA-2, PE-3.

References: None.

CA-9 INTERNAL SYSTEM CONNECTIONS

Control:

a. Authorize internal connections of [*Assignment: organization-defined system components or classes of components*] to the system; and

b. Document, for each internal connection, the interface characteristics, security and privacy requirements, and the nature of the information communicated.

Supplemental Guidance: This control applies to connections between organizational systems and separate constituent system components. These intra-system connections, include, for example, system connections with mobile devices, notebook computers, desktop computers, workstations, printers, copiers, facsimile machines, scanners, sensors, and servers. Instead of authorizing each individual internal system connection, organizations can authorize internal connections for a class of system components with common characteristics and/or configurations. This can include, for example, all digital printers, scanners, and copiers with a specified processing, transmission, and storage capability or all smart phones with a specific baseline configuration.

Related Controls: AC-3, AC-4, AC-18, AC-19, CM-2, IA-3, SC-7, SI-12.

Control Enhancements:

(1) INTERNAL SYSTEM CONNECTIONS | COMPLIANCE CHECKS

Perform security and privacy compliance checks on constituent system components prior to the establishment of the internal connection.

Supplemental Guidance: Compliance checks may include, for example, verification of the relevant baseline configuration.

Related Controls: CM-6.

References: NIST Special Publication 800-124; NIST Interagency Report 8023.

3.1 CONFIGURATION MANAGEMENT

Quick link to Configuration Management summary table

CM-1 CONFIGURATION MANAGEMENT POLICY AND PROCEDURES

Control:

a. Develop, document, and disseminate to [*Assignment: organization-defined personnel or roles*]:

   1. A configuration management policy that:

     (a) Addresses purpose, scope, roles, responsibilities, management commitment, coordination among organizational entities, and compliance; and

     (b) Is consistent with applicable laws, Executive Orders, directives, regulations, policies, standards, and guidelines; and

   2. Procedures to facilitate the implementation of the configuration management policy and the associated configuration management controls;

b. Designate an [*Assignment: organization-defined senior management official*] to manage configuration management policy and procedures;

c. Review and update the current configuration management:

   1. Policy [*Assignment: organization-defined frequency*]; and

   2. Procedures [*Assignment: organization-defined frequency*];

d. Ensure that the configuration management procedures implement the configuration management policy and controls; and

e. Develop, document, and implement remediation actions for violations of the configuration management policy.

Supplemental Guidance: This control addresses the establishment of policy and procedures for the effective implementation of the controls and control enhancements in the CM family. The risk management strategy is an important factor in establishing policy and procedures. Comprehensive policy and procedures help provide security and privacy assurance. Security and privacy program policies and procedures at the organization level may make the need for system-specific policies and procedures unnecessary. The policy can be included as part of the general security and privacy policy or can be represented by multiple policies reflecting the complex nature of organizations. The procedures can be established for security and privacy programs and for systems, if needed. Procedures describe how policies or controls are implemented and can be directed at the personnel or role that is the object of the procedure. Procedures can be documented in system security and privacy plans or in one or more separate documents. It is important to recognize that restating controls does not constitute an organizational policy or procedure.

Related Controls: PM-9, PS-8, SI-12.

Control Enhancements: None.

References: NIST Special Publications 800-12, 800-30, 800-39, 800-100.

CM-2 BASELINE CONFIGURATION

Control:

a. Develop, document, and maintain under configuration control, a current baseline configuration of the system; and

b. Review and update the baseline configuration of the system:

1. [*Assignment: organization-defined frequency*];

2. When required due to [*Assignment organization-defined circumstances*]; and

3. When system components are installed or upgraded.

Supplemental Guidance: This control establishes baseline configurations for systems and system components including communications and connectivity-related aspects of systems. Baseline configurations are documented, formally reviewed and agreed-upon sets of specifications for systems or configuration items within those systems. Baseline configurations serve as a basis for future builds, releases, and/or changes to systems. Baseline configurations include information about system components, network topology, and the logical placement of those components within the system architecture. Maintaining baseline configurations requires creating new baselines as organizational systems change over time. Baseline configurations of systems reflect the current enterprise architecture.

Related Controls: AC-19, AU-6, CA-9, CM-1, CM-3, CM-5, CM-6, CM-8, CM-9, CP-9, CP-10, CP-12, PL-8, PM-5, SA-10, SC-18.

Control Enhancements:

(1) BASELINE CONFIGURATION | REVIEWS AND UPDATES
[Withdrawn: Incorporated into CM-2].

(2) BASELINE CONFIGURATION | AUTOMATION SUPPORT FOR ACCURACY AND CURRENCY
Employ automated mechanisms to maintain an up-to-date, complete, accurate, and readily available baseline configuration of the system.

Supplemental Guidance: Automated mechanisms that help organizations maintain consistent baseline configurations for systems include, for example, hardware and software inventory tools, configuration management tools, and network management tools. Such tools can be deployed and/or allocated as common controls, at the system level, or at the operating system or component level including, for example, on workstations, servers, notebook computers, network components, or mobile devices. Tools can be used, for example, to track version numbers on operating systems, applications, types of software installed, and current patch levels. This control enhancement can be satisfied by the implementation of CM-8(2) for organizations that choose to combine system component inventory and baseline configuration activities.

Related Controls: CM-7, IA-3, RA-5.

(3) BASELINE CONFIGURATION | RETENTION OF PREVIOUS CONFIGURATIONS
Retain [*Assignment: organization-defined previous versions of baseline configurations of the system*] to support rollback.

Supplemental Guidance: Retaining previous versions of baseline configurations to support rollback may include, for example, hardware, software, firmware, configuration files, and configuration records.

Related Controls: None.

(4) BASELINE CONFIGURATION | UNAUTHORIZED SOFTWARE
[Withdrawn: Incorporated into CM-7(4)].

(5) BASELINE CONFIGURATION | AUTHORIZED SOFTWARE
[Withdrawn: Incorporated into CM-7(5)].

(6) BASELINE CONFIGURATION | DEVELOPMENT AND TEST ENVIRONMENTS
Maintain a baseline configuration for system development and test environments that is managed separately from the operational baseline configuration.

Supplemental Guidance: Establishing separate baseline configurations for development, testing, and operational environments helps protect systems from unplanned/unexpected events related to development and testing activities. Separate baseline configurations allow organizations to apply the configuration management that is most appropriate for each type of configuration. For example, management of operational configurations typically emphasizes the need for stability while management of development/test configurations requires greater flexibility. Configurations in the test environment mirror the configurations in the operational environment to the extent practicable so that the results of the testing are representative of the proposed changes to the operational systems. This control enhancement requires separate configurations but not necessarily separate physical environments.

Related Controls: CM-4, SC-3, SC-7.

(7) BASELINE CONFIGURATION | CONFIGURE SYSTEMS AND COMPONENTS FOR HIGH-RISK AREAS

(a) Issue [*Assignment: organization-defined systems or system components*] with [*Assignment: organization-defined configurations*] to individuals traveling to locations that the organization deems to be of significant risk; and

(b) Apply [*Assignment: organization-defined security safeguards*] to the components when the individuals return from travel.

Supplemental Guidance: When it is known that systems or system components will be in high-risk areas, additional controls may be implemented to counter the increased threat in such areas. For example, organizations can take specific actions for notebook computers used by individuals departing on and returning from travel. These actions can include, for example, determining which locations are of concern, defining required configurations for the devices, ensuring that the devices are configured as intended before travel is initiated, and applying specific safeguards to the component after travel is completed. Specially configured notebook computers include, for example, computers with sanitized hard drives, limited applications, and more stringent configuration settings. Specified safeguards applied to mobile devices upon return from travel include, for example, examining the device for signs of physical tampering; and purging and reimaging the hard disk drive. Protecting information residing on mobile devices is covered in the media protection family.

Related Controls: None.

References: NIST Special Publications 800-124, 800-128.

CM-3 CONFIGURATION CHANGE CONTROL

Control:

a. Determine the types of changes to the system that are configuration-controlled;

b. Review proposed configuration-controlled changes to the system and approve or disapprove such changes with explicit consideration for security impact analyses;

c. Document configuration change decisions associated with the system;

d. Implement approved configuration-controlled changes to the system;

e. Retain records of configuration-controlled changes to the system for [*Assignment: organization-defined time-period*];

f. Monitor and review activities associated with configuration-controlled changes to the system; and

g. Coordinate and provide oversight for configuration change control activities through [*Assignment: organization-defined configuration change control element*] that convenes [*Selection (one or more): [Assignment: organization-defined frequency*]; [*Assignment: organization-defined configuration change conditions*]].

Supplemental Guidance: Configuration change controls for organizational systems involve the systematic proposal, justification, implementation, testing, review, and disposition of changes to the systems, including system upgrades and modifications. Configuration change control includes changes to baseline configurations for components and configuration items of systems; changes to configuration settings for component products; unscheduled or unauthorized changes; and changes to remediate vulnerabilities. Configuration change control elements can include such entities as committees or boards. Typical processes for managing configuration changes to systems include, for example, Configuration Control Boards or Change Advisory Boards that review and approve proposed changes to systems. For new development systems or systems undergoing major upgrades, organizations consider including representatives from development organizations on the Configuration Control Boards or Change Advisory Boards. Auditing of changes includes activities before and after changes are made to organizational systems and the auditing activities required to implement such changes.

Related Controls: CA-7, CM-2, CM-4, CM-5, CM-6, CM-9, CM-11, IA-3, MA-2, PE-16, SA-10, SA-19, SC-28, SC-34, SC-37, SI-2, SI-3, SI-4, SI-7, SI-10.

Control Enhancements:

(1) CONFIGURATION CHANGE CONTROL | AUTOMATED DOCUMENTATION, NOTIFICATION, AND PROHIBITION OF CHANGES

Employ automated mechanisms to:

(a) Document proposed changes to the system;

(b) Notify [*Assignment: organized-defined approval authorities*] of proposed changes to the system and request change approval;

(c) Highlight proposed changes to the system that have not been approved or disapproved by [*Assignment: organization-defined time-period*];

(d) Prohibit changes to the system until designated approvals are received;

(e) Document all changes to the system; and

(f) Notify [*Assignment: organization-defined personnel*] when approved changes to the system are completed.

Supplemental Guidance: None.

Related Controls: None.

(2) CONFIGURATION CHANGE CONTROL | TESTING, VALIDATION, AND DOCUMENTATION OF CHANGES

Test, validate, and document changes to the system before fully implementing the changes on the system.

Supplemental Guidance: Changes to systems include modifications to hardware, software, or firmware components and configuration settings defined in CM-6. Organizations ensure that testing does not interfere with system operations. Individuals or groups conducting tests understand organizational security and privacy policies and procedures, system security and privacy policies and procedures, and the health, safety, and environmental risks associated with specific facilities or processes. Operational systems may need to be taken off-line, or replicated to the extent feasible, before testing can be conducted. If systems must be taken off-line for testing, the tests are scheduled to occur during planned system outages whenever possible. If the testing cannot be conducted on operational systems, organizations employ compensating controls.

Related Controls: None.

(3) CONFIGURATION CHANGE CONTROL | AUTOMATED CHANGE IMPLEMENTATION

Employ automated mechanisms to implement changes to the current system baseline and deploy the updated baseline across the installed base.

Supplemental Guidance: None.

Related Controls: None.

(4) CONFIGURATION CHANGE CONTROL | SECURITY REPRESENTATIVE

Require an [*Assignment: organization-defined* information security representative] to be a member of the [*Assignment: organization-defined configuration change control element*].

Supplemental Guidance: Information security representatives can include, for example, Senior Agency Information Security Officers, system security officers, or system security managers. Representation by personnel with information security expertise is important because changes to system configurations can have unintended side effects, some of which may be security-relevant. Detecting such changes early in the process can help avoid unintended, negative consequences that could ultimately affect the security state of organizational systems. The configuration change control element in this control enhancement reflects the change control elements defined by organizations in CM-3.

(5) CONFIGURATION CHANGE CONTROL | AUTOMATED SECURITY RESPONSE

Implement [*Assignment: organization-defined security responses*] automatically if baseline configurations are changed in an unauthorized manner.

Supplemental Guidance: Security responses include, for example, halting system processing, halting selected system functions, or issuing alerts or notifications to organizational personnel when there is an unauthorized modification of a configuration item.

Related Controls: None.

(6) CONFIGURATION CHANGE CONTROL | CRYPTOGRAPHY MANAGEMENT

Ensure that cryptographic mechanisms used to provide [*Assignment: organization-defined security safeguards*] are under configuration management.

Supplemental Guidance: Regardless of the cryptographic means employed, organizations ensure that there are processes and procedures in place to manage those means. For example, if devices use certificates for identification and authentication, a process is implemented to address the expiration of those certificates.

Related Controls: SC-12.

References: NIST Special Publications 800-124, 800-128; NIST Interagency Report 8062.

CM-4 SECURITY AND PRIVACY IMPACT ANALYSES

Control: Analyze changes to the system to determine potential security and privacy impacts prior to change implementation.

Supplemental Guidance: Organizational personnel with security or privacy responsibilities conduct impact analyses. Individuals conducting impact analyses possess the necessary skills and technical expertise to analyze the changes to systems and the associated security or privacy ramifications. Security and privacy impact analyses include, for example, reviewing security and privacy plans, policies, and procedures to understand security and privacy control requirements; reviewing system design documentation to understand control implementation and how specific changes might affect the controls; and determining how potential changes to a system create new risks to the privacy of individuals and the ability of implemented controls to mitigate those risks. Impact analyses may also include assessments of risk to better understand the impact of the changes and to determine if additional security or privacy controls are required.

Related Controls: CA-7, CM-3, CM-8, CM-9, MA-2, RA-5, SA-5, SA-10, SI-2.

Control Enhancements:

(1) SECURITY AND PRIVACY IMPACT ANALYSES | SEPARATE TEST ENVIRONMENTS

Analyze changes to the system in a separate test environment before implementation in an operational environment, looking for security and privacy impacts due to flaws, weaknesses, incompatibility, or intentional malice.

Supplemental Guidance: Separate test environment in this context means an environment that is physically or logically isolated and distinct from the operational environment. The separation is sufficient to ensure that activities in the test environment do not impact activities in the operational environment, and information in the operational environment is not inadvertently transmitted to the test environment. Separate environments can be achieved by physical or logical means. If physically separate test environments are not used, organizations determine the strength of mechanism required when implementing logical separation.

Related Controls: SA-11, SC-7.

(2) SECURITY AND PRIVACY IMPACT ANALYSES | VERIFICATION OF SECURITY AND PRIVACY FUNCTIONS

Check the security and privacy functions after system changes, to verify that the functions are implemented correctly, operating as intended, and producing the desired outcome with regard to meeting the security and privacy requirements for the system.

Supplemental Guidance: Implementation in this context refers to installing changed code in the operational system.

Related Controls: SA-11, SC-3, SI-6.

References: NIST Special Publication 800-128.

CM-5 ACCESS RESTRICTIONS FOR CHANGE

Control: Define, document, approve, and enforce physical and logical access restrictions associated with changes to the system.

Supplemental Guidance: Any changes to the hardware, software, and/or firmware components of systems can potentially have significant effects on the overall security of the systems. Therefore, organizations permit only qualified and authorized individuals to access systems for purposes of initiating changes, including upgrades and modifications. Access restrictions for change also include software libraries. Access restrictions include, for example, physical and logical access controls (see AC-3 and PE-3), workflow automation, media libraries, abstract layers (i.e., changes implemented into external interfaces rather than directly into systems), and change windows (i.e., changes occur only during specified times).

Related Controls: AC-3, AC-5, AC-6, CM-9, PE-3, SC-28, SC-34, SC-37, SI-2, SI-10.

Control Enhancements:

(1) ACCESS RESTRICTIONS FOR CHANGE | AUTOMATED ACCESS ENFORCEMENT AND AUDITING

   (a) Enforce access restrictions; and

   (b) Generate audit records of the enforcement actions.

   Supplemental Guidance: Organizations log access records associated with applying configuration changes to ensure that configuration change control is implemented and to support after-the-fact actions should organizations discover any unauthorized changes.

   Related Controls: AU-2, AU-6, AU-7, AU-12, CM-6, CM-11, SI-12.

(2) ACCESS RESTRICTIONS FOR CHANGE | REVIEW SYSTEM CHANGES

   Review system changes [*Assignment: organization-defined frequency*] and [*Assignment: organization-defined circumstances*] to determine whether unauthorized changes have occurred.

   Supplemental Guidance: Indications that warrant review of system changes and the specific circumstances justifying such reviews may be obtained from activities carried out by organizations during the configuration change process.

   Related Controls: AU-6, AU-7, CM-3.

(3) ACCESS RESTRICTIONS FOR CHANGE | SIGNED COMPONENTS

   Prevent the installation of [*Assignment: organization-defined software and firmware components*] without verification that the component has been digitally signed using a certificate that is recognized and approved by the organization.

   Supplemental Guidance: Software and firmware components prevented from installation unless signed with recognized and approved certificates include, for example, software and firmware version updates, patches, service packs, device drivers, and basic input output system (BIOS) updates. Organizations can identify applicable software and firmware components by type, by specific items, or a combination of both. Digital signatures and organizational verification of such signatures, is a method of code authentication.

   Related Controls: CM-7, SC-13, SI-7.

(4) ACCESS RESTRICTIONS FOR CHANGE | DUAL AUTHORIZATION

   Enforce dual authorization for implementing changes to [*Assignment: organization-defined system components and system-level information*].

   Supplemental Guidance: Organizations employ dual authorization to ensure that any changes to selected system components and information cannot occur unless two qualified individuals implement such changes. The two individuals possess sufficient skills and expertise to determine if the proposed changes are correct implementations of approved changes. Dual authorization may also be known as two-person control.

   Related Controls: AC-2, AC-5, CM-3.

(5)   ACCESS RESTRICTIONS FOR CHANGE | PRIVILEGE LIMITATION FOR PRODUCTION AND OPERATION

(a)   Limit privileges to change system components and system-related information within a production or operational environment; and

(b)   Review and reevaluate privileges [*Assignment: organization-defined frequency*].

Supplemental Guidance: In many organizations, systems support many missions and business functions. Limiting privileges to change system components with respect to operational systems is necessary because changes to a system component may have far-reaching effects on mission and business processes supported by the system. The complex, many-to-many relationships between systems and mission/business processes are in some cases, unknown to developers.

Related Controls: AC-2.

(6)   ACCESS RESTRICTIONS FOR CHANGE | LIMIT LIBRARY PRIVILEGES
       Limit privileges to change software resident within software libraries.

Supplemental Guidance: Software libraries include privileged programs.

Related Controls: AC-2.

(7)   ACCESS RESTRICTIONS FOR CHANGE | AUTOMATIC IMPLEMENTATION OF SECURITY SAFEGUARDS
       [Withdrawn: Incorporated into SI-7].

References: FIPS Publications 140-2, 186-4.

CM-6   CONFIGURATION SETTINGS

Control:

a.   Establish and document configuration settings for components employed within the system using [*Assignment: organization-defined common secure configurations*] that reflect the most restrictive mode consistent with operational requirements;

b.   Implement the configuration settings;

c.   Identify, document, and approve any deviations from established configuration settings for [*Assignment: organization-defined system components*] based on [*Assignment: organization-defined operational requirements*]; and

d.   Monitor and control changes to the configuration settings in accordance with organizational policies and procedures.

Supplemental Guidance: Configuration settings are the parameters that can be changed in hardware, software, or firmware components of the system that affect the security posture or functionality of the system. Information technology products for which security-related configuration settings can be defined include, for example, mainframe computers, servers, workstations, input/output devices, network devices, operating systems, and applications. Security-related parameters are those parameters impacting the security state of systems including the parameters required to satisfy other security control requirements. Security-related parameters include, for example, registry settings; account, file, directory permission settings; and settings for functions, ports, protocols, and remote connections. Organizations establish organization-wide configuration settings and subsequently derive specific configuration settings for systems. The established settings become part of the systems configuration baseline.

Common secure configurations (also referred to as security configuration checklists, lockdown and hardening guides, security reference guides, security technical implementation guides) provide recognized, standardized, and established benchmarks that stipulate secure configuration settings for specific information technology platforms/products and instructions for configuring those system components to meet operational requirements. Common secure configurations can be developed by a variety of organizations including, for example, information technology product developers, manufacturers, vendors, consortia, academia, industry, federal agencies, and other organizations in the public and private sectors. Implementation of a specific common secure configuration may be mandated at the organizational or mission/business process level or may be mandated at a higher level including, for example, by a regulatory agency. Common secure configurations include the United States Government Configuration Baseline (USGCB) which affects the implementation of CM-6 and other controls such as AC-19 and CM-7. The Security Content Automation Protocol (SCAP) and the defined standards within the protocol provide an effective method to uniquely identify, track, and control configuration settings.

Related Controls: AC-3, AC-19, AU-2, AU-6, CA-9, CM-2, CM-3, CM-5, CM-7, CM-11, CP-7, CP-9, CP-10, IA-3, IA-5, PL-8, RA-5, SA-4, SA-5, SA-9, SC-18, SC-19, SC-28, SC-43, SI-2, SI-4, SI-6.

Control Enhancements:

(1) CONFIGURATION SETTINGS | AUTOMATED MANAGEMENT, APPLICATION, AND VERIFICATION

Employ automated mechanisms to centrally manage, apply, and verify configuration settings for [*Assignment: organization-defined system components*].

Supplemental Guidance:

Related Controls: CA-7.

(2) CONFIGURATION SETTINGS | RESPOND TO UNAUTHORIZED CHANGES

Employ [*Assignment: organization-defined security safeguards*] to respond to unauthorized changes to [*Assignment: organization-defined configuration settings*].

Supplemental Guidance: Responses to unauthorized changes to configuration settings can include, for example, alerting designated organizational personnel, restoring established configuration settings, or in extreme cases, halting affected system processing.

Related Controls: IR-4, IR-6, SI-7.

(3) CONFIGURATION SETTINGS | UNAUTHORIZED CHANGE DETECTION

[Withdrawn: Incorporated into SI-7].

(4) CONFIGURATION SETTINGS | CONFORMANCE DEMONSTRATION

[Withdrawn: Incorporated into CM-4].

References: NIST Special Publications 800-70, 800-126, 800-128; US Government Configuration Baselines; National Checklist Repository.

CM-7   LEAST FUNCTIONALITY

Control:

a.   Configure the system to provide only essential capabilities; and

b.   Prohibit or restrict the use of the following functions, ports, protocols, and/or services: [*Assignment: organization-defined prohibited or restricted functions, ports, protocols, and/or services*].

Supplemental Guidance: Systems provide a wide variety of functions and services. Some of the functions and services routinely provided by default, may not be necessary to support essential organizational missions, functions, or operations. Additionally, it is sometimes convenient to provide multiple services from a single system component, but doing so increases risk over limiting the services provided by that single component. Where feasible, organizations limit component functionality to a single function per component. Organizations review functions and services provided by systems or components of systems, to determine which functions and services are candidates for elimination. Organizations consider disabling unused or unnecessary physical and logical ports and protocols to prevent unauthorized connection of devices, transfer of information, and tunneling. Organizations employ network scanning tools, intrusion detection and prevention systems, and end-point protection technologies such as firewalls and host-based intrusion detection systems to identify and prevent the use of prohibited functions, protocols, ports, and services.

Related Controls: AC-3, AC-4, CM-2, CM-5, CM-11, RA-5, SA-4, SA-5, SA-9, SA-15, SC-7, SC-37, SI-4.

Control Enhancements:

(1) LEAST FUNCTIONALITY | PERIODIC REVIEW

(a) Review the system [*Assignment: organization-defined frequency*] to identify unnecessary and/or nonsecure functions, ports, protocols, and services; and

(b) Disable [*Assignment: organization-defined functions, ports, protocols, and services within the system deemed to be unnecessary and/or nonsecure*].

Supplemental Guidance: Organizations can either decide the relative security of the function, port, protocol, and/or service or base the security decision on the assessment of other entities. Bluetooth, FTP, and peer-to-peer networking are examples of less than secure protocols.

Related Controls: AC-18.

(2) LEAST FUNCTIONALITY | PREVENT PROGRAM EXECUTION

Prevent program execution in accordance with [*Selection (one or more): [Assignment: organization-defined policies regarding software program usage and restrictions]; rules authorizing the terms and conditions of software program usage*].

Supplemental Guidance: This control enhancement addresses organizational policies restricting software usage as well as the terms and conditions imposed by the developer or manufacturer including, for example, software licensing and copyrights. Restrictions include, for example, restricting the roles allowed to approve program execution; prohibiting auto-execute; program blacklisting and whitelisting; or restricting the number of program instances executed at the same time.

Related Controls: CM-8, PM-5.

(3) LEAST FUNCTIONALITY | REGISTRATION COMPLIANCE

Ensure compliance with [*Assignment: organization-defined registration requirements for functions, ports, protocols, and services*].

Supplemental Guidance: Organizations use the registration process to manage, track, and provide oversight for systems and implemented functions, ports, protocols, and services.

Related Controls: None.

(4) LEAST FUNCTIONALITY | UNAUTHORIZED SOFTWARE — BLACKLISTING

(a) Identify [*Assignment: organization-defined software programs not authorized to execute on the system*];

(b) Employ an allow-all, deny-by-exception policy to prohibit the execution of unauthorized software programs on the system; and

(c) Review and update the list of unauthorized software programs [*Assignment: organization-defined frequency*].

Supplemental Guidance: The process used to identify specific software programs or entire categories of software programs that are not authorized to execute on organizational systems is commonly referred to as *blacklisting*. Organizations can implement CM-7(5) instead of this control enhancement if whitelisting (the stronger of the two policies) is the preferred approach for restricting software program execution.

Related Controls: CM-6, CM-8, CM-10, PM-5.

(5) LEAST FUNCTIONALITY | AUTHORIZED SOFTWARE — WHITELISTING

(a) Identify [*Assignment: organization-defined software programs authorized to execute on the system*];

(b) Employ a deny-all, permit-by-exception policy to allow the execution of authorized software programs on the system; and

(c) Review and update the list of authorized software programs [*Assignment: organization-defined frequency*].

Supplemental Guidance: The process used to identify specific software programs or entire categories of software programs that are authorized to execute on organizational systems is commonly referred to as *whitelisting*. To effect comprehensive whitelisting and increase the strength of protection for attacks that bypass application level whitelisting, software programs may be decomposed into and monitored at multiple levels of detail. Software program levels of detail include, for example, applications, application programming interfaces, application modules, scripts, system processes, system services, kernel actions, registries, drivers, and dynamic link libraries. The concept of whitelisting may also be applied to user actions, ports, IP addresses, and media access control (MAC) addresses. Organizations consider verifying the integrity of white-listed software programs using, for example, cryptographic checksums, digital signatures, or hash functions. Verification of white-listed software can occur either prior to execution or at system startup.

Related Controls: CM-2, CM-6, CM-8, CM-10, PM-5, SA-10, SC-34, SI-7.

References: FIPS Publications 140-2, 180-4, 186-4, 202; NIST Special Publication 800-167.

CM-8   SYSTEM COMPONENT INVENTORY

Control:

a. Develop and document an inventory of system components that:

1. Accurately reflects the current system;

2. Includes all components within the authorization boundary of the system;

3. Is at the level of granularity deemed necessary for tracking and reporting; and

4. Includes [*Assignment: organization-defined information deemed necessary to achieve effective system component accountability*]; and

b. Review and update the system component inventory [*Assignment: organization-defined frequency*].

Supplemental Guidance: System components are discrete identifiable information technology assets that represent a building block of a system and include hardware, software, firmware, and virtual machines. Organizations may choose to implement centralized system component inventories that include components from all organizational systems. In such situations, organizations ensure that the inventories include system-specific information required for proper component accountability. Information necessary for effective accountability of system components includes, for example, hardware inventory specifications; software license information; software component owners; version numbers; and for networked components or devices, the machine names and network addresses. Inventory specifications include, for example, manufacturer; device type; model; serial number; and physical location.

Related Controls: CM-2, CM-7, CM-9, CM-10, CM-11, CP-2, CP-9, MA-6, PE-20, PM-5, PM-29, SA-4, SA-5, SI-2.

Control Enhancements:

(1) SYSTEM COMPONENT INVENTORY | UPDATES DURING INSTALLATION AND REMOVAL

Update the inventory of system components as an integral part of component installations, removals, and system updates.

Supplemental Guidance: None.

Related Controls: None.

(2) SYSTEM COMPONENT INVENTORY | AUTOMATED MAINTENANCE

Employ automated mechanisms to help maintain an up-to-date, complete, accurate, and readily available inventory of system components.

Supplemental Guidance: Organizations maintain system inventories to the extent feasible. Virtual machines, for example, can be difficult to monitor because such machines are not visible to the network when not in use. In such cases, organizations maintain as up-to-date, complete, and accurate an inventory as is deemed reasonable. This control enhancement can be satisfied by the implementation of CM-2 (2) for organizations that choose to combine system component inventory and baseline configuration activities.

Related Controls: None.

(3) SYSTEM COMPONENT INVENTORY | AUTOMATED UNAUTHORIZED COMPONENT DETECTION

  (a) Employ automated mechanisms [*Assignment: organization-defined frequency*] to detect the presence of unauthorized hardware, software, and firmware components within the system; and

  (b) Take the following actions when unauthorized components are detected: [*Selection (one or more): disable network access by such components; isolate the components; notify [Assignment: organization-defined personnel or roles]*].

Supplemental Guidance: This control enhancement is applied in addition to the monitoring for unauthorized remote connections and mobile devices. Monitoring for unauthorized system components may be accomplished on an ongoing basis or by the periodic scanning of systems for that purpose. Automated mechanisms can be implemented within systems or in other separate devices. Isolation can be achieved, for example, by placing unauthorized system components in separate domains or subnets or otherwise quarantining such components. This type of component isolation is commonly referred to as sandboxing.

Related Controls: AC-19, CA-7, RA-5, SI-3, SI-4, SI-7.

(4) SYSTEM COMPONENT INVENTORY | ACCOUNTABILITY INFORMATION

Includes in the system component inventory information, a means for identifying by [*Selection (one or more): name; position; role*], individuals responsible and accountable for administering those components.

Supplemental Guidance: Identifying individuals who are both responsible and accountable for administering system components helps to ensure that the assigned components are properly administered and organizations can contact those individuals if some action is required, for example, the component is determined to be the source of a breach; the component needs to be recalled or replaced; or the component needs to be relocated.

Related Controls: None.

(5) SYSTEM COMPONENT INVENTORY | NO DUPLICATE ACCOUNTING OF COMPONENTS

  (a) Verify that all components within the authorization boundary of the system are not duplicated in other system component inventories; or

  (b) If a centralized component inventory is used, verify components are not assigned to multiple systems.

Supplemental Guidance: This control enhancement addresses the potential problem of duplicate accounting of system components in large or complex interconnected systems.

Related Controls: None.

(6) SYSTEM COMPONENT INVENTORY | ASSESSED CONFIGURATIONS AND APPROVED DEVIATIONS

Include assessed component configurations and any approved deviations to current deployed configurations in the system component inventory.

Supplemental Guidance: This control enhancement focuses on configuration settings established by organizations for system components, the specific components that have been assessed to determine compliance with the required configuration settings, and any approved deviations from established configuration settings.

Related Controls: None.

(7) SYSTEM COMPONENT INVENTORY | CENTRALIZED REPOSITORY

Provide a centralized repository for the inventory of system components.

Supplemental Guidance: Organizations may choose to implement centralized system component inventories that include components from all organizational systems. Centralized repositories of system component inventories provide opportunities for efficiencies in accounting for organizational hardware, software, and firmware assets. Such repositories may also help organizations rapidly identify the location and responsible individuals of system components that have been compromised, breached, or are otherwise in need of mitigation actions. Organizations ensure that the resulting centralized inventories include system-specific information required for proper component accountability.

Related Controls: None.

(8) SYSTEM COMPONENT INVENTORY | AUTOMATED LOCATION TRACKING

Employ automated mechanisms to support tracking of system components by geographic location.

Supplemental Guidance: The use of automated mechanisms to track the location of system components can increase the accuracy of component inventories. Such capability may also help organizations rapidly identify the location and responsible individuals of system components that have been compromised, breached, or are otherwise in need of mitigation actions.

Related Controls: None.

(9) SYSTEM COMPONENT INVENTORY | ASSIGNMENT OF COMPONENTS TO SYSTEMS

   (a) **Assign [*Assignment: organization-defined acquired system components*] to a system; and**

   (b) **Receive an acknowledgement from [*Assignment: organization-defined personnel or roles*] of this assignment.**

Supplemental Guidance: Organizations determine the types of system components that are subject to this control enhancement.

Related Controls: None.

(10) SYSTEM COMPONENT INVENTORY | DATA ACTION MAPPING

Develop and document a system map of data actions that process personally identifiable information.

Supplemental Guidance: Data actions are system operations that process personally identifiable information. Such processing encompasses the full information life cycle which includes collection, generation, transformation, use, disclosure, retention, disposal. Creating a system map of data actions supports a privacy risk assessment. The development of this map may necessitate coordination between the privacy and security programs regarding the covered data actions, the system components, and the definition of the authorization boundary.

Related Controls: PM-30, CM-4.

References: NIST Special Publications 800-57-1, 800-57-2, 800-57-3, 800-128; NIST Interagency Report 8062.

CM-9 CONFIGURATION MANAGEMENT PLAN

Control: Develop, document, and implement a configuration management plan for the system that:

a. Addresses roles, responsibilities, and configuration management processes and procedures;

b. Establishes a process for identifying configuration items throughout the system development life cycle and for managing the configuration of the configuration items;

c. Defines the configuration items for the system and places the configuration items under configuration management;

d. Is reviewed and approved by [*Assignment: organization-defined personnel or roles*]; and

e. Protects the configuration management plan from unauthorized disclosure and modification.

Supplemental Guidance: Configuration management plans satisfy the requirements in configuration management policies while being tailored to individual systems. Such plans define processes and procedures for how configuration management is used to support system development life cycle activities. Configuration management plans are typically developed during the development and acquisition phase of the system development life cycle. The plans describe how to move changes through change management processes, how to update configuration settings and baselines, how to maintain system component inventories, how to control development, test, and operational environments, and how to develop, release, and update key documents. Organizations can employ templates to help ensure consistent and timely development and implementation of configuration management plans. Such templates can represent a master configuration management plan for the organization with subsets of the plan implemented on a system by system basis. Configuration management approval processes include designation of key management stakeholders responsible the monitoring and analysis ... ministration changes occurring, and personnel that conduct security impact analyses prior to the implementation of changes to the systems. Configuration items are the system components (i.e., hardware, software, firmware, and documentation) to be configuration-managed. As systems continue through the system development life cycle, new configuration items may be identified and some existing configuration items may no longer need to be under configuration control.

Related Controls: CM-2, CM-3, CM-4, CM-5, CM-8, PL-2, SA-10, SI-12.

Control Enhancements:

(1) CONFIGURATION MANAGEMENT PLAN | ASSIGNMENT OF RESPONSIBILITY
Assign responsibility for developing the configuration management process to organizational personnel that are not directly involved in system development.

Supplemental Guidance: In the absence of dedicated configuration management teams assigned within organizations, system developers may be tasked to develop configuration management processes using personnel who are not directly involved in system development or integration. This separation of duties ensures that organizations establish and maintain a sufficient degree of independence between the system development and integration processes and configuration management processes to facilitate quality control and more effective oversight.

Related Controls: None.

References: NIST Special Publication 800-128.

CM-10 SOFTWARE USAGE RESTRICTIONS

Control:

a. Use software and associated documentation in accordance with contract agreements and copyright laws;

b. Track the use of software and associated documentation protected by quantity licenses to control copying and distribution; and

c. Control and document the use of peer-to-peer file sharing technology to ensure that this capability is not used for the unauthorized distribution, display, performance, or reproduction of copyrighted work.

Supplemental Guidance: Software license tracking can be accomplished by manual methods or automated methods depending on organizational needs.

Related Controls: AC-17, AU-6, CM-7, CM-8, SC-7.

Control Enhancements:

(1) SOFTWARE USAGE RESTRICTIONS | OPEN SOURCE SOFTWARE
Establish the following restrictions on the use of open source software: [*Assignment: organization-defined restrictions*].

Supplemental Guidance: Open source software refers to software that is available in source code form. Certain software rights normally reserved for copyright holders are routinely provided under software license agreements that permit individuals to study, change, and improve the software. From a security perspective, the major advantage of open source software is that it provides organizations with the ability to examine the source code. However, there are also various licensing issues associated with open source software including, for example, the constraints on derivative use of such software.

Related Controls: SI-7.

References: None.

CM-11 USER-INSTALLED SOFTWARE

Control:

a. Establish [*Assignment: organization-defined policies*] governing the installation of software by users;

b. Enforce software installation policies through the following methods: [*Assignment: organization-defined methods*]; and

c. Monitor policy compliance at [*Assignment: organization-defined frequency*].

Supplemental Guidance: If provided the necessary privileges, users have the ability to install software in organizational systems. To maintain control over the types of software installed, organizations identify permitted and prohibited actions regarding software installation. Permitted software installations may include, for example, updates and security patches to existing software and downloading applications from organization-approved "app stores." Prohibited software installations may include, for example, software with unknown or suspect pedigrees or software that organizations consider potentially malicious. The policies organizations select governing user-installed software may be organization-developed or provided by some external entity. Policy enforcement methods include procedural methods, automated methods, or both.

Related Controls: AC-3, AU-6, CM-2, CM-3, CM-5, CM-6, CM-7, CM-8, PL-4, SI-7.

Control Enhancements:

(1) USER-INSTALLED SOFTWARE | ALERTS FOR UNAUTHORIZED INSTALLATIONS
[Withdrawn: Incorporated into CM-8(3)].

(2) SOFTWARE INSTALLATION WITH PRIVILEGED STATUS
Allow user installation of software only with explicit privileged status.

Supplemental Guidance: Privileged status can be obtained, for example, by serving in the role of system administrator.

Related Controls: AC-5, AC-6.

References: None.

CM-12 INFORMATION LOCATION

Control:

a. Identify the location of [*Assignment: organization-defined information*] and the specific system components on which the information resides;

b. Identify and document the users who have access to the system and system components where the information resides; and

c. Document changes to the location (i.e., system or system components) where the information resides.

Supplemental Guidance: This control addresses the need to understand where information is being processed and stored and is typically applied with respect to Controlled Unclassified Information (CUI). The National Archives and Records Administration defines the types of information that are categorized as CUI. Information location includes identifying where specific information types and associated information reside in the system components that compose organizational systems; and how information is being processed so that information flow can be understood and adequate protection and policy management provided for such information and system components.

Related Controls: AC-3, AC-4, AC-6, AC-23, CM-8, PM-29, SC-4, SC-16, SC-28, SI-4, SI-7.

Control Enhancements:

(1) INFORMATION LOCATION | AUTOMATED TOOLS TO SUPPORT INFORMATION LOCATION

Use automated tools to identify [*Assignment: organization-defined information by information type*] on [*Assignment: organization-defined system components*] to ensure adequate security and privacy controls are in place to protect organizational information and individual privacy.

Supplemental Guidance: This control enhancement gives organizations the capability to check systems and selected system components for types of information to confirm such information resides on the component and to ensure that the required protection measures are in place for that component.

Related Controls: None.

References: FIPS Publication 199; NIST Special Publication 800-60-1, 800-60-2.

3.6 CONTINGENCY PLANNING

<u>Quick link to Contingency Planning summary table</u>

CP-1 CONTINGENCY PLANNING POLICY AND PROCEDURES

<u>Control</u>

a. Develop, document, and disseminate to [*Assignment: organization-defined personnel or roles*]:

1. A contingency planning policy that:

   (a) Addresses purpose, scope, roles, responsibilities, management commitment, coordination among organizational entities, and compliance; and

   (b) Is consistent with applicable laws, Executive Orders, directives, regulations, policies, standards, and guidelines; and

2. Procedures to facilitate the implementation of the contingency planning policy and the associated contingency planning controls;

b. Designate an [*Assignment: organization-defined senior management official*] to manage the contingency planning policy and procedures;

c. Review and update the current contingency planning:

1. Policy [*Assignment: organization-defined frequency*]; and

2. Procedures [*Assignment: organization-defined frequency*];

d. Ensure that the contingency planning procedures implement the contingency planning policy and controls; and

e. Develop, document, and implement remediation actions for violations of the contingency planning policy.

<u>Supplemental Guidance</u>: This control addresses the establishment of policy and procedures for the effective implementation of the controls and control enhancements in the CP family. The risk management strategy is an important factor in establishing policy and procedures. Comprehensive policy and procedures help provide security and privacy assurance. Security and privacy program policies and procedures at the organization level may make the need for system-specific policies and procedures unnecessary. The policy can be included as part of the general security and privacy policy or can be represented by multiple policies reflecting the complex nature of organizations. The procedures can be established for security and privacy programs and for systems, if needed. Procedures describe how policies or controls are implemented and can be directed at the personnel or role that is the object of the procedure. Procedures can be documented in system security and privacy plans or in one or more separate documents. It is important to recognize that restating controls does not constitute an organizational policy or procedure.

<u>Related Controls</u>: PM-9, PS-8, SI-12.

<u>Control Enhancements</u>: None.

<u>References</u>: NIST Special Publications <u>800-12</u>, <u>800-30</u>, <u>800-34</u>, <u>800-39</u>, <u>800-100</u>.

CP-2 CONTINGENCY PLAN

<u>Control</u>:

a. Develop a contingency plan for the system that:

1. Identifies essential missions and business functions and associated contingency requirements;

      2. Provides recovery objectives, restoration priorities, and metrics;

      3. Addresses contingency roles, responsibilities, assigned individuals with contact information;

      4. Addresses maintaining essential missions and business functions despite a system disruption, compromise, or failure;

      5. Addresses eventual, full system restoration without deterioration of the security and privacy controls originally planned and implemented; and

      6. Is reviewed and approved by [*Assignment: organization-defined personnel or roles*];

  b. Distributes copies of the contingency plan to [*Assignment: organization-defined key contingency personnel (identified by name and/or by role) and organizational elements*];

  c. Coordinates contingency planning activities with incident handling activities;

  d. Reviews the contingency plan for the system [*Assignment: organization-defined frequency*];

  e. Updates the contingency plan to address changes to the organization, system, or environment of operation and problems encountered during contingency plan implementation, execution, or testing;

  f. Communicates contingency plan changes to [*Assignment: organization-defined key contingency personnel (identified by name and/or by role) and organizational elements*]; and

  g. Protects the contingency plan from unauthorized disclosure and modification.

Supplemental Guidance: Contingency planning for systems is part of an overall organizational program for achieving continuity of operations for mission/business functions. Contingency planning addresses system restoration and implementation of alternative mission or business processes when systems are compromised or breached. The effectiveness of contingency planning is maximized by considering such planning throughout the system development life cycle. Performing contingency planning on hardware, software, and firmware development can be an effective means of achieving system resiliency. Contingency plans reflect the degree of restoration required for organizational systems since not all systems need to fully recover to achieve the level of continuity of operations desired. System recovery objectives reflect applicable laws, Executive Orders, directives, policies, standards, regulations, and guidelines. In addition to availability, contingency plans address other security-related events resulting in a reduction in mission or business effectiveness, such as malicious attacks compromising the confidentiality or integrity of systems. Actions addressed in contingency plans include, for example, orderly and graceful degradation, system shutdown, fallback to a manual mode, alternate information flows, and operating in modes reserved for when systems are under attack. By coordinating contingency planning with incident handling activities, organizations can ensure that the necessary planning activities are in place and activated in the event of a security incident.

Related Controls: CP-3, CP-4, CP-6, CP-7, CP-8, CP-9, CP-10, CP-11, CP-13, IR-4, IR-6, IR-8, IR-9, MA-6, MP-2, MP-4, MP-5, PL-2, PM-8, PM-11, SA-15, SA-20, SC-7, SC-23, SI-12.

Control Enhancements:

(1) CONTINGENCY PLAN | COORDINATE WITH RELATED PLANS

Coordinate contingency plan development with organizational elements responsible for related plans.

Supplemental Guidance: Plans related to contingency plans for organizational systems include, for example, Business Continuity Plans, Disaster Recovery Plans, Continuity of Operations Plans, Crisis Communications Plans, Critical Infrastructure Plans, Cyber Incident Response Plans, Insider Threat Implementation Plan, and Occupant Emergency Plans.

Related Controls: None.

(2) CONTINGENCY PLAN | CAPACITY PLANNING

Conduct capacity planning so that necessary capacity for information processing, telecommunications, and environmental support exists during contingency operations.

Supplemental Guidance: Capacity planning is needed because different types of threats can result in a reduction of the available processing, telecommunications, and support services intended to support the organizational missions and business functions. Organizations need to anticipate degraded operations during contingency operations and factor such degradation into capacity planning. With respect to capacity planning, environmental support refers to any environmental support factor for which the organization determines that it needs to provide support in a contingency situation, even if in a degraded state. As always, such determinations are based on an assessment of risk, system categorization (impact level), and organizational risk tolerance.

Related Controls: PE-11, PE-12, PE-13, PE-14, PE-18, SC-5.

(3) CONTINGENCY PLAN | RESUME ESSENTIAL MISSIONS AND BUSINESS FUNCTIONS

Plan for the resumption of essential missions and business functions within [*Assignment: organization-defined time-period*] of contingency plan activation.

Supplemental Guidance: Organizations may choose to carry out the contingency planning activities in this control enhancement as part of organizational business continuity planning including, for example, as part of business impact analyses. The time-period for resumption of essential missions and business functions may be dependent on the severity and extent of the disruptions to the system and its supporting infrastructure.

Related Controls: None.

(4) CONTINGENCY PLAN | RESUME ALL MISSIONS AND BUSINESS FUNCTIONS

Plan for the resumption of all missions and business functions within [*Assignment: organization-defined time-period*] of contingency plan activation.

Supplemental Guidance: Organizations may choose to carry out the contingency planning activities in this control enhancement as part of organizational business continuity planning including, for example, as part of business impact analyses. The time-period for resumption of missions and business functions may be dependent on the severity and extent of disruptions to the system and its supporting infrastructure.

Related Controls: None.

(5) CONTINGENCY PLAN | CONTINUE ESSENTIAL MISSIONS AND BUSINESS FUNCTIONS

Plan for the continuance of essential missions and business functions with little or no loss of operational continuity and sustains that continuity until full system restoration at primary processing and/or storage sites.

Supplemental Guidance: Organizations may choose to carry out the contingency planning activities in this control enhancement as part of organizational business continuity planning including, for example, as part of business impact analyses. Primary processing and/or storage sites defined by organizations as part of contingency planning may change depending on the circumstances associated with the contingency.

Related Controls: None.

(6) CONTINGENCY PLAN | ALTERNATE PROCESSING AND STORAGE SITE

Plan for the transfer of essential missions and business functions to alternate processing and/or storage sites with little or no loss of operational continuity and sustain that continuity through system restoration to primary processing and/or storage sites.

Supplemental Guidance: Organizations may choose to carry out the contingency planning activities in this control enhancement as part of organizational business continuity planning including, for example, as part of business impact analyses. Primary processing and/or storage sites defined by organizations as part of contingency planning may change depending on the circumstances associated with the contingency.

Related Controls: None.

(7) CONTINGENCY PLAN | COORDINATE WITH EXTERNAL SERVICE PROVIDERS

Coordinate the contingency plan with the contingency plans of external service providers to
ensure that contingency requirements can be satisfied.

Supplemental Guidance: When the capability of an organization to successfully carry out its
core missions and business functions is dependent on external service providers, developing a
timely and comprehensive contingency plan may become more challenging. In this situation,
organizations coordinate contingency planning activities with the external entities to ensure
that the individual plans reflect the overall contingency needs of the organization.

Related Controls: SA-9.

(8) CONTINGENCY PLAN | IDENTIFY CRITICAL ASSETS

Identify critical system assets supporting essential missions and business functions.

Supplemental Guidance: Organizations may choose to carry out the contingency planning
activities in this control enhancement as part of organizational criticality analysis or business
continuity planning including, for example, as part of business impact analyses. Organizations
identify critical system assets so additional safeguards and countermeasures can be employed
(beyond those safeguards and countermeasures routinely implemented) to help ensure that
organizational missions/business functions can continue to be conducted during contingency
operations. The identification of critical information assets also facilitates the prioritization of
organizational resources. Critical system assets include both technical and operational aspects.
Technical aspects include, for example, information technology services, system components,
information technology products, and mechanisms. Operational aspects include, for example,
procedures (manually executed operations) and personnel (individuals operating technical
safeguards and/or executing manual procedures). Organizational program protection plans can
aid in identifying critical assets.

Related Controls: CM-8, RA-9.

References: NIST Special Publication 800-34; NIST Interagency Report 8179.

CP-3 CONTINGENCY TRAINING

Control: Provide contingency training to system users consistent with assigned roles and
responsibilities:

a. Within [*Assignment: organization-defined time-period*] of assuming a contingency role or
responsibility;

b. When required by system changes; and

c. [*Assignment: organization-defined frequency*] thereafter.

Supplemental Guidance: Contingency training provided by organizations is linked to the assigned
roles and responsibilities of organizational personnel to ensure that the appropriate content and
level of detail is included in such training. For example, regular users may only need to know
when and where to report for duty during contingency operations and if normal duties are affected;
system administrators may require additional training on how to set up systems at alternate
processing and storage sites; and managers/senior leaders may receive more specific training on
how to conduct mission-essential functions in designated off-site locations and how to establish
communications with other governmental entities for purposes of coordination on contingency-
related activities. Training for contingency roles/responsibilities reflects the specific continuity
requirements in the contingency plan.

Related Controls: AT-2, AT-3, AT-4, CP-2, CP-4, CP-8, IR-2, IR-4, IR-9.

Control Enhancements:

(1) CONTINGENCY TRAINING | SIMULATED EVENTS

Incorporate simulated events into contingency training to facilitate effective response by personnel
in crisis situations.

Supplemental Guidance: None.

Related Controls: None.

    (2) CONTINGENCY TRAINING | AUTOMATED TRAINING ENVIRONMENTS

    Employ automated mechanisms to provide a more thorough and realistic contingency training environment.

    Supplemental Guidance: None.

    Related Controls: None.

References. NIST Special Publication 800-50.

CP-4   CONTINGENCY PLAN TESTING

Control:

a. Test the contingency plan for the system [*Assignment: organization-defined frequency*] using [*Assignment: organization-defined tests*] to determine the effectiveness of the plan and the organizational readiness to execute the plan;

b. Review the contingency plan test results; and

c. Initiate corrective actions, if needed.

Supplemental Guidance: Methods for testing contingency plans to determine the effectiveness of the plans and to identify potential weaknesses in the plans include, for example, walk-through and tabletop exercises, checklists, simulations (parallel, full interrupt), and comprehensive exercises. Organizations conduct testing based on the continuity requirements in contingency plans and include a determination of the effects on organizational operations, assets, and individuals arising due to contingency operations. Organizations have flexibility and discretion in the breadth, depth, and timelines of corrective actions.

Related Controls: AT-3, CP-2, CP-3, CP-8, CP-9, IR-3, IR-4, PL-2, PM-14.

Control Enhancements:

    (1) CONTINGENCY PLAN TESTING | COORDINATE WITH RELATED PLANS

    Coordinate contingency plan testing with organizational elements responsible for related plans.

    Supplemental Guidance: Plans related to contingency plans for organizational systems include, for example, business continuity plans, disaster recovery plans, continuity of operations plans, crisis communications plans, critical infrastructure plans, cyber incident response plans, and occupant emergency plans. This control enhancement does not require organizations to create organizational elements to handle related plans or to align such elements with specific plans. It does require, however, that if such organizational elements are responsible for related plans, organizations should coordinate with those elements.

    Related Controls: IR-8, PM-8.

    (2) CONTINGENCY PLAN TESTING | ALTERNATE PROCESSING SITE

    Test the contingency plan at the alternate processing site:

      (a) To familiarize contingency personnel with the facility and available resources; and

      (b) To evaluate the capabilities of the alternate processing site to support contingency operations.

    Supplemental Guidance: None.

    Related Controls: CP-7.

    (3) CONTINGENCY PLAN TESTING | AUTOMATED TESTING

    Employ automated mechanisms to more thoroughly and effectively test the contingency plan.

    Supplemental Guidance: Automated mechanisms facilitate more thorough and effective testing of contingency plans. This occurs by providing more complete coverage of contingency issues; by selecting more realistic test scenarios and environments; and by effectively stressing the system and supported missions and business operations.

    Related Controls: None.

(4) CONTINGENCY PLAN TESTING | FULL RECOVERY AND RECONSTITUTION

Include a full recovery and reconstitution of the system to a known state as part of contingency plan testing.

Supplemental Guidance: None.

Related Controls: CP-10, SC-24.

References: FIPS Publication 199; NIST Special Publications 800-34, 800-84.

CP-5   CONTINGENCY PLAN UPDATE

[Withdrawn: Incorporated into CP-2].

CP-6   ALTERNATE STORAGE SITE

Control:

a.   Establish an alternate storage site including necessary agreements to permit the storage and retrieval of system backup information; and

b.   Ensure that the alternate storage site provides security controls equivalent to that of the primary site.

Supplemental Guidance: Alternate storage sites are sites that are geographically distinct from primary storage sites. An alternate storage site maintains duplicate copies of information and data if the primary storage site is not available. Items covered by alternate storage site agreements include, for example, environmental conditions at alternate sites, access rules, physical and environmental protection requirements, and coordination of delivery/retrieval of backup media. Alternate storage sites reflect the requirements in contingency plans so that organizations can maintain essential missions and business functions despite disruption, compromise, or failure in organizational systems.

Related Controls: CP-2, CP-7, CP-8, CP-9, CP-10, MP-4, MP-5, PE-3, SC-36, SI-13.

Control Enhancements:

(1) ALTERNATE STORAGE SITE | SEPARATION FROM PRIMARY SITE

Identify an alternate storage site that is separated from the primary storage site to reduce susceptibility to the same threats.

Supplemental Guidance: Threats that affect alternate storage sites are defined in organizational assessments of risk and include, for example, natural disasters, structural failures, hostile attacks, and errors of omission or commission. Organizations determine what is considered a sufficient degree of separation between primary and alternate storage sites based on the types of threats that are of concern. For threats such as hostile attacks, the degree of separation between sites is less relevant.

Related Controls: RA-3.

(2) ALTERNATE STORAGE SITE | RECOVERY TIME AND RECOVERY POINT OBJECTIVES

Configure the alternate storage site to facilitate recovery operations in accordance with recovery time and recovery point objectives.

Supplemental Guidance: None.

Related Controls: None.

(3) ALTERNATE STORAGE SITE | ACCESSIBILITY

Identify potential accessibility problems to the alternate storage site in the event of an area-wide disruption or disaster and outlines explicit mitigation actions.

Supplemental Guidance: Area-wide disruptions refer to those types of disruptions that are broad in geographic scope with such determinations made by organizations based on organizational assessments of risk. Explicit mitigation actions include, for example, duplicating backup information at other alternate storage sites if access problems occur at originally designated alternate sites; or planning for physical access to retrieve backup information if electronic accessibility to the alternate site is disrupted.

Related Controls: RA-3.

References: NIST Special Publication 800-34.

CP-7   ALTERNATE PROCESSING SITE

Control:

a. Establish an alternate processing site including necessary agreements to permit the transfer and resumption of [*Assignment: organization-defined system operations*] for essential missions and business functions within [*Assignment: organization-defined time-period consistent with recovery time and recovery point objectives*] when the primary processing capabilities are unavailable;

b. Make available at the alternate processing site, the equipment and supplies required to transfer and resume operations or put contracts in place to support delivery to the site within the organization-defined time-period for transfer and resumption; and

c. Provide information security and privacy safeguards at the alternate processing site that are equivalent to those at the primary site.

Supplemental Guidance: Alternate processing sites are sites that are geographically distinct from primary processing sites. An alternate processing site provides processing capability if the primary processing site is not available. Geographically distributed architectures may also be considered as alternate processing sites. Safeguards that are covered by alternate processing site agreements include, for example, environmental conditions at alternate sites; access rules; physical and environmental protection requirements; and the coordination for the transfer and assignment of personnel. Requirements are specifically allocated to alternate processing sites that reflect the requirements in contingency plans to maintain essential missions and business functions despite disruption, compromise, or failure in organizational systems.

Related Controls: CP-2, CP-6, CP-8, CP-9, CP-10, MA-6, PE-3, PE-11, PE-12, PE-17, SC-36, SI-13.

Control Enhancements:

(1) ALTERNATE PROCESSING SITE | SEPARATION FROM PRIMARY SITE

Identify an alternate processing site that is separated from the primary processing site to reduce susceptibility to the same threats.

Supplemental Guidance: Threats that affect alternate processing sites are typically defined in organizational assessments of risk and include, for example, natural disasters, structural failures, hostile attacks, and errors of omission/commission. Organizations determine what is considered a sufficient degree of separation between primary and alternate processing sites based on the types of threats that are of concern. For threats such as hostile attacks, the degree of separation between sites is less relevant.

Related Controls: RA-3.

(2) ALTERNATE PROCESSING SITE | ACCESSIBILITY

Identify potential accessibility problems to the alternate processing site in the event of an area-wide disruption or disaster and outlines explicit mitigation actions.

Supplemental Guidance: Area-wide disruptions refer to those types of disruptions that are broad in geographic scope with such determinations made by organizations based on organizational assessments of risk.

Related Controls: RA-3.

(3) ALTERNATE PROCESSING SITE | PRIORITY OF SERVICE

Develop alternate processing site agreements that contain priority-of-service provisions in accordance with organizational availability requirements (including recovery time objectives).

Supplemental Guidance: Priority-of-service agreements refer to negotiated agreements with
service providers that ensure that organizations receive priority treatment consistent with their
availability requirements and the availability of information resources at the alternate
processing site.

Related Controls: None.

(4) ALTERNATE PROCESSING SITE | PREPARATION FOR USE

**Prepare the alternate processing site so that the site is ready to be used as the operational site
supporting essential missions and business functions.**

Supplemental Guidance: Site preparation includes, for example, establishing configuration
settings for system components at the alternate processing site consistent with the
requirements for such settings at the primary site and ensuring that essential supplies and
other logistical considerations are in place.

Related Controls: CM-2, CM-6, CP-4.

(5) ALTERNATE PROCESSING SITE | EQUIVALENT INFORMATION SECURITY SAFEGUARDS

[Withdrawn: Incorporated into CP-7].

(6) ALTERNATE PROCESSING SITE | INABILITY TO RETURN TO PRIMARY SITE

Plan and prepare for circumstances that preclude returning to the primary processing site.

Supplemental Guidance: None.

Related Controls: None.

References: NIST Special Publication 800-34.

CP-8   TELECOMMUNICATIONS SERVICES

Control: Establish alternate telecommunications services including necessary agreements to permit
the resumption of [*Assignment: organization-defined system operations*] for essential missions and
business functions within [*Assignment: organization-defined time-period*] when the primary
telecommunications capabilities are unavailable at either the primary or alternate processing or
storage sites.

Supplemental Guidance: This control applies to telecommunications services (data and voice) for
primary and alternate processing and storage sites. Alternate telecommunications services reflect
the continuity requirements in contingency plans to maintain essential missions and business
functions despite the loss of primary telecommunications services. Organizations may specify
different time-periods for primary/alternate sites. Alternate telecommunications services include,
for example, additional organizational or commercial ground-based circuits/lines or satellites in
lieu of ground-based communications. Organizations consider factors such as availability, quality
of service, and access when entering alternate telecommunications agreements.

Related Controls: CP-2, CP-6, CP-7, CP-11, SC-7.

Control Enhancements:

(1) TELECOMMUNICATIONS SERVICES | PRIORITY OF SERVICE PROVISIONS

(a) **Develop primary and alternate telecommunications service agreements that contain priority-
of-service provisions in accordance with organizational availability requirements (including
recovery time objectives); and**

(b) **Request Telecommunications Service Priority for all telecommunications services used for
national security emergency preparedness if the primary and/or alternate telecommunications
services are provided by a common carrier.**

Supplemental Guidance: Organizations consider the potential mission/business impact in
situations where telecommunications service providers are servicing other organizations with
similar priority-of-service provisions.

Related Controls: None.

(2) TELECOMMUNICATIONS SERVICES | SINGLE POINTS OF FAILURE

Obtain alternate telecommunications services to reduce the likelihood of sharing a single point of failure with primary telecommunications services.

Supplemental Guidance: None.

Related Controls: None.

(3) TELECOMMUNICATIONS SERVICES | SEPARATION OF PRIMARY AND ALTERNATE PROVIDERS

Obtain alternate telecommunications services from providers that are separated from primary service providers to reduce susceptibility to the same threats.

Supplemental Guidance: Threats that affect telecommunications services are typically defined in organizational assessments of risk and include, for example, natural disasters, structural failures, hostile cyber/physical attacks, and errors of omission/commission. Organizations seek to reduce common susceptibilities by, for example, minimizing shared infrastructure among telecommunications service providers and achieving sufficient geographic separation between services. Organizations may consider using a single service provider in situations where the service provider can provide alternate telecommunications services meeting the separation needs addressed in the risk assessment.

Related Controls: None.

(4) TELECOMMUNICATIONS SERVICES | PROVIDER CONTINGENCY PLAN

(a) **Require primary and alternate telecommunications service providers to have contingency plans;**

(b) **Review provider contingency plans to ensure that the plans meet organizational contingency requirements; and**

(c) **Obtain evidence of contingency testing and training by providers [*Assignment: organization-defined frequency*].**

Supplemental Guidance: Reviews of provider contingency plans consider the proprietary nature of such plans. In some situations, a summary of provider contingency plans may be sufficient evidence for organizations to satisfy the review requirement. Telecommunications service providers may also participate in ongoing disaster recovery exercises in coordination with the Department of Homeland Security, state, and local governments. Organizations may use these types of activities to satisfy evidentiary requirements related to service provider contingency plan reviews, testing, and training.

Related Controls: CP-3, CP-4.

(5) TELECOMMUNICATIONS SERVICES | ALTERNATE TELECOMMUNICATION SERVICE TESTING

Test alternate telecommunication services [*Assignment: organization-defined frequency*].

Supplemental Guidance: CP-3.

Related Controls: None.

References: NIST Special Publication 800-34.

CP-9   SYSTEM BACKUP

Control:

a. Conduct backups of user-level information contained in the system [*Assignment: organization-defined frequency consistent with recovery time and recovery point objectives*];

b. Conduct backups of system-level information contained in the system [*Assignment: organization-defined frequency consistent with recovery time and recovery point objectives*];

c. Conduct backups of system documentation including security-related documentation [*Assignment: organization-defined frequency consistent with recovery time and recovery point objectives*]; and

d. Protect the confidentiality, integrity, and availability of backup information at storage locations.

Supplemental Guidance: [illegible] System-level information includes, for example, system state information, operating system software, application software, and licenses. User-level information includes any information other than system-level information. Mechanisms employed to protect the integrity of system backups include, for example, digital signatures and cryptographic hashes. Protection of backup information while in transit is beyond the scope of this control. System backups reflect the requirements in contingency plans as well as other organizational requirements for backing up information.

Related Controls: CP-2, CP-6, CP-10, MP-4, MP-5, SC-13, SI-4, SI-13.

Control Enhancements:

(1) SYSTEM BACKUP | TESTING FOR RELIABILITY AND INTEGRITY

Test backup information [*Assignment: organization-defined frequency*] to verify media reliability and information integrity.

Supplemental Guidance: None.

Related Controls: CP-4.

(2) SYSTEM BACKUP | TEST RESTORATION USING SAMPLING

Use a sample of backup information in the restoration of selected system functions as part of contingency plan testing.

Supplemental Guidance:

Related Controls: CP-4.

(3) SYSTEM BACKUP | SEPARATE STORAGE FOR CRITICAL INFORMATION

Store backup copies of [*Assignment: organization-defined critical system software and other security-related information*] in a separate facility or in a fire-rated container that is not collocated with the operational system.

Supplemental Guidance: Critical system software includes, for example, operating systems, cryptographic key management systems, and intrusion detection/prevention systems. Security-related information includes, for example, organizational inventories of hardware, software, and firmware components. Alternate storage sites typically serve as separate storage facilities for organizations.

Related Controls: CM-2, CM-6, CM-8.

(4) SYSTEM BACKUP | PROTECTION FROM UNAUTHORIZED MODIFICATION

[Withdrawn: Incorporated into CP-9].

(5) SYSTEM BACKUP | TRANSFER TO ALTERNATE STORAGE SITE

Transfer system backup information to the alternate storage site [*Assignment: organization-defined time-period and transfer rate consistent with the recovery time and recovery point objectives*].

Supplemental Guidance: System backup information can be transferred to alternate storage sites either electronically or by physical shipment of storage media.

Related Controls: CP-7, MP-3, MP-4, MP-5.

(6) SYSTEM BACKUP | REDUNDANT SECONDARY SYSTEM

Conduct system backup by maintaining a redundant secondary system that is not collocated with the primary system and that can be activated without loss of information or disruption to operations.

Supplemental Guidance:

Related Controls: CP-7.

(7) SYSTEM BACKUP | DUAL AUTHORIZATION

Enforce dual authorization for the deletion or destruction of [*Assignment: organization-defined backup information*].

Supplemental Guidance: Dual authorization ensures that the deletion or destruction of backup information cannot occur unless two qualified individuals carry out the task. Individuals deleting/destroying backup information possess sufficient skills/expertise to determine if the proposed deletion/destruction of backup information reflects organizational policies and procedures. Dual authorization may also be known as two-person control.

Related Controls: AC-3, AC-5, MP-2.

(8) SYSTEM BACKUP | CRYPTOGRAPHIC PROTECTION

Implement cryptographic mechanisms to prevent unauthorized disclosure and modification of [*Assignment: organization-defined backup information*].

Supplemental Guidance: The selection of cryptographic mechanisms is based on the need to protect the confidentiality and integrity of backup information. The strength of mechanism is commensurate with the security category and/or classification of the information. This control enhancement applies to system backup information in storage at primary and alternate locations. Organizations implementing cryptographic mechanisms to protect information at rest also consider cryptographic key management solutions.

Related Controls: SC-12, SC-13, SC-28.

References: FIPS Publications 140-2, 186-4; NIST Special Publications 800-34, 800-130, 800-152.

CP-10 SYSTEM RECOVERY AND RECONSTITUTION

Control: Provide for the recovery and reconstitution of the system to a known state after a disruption, compromise, or failure within [*Assignment: organization-defined time-period consistent with recovery time and recovery point objectives*].

Supplemental Guidance: Recovery is executing contingency plan activities to restore organizational missions and business functions. Reconstitution takes place following recovery and includes activities for returning systems to fully operational states. Recovery and reconstitution operations reflect mission and business priorities, recovery point, time, and reconstitution objectives, and established organizational metrics consistent with contingency plan requirements. Reconstitution includes the deactivation of any interim system capabilities that may have been needed during recovery operations. Reconstitution also includes assessments of fully restored system capabilities, reestablishment of continuous monitoring activities, system reauthorizations (if required), and activities to prepare the systems against future disruptions, compromises, or failures. Recovery and reconstitution capabilities employed by organizations can include both automated mechanisms and manual procedures.

Related Controls: CP-2, CP-4, CP-6, CP-7, CP-9, IR-4, SC-24, SI-13.

Control Enhancements:

(1) SYSTEM RECOVERY AND RECONSTITUTION | CONTINGENCY PLAN TESTING

[Withdrawn: Incorporated into CP-4].

(2) SYSTEM RECOVERY AND RECONSTITUTION | TRANSACTION RECOVERY

Implement transaction recovery for systems that are transaction-based.

Supplemental Guidance: Transaction-based systems include, for example, database management systems and transaction processing systems. Mechanisms supporting transaction recovery include, for example, transaction rollback and transaction journaling.

Related Controls: None.

(3) SYSTEM RECOVERY AND RECONSTITUTION | COMPENSATING SECURITY CONTROLS

[Withdrawn: Addressed through tailoring procedures].

(4) SYSTEM RECOVERY AND RECONSTITUTION | RESTORE WITHIN TIME-PERIOD

Provide the capability to restore system components within [*Assignment: organization-defined restoration time-periods*] from configuration-controlled and integrity-protected information representing a known, operational state for the components.

Supplemental Guidance: Restoration of system components includes, for example, reimaging which restores components to known, operational states.

Related Controls: CM-2, CM-6.

(5) SYSTEM RECOVERY AND RECONSTITUTION | TRANSACTION RECOVERY
     [Withdrawn: Incorporated into SI-13].

(6) SYSTEM RECOVERY AND RECONSTITUTION | COMPONENT PROTECTION
     Protect system components used for backup and restoration.

     Supplemental Guidance: Protection of system backup and restoration components (hardware,
     firmware, and software) includes both physical and technical safeguards. Backup and
     restoration software includes, for example, router tables, compilers, and other security-
     relevant system software.

     Related Controls: AC-3, AC-6, MP-2, MP-4, PE-3, PE-6.

References: NIST Special Publication 800-34.

CP-11 ALTERNATE COMMUNICATIONS PROTOCOLS

Control: Provide the capability to employ [*Assignment: organization-defined alternative
communications protocols*] in support of maintaining continuity of operations.

Supplemental Guidance: Contingency plans and the training/testing associated with those plans,
incorporate an alternate communications protocol capability as part of establishing resilience in
organizational systems. Alternate communications protocols include, for example, switching from
TCP/IP Version 4 to TCP/IP Version 6. Switching communications protocols may affect software
applications and operational aspects of systems. Organizations assess the potential side effects of
introducing such alternate communications protocols prior to implementation.

Related Controls: CP-2, CP-8, CP-13.

Control Enhancements: None.

References: None.

CP-12 SAFE MODE

Control: When [*Assignment: organization-defined conditions*] are detected, enter a safe mode of
operation with [*Assignment: organization-defined restrictions of safe mode of operation*].

Supplemental Guidance: For systems supporting critical missions and business functions including,
for example, military operations and weapons systems, civilian space operations, nuclear power
plant operations, and air traffic control operations (especially real-time operational environments),
organizations can identify certain conditions under which those systems revert to a predefined safe
mode of operation. The safe mode of operation, which can be activated automatically or manually,
restricts the activities or operations systems can execute when those conditions are encountered.
Restriction includes, for example, allowing only certain functions that can be carried out under
limited power or with reduced communications bandwidth.

Related Controls: CM-2, SC-24, SI-13, SI-17.

Control Enhancements: None.

References: None.

CP-13 ALTERNATIVE SECURITY MECHANISMS

Control: Employ [*Assignment: organization-defined alternative or supplemental security
mechanisms*] for satisfying [*Assignment: organization-defined security functions*] when the
primary means of implementing the security function is unavailable or compromised.

Supplemental Guidance: This control supports system resiliency, contingency planning, and
continuity of operations. To ensure mission and business continuity, organizations can implement
alternative or supplemental security mechanisms. These mechanisms may be less effective than
the primary mechanisms. However, having the capability to readily employ these alternative or

supplemental mechanisms, enhances mission and business continuity that might otherwise be adversely impacted if operations had to be curtailed until the primary means of implementing the functions was restored. Given the cost and level of effort required to provide such alternative capabilities, this control is typically applied only to critical security capabilities provided by systems, system components, or system services. For example, an organization may issue to senior executives and system administrators one-time pads if multifactor tokens, the standard means for secure remote authentication, is compromised.

Related Controls: CP-2 CP-11, SI-13.

Control Enhancements: None.

References: None.

3.7 IDENTIFICATION AND AUTHENTICATION

Quick link to Identification and Authentication summary table

IA-1 IDENTIFICATION AND AUTHENTICATION POLICY AND PROCEDURES

Control:

a. Develop, document, and disseminate to [*Assignment: organization-defined personnel or roles*]:

1. An identification and authentication policy that:

(a) Addresses purpose, scope, roles, responsibilities, management commitment, coordination among organizational entities, and compliance; and

(b) Is consistent with applicable laws, Executive Orders, directives, regulations, policies, standards, and guidelines; and

2. Procedures to facilitate the implementation of the identification and authentication policy and the associated identification and authentication controls;

b. Designate an [*Assignment: organization-defined senior management official*] to manage the identification and authentication policy and procedures;

c. Review and update the current identification and authentication:

1. Policy [*Assignment: organization-defined frequency*]; and

2. Procedures [*Assignment: organization-defined frequency*];

d. Ensure that the identification and authentication procedures implement the identification and authentication policy and controls; and

e. Develop, document, and implement remediation actions for violations of the identification and authentication policy.

Supplemental Guidance: This control addresses the establishment of policy and procedures for the effective implementation of the controls and control enhancements in the IA family. The risk management strategy is an important factor in establishing policy and procedures. Comprehensive policy and procedures help provide security and privacy assurance. Security and privacy program policies and procedures at the organization level may make the need for system-specific policies and procedures unnecessary. The policy can be included as part of the general security and privacy policy or can be represented by multiple policies reflecting the complex nature of organizations. The procedures can be established for security and privacy programs and for systems, if needed. Procedures describe how policies or controls are implemented and can be directed at the personnel or role that is the object of the procedure. Procedures can be documented in system security and privacy plans or in one or more separate documents. It is important to recognize that restating controls does not constitute an organizational policy or procedure.

Related Controls: AC-1, PM-9, PS-8, SI-12.

Control Enhancements: None.

References: FIPS Publication 201; NIST Special Publications 800-12, 800-30, 800-39, 800-63, 800-73, 800-76, 800-78, 800-100; NIST Interagency Report 7874.

IA-2 IDENTIFICATION AND AUTHENTICATION (ORGANIZATIONAL USERS)

Control: Uniquely identify and authenticate organizational users or processes acting on behalf of organizational users.

Supplemental Guidance: Organizations can satisfy the identification and authentication requirements in this control by complying with the requirements in Homeland Security Presidential Directive 12. Organizational users include employees or individuals that organizations consider having the equivalent status of employees including, for example, contractors and guest researchers. This control applies to all accesses other than accesses that are explicitly identified in AC-14 and that occur through the authorized use of group authenticators without individual authentication. Organizations may require unique identification of individuals in group accounts or for detailed accountability of individual activity. Organizations employ passwords, physical authenticators, or biometrics to authenticate user identities, or in the case of multifactor authentication, some combination thereof. Access to organizational systems is defined as either local access or network access. Local access is any access to organizational systems by users or processes acting on behalf of users, where such access is obtained through direct connections without the use of networks. Network access is access to organizational systems by users (or processes acting on behalf of users) where such access is obtained through network connections (i.e., nonlocal accesses). Remote access is a type of network access that involves communication through external networks. Internal networks include local area networks and wide area networks. The use of encrypted virtual private networks for network connections between organization-controlled endpoints and non-organization controlled endpoints may be treated as internal networks with respect to protecting the confidentiality and integrity of information traversing the network. Identification and authentication requirements for non-organizational users are described in IA-8.

Related Controls: AC-2, AC-3, AC-4, AC-14, AC-17, AC-18, AU-1, AU-6, IA-4, IA-5, IA-8, MA-4, MA-5, PE-2, PL-4, SA-4.

Control Enhancements:

(1) IDENTIFICATION AND AUTHENTICATION (ORGANIZATIONAL USERS) | MULTIFACTOR AUTHENTICATION TO PRIVILEGED ACCOUNTS

Implement multifactor authentication for access to privileged accounts.

Supplemental Guidance: Multifactor authentication requires the use of two or more different factors to achieve authentication. Factors are defined as follows: something you know, for example, a password or personal identification number (PIN); something you have, for example, a physical authenticator or cryptographic identification device; or something you are, for example, a biometric. Multifactor solutions that feature physical authenticators include, for example, hardware authenticators providing time-based or challenge-response authenticators and smart cards such as the U.S. Government Personal Identity Verification card or the DoD common access card. In addition to authenticating users at the system level (i.e., at logon), organizations may also employ authentication mechanisms at the application level, at their discretion, to provide increased information security. Regardless of the type of access (i.e., local, network, or remote) privileged accounts are always authenticated using multifactor options appropriate for the level of risk. Organizations can add additional security measures, such as additional or more rigorous authentication mechanisms, for specific types of access.

Related Controls: AC-5, AC-6.

(2) IDENTIFICATION AND AUTHENTICATION (ORGANIZATIONAL USERS) | MULTIFACTOR AUTHENTICATION TO NON-PRIVILEGED ACCOUNTS

Implement multifactor authentication for access to non-privileged accounts.

Supplemental Guidance: Multifactor authentication requires the use of two or more different factors to achieve authentication. Factors are defined as follows: something you know, for example, a personal identification number (PIN); something you have, for example, a physical authenticator or cryptographic private key stored in hardware or software; or something you are, for example, a biometric. Multifactor solutions that feature physical authenticators include, for example, hardware authenticators providing time-based or challenge-response authenticators and smart cards such as the U.S. Government Personal Identity Verification card or the DoD common access card. In addition to authenticating users at the system level, organizations may also employ authentication mechanisms at the application level, at their discretion to provide increased information security. Organizations can also provide additional security measures, such as additional or more rigorous authentication mechanisms, for specific types of access.

Related Controls: AC-5.

(3) IDENTIFICATION AND AUTHENTICATION (ORGANIZATIONAL USERS) | LOCAL ACCESS TO PRIVILEGED ACCOUNTS

[Withdrawn: Incorporated into IA-2(1)(2)].

(4) IDENTIFICATION AND AUTHENTICATION (ORGANIZATIONAL USERS) | LOCAL ACCESS TO NON-PRIVILEGED ACCOUNTS

[Withdrawn: Incorporated into IA-2(1)(2)].

(5) IDENTIFICATION AND AUTHENTICATION (ORGANIZATIONAL USERS) | INDIVIDUAL AUTHENTICATION WITH GROUP AUTHENTICATION

When shared accounts or authenticators are employed, require users to be individually authenticated before granting access to the shared accounts or resources.

Supplemental Guidance: Individual authentication prior to the shared group authentication helps organizations to mitigate the risk of using group accounts or authenticators.

Related Controls: None.

(6) IDENTIFICATION AND AUTHENTICATION (ORGANIZATIONAL USERS) | NETWORK ACCESS TO PRIVILEGED ACCOUNTS — SEPARATE DEVICE

[Withdrawn: Incorporated into IA-2(1)(2)].

(7) IDENTIFICATION AND AUTHENTICATION (ORGANIZATIONAL USERS) | NETWORK ACCESS TO NON-PRIVILEGED ACCOUNTS — SEPARATE DEVICE

[Withdrawn: Incorporated into IA-2(1)(2)].

(8) IDENTIFICATION AND AUTHENTICATION (ORGANIZATIONAL USERS) | ACCESS TO ACCOUNTS - REPLAY RESISTANT

Implement replay-resistant authentication mechanisms for access to [*Selection (one or more): privileged accounts; non-privileged accounts*].

Supplemental Guidance: Authentication processes resist replay attacks if it is impractical to achieve successful authentications by replaying previous authentication messages. Replay-resistant techniques include, for example, protocols that use nonces or challenges such as time synchronous or challenge-response one-time authenticators.

Related Controls: None.

(9) IDENTIFICATION AND AUTHENTICATION (ORGANIZATIONAL USERS) | NETWORK ACCESS TO NON-PRIVILEGED ACCOUNTS — REPLAY RESISTANT

[Withdrawn: Incorporated into IA-2(8)].

(10) IDENTIFICATION AND AUTHENTICATION (ORGANIZATIONAL USERS) | SINGLE SIGN-ON

Provide a single sign-on capability for [*Assignment: organization-defined system accounts and services*].

Supplemental Guidance: Single sign-on enables users to log in once and gain access to multiple system resources. Organizations consider the operational efficiencies provided by single sign-on capabilities with the risk introduced by allowing access to multiple systems via a single authentication event. Single sign-on can present opportunities to improve system security, for example by providing the ability to add multifactor authentication for applications that may not be able to natively support this function. This situation may occur in legacy applications or systems.

Related Controls: None.

(11) IDENTIFICATION AND AUTHENTICATION (ORGANIZATIONAL USERS) | REMOTE ACCESS — SEPARATE DEVICE

[Withdrawn: Incorporated into IA-2(1)(2)].

(12) IDENTIFICATION AND AUTHENTICATION (ORGANIZATIONAL USERS) | ACCEPTANCE OF PIV CREDENTIALS

Accept and electronically verify Personal Identity Verification credentials.

Supplemental Guidance: This control enhancement applies to organizations implementing logical access control and physical access control systems. Personal Identity Verification (PIV) credentials are those credentials issued by federal agencies that conform to FIPS Publication 201 and supporting guidance documents. The adequacy and reliability of PIV card issuers are addressed and authorized using NIST Special Publication 800-79. Acceptance of PIV credentials includes derived PIV credentials, the use of which is addressed in NIST Special Publication 800-166.

Related Controls: None.

(13) IDENTIFICATION AND AUTHENTICATION (ORGANIZATIONAL USERS) | OUT-OF-BAND AUTHENTICATION

[Withdrawn: Incorporated into IA-2(1)(2)].

References: FIPS Publications 140-2, 201, 202; NIST Special Publications 800-63, 800-73, 800-76, 800-78, 800-79, 800-156, 800-166; NIST Interagency Reports 7539, 7676, 7817, 7849, 7870, 7874, 7966.

IA-3   DEVICE IDENTIFICATION AND AUTHENTICATION

Control: Uniquely identify and authenticate [*Assignment: organization-defined specific and/or types of devices*] before establishing a [*Selection (one or more): local; remote; network*] connection.

Supplemental Guidance: Devices requiring unique device-to-device identification and authentication are defined by type, by device, or by a combination of type and device. Organization-defined device types may include devices that are not owned by the organization. Systems use shared known information (e.g., Media Access Control [MAC] or Transmission Control Protocol/Internet Protocol [TCP/IP] addresses) for device identification or organizational authentication solutions (e.g., IEEE 802.1x and Extensible Authentication Protocol [EAP], RADIUS server with EAP-Transport Layer Security [TLS] authentication, Kerberos) to identify and authenticate devices on local and wide area networks. Organizations determine the required strength of authentication mechanisms based on the security categories of systems and mission/business requirements. Because of the challenges of implementing this control on large scale, organizations can restrict the application of the control to a limited number (and type) of devices based on organizational need.

Related Controls: AC-17, AC-18, AC-19, AU-6, CA-3, CA-9, IA-4, IA-5, IA-9, IA-11, SI-4.

Control Enhancements:

(1) DEVICE IDENTIFICATION AND AUTHENTICATION | CRYPTOGRAPHIC BIDIRECTIONAL AUTHENTICATION

Authenticate [*Assignment: organization-defined specific devices and/or types of devices*] before establishing [*Selection (one or more): local; remote; network*] connection using bidirectional authentication that is cryptographically based.

Supplemental Guidance: A local connection is any connection with a device communicating without the use of a network. A network connection is any connection with a device that communicates through a network. A remote connection is any connection with a device communicating through an external network. Bidirectional authentication provides stronger safeguards to validate the identity of other devices for connections that are of greater risk.

Related Controls: SC-8, SC-12, SC-13.

(2) DEVICE IDENTIFICATION AND AUTHENTICATION | CRYPTOGRAPHIC BIDIRECTIONAL NETWORK AUTHENTICATION

[Withdrawn: Incorporated into IA-3(1)].

(3) DEVICE IDENTIFICATION AND AUTHENTICATION | DYNAMIC ADDRESS ALLOCATION

(a) Where addresses are allocated dynamically, standardize dynamic address allocation lease information and the lease duration assigned to devices in accordance with [*Assignment: organization-defined lease information and lease duration*]; and

(b) Audit lease information when assigned to a device.

Supplemental Guidance: DHCP and DHCPv6 are applications that enable clients to dynamically obtain Internet Protocol address leases from DHCP servers.

Related Controls: None.

(4) DEVICE IDENTIFICATION AND AUTHENTICATION | DEVICE ATTESTATION

Handle device identification and authentication based on attestation by [*Assignment: organization-defined configuration management process*].

Supplemental Guidance: Device attestation refers to the identification and authentication of a device based on its configuration and known operating state. This might be determined via some cryptographic hash of the device. If device attestation is the means of identification and authentication, then it is important that patches and updates to the device are handled via a configuration management process such that the patches and updates are done securely and at the same time do not disrupt the identification and authentication to other devices.

Related Controls: CM-2, CM-3, CM-6.

References: None.

IA-4   IDENTIFIER MANAGEMENT

Control: Manage system identifiers by:

a.   Receiving authorization from [*Assignment: organization-defined personnel or roles*] to assign an individual, group, role, or device identifier;

b.   Selecting an identifier that identifies an individual, group, role, or device;

c.   Assigning the identifier to the intended individual, group, role, or device; and

d.   Preventing reuse of identifiers for [*Assignment: organization-defined time-period*].

Supplemental Guidance: Common device identifiers include, for example, media access control (MAC), Internet Protocol addresses, or device-unique token identifiers. Management of individual identifiers is not applicable to shared system accounts. Typically, individual identifiers are the user names of the system accounts assigned to those individuals. In such instances, the account management activities of AC-2 use account names provided by IA-4. This control also addresses individual identifiers not necessarily associated with system accounts. Preventing the reuse of identifiers implies preventing the assignment of previously used individual, group, role, or device identifiers to different individuals, groups, roles, or devices.

Related Controls: IA-2, IA-3, IA-5, IA-8, IA-9, MA-4, PE-2, PE-3, PE-4, PL-4, PM-12, PS-3, PS-4, PS-5, SC-37.

Control Enhancements:

(1) IDENTIFIER MANAGEMENT | PROHIBIT ACCOUNT IDENTIFIERS AS PUBLIC IDENTIFIERS

Prohibit the use of system account identifiers that are the same as public identifiers for individual electronic mail accounts.

Supplemental Guidance: Prohibiting the use of systems account identifiers that are the same as some public identifier such as the individual identifier section of an electronic mail address, makes it more difficult for adversaries to guess user identifiers on organizational systems. The use of this control alone only complicates guessing of identifiers and must be combined with appropriate protections for authenticators and attributes to protect the account as a whole.

Related Controls: AT-2.

(2) IDENTIFIER MANAGEMENT | SUPERVISOR AUTHORIZATION
[Withdrawn: Incorporated into IA-12(1)].

(3) IDENTIFIER MANAGEMENT | MULTIPLE FORMS OF CERTIFICATION
[Withdrawn: Incorporated into IA-12(2)].

(4) IDENTIFIER MANAGEMENT | IDENTIFY USER STATUS

Manage individual identifiers by uniquely identifying each individual as [*Assignment: organization-defined characteristic identifying individual status*].

Supplemental Guidance: Characteristics identifying the status of individuals include, for example, contractors and foreign nationals. Identifying the status of individuals by specific characteristics provides additional information about the people with whom organizational personnel are communicating. For example, it might be useful for a government employee to know that one of the individuals on an email message is a contractor.

Related Controls: None.

(5) IDENTIFIER MANAGEMENT | DYNAMIC MANAGEMENT

Manage individual identifiers dynamically.

Supplemental Guidance: In contrast to conventional approaches to identification which presume static accounts for preregistered users, many distributed systems establish identifiers at run time for entities that were previously unknown. In these situations, organizations anticipate and provision for the dynamic establishment of identifiers. Pre-established trust relationships and mechanisms with appropriate authorities to validate identities and related credentials are essential.

Related Controls: AC-16.

(6) IDENTIFIER MANAGEMENT | CROSS-ORGANIZATION MANAGEMENT

Coordinate with [*Assignment: organization-defined external organizations*] for cross-organization management of identifiers.

Supplemental Guidance: Cross-organization identifier management provides the capability for organizations to appropriately identify individuals, groups, roles, or devices when conducting cross-organization activities involving the processing, storage, or transmission of information.

Related Controls: AU-16, IA-2, IA-5.

(7) IDENTIFIER MANAGEMENT | IN-PERSON REGISTRATION

[Withdrawn: Incorporated into IA-12(4)].

(8) IDENTIFIER MANAGEMENT | PAIRWISE PSEUDONYMOUS IDENTIFIERS

Generate pairwise pseudonymous identifiers.

Supplemental Guidance: Generating distinct pairwise pseudonymous identifiers, with no identifying information about a subscriber, discourages subscriber activity tracking and profiling beyond the operational requirements established by an organization. The pairwise pseudonymous identifiers are unique to each relying party, except in situations where relying parties show a demonstrable relationship justifying an operational need for correlation, or all parties consent to being correlated in such a manner.

Related Controls: IA-5.

References: FIPS Publication 201; NIST Special Publications 800-63, 800-73, 800-76, 800-78.

IA-5 AUTHENTICATOR MANAGEMENT

Control: Manage system authenticators by:

a. Verifying, as part of the initial authenticator distribution, the identity of the individual, group, role, or device receiving the authenticator;

b. Establishing initial authenticator content for any authenticators issued by the organization;

c. Ensuring that authenticators have sufficient strength of mechanism for their intended use;

d. Establishing and implementing administrative procedures for initial authenticator distribution, for lost/compromised or damaged authenticators, and for revoking authenticators;

e. Establishing minimum and maximum lifetime restrictions and reuse conditions for authenticators;

f. Changing/refreshing authenticators [*Assignment: organization-defined time-period by authenticator type*];

g. Protecting authenticator content from unauthorized disclosure and modification;

h. Requiring individuals to take, and having devices implement, specific security controls to protect authenticators; and

i. Changing authenticators for group/role accounts when membership to those accounts changes.

Supplemental Guidance: Examples of individual authenticators include passwords, cryptographic devices, one-time password devices, and key cards. The initial authenticator content is the actual content of the authenticator, for example, the initial password. In contrast, the requirements about authenticator content include, for example, the minimum password length. Developers may ship system components with factory default authentication credentials to allow for initial installation and configuration. Default authentication credentials are often well known, easily discoverable, and present a significant security risk. The requirement to protect individual authenticators may be implemented via control PL-4 or PS-6 for authenticators in the possession of individuals and by controls AC-3, AC-6, and SC-28 for authenticators stored in organizational systems including, for example, passwords stored in hashed or encrypted formats or files containing encrypted or hashed passwords accessible with administrator privileges. Systems support authenticator management by organization-defined settings and restrictions for various authenticator characteristics including, for example, minimum password length, validation time window for time synchronous one-time tokens, and number of allowed rejections during the verification stage of biometric authentication. Actions that can be taken to safeguard individual authenticators include, for example, maintaining possession of authenticators, not loaning or sharing authenticators with others, and reporting lost, stolen, or compromised authenticators immediately. Authenticator management includes issuing and revoking, when no longer needed, authenticators for temporary access such as that required for remote maintenance. Device authenticators include, for example, certificates and passwords.

Related Controls: AC-3, AC-6, CM-6, IA-2, IA-4, IA-7, IA-8, IA-9, MA-4, PE-2, PL-4.

Control Enhancements:

(1) AUTHENTICATOR MANAGEMENT | PASSWORD-BASED AUTHENTICATION

For password-based authentication:

(a) Maintain a list of commonly-used, expected, or compromised passwords and update the list [*Assignment: organization-defined frequency*] and when organizational passwords are suspected to have been compromised directly or indirectly;

(b) Verify, when users create or update passwords, that the passwords are not found on the organization-defined list of commonly-used, expected, or compromised passwords;

(c) Transmit only cryptographically-protected passwords;

(d) Store passwords using an approved hash algorithm and salt, preferably using a keyed hash;

(e) Require immediate selection of a new password upon account recovery;

(f) Allow user selection of long passwords and passphrases, including spaces and all printable characters; and

(g) Employ automated tools to assist the user in selecting strong password authenticators.

Supplemental Guidance: This control enhancement applies to passwords regardless of whether they are used in single-factor or multi-factor authentication. Long passwords or passphrases are preferable over shorter passwords. Enforced composition rules provide marginal security benefit while decreasing usability. Account recovery can occur, for example, in situations when a password is forgotten. Cryptographically-protected passwords include, for example, salted one-way cryptographic hashes of passwords. The list of commonly-used, expected, or compromised passwords may include, for example, passwords obtained from previous breach corpuses, dictionary words, and repetitive or sequential characters. Examples include aaaaaaa, 1234abcd, and qwertyuiop. The list can also include context specific words, for example, the name of the service, username, and derivatives thereof.

Related Controls: IA-6.

(2) AUTHENTICATOR MANAGEMENT | PUBLIC KEY-BASED AUTHENTICATION

For public key-based authentication:

(a) Enforce authorized access to the corresponding private key; and

(b) Map the authenticated identity to the account of the individual or group; and

When public key infrastructure (PKI) is used:

(c) Validate certificates by constructing and verifying a certification path to an accepted trust anchor including checking certificate status information; and

(d) Implement a local cache of revocation data to support path discovery and validation.

Supplemental Guidance: Public key cryptography is a valid authentication mechanism for individuals and machines/devices. When PKI is leveraged, status information for certification paths includes, for example, certificate revocation lists or certificate status protocol responses. For PIV cards, the validation of certificates involves the construction and verification of a certification path to the Common Policy Root trust anchor which includes certificate policy processing. Implementing a local cache of revocation data to support path discovery and validation supports system availability in situations where organizations are unable to access revocation information via the network

Related Controls: IA-3, SC-17.

(3) AUTHENTICATOR MANAGEMENT | IN-PERSON OR TRUSTED EXTERNAL PARTY REGISTRATION

[Withdrawn: Incorporated into IA-12(4)].

(4) AUTHENTICATOR MANAGEMENT | AUTOMATED SUPPORT FOR PASSWORD STRENGTH DETERMINATION

[Withdrawn: Incorporated into IA-5(1)].

(5) AUTHENTICATOR MANAGEMENT | CHANGE AUTHENTICATORS PRIOR TO DELIVERY

Require developers and installers of system components to provide unique authenticators or change default authenticators prior to delivery and installation.

Supplemental Guidance: This control enhancement extends the requirement for organizations to change default authenticators upon system installation, by requiring developers and/or installers to provide unique authenticators or change default authenticators for system components prior to delivery and/or installation. However, it typically does not apply to the developers of commercial off-the-shelf information technology products. Requirements for unique authenticators can be included in acquisition documents prepared by organizations when procuring systems or system components.

Related Controls: None.

(6) AUTHENTICATOR MANAGEMENT | PROTECTION OF AUTHENTICATORS

Protect authenticators commensurate with the security category of the information to which use of the authenticator permits access.

Supplemental Guidance: For systems containing multiple security categories of information without reliable physical or logical separation between categories, authenticators used to grant access to the systems are protected commensurate with the highest security category of information on the systems. Security categories of information are determined as part of the security categorization process.

Related Controls: RA-2.

(7) AUTHENTICATOR MANAGEMENT | NO EMBEDDED UNENCRYPTED STATIC AUTHENTICATORS

Ensure that unencrypted static authenticators are not embedded in applications or access scripts or stored on function keys.

Supplemental Guidance: Organizations exercise caution in determining whether embedded or stored authenticators are in encrypted or unencrypted form. If authenticators are used in the manner stored, then those representations are considered unencrypted authenticators. This is irrespective of whether that representation is perhaps an encrypted version of something else.

Related Controls: None.

(8) AUTHENTICATOR MANAGEMENT | MULTIPLE SYSTEM ACCOUNTS

Implement [Assignment: organization-defined security safeguards] to manage the risk of compromise due to individuals having accounts on multiple systems.

Supplemental Guidance: When individual class accounts for multiple systems, risks to the risk then a compromise of one account may lead to the compromise of other accounts if individuals use the same authenticators. Possible alternatives include: having different authenticators on all systems; employing some form of single sign-on mechanism; or using some form of one-time passwords on all systems.

Related Controls: None.

(9) AUTHENTICATOR MANAGEMENT | FEDERATED CREDENTIAL MANAGEMENT

Use [*Assignment: organization-defined external organizations*] to federate authenticators.

Supplemental Guidance: Federation provides the capability for organizations to appropriately authenticate individuals and devices when conducting cross-organization activities involving the processing, storage, or transmission of information.

Related Controls: AU-7, AU-16.

(10) AUTHENTICATOR MANAGEMENT | DYNAMIC CREDENTIAL BINDING

Bind identities and authenticators dynamically.

Supplemental Guidance: Authentication requires some form of binding between an identity and the authenticator used to confirm the identity. In conventional approaches, this binding is established by pre-provisioning both the identity and the authenticator to the system. For example, the binding between a username (i.e., identity) and a password (i.e., authenticator) is accomplished by provisioning the identity and authenticator as a pair in the system. New authentication techniques allow the binding between the identity and the authenticator to be implemented outside a system. For example, with smartcard credentials, the identity and the authenticator are bound together on the smartcard. Using these credentials, systems can authenticate identities that have not been pre-provisioned, dynamically provisioning the identity after authentication. In these situations, organizations can anticipate the dynamic provisioning of identities. Pre-established trust relationships and mechanisms with appropriate authorities to validate identities and related credentials are essential.

Related Controls: AU-16, IA-5.

(11) AUTHENTICATOR MANAGEMENT | HARDWARE TOKEN-BASED AUTHENTICATION

[Withdrawn: Incorporated into IA-2(1)(2)].

(12) AUTHENTICATOR MANAGEMENT | BIOMETRIC AUTHENTICATION PERFORMANCE

For biometric-based authentication, employ mechanisms that satisfy [*Assignment: organization-defined biometric quality requirements*].

Supplemental Guidance: Unlike password-based authentication which provides exact matches of user-input passwords to stored passwords, biometric authentication does not provide such exact matches. Depending upon the type of biometric and the type of collection mechanism, there is likely to be some divergence from the presented biometric and stored biometric which serves as the basis of comparison. The matching performance is the rate at which a biometric algorithm correctly results in a match for a genuine user and rejects other users. Biometric performance requirements include, for example, the match rate as this reflects the accuracy of the biometric matching algorithm being used by a system.

Related Controls: AC-7.

(13) AUTHENTICATOR MANAGEMENT | EXPIRATION OF CACHED AUTHENTICATORS

Prohibit the use of cached authenticators after [*Assignment: organization-defined time-period*].

Supplemental Guidance: None.

Related Controls: None.

(14) AUTHENTICATOR MANAGEMENT | MANAGING CONTENT OF PKI TRUST STORES

For PKI-based authentication, employ a deliberate organization-wide methodology for managing the content of PKI trust stores installed across all platforms including networks, operating systems, browsers, and applications.

Supplemental Guidance: None.

Related Controls: None.

(15) AUTHENTICATOR MANAGEMENT | GSA-APPROVED PRODUCTS AND SERVICES

Use only General Services Administration-approved and validated products and services.

Supplemental Guidance: General Services Administration (GSA)-approved products and services are the products and services that have been approved through the GSA conformance program, where applicable, and posted to the GSA Approved Products List.

Related Controls: None.

(16) AUTHENTICATOR MANAGEMENT | IN-PERSON OR TRUSTED EXTERNAL PARTY AUTHENTICATOR ISSUANCE

Require that the issuance of [*Assignment: organization-defined types of and/or specific authenticators*] be conducted [*Selection: in person; by a trusted external party*] before [*Assignment: organization-defined registration authority*] with authorization by [*Assignment: organization-defined personnel or roles*].

Supplemental Guidance: None.

Related Controls: IA-12.

(17) AUTHENTICATOR MANAGEMENT | PRESENTATION ATTACK DETECTION FOR BIOMETRIC AUTHENTICATORS

Employ presentation attack detection mechanisms for biometric-based authentication.

Supplemental Guidance: Biometric characteristics do not constitute secrets. Such characteristics can be obtained by online web accesses; taking a picture of someone with a camera phone to obtain facial images with or without their knowledge; lifting from objects that someone has touched, for example, a latent fingerprint; or capturing a high-resolution image, for example, an iris pattern. Presentation attack detection technologies including, for example, liveness detection, can mitigate the risk of these types of attacks by making it more difficult to produce artifacts intended to defeat the biometric sensor.

Related Controls: AC-7.

References: FIPS Publications 140-2, 180-4, 201, 202; NIST Special Publications 800-73, 800-63, 800-76, 800-78; NIST Interagency Reports 7539, 7817, 7849, 7870, 8040.

IA-6   AUTHENTICATOR FEEDBACK

Control: Obscure feedback of authentication information during the authentication process to protect the information from possible exploitation and use by unauthorized individuals.

Supplemental Guidance: The feedback from systems does not provide information that would allow unauthorized individuals to compromise authentication mechanisms. For some types of systems or system components, for example, desktops/notebooks with relatively large monitors, the threat (referred to as shoulder surfing) may be significant. For other types of systems or components, for example, mobile devices with small displays, this threat may be less significant, and is balanced against the increased likelihood of typographic input errors due to the small keyboards. Therefore, the means for obscuring authenticator feedback is selected accordingly. Obscuring authenticator feedback includes, for example, displaying asterisks when users type passwords into input devices, or displaying feedback for a very limited time before fully obscuring it.

Related Controls: AC-3.

Control Enhancements: None.

References: None.

IA-7   CRYPTOGRAPHIC MODULE AUTHENTICATION

Control: Implement mechanisms for authentication to a cryptographic module that meet the requirements of applicable laws, Executive Orders, directives, policies, regulations, standards, and guidelines for such authentication.

Supplemental Guidance: Individuals often transmit data not required within a cryptographic module to authenticate an operator accessing the module and to verify that the operator is authorized to assume the requested role and perform services within that role.

Related Controls: AC-3, IA-5, SA-4, SC-12, SC-13.

Control Enhancements: None.

References: FIPS Publication 140-2.

IA-8 IDENTIFICATION AND AUTHENTICATION (NON-ORGANIZATIONAL USERS)

Control: Uniquely identify and authenticate non-organizational users or processes acting on behalf of non-organizational users.

Supplemental Guidance: Non-organizational users include system users other than organizational users explicitly covered by IA-2. These individuals are uniquely identified and authenticated for accesses other than those accesses explicitly identified and documented in AC-14. Identification and authentication of non-organizational users accessing federal systems may be required to protect federal, proprietary, or privacy-related information (with exceptions noted for national security systems). Organizations consider many factors including scalability, practicality, security, and privacy in balancing the need to ensure ease of use for access to federal information and systems with the need to protect and adequately mitigate risk.

Related Controls: AC-2, AC-6, AC-14, AC-17, AC-18, AU-6, IA-2, IA-4, IA-5, IA-10, IA-11, MA-4, RA-3, SA-4, SA-12, SC-8.

Control Enhancements:

(1) IDENTIFICATION AND AUTHENTICATION (NON-ORGANIZATIONAL USERS) | ACCEPTANCE OF PIV CREDENTIALS FROM OTHER AGENCIES

Accept and electronically verify Personal Identity Verification credentials from other federal agencies.

Supplemental Guidance: This control enhancement applies to both logical and physical access control systems. Personal Identity Verification (PIV) credentials are those credentials issued by federal agencies that conform to FIPS Publication 201 and supporting guidelines. The adequacy and reliability of PIV card issuers are addressed and authorized using NIST Special Publication 800-79.

Related Controls: PE-3.

(2) IDENTIFICATION AND AUTHENTICATION (NON-ORGANIZATIONAL USERS) | ACCEPTANCE OF EXTERNAL CREDENTIALS

Accept only external credentials that are NIST compliant.

Supplemental Guidance: This control enhancement applies to organizational systems that are accessible to the public, for example, public-facing websites. External credentials are those credentials issued by nonfederal government entities. Such credentials are certified as compliant with NIST Special Publication 800-63 by an approved accreditation authority. Approved external credentials meet or exceed the set of minimum federal government-wide technical, security, privacy, and organizational maturity requirements. This allows federal government relying parties to trust such credentials at their approved assurance levels.

Related Controls: None.

(3) IDENTIFICATION AND IDENTIFICATION AND AUTHENTICATION (NON-ORGANIZATIONAL USERS) | USE OF FICAM-APPROVED PRODUCTS

[Withdrawn: Incorporated into IA-8(2)].

(4) IDENTIFICATION AND AUTHENTICATION (NON-ORGANIZATIONAL USERS) | USE OF NIST-ISSUED PROFILES

Conform to NIST-issued profiles for identity management.

Supplemental Guidance: This control enhancement addresses open identity management standards. To ensure that these identity management standards are viable, robust, reliable, sustainable, and interoperable as documented, the United States Government assesses and scopes the standards and technology implementations against applicable laws, Executive Orders, directives, policies, regulations, standards, and guidelines. The result is NIST-issued implementation profiles of approved protocols.

Related Controls: None.

(5) IDENTIFICATION AND AUTHENTICATION (NON-ORGANIZATIONAL USERS) | ACCEPTANCE OF PIV-I CREDENTIALS

Accept and electronically verify Personal Identity Verification-I (PIV-I) credentials.

Supplemental Guidance: This control enhancement applies to both logical access control and physical access control systems. It addresses Nonfederal Issuers of identity cards that desire to interoperate with United States Government Personal Identity Verification (PIV) systems and that can be trusted by federal government-relying parties. The X.509 certificate policy for the Federal Bridge Certification Authority (FBCA) addresses PIV-I requirements. The PIV-I card is commensurate with the PIV credentials as defined in cited references. PIV-I credentials are the credentials issued by a PIV-I provider whose PIV-I certificate policy maps to the Federal Bridge PIV-I Certificate Policy. A PIV-I provider is cross-certified with the FBCA (directly or through another PKI bridge) with policies that have been mapped and approved as meeting the requirements of the PIV-I policies defined in the FBCA certificate policy.

Related Controls: None.

(6) IDENTIFICATION AND AUTHENTICATION (NON-ORGANIZATIONAL USERS) | DISASSOCIABILITY

Implement [*Assignment: organization-defined measures*] to disassociate user attributes or credential assertion relationships among individuals, credential service providers, and relying parties.

Supplemental Guidance: Federated identity solutions can create increased privacy risks due to tracking and profiling of individuals. Using identifier mapping tables or privacy-enhancing cryptographic techniques to blind credential service providers and relying parties from each other or to make identity attributes less visible to transmitting parties can reduce these privacy risks.

Related Controls: None.

References: FIPS Publication 201; NIST Special Publications 800-63, 800-79, 800-116; NIST Interagency Report 8062.

IA-9   SERVICE IDENTIFICATION AND AUTHENTICATION

Control: Identify and authenticate [*Assignment: organization-defined system services and applications*] before establishing communications with devices, users, or other services or applications.

Supplemental Guidance: Services that may require identification and authentication include, for example, web applications using digital certificates or services/applications that query a database. Identification and authentication methods for system services/applications include, for example, information or code signing, provenance graphs, and/or electronic signatures indicating the sources of services.

Related Controls: IA-3, IA-4, IA-5.

Control Enhancements:

(1) SERVICE IDENTIFICATION AND AUTHENTICATION | INFORMATION EXCHANGE

Ensure that service providers receive, validate, and transmit identification and authentication information.

Supplemental Guidance: None.

Related Controls: None.

(b) SERVICE IDENTIFICATION AND AUTHENTICATION | TRANSMISSION OF DECISIONS

Transmit identification and authentication decisions between [*Assignment: organization-defined services*] consistent with organizational policies.

Supplemental Guidance: For distributed architectures, the decisions regarding the validation of identification and authentication claims may be made by services separate from the services acting on those decisions. In such situations, it is necessary to provide the identification and authentication decisions (instead of the actual identifiers and authenticators) to the services that need to act on those decisions.

Related Controls: SC-8.

References: None.

IA-10 ADAPTIVE AUTHENTICATION

Control: Require individuals accessing the system to employ [*Assignment: organization-defined supplemental authentication techniques or mechanisms*] under specific [*Assignment: organization-defined circumstances or situations*].

Supplemental Guidance: Adversaries may compromise individual authentication mechanisms and subsequently attempt to impersonate legitimate users. This situation can potentially occur with any authentication mechanisms employed by organizations. To address this threat, organizations may employ specific techniques or mechanisms and establish protocols to assess suspicious behavior. Such behavior may include, for example, accessing information that individuals do not typically access as part of their duties, roles, or responsibilities; accessing greater quantities of information than the individuals would routinely access; or attempting to access information from suspicious network addresses. In situations when pre-established conditions or triggers occur, organizations can require individuals to provide additional authentication information. Another potential use for adaptive authentication is to increase the strength of mechanism based on the number and/or types of records being accessed. Adaptive authentication does not replace and is not used to avoid multifactor mechanisms, but can augment implementations of these controls.

Related Controls: IA-2, IA-8.

Control Enhancements: None.

References: NIST Special Publication 800-63.

IA-11 RE-AUTHENTICATION

Control: Require users to re-authenticate when [*Assignment: organization-defined circumstances or situations requiring re-authentication*].

Supplemental Guidance: In addition to the re-authentication requirements associated with device locks, organizations may require re-authentication of individuals in certain situations including, for example, when authenticators or roles change; when security categories of systems change; when the execution of privileged functions occurs; after a fixed time-period; or periodically.

Related Controls: AC-3, AC-11, IA-2, IA-3, IA-8.

Control Enhancements: None.

References: None.

IA-12 IDENTITY PROOFING

Control:

a. Identity proof users that require accounts for logical access to systems based on appropriate identity assurance level requirements as specified in applicable standards and guidelines;

b. Resolve user identities to a unique individual; and

c. Collect, validate, and verify identity evidence.

Supplemental Guidance: Identity proofing is the process of collecting, validating, and verifying user's identity information for the purposes of issuing credentials for accessing a system. This control is intended to mitigate threats to the registration of users and the establishment of their accounts. Standards and guidelines specifying identity assurance levels for identity proofing include NIST Special Publications 800-63 and 800-63A.

Related Controls: IA-1, IA-2, IA-3, IA-4, IA-5, IA-6, IA-8.

(1) IDENTITY PROOFING | SUPERVISOR AUTHORIZATION

Require that the registration process to receive an account for logical access includes supervisor or sponsor authorization.

Supplemental Guidance: None.

Related Controls: None.

(2) IDENTITY PROOFING | IDENTITY EVIDENCE

Require evidence of individual identification be presented to the registration authority.

Supplemental Guidance: Requiring identity evidence, such as documentary evidence or a combination of documents and biometrics, reduces the likelihood of individuals using fraudulent identification to establish an identity, or at least increases the work factor of potential adversaries. Acceptable forms of evidence are consistent with the risk to the systems, roles, and privileges associated with the user's account.

Related Controls: None.

(3) IDENTITY PROOFING | IDENTITY EVIDENCE VALIDATION AND VERIFICATION

Require that the presented identity evidence be validated and verified through [*Assignment: organizational defined methods of validation and verification*].

Supplemental Guidance: Validating and verifying identity evidence increases the assurance that that accounts, identifiers, and authenticators are being issued to the correct user. Validation refers to the process of confirming that the evidence is genuine and authentic and that the data contained in the evidence is correct, current, and related to an actual person or individual. Verification confirms and establishes a linkage between the claimed identity and the actual existence of the user presenting the evidence. Acceptable methods for validating and verifying identity evidence are consistent with the risk to the systems, roles, and privileges associated with the users account

Related Controls: None.

(4) IDENTITY PROOFING | IN-PERSON VALIDATION AND VERIFICATION

Require that the validation and verification of identity evidence be conducted in person before a designated registration authority.

Supplemental Guidance: In-person proofing reduces the likelihood of fraudulent credentials being issued because it requires the physical presence of individuals, the presentation of physical identity documents, and actual face-to-face interactions with designated registration authorities.

Related Controls: None.

(5) IDENTITY PROOFING | ADDRESS CONFIRMATION

Require that a [*Selection: registration code; notice of proofing*] be delivered through an out-of-band channel to verify the users address (physical or digital) of record.

Supplemental Guidance: To make it more difficult for adversaries to pose as legitimate users during the identity proofing process, organizations can use out-of-band methods to increase assurance that the individual associated with an address of record was the same person that participated in the registration. Confirmation can take the form of a temporary enrollment code or a notice of proofing. The delivery address for these artifacts are obtained from records and not self-asserted by the user. The address can include a physical or a digital address. A home address is an example of a physical address. Email addresses and telephone numbers are examples of digital addresses.

Related Controls: IA-12.

(6) IDENTITY PROOFING | ACCEPT EXTERNALLY-PROOFED IDENTITIES

Accept externally-proofed identities at [*Assignment: organization-defined identity assurance level*].

Supplemental Guidance: To limit unnecessary re-proofing of identities, particularly of non-PIV users, organizations accept proofing conducted at a commensurate level of assurance by other agencies or organizations. Proofing is consistent with organizational security policy and with the identity assurance level appropriate for the system, application, or information accessed. This is a core component of managing federated identities across agencies and organizations.

Related Controls: IA-3, IA-4, IA-5, IA-8.

References: FIPS Publication 201; NIST Special Publications 800-63, 800-63A.

3.8 INDIVIDUAL PARTICIPATION

Quick link to Individual Participation summary table

IP-1   INDIVIDUAL PARTICIPATION POLICY AND PROCEDURES

Control:

a. Develop, document, and disseminate to [*Assignment: organization-defined personnel or roles*]:

   1. An individual participation policy that:

      (a) Addresses purpose, scope, roles, responsibilities, management commitment, coordination among organizational entities, and compliance; and

      (b) Is consistent with applicable laws, Executive Orders, directives, regulations, policies, standards, and guidelines; and

   2. Procedures to facilitate the implementation of the individual participation policy and the associated individual participation controls;

b. Designate an [*Assignment: organization-defined senior management official*] to manage the individual participation policy and procedures;

c. Review and update the current individual participation:

   1. Policy [*Assignment: organization-defined frequency*]; and

   2. Procedures [*Assignment: organization-defined frequency*];

d. Ensure that the individual participation procedures implement the individual participation policy and controls; and

e. Develop, document, and implement remediation actions for violations of the individual participation policy.

Supplemental Guidance: This control addresses the establishment of policy and procedures for the effective implementation of the controls and control enhancements in the IP family. The risk management strategy is an important factor in establishing policy and procedures. Comprehensive policy and procedures help provide security and privacy assurance. Security and privacy program policies and procedures at the organization level may make the need for system-specific policies and procedures unnecessary. The policy can be included as part of the general security and privacy policy or can be represented by multiple policies reflecting the complex nature of organizations. The procedures can be established for security and privacy programs and for systems, if needed. Procedures describe how policies or controls are implemented and can be directed at the personnel or role that is the object of the procedure. Procedures can be documented in system security and privacy plans or in one or more separate documents. It is important to recognize that restating controls does not constitute an organizational policy or procedure.

Related Controls: PM-9, PS-8, SI-12.

Control Enhancements: None.

References: NIST Special Publications 800-12, 800-30, 800-39, 800-100.

IP-2   CONSENT

Control: Implement [*Assignment: organization-defined tools or mechanisms*] for users to authorize the processing of their personally identifiable information prior to its collection that:

a. Use plain language and provide examples to illustrate the potential privacy risks of the authorization; and

b.   Provide a means for users to decline the authorization.

Supplemental Guidance: This control transfers risk that arises from the processing of personally identifiable information from the organization to an individual. It is only selected as required by law or regulation or when individuals can be reasonably expected to understand and accept any privacy risks arising from their authorization. Organizations consider whether other controls may more effectively mitigate privacy risk either alone or in conjunction with consent.

To help users understand the risks being accepted when providing consent, organizations write materials in plain language and avoid technical jargon. The examples required in IP-2 a. focus on key points necessary for user decision-making. When developing or purchasing consent tools, organizations consider the application of good information design procedures in all user-facing consent materials; use of active voice and conversational style; logical sequencing of main points; consistent use of the same word (rather than synonyms) to avoid confusion; the use of bullets, numbers, and formatting where appropriate to aid readability; and legibility of text, such as font style, size, color, and contrast with surrounding background.

Related Controls: AC-16, IP-4.

Control Enhancements:

(1)   CONSENT | ATTRIBUTE MANAGEMENT

Allow data subjects to tailor use permissions to selected attributes.

Supplemental Guidance: Allowing individuals to select how specific data attributes may be further used or disclosed beyond the original use may help reduce privacy risk arising from the most sensitive of the data attributes while maintaining utility of the data.

Related Controls: None.

(2)   CONSENT | JUST-IN-TIME NOTICE OF CONSENT

Present authorizations to process personally identifiable information in conjunction with the data action or [*Assignment: organization-defined frequency*].

Supplemental Guidance: If the circumstances under which an individual gave consent have changed or a significant amount of time has passed since an individual gave consent for the processing of his or her personally identifiable information, the data subject's assumption about how the information is being processed might no longer be accurate or reliable. Just-in-time notice can help maintain individual satisfaction with how the personally identifiable information is being processed.

Related Controls: None.

References: NIST Special Publication 800-63; NIST Interagency Report 8062.

IP-3   REDRESS

Control:

a.   Establish and implement a process for individuals to have inaccurate personally identifiable information maintained by the organization corrected or amended; and

b.   Establish and implement a process for disseminating corrections or amendments of personally identifiable information to other authorized users of the personally identifiable information.

Supplemental Guidance: Redress supports the ability of individuals to ensure the accuracy of their personally identifiable information held by organizations. Effective redress processes demonstrate organizational commitment to data quality especially in those business functions where inaccurate data may result in inappropriate decisions or the denial of benefits and services to individuals. Organizations use discretion in determining if records are to be corrected or amended, based on the scope of redress requests, the changes sought, and the impact of the changes. Other authorized users of personally identifiable information include, for example, external information-sharing partners.

An effective redress process includes: providing effective notice of the existence of a personally identifiable information collection; providing plain language explanations of the processes and mechanisms for requesting access to records; establishing the criteria for submitting requests for correction or amendment of records; implementing resources to analyze and adjudicate requests; implementing means of correcting or amending data collections; and reviewing any decisions that may have been the result of inaccurate information.

Related Controls: IP-4, IP-6, IR-7, PM-28.

Control Enhancements:

(1) REDRESS | NOTICE OF CORRECTION OR AMENDMENT
Notify affected individuals if their personally identifiable information has been corrected or amended.

Supplemental Guidance: Where personally identifiable information is corrected or amended, organizations take steps to ensure that all authorized recipients of such information and the individual with which the information is associated, are informed of the corrected or amended information.

Related Controls: None.

(2) REDRESS | APPEAL
Provide [*Assignment: organization-defined process*] for individuals to appeal an adverse decision and have incorrect information amended.

Supplemental Guidance: The Senior Agency Official for Privacy ensures that practical means and mechanisms exist and are accessible for individuals to seek the correction or amendment of their personally identifiable information. Redress processes are clearly defined and publicly available. Additionally, redress processes include the provision of responses to individuals of decisions to deny requests for correction or amendment. The responses include the reasons for the decisions, a means to record individual objections to the decisions, and finally, a means of requesting reviews of the initial determinations.

Related Controls: None.

References: None.

IP-4   PRIVACY NOTICE

Control:

a. Make privacy notice(s) available to individuals upon first interacting with an organization, and subsequently [*Assignment: organization-defined frequency*].

b. Ensure that privacy notices are clear and easy-to-understand, expressing information about personally identifiable information processing in plain language.

Supplemental Guidance: To help users understand how their information is being processed, organizations write materials in plain language and avoid technical jargon. When developing privacy notices, organizations consider the application of good information design procedures in all user-facing materials; use of active voice and conversational style; logical sequencing of main points; consistent use of the same word (rather than synonyms) to avoid confusion; use of bullets, numbers, and formatting where appropriate to aid readability; and legibility of text, such as font style, size, color, and contrast with surrounding background.

Related Controls: IP-2, IP-3, IP-4, IP-5, PA-2, PA-3, PA-4, PM-21.

Control Enhancements:

(1) PRIVACY NOTICE | JUST-IN-TIME NOTICE OF PRIVACY AUTHORIZATION
Present authorizations to process personally identifiable information in conjunction with the data action, or [*Assignment: organization-defined frequency*].

Supplemental Guidance: If the circumstances under which an individual gave consent have changed or a significant amount of time has passed since an individual gave consent for the processing of the of the personally identifiable information, the data subject's assumption about how the information is being processed might no longer be accurate or reliable. Just-in-time notice can help maintain individual satisfaction with or ability to participate in how the personally identifiable information is being processed.

Related Controls: IP-2, IP-3, IP-5, PA-3, PA-4, PM-22.

References: NIST Interagency Report 8062.

IP-5   PRIVACY ACT STATEMENTS

Control:

a.   Include Privacy Act Statements on organizational forms that collect personally identifiable information, or on separate forms that can be retained by individuals; or

b.   Read a Privacy Act Statement to the individual prior to initiating the collection of personally identifiable information verbally.

Supplemental Guidance: Privacy Act Statements provide additional formal notice to individuals from whom the information is being collected, notice of the authority of organizations to collect personally identifiable information; whether providing personally identifiable information is mandatory or optional; the principal purpose or purposes for which the personally identifiable information is to be used; the intended disclosures or routine uses of the information; and the consequences of not providing all or some portion of the information requested. Personally identifiable information may be collected verbally, for example, when conducting telephone interviews or surveys.

Related Controls: IP-4, PA-3, PM-20, PM-21.

Control Enhancements: None.

References: None.

IP-6   INDIVIDUAL ACCESS

Control: Provide individuals the ability to access their personally identifiable information maintained in organizational systems of records.

Supplemental Guidance: Access affords individuals the ability to review personally identifiable information about them held within organizational systems of records. Access includes timely, simplified, and inexpensive access to data. Organizational processes for allowing access to records may differ based on resources, legal requirements, or other factors. The Senior Agency Official for Privacy is responsible for the content of Privacy Act regulations and record request processing, in consultation with legal counsel. Access to certain types of records may not be appropriate, and heads of agencies may promulgate rules exempting specific systems from the access provision of the Privacy Act. When feasible, those rules will be publicly available. In addition, individuals are not entitled to access to information compiled in reasonable anticipation of a civil action or proceeding.

Related Controls: IP-3, PA-3, PM-27.

Control Enhancements: None.

References: NIST Interagency Report 8062.

3.9 INCIDENT RESPONSE

Quick link to Incident Response summary table

IR-1 INCIDENT RESPONSE POLICY AND PROCEDURES

Control:

a. Develop, document, and disseminate to [*Assignment: organization-defined personnel or roles*]:

   1. An incident response policy that:

      (a) Addresses purpose, scope, roles, responsibilities, management commitment, coordination among organizational entities, and compliance; and

      (b) Is consistent with applicable laws, Executive Orders, directives, regulations, policies, standards, and guidelines; and

   2. Procedures to facilitate the implementation of the incident response policy and the associated incident response controls;

b. Designate an [*Assignment: organization-defined senior management official*] to manage the incident response policy and procedures;

c. Review and update the current incident response:

   1. Policy [*Assignment: organization-defined frequency*]; and

   2. Procedures [*Assignment: organization-defined frequency*];

d. Ensure that the incident response procedures implement the incident response policy and controls; and

e. Develop, document, and implement remediation actions for violations of the incident response policy.

Supplemental Guidance: This control addresses the establishment of policy and procedures for the effective implementation of the controls and control enhancements in the IR family. The risk management strategy is an important factor in establishing policy and procedures. Comprehensive policy and procedures help provide security and privacy assurance. Security and privacy program policies and procedures at the organization level may make the need for system-specific policies and procedures unnecessary. The policy can be included as part of the general security and privacy policy or can be represented by multiple policies reflecting the complex nature of organizations. The procedures can be established for security and privacy programs and for systems, if needed. Procedures describe how policies or controls are implemented and can be directed at the personnel or role that is the object of the procedure. Procedures can be documented in system security and privacy plans or in one or more separate documents. It is important to recognize that restating controls does not constitute an organizational policy or procedure.

Related Controls: PM-9, PS-8, SI-12.

Control Enhancements: None.

References: NIST Special Publications 800-12, 800-30, 800-39, 800-61, 800-83, 800-100.

IR-2 INCIDENT RESPONSE TRAINING

Control: Provide incident response training to system users consistent with assigned roles and responsibilities:

a. Within [*Assignment: organization-defined time-period*] of assuming an incident response role or responsibility;

b. When required by ....; and

c. [*Assignment: organization-defined frequency*] thereafter.

<u>Supplemental Guidance</u>: Incident response training is linked to assigned roles and responsibilities of organizational personnel to ensure the appropriate content and level of detail is included in such training. For example, users may only need to know who to call or how to recognize an incident; system administrators may require additional training on how to handle and remediate incidents; and finally, incident responders may receive more specific training on forensics, reporting, system recovery, and restoration. Incident response training includes user training in the identification and reporting of suspicious activities, both from external and internal sources.

<u>Related Controls</u>: AT-2, AT-4, AT-3, CP-3, IR-3, IR-4, IR-8, IR-9.

<u>Control Enhancements</u>:

(1) INCIDENT RESPONSE TRAINING | SIMULATED EVENTS

Incorporate simulated events into incident response training to facilitate effective response by personnel in crisis situations.

<u>Supplemental Guidance</u>: None.

<u>Related Controls</u>: None.

(2) INCIDENT RESPONSE TRAINING | AUTOMATED TRAINING ENVIRONMENTS

Employ automated mechanisms to provide a more thorough and realistic incident response training environment.

<u>Supplemental Guidance</u>: None.

<u>Related Controls</u>: None.

<u>References</u>: NIST Special Publication 800-50.

IR-3 INCIDENT RESPONSE TESTING

<u>Control</u>: Test the incident response capability for the system [*Assignment: organization-defined frequency*] using [*Assignment: organization-defined tests*] to determine the incident response effectiveness and documents the results.

<u>Supplemental Guidance</u>: Organizations test incident response capabilities to determine the overall effectiveness of the capabilities and to identify potential weaknesses or deficiencies. Incident response testing includes, for example, the use of checklists, walk-through or tabletop exercises, simulations (parallel/full interrupt), and comprehensive exercises. Incident response testing can also include a determination of the effects on organizational operations, organizational assets, and individuals due to incident response. Use of qualitative and quantitative data aids in determining the effectiveness of incident response processes.

<u>Related Controls</u>: CP-3, CP-4, IR-2, IR-4, IR-8, PM-14.

<u>Control Enhancements</u>:

(1) INCIDENT RESPONSE TESTING | AUTOMATED TESTING

Employ automated mechanisms to more thoroughly and effectively test the incident response capability.

<u>Supplemental Guidance</u>: Organizations use automated mechanisms to more thoroughly and effectively test incident response capabilities. This can be accomplished, for example, by providing more complete coverage of incident response issues; by selecting more realistic test scenarios and test environments; and by stressing the response capability.

<u>Related Controls</u>: None.

(2) INCIDENT RESPONSE TESTING | COORDINATION WITH RELATED PLANS

Coordinate incident response testing with organizational elements responsible for related plans.

<u>Supplemental Guidance</u>: Organizational plans related to incident response testing include, for example, Business Continuity Plans, Contingency Plans, Disaster Recovery Plans, Continuity

of Operations Plans, Crisis Communications Plans, Occupant Emergency Plans, and Critical Infrastructure Plans.

Related Controls: None.

(3) INCIDENT RESPONSE TESTING | CONTINUOUS IMPROVEMENT

Use qualitative and quantitative data from testing to:

(a) Determine the effectiveness of incident response processes;

(b) Continuously improve incident response processes incorporating advanced information security practices; and

(c) Provide incident response measures and metrics that are accurate, consistent, and in a reproducible format.

Supplemental Guidance: To help incident response activities function as intended, organizations may use of metrics and evaluation criteria to assess incident response programs as part of an effort to continually improve response performance. These efforts facilitate improvement in incident response efficacy and lessen the impact of incidents.

Related Controls: None.

References: NIST Special Publications 800-84, 800-115.

IR-4   INCIDENT HANDLING

Control:

a. Implement an incident handling capability for security and privacy incidents that includes preparation, detection and analysis, containment, eradication, and recovery;

b. Coordinate incident handling activities with contingency planning activities;

c. Incorporate lessons learned from ongoing incident handling activities into incident response procedures, training, and testing, and implement the resulting changes accordingly; and

d. Ensure the rigor, intensity, scope, and results of incident handling activities are comparable and predictable across the organization.

Supplemental Guidance: Organizations recognize that incident response capability is dependent on the capabilities of organizational systems and the mission/business processes being supported by those systems. Therefore, organizations consider incident response as part of the definition, design, and development of mission/business processes and systems. Incident-related information can be obtained from a variety of sources including, for example, audit monitoring, network monitoring, physical access monitoring, user/administrator reports, and reported supply chain events. Effective incident handling capability includes coordination among many organizational entities including, for example, mission/business owners, system owners, authorizing officials, human resources offices, physical and personnel security offices, legal departments, operations personnel, procurement offices, and the risk executive (function).

Related Controls: AC-19, AU-6, AU-7, CM-6, CP-2, CP-3, CP-4, IR-2, IR-3, IR-8, PE-6, PL-2, PM-12, SA-12, SC-5, SC-7, SI-3, SI-4, SI-7.

Control Enhancements:

(1) INCIDENT HANDLING | AUTOMATED INCIDENT HANDLING PROCESSES

Employ automated mechanisms to support the incident handling process.

Supplemental Guidance: Automated mechanisms supporting incident handling processes include, for example, online incident management systems; and tools that support collection of live response data, full network packet capture, and forensic analysis.

Related Controls: None.

(2) INCIDENT HANDLING | DYNAMIC RECONFIGURATION

Include dynamic reconfiguration of [Assignment: organization-defined system components] as part of the incident response capability.

rules, access control lists, intrusion detection/prevention system parameters, and filter rules for firewalls and gateways. Organizations perform dynamic reconfiguration of systems, for example, to stop attacks, to misdirect attackers, and to isolate components of systems, thus limiting the extent of the damage from breaches or compromises. Organizations include time frames for achieving the reconfiguration of systems in the definition of the reconfiguration capability, considering the potential need for rapid response to effectively address cyber threats.

Related Controls: AC-2, AC-4, CM-2.

(3) INCIDENT HANDLING | CONTINUITY OF OPERATIONS

Identify [*Assignment: organization-defined classes of incidents*] and [*Assignment: organization-defined actions to take in response to classes of incidents*] to ensure continuation of organizational missions and business functions.

Supplemental Guidance: Classes of incidents include, for example, malfunctions due to design/implementation errors and omissions, targeted malicious attacks, and untargeted malicious attacks. Appropriate incident response actions include, for example, graceful degradation, system shutdown, fall back to manual mode/alternative technology whereby the system operates differently, employing deceptive measures, alternate information flows, or operating in a mode that is reserved solely for when systems are under attack.

Related Controls: None.

(4) INCIDENT HANDLING | INFORMATION CORRELATION

Correlate incident information and individual incident responses to achieve an organization-wide perspective on incident awareness and response.

Supplemental Guidance: Sometimes the nature of a threat event, for example, a hostile attack, is such that it can only be observed by bringing together information from different sources including various reports and reporting procedures established by organizations.

Related Controls: None.

(5) INCIDENT HANDLING | AUTOMATIC DISABLING OF SYSTEM

Implement a configurable capability to automatically disable the system if [*Assignment: organization-defined security violations*] are detected.

Supplemental Guidance: None.

Related Controls: None.

(6) INCIDENT HANDLING | INSIDER THREATS — SPECIFIC CAPABILITIES

Implement an incident handling capability for incidents involving insider threats.

Supplemental Guidance: While many organizations address insider threat incidents as an inherent part of their organizational incident response capability, this control enhancement provides additional emphasis on this type of threat and the need for specific incident handling capabilities (as defined within organizations) to provide appropriate and timely responses.

Related Controls: None.

(7) INCIDENT HANDLING | INSIDER THREATS — INTRA-ORGANIZATION COORDINATION

Coordinate an incident handling capability for insider threats across [*Assignment: organization-defined components or elements of the organization*].

Supplemental Guidance: Incident handling for insider threat incidents (including preparation, detection and analysis, containment, eradication, and recovery) requires close coordination among a variety of organizational components or elements to be effective. These components or elements include, for example, mission/business owners, system owners, human resources offices, procurement offices, personnel/physical security offices, operations personnel, and risk executive (function). In addition, organizations may require external support from federal, state, and local law enforcement agencies.

Related Controls: None.

(8) INCIDENT HANDLING | CORRELATION WITH EXTERNAL ORGANIZATIONS

Coordinate with [*Assignment: organization-defined external organizations*] to correlate and share [*Assignment: organization-defined incident information*] to achieve a cross-organization perspective on incident awareness and more effective incident responses.

Supplemental Guidance: The coordination of incident information with external organizations including, for example, mission/business partners, military/coalition partners, customers, and multi-tiered developers, can provide significant benefits. Cross-organizational coordination with respect to incident handling can serve as an important risk management capability. This capability allows organizations to leverage critical information from a variety of sources to effectively respond to information security-related incidents potentially affecting the organization's operations, assets, and individuals.

Related Controls: AU-16, PM-16.

(9) INCIDENT HANDLING | DYNAMIC RESPONSE CAPABILITY

Employ [*Assignment: organization-defined dynamic response capabilities*] to effectively respond to security incidents.

Supplemental Guidance: This control enhancement addresses the timely deployment of new or replacement organizational capabilities in response to security and privacy incidents. This includes capabilities implemented at the mission and business process level and at the system level.

Related Controls: None.

(10) INCIDENT HANDLING | SUPPLY CHAIN COORDINATION

Coordinate incident handling activities involving supply chain events with other organizations involved in the supply chain.

Supplemental Guidance: Organizations involved in supply chain activities include, for example, system/product developers, integrators, manufacturers, packagers, assemblers, distributors, vendors, and resellers. Supply chain incidents include, for example, compromises/breaches involving system components, information technology products, development processes or personnel, and distribution processes or warehousing facilities.

Related Controls: MA-2, SA-9.

References: NIST Special Publications 800-61, 800-101, 800-86; NIST Interagency Report 7599.

IR-5   INCIDENT MONITORING

Control: Track and document system security and privacy incidents.

Supplemental Guidance: Documenting system security and privacy incidents includes, for example, maintaining records about each incident, the status of the incident, and other pertinent information necessary for forensics; and evaluating incident details, trends, and handling. Incident information can be obtained from a variety of sources including, for example, network monitoring; incident reports; incident response teams; user complaints; audit monitoring; physical access monitoring; and user and administrator reports.

Related Controls: AU-6, AU-7, IR-8, PE-6, PM-29, SC-5, SC-7, SI-3, SI-4, SI-7.

Control Enhancements:

(1) INCIDENT MONITORING | AUTOMATED TRACKING, DATA COLLECTION, AND ANALYSIS

Employ automated mechanisms to assist in the tracking of security and privacy incidents and in the collection and analysis of incident information.

Supplemental Guidance: Automated mechanisms for tracking incidents and for collecting and analyzing incident information include, for example, Computer Incident Response Centers or other electronic databases of incidents and network monitoring devices.

Related Controls: AU-7, IR-4.

References: NIST Special Publication 800-61.

IR-6   INCIDENT REPORTING

Control:

a. Require personnel to report suspected security and privacy incidents to the organizational incident response capability within [*Assignment: organization-defined time-period*]; and

b. Report security, privacy, and supply chain incident information to [*Assignment: organization-defined authorities*].

Supplemental Guidance: The intent of this control is to address both specific incident reporting requirements within an organization and the incident reporting requirements for organizations. Suspected security incidents include, for example, the receipt of suspicious email communications that can potentially contain malicious code. Suspected privacy incidents include, for example a suspected breach of personally identifiable information or the recognition that the processing of personally identifiable information creates potential privacy risk. The types of incidents reported, the content and timeliness of the reports, and the designated reporting authorities reflect applicable laws, Executive Orders, directives, regulations, policies, standards, and guidelines.

Related Controls: CM-6, CP-2, IR-4, IR-5, IR-8, IR-9.

Control Enhancements:

(1) INCIDENT REPORTING | AUTOMATED REPORTING

Employ automated mechanisms to assist in the reporting of security and privacy incidents.

Supplemental Guidance: None.

Related Controls: IR-7.

(2) INCIDENT REPORTING | VULNERABILITIES RELATED TO INCIDENTS

Report system vulnerabilities associated with reported security and privacy incidents to [*Assignment: organization-defined personnel or roles*].

Supplemental Guidance: None.

Related Controls: None.

(3) INCIDENT REPORTING | SUPPLY CHAIN COORDINATION

Provide security and privacy incident information to the provider of the product or service and other organizations involved in the supply chain for systems or system components related to the incident.

Supplemental Guidance: Organizations involved in supply chain activities include, for example, system/product developers, integrators, manufacturers, packagers, assemblers, distributors, vendors, and resellers. Supply chain incidents include, for example, compromises/breaches involving system components, information technology products, development processes or personnel, and distribution processes or warehousing facilities. Organizations determine the appropriate information to share considering the value gained from support by external organizations with the potential for harm due to controlled unclassified information being released to outside organizations of perhaps questionable trustworthiness.

Related Controls: SA-12.

References: NIST Special Publication 800-61.

IR-7   INCIDENT RESPONSE ASSISTANCE

Control: Provide an incident response support resource, integral to the organizational incident response capability that offers advice and assistance to users of the system for the handling and reporting of security and privacy incidents.

Supplemental Guidance: Incident response support resources provided by organizations include, for example, help desks, assistance groups, and access to forensics services or consumer redress services, when required.

Related Controls: AT-2, AT-3, IP-3, IR-4, IR-6, IR-8, PM-28, SA-9.

Control Enhancements:

(1) INCIDENT RESPONSE ASSISTANCE | AUTOMATION SUPPORT FOR AVAILABILITY OF INFORMATION AND SUPPORT

Employ automated mechanisms to increase the availability of incident response-related information and support.

Supplemental Guidance: Automated mechanisms can provide a push and/or pull capability for users to obtain incident response assistance. For example, individuals might have access to a website to query the assistance capability, or the assistance capability can proactively send information to users (general distribution or targeted) as part of increasing understanding of current response capabilities and support.

Related Controls: None.

(2) INCIDENT RESPONSE ASSISTANCE | COORDINATION WITH EXTERNAL PROVIDERS

(a) **Establish a direct, cooperative relationship between its incident response capability and external providers of system protection capability; and**

(b) **Identify organizational incident response team members to the external providers.**

Supplemental Guidance: External providers of a system protection capability include, for example, the Computer Network Defense program within the U.S. Department of Defense. External providers help to protect, monitor, analyze, detect, and respond to unauthorized activity within organizational information systems and networks.

Related Controls: None.

References: NIST Interagency Report 7559.

IR-8 INCIDENT RESPONSE PLAN

Control:

a. Develop an incident response plan that:

1. Provides the organization with a roadmap for implementing its incident response capability;

2. Describes the structure and organization of the incident response capability;

3. Provides a high-level approach for how the incident response capability fits into the overall organization;

4. Meets the unique requirements of the organization, which relate to mission, size, structure, and functions;

5. Defines reportable incidents;

6. Provides metrics for measuring the incident response capability within the organization;

7. Defines the resources and management support needed to effectively maintain and mature an incident response capability;

8. Is reviewed and approved by [*Assignment: organization-defined personnel or roles*] [*Assignment: organization-defined frequency*]; and

9. Explicitly designates responsibility for incident response to [*Assignment: organization-defined entities, personnel, or roles*].

b. Distribute copies of the incident response plan to [*Assignment: organization-defined incident response personnel (identified by name and/or by role) and organizational elements*];

c. Update the incident response plan to address system and organizational changes or problems encountered during plan implementation, execution, or testing;

d. Communicate incident response plan changes to [*Assignment: organization-defined incident response personnel (identified by name and/or by role) and organizational elements*]; and

~~Protect the incident response plan from unauthorized disclosure and modification.~~

Supplemental Guidance: It is important that organizations develop and implement a coordinated approach to incident response. Organizational missions, business functions, strategies, goals, and objectives for incident response help to determine the structure of incident response capabilities. As part of a comprehensive incident response capability, organizations consider the coordination and sharing of information with external organizations, including, for example, external service providers and organizations involved in the supply chain for organizational systems. For incidents involving personally identifiable information, include a process to determine whether notice to oversight organizations or affected individuals is appropriate and provide that notice accordingly.

Related Controls: AC-2, CP-2, CP-4, IR-4, IR-7, IR-9, PE-6, PL-2, SA-12, SA-15, SI-12.

Control Enhancements:

(1) INCIDENT RESPONSE PLAN | PERSONALLY IDENTIFIABLE INFORMATION PROCESSES

Include the following additional processes in the Incident Response Plan for incidents involving personally identifiable information:

(a) A process to determine if notice to oversight organizations is appropriate and to provide that notice, if appropriate;

(b) An assessment process to determine the extent of the harm, embarrassment, inconvenience, or unfairness to affected individuals; and

(c) A process to ensure prompt reporting by organizational users of any privacy incident to [Assignment: organization-defined roles].

Supplemental Guidance: Some organizations may be required by law or policy to provide notice to oversight organizations in the event of a privacy-related incident. Organization-defined roles to which privacy incidents may be reported include, for example, the Senior Agency Official for Privacy, Senior Agency Information Security Officer, Authorizing Official, and System Owner.

Related Controls: None.

References: NIST Special Publication 800-61.

IR-9 INFORMATION SPILLAGE RESPONSE

Control: Respond to information spills by:

a. Identifying the specific information involved in the system contamination;

b. Alerting [Assignment: organization-defined personnel or roles] of the information spill using a method of communication not associated with the spill;

c. Isolating the contaminated system or system component;

d. Eradicating the information from the contaminated system or component;

e. Identifying other systems or system components that may have been subsequently contaminated; and

f. Performing the following additional actions: [Assignment: organization-defined actions].

Supplemental Guidance: Information spillage refers to instances where either classified or controlled unclassified information is inadvertently placed on systems that are not authorized to process such information. Such information spills occur when information that is initially thought to be of lower sensitivity is transmitted to a system and then subsequently determined to be of higher sensitivity. At that point, corrective action is required. The nature of the organizational response is generally based upon the degree of sensitivity of the spilled information, the security capabilities of the system, the specific nature of contaminated storage media, and the access authorizations of individuals with authorized access to the contaminated system. The methods used to communicate information about the spill after the fact do not involve methods directly associated with the actual spill to minimize the risk of further spreading the contamination before such contamination is isolated and eradicated.

Related Controls: CP-2, IR-6, PM-28, PM-30, RA-7.

Control Enhancements:

(1) INFORMATION SPILLAGE RESPONSE | RESPONSIBLE PERSONNEL

Assign [*Assignment: organization-defined personnel or roles*] with responsibility for responding to information spills.

Supplemental Guidance: None.

Related Controls: None.

(2) INFORMATION SPILLAGE RESPONSE | TRAINING

Provide information spillage response training [*Assignment: organization-defined frequency*].

Supplemental Guidance: None.

Related Controls: AT-2, AT-3, CP-3, IR-2.

(3) INFORMATION SPILLAGE RESPONSE | POST-SPILL OPERATIONS

Implement [*Assignment: organization-defined procedures*] to ensure that organizational personnel impacted by information spills can continue to carry out assigned tasks while contaminated systems are undergoing corrective actions.

Supplemental Guidance: Correction actions for systems contaminated due to information spillages may be very time-consuming. During those periods, personnel may not have access to the contaminated systems, which may potentially affect their ability to conduct organizational business.

Related Controls: None.

(4) INFORMATION SPILLAGE RESPONSE | EXPOSURE TO UNAUTHORIZED PERSONNEL

Employ [*Assignment: organization-defined security safeguards*] for personnel exposed to information not within assigned access authorizations.

Supplemental Guidance: Security safeguards include, for example, ensuring that personnel who are exposed to spilled information are made aware of the laws, Executive Orders, directives, regulations, policies, standards, and guidelines regarding the information and the restrictions imposed based on exposure to such information.

Related Controls: None.

References: None.

IR-10 INTEGRATED INFORMATION SECURITY ANALYSIS TEAM

Control: Establish an integrated team of forensic and malicious code analysts, tool developers, and real-time operations personnel to handle incidents.

Supplemental Guidance: Having an integrated team for incident response facilitates information sharing. Such capability allows organizational personnel, including developers, implementers, and operators, to leverage the team knowledge of the threat to implement defensive measures that will enable organizations to deter intrusions more effectively. Moreover, integrated teams promote the rapid detection of intrusions, development of appropriate mitigations, and the deployment of effective defensive measures. For example, when an intrusion is detected, the integrated analysis team can rapidly develop an appropriate response for operators to implement, correlate the new incident with information on past intrusions, and augment ongoing intelligence development. This enables the team to identify adversary tactics, techniques, and procedures that are linked to the operations tempo or to specific missions and business functions, and to define responsive actions in a way that does not disrupt those missions and business functions. Information security analysis teams are distributed within organizations to make the capability more resilient.

Related Controls: AT-3.

Control Enhancements: None.

References: NIST Special Publication 800-150; NIST Interagency Report 7559.

3.10 MAINTENANCE

Quick link to Maintenance summary table

MA-1 SYSTEM MAINTENANCE POLICY AND PROCEDURES

Control:

a. Develop, document, and disseminate to [*Assignment: organization-defined personnel or roles*]:

1. A system maintenance policy that:

   (a) Addresses purpose, scope, roles, responsibilities, management commitment, coordination among organizational entities, and compliance; and

   (b) Is consistent with applicable laws, Executive Orders, directives, regulations, policies, standards, and guidelines; and

2. Procedures to facilitate the implementation of the system maintenance policy and the associated system maintenance controls;

b. Designate an [*Assignment: organization-defined senior management official*] to manage the system maintenance policy and procedures;

c. Review and update the current system maintenance:

1. Policy [*Assignment: organization-defined frequency*]; and

2. Procedures [*Assignment: organization-defined frequency*];

d. Ensure that the system maintenance procedures implement the system maintenance policy and controls; and

e. Develop, document, and implement remediation actions for violations of the maintenance policy.

Supplemental Guidance: This control addresses the establishment of policy and procedures for the effective implementation of the controls and control enhancements in the MA family. The risk management strategy is an important factor in establishing policy and procedures. Comprehensive policy and procedures help provide security and privacy assurance. Security and privacy program policies and procedures at the organization level may make the need for system-specific policies and procedures unnecessary. The policy can be included as part of the general security and privacy policy or can be represented by multiple policies reflecting the complex nature of organizations. The procedures can be established for security and privacy programs and for systems, if needed. Procedures describe how policies or controls are implemented and can be directed at the personnel or role that is the object of the procedure. Procedures can be documented in system security and privacy plans or in one or more separate documents. It is important to recognize that restating controls does not constitute an organizational policy or procedure.

Related Controls: PM-9, PS-8, SI-12.

Control Enhancements: None.

References: NIST Special Publications 800-12, 800-30, 800-39, 800-100.

MA-2 CONTROLLED MAINTENANCE

Control:

a. Schedule, document, and review records of maintenance, repair, or replacement on system components in accordance with manufacturer or vendor specifications and/or organizational requirements;

b. Approve and monitor all maintenance activities, whether performed on site or remotely and whether the system or system components are serviced on site or removed to another location;

c. Require that [*Assignment: organization-defined personnel or roles*] explicitly approve the removal of the system or system components from organizational facilities for off-site maintenance, repair, or replacement;

d. Sanitize equipment to remove all information from associated media prior to removal from organizational facilities for off-site maintenance, repair, or replacement;

e. Check all potentially impacted security and privacy controls to verify that the controls are still functioning properly following maintenance, repair, or replacement actions; and

f. Include [*Assignment: organization-defined maintenance-related information*] in organizational maintenance records.

Supplemental Guidance: This control addresses the information security aspects of the system maintenance program and applies to all types of maintenance to any system component (hardware, firmware, applications) conducted by any local or nonlocal entity. System maintenance also includes those components not directly associated with information processing and/or data or information retention such as scanners, copiers, and printers. Information necessary for creating effective maintenance records includes, for example, date and time of maintenance; name of individuals or group performing the maintenance; name of escort, if necessary; a description of the maintenance performed; and system components or equipment removed or replaced (including identification numbers, if applicable). The level of detail included in maintenance records can be informed by the security categories of organizational systems. Organizations consider supply chain issues associated with replacement components for systems.

Related Controls: CM-3, CM-4, CM-5, MA-4, MP-6, PE-16, SA-12, SA-19, SI-2.

Control Enhancements:

(1) CONTROLLED MAINTENANCE | RECORD CONTENT
[Withdrawn: Incorporated into MA-2].

(2) CONTROLLED MAINTENANCE | AUTOMATED MAINTENANCE ACTIVITIES

(a) Employ automated mechanisms to schedule, conduct, and document maintenance, repair, and replacement actions for the system or system components; and

(b) Produce up-to date, accurate, and complete records of all maintenance, repair, and replacement actions requested, scheduled, in process, and completed.

Supplemental Guidance: None.

Related Controls: MA-3.

References: NIST Interagency Report 8023.

MA-3 MAINTENANCE TOOLS

Control:

a. Approve, control, and monitor the use of system maintenance tools; and

b. Review previously approved system maintenance tools [*Assignment: organization-defined frequency*].

Supplemental Guidance: This control addresses security-related issues associated with maintenance tools that are not within organizational system boundaries but are used specifically for diagnostic and repair actions on organizational systems. Organizations have flexibility in determining roles for approval of maintenance tools and how that approval is documented. Periodic review of system maintenance tools facilitates withdrawal of the approval for outdated, unsupported, irrelevant, or no-longer-used tools. Maintenance tools can include hardware, software, and firmware items. Maintenance tools are potential vehicles for transporting malicious code, intentionally or unintentionally, into a facility and subsequently into systems. Maintenance tools can include, for example, hardware/software diagnostic test equipment and hardware and software procedures. This control does not cover hardware or software components that support system maintenance and are a part of the system, for example, the software implementing "ping," "ls," "ipconfig," or the hardware and software implementing the monitoring port of an Ethernet switch.

Related Controls: MA-2, PE-16.

Control Enhancements:

(1) MAINTENANCE TOOLS | INSPECT TOOLS

Inspect the maintenance tools carried into a facility by maintenance personnel for improper or unauthorized modifications.

Supplemental Guidance: If, upon inspection of maintenance tools, organizations determine that the tools have been modified in an improper/unauthorized manner or contain malicious code, the incident is handled consistent with organizational policies and procedures for incident handling.

Related Controls: SI-7.

(2) MAINTENANCE TOOLS | INSPECT MEDIA

Check media containing diagnostic and test programs for malicious code before the media are used in the system.

Supplemental Guidance: If, upon inspection of media containing maintenance diagnostic and test programs, organizations determine that the media contain malicious code, the incident is handled consistent with organizational incident handling policies and procedures.

Related Controls: SI-3.

(3) MAINTENANCE TOOLS | PREVENT UNAUTHORIZED REMOVAL

Prevent the removal of maintenance equipment containing organizational information by:
  (a) Verifying that there is no organizational information contained on the equipment;
  (b) Sanitizing or destroying the equipment;
  (c) Retaining the equipment within the facility; or
  (d) Obtaining an exemption from [Assignment: organization-defined personnel or roles] explicitly authorizing removal of the equipment from the facility.

Supplemental Guidance: Organizational information includes all information specifically owned by organizations and information provided to organizations in which organizations serve as information stewards.

Related Controls: MP-6.

(4) MAINTENANCE TOOLS | RESTRICTED TOOL USE

Restrict the use of maintenance tools to authorized personnel only.

Supplemental Guidance: This control enhancement applies to systems that are used to carry out maintenance functions.

Related Controls: AC-3, AC-5, AC-6.

References: NIST Special Publication 800-88.

MA-4 NONLOCAL MAINTENANCE

Control:

a. Approve and monitor nonlocal maintenance and diagnostic activities;

b. Allow the use of nonlocal maintenance and diagnostic tools only as consistent with organizational policy and documented in the security plan for the system;

c. Employ strong authenticators in the establishment of nonlocal maintenance and diagnostic sessions;

d. Maintain records for nonlocal maintenance and diagnostic activities; and

e. Terminate session and network connections when nonlocal maintenance is completed.

Supplemental Guidance: Nonlocal maintenance and diagnostic activities are those activities conducted by individuals communicating through a network, either an external network or an internal network. Local maintenance and diagnostic activities are those activities carried out by individuals physically present at the system or system component and not communicating across a network connection. Authentication techniques used in the establishment of nonlocal maintenance and diagnostic sessions reflect the network access requirements in IA-2. Strong authentication requires authenticators that are resistant to replay attacks and employ multifactor authentication. Strong authenticators include, for example, PKI where certificates are stored on a token protected by a password, passphrase, or biometric. Enforcing requirements in MA-4 is accomplished in part by other controls.

Related Controls: AC-2, AC-3, AC-6, AC-17, AU-2, AU-3, IA-2, IA-4, IA-5, IA-8, MA-2, MA-5, PL-2, SC-7, SC-10.

Control Enhancements:

(1) NONLOCAL MAINTENANCE | AUDITING AND REVIEW

    (a) Audit [*Assignment: organization-defined audit events*] for nonlocal maintenance and diagnostic sessions; and

    (b) Review the records of the maintenance and diagnostic sessions.

Supplemental Guidance: None.

Related Controls: AU-6, AU-12.

(2) NONLOCAL MAINTENANCE | DOCUMENT NONLOCAL MAINTENANCE

[Withdrawn: Incorporated into MA-1 and MA-4]

(3) NONLOCAL MAINTENANCE | COMPARABLE SECURITY AND SANITIZATION

    (a) Require that nonlocal maintenance and diagnostic services be performed from a system that implements a security capability comparable to the capability implemented on the system being serviced; or

    (b) Remove the component to be serviced from the system prior to nonlocal maintenance or diagnostic services; sanitize the component (for organizational information) before removal from organizational facilities; and after the service is performed, inspect and sanitize the component (for potentially malicious software) before reconnecting the component to the system.

Supplemental Guidance: Comparable security capability on systems, diagnostic tools, and equipment providing maintenance services implies that the implemented security controls on those systems, tools, and equipment are at least as comprehensive as the controls on the system being serviced.

Related Controls: MP-6, SI-3, SI-7.

(4) NONLOCAL MAINTENANCE | AUTHENTICATION AND SEPARATION OF MAINTENANCE SESSIONS

Protect nonlocal maintenance sessions by:

    (a) Employing [*Assignment: organization-defined authenticators that are replay resistant*]; and

    (b) Separating the maintenance sessions from other network sessions with the system by either:

        (1) Physically separated communications paths; or

        (2) Logically separated communications paths based upon encryption.

Supplemental Guidance: None.

Related Controls: None.

(5) NONLOCAL MAINTENANCE | APPROVALS AND NOTIFICATIONS

    (a) Require the approval of each nonlocal maintenance session by [*Assignment: organization-defined personnel or roles*]; and

    (b) Notify [*Assignment: organization-defined personnel or roles*] of the date and time of planned nonlocal maintenance.

Supplemental Guidance: Notification may be performed by maintenance personnel. Approval of nonlocal maintenance sessions is accomplished by organizational personnel with sufficient information security and system knowledge to determine the appropriateness of the proposed maintenance.

Related Controls: None.

(6) NONLOCAL MAINTENANCE | CRYPTOGRAPHIC PROTECTION

Implement cryptographic mechanisms to protect the integrity and confidentiality of nonlocal maintenance and diagnostic communications.

Supplemental Guidance: None.

Related Controls: SC-8, SC-13.

(7) NONLOCAL MAINTENANCE | REMOTE DISCONNECT VERIFICATION

Implement remote disconnect verification at the termination of nonlocal maintenance and diagnostic sessions.

Supplemental Guidance: Remote disconnect verification ensures that remote connections from nonlocal maintenance sessions have been terminated and are no longer available for use.

Related Controls: AC-12.

References: FIPS Publications 140-2, 197, 201; NIST Special Publications 800-63, 800-88.

MA-5 MAINTENANCE PERSONNEL

Control:

a. Establish a process for maintenance personnel authorization and maintains a list of authorized maintenance organizations or personnel;

b. Verify that non-escorted personnel performing maintenance on the system possess the required access authorizations; and

c. Designate organizational personnel with required access authorizations and technical competence to supervise the maintenance activities of personnel who do not possess the required access authorizations.

Supplemental Guidance: This control applies to individuals performing hardware or software maintenance on organizational systems, while PE-2 addresses physical access for individuals whose maintenance duties place them within the physical protection perimeter of the systems. Technical competence of supervising individuals relates to the maintenance performed on the systems while having required access authorizations refers to maintenance on and near the systems. Individuals not previously identified as authorized maintenance personnel, such as information technology manufacturers, vendors, systems integrators, and consultants, may require privileged access to organizational systems, for example, when required to conduct maintenance activities with little or no notice. Based on organizational assessments of risk, organizations may issue temporary credentials to these individuals. Temporary credentials may be for one-time use or for very limited time-periods.

Related Controls: AC-2, AC-3, AC-5, AC-6, IA-2, IA-8, MA-4, MP-2, PE-2, PE-3, PS-7, RA-3.

Control Enhancements:

(1) MAINTENANCE PERSONNEL | INDIVIDUALS WITHOUT APPROPRIATE ACCESS

(a) Implement procedures for the use of maintenance personnel that lack appropriate security clearances or are not U.S. citizens, that include the following requirements:

(1) Maintenance personnel who do not have needed access authorizations, clearances, or formal access approvals are escorted and supervised during the performance of maintenance and diagnostic activities on the system by approved organizational personnel who are fully cleared, have appropriate access authorizations, and are technically qualified;

(2) Prior to initiating maintenance or diagnostic activities by personnel who do not have needed access authorizations, clearances or formal access approvals, all volatile information storage components within the system are sanitized and all nonvolatile storage media are removed or physically disconnected from the system and secured; and

(b) Develop and implement alternate security safeguards in the event a system component cannot be sanitized, removed, or disconnected from the system.

Supplemental Guidance: This control enhancement denies individuals who lack appropriate security clearances or who are not U.S. citizens, visual and electronic access to any classified or controlled unclassified information contained on organizational systems. Procedures for the use of maintenance personnel can be documented in security plans for the systems.

Related Controls: MP-6, PL-2.

(2) MAINTENANCE PERSONNEL | SECURITY CLEARANCES FOR CLASSIFIED SYSTEMS

Verify that personnel performing maintenance and diagnostic activities on a system processing, storing, or transmitting classified information possess security clearances and formal access approvals for at least the highest classification level and for all compartments of information on the system.

Supplemental Guidance: None.

Related Controls: PS-3.

(3) MAINTENANCE PERSONNEL | CITIZENSHIP REQUIREMENTS FOR CLASSIFIED SYSTEMS

Verify that personnel performing maintenance and diagnostic activities on a system processing, storing, or transmitting classified information are U.S. citizens.

Supplemental Guidance: None.

Related Controls: PS-3.

(4) MAINTENANCE PERSONNEL | FOREIGN NATIONALS

Verify that:

(a) Foreign nationals with appropriate security clearances are used to conduct maintenance and diagnostic activities on classified systems only when the systems are jointly owned and operated by the United States and foreign allied governments, or owned and operated solely by foreign allied governments; and

(b) Approvals, consents, and detailed operational conditions regarding the use of foreign nationals to conduct maintenance and diagnostic activities on classified systems are fully documented within Memoranda of Agreements.

Supplemental Guidance: None.

Related Controls: PS-3.

(5) MAINTENANCE PERSONNEL | NON-SYSTEM MAINTENANCE

Verify that non-escorted personnel performing maintenance activities not directly associated with the system but in the physical proximity of the system, have required access authorizations.

Supplemental Guidance: Personnel performing maintenance activities in other capacities not directly related to the system include, for example, physical plant personnel and janitorial personnel.

Related Controls: None.

References: None.

MA-6   TIMELY MAINTENANCE

Control: Obtain maintenance support and/or spare parts for [*Assignment: organization-defined system components*] within [*Assignment: organization-defined time-period*] of failure.

Supplemental Guidance: Organizations specify the system components that result in increased risk to organizational operations and assets, individuals, other organizations, or the Nation when the functionality provided by those components is not operational. Organizational actions to obtain maintenance support typically include having appropriate contracts in place.

Related Controls: CM-8, CP-2, CP-7, RA-7, SA-12, SA-15, SI-13.

Control Enhancements:

(1) TIMELY MAINTENANCE | PREVENTIVE MAINTENANCE

Perform preventive maintenance on [*Assignment: organization-defined system components*] at [*Assignment: organization-defined time intervals*].

Supplemental Guidance: Preventive maintenance includes protective care and servicing of system components to maintain equipment and facilities in satisfactory operating condition. Such maintenance provides for the systematic inspection, tests, measurements, adjustments, parts replacement, detection, and correction of incipient failures either before they occur or before they develop into major defects. The primary goal of preventive maintenance is to avoid/mitigate the consequences of equipment failures. Preventive maintenance is designed to preserve and restore equipment reliability by replacing worn components before they fail. Methods of determining what preventive (or other) failure management policies to apply include, for example, original equipment manufacturer recommendations, statistical failure records, requirements of codes, legislation, or regulations within a jurisdiction, expert opinion, maintenance that has already been conducted on similar equipment, or measured values and performance indications.

Related Controls: None.

(2) TIMELY MAINTENANCE | PREDICTIVE MAINTENANCE

Perform predictive maintenance on [*Assignment: organization-defined system components*] at [*Assignment: organization-defined time intervals*].

Supplemental Guidance: Predictive maintenance, or condition-based maintenance, attempts to evaluate the condition of equipment by performing periodic or continuous (online) equipment condition monitoring. The goal of predictive maintenance is to perform maintenance at a scheduled point in time when the maintenance activity is most cost-effective and before the equipment loses performance within a threshold. The predictive component of predictive maintenance stems from the goal of predicting the future trend of the equipment's condition. This approach uses principles of statistical process control to determine at what point in the future maintenance activities will be appropriate. Most predictive maintenance inspections are performed while equipment is in service, thereby minimizing disruption of normal system operations. Predictive maintenance can result in substantial cost savings and higher system reliability. Predictive maintenance tends to include measurement of the item. To evaluate equipment condition, predictive maintenance utilizes nondestructive testing technologies such as infrared, acoustic (partial discharge and airborne ultrasonic), corona detection, vibration analysis, sound level measurements, oil analysis, and other specific online tests.

Related Controls: None.

(3) TIMELY MAINTENANCE | AUTOMATED SUPPORT FOR PREDICTIVE MAINTENANCE

Employ automated mechanisms to transfer predictive maintenance data to a computerized maintenance management system.

Supplemental Guidance: A computerized maintenance management system maintains a database of information about the maintenance operations of organizations and automates processing equipment condition data to trigger maintenance planning, execution, and reporting.

Related Controls: None.

(4) TIMELY MAINTENANCE | ADEQUATE SUPPLY

Employ [*Assignment: organization-defined security safeguards*] to ensure an adequate supply of [*Assignment: organization-defined critical system components*].

Supplemental Guidance: Adversaries can attempt to impede organizational operations by disrupting the supply of critical system components or corrupting supplier operations. Organizations may track systems and component mean time to failure to mitigate the loss of temporary or permanent system function. Safeguards to ensure that adequate supplies of critical system components include, for example, the use of multiple suppliers throughout the supply chain for the identified critical components; stockpiling spare components to ensure operation during mission-critical times, and the identification of functionally-identical or similar components which may be used, if necessary.

Related Controls: SA-12, SA-19.

References: None.

3.11 MEDIA PROTECTION

<u>Quick link to Media Protection summary table</u>

MP-1 MEDIA PROTECTION POLICY AND PROCEDURES

<u>Control</u>:

a. Develop, document, and disseminate to [*Assignment: organization-defined personnel or roles*]:

   1. A media protection policy that:

      (a) Addresses purpose, scope, roles, responsibilities, management commitment, coordination among organizational entities, and compliance; and

      (b) Is consistent with applicable laws, Executive Orders, directives, regulations, policies, standards, and guidelines; and

   2. Procedures to facilitate the implementation of the media protection policy and the associated media protection controls;

b. Designate an [*Assignment: organization-defined senior management official*] to manage the media protection policy and procedures;

c. Review and update the current media protection:

   1. Policy [*Assignment: organization-defined frequency*]; and

   2. Procedures [*Assignment: organization-defined frequency*];

d. Ensure that the media protection procedures implement the media protection policy and controls; and

e. Develop, document, and implement remediation actions for violations of the media protection policy.

<u>Supplemental Guidance</u>: This control addresses the establishment of policy and procedures for the effective implementation of the controls and control enhancements in the MP family. The risk management strategy is an important factor in establishing policy and procedures. Comprehensive policy and procedures help provide security and privacy assurance. Security and privacy program policies and procedures at the organization level may make the need for system-specific policies and procedures unnecessary. The policy can be included as part of the general security and privacy policy or can be represented by multiple policies reflecting the complex nature of organizations. The procedures can be established for security and privacy programs and for systems, if needed. Procedures describe how policies or controls are implemented and can be directed at the personnel or role that is the object of the procedure. Procedures can be documented in system security and privacy plans or in one or more separate documents. It is important to recognize that restating controls does not constitute an organizational policy or procedure.

<u>Related Controls</u>: PM-9, PS-8, SI-12.

<u>Control Enhancements</u>: None.

<u>References</u>: NIST Special Publications <u>800-12</u>, <u>800-30</u>, <u>800-39</u>, <u>800-100</u>.

MP-2 MEDIA ACCESS

<u>Control</u>: Restrict access to [*Assignment: organization-defined types of digital and/or non-digital media*] to [*Assignment: organization-defined personnel or roles*].

<u>Supplemental Guidance</u>: System media includes both digital and non-digital media. Digital media includes, for example, diskettes, magnetic tapes, external/removable hard disk drives, flash drives,

compact disks and digital video disks. Non-digital media includes, for example, paper and microfilm. Restricting non-digital media access includes, for example, denying access to patient medical records in a community hospital unless the individuals seeking access to such records are authorized healthcare providers. Restricting access to digital media includes, for example, limiting access to design specifications stored on compact disks in the media library to the project leader and the individuals on the development team.

Related Controls: AC-19, AU-9, CP-2, CP-9, CP-10, MA-5, MP-6, MP-4, PE-2, PE-3, SC-13, SC-34, SI-12.

Control Enhancements:

(1) MEDIA ACCESS | AUTOMATED RESTRICTED ACCESS
[Withdrawn: Incorporated into MP-4(2)].

(2) MEDIA ACCESS | CRYPTOGRAPHIC PROTECTION
[Withdrawn: Incorporated into SC-28(1)].

References: FIPS Publication 199; NIST Special Publication 800-111.

MP-3 MEDIA MARKING

Control:

a. Mark system media indicating the distribution limitations, handling caveats, and applicable security markings (if any) of the information; and

b. Exempt [*Assignment: organization-defined types of system media*] from marking if the media remain within [*Assignment: organization-defined controlled areas*].

Supplemental Guidance: Security marking refers to the application or use of human-readable security attributes. Security labeling refers to the application or use of security attributes regarding internal data structures within systems. System media includes both digital and non-digital media. Digital media includes, for example, diskettes, magnetic tapes, external or removable disk drives, flash drives, compact disks, and digital video disks. Non-digital media includes, for example, paper and microfilm. Security marking is generally not required for media containing information determined by organizations to be in the public domain or to be publicly releasable. However, some organizations may require markings for public information indicating that the information is publicly releasable. Marking of system media reflects applicable laws, Executive Orders, directives, policies, regulations, standards, and guidelines.

Related Controls: AC-16, CP-9, MP-5, PE-22, SI-12.

Control Enhancements: None.

References: FIPS Publication 199.

MP-4 MEDIA STORAGE

Control:

a. Physically control and securely store [*Assignment: organization-defined types of digital and/or non-digital media*] within [*Assignment: organization-defined controlled areas*]; and

b. Protect system media until the media are destroyed or sanitized using approved equipment, techniques, and procedures.

Supplemental Guidance: System media includes both digital and non-digital media. Digital media includes, for example, diskettes, magnetic tapes, external or removable hard disk drives, flash drives, compact disks, and digital video disks. Non-digital media includes, for example, paper and microfilm. Physically controlling system media includes, for example, conducting inventories, ensuring procedures are in place to allow individuals to check out and return media to the media library, and maintaining accountability for stored media. Secure storage includes, for example, a locked drawer, desk, or cabinet; or a controlled media library. The type of media storage employed by organizations is commensurate with the security category or classification of the information residing on the media. Controlled areas are areas that provide sufficient physical and procedural safeguards to meet the requirements established for protecting information and systems. For media containing information determined to be in the public domain, to be publicly releasable, or to have limited or no adverse impact on organizations or individuals if accessed by other than authorized personnel, fewer safeguards may be needed. In these situations, physical access controls provide adequate protection.

Related Controls: AC-19, CP-2, CP-6, CP-9, CP-10, MP-2, MP-7, PE-3, PL-2, SC-13, SC-28, SC-34, SI-12.

Control Enhancements:

(1) MEDIA STORAGE | CRYPTOGRAPHIC PROTECTION
[Withdrawn: Incorporated into SC-28(1)].

(2) MEDIA STORAGE | AUTOMATED RESTRICTED ACCESS
Employ automated mechanisms to restrict access to media storage areas and to audit access attempts and access granted.

Supplemental Guidance: Automated mechanisms can include, for example, keypads or card readers on the external entries to media storage areas.

Related Controls: AC-3, AU-2, AU-6, AU-9, AU-12, PE-3.

References: FIPS Publication 199; NIST Special Publications 800-56A, 800-56B, 800-56C, 800-57-1, 800-57-2, 800-57-3, 800-111.

MP-5   MEDIA TRANSPORT

Control:

a. Protect and control [*Assignment: organization-defined types of system media*] during transport outside of controlled areas using [*Assignment: organization-defined security safeguards*];

b. Maintain accountability for system media during transport outside of controlled areas;

c. Document activities associated with the transport of system media; and

d. Restrict the activities associated with the transport of system media to authorized personnel.

Supplemental Guidance: System media includes both digital and non-digital media. Digital media includes, for example, diskettes, magnetic tapes, external/removable hard disk drives, flash drives, compact disks, and digital video disks. Non-digital media includes, for example, microfilm and paper. Controlled areas are areas or spaces for which organizations provide sufficient physical or procedural safeguards to meet requirements established for protecting information and systems.

Physical and technical safeguards for media are commensurate with the security category or classification of the information residing on the media. Safeguards to protect media during transport include, for example, locked containers and cryptography. Cryptographic mechanisms can provide confidentiality and integrity protections depending upon the mechanisms used. Activities associated with transport include the actual transport as well as those activities such as releasing media for transport and ensuring that media enters the appropriate transport processes. For the actual transport, authorized transport and courier personnel may include individuals from outside the organization. Maintaining accountability of media during transport includes, for example, restricting transport activities to authorized personnel, and tracking and/or obtaining explicit records of transport activities as the media moves through the transportation system to prevent and detect loss, destruction, or tampering. Organizations establish documentation requirements for activities associated with the transport of system media in accordance with organizational assessments of risk to include the flexibility to define different record-keeping methods for the different types of media transport as part of an overall system of transport-related records.

Related Controls: AC-7, AC-19, CP-2, CP-9, MP-3, MP-4, PE-16, PL-2, SC-13, SC-28, SC-34.

Control Enhancements:

(1) MEDIA TRANSPORT | PROTECTION OUTSIDE OF CONTROLLED AREAS
[Withdrawn: Incorporated into MP-5].

(2) MEDIA TRANSPORT | DOCUMENTATION OF ACTIVITIES
[Withdrawn: Incorporated into MP-5].

(3) MEDIA TRANSPORT | CUSTODIANS
Employ an identified custodian during transport of system media outside of controlled areas.

Supplemental Guidance: Identified custodians provide organizations with specific points of contact during the media transport process and facilitate individual accountability. Custodial responsibilities can be transferred from one individual to another if an unambiguous custodian is identified at all times.

Related Controls: None.

(4) MEDIA TRANSPORT | CRYPTOGRAPHIC PROTECTION
[Withdrawn: Incorporated into SC-28(1)].

References: FIPS Publication 199; NIST Special Publication 800-60-1, 800-60-2.

MP-6 MEDIA SANITIZATION

Control:

a. Sanitize [*Assignment: organization-defined system media*] prior to disposal, release out of organizational control, or release for reuse using [*Assignment: organization-defined sanitization techniques and procedures*]; and

b. Employ sanitization mechanisms with the strength and integrity commensurate with the security category or classification of the information.

Supplemental Guidance: This control applies to all system media, both digital and non-digital, subject to disposal or reuse, whether or not the media is considered removable. Examples include: digital media found in scanners, copiers, printers, notebook computers, workstations, network components, mobile devices; and non-digital media such as paper and microfilm. The sanitization process removes information from the media such that the information cannot be retrieved or reconstructed. Sanitization techniques, including clearing, purging, cryptographic erase, and destruction, prevent the disclosure of information to unauthorized individuals when such media is reused or released for disposal. Organizations determine the appropriate sanitization methods recognizing that destruction is sometimes necessary when other methods cannot be applied to media requiring sanitization. Organizations use discretion on the employment of approved sanitization techniques and procedures for media containing information deemed to be in the public domain or publicly releasable, or deemed to have no adverse impact on organizations or individuals if released for reuse or disposal. Sanitization of non-digital media includes, for example, destruction, removing a classified appendix from an otherwise unclassified document, or redacting selected sections or words from a document by obscuring the redacted sections or words in a manner equivalent in effectiveness to removing them from the document. NARA policy and guidance control the sanitization process for controlled unclassified information. NSA standards and policies control the sanitization process for media containing classified information.

Related Controls: AC-3, AC-7, AU-11, MA-2, MA-3, MA-4, MA-5, SI-12, SI-18.

Control Enhancements:

(1) MEDIA SANITIZATION | REVIEW, APPROVE, TRACK, DOCUMENT, AND VERIFY
Review, approve, track, document, and verify media sanitization and disposal actions.

Supplemental Guidance: Organizations review and approve media to be sanitized to ensure compliance with records-retention policies. Tracking and documenting actions include, for example, listing personnel who reviewed and approved sanitization and disposal actions; types of media sanitized; specific files stored on the media; sanitization methods used; date and time of the sanitization actions; personnel who performed the sanitization; verification actions taken; personnel who performed the verification; and the disposal actions taken. Organizations verify that the sanitization of the media was effective prior to disposal.

Related Controls: None.

(2) MEDIA SANITIZATION | EQUIPMENT TESTING

Test sanitization equipment and procedures [*Assignment: organization-defined frequency*] to verify that the intended sanitization is being achieved.

Supplemental Guidance: Testing of sanitization equipment and procedures may be conducted by qualified and authorized external entities including, for example, federal agencies or external service providers.

Related Controls: None.

(3) MEDIA SANITIZATION | NONDESTRUCTIVE TECHNIQUES

Apply nondestructive sanitization techniques to portable storage devices prior to connecting such devices to the system under the following circumstances: [*Assignment: organization-defined circumstances requiring sanitization of portable storage devices*].

Supplemental Guidance: Portable storage devices can be the source of malicious code insertions into organizational systems. Many of these devices are obtained from untrustworthy sources and may contain malicious code that can be readily transferred to systems through USB ports or other entry portals. While scanning storage devices is recommended, sanitization provides additional assurance that such devices are free of malicious code. Organizations consider nondestructive sanitization of portable storage devices when these devices are purchased from manufacturers or vendors prior to initial use or when organizations cannot maintain a positive chain of custody for the devices.

Related Controls: None.

(4) MEDIA SANITIZATION | CONTROLLED UNCLASSIFIED INFORMATION

[Withdrawn: Incorporated into MP-6].

(5) MEDIA SANITIZATION | CLASSIFIED INFORMATION

[Withdrawn: Incorporated into MP-6].

(6) MEDIA SANITIZATION | MEDIA DESTRUCTION

[Withdrawn: Incorporated into MP-6].

(7) MEDIA SANITIZATION | DUAL AUTHORIZATION

Enforce dual authorization for the sanitization of [*Assignment: organization-defined system media*].

Supplemental Guidance: Organizations employ dual authorization to ensure that system media sanitization cannot occur unless two technically qualified individuals conduct the designated task. Individuals sanitizing system media possess sufficient skills and expertise to determine if the proposed sanitization reflects applicable federal and organizational standards, policies, and procedures. Dual authorization also helps to ensure that sanitization occurs as intended, both protecting against errors and false claims of having performed the sanitization actions. Dual authorization may also be known as two-person control.

Related Controls: AC-3, MP-2.

(8) MEDIA SANITIZATION | REMOTE PURGING OR WIPING OF INFORMATION

Provide the capability to purge or wipe information from [*Assignment: organization-defined systems or system components*] either remotely or under the following conditions: [*Assignment: organization-defined conditions*].

Supplemental Guidance: This control enhancement protects data/information on organizational systems and system components if such systems or components are obtained by unauthorized individuals. Remote purge/wipe commands require strong authentication to mitigate the risk of unauthorized individuals purging/wiping the system/component/device. The purge or wipe function can be implemented in a variety of ways including, for example, by overwriting data/information multiple times or by destroying the key necessary to decrypt encrypted data.

Related Controls: None

(9) MEDIA SANITIZATION | DESTRUCTION OF PERSONALLY IDENTIFIABLE INFORMATION

Facilitate the destruction of personally identifiable information by:

(a) De-identifying the personally identifiable information;

(b) Proactively reviewing media to actively find personally identifiable information and removing such information; and

(c) Reviewing media as it is being archived or disposed to find and remove personally identifiable information.

Supplemental Guidance: Disposal or destruction of media containing personally identifiable information applies to originals, copies, and archived records, including system logs that may contain such information. De-identification is the general term for any process of removing the association between a set of identifying data and the data subject and is accomplished in a manner that prevents loss, theft, misuse, or unauthorized access.

Related Controls: SI-20.

References: FIPS Publication 199; NIST Special Publications 800-60-1, 800-60-2, 800-88, 800-124; NIST Interagency Report 8023.

MP-7 MEDIA USE

Control:

a. [Selection: Restrict; Prohibit] the use of [Assignment: organization-defined types of system media] on [Assignment: organization-defined systems or system components] using [Assignment: organization-defined security safeguards]; and

b. Prohibit the use of portable storage devices in organizational systems when such devices have no identifiable owner.

Supplemental Guidance: System media includes digital and non-digital media. Digital media includes, for example, diskettes, magnetic tapes, external or removable hard disk drives, flash drives, compact disks, and digital video disks. Non-digital media includes, for example, paper and microfilm. This control also applies to mobile devices with information storage capability. In contrast to MP-2, which restricts user access to media, this control restricts the use of certain types of media on systems, for example, restricting/prohibiting the use of flash drives or external hard disk drives. Organizations can employ technical and nontechnical safeguards to restrict the use of system media. Organizations may restrict the use of portable storage devices, for example, by using physical cages on workstations to prohibit access to certain external ports, or disabling or removing the ability to insert, read or write to such devices. Organizations may also limit the use of portable storage devices to only approved devices including, for example, devices provided by the organization, devices provided by other approved organizations, and devices that are not personally owned. Finally, organizations may restrict the use of portable storage devices based on the type of device, for example, prohibiting the use of writeable, portable storage devices, and implementing this restriction by disabling or removing the capability to write to such devices. Requiring identifiable owners for portable storage devices reduces the risk of using such devices by allowing organizations to assign responsibility for addressing known vulnerabilities in the devices.

Related Controls: AC-19, AC-20, PL-4, PM-12, SC-34, SC-41.

Control Enhancements:

(1) MEDIA USE | PROHIBIT USE WITHOUT OWNER

[Withdrawn: Incorporated into MP-7].

(2) MEDIA USE | PROHIBIT USE OF SANITIZATION-RESISTANT MEDIA

Prohibit the use of sanitization-resistant media in organizational systems.

Supplemental Guidance: Sanitization-resistance refers to non-destructive sanitization techniques and applies to the capability to purge information from media. Certain types of media do not support sanitize commands, or if supported, the interfaces are not supported in a standardized way across these devices. Sanitization-resistant media include, for example, compact flash, embedded flash on boards and devices, solid state drives, and USB removable media.

Related Controls: MP-6.

References: FIPS Publication 199; NIST Special Publication 800-111.

MP-8   MEDIA DOWNGRADING

Control:

a. Establish [*Assignment: organization-defined system media downgrading process*] that includes employing downgrading mechanisms with strength and integrity commensurate with the security category or classification of the information;

b. Verify that the system media downgrading process is commensurate with the security category and/or classification level of the information to be removed and the access authorizations of the potential recipients of the downgraded information;

c. Identify [*Assignment: organization-defined system media requiring downgrading*]; and

d. Downgrade the identified system media using the established process.

Supplemental Guidance: This control applies to all system media, digital and non-digital, subject to release outside of the organization, whether the media is considered removable or not removeable. The downgrading process, when applied to system media, removes information from the media, typically by security category or classification level, such that the information cannot be retrieved or reconstructed. Downgrading of media includes redacting information to enable wider release and distribution. It also ensures that empty space on the media is devoid of information.

Control Enhancements:

(1) MEDIA DOWNGRADING | DOCUMENTATION OF PROCESS
     Document system media downgrading actions.

     Supplemental Guidance: Organizations can document the media downgrading process by providing information such as the downgrading technique employed, the identification number of the downgraded media, and the identity of the individual that authorized and/or performed the downgrading action.

     Related Controls: None.

(2) MEDIA DOWNGRADING | EQUIPMENT TESTING
     Test downgrading equipment and procedures [*Assignment: organization-defined frequency*] to verify that intended downgrading actions are being achieved.

     Supplemental Guidance: None.

     Related Controls: None.

(3) MEDIA DOWNGRADING | CONTROLLED UNCLASSIFIED INFORMATION
     Downgrade system media containing [*Assignment: organization-defined Controlled Unclassified Information (CUI)*] prior to public release.

     Supplemental Guidance: None.

     Related Controls: None.

(4) MEDIA DOWNGRADING | CLASSIFIED INFORMATION
     Downgrade system media containing classified information prior to release to individuals without required access authorizations.

     Supplemental Guidance: Downgrading of classified information uses approved sanitization tools, techniques, and procedures to transfer information confirmed to be unclassified from classified systems to unclassified media.

     Related Controls: None.

References: None.

3.12 PRIVACY AUTHORIZATION

Quick link to Privacy Authorization summary table

PA-1 PRIVACY AUTHORIZATION POLICY AND PROCEDURES

Control:

a. Develop, document, and disseminate to [*Assignment: organization-defined personnel or roles*]:

  1. A privacy authorization policy that:

     (a) Addresses purpose, scope, roles, responsibilities, management commitment, coordination among organizational entities, and compliance; and

     (b) Is consistent with applicable laws, Executive Orders, directives, regulations, policies, standards, and guidelines; and

  2. Procedures to facilitate the implementation of the privacy authorization policy and the associated privacy authorization controls;

b. Designate an [*Assignment: organization-defined senior management official*] to manage the privacy authorization policy and procedures;

c. Review and update the current privacy authorization:

  1. Policy [*Assignment: organization-defined frequency*]; and

  2. Procedures [*Assignment: organization-defined frequency*];

d. Ensure that the privacy authorization procedures implement the privacy authorization policy and controls; and

e. Develop, document, and implement remediation actions for violations of the privacy authorization policy.

Supplemental Guidance: This control addresses the establishment of policy and procedures for the effective implementation of the controls and control enhancements in the PA family. The risk management strategy is an important factor in establishing policy and procedures. Comprehensive policy and procedures help provide security and privacy assurance. Security and privacy program policies and procedures at the organization level may make the need for system-specific policies and procedures unnecessary. The policy can be included as part of the general security and privacy policy or can be represented by multiple policies reflecting the complex nature of organizations. The procedures can be established for security and privacy programs and for systems, if needed. Procedures describe how policies or controls are implemented and can be directed at the personnel or role that is the object of the procedure. Procedures can be documented in system security and privacy plans or in one or more separate documents. It is important to recognize that restating controls does not constitute an organizational policy or procedure.

Related Controls: PA-2, PM-9, PS-8, SI-12.

Control Enhancements: None.

References: NIST Special Publications 800-12, 800-30, 800-39, 800-100.

PA-2 AUTHORITY TO COLLECT

Control: Determine and document the legal authority that permits the collection, use, maintenance, and sharing of personally identifiable information, either generally or in support of a specific program or system need.

Supplemental Guidance: Prior to collecting personally identifiable information, organizations determine whether the collection of such information is legally authorized. Organizational officials consult with the Senior Agency Official for Privacy and legal counsel regarding the authority of any program or activity to collect personally identifiable information. The authority to collect personally identifiable information is documented in the System of Records Notice and/or Privacy Impact Assessment or other applicable documentation such as Privacy Act Statements or Computer Matching Agreements.

Related Controls: IP-4, IP-6, PA-1, PA-3, PM-9, PM-20, PM-25, RA-8, SI-12.

Control Enhancements: None.

References: None.

PA-3 PURPOSE SPECIFICATION

Control: Identify and document the purpose(s) for which personally identifiable information is collected, used, maintained, and shared in its privacy notices.

Supplemental Guidance: Statutory language often expressly authorizes specific collections and uses of personally identifiable information. When statutory language is written broadly and thus subject to interpretation, organizations consult with the Senior Agency Official for Privacy and legal counsel to verify that there is a close nexus between the general authorization and any specific collection of personally identifiable information. Once the specific purpose has been identified, the purpose is clearly described in the related privacy compliance documentation, including, for example, Privacy Impact Assessments, System of Records Notices, and Privacy Act Statements provided at the time of collection including, for example, on forms organizations use to collect personally identifiable information. Further, in order to avoid unauthorized collections or uses of personally identifiable information, personnel who manage such information receive role-based training as specified in AT-3.

Related Controls: IP-4, IP-5, IP-6, PA-2, PA-4, PM-9, PM-20, PM-26, RA-8, SC-43, SI-12.

Control Enhancements:

(1) PURPOSE SPECIFICATION | USAGE RESTRICTIONS OF PERSONALLY IDENTIFIABLE INFORMATION

Restrict the use of personally identifiable information to only the authorized purpose(s) consistent with applicable laws or regulations and/or in public notices.

Supplemental Guidance: Organizations take steps to help ensure that personally identifiable information is used only for legally authorized purposes and in a manner, compatible with the uses identified in the Privacy Act and/or in public notices. These steps include, for example, monitoring and auditing organizational use of personally identifiable information and training organizational personnel on the authorized uses of such information. With guidance from the Senior Agency Official for Privacy and where appropriate, legal counsel, organizations document the processes and procedures for evaluating the proposed new uses of personally identifiable information to assess whether such uses fall within the scope of the organizational authorities. Where appropriate, organizations obtain consent from individuals for the new uses of personally identifiable information.

Related Controls: None.

(2) PURPOSE SPECIFICATION | AUTOMATION

Employ automated mechanisms to support records management of authorizing policies and procedures for personally identifiable information.

Supplemental Guidance: Automated mechanisms may be used to support records management of authorizing policies and procedures for personally identifiable information. Automated mechanisms augment verification that organizational policies and procedures are enforced for the management and tracking of personally identifiable information within an organization's systems.

Related Controls: CA-6, CM-12, IP-5, PM-29, PM-23, SC-16, SC-43, SI-12, SI-10, SI-15, SI-20, SI-19.

_____

Historical Note

PA-4 INFORMATION SHARING WITH EXTERNAL PARTIES

Control:

a. Develop, document, and disseminate guidelines to [*Assignment: organization-defined personnel or roles*] for the sharing of personally identifiable information externally, only for the authorized purposes identified in the Privacy Act and/or described in its notices, or for a purpose that is compatible with those purposes;

b. Evaluate proposed new instances of sharing personally identifiable information with external parties to assess whether:

    1. The sharing is authorized; and

    2. Additional or new public notice is required;

c. Enter into information sharing agreements with external parties that specifically:

    1. Describe the personally identifiable information covered;

    2. Enumerate the purpose(s) for which the personally identifiable information may be used; and

    3. Include security requirements consistent with the information being shared; and

d. Monitor and audit the authorized sharing of personally identifiable information with external parties.

Supplemental Guidance: The Senior Agency Official for Privacy and where appropriate, legal counsel, review and approve proposed external sharing of personally identifiable information, including with other public, international, or private sector entities, for consistency with the uses described in the existing organizational public notice(s). Formal agreements for information sharing include, for example, Memoranda of Understanding, Letters of Intent, Memoranda of Agreement, and Computer Matching Agreements. When a proposed new instance of external sharing of personally identifiable information is not currently authorized by the Privacy Act and/or specified in a notice, organizations evaluate whether the proposed external sharing is compatible with the purpose(s) specified in the notice. If the proposed sharing is compatible, organizations review, update, and republish the Privacy Impact Assessments, System of Records Notices, website privacy policies, and other public notices, if any, to include specific descriptions of the new use(s) and obtain consent where appropriate and feasible.

Related Controls: IP-4, PM-25.

Control Enhancements: None.

References: None.

3.13 PHYSICAL AND ENVIRONMENTAL PROTECTION

Quick link to Physical and Environmental Protection summary table

PE-1 PHYSICAL AND ENVIRONMENTAL PROTECTION POLICY AND PROCEDURES

Control:

a. Develop, document, and disseminate to [*Assignment: organization-defined personnel or roles*]:

1. A physical and environmental protection policy that:

    (a) Addresses purpose, scope, roles, responsibilities, management commitment, coordination among organizational entities, and compliance; and

    (b) Is consistent with applicable laws, Executive Orders, directives, regulations, policies, standards, and guidelines; and

2. Procedures to facilitate the implementation of the physical and environmental protection policy and the associated physical and environmental protection controls;

b. Designate an [*Assignment: organization-defined senior management official*] to manage the physical and environmental protection policy and procedures;

c. Review and update the current physical and environmental protection:

1. Policy [*Assignment: organization-defined frequency*]; and

2. Procedures [*Assignment: organization-defined frequency*];

d. Ensure that the physical and environmental protection procedures implement the physical and environmental protection policy and controls; and

e. Develop, document, and implement remediation actions for violations of the physical and environmental protection policy.

Supplemental Guidance: This control addresses the establishment of policy and procedures for the effective implementation of the controls and control enhancements in the PE family. The risk management strategy is an important factor in establishing policy and procedures. Comprehensive policy and procedures help provide security and privacy assurance. Security and privacy program policies and procedures at the organization level may make the need for system-specific policies and procedures unnecessary. The policy can be included as part of the general security and privacy policy or can be represented by multiple policies reflecting the complex nature of organizations. The procedures can be established for security and privacy programs and for systems, if needed. Procedures describe how policies or controls are implemented and can be directed at the personnel or role that is the object of the procedure. Procedures can be documented in system security and privacy plans or in one or more separate documents. It is important to recognize that restating controls does not constitute an organizational policy or procedure.

Related Controls: AT-3, PM-9, PS-8, SI-12.

Control Enhancements: None.

References: NIST Special Publications 800-12, 800-30, 800-39, 800-100.

PE-2 PHYSICAL ACCESS AUTHORIZATIONS

Control:

a. Develop, approve, and maintain a list of individuals with authorized access to the facility where the system resides;

b. Issue authorization credentials for facility access;

c. *Review the access list detailing authorized facility access by individuals [Assignment: organization-defined frequency]*; and

d. Remove individuals from the facility access list when access is no longer required.

Supplemental Guidance: This control applies to employees and visitors. Individuals with permanent physical access authorization credentials are not considered visitors. Authorization credentials include, for example, badges, identification cards, and smart cards. Organizations determine the strength of authorization credentials needed consistent with applicable laws, Executive Orders, directives, regulations, policies, standards, and guidelines. This control only applies to areas within facilities that have not been designated as publicly accessible.

Related Controls: AT-3, AU-9, IA-4, MA-5, MP-2, PE-3, PE-4, PE-5, PE-8, PM-12, PS-3, PS-4, PS-5, PS-6.

Control Enhancements:

(1) PHYSICAL ACCESS AUTHORIZATIONS | ACCESS BY POSITION OR ROLE

Authorize physical access to the facility where the system resides based on position or role.

Supplemental Guidance: None.

Related Controls: AC-2, AC-3, AC-6.

(2) PHYSICAL ACCESS AUTHORIZATIONS | TWO FORMS OF IDENTIFICATION

Require two forms of identification from [Assignment: organization-defined list of acceptable forms of identification] for visitor access to the facility where the system resides.

Supplemental Guidance: Acceptable forms of identification include, for example, passports, Personal Identity Verification (PIV) cards, and drivers' licenses. For gaining access to facilities using automated mechanisms, organizations may use PIV cards, key cards, PINs, and biometrics.

Related Controls: IA-2, IA-4, IA-5.

(3) PHYSICAL ACCESS AUTHORIZATIONS | RESTRICT UNESCORTED ACCESS

Restrict unescorted access to the facility where the system resides to personnel with [Selection (one or more): security clearances for all information contained within the system; formal access authorizations for all information contained within the system; need for access to all information contained within the system; [Assignment: organization-defined credentials]].

Supplemental Guidance: Due to the highly sensitive nature of classified information stored within certain facilities, it is important that individuals lacking sufficient security clearances, access approvals, or need to know, be escorted by individuals with appropriate credentials to ensure that such information is not exposed or otherwise compromised.

Related Controls: PS-2, PS-6.

References: FIPS Publication 201; NIST Special Publications 800-76, 800-73, 800-78.

PE-3   PHYSICAL ACCESS CONTROL

Control:

a. Enforce physical access authorizations at *[Assignment: organization-defined entry and exit points to the facility where the system resides]* by;

  1. Verifying individual access authorizations before granting access to the facility; and

  2. Controlling ingress and egress to the facility using *[Selection (one or more): [Assignment: organization-defined physical access control systems or devices]; guards]*;

b. Maintain physical access audit logs for *[Assignment: organization-defined entry/exit points]*;

c. Provide *[Assignment: organization-defined security safeguards]* to control access to areas within the facility designated as publicly accessible;

d. Escort visitors and monitor visitor activity *[Assignment: organization-defined circumstances requiring visitor escorts and monitoring]*;

e. Secure keys, combinations, and other physical access devices;

f. Inventory [*Assignment: organization-defined physical access devices*] every [*Assignment: organization-defined frequency*]; and

g. Change combinations and keys [*Assignment: organization-defined frequency*] and/or when keys are lost, combinations are compromised, or individuals are transferred or terminated.

Supplemental Guidance: This control applies to employees and visitors. Individuals with permanent physical access authorization credentials are not considered visitors. Organizations determine the types of facility guards needed including, for example, professional security staff, administrative staff, or system users. Physical access devices include, for example, keys, locks, combinations, and card readers. Physical access control systems comply with applicable laws, Executive Orders, directives, policies, regulations, standards, and guidelines. Organizations have flexibility in the types of audit logs employed. Audit logs can be procedural, automated, or some combination thereof. Physical access points can include facility access points, interior access points to systems or system components requiring supplemental access controls, or both. Components of systems may be in areas designated as publicly accessible with organizations safeguarding access to such devices.

Related Controls: AT-3, AU-2, AU-6, AU-9, AU-13, CP-10, IA-3, IA-8, MA-5, MP-2, MP-4, PE-2, PE-4, PE-5, PE-8, PS-2, PS-3, PS-7, RA-3, SA-19, SC-28, SI-4.

Control Enhancements:

(1) PHYSICAL ACCESS CONTROL | SYSTEM ACCESS

   Enforce physical access authorizations to the system in addition to the physical access controls for the facility at [*Assignment: organization-defined physical spaces containing one or more components of the system*].

   Supplemental Guidance: This control enhancement provides additional physical security for those areas within facilities where there is a concentration of system components.

   Related Controls: PS-2.

(2) PHYSICAL ACCESS CONTROL | FACILITY AND SYSTEM BOUNDARIES

   Perform security checks [*Assignment: organization-defined frequency*] at the physical boundary of the facility or system for exfiltration of information or removal of system components.

   Supplemental Guidance: Organizations determine the extent, frequency, and/or randomness of security checks to adequately mitigate risk associated with exfiltration.

   Related Controls: AC-4, SC-7.

(3) PHYSICAL ACCESS CONTROL | CONTINUOUS GUARDS

   Employ guards to control [Assignment: organization-defined physical access points] to the facility where the system resides 24 hours per day, 7 days per week.

   Supplemental Guidance: None.

   Related Controls: CP-6, CP-7, PE-6.

(4) PHYSICAL ACCESS CONTROL | LOCKABLE CASINGS

   Use lockable physical casings to protect [*Assignment: organization-defined system components*] from unauthorized physical access.

   Supplemental Guidance: None.

   Related Controls: None.

(5) PHYSICAL ACCESS CONTROL | TAMPER PROTECTION

   Employ [*Assignment: organization-defined security safeguards*] to [*Selection (one or more): detect; prevent*] physical tampering or alteration of [*Assignment: organization-defined hardware components*] within the system.

   Supplemental Guidance: Organizations implement tamper detection and prevention at selected hardware components or tamper detection at some components and tamper prevention at other components. Such detection and prevention activities can employ many types of anti-tamper technologies including, for example, tamper-detection seals and anti-tamper coatings. Anti-

~~Iamaaoi oioi oioio lo lpi oi oi oi oi oi oiambo oio aioi oioioioi oi Moaatiah oounturtaiting and oilio oi oioly~~
~~chain-related risks.~~

Related Controls: SA-12, SA-16, SA-18.

(6) PHYSICAL ACCESS CONTROL | FACILITY PENETRATION TESTING

[Withdrawn: Incorporated into CA-8].

(7) PHYSICAL ACCESS CONTROL | PHYSICAL BARRIERS

Limit access using physical barriers.

Supplemental Guidance: Physical barriers include, for example, bollards, concrete slabs, jersey walls, and hydraulic active vehicle barriers.

Related Controls: None.

References: FIPS Publication 201; NIST Special Publications 800-73, 800-76, 800-78, 800-116.

PE-4 ACCESS CONTROL FOR TRANSMISSION

Control: Control physical access to [*Assignment: organization-defined system distribution and transmission lines*] within organizational facilities using [*Assignment: organization-defined security safeguards*].

Supplemental Guidance: Security safeguards applied to system distribution and transmission lines prevent accidental damage, disruption, and physical tampering. Such safeguards may also be necessary to help prevent eavesdropping or modification of unencrypted transmissions. Safeguards used to control physical access to system distribution and transmission lines include, for example, locked wiring closets; disconnected or locked spare jacks; protection of cabling by conduit or cable trays; and wiretapping sensors.

Related Controls: AT-3, IA-4, MP-2, MP-4, PE-2, PE-3, PE-5, PE-9, SC-7, SC-8.

Control Enhancements: None.

References: None.

PE-5 ACCESS CONTROL FOR OUTPUT DEVICES

Control: Control physical access to output from [*Assignment: organization-defined output devices*] to prevent unauthorized individuals from obtaining the output.

Supplemental Guidance: Controlling physical access to output devices includes, for example, placing output devices in locked rooms or other secured areas and allowing access to authorized individuals only; placing output devices in locations that can be monitored by organizational personnel; installing monitor or screen filters; and using headphones. Output devices include, for example, monitors, printers, copiers, scanners, facsimile machines, and audio devices.

Related Controls: PE-2, PE-3, PE-4, PE-18.

Control Enhancements:

(1) ACCESS CONTROL FOR OUTPUT DEVICES | ACCESS TO OUTPUT BY AUTHORIZED INDIVIDUALS
Verify that only authorized individuals receive output from output devices.

Supplemental Guidance: Methods to ensure only authorized individuals receive output from output devices include, for example, placing printers, copiers, and facsimile machines in controlled areas with keypad or card reader access controls; and limiting access to individuals with certain types of badges.

Related Controls: None.

(2) ACCESS CONTROL FOR OUTPUT DEVICES | ACCESS TO OUTPUT BY INDIVIDUAL IDENTITY
Link individual identity to receipt of output from output devices.

Supplemental Guidance: Methods to link individual identity to receipt of output from output devices include, for example, installing security functionality on facsimile machines, copiers, and printers. Such functionality allows organizations to implement authentication on output devices prior to the release of output to individuals.

Related Controls: None.

(3) ACCESS CONTROL FOR OUTPUT DEVICES | MARKING OUTPUT DEVICES

Mark [*Assignment: organization-defined system output devices*] indicating the appropriate security marking of the information permitted to be output from the device.

Supplemental Guidance: Outputs devices include, for example, printers, monitors, facsimile machines, scanners, copiers, and audio devices.

Related Controls: None.

References: NIST Interagency Report 8023.

PE-6 MONITORING PHYSICAL ACCESS

Control:

a. Monitor physical access to the facility where the system resides to detect and respond to physical security incidents;

b. Review physical access logs [*Assignment: organization-defined frequency*] and upon occurrence of [*Assignment: organization-defined events or potential indications of events*]; and

c. Coordinate results of reviews and investigations with the organizational incident response capability.

Supplemental Guidance: Monitoring of physical access includes publicly accessible areas within organizational facilities. This can be accomplished for example, by the employment of guards; the use of video surveillance equipment such as cameras; or the use of sensor devices. Organizational incident response capabilities include investigations of and responses to detected physical security incidents. Security incidents include, for example, security violations or suspicious physical access activities. Suspicious physical access activities include, for example, accesses outside of normal work hours; repeated accesses to areas not normally accessed; accesses for unusual lengths of time; and out-of-sequence accesses.

Related Controls: AU-6, AU-9, CA-7, CP-10, IR-4, IR-8.

Control Enhancements:

(1) MONITORING PHYSICAL ACCESS | INTRUSION ALARMS AND SURVEILLANCE EQUIPMENT

Monitor physical access to the facility where the system resides using physical intrusion alarms and surveillance equipment.

Supplemental Guidance: None.

Related Controls: None.

(2) MONITORING PHYSICAL ACCESS | AUTOMATED INTRUSION RECOGNITION AND RESPONSES

Employ automated mechanisms to recognize [*Assignment: organization-defined classes or types of intrusions*] and initiate [*Assignment: organization-defined response actions*].

Supplemental Guidance: None.

Related Controls: SI-4.

(3) MONITORING PHYSICAL ACCESS | VIDEO SURVEILLANCE

Employ video surveillance of [*Assignment: organization-defined operational areas*] and retain video recordings for [*Assignment: organization-defined time-period*].

Supplemental Guidance: This control enhancement focuses on recording surveillance video for purposes of subsequent review, if circumstances so warrant. It does not require monitoring surveillance video although organizations may choose to do so. Note that there may be legal considerations when performing and retaining video surveillance, especially if such surveillance is in a public location.

Related Controls: None.

(4) MONITORING PHYSICAL ACCESS | MONITORING PHYSICAL ACCESS TO SYSTEMS

Monitor physical access to the system in addition to the physical access monitoring of the facility at [*Assignment: organization-defined physical spaces containing one or more components of the system*].

Supplemental Guidance: This control enhancement provides additional monitoring for those areas within facilities where there is a concentration of system components including, for example, server rooms, media storage areas, and communications centers.

Related Controls: None.

References: None.

PE-7 VISITOR CONTROL

[Withdrawn: Incorporated into PE-2 and PE-3].

PE-8 VISITOR ACCESS RECORDS

Control:

a. Maintain visitor access records to the facility where the system resides for [*Assignment: organization-defined time-period*]; and

b. Review visitor access records [*Assignment: organization-defined frequency*].

Supplemental Guidance: Visitor access records include, for example, names and organizations of persons visiting; visitor signatures; forms of identification; dates of access; entry and departure times; purpose of visits; and names and organizations of persons visited. Access records are not required for publicly accessible areas.

Control Enhancements:

(1) VISITOR ACCESS RECORDS | AUTOMATED RECORDS MAINTENANCE AND REVIEW

Employ automated mechanisms to facilitate the maintenance and review of visitor access records.

Supplemental Guidance: None.

Related Controls: None.

(2) VISITOR ACCESS RECORDS | PHYSICAL ACCESS RECORDS

[Withdrawn: Incorporated into PE-2].

References: None.

PE-9 POWER EQUIPMENT AND CABLING

Control: Protect power equipment and power cabling for the system from damage and destruction.

Supplemental Guidance: Organizations determine the types of protection necessary for the power equipment and cabling employed at different locations both internal and external to organizational facilities and environments of operation. This includes, for example, generators and power cabling outside of buildings; internal cabling and uninterruptable power sources within an office or data center; and power sources for self-contained entities such as vehicles and satellites.

Related Controls: PE-4.

Control Enhancements:

(1) POWER EQUIPMENT AND CABLING | REDUNDANT CABLING

Employ redundant power cabling paths that are physically separated by [*Assignment: organization-defined distance*].

Supplemental Guidance: Physically separate and redundant power cables ensure that power continues to flow in the event one of the cables is cut or otherwise damaged.

Related Controls: None.

(2) POWER EQUIPMENT AND CABLING | AUTOMATIC VOLTAGE CONTROLS

Employ automatic voltage controls for [*Assignment: organization-defined critical system components*].

Supplemental Guidance: Automatic voltage controls can monitor and control voltage. Such controls include, for example, voltage regulators, voltage conditioners, and voltage stabilizers.

Related Controls: None.

References: None.

PE-10 EMERGENCY SHUTOFF

Control:

a. Provide the capability of shutting off power to the system or individual system components in emergency situations;

b. Place emergency shutoff switches or devices in [*Assignment: organization-defined location by system or system component*] to facilitate safe and easy access for personnel; and

c. Protect emergency power shutoff capability from unauthorized activation.

Supplemental Guidance: This control applies primarily to facilities containing concentrations of system resources including, for example, data centers, server rooms, rooms/buildings containing computer-controlled machinery, and mainframe computer rooms.

Related Controls: PE-15.

Control Enhancements:

(1) EMERGENCY SHUTOFF | ACCIDENTAL AND UNAUTHORIZED ACTIVATION

[Withdrawn: Incorporated into PE-10].

References: None.

PE-11 EMERGENCY POWER

Control: Provide a short-term uninterruptible power supply to facilitate [*Selection (one or more): an orderly shutdown of the system; transition of the system to long-term alternate power*] in the event of a primary power source loss.

Supplemental Guidance: None.

Related Controls: AT-3, CP-2, CP-7.

Control Enhancements:

(1) EMERGENCY POWER | LONG-TERM ALTERNATE POWER SUPPLY — MINIMAL OPERATIONAL CAPABILITY

Provide a long-term alternate power supply for the system that can maintain minimally required operational capability in the event of an extended loss of the primary power source.

Supplemental Guidance: This control enhancement can be satisfied, for example, by using a secondary commercial power supply or other external power supply. The long-term alternate power supplies for organizational systems are either manually or automatically activated.

Related Controls: None.

(2) EMERGENCY POWER | LONG-TERM ALTERNATE POWER SUPPLY — SELF-CONTAINED

Provide a long-term alternate power supply for the system that is:

(a) **Self-contained;**

(b) **Not reliant on external power generation; and**

(4) ~~Supply or maintaining [delay from minimum required operational capability, full maintenance capability] in the event of an extended loss of the primary power source~~

Supplemental Guidance: This control enhancement can be satisfied, for example, by using one or more generators with sufficient capacity to meet the needs of the organization. Long-term alternate power supplies for organizational systems are either manually or automatically activated.

Related Controls: None.

References: None.

PE-12   EMERGENCY LIGHTING

Control: Employ and maintain automatic emergency lighting for the system that activates in the event of a power outage or disruption and that covers emergency exits and evacuation routes within the facility.

Supplemental Guidance: This control applies primarily to facilities containing concentrations of system resources including, for example, data centers, server rooms, and mainframe computer rooms.

Related Controls: CP-2, CP-7.

Control Enhancements:

(1) EMERGENCY LIGHTING | ESSENTIAL MISSIONS AND BUSINESS FUNCTIONS

Provide emergency lighting for all areas within the facility supporting essential missions and business functions.

Supplemental Guidance: None.

Related Controls: None.

References: None.

PE-13   FIRE PROTECTION

Control: Employ and maintain fire suppression and detection devices/systems for the system that are supported by an independent energy source.

Supplemental Guidance: This control applies primarily to facilities containing concentrations of system resources including, for example, data centers, server rooms, and mainframe computer rooms. Fire suppression and detection devices or systems that may require an independent energy source include, for example, sprinkler systems, fixed fire hoses, and smoke detectors.

Related Controls: AT-3.

Control Enhancements:

(1) FIRE PROTECTION | DETECTION DEVICES AND SYSTEMS

Employ fire detection devices/systems for the system that activate automatically and notify [*Assignment: organization-defined personnel or roles*] and [*Assignment: organization-defined emergency responders*] in the event of a fire.

Supplemental Guidance: Organizations can identify specific personnel, roles, and emergency responders if individuals on the notification list need to have appropriate access authorizations and/or clearances, for example, to obtain access to facilities where classified operations are taking place or where there are systems containing classified information.

Related Controls: None.

(2) FIRE PROTECTION | AUTOMATIC SUPPRESSION DEVICES AND SYSTEMS

(a) **Employ fire suppression devices/systems for the system that provide automatic notification of any activation to [*Assignment: organization-defined personnel or roles*] and [*Assignment: organization-defined* emergency responders]; and**

(b) **Employ an automatic fire suppression capability for the system when the facility is not staffed on a continuous basis.**

Supplemental Guidance: Organizations can identify specific personnel, roles, and emergency responders if individuals on the notification list need to have appropriate access authorizations and/or clearances, for example, to obtain access to facilities where classified operations are taking place or where there are systems containing classified information.

Related Controls: None.

(3) FIRE PROTECTION | AUTOMATIC FIRE SUPPRESSION

[Withdrawn: Incorporated into PE-13(2)].

(4) FIRE PROTECTION | INSPECTIONS

Verify that the facility undergoes [*Assignment: organization-defined frequency*] fire protection inspections by authorized and qualified inspectors and resolves identified deficiencies within [*Assignment: organization-defined time-period*].

Supplemental Guidance: None.

Related Controls: None.

References: None.

PE-14   TEMPERATURE AND HUMIDITY CONTROLS

Control:

a.   Maintain temperature and humidity levels within the facility where the system resides at [*Assignment: organization-defined acceptable levels*]; and

b.   Monitor temperature and humidity levels [*Assignment: organization-defined frequency*].

Supplemental Guidance: This control applies primarily to facilities containing concentrations of system resources, for example, data centers, server rooms, and mainframe computer rooms.

Related Controls: AT-3, CP-2.

Control Enhancements:

(1) TEMPERATURE AND HUMIDITY CONTROLS | AUTOMATIC CONTROLS

Employs automatic temperature and humidity controls in the facility to prevent fluctuations potentially harmful to the system.

Supplemental Guidance: None.

Related Controls: None.

(2) TEMPERATURE AND HUMIDITY CONTROLS | MONITORING WITH ALARMS AND NOTIFICATIONS

Employ temperature and humidity monitoring that provides an alarm or notification of changes potentially harmful to personnel or equipment to [*Assignment: organization-defined personnel or roles*].

Supplemental Guidance: None.

Related Controls: None.

References: None.

PE-15   WATER DAMAGE PROTECTION

Control: Protect the system from damage resulting from water leakage by providing master shutoff or isolation valves that are accessible, working properly, and known to key personnel.

Supplemental Guidance: This control applies primarily to facilities containing concentrations of system resources including, for example, data centers, server rooms, and mainframe computer rooms. Isolation valves can be employed in addition to or in lieu of master shutoff valves to shut off water supplies in specific areas of concern, without affecting entire organizations.

Related Controls: AT-3, PE-10.

Control Enhancements:

(1) WATER DAMAGE PROTECTION | AUTOMATION SUPPORT

Employ automated mechanisms to detect the presence of water near the system and alert [*Assignment: organization-defined personnel or roles*].

Supplemental Guidance: Automated mechanisms include, for example, water detection sensors, alarms, and notification systems.

Related Controls: None.

References: None.

PE-16 DELIVERY AND REMOVAL

Control: Authorize, monitor, and control [*Assignment: organization-defined types of system components*] entering and exiting the facility and maintain records of those items.

Supplemental Guidance: Enforcing authorizations for entry and exit of system components may require restricting access to delivery areas and isolating the areas from the system and media libraries.

Related Controls: CM-3, MA-2, MA-3, MP-5, SA-12.

Control Enhancements: None.

References: None.

PE-17 ALTERNATE WORK SITE

Control:

a. Determine and document the [*Assignment: organization-defined alternate work sites*] allowed for use by employees;

b. Employ [*Assignment: organization-defined security and privacy controls*] at alternate work sites;

c. Assess the effectiveness of security and privacy controls at alternate work sites; and

d. Provide a means for employees to communicate with information security and privacy personnel in case of security or privacy incidents or problems.

Supplemental Guidance: Alternate work sites include, for example, government facilities or private residences of employees. While distinct from alternative processing sites, alternate work sites can provide readily available alternate locations during contingency operations. Organizations can define different sets of controls for specific alternate work sites or types of sites depending on the work-related activities conducted at those sites. This control supports the contingency planning activities of organizations.

Related Controls: AC-17, AC-18, CP-7.

Control Enhancements: None.

References: NIST Special Publication 800-46.

PE-18 LOCATION OF SYSTEM COMPONENTS

Control: Position system components within the facility to minimize potential damage from [*Assignment: organization-defined physical and environmental hazards*] and to minimize the opportunity for unauthorized access.

Supplemental Guidance: Physical and environmental hazards include, for example, flooding, fire, tornados, earthquakes, hurricanes, acts of terrorism, vandalism, electromagnetic pulse, electrical interference, and other forms of incoming electromagnetic radiation. Organizations also consider the location of entry points where unauthorized individuals, while not being granted access, might nonetheless be near systems. Such proximity can increase the risk of unauthorized access to organizational communications, including, for example, using wireless sniffers or microphones.

Related Controls: CP-2, PE-5, PE-19, PE-20, RA-3.

Control Enhancements:

(1) LOCATION OF SYSTEM COMPONENTS | FACILITY SITE

   (a) Plan the location or site of the facility where the system resides considering physical and environmental hazards; and

   (b) For existing facilities, consider the physical and environmental hazards in the organizational risk management strategy.

   Supplemental Guidance: None.

   Related Controls: PM-8.

References: None.

PE-19 INFORMATION LEAKAGE

Control: Protect the system from information leakage due to electromagnetic signals emanations.

Supplemental Guidance: Information leakage is the intentional or unintentional release of data or information to an untrusted environment from electromagnetic signals emanations. The security categories or classifications of systems (with respect to confidentiality), organizational security policies, and risk tolerance guide the selection of controls employed to protect systems against information leakage due to electromagnetic signals emanations.

Related Controls: AC-18, PE-18, PE-20.

Control Enhancements:

(1) INFORMATION LEAKAGE | NATIONAL EMISSIONS AND TEMPEST POLICIES AND PROCEDURES

   Protect system components, associated data communications, and networks in accordance with national Emissions Security policies and procedures based on the security category or classification of the information.

   Supplemental Guidance: Emissions Security (EMSEC) policies include the former TEMPEST policies.

   Related Controls: None.

References: FIPS Publication 199.

PE-20 ASSET MONITORING AND TRACKING

Control: Employ [Assignment: organization-defined asset location technologies] to track and monitor the location and movement of [Assignment: organization-defined assets] within [Assignment: organization-defined controlled areas].

Supplemental Guidance: Asset location technologies can help organizations ensure that critical assets, including, for example, vehicles, equipment, or essential system components remain in authorized locations. Organizations consult with the Office of the General Counsel and the Senior Agency Official for Privacy regarding the deployment and use of asset location technologies to address potential privacy concerns.

Related Controls: CM-8, PM-8.

Control Enhancements: None.

References: None.

PE-21 ELECTROMAGNETIC PULSE PROTECTION

Control: Employ [Assignment: organization-defined security safeguards] against electromagnetic pulse damage for [Assignment: organization-defined systems and system components].

Supplemental Guidance: An electromagnetic pulse (EMP) is a short burst of electromagnetic energy that is spread over a range of frequencies. Such energy bursts may be natural or man-made. EMP interference may be disruptive or damaging to electronic equipment. Protective measures used to mitigate EMP risk include shielding, surge suppressors, ferro-resonant transformers, and earth grounding.

Related Controls: PE-18, PE-19.

Control Enhancements: None.

References: None.

PE-22   COMPONENT MARKING

Control: Mark [*Assignment: organization-defined system hardware components*] indicating the impact or classification level of the information permitted to be processed, stored, or transmitted by the hardware component.

Supplemental Guidance: Hardware components that may require marking include, for example, input devices marked to indicate the classification of the network to which they are connected or a multifunction function printer or copier residing in a classified area. Security marking refers to the application or use of human-readable security attributes. Security labeling refers to the application or use of security attributes regarding internal data structures within systems. Security marking is generally not required for hardware components processing, storing, or transmitting information determined by organizations to be in the public domain or to be publicly releasable. However, organizations may require markings for hardware components processing, storing, or transmitting public information indicating that such information is publicly releasable. The marking of system hardware components reflects applicable laws, Executive Orders, directives, policies, regulations, standards, and guidelines.

Related Controls: AC-16, MP-3.

Control Enhancements: None.

References: None.

3.14 PLANNING

Quick link to Planning summary table

PL-1 PLANNING POLICY AND PROCEDURES

Control:

a. Develop, document, and disseminate to [*Assignment: organization-defined personnel or roles*]:

   1. Security and privacy planning policies that:

      (a) Address purpose, scope, roles, responsibilities, management commitment, coordination among organizational entities, and compliance; and

      (b) Are consistent with applicable laws, Executive Orders, directives, regulations, policies, standards, and guidelines; and

   2. Procedures to facilitate the implementation of the security and privacy planning policies and the associated security and privacy planning controls;

b. Designate an [*Assignment: organization-defined senior management official*] to manage the security and privacy planning policies and procedures;

c. Review and update the current security and privacy planning:

   1. Policies [*Assignment: organization-defined frequency*]; and

   2. Procedures [*Assignment: organization-defined frequency*];

d. Ensure that the security and privacy planning procedures implement the security and privacy planning policies and controls; and

e. Develop, document, and implement remediation actions for violations of the planning policy.

Supplemental Guidance: This control addresses the establishment of policy and procedures for the effective implementation of the controls and control enhancements in the PL family. The risk management strategy is an important factor in establishing policy and procedures. Comprehensive policy and procedures help provide security and privacy assurance. Security and privacy program policies and procedures at the organization level may make the need for system-specific policies and procedures unnecessary. The policy can be included as part of the general security and privacy policies or can be represented by multiple policies reflecting the complex nature of organizations. The procedures can be established for security and privacy programs and for systems, if needed. Procedures describe how policies or controls are implemented and can be directed at the personnel or role that is the object of the procedure. Procedures can be documented in system security and privacy plans or in one or more separate documents. It is important to recognize that restating controls does not constitute an organizational policy or procedure.

Related Controls: PM-9, PS-8, SI-12.

Control Enhancements: None.

References: NIST Special Publications 800-12, 800-18, 800-30, 800-39, 800-100.

PL-2 SECURITY AND PRIVACY PLANS

Control:

a. Develop security and privacy plans for the system that:

   1. Are consistent with the organization's enterprise architecture;

   2. Explicitly define the authorization boundary for the system;

3. ~~Describe the operational environment for the system in terms of missions and business~~
processes.

4. Provide the security categorization of the system including supporting rationale;

5. Describe the operational environment for the system and relationships with or connections to other systems;

6. Provide an overview of the security and privacy requirements for the system;

7. Identify any relevant overlays, if applicable;

8. Describe the security and privacy controls in place or planned for meeting those requirements including a rationale for the tailoring decisions; and

9. Are reviewed and approved by the authorizing official or designated representative prior to plan implementation;

b. Distribute copies of the security and privacy plans and communicate subsequent changes to the plans to [*Assignment: organization-defined personnel or roles*];

c. Review the security and privacy plans [*Assignment: organization-defined frequency*];

d. Update the security and privacy plans to address changes to the system and environment of operation or problems identified during plan implementation or security and privacy control assessments; and

e. Protect the security and privacy plans from unauthorized disclosure and modification.

<u>Supplemental Guidance</u>: Security and privacy plans relate security and privacy requirements to a set of security and privacy controls and control enhancements. The plans describe how the security and privacy controls and control enhancements meet those security and privacy requirements, but do not provide detailed, technical descriptions of the specific design or implementation of the controls and control enhancements. Security and privacy plans contain sufficient information (including the specification of parameter values for assignment and selection statements either explicitly or by reference) to enable a design and implementation that is unambiguously compliant with the intent of the plans and subsequent determinations of risk to organizational operations and assets, individuals, other organizations, and the Nation if the plan is implemented as intended. Organizations can also apply tailoring guidance to the control baselines in Appendix D to develop *overlays* for community-wide use or to address specialized requirements, technologies, missions, business applications, or environments of operation.

Security and privacy plans need not be single documents. The plans can be a collection of various documents including documents that already exist. Effective security and privacy plans make extensive use of references to policies, procedures, and additional documents including, for example, design and implementation specifications where more detailed information can be obtained. This reduces the documentation associated with security and privacy programs and maintains the security- and privacy-related information in other established management and operational areas including, for example, enterprise architecture, system development life cycle, systems engineering, and acquisition. Thus, security and privacy plans do not contain detailed contingency plan or incident response plan information but instead provide explicitly or by reference, sufficient information to define what needs to be accomplished by those plans.

<u>Related Controls</u>: AC-2, AC-6, AC-14, AC-17, AC-20, CA-2, CA-3, CA-7, CM-9, CP-2, IR-8, MA-4, MA-5, MP-4, MP-5, PL-7, PL-8, PM-1, PM-7, PM-8, PM-9, PM-10, PM-11, RA-3, RA-9, SA-5, SA-17, SA-22, SI-12.

<u>Control Enhancements</u>:

(1) SECURITY AND PRIVACY PLANS | CONCEPT OF OPERATIONS
[Withdrawn: Incorporated into PL-7].

(2) SECURITY AND PRIVACY PLANS | FUNCTIONAL ARCHITECTURE
[Withdrawn: Incorporated into PL-8].

   (3) SECURITY AND PRIVACY PLANS | PLAN AND COORDINATE WITH OTHER ORGANIZATIONAL ENTITIES

Plan and coordinate security- and privacy-related activities affecting the system with [*Assignment: organization-defined individuals or groups*] before conducting such activities to reduce the impact on other organizational entities.

Supplemental Guidance: Security- and privacy-related activities include, for example, security and privacy assessments, audits and inspections, hardware and software maintenance, patch management, and contingency plan testing. Planning and coordination includes emergency and nonemergency (i.e., planned or non-urgent unplanned) situations. The process defined by organizations to plan and coordinate security- and privacy-related activities can be included in security and privacy plans for systems or other documents, as appropriate.

Related Controls: CP-4, IR-4.

References: NIST Special Publication 800-18.

PL-3 SYSTEM SECURITY PLAN UPDATE

[Withdrawn: Incorporated into PL-2].

PL-4 RULES OF BEHAVIOR

Control:

a. Establish and provide to individuals requiring access to the system, the rules that describe their responsibilities and expected behavior for information and system usage, security, and privacy;

b. Receive a documented acknowledgment from such individuals, indicating that they have read, understand, and agree to abide by the rules of behavior, before authorizing access to information and the system;

c. Review and update the rules of behavior [*Assignment: organization-defined frequency*]; and

d. Require individuals who have signed a previous version of the rules of behavior to read and re-sign [*Selection (one or more): [Assignment: organization-defined frequency]; when the rules are revised or updated.*]

Supplemental Guidance: This control enhancement applies to organizational users. Organizations consider rules of behavior based on individual user roles and responsibilities, differentiating, for example, between rules that apply to privileged users and rules that apply to the general user population. Establishing rules of behavior for some types of non-organizational users including, for example, individuals who simply receive data or information from federal systems, is often not feasible given the large number of such users and the limited nature of their interactions with the systems. Rules of behavior for organizational and non-organizational users can also be established in AC-8, System Use Notification. PL-4b, the documented acknowledgment portion of the control, may be satisfied by the security and privacy awareness training and the role-based security and privacy training programs conducted by organizations if such training includes rules of behavior. Documented acknowledgements for rules of behavior may include, for example, electronic or physical signatures; and electronic agreement check boxes/radio buttons.

Related Controls: AC-2, AC-6, AC-8, AC-9, AC-17, AC-18, AC-19, AC-20, AT-2, AT-3, CM-11, IA-2, IA-4, IA-5, MP-7, PS-6, PS-8, SA-5, SI-12.

Control Enhancements:

(1) RULES OF BEHAVIOR | SOCIAL MEDIA AND NETWORKING RESTRICTIONS

Include in the rules of behavior, explicit restrictions on the use of social media and networking sites and posting organizational information on public websites.

Supplemental Guidance: This control enhancement addresses rules of behavior related to the use of social media and networking sites when organizational personnel are using such sites for official duties or in the conduct of official business; when organizational information is involved in social media and networking transactions; and when personnel are accessing

...and retain information and for revoking rules from organizational systems. Organizations also address specific rules that prevent unauthorized entities from obtaining, either directly or through inference, non-public organizational information from social media and networking sites. Examples of non-public information include system account information and personally identifiable information.

Related Controls: None.

References: NIST Special Publication 800-18.

PL-5 PRIVACY IMPACT ASSESSMENT

[Withdrawn: Incorporated into RA-8].

PL-6 SECURITY-RELATED ACTIVITY PLANNING

[Withdrawn: Incorporated into PL-2].

PL-7 CONCEPT OF OPERATIONS

Control:

a. Develop a Concept of Operations (CONOPS) for the system describing how the organization intends to operate the system from the perspective of information security and privacy; and

b. Review and update the CONOPS [Assignment: organization-defined frequency].

Supplemental Guidance: The security and privacy CONOPS may be included in the security or privacy plans for the system or in other system development life cycle documents, as appropriate. Changes to the CONOPS are reflected in ongoing updates to the security and privacy plans, the security and privacy architectures, and other appropriate organizational documents, including, for example, system development life cycle documents, procurement specifications, and systems engineering documents.

Related Controls. PL-2, SA-2, SI-12.

Control Enhancements: None.

References: None.

PL-8 SECURITY AND PRIVACY ARCHITECTURES

Control:

a. Develop security and privacy architectures for the system that:

   1. Describe the philosophy, requirements, and approach to be taken for protecting the confidentiality, integrity, and availability of organizational information;

   2. Describe the philosophy, requirements, and approach to be taken for processing personally identifiable information;

   3. Describe how the security and privacy architectures are integrated into and support the enterprise architecture; and

   4. Describe any security- and privacy-related assumptions about, and dependencies on, external services;

b. Review and update the security and privacy architectures [Assignment: organization-defined frequency] to reflect updates in the enterprise architecture; and

c. Reflect planned security and privacy architecture changes in the security and privacy plans, the Concept of Operations (CONOPS), and organizational procurements and acquisitions.

Supplemental Guidance: This control addresses actions taken by organizations in the design and development of systems. The security and privacy architectures at the system level are consistent with and complement the organization-wide security and privacy architectures described in PM-7 that are integral to and developed as part of the enterprise architecture. The security and privacy architectures include an architectural description, the placement and allocation of security and privacy functionality (including security and privacy controls), security- and privacy-related information for external interfaces, information being exchanged across the interfaces, and the protection mechanisms associated with each interface. In addition, the security and privacy architectures can include other information, for example, user roles and the access privileges assigned to each role, unique security and privacy requirements, types of information processed, stored, and transmitted by the system, restoration priorities of information and system services, and any other specific protection needs.

In today's modern computing architectures, it is becoming less common for organizations to control all information resources. There may be key dependencies on external information services and service providers. Describing such dependencies in the security and privacy architectures is important to developing a comprehensive mission and business protection strategy. Establishing, developing, documenting, and maintaining under configuration control, a baseline configuration for organizational systems is critical to implementing and maintaining effective security and privacy architectures. The development of the security and privacy architectures is coordinated with the Senior Agency Information Security Officer and the Senior Agency Official for Privacy to ensure that security and privacy controls needed to support security and privacy requirements are identified and effectively implemented. PL-8 is primarily directed at organizations to ensure that they develop security and privacy architectures for the system, and that the architectures are integrated with or tightly coupled to the enterprise architecture through the organization-wide security and privacy architectures. In contrast, SA-17 is primarily directed at external information technology product and system developers and integrators. SA-17, which is complementary to PL-8, is selected when organizations outsource the development of systems or system components to external entities, and there is a need to demonstrate consistency with the organization's enterprise architecture and security and privacy architectures.

Related Controls: CM-2, CM-6, PL-2, PL-7, PL-9, PM-7, PM-29, RA-9, SA-3, SA-5, SA-8, SA-17.

Control Enhancements:

(1) SECURITY AND PRIVACY ARCHITECTURES | DEFENSE-IN-DEPTH

Design the security and privacy architectures for the system using a defense-in-depth approach that:

(a) Allocates [*Assignment: organization-defined security and privacy safeguards*] to [*Assignment: organization-defined locations and architectural layers*]; and

(b) Ensures that the allocated security and privacy safeguards operate in a coordinated and mutually reinforcing manner.

Supplemental Guidance: Organizations strategically allocate security safeguards (procedural, technical, or both) in the security architecture so that adversaries must overcome multiple safeguards to achieve their objective. Requiring adversaries to defeat multiple mechanisms makes it more difficult to successfully attack critical information resources by increasing the work factor of the adversary. It also increases the likelihood of detection. The coordination of allocated safeguards is essential to ensure that an attack that involves one safeguard does not create adverse unintended consequences by interfering with other safeguards. Examples of such unintended consequences include system lockout and cascading alarms. Placement of security safeguards is an important activity requiring thoughtful analysis. The criticality or value of the organizational asset is a key consideration in providing additional layering.

Related Controls: SC-29, SC-36.

(2) SECURITY AND PRIVACY ARCHITECTURES | SUPPLIER DIVERSITY

Require that [*Assignment: organization-defined security and privacy safeguards*] allocated to [*Assignment: organization-defined locations and architectural layers*] are obtained from different suppliers.

Supplemental Guidance: Different information technology products have different strengths and weaknesses. Providing a broad spectrum of products complements the individual offerings. For example, vendors offering malicious code protection typically update their products at different times, often developing solutions for unknown requirements. Teams or teams based on their priorities and development schedules. By having different products at different locations there is an increased likelihood that at least one will detect the malicious code.

Related Controls: SA-12, SC-29.

References: None.

PL-9 CENTRAL MANAGEMENT

Control: Centrally manage [*Assignment: organization-defined security and privacy controls and related processes*].

Supplemental Guidance: Central management refers to the organization-wide management and implementation of selected security and privacy controls and related processes. This includes planning, implementing, assessing, authorizing, and monitoring the organization-defined, centrally managed controls and processes. As the central management of security and privacy controls is generally associated with the concept of common controls, such management promotes and facilitates standardization of control implementations and management and judicious use of organizational resources. Centrally-managed controls and processes may also meet independence requirements for assessments in support of initial and ongoing authorizations to operate and as part of organizational continuous monitoring. As part of the security and privacy control selection processes, organizations determine which controls may be suitable for central management based on organizational resources and capabilities. It is not always possible to centrally manage every aspect of a security or privacy control. In such cases, the control can be treated as a hybrid control with the control managed and implemented centrally or at the system level. Those controls and control enhancements that are candidates for full or partial central management include, but are not limited to: AC-2 (1) (2) (3) (4); AC-17 (1) (2) (3) (9); AC-18 (1) (3) (4) (5); AC-19 (4); AC-22; AC-23; AT-2 (1) (2); AT-3 (1) (2) (3); AT-4; AU-6 (1) (3) (5) (6) (9); AU-7 (1) (2); AU-11, AU-13, AU-16, CA-2 (1) (2) (3); CA-3 (1) (2) (3); CA-7 (1); CA-9; CM-2 (1) (2); CM-3 (1) (4); CM-4; CM-6 (1); CM-7 (4) (5); CM-8 (all); CM-9 (1); CM-10; CM-11; CP-7 (all); CP-8 (all); SC-43; SI-2; SI-3; SI-7; and SI-8.

Related Controls: PL-8, PM-9.

Control Enhancements: None.

References: NIST Special Publication 800-37.

PL-10 BASELINE SELECTION

Control: Select a control baseline for the system.

Supplemental Guidance: The selection of an appropriate control baseline is determined by the needs of organizational stakeholders. Stakeholder needs and concerns consider mission and business requirements and mandates imposed by applicable laws, Executive Orders, directives, policies, regulations, standards, and guidelines. For example, the three control baselines in Appendix D are based on the requirements from the Federal Information Security Modernization Act (FISMA) and the Privacy Act. These requirements, along with the NIST standards and guidelines implementing the legislation, require organizations to select one of the control baselines after the reviewing the information types and the information that is processed, stored, and transmitted on organizational systems; analyzing the potential adverse impact or consequences of the loss or compromise of the system or information on the organization's operations and assets, individuals, other organizations or the Nation; and considering the results from organizational and system assessments of risk. Nonfederal organizations that are part of other communities of interest including the U.S. critical infrastructure sectors, can develop similar control baselines (using the controls in Chapter Three) that represent the needs and concerns of those entities.

Related Controls: PL-11, RA-2, RA-3, SA-8.

Control Enhancements: None.

References: FIPS Publications <u>199</u>, <u>200</u>; NIST Special Publications <u>800-30</u>, <u>800-37</u>, <u>800-39</u>, <u>800-60-1</u>, <u>800-60-2</u>, <u>800-160</u>.

PL-11   BASELINE TAILORING

Control: Tailor the selected control baseline by applying specified tailoring actions.

Supplemental Guidance: The concept of tailoring allows organizations to specialize or customize a set of baseline controls by applying a defined set of tailoring actions. These actions facilitate such specialization and customization by allowing organizations to develop security and privacy plans that reflect their specific missions and business functions, the environments where their systems operate, the threats and vulnerabilities that can affect their systems, and any other conditions or situations that can impact their mission or business success. The tailoring actions are described in Appendix G. Tailoring a control baseline is accomplished by identifying and designating common controls; applying scoping considerations; selecting compensating controls; assigning values to control parameters; supplementing the control baseline with additional controls, as needed; and providing information for control implementation. The general tailoring actions in Appendix G can be supplemented with additional actions based on the needs of organizations. Tailoring actions can be applied to the baselines in Appendix D in accordance with the security requirements from the Federal Information Security Modernization Act (FISMA) and the privacy requirements from the Privacy Act. Alternatively, other communities of interest adopting different control baselines can apply the tailoring actions in Appendix G to specialize or customize the controls that represent the specific needs and concerns of those entities.

Related Controls: PL-10, RA-2, RA-3, RA-9, SA-8, SA-12.

Control Enhancements: None.

References: FIPS Publications <u>199</u>, <u>200</u>; NIST Special Publications <u>800-30</u>, <u>800-37</u>, <u>800-39</u>, <u>800-160</u>.

3.14 PROGRAM MANAGEMENT

Quick link to Program Management summary table

PM-1 INFORMATION SECURITY PROGRAM PLAN

Control:

a. Develop and disseminate an organization-wide information security program plan that:

1. Provides an overview of the requirements for the security program and a description of the security program management controls and common controls in place or planned for meeting those requirements;

2. Includes the identification and assignment of roles, responsibilities, management commitment, coordination among organizational entities, and compliance;

3. Reflects the coordination among organizational entities responsible for information security; and

4. Is approved by a senior official with responsibility and accountability for the risk being incurred to organizational operations (including mission, functions, image, and reputation), organizational assets, individuals, other organizations, and the Nation;

b. Review the organization-wide information security program plan [*Assignment: organization-defined frequency*];

c. Update the information security program plan to address organizational changes and problems identified during plan implementation or control assessments; and

d. Protect the information security program plan from unauthorized disclosure and modification.

Supplemental Guidance: Information security program plans can be represented in single documents or compilations of documents at the discretion of organizations. The plans document the program management controls and organization-defined common controls. Information security program plans provide sufficient information about the program management controls/common controls (including specification of parameters for any assignment and selection statements either explicitly or by reference) to enable implementations that are unambiguously compliant with the intent of the plans and a determination of the risk to be incurred if the plans are implemented as intended. Security plans for individual systems and the organization-wide information security program plan, provide complete coverage for all security controls employed within the organization. Common controls are documented in an appendix to the organization's information security program plan unless the controls are included in a separate security plan for a system. The organization-wide information security program plan will indicate which separate security plans contain descriptions of common controls.

Organizations have the flexibility to describe common controls in a single document or in multiple documents. For multiple documents, the documents describing common controls are included as attachments to the information security program plan. If the information security program plan contains multiple documents, the organization specifies in each document the organizational official or officials responsible for the development, implementation, assessment, authorization, and monitoring of the respective common controls. For example, the Facilities Management Office may develop, implement, assess, authorize, and continuously monitor common physical and environmental protection controls from the PE family when such controls are not associated with a particular system but instead, support multiple systems.

Related Controls: PL-2, PM-8, PM-12, RA-9, SA-12, SI-12.

Control Enhancements: None.

References: None.

PM-2   INFORMATION SECURITY PROGRAM ROLES

Control:

a.   Appoint a Senior Agency Information Security Officer with the mission and resources to coordinate, develop, implement, and maintain an organization-wide information security program;

b.   Appoint a Senior Accountable Official for Risk Management to align information security management proceeses with strategic, operational, and budgetary planning procceses; and

c.   Appoint a Risk Executive (function) to view and analyze risk from an organization-wide perspective and ensure management of risk is consistent across the organization.

Supplemental Guidance: The senior information security officer is an organizational official. For federal agencies (as defined by applicable laws, Executive Orders, regulations, directives, policies, and standards), this official is the Senior Agency Information Security Officer. Organizations may also refer to this official as the Senior Information Security Officer or Chief Information Security Officer. The senior accountable official for risk management leads the risk executive (function) in organization-wide risk management activities.

Related Controls: None.

Control Enhancements: None.

References: NIST Special Publications 800-37, 800-39; OMB Memorandum 17-25.

PM-3   INFORMATION SECURITY AND PRIVACY RESOURCES

Control:

a.   Include the resources needed to implement the information security and privacy programs in capital planning and investment requests and document all exceptions to this requirement;

b.   Prepare documentation required for addressing information security and privacy programs in capital planning and investment requests in accordance with applicable laws, Executive Orders, directives, policies, regulations, standards; and

c.   Make available for expenditure, the planned information security and privacy resources.

Supplemental Guidance: Organizations consider establishing champions for information security and privacy efforts and as part of including the necessary resources, assign specialized expertise and resources as needed. Organizations may designate and empower an Investment Review Board or similar group to manage and provide oversight for the information security-and privacy-related aspects of the capital planning and investment control process.

Related Controls: PM-4, SA-2.

Control Enhancements: None.

References: NIST Special Publication 800-65.

PM-4   PLAN OF ACTION AND MILESTONES PROCESS

Control:

a.   Implement a process to ensure that plans of action and milestones for the security and privacy programs and associated organizational systems:

1.   Are developed and maintained;

2.   Document the remedial information security and privacy actions to adequately respond to risk to organizational operations and assets, individuals, other organizations, and the Nation; and

3.   Are reported in accordance with established reporting requirements.

b. Review plans of action and milestones for consistency with the organizational risk
management strategy and organization-wide priorities for risk response actions.

Supplemental Guidance: The plan of action and milestones is a key document in the information
security and privacy programs and is subject to reporting requirements established by the Office of
Management and Budget. Organizations view plans of action and milestones from an enterprise-
wide perspective, prioritizing risk response actions and ensuring consistency with the goals and
objectives of the organization. Plan of action and milestones updates are based on findings from
control assessments and continuous monitoring activities.

Related Controls: CA-5; CA-7, PM-3, RA-7, SI-12.

Control Enhancements: None.

References: NIST Special Publications 800-37.

PM-5   SYSTEM INVENTORY

Control: Develop and maintain an inventory of organizational systems.

Supplemental Guidance: OMB provides guidance on developing systems inventories and associated
reporting requirements. This control refers to an organization-wide inventory of systems, not
system components as described in CM-8.

Related Controls: None.

Control Enhancements: None.

References: None.

PM-6   MEASURES OF PERFORMANCE

Control: Develop, monitor, and report on the results of information security and privacy measures
of performance.

Supplemental Guidance: Measures of performance are outcome-based metrics used by an
organization to measure the effectiveness or efficiency of the information security and privacy
programs and the security and privacy controls employed in support of the program.

Related Controls: CA-7.

Control Enhancements: None.

References: NIST Special Publications 800-55, 800-137.

PM-7   ENTERPRISE ARCHITECTURE

Control: Develop an enterprise architecture with consideration for information security, privacy,
and the resulting risk to organizational operations and assets, individuals, other organizations, and
the Nation.

Supplemental Guidance: The integration of security and privacy requirements and controls into the
enterprise architecture ensures that security and privacy considerations are addressed early in the
system development life cycle and are directly and explicitly related to the organization's mission
and business processes. The process of security and privacy requirements integration also embeds
into the enterprise architecture, the organization's security and privacy architectures consistent
with the organizational risk management and information security and privacy strategies. For PM-
7, the security and privacy architectures are developed at a system-of-systems level, representing
all organizational systems. For PL-8, the security and privacy architectures are developed at a
level representing an individual system. The system-level architectures are consistent with the
security and privacy architectures defined for the organization. Security and privacy requirements
and control integration are most effectively accomplished through the rigorous application of the
Risk Management Framework and supporting security standards and guidelines.

Related Controls: AU-6, PL-2, PL-8, PM-11, RA-2, SA-3, SA-8, SA-17.

Control Enhancements: None.

References: NIST Special Publication 800-39.

PM-8 CRITICAL INFRASTRUCTURE PLAN

Control: Address information security and privacy issues in the development, documentation, and updating of a critical infrastructure and key resources protection plan.

Supplemental Guidance: Protection strategies are based on the prioritization of critical assets and resources. The requirement and guidance for defining critical infrastructure and key resources and for preparing an associated critical infrastructure protection plan are found in applicable laws, Executive Orders, directives, policies, regulations, standards, and guidelines.

Related Controls: CP-2, CP-4, PE-18, PL-2, PM-1, PM-9, PM-11, PM-18, RA-3, SI-12.

Control Enhancements: None.

References: HSPD 7; National Infrastructure Protection Plan.

PM-9 RISK MANAGEMENT STRATEGY

Control:

a. Develops a comprehensive strategy to manage:

1. Security risk to organizational operations and assets, individuals, other organizations, and the Nation associated with the operation and use of organizational systems;

2. Privacy risk to individuals resulting from the collection, sharing, storing, transmitting, use, and disposal of personally identifiable information; and

3. Supply chain risks associated with the development, acquisition, maintenance, and disposal of systems, system components, and system services;

b. Implement the risk management strategy consistently across the organization; and

c. Review and update the risk management strategy [*Assignment: organization-defined frequency*] or as required, to address organizational changes.

Supplemental Guidance: An organization-wide risk management strategy includes, for example, an expression of the security, privacy, and supply chain risk tolerance for the organization; acceptable risk assessment methodologies; security, privacy, and supply chain risk mitigation strategies; a process for consistently evaluating security, privacy, and supply chain risk across the organization with respect to the organization's risk tolerance; and approaches for monitoring risk over time. The senior accountable official for risk management (agency head or designated official) aligns information security management proceeses with strategic, operational, and budgetary planning proceeses. The use of a risk executive function, led by the senior accountable official for risk management, can facilitate consistent application of the risk management strategy organization-wide. The organization-wide risk management strategy can be informed by security, privacy, and supply chain risk-related inputs from other sources, internal and external to the organization, to ensure the strategy is both broad-based and comprehensive.

Related Controls: All XX-1 Controls, CA-2, CA-5, CA-6, CA-7, IP-1, PA-1, PA-2, PA-3, PL-2, PM-8, PM-18, PM-31, PM-32, RA-3, RA-9, SA-4, SA-12, SC-38, SI-12.

Control Enhancements: None.

References: NIST Special Publications 800-30, 800-39, 800-161; NIST Interagency Report 8023.

PM-10 AUTHORIZATION PROCESS

Control:

a. Manage the security and privacy state of organizational systems and the environments in which those systems operate through authorization processes;

b. Designate individuals to fulfill specific roles and responsibilities within the organizational risk management process; and

c. Integrate the authorization processes into an organization-wide risk management program.

Supplemental Guidance: Authorization processes for organizational systems and environments of operation require the implementation of an organization-wide risk management process, a Risk Management Framework, and associated security and privacy standards and guidelines. Specific roles for risk management processes include a risk executive (function) and designated authorizing officials for each organizational system and common control provider. The organizational authorization processes are integrated with continuous monitoring processes to facilitate ongoing understanding and acceptance of security and privacy risks to organizational operations and assets, individuals, other organizations, and the Nation.

Related Controls: CA-6, CA-7, PL-2.

Control Enhancements: None.

References: NIST Special Publications 800-37, 800-39.

PM-11 MISSION AND BUSINESS PROCESS DEFINITION

Control:

a. Define organizational mission and business processes with consideration for information security and privacy and the resulting risk to organizational operations, organizational assets, individuals, other organizations, and the Nation; and

b. Determine information protection and personally identifiable information processing needs arising from the defined mission and business processes; and

c. Review and revise the mission and business processes [*Assignment: organization-defined frequency*], until achievable protection and personally identifiable information processing needs are obtained.

Supplemental Guidance: Protection needs are technology-independent, required capabilities to counter threats to organizations, individuals, systems, and the Nation through the compromise of information (i.e., loss of confidentiality, integrity, availability, or privacy). Information protection and personally identifiable information processing needs are derived from mission and business needs defined by the stakeholders in organizations, the mission and business processes defined to meet those needs, and the organizational risk management strategy. Information protection and personally identifiable information processing needs determine the required security and privacy controls for the organization and the systems supporting the mission and business processes. Inherent in defining the protection and personally identifiable information processing needs, is an understanding of adverse impact or consequences that could result if a compromise of information occurs. The categorization process is used to make such potential impact determinations. Privacy risks to individuals can arise from the compromise of personally identifiable information, but they can also arise as unintended consequences or a byproduct of authorized processing of information at any stage of the data life cycle. Privacy risk assessments are used to prioritize the risks that are created for individuals from system processing of personally identifiable information. These risk assessments enable the selection of the required privacy controls for the organization and systems supporting the mission and business processes. Mission and business process definitions and the associated protection requirements are documented in accordance with organizational policy and procedures.

Related Controls: CP-2, PL-2, PM-7, PM-8, RA-2, SA-2.

Control Enhancements: None.

References: FIPS Publication 199; NIST Special Publication 800-60-1, 800-60-2.

PM-12 INSIDER THREAT PROGRAM

Control: Implement an insider threat program that includes a cross-discipline insider threat incident handling team.

Supplemental Guidance: Organizations handling classified information are required, under Executive Order 13587 and the National Policy on Insider Threat, to establish insider threat programs. The standards and guidelines that apply to insider threat programs in classified environments can also be employed effectively to improve the security of Controlled Unclassified Information in non-national security systems. Insider threat programs include controls to detect and prevent malicious insider activity through the centralized integration and analysis of both technical and non-technical information to identify potential insider threat concerns. A senior official is designated by the department or agency head as the responsible individual to implement and provide oversight for the program. In addition to the centralized integration and analysis capability, insider threat programs as a minimum, prepare department or agency insider threat policies and implementation plans; conduct host-based user monitoring of individual employee activities on government-owned classified computers; provide insider threat awareness training to employees; receive access to information from all offices within the department or agency for insider threat analysis; and conduct self-assessments of department or agency insider threat posture.

Insider threat programs can leverage the existence of incident handling teams that organizations may already have in place, such as computer security incident response teams. Human resources records are especially important in this effort, as there is compelling evidence to show that some types of insider crimes are often preceded by nontechnical behaviors in the workplace including, for example, ongoing patterns of disgruntled behavior and conflicts with coworkers and other colleagues. These precursors can better inform and guide organizational officials in more focused, targeted monitoring efforts. However, the use of human resource records could raise significant concerns for privacy. The participation of a comprehensive legal team, including consultation with the senior agency officer for privacy (SAOP), ensures that all monitoring activities are performed in accordance with applicable laws, Executive Orders, directives, regulations, policies, standards, and guidelines.

Related Controls: AC-6, AT-2, AU-6, AU-7, AU-10, AU-12, AU-13, CA-7, IA-4, IR-4, MP-7, PE-2, PM-16, PS-3, PS-4, PS-5, PS-7, PS-8, SC-7, SC-38, SI-4, PM-1, PM-14.

Control Enhancements: None.

References: None.

PM-13 SECURITY AND PRIVACY WORKFORCE

Control: Establish a security and privacy workforce development and improvement program.

Supplemental Guidance: Security and privacy workforce development and improvement programs include, for example, defining the knowledge, skills, and abilities needed to perform security and privacy duties and tasks; developing role-based training programs for individuals assigned security and privacy roles and responsibilities; and providing standards and guidelines for measuring and building individual qualifications for incumbents and applicants for security- and privacy-related positions. Such workforce development and improvement programs can also include security and privacy career paths to encourage security and privacy professionals to advance in the field and fill positions with greater responsibility. The programs encourage organizations to fill security- and privacy-related positions with qualified personnel. Security and privacy workforce development and improvement programs are complementary to organizational security awareness and training programs and focus on developing and institutionalizing the core security and privacy capabilities of personnel needed to protect organizational operations, assets, and individuals.

Related Controls: AT-2, AT-3.

Control Enhancements: None.

References: NIST Cyber Workforce Framework.

PM-14 TESTING, TRAINING, AND MONITORING

Control:

a. Implement a process for ensuring that organizational plans for conducting security and privacy testing, training, and monitoring activities associated with organizational systems:

    1. Are developed and maintained; and

    2. Continue to be executed in a timely manner;

b. Review testing, training, and monitoring plans for consistency with the organizational risk management strategy and organization-wide priorities for risk response actions.

Supplemental Guidance: This control ensures that organizations provide oversight for the security and privacy testing, training, and monitoring activities conducted organization-wide and that those activities are coordinated. With the growing importance of continuous monitoring programs, the implementation of information security and privacy across the three tiers of the risk management hierarchy and the widespread use of common controls, organizations coordinate and consolidate the testing and monitoring activities that are routinely conducted as part of ongoing organizational assessments supporting a variety of security and privacy controls. Security and privacy training activities, while focused on individual systems and specific roles, also necessitate coordination across all organizational elements. Testing, training, and monitoring plans and activities are informed by current threat and vulnerability assessments.

Related Controls: AT-2, AT-3, CA-7, CP-4, IR-3, PM-12, SI-4.

Control Enhancements: None.

References: NIST Special Publications 800-37, 800-39; 800-53A, 800-137.

PM-15 CONTACTS WITH GROUPS AND ASSOCIATIONS

Control: Establish and institutionalize contact with selected groups and associations within the security and privacy communities:

a. To facilitate ongoing security and privacy education and training for organizational personnel;

b. To maintain currency with recommended security and privacy practices, techniques, and technologies; and

c. To share current security- and privacy-related information including threats, vulnerabilities, and incidents.

Supplemental Guidance: Ongoing contact with security and privacy groups and associations is of paramount importance in an environment of rapidly changing technologies and threats. Security and privacy groups and associations include, for example, special interest groups, professional associations, forums, news groups, and peer groups of security and privacy professionals in similar organizations. Organizations select groups and associations based on organizational missions and business functions. Organizations share threat, vulnerability, privacy problems, contextual insights, compliance techniques, and incident information consistent with applicable laws, Executive Orders, directives, policies, regulations, standards, and guidelines.

Related Controls: SA-11, SI-5.

Control Enhancements: None.

References: None.

PM-16 THREAT AWARENESS PROGRAM

Control: Implement a threat awareness program that includes a cross-organization information-sharing capability.

Supplemental Guidance: Because of the constantly changing and increasing sophistication of adversaries, especially the advanced persistent threat (APT), it may be more likely that adversaries can successfully breach or compromise organizational systems. One of the best techniques to address this concern is for organizations to share threat information. This can include sharing threat events (i.e., tactics, techniques, and procedures) that organizations have experienced, mitigations that organizations have found are effective against certain types of threats, and threat intelligence (i.e., indications and warnings about threats that can occur). Threat information sharing may be bilateral or multilateral. Examples of bilateral threat sharing include government-commercial cooperatives and government-government cooperatives. An example of multilateral sharing includes organizations taking part in threat-sharing consortia. Threat information may be highly sensitive requiring special agreements and protection, or less sensitive and freely shared.

Related Controls: IR-4, PM-12.

Control Enhancements:

(1) THREAT AWARENESS PROGRAM | AUTOMATED MEANS FOR SHARING THREAT INTELLIGENCE

Utilize automated means to maximize the effectiveness of sharing threat intelligence information.

Supplemental Guidance: To maximize the effectiveness of monitoring, it is important to know what threat observables and indicators the sensors need to be searching for. By utilizing well established frameworks, services, and automated tools, organizations greatly improve their ability to rapidly share and feed into monitoring tools, the relevant threat detection signatures.

Related Controls: None.

References: None.

PM-17 PROTECTING CONTROLLED UNCLASSIFIED INFORMATION ON EXTERNAL SYSTEMS

Control:

a. Establish policy and procedures to ensure that the requirements for the protection of Controlled Unclassified Information processed, stored or transmitted on external systems, are implemented in accordance with applicable laws, Executive Orders, directives, policies, regulations, and standards.

b. Update the policy and procedures [Assignment: organization-defined frequency].

Supplemental Guidance: The protection of Controlled Unclassified Information (CUI) in nonfederal organizations and systems is critical to the security of federal operations and assets and the privacy of individuals. CUI is defined by the National Archives and Records Administration along with the appropriate safeguarding and dissemination requirements for such information and is codified in 32 CFR 2002, Controlled Unclassified Information and specifically, for systems external to the federal organization, in 32 CFR 2002.14h. The policy prescribes the specific use and conditions to be implemented in accordance with organizational procedures including, for example, via its contracting processes.

Related Controls: CA-6, PM-10.

Control Enhancements: None.

References: 32 CFR 2002; NIST Special Publication 800-171; NARA CUI Registry.

PM-18 PRIVACY PROGRAM PLAN

Control:

a. Develop and disseminate an organization-wide privacy program plan that provides an overview of the agency's privacy program, and:

1. Includes a description of the structure of the privacy program and the resources dedicated to the privacy program;

2. Provides an overview of the requirements for the privacy program and a description of the privacy program management controls and common controls in place or planned for meeting those requirements;

3. Includes the role of the Senior Agency Official for Privacy and the identification and assignment of roles of other privacy officials and staff and their responsibilities;

4. Describes management commitment, compliance, and the strategic goals and objectives of the privacy program;

5. Reflects coordination among organizational entities responsible for the different aspects of privacy; and

6. Is approved by a senior official with responsibility and accountability for the privacy risk being incurred to organizational operations (including mission, functions, image, and reputation), organizational assets, individuals, other organizations, and the Nation; and

b. Update the plan to address changes in federal privacy laws and policy and organizational changes and problems identified during plan implementation or privacy control assessments.

Supplemental Guidance: A Privacy program plan is a formal document that provides an overview of an organization's privacy program, including a description of the structure of the privacy program, the resources dedicated to the privacy program, the role of the Senior Agency Official for Privacy and other privacy officials and staff, the strategic goals and objectives of the privacy program, and the program management and common controls in place or planned for meeting applicable privacy requirements and managing privacy risks.

Privacy program plans can be integrated with information security plans or can be represented independently, either in a single document or in compilations of documents at the discretion of organizations. The plans document the program management controls and organization-defined common controls. Privacy program plans provide sufficient information about the program management and common controls (including specification of parameters and assignment and selection statements either explicitly or by reference) to enable control implementations that are unambiguously compliant with the intent of the plans and a determination of the risk incurred if the plans are implemented as intended.

The privacy plans for individual systems and the organization-wide privacy program plan together provide complete coverage for all privacy controls employed within the organization. Common controls are documented in an appendix to the organization's privacy program plan unless the controls are included in a separate privacy plan for a system. The organization-wide privacy program plan indicates which separate privacy plans contain descriptions of privacy controls.

Organizations have the flexibility to describe common controls in a single document or in multiple documents. In the case of multiple documents, the documents describing common controls are included as attachments to the privacy program plan. If the privacy program plan contains multiple documents, the organization specifies in each document, the organizational official or officials responsible for the development, implementation, assessment, authorization, and monitoring of the respective common controls.

Related Controls: PM-8, PM-9, PM-19.

Control Enhancements: None.

References: None.

PM-19 PRIVACY PROGRAM ROLES

Control: Appoint a Senior Agency Official for Privacy with the authority, mission, accountability, and resources to coordinate, develop, and implement, applicable privacy requirements and manage privacy risks through the organization-wide privacy program.

Supplemental Guidance: The privacy officer described in this control is an organizational official. For federal agencies, as defined by applicable laws, Executive Orders, directives, regulations, policies, standards, and guidelines, this official is designated as the Senior Agency Official for Privacy. Organizations may also refer to this official as the Chief Privacy Officer.

Related Controls: PM-18, PM-21.

Control Enhancements: None.

References: None.

PM-20 SYSTEM OF RECORDS NOTICE

Control:

a.   Publish System of Records Notices in the Federal Register, subject to required oversight processes, for systems containing personally identifiable information; and

b.   Keep System of Records Notices current.

Supplemental Guidance: Organizations issue System of Records Notices to provide the public notice regarding personally identifiable information collected in a system of records. The Privacy Act defines a system of records as a group of any records under the control of any agency from which information is retrieved by the name of an individual or by some identifying number, symbol, or other identifier. System of Records Notices explain how the information is used, retained, and may be corrected, and whether certain portions of the system are subject to Privacy Act exemptions for law enforcement or national security reasons.

Related Controls: IP-5, PA-2, PA-3.

Control Enhancements: None.

References: None.

PM-21 DISSEMINATION OF PRIVACY PROGRAM INFORMATION

Control:

a.   Ensure that the public has access to information about organizational privacy activities and can communicate with its Senior Agency Official for Privacy;

b.   Ensure that organizational privacy practices are publicly available through organizational websites or otherwise; and

c.   Employ publicly facing email addresses and/or phone lines to enable the public to provide feedback and/or direct questions to privacy offices regarding privacy practices.

Supplemental Guidance: Organizations employ different mechanisms for informing the public about their privacy practices including, for example, Privacy Impact Assessments, System of Records Notices, privacy reports, publicly available web pages, email distributions, blogs, and periodic publications, including, for example, quarterly newsletters.

Related Controls: IP-4, IP-5, PM-19.

Control Enhancements: None.

References: None.

PM-11 ACCOUNTING OF DISCLOSURES

Control:

a. Develop and maintain an accounting of disclosures of personally identifiable information held in each system of records under its control, including:

 1. Date, nature, and purpose of each disclosure of a record; and

 2. Name and address of the person or organization to which the disclosure was made;

b. Retain the accounting of disclosures for the life of the record or five years after the disclosure is made, whichever is longer; and

c. Make the accounting of disclosures available to the person named in the record upon request.

Supplemental Guidance: This control addresses disclosure accounting requirements in the Privacy Act. The purpose of disclosure accounting requirements is to allow individuals to learn to whom records about them have been disclosed; to provide a basis for subsequently advising recipients of records of any corrected or disputed records; and to provide an audit trail for subsequent reviews of organizational compliance with conditions for disclosures. Organizations can use any system for keeping notations of disclosures, if it can construct from such a system, a document listing of all disclosures. Automated mechanisms can be used by organizations to determine when such information is disclosed, including, for example, commercial services providing notifications and alerts. Accounting of disclosures may also be used to help organizations verify compliance with applicable privacy statutes and policies governing disclosure or dissemination of information and dissemination restrictions.

Related Controls: AU-2.

Control Enhancements: None.

References: None.

PM-23 DATA QUALITY MANAGEMENT

Control: Issue guidelines ensuring and maximizing the quality, utility, objectivity, integrity, impact determination, and de-identification of personally identifiable information across the information life cycle.

Supplemental Guidance: Data quality management guidelines include the reasonable steps that organizations take to confirm the accuracy and relevance of personally identifiable information throughout the information life cycle. The information life cycle includes the creation, collection, use, processing, storage, maintenance, dissemination, disclosure, and disposition of personally identifiable information. Such steps may include, for example, editing and validating addresses as they are collected or entered into systems using automated address verification look-up application programming interfaces. The measures taken to protect data quality are based on the nature and context of the personally identifiable information, how it is to be used, how it was obtained, the impact level of the personally identifiable information obtained, and potential de-identification methods employed. Measures taken to validate the accuracy of personally identifiable information that is used to make determinations about the rights, benefits, or privileges of individuals under federal programs may be more comprehensive than those used to validate less sensitive personally identifiable information. Additional steps may be necessary to validate personally identifiable information that is obtained from sources other than individuals or the authorized representatives of individuals.

Related Controls: PM-24, SI-20.

Control Enhancements:

(1) DATA QUALITY MANAGEMENT | AUTOMATION

 Issue technical guidelines and documentation to support automated evaluation of data quality across the information life cycle.

Supplemental Guidance: As data is obtained and used across the information life cycle, it is important to confirm the accuracy and relevance of personally identifiable information. Automated tools and techniques can augment existing process and procedures and enable an organization to better identify and manage personally identifiable information in large-scale systems. For example, automated tools can greatly improve efforts to consistently normalize data or identify malformed data. Automated tools can also be used to improve auditing of data, to track how data is used across the information life cycle, and to detect errors that may incorrectly alter personally identifiable information or incorrectly associate such information with the wrong individual. These automated capabilities backstop processes and procedures at-scale. They also enable more fine-grained detection and correction of data quality errors.

Related Controls: None.

(2) DATA QUALITY MANAGEMENT | DATA TAGGING

Issue data modeling guidelines to support tagging of personally identifiable information.

Supplemental Guidance: Data tagging includes, for example, tags noting the authority to collect, usage, presence of personally identifiable information, de-identification, impact level, and information life cycle stage.

Related Controls: SC-16.

(3) DATA QUALITY MANAGEMENT | UPDATING PERSONALLY IDENTIFIABLE INFORMATION

When managing personally identifiable information, develop procedures and incorporate mechanisms to identify and record the method under which the information is updated, and the frequency that such updates occur.

Supplemental Guidance: When managing personally identifiable information including, for example, health information and financial information, it is important to carefully track updates or changes to such data. Having the ability to track both the method and frequency of updates enhances transparency and individual participation. It also enables individuals to better understand how and when their information is changed and helps both individuals and the responsible organizations to know how and what personally identifiable information was changed should erroneous information be identified.

Related Controls: None.

References: NIST Special Publication 800-188.

PM-24 DATA MANAGEMENT BOARD

Control:

a. Establish a written charter for a Data Management Board;

b. Establish the Data Management Board consisting of [*Assignment: organization-defined roles*] with the following responsibilities:

   1. Develop and implement guidelines supporting data modeling, quality, integrity, and de-identification needs of personally identifiable information across the information life cycle;

   2. Review and approve applications to release data outside of the organization, archiving the applications and the released data, and performing post-release monitoring to ensure that the assumptions made as part of the data release continue to be valid;

c. Include requirements for personnel interaction with the Data Management Board in security and privacy awareness and/or role-based training.

Supplemental Guidance: The guidelines established by Data Management Board establish policies, procedures, and standards that enable data governance so that personally identifiable information is managed and maintained in accordance with any relevant statutes, regulations, and guidance. Members may include the Chief Information Officer, Senior Agency Information Security Officer, and Senior Agency Official for Privacy. With respect to data modeling, and the quality, integrity, and de-identification of personally identifiable information, data and information needs are met through organization-wide data governance policies that establish the roles, responsibilities and procedures by which personnel manage information as an asset across the information life cycle. The information life cycle includes creation, collection, use, processing, storage, maintenance, dissemination, disclosure, and disposition. Members may include the Chief Information Officer, Senior Agency Official for Privacy, and Senior Agency Information Security Officer.

Related Controls: AT-2, AT-3, PM-23, PM-25, SI-4, SI-20.

Control Enhancements: None.

References: NIST Special Publication 800-188.

PM-25 DATA INTEGRITY BOARD

Control: Establish a Data Integrity Board to oversee organizational Computer Matching Agreements.

Supplemental Guidance: Organizations executing Computer Matching Agreements or participating in such agreements with other organizations regarding applicants for and recipients of financial assistance or payments under federal benefit programs or certain computerized comparisons involving federal personnel or payroll records, establish a Data Integrity Board to oversee and coordinate the implementation of those matching agreements. As data is obtained and used across the information life cycle, it is important to confirm the accuracy and relevance of personally identifiable information. Organizations may integrate the function of the Data Integrity Board into the responsibilities of the Data Management Board under PM-24. In many organizations, the Data Integrity Board is led by the Senior Agency Official for Privacy.

Related Controls: AC-1, AC-3, AC-4, AU-2, AU-3, AU-6, AU-11, PA-2, PA-4, PM-24, SC-8, SC-28, SI-19, SI-20.

Control Enhancements:

(1) DATA INTEGRITY BOARD | PUBLISH AGREEMENTS ON WEBSITE
 Publish Computer Matching Agreements on the public website of the organization.
 Supplemental Guidance: None.
 Related Controls: None.

References: None.

PM-26 MINIMIZATION OF PERSONALLY IDENTIFIABLE INFORMATION USED IN TESTING, TRAINING, AND RESEARCH

Control:

a. Develop and implement policies and procedures that address the use of personally identifiable information for internal testing, training, and research;

b. Take measures to limit or minimize the amount of personally identifiable information used for internal testing, training, and research purposes; and

c. Authorize the use of personally identifiable information when such information is required for internal testing, training, and research.

Supplemental Guidance: Organizations often use personally identifiable information for testing new applications or systems prior to deployment, for research purposes, and for training. The use of personally identifiable information in testing, research, and training increases risk of unauthorized disclosure or misuse of such information. Organizations consult with the Senior Agency Official for Privacy and legal counsel to ensure that the use of personally identifiable information in testing, training, and research is compatible with the original purpose for which it was collected. When possible, organizations use placeholder data to avoid exposure of personally identifiable information when conducting testing, training, and research.

Related Controls: PA-3.

Control Enhancements: None.

References: None.

PM-27 INDIVIDUAL ACCESS CONTROL

Control:

a. Publish:

1. Policies governing how individuals may request access to records maintained in a Privacy Act system of records; and

2. Access procedures in System of Records Notices; and

b. Ensure that the published policies and access procedures are consistent with Privacy Act requirements and Office of Management and Budget policies and guidance for the proper processing of Privacy Act requests.

Supplemental Guidance: Access affords individuals the ability to review personally identifiable information about them held within organizational systems of records. Access includes timely, simplified, and inexpensive access to data. Organizational processes for allowing access to records may differ based on resources, legal requirements, or other factors. The Senior Agency Official for Privacy is responsible for the content of Privacy Act regulations and record request processing, in consultation with the organization's legal counsel. Access to certain types of records may not be appropriate, however, and heads of agencies may promulgate rules exempting particular systems from the access provision of the Privacy Act.

Related Controls: IP-6.

Control Enhancements: None.

References: None.

PM-28 COMPLAINT MANAGEMENT

Control: Implement a process for receiving and responding to complaints, concerns, or questions from individuals about the organizational privacy practices that includes:

a. Mechanisms that are easy to use and readily accessible by the public;

b. All information necessary for successfully filing complaints; and

c. Tracking mechanisms to ensure all complaints received are reviewed and appropriately addressed in a timely manner.

Supplemental Guidance: Complaints, concerns, and questions from individuals can serve as a valuable source of external input that ultimately improves operational models, uses of technology, data collection practices, and privacy and security controls. Mechanisms that can be used by the public may include, for example, e-mail, telephone hotline, or web-based forms. Information necessary for successfully filing complaints includes, for example, contact information for the Senior Agency Official for Privacy or other official designated to receive complaints.

Related Controls: IP-3, IR-7, IR-9.

Control Enhancements: None.

References: None.

PM-29 INVENTORY OF PERSONALLY IDENTIFIABLE INFORMATION

Control:

a. Establish, maintain, and update [*Assignment: organization-defined frequency*] an inventory of all programs and systems that create, collect, use, process, store, maintain, disseminate, disclose, or dispose of personally identifiable information;

b. Provide updates of the personally identifiable information inventory to the Chief Information Officer, Senior Agency Official for Privacy, and Senior Agency Information Security Officer [*Assignment: organization-defined frequency*];

c. Use the personally identifiable information inventory to support the establishment of information security and privacy requirements for all new or modified systems containing personally identifiable information;

d. Review the personally identifiable information inventory [*Assignment: organization-defined frequency*];

e. Ensure to the extent practicable, that personally identifiable information is accurate, relevant, timely, and complete; and

f. Reduce personally identifiable information to the minimum necessary for the proper performance of authorized organizational functions.

Supplemental Guidance: Organizations coordinate with federal records officers to ensure that reductions in organizational holdings of personally identifiable information are consistent with National Archives and Records Administration retention schedules. By performing periodic assessments, organizations ensure that only the data specified in the notice is collected, and that the data collected is still relevant and necessary for the purpose specified in privacy notices. The set of personally identifiable information elements required to support an organizational mission or business process may be a subset of the personally identifiable information the organization is authorized to collect.

Related Controls: CM-8, PL-8.

Control Enhancements:

(1) INVENTORY OF PERSONALLY IDENTIFIABLE INFORMATION | AUTOMATION SUPPORT

Employ automated mechanisms to determine if personally identifiable information is maintained in electronic form.

Supplemental Guidance: Automated mechanisms include, for example, commercial services providing notifications and alerts to organizations about where personally identifiable information is stored.

Related Controls: None.

References: None.

PM-30 PRIVACY REPORTING

Control: Develop, disseminate, and update privacy reports to:

a. The Office of Management and Budget, Congress, and other oversight bodies to demonstrate accountability with statutory and regulatory privacy program mandates; and

b. [*Assignment: organization-defined officials*] and other personnel with responsibility for monitoring privacy program progress and compliance.

Supplemental Guidance: Through internal and external privacy reporting, organizations promote accountability and transparency in organizational privacy operations. Reporting can also help organizations to determine progress in meeting privacy compliance requirements and privacy controls, compare performance across the federal government, identify vulnerabilities and gaps in policy and implementation, and identify success models. Privacy reports include, for example, annual Senior Agency Official for Privacy reports to OMB; reports to Congress required by the Implementing Regulations of the 9/11 Commission Act; and other public reports required by specific statutory mandates or internal policies of organizations. The Senior Agency Official for Privacy consults with legal counsel, where appropriate, to ensure that organizations meet all applicable privacy reporting requirements.

Related Controls: IR-9, PM-19.

Control Enhancements: None.

References: None.

PM-31 SUPPLY CHAIN RISK MANAGEMENT PLAN

Control:

a. Develop a plan for managing supply chain risks associated with the development, acquisition, maintenance, and disposal of systems, system components, and system services;

b. Implement the supply chain risk management plan consistently across the organization; and

c. Review and update the supply chain risk management plan [*Assignment: organization-defined frequency*] or as required, to address organizational changes.

Supplemental Guidance: An organization-wide supply chain risk management plan includes, for example, an unambiguous expression of the supply chain risk tolerance for the organization, acceptable supply chain risk mitigation strategies or controls, a process for consistently evaluating and monitoring supply chain risk, approaches for implementing and communicating the supply chain risk management plan, and associated roles and responsibilities. The organization-wide supply chain risk management plan can be incorporated into the organization's risk management strategy and be used to inform the system-level supply chain risk management plan. The use of a risk executive function can facilitate consistent, organization-wide application of the supply chain risk management plan.

Related Controls: PM-9, SA-12.

Control Enhancements: None.

References: NIST Special Publication 800-161.

PM-32 RISK FRAMING

Control:

a. Identify assumptions affecting risk assessments, risk response, and risk monitoring;

b. Identify constraints affecting risk assessments, risk response, and risk monitoring;

c. Identify the organizational risk tolerance; and

d. Identify priorities and trade-offs considered by the organization for managing risk.

Supplemental Guidance: Risk framing is most effectively conducted at the organization-wide level. The assumptions, constraints, organizational risk tolerance, and priorities and trade-offs identified for this control inform the organizational risk management strategy which in turn, informs the conduct of risk assessment, risk response, and risk monitoring.

Related Controls: CA-7, PM-9, RA-3, RA-7.

Control Enhancements: None.

References: NIST Special Publication 800-39.

9.10 PERSONNEL SECURITY

Quick link to Personnel Security summary table

PS-1 PERSONNEL SECURITY POLICY AND PROCEDURES

Control:

a. Develop, document, and disseminate to [*Assignment: organization-defined personnel or roles*]:

1. A personnel security policy that:

    (a) Addresses purpose, scope, roles, responsibilities, management commitment, coordination among organizational entities, and compliance; and

    (b) Is consistent with applicable laws, Executive Orders, directives, regulations, policies, standards, and guidelines; and

2. Procedures to facilitate the implementation of the personnel security policy and the associated personnel security controls;

b. Designate an [*Assignment: organization-defined senior management official*] to manage the personnel security policy and procedures;

c. Review and update the current personnel security:

1. Policy [*Assignment: organization-defined frequency*]; and

2. Procedures [*Assignment: organization-defined frequency*];

d. Ensure that the personnel security procedures implement the personnel security policy and controls; and

e. Develop, document, and implement remediation actions for violations of the personnel security policy.

Supplemental Guidance: This control addresses the establishment of policy and procedures for the effective implementation of the controls and control enhancements in the PS family. The risk management strategy is an important factor in establishing policy and procedures. Comprehensive policy and procedures help provide security and privacy assurance. Security and privacy program policies and procedures at the organization level may make the need for system-specific policies and procedures unnecessary. The policy can be included as part of the general security and privacy policy or can be represented by multiple policies reflecting the complex nature of organizations. The procedures can be established for security and privacy programs and for systems, if needed. Procedures describe how policies or controls are implemented and can be directed at the personnel or role that is the object of the procedure. Procedures can be documented in system security and privacy plans or in one or more separate documents. It is important to recognize that restating controls does not constitute an organizational policy or procedure.

Related Controls: PM-9, PS-8, SI-12.

Control Enhancements: None.

References: NIST Special Publications 800-12, 800-30, 800-39, 800-100.

PS-2 POSITION RISK DESIGNATION

Control:

a. Assign a risk designation to all organizational positions;

b. Establish screening criteria for individuals filling those positions; and

c. Review and update position risk designations [*Assignment: organization-defined frequency*].

Supplemental Guidance: Position risk designations reflect Office of Personnel Management policy and guidance. Risk designations can guide and inform the types of authorizations individuals receive when accessing organizational information and systems. Position screening criteria include explicit information security role appointment requirements.

Related Controls: AC-5, AT-3, PE-2, PE-3, PL-2, PS-3, PS-6, SA-5, SA-21, SI-12.

Control Enhancements: None.

References: 5 C.F.R. 731.106.

PS-3   PERSONNEL SCREENING

Control:

a. Screen individuals prior to authorizing access to the system; and

b. Rescreen individuals in accordance with [*Assignment: organization-defined conditions requiring rescreening and, where rescreening is so indicated, the frequency of rescreening*].

Supplemental Guidance: Personnel screening and rescreening activities reflect applicable laws, Executive Orders, directives, regulations, policies, standards, guidelines, and specific criteria established for the risk designations of assigned positions. Organizations may define different rescreening conditions and frequencies for personnel accessing systems based on types of information processed, stored, or transmitted by the systems.

Related Controls: AC-2, IA-4, MA-5, PE-2, PM-12, PS-2, PS-6, PS-7, SA-21.

Control Enhancements:

(1) PERSONNEL SCREENING | CLASSIFIED INFORMATION

Verify that individuals accessing a system processing, storing, or transmitting classified information are cleared and indoctrinated to the highest classification level of the information to which they have access on the system.

Supplemental Guidance: None.

Related Controls: AC-3, AC-4.

(2) PERSONNEL SCREENING | FORMAL INDOCTRINATION

Verify that individuals accessing a system processing, storing, or transmitting types of classified information which require formal indoctrination, are formally indoctrinated for all the relevant types of information to which they have access on the system.

Supplemental Guidance: Types of classified information requiring formal indoctrination include, for example, Special Access Program (SAP), Restricted Data (RD), and Sensitive Compartment Information (SCI).

Related Controls: AC-3, AC-4.

(3) PERSONNEL SCREENING | INFORMATION WITH SPECIAL PROTECTION MEASURES

Verify that individuals accessing a system processing, storing, or transmitting information requiring special protection:

(a) **Have valid access authorizations that are demonstrated by assigned official government duties; and**

(b) **Satisfy [*Assignment: organization-defined additional personnel screening criteria*].**

Supplemental Guidance: Organizational information requiring special protection includes, for example, Controlled Unclassified Information (CUI). Personnel security criteria include, for example, position sensitivity background screening requirements.

Related Controls: None.

(4) PERSONNEL SCREENING | CITIZENSHIP REQUIREMENTS

Verify that individuals accessing a system processing, storing, or transmitting [*Assignment: organization-defined information types*] meet [*Assignment: organization-defined citizenship requirements*].

Related Controls: None.

References: FIPS Publications 199, 201; NIST Special Publications 800-60-1, 800-60-2, 800-73, 800-76, 800-78.

PS-4 PERSONNEL TERMINATION

Control: Upon termination of individual employment:

a. Disable system access within [*Assignment: organization-defined time-period*];

b. Terminate or revoke any authenticators and credentials associated with the individual;

c. Conduct exit interviews that include a discussion of [*Assignment: organization-defined information security topics*];

d. Retrieve all security-related organizational system-related property;

e. Retain access to organizational information and systems formerly controlled by terminated individual; and

f. Notify [*Assignment: organization-defined personnel or roles*] within [*Assignment: organization-defined time-period*].

Supplemental Guidance: System-related property includes, for example, hardware authentication tokens, system administration technical manuals, keys, identification cards, and building passes. Exit interviews ensure that terminated individuals understand the security constraints imposed by being former employees and that proper accountability is achieved for system-related property. Security topics of interest at exit interviews can include, for example, reminding terminated individuals of nondisclosure agreements and potential limitations on future employment. Exit interviews may not be possible for some terminated individuals, for example, in cases related to job abandonment, illnesses, and unavailability of supervisors. Exit interviews are important for individuals with security clearances. Timely execution of termination actions is essential for individuals terminated for cause. In certain situations, organizations consider disabling the system accounts of individuals that are being terminated prior to the individuals being notified.

Related Controls: AC-2, IA-4, PE-2, PM-12, PS-6, PS-7.

Control Enhancements:

(1) PERSONNEL TERMINATION | POST-EMPLOYMENT REQUIREMENTS

    (a) **Notify terminated individuals of applicable, legally binding post-employment requirements for the protection of organizational information; and**

    (b) **Require terminated individuals to sign an acknowledgment of post-employment requirements as part of the organizational termination process.**

    Supplemental Guidance: Organizations consult with the Office of the General Counsel regarding matters of post-employment requirements on terminated individuals.

    Related Controls: None.

(2) PERSONNEL TERMINATION | AUTOMATED NOTIFICATION

    Employ automated mechanisms to notify [*Assignment: organization-defined personnel or roles*] upon termination of an individual.

    Supplemental Guidance: In organizations with many employees, not all personnel who need to know about termination actions receive the appropriate notifications—or, if such notifications are received, they may not occur in a timely manner. Automated mechanisms can be used to send automatic alerts or notifications to specific organizational personnel or roles when individuals are terminated. Such automatic alerts or notifications can be conveyed in a variety of ways, including, for example, telephonically, via electronic mail, via text message, or via websites.

    Related Controls: None.

<u>References</u>: None.

PS-5   PERSONNEL TRANSFER

<u>Control</u>:

a. Review and confirm ongoing operational need for current logical and physical access authorizations to systems and facilities when individuals are reassigned or transferred to other positions within the organization;

b. Initiate [*Assignment: organization-defined transfer or reassignment actions*] within [*Assignment: organization-defined time-period following the formal transfer action*];

c. Modify access authorization as needed to correspond with any changes in operational need due to reassignment or transfer; and

d. Notify [*Assignment: organization-defined personnel or roles*] within [*Assignment: organization-defined time-period*].

<u>Supplemental Guidance</u>: This control applies when reassignments or transfers of individuals are permanent or of such extended durations as to make the actions warranted. Organizations define actions appropriate for the types of reassignments or transfers, whether permanent or extended. Actions that may be required for personnel transfers or reassignments to other positions within organizations include, for example, returning old and issuing new keys, identification cards, and building passes; closing system accounts and establishing new accounts; changing system access authorizations (i.e., privileges); and providing for access to official records to which individuals had access at previous work locations and in previous system accounts.

<u>Related Controls</u>: AC-2, IA-4, PE-2, PM-12, PS-4, PS-7.

<u>Control Enhancements</u>: None.

<u>References</u>: None.

PS-6   ACCESS AGREEMENTS

<u>Control</u>:

a. Develop and document access agreements for organizational systems;

b. Review and update the access agreements [*Assignment: organization-defined frequency*]; and

c. Verify that individuals requiring access to organizational information and systems:

    1. Sign appropriate access agreements prior to being granted access; and

    2. Re-sign access agreements to maintain access to organizational systems when access agreements have been updated or [*Assignment: organization-defined frequency*].

<u>Supplemental Guidance</u>: Access agreements include, for example, nondisclosure agreements, acceptable use agreements, rules of behavior, and conflict-of-interest agreements. Signed access agreements include an acknowledgement that individuals have read, understand, and agree to abide by the constraints associated with organizational systems to which access is authorized. Organizations can use electronic signatures to acknowledge access agreements unless specifically prohibited by organizational policy.

<u>Related Controls</u>: AC-17, PE-2, PL-4, PS-2, PS-3, PS-7, PS-8, SA-21, SI-12.

<u>Control Enhancements</u>:

(1) ACCESS AGREEMENTS | INFORMATION REQUIRING SPECIAL PROTECTION
     [Withdrawn: Incorporated into PS-3].

(2) ACCESS AGREEMENTS | CLASSIFIED INFORMATION REQUIRING SPECIAL PROTECTION
     Verify that access to classified information requiring special protection is granted only to individuals who:

(a) Have a valid access authorization that is demonstrated by assigned official government duties;

(b) **Satisfy associated personnel security criteria; and**

(c) **Have read, understood, and signed a nondisclosure agreement.**

Supplemental Guidance: Classified information requiring special protection includes, for example, collateral information, Special Access Program (SAP) information, and Sensitive Compartmented Information (SCI). Personnel security criteria reflect applicable laws, Executive Orders, directives, regulations, policies, standards, and guidelines.

Related Controls: None.

(3) ACCESS AGREEMENTS | POST-EMPLOYMENT REQUIREMENTS

(a) **Notify individuals of applicable, legally binding post-employment requirements for protection of organizational information; and**

(b) **Require individuals to sign an acknowledgment of these requirements, if applicable, as part of granting initial access to covered information.**

Supplemental Guidance: Organizations consult with the Office of the General Counsel regarding matters of post-employment requirements on terminated individuals.

Related Controls: PS-4.

References: None.

PS-7   EXTERNAL PERSONNEL SECURITY

Control:

a. Establish personnel security requirements including security roles and responsibilities for external providers;

b. Require external providers to comply with personnel security policies and procedures established by the organization;

c. Document personnel security requirements;

d. Require external providers to notify [*Assignment: organization-defined personnel or roles*] of any personnel transfers or terminations of external personnel who possess organizational credentials and/or badges, or who have system privileges within [*Assignment: organization-defined time-period*]; and

e. Monitor provider compliance.

Supplemental Guidance: External provider refers to organizations other than the organization operating or acquiring the system. External providers include, for example, service bureaus, contractors, and other organizations providing system development, information technology services, outsourced applications, testing/assessment services, and network and security management. Organizations explicitly include personnel security requirements in acquisition-related documents. External providers may have personnel working at organizational facilities with credentials, badges, or system privileges issued by organizations. Notifications of external personnel changes ensure appropriate termination of privileges and credentials. Organizations define the transfers and terminations deemed reportable by security-related characteristics that include, for example, functions, roles, and nature of credentials/privileges associated with individuals transferred or terminated.

Related Controls: AT-2, AT-3, MA-5, PE-3, PS-2, PS-3, PS-4, PS-5, PS-6, SA-5, SA-9, SA-21.

Control Enhancements: None.

References: NIST Special Publication 800-35.

PS-8 PERSONNEL SANCTIONS

Control:

a. Employ a formal sanctions process for individuals failing to comply with established information security policies and procedures; and

b. Notify [*Assignment: organization-defined personnel or roles*] within [*Assignment: organization-defined time-period*] when a formal employee sanctions process is initiated, identifying the individual sanctioned and the reason for the sanction.

Supplemental Guidance: Organizational sanctions processes reflect applicable laws, Executive Orders, directives, regulations, policies, standards, and guidelines. Sanctions processes are described in access agreements and can be included as part of general personnel policies and procedures for organizations. Organizations consult with the Office of the General Counsel regarding matters of employee sanctions.

Related Controls: All XX-1 Controls, IP-1, PL-4, PM-12, PS-6.

Control Enhancements: None.

References: None.

3.17 RISK ASSESSMENT

Quick link to Risk Assessment summary table

RA-1   RISK ASSESSMENT POLICY AND PROCEDURES

<u>Control</u>:

a. Develop, document, and disseminate to [*Assignment: organization-defined personnel or roles*]:

    1. A risk assessment policy that:

        (a) Addresses purpose, scope, roles, responsibilities, management commitment, coordination among organizational entities, and compliance; and

        (b) Is consistent with applicable laws, Executive Orders, directives, regulations, policies, standards, and guidelines; and

    2. Procedures to facilitate the implementation of the risk assessment policy and the associated risk assessment controls;

b. Designate an [*Assignment: organization-defined senior management official*] to manage the risk assessment policy and procedures;

c. Review and update the current risk assessment:

    1. Policy [*Assignment: organization-defined frequency*]; and

    2. Procedures [*Assignment: organization-defined frequency*];

d. Ensure that the risk assessment procedures implement the risk assessment policy and controls; and

e. Develop, document, and implement remediation actions for violations of the risk assessment policy.

<u>Supplemental Guidance</u>: This control addresses the establishment of policy and procedures for the effective implementation of the controls and control enhancements in the RA family. The risk management strategy is an important factor in establishing policy and procedures. Comprehensive policy and procedures help provide security and privacy assurance. Security and privacy program policies and procedures at the organization level may make the need for system-specific policies and procedures unnecessary. The policy can be included as part of the general security and privacy policy or can be represented by multiple policies reflecting the complex nature of organizations. The procedures can be established for security and privacy programs and for systems, if needed. Procedures describe how policies or controls are implemented and can be directed at the personnel or role that is the object of the procedure. Procedures can be documented in system security and privacy plans or in one or more separate documents. It is important to recognize that restating controls does not constitute an organizational policy or procedure.

<u>Related Controls</u>: PM-9, PS-8, SI-12.

<u>Control Enhancements</u>: None.

<u>References</u>: NIST Special Publications <u>800-12</u>, <u>800-30</u>, <u>800-39</u>, <u>800-100</u>.

RA-2   SECURITY CATEGORIZATION

<u>Control</u>:

a. Categorize the system and information it processes, stores, and transmits;

b. Document the security categorization results including supporting rationale, in the security plan for the system; and

c.   Verify that the authorizing official or authorizing official designated representative reviews and approves the security categorization decision.

Supplemental Guidance: Clearly defined authorization boundaries are a prerequisite for effective security categorization decisions. Security categories describe the potential adverse impacts to organizational operations, organizational assets, and individuals if organizational information and systems are comprised through a loss of confidentiality, integrity, or availability. Organizations conduct the security categorization process as an organization-wide activity with the involvement of Chief Information Officers, Senior Agency Information Security Officers, system owners, mission and business owners, and information owners/stewards. Organizations also consider the potential adverse impacts to other organizations and, in accordance with the USA PATRIOT Act of 2001 and Homeland Security Presidential Directives, potential national-level adverse impacts. Security categorization processes facilitate the development of inventories of information assets, and along with CM-8, mappings to specific system components where information is processed, stored, or transmitted.

Related Controls: CM-8, MP-4, PL-2, PL-10, PL-11, PM-7, RA-3, RA-5, RA-7, SC-7, SC-38, SI-12.

Control Enhancements:

(1)   SECURITY CATEGORIZATION | SECOND-LEVEL CATEGORIZATION

Conduct a second-level categorization of organizational systems to obtain additional granularity on system impact levels.

Supplemental Guidance: Organizations apply the "high water mark" concept to each of their systems categorized in accordance with FIPS Publication 199. This process results in systems designated as low impact, moderate impact, or high impact. Organizations desiring additional granularity in the system impact designations for risk-based decision making, can further partition the systems into sub-categories of the initial, first-level system categorization. For example, a second-level categorization on a moderate-impact system can produce three new sub-categories: low-moderate systems, moderate-moderate systems, and high-moderate systems. This secondary categorization and the resulting sub-categories of the system give organizations an opportunity to further prioritize their investments related to security control selection and the tailoring of control baselines in responding to identified risks. Second-level categorization can also be used to determine those systems that are exceptionally critical to organizational missions and business operations. These systems are sometimes described as high-value assets and thus, organizations may be more focused on complexity, aggregation, and interconnections. Such systems can be identified by partitioning high-impact systems into low-high systems, moderate-high systems, and high-high systems.

Related Controls: None.

References: FIPS Publications 199, 200; NIST Special Publications 800-30, 800-39, 800-60-1, 800-60-2.

RA-3   RISK ASSESSMENT

Control:

a.   Conduct a risk assessment, including the likelihood and magnitude of harm, from:

1.   The unauthorized access, use, disclosure, disruption, modification, or destruction of the system, the information it processes, stores, or transmits, and any related information; and

2.   Privacy-related problems for individuals arising from the intentional processing of personally identifiable information;

b.   Integrate risk assessment results and risk management decsions from the organization and missions/business process perspectives with system-level risk assessments;

c.   Document risk assessment results in [Selection: security and privacy plans; risk assessment report; [Assignment: organization-defined document]];

d.   Review risk assessment results [*Assignment: organization-defined frequency*];

e.   Disseminate risk assessment results to [*Assignment: organization-defined personnel or roles*]; and

f.   Update the risk assessment [*Assignment: organization-defined frequency*] or when there are significant changes to the system, its environment of operation, or other conditions that may impact the security or privacy state of the system.

Supplemental Guidance: Clearly defined authorization boundaries are a prerequisite for effective risk assessments. Risk assessments consider threats, vulnerabilities, likelihood, and impact to organizational operations and assets, individuals, other organizations, and the Nation based on the operation and use of systems. Risk assessments also take into account risk from external parties including, for example, individuals accessing organizational systems; contractors operating systems on behalf of the organization; service providers; and outsourcing entities.

Organizations can conduct risk assessments, either formal or informal, at all three tiers in the risk management hierarchy (i.e., organization level, mission/business process level, or system level) and at any phase in the system development life cycle. Risk assessments can also be conducted at various steps in the Risk Management Framework, including categorization, control selection, control implementation, control assessment, system authorization, and control monitoring. In addition to the information processed, stored, and transmitted by the system, risk assessments can also address any information related to the system including, for example, system design, the intended use of the system, testing results, and other supply chain-related information or artifacts. Assessments of risk can play an important role in security and privacy control selection processes, particularly during the application of tailoring guidance.

Related Controls: CA-3, CP-6, CP-7, IA-8, MA-5, PE-3, PE-18, PL-2, PL-10, PL-11, PM-8, PM-9, PM-32, RA-2, RA-5, RA-7, SA-9, SC-38, SI-12.

Control Enhancements:

(1)   RISK ASSESSMENT | SUPPLY CHAIN RISK ASSESSMENT

   (a)   Assess supply chain risks associated with [*Assignment: organization-defined systems, system components, and system services*]; and

   (b)   Update the supply chain risk assessment [*Assignment: organization-defined frequency*], when there are significant changes to the relevant supply chain, or when changes to the system, environments of operation, or other conditions may necessitate a change in the supply chain.

   Supplemental Guidance: Supply chain-related events include, for example, disruption, theft, use of defective components, insertion of counterfeits, malicious development practices, improper delivery practices, and insertion of malicious code. These events can have a significant impact on the confidentiality, integrity, or availability of a system and its information and therefore, can also adversely impact organizational operations (including mission, functions, image, or reputation), organizational assets, individuals, other organizations, and the Nation. The supply chain-related events may be unintentional or malicious and can occur at any point during the system life cycle. An analysis of supply chain risk can help an organization identify systems or components for which additional supply chain risk mitigations are required.

   Related Controls: RA-2, RA-9, PM-17, SA-12.

References: NIST Special Publications 800-30, 800-39, 800-161; NIST Interagency Report 8023.

RA-4   RISK ASSESSMENT UPDATE

[Withdrawn: Incorporated into RA-3].

RA-5 VULNERABILITY SCANNING

Control:

a. Scan for vulnerabilities in the system and hosted applications [*Assignment: organization-defined frequency and/or randomly in accordance with organization-defined process*] and when new vulnerabilities potentially affecting the system are identified and reported;

b. Employ vulnerability scanning tools and techniques that facilitate interoperability among tools and automate parts of the vulnerability management process by using standards for:

   1. Enumerating platforms, software flaws, and improper configurations;

   2. Formatting checklists and test procedures; and

   3. Measuring vulnerability impact;

c. Analyze vulnerability scan reports and results from control assessments;

d. Remediate legitimate vulnerabilities [*Assignment: organization-defined response times*] in accordance with an organizational assessment of risk;

e. Share information obtained from the vulnerability scanning process and control assessments with [*Assignment: organization-defined personnel or roles*] to help eliminate similar vulnerabilities in other systems; and

f. Employ vulnerability scanning tools that include the capability to readily update the vulnerabilities to be scanned.

Supplemental Guidance: Security categorization of information and systems guides the frequency and comprehensiveness of vulnerability scans. Organizations determine the required vulnerability scanning for system components, ensuring that the potential sources of vulnerabilities such as networked printers, scanners, and copiers are not overlooked. The vulnerabilities to be scanned need to be readily updated as new vulnerabilities are discovered, announced, and scanning methods developed. This process helps to ensure that potential vulnerabilities in the system are identified and addressed as quickly as possible. Vulnerability analyses for custom software may require additional approaches such as static analysis, dynamic analysis, binary analysis, or a hybrid of the three approaches. Organizations can use these analysis approaches in source code reviews and in a variety of tools including, for example, web-based application scanners, static analysis tools, and binary analyzers. Vulnerability scanning includes, for example, scanning for patch levels; scanning for functions, ports, protocols, and services that should not be accessible to users or devices; and scanning for improperly configured or incorrectly operating information flow control mechanisms. Scanning tools that facilitate interoperability include, for example, products that are Security Content Automated Protocol (SCAP) validated. Thus, organizations consider using scanning tools that express vulnerabilities in the Common Vulnerabilities and Exposures (CVE) naming convention and that use the Open Vulnerability Assessment Language (OVAL) to determine the presence of vulnerabilities. Sources for vulnerability information include, for example, the Common Weakness Enumeration (CWE) listing and the National Vulnerability Database (NVD). Control assessments such as red team exercises provide additional sources of potential vulnerabilities for which to scan. Organizations also consider using scanning tools that express vulnerability impact by the Common Vulnerability Scoring System (CVSS).

Related Controls: CA-2, CA-7, CM-2, CM-4, CM-6, CM-8, RA-2, RA-3, SA-11, SA-12, SA-15, SC-38, SI-2, SI-3, SI-4, SI-7.

Control Enhancements:

(1) VULNERABILITY SCANNING | UPDATE TOOL CAPABILITY

   [Withdrawn: Incorporated into RA-5].

(2) VULNERABILITY SCANNING | UPDATE BY FREQUENCY, PRIOR TO NEW SCAN, OR WHEN IDENTIFIED

   Update the system vulnerabilities to be scanned [*Selection (one or more):* [*Assignment: organization-defined frequency*]; *prior to a new scan; when new vulnerabilities are identified and reported*].

⁹⁰⁰⁹⁰⁰⁰⁰⁰⁰⁰⁰⁰⁰⁰⁰ ⁰⁰⁰⁰⁰⁰⁰⁰ ⁰⁰⁰⁰⁰,

Related Controls: SI-5.

(3) VULNERABILITY SCANNING | BREADTH AND DEPTH OF COVERAGE

Employ vulnerability scanning procedures that can identify the breadth and depth of coverage.

Supplemental Guidance: The identification of the breadth and depth of coverage can include, for example, the system components scanned and the vulnerabilities checked.

Related Controls: None.

(4) VULNERABILITY SCANNING | DISCOVERABLE INFORMATION

Determine unintended discoverable information about the system and take [*Assignment: organization-defined corrective actions*].

Supplemental Guidance: Discoverable information includes information that adversaries could obtain without directly compromising or breaching the system, for example, by collecting information the system is exposing or by conducting extensive searches of the web. Corrective actions can include, for example, notifying appropriate organizational personnel, removing designated information, or changing the system to make designated information less relevant or attractive to adversaries.

Related Controls: AU-13.

(5) VULNERABILITY SCANNING | PRIVILEGED ACCESS

Implements privileged access authorization to [*Assignment: organization-identified system components*] for [*Assignment: organization-defined vulnerability scanning activities*].

Supplemental Guidance: In certain situations, the nature of the vulnerability scanning may be more intrusive or the system component that is the subject of the scanning may contain classified or controlled unclassified information. Privileged access authorization to selected system components facilitates more thorough vulnerability scanning and protects the sensitive nature of such scanning.

Related Controls: None.

(6) VULNERABILITY SCANNING | AUTOMATED TREND ANALYSES

Employ automated mechanisms to compare the results of vulnerability scans over time to determine trends in system vulnerabilities.

Supplemental Guidance: None.

Related Controls: None.

(7) VULNERABILITY SCANNING | AUTOMATED DETECTION AND NOTIFICATION OF UNAUTHORIZED COMPONENTS
[Withdrawn: Incorporated into CM-8].

(8) VULNERABILITY SCANNING | REVIEW HISTORIC AUDIT LOGS

Review historic audit logs to determine if a vulnerability identified in the system has been previously exploited.

Supplemental Guidance: None.

Related Controls: AU-6, AU-11.

(9) VULNERABILITY SCANNING | PENETRATION TESTING AND ANALYSES
[Withdrawn: Incorporated into CA-8].

(10) VULNERABILITY SCANNING | CORRELATE SCANNING INFORMATION

Correlate the output from vulnerability scanning tools to determine the presence of multi-vulnerability and multi-hop attack vectors.

Supplemental Guidance: None.

Related Controls: None.

References: NIST Special Publications 800-40, 800-70, 800-115, 800-126; NIST Interagency Reports 7788, 8023.

RA-6   TECHNICAL SURVEILLANCE COUNTERMEASURES SURVEY

<u>Control</u>: Employ a technical surveillance countermeasures survey at [*Assignment: organization-defined locations*] [*Selection (one or more)*: [*Assignment: organization-defined frequency*]; [*Assignment: organization-defined events or indicators occur*]].

<u>Supplemental Guidance</u>: Technical surveillance countermeasures surveys are performed by qualified personnel. Organizations use such surveys to detect the presence of technical surveillance devices and hazards and to identify technical security weaknesses that could aid in the conduct of technical penetrations of surveyed facilities. In addition, technical surveillance countermeasures surveys provide evaluations of the technical security posture of organizations and facilities and include thorough visual, electronic, and physical examinations of surveyed facilities, both internally and externally. The surveys also provide useful input for organizational risk assessments and critical information regarding organizational exposure to potential adversaries.

<u>Related Controls</u>: None.

<u>Control Enhancements</u>: None.

<u>References</u>: None.

RA-7   RISK RESPONSE

<u>Control</u>: Respond to findings from security and privacy assessments, monitoring, and audits.

<u>Supplemental Guidance</u>: Organizations have a variety of options for responding to risk including: mitigating the risk by implementing new controls or strengthening existing controls; accepting the risk with appropriate justification or rationale; sharing or transferring the risk; or rejecting the risk. Organizational risk tolerance influences risk response decisions and actions. Risk response is also known as risk treatment. This control addresses the need to determine an appropriate response to risk before a plan of action and milestones entry is generated. For example, the response may be to accept risk or reject risk, or it may be possible to mitigate the risk immediately so a plan of action and milestones entry is not needed. However, if the risk response is to mitigate the risk and the mitigation cannot be completed immediately, a plan of action and milestones entry is generated.

<u>Related Controls</u>: CA-5, IR-9, PM-4, PM-32, RA-2, RA-3.

<u>Control Enhancements</u>: None.

<u>References</u>: FIPS Publications <u>199</u>, <u>200</u>; NIST Special Publications <u>800-30</u>, <u>800-37</u>, <u>800-39</u>, <u>800-160</u>.

RA-8   PRIVACY IMPACT ASSESSMENTS

<u>Control</u>: Conduct privacy impact assessments for systems, programs, or other activities that pose a privacy risk before:

a.   Developing or procuring information technology that collects, maintains, or disseminates information that is in an identifiable form; and

b.   Initiating a new collection of information that:

   1.   Will be collected, maintained, or disseminated using information technology; and

   2.   Includes information in an identifiable form permitting the physical or online contacting of a specific individual, if identical questions have been posed to, or identical reporting requirements imposed on, ten or more persons, other than agencies, instrumentalities, or employees of the Federal Government.

<u>Supplemental Guidance</u>: Privacy impact assessments are an analysis of how information is managed to ensure that such management conforms to applicable legal, regulatory, and policy requirements regarding privacy; to determine the associated privacy risks and effects of creating, collecting, using, processing, storing, maintaining, disseminating, disclosing, and disposing of information in

identifiable form in a system and to examine and evaluate the protections and alternate processes for managing information to mitigate potential privacy concerns. A privacy impact assessment is an analysis and a formal document detailing the process and outcome of the analysis. To conduct the analysis, organizations use risk assessment processes. Although privacy impact assessments may be required by law, organizations may develop policies to require privacy impact assessments in circumstances where a privacy impact assessment would not be required by law.

Related Controls: IP-4, PA-2, PA-3, RA-1, RA-3, RA-7.

Control Enhancements: None.

References: None.

RA-9   CRITICALITY ANALYSIS

Control: Identify critical system components and functions by performing a criticality analysis for [*Assignment: organization-defined systems, system components, or system services*] at [*Assignment: organization-defined decision points in the system development life cycle*].

Supplemental Guidance: Not all system components, functions, or services necessarily require significant protections. Criticality analysis is a key tenet of, for example, supply chain risk management, and informs the prioritization of protection activities. The identification of critical system components and functions considers applicable regulations, directives, policies, standards, and guidelines, system functionality requirements, system and component interfaces, and system and component dependencies. Systems engineers conduct an end-to-end functional decomposition of a system to identify mission-critical functions and components. The functional decomposition includes the identification of core organizational missions supported by the system, decomposition into the specific functions to perform those missions, and traceability to the hardware, software, and firmware components that implement those functions, including when the functions are shared by many components within and beyond the system boundary.

The operational environment of a system or component may impact the criticality including, for example, the connections to and dependencies on cyber-physical systems, devices, system-of-systems, and outsourced IT services. System components that allow unmediated access to critical system components or functions are considered critical due to the inherent vulnerabilities such components create. Component and function criticality are assessed in terms of the impact of a component or function failure on the organizational missions supported by the system containing those components and functions. A criticality analysis is performed when an architecture or design is being developed, modified, or upgraded. If done early in the system life cycle, organizations may consider modifying the system design to reduce the critical nature of these components and functions by, for example, adding redundancy or alternate paths into the system design.

Related Controls: CP-2, PL-2, PL-8, PL-11, PM-1, SA-8, SA-12, SA-15, SA-20.

Control Enhancements: None.

References: None.

3.18 SYSTEM AND SERVICES ACQUISITION

Quick link to System and Services Acquisition summary table

SA-1 SYSTEM AND SERVICES ACQUISITION POLICY AND PROCEDURES

Control:

a. Develop, document, and disseminate to [*Assignment: organization-defined personnel or roles*]:

   1. A system and services acquisition policy that:

      (a) Addresses purpose, scope, roles, responsibilities, management commitment, coordination among organizational entities, and compliance; and

      (b) Is consistent with applicable laws, Executive Orders, directives, regulations, policies, standards, and guidelines; and

   2. Procedures to facilitate the implementation of the system and services acquisition policy and the associated system and services acquisition controls;

b. Designate an [*Assignment: organization-defined senior management official*] to manage the system and services acquisition policy and procedures;

c. Review and update the current system and services acquisition:

   1. Policy [*Assignment: organization-defined frequency*]; and

   2. Procedures [*Assignment: organization-defined frequency*];

d. Ensure that the system and services acquisition procedures implement the system and services acquisition policy and controls; and

e. Develop, document, and implement remediation actions for violations of the system and services acquisition policy.

Supplemental Guidance: This control addresses the establishment of policy and procedures for the effective implementation of the controls and control enhancements in the SA family. The risk management strategy is an important factor in establishing policy and procedures. Comprehensive policy and procedures help provide security and privacy assurance. Security and privacy program policies and procedures at the organization level may make the need for system-specific policies and procedures unnecessary. The policy can be included as part of the general security and privacy policy or can be represented by multiple policies reflecting the complex nature of organizations. The procedures can be established for security and privacy programs and for systems, if needed. Procedures describe how policies or controls are implemented and can be directed at the personnel or role that is the object of the procedure. Procedures can be documented in system security and privacy plans or in one or more separate documents. It is important to recognize that restating controls does not constitute an organizational policy or procedure.

Related Controls: PM-9, PS-8, SI-12.

Control Enhancements: None.

References: NIST Special Publications 800-12, 800-30, 800-39, 800-100.

SA-2 ALLOCATION OF RESOURCES

Control:

a. Determine information security and privacy requirements for the system or system service in mission and business process planning;

b. Determine, document, and allocate the resources required to protect the system or system service as part of the organizational capital planning and investment control process; and

c. Establish a discrete line item for information security and privacy in organizational programming and budgeting documentation.

Supplemental Guidance: Resource allocation for information security and privacy includes funding for system or service acquisition, sustainment, and supply chain concerns throughout the system development life cycle.

Related Controls: PL-7, PM-3, PM-11, SA-9.

Control Enhancements: None.

References: NIST Special Publication 800-65.

SA-3   SYSTEM DEVELOPMENT LIFE CYCLE

Control:

a. Manage the system using [*Assignment: organization-defined system development life cycle*] that incorporates information security and privacy considerations;

b. Define and document information security and privacy roles and responsibilities throughout the system development life cycle;

c. Identify individuals having information security and privacy roles and responsibilities; and

d. Integrate the organizational information security and privacy risk management process into system development life cycle activities.

Supplemental Guidance: A system development life cycle process provides the foundation for the successful development, implementation, and operation of organizational systems. To apply the required security and privacy controls within the system development life cycle requires a basic understanding of information security and privacy, threats, vulnerabilities, adverse impacts, and risk to critical missions and business functions. The security engineering principles in SA-8 help individuals properly design, code, and test systems and system components. Organizations include qualified personnel including, for example, chief information security officers, security architects, security engineers, system security officers, and chief privacy officers in system development life cycle processes to ensure that established security and privacy requirements are incorporated into organizational systems. It is also important that developers include individuals on the development team that possess the requisite security and privacy expertise and skills to ensure that the needed security and privacy capabilities are effectively integrated into the system. Role-based security and privacy training programs can ensure that individuals having key security and privacy roles and responsibilities have the experience, skills, and expertise to conduct assigned system development life cycle activities. The effective integration of security and privacy requirements into enterprise architecture also ensures that important security and privacy considerations are addressed early in the system life cycle and that those considerations are directly related to organizational mission and business processes. This process also facilitates the integration of the information security and privacy architectures into the enterprise architecture, consistent with risk management strategy of the organization. Because the development life cycle of a system involves multiple organizations, including, for example, external suppliers, developers, integrators, and service providers, it is important to recognize that acquisition and supply chain risk management functions and controls play a significant role in the overall effective management of the system during that life cycle.

Related Controls: AT-3, PL-8, PM-7, SA-4, SA-5, SA-8, SA-11, SA-12, SA-15, SA-17, SA-18, SA-22.

Control Enhancements:

(1) SYSTEM DEVELOPMENT LIFE CYCLE | MANAGE DEVELOPMENT ENVIRONMENT

Protect system development, test, and integration environments commensurate with risk throughout the system development life cycle for the system, system component, or system service.

Supplemental Guidance: None.

Related Controls: CM-2, CM-4, RA-3, SA-4.

(2) SYSTEM DEVELOPMENT LIFE CYCLE | USE OF LIVE DATA

(a) **Approve, document, and control the use of live data in development, test, and integration environments for the system, system component, or system service; and**

(b) **Ensure development, test, and integration environments for the system, system component, or system service are protected at the same impact or classification level as any live data used.**

Supplemental Guidance: Live data is also referred to as operational data. The use of live data in preproduction environments can result in significant risk to organizations. Organizations can minimize such risk by using test or dummy data during the design, development, and testing of systems, system components, and system services.

Related Controls: RA-3.

(3) SYSTEM DEVELOPMENT LIFE CYCLE | TECHNOLOGY REFRESH

Plan for and implement a technology refresh schedule to support the system throughout the system development life cycle.

Supplemental Guidance: Technology refresh planning may encompass hardware, software, firmware, processes, personnel skill sets, suppliers, service providers, and facilities. The use of obsolete or nearing obsolete technology may increase security and privacy risks associated with, for example, unsupported components, components unable to implement security or privacy requirements, counterfeit or re-purposed components, slow or inoperable components, components from untrusted sources, inadvertent personnel error, or increased complexity.

Related Controls: None.

References: NIST Special Publications 800-30, 800-37, 800-64.

SA-4   ACQUISITION PROCESS

Control: Include the following requirements, descriptions, and criteria, explicitly or by reference, in the acquisition contract for the system, system component, or system service:

a. Security and privacy functional requirements;

b. Strength of mechanism requirements;

c. Security and privacy assurance requirements;

d. Security and privacy documentation requirements;

e. Requirements for protecting security and privacy documentation;

f. Description of the system development environment and environment in which the system is intended to operate;

g. Allocation of responsibility or identification of parties responsible for information security, privacy, and supply chain risk management; and

h. Acceptance criteria.

Supplemental Guidance: System components are discrete, identifiable information technology assets including, for example, hardware, software, or firmware. These components represent the building blocks of a system. System components typically consist of commercial information technology products. Security and privacy functional requirements include security and privacy capabilities, functions, and mechanisms. Strength requirements associated with such capabilities, functions, and mechanisms include integrity protection measures, limitations to tampering or bypass, and resistance to direct attack. Security and privacy assurance requirements include development processes, procedures, practices, and methodologies; and the evidence from development and assessment activities providing grounds for confidence that the required security and privacy functionality is implemented and possesses the required strength of mechanism. Security and privacy documentation requirements address all phases of the system development life cycle.

Security and privacy requirements are expressed in terms of security and privacy controls and control enhancements that have been selected through the tailoring process. The tailoring process includes, for example, the specification of parameter values using assignment and selection statements and platform dependencies and implementation information. Security and privacy documentation provides user and administrator guidance regarding the implementation and operation of security and privacy controls. The level of detail required in such documentation is based on the security categorization or classification level of the system and the degree to which organizations depend on the stated security or privacy capabilities, functions, or mechanisms to meet overall risk response expectations. Security and privacy requirements can include mandated configuration settings specifying allowed functions, ports, protocols, and services. Acceptance criteria for systems, system components, and system services are defined in the same manner as such criteria for any organizational acquisition or procurement.

Related Controls: CM-6, CM-8, PS-7, SA-3, SA-5, SA-8, SA-11, SA-12, SA-15, SA-16, SA-17, SA-21.

Control Enhancements:

(1) ACQUISITION PROCESS | FUNCTIONAL PROPERTIES OF CONTROLS

Require the developer of the system, system component, or system service to provide a description of the functional properties of the controls to be implemented.

Supplemental Guidance: Functional properties of security and privacy controls describe the functionality (i.e., security or privacy capability, functions, or mechanisms) visible at the interfaces of the controls and specifically exclude functionality and data structures internal to the operation of the controls.

Related Controls: None.

(2) ACQUISITION PROCESS | DESIGN AND IMPLEMENTATION INFORMATION FOR CONTROLS

Require the developer of the system, system component, or system service to provide design and implementation information for the selected controls that includes: [Selection (one or more): security-relevant external system interfaces; high-level design; low-level design; source code or hardware schematics; [Assignment: organization-defined design and implementation information]] at [Assignment: organization-defined level of detail].

Supplemental Guidance: Organizations may require different levels of detail in design and implementation documentation for controls implemented in organizational systems, system components, or system services based on mission and business requirements; requirements for trustworthiness and resiliency; and requirements for analysis and testing. Systems can be partitioned into multiple subsystems. Each subsystem within the system can contain one or more modules. The high-level design for the system is expressed in terms of subsystems and the interfaces between subsystems providing security-relevant functionality. The low-level design for the system is expressed in terms of modules and the interfaces between modules providing security-relevant functionality. Design and implementation documentation may include information such as manufacturer, version, serial number, verification hash signature, software libraries used, date of purchase or download, and the vendor or download source. Source code and hardware schematics are referred to as the implementation representation of the system.

Related Controls: None.

(3) ACQUISITION PROCESS | DEVELOPMENT METHODS, TECHNIQUES, AND PRACTICES

Require the developer of the system, system component, or system service to demonstrate the use of a system development life cycle process that includes [Assignment: organization-defined systems engineering methods; [Selection (one or more): systems security engineering methods;

privacy engineering methods]; software development methods; testing, evaluation, assessment, verification, and validation methods; and quality control processes].

Supplemental Guidance: Following a system development life cycle that includes state-of-the-practice software development methods, systems engineering methods, systems security and privacy engineering methods, and quality control processes helps to reduce the number and severity of latent errors within systems, system components, and system services. Reducing the number and severity of such errors reduces the number of vulnerabilities in those systems, components, and services.

Related Controls: None.

(4) ACQUISITION PROCESS | ASSIGNMENT OF COMPONENTS TO SYSTEMS

[Withdrawn: Incorporated into CM-8(9)].

(5) ACQUISITION PROCESS | SYSTEM, COMPONENT, AND SERVICE CONFIGURATIONS

Require the developer of the system, system component, or system service to:

(d) Deliver the system, component, or service with [*Assignment: organization-defined security configurations*] implemented; and

(e) Use the configurations as the default for any subsequent system, component, or service reinstallation or upgrade.

Supplemental Guidance: Security configurations include, for example, the U.S. Government Configuration Baseline (USGCB) and any limitations on functions, ports, protocols, and services. Security characteristics include, for example, requiring that default passwords have been changed.

Related Controls: None.

(6) ACQUISITION PROCESS | USE OF INFORMATION ASSURANCE PRODUCTS

(a) Employ only government off-the-shelf or commercial off-the-shelf information assurance and information assurance-enabled information technology products that compose an NSA-approved solution to protect classified information when the networks used to transmit the information are at a lower classification level than the information being transmitted; and

(b) Ensure that these products have been evaluated and/or validated by NSA or in accordance with NSA-approved procedures.

Supplemental Guidance: Commercial off-the-shelf IA or IA-enabled information technology products used to protect classified information by cryptographic means may be required to use NSA-approved key management.

Related Controls: SC-8, SC-12, SC-13.

(7) ACQUISITION PROCESS | NIAP-APPROVED PROTECTION PROFILES

(a) Limit the use of commercially provided information assurance and information assurance-enabled information technology products to those products that have been successfully evaluated against a National Information Assurance partnership (NIAP)-approved Protection Profile for a specific technology type, if such a profile exists; and

(b) Require, if no NIAP-approved Protection Profile exists for a specific technology type but a commercially provided information technology product relies on cryptographic functionality to enforce its security policy, that the cryptographic module is FIPS-validated or NSA-approved.

Supplemental Guidance: None.

Related Controls: IA-7, SC-12, SC-13.

(8) ACQUISITION PROCESS | CONTINUOUS MONITORING PLAN FOR CONTROLS

Require the developer of the system, system component, or system service to produce a plan for continuous monitoring of security and privacy control effectiveness that contains the following: [*Assignment: organization-defined level of detail*].

Supplemental Guidance: The objective of continuous monitoring plans is to determine if the complete set of planned, required, and deployed security and privacy controls within the system, system component, or system service continue to be effective over time based on the inevitable changes that occur. Developer continuous monitoring plans include a sufficient level of detail such that the information can be incorporated into the continuous monitoring strategies and programs implemented by organizations.

Related Controls: CA-7.

(9) ACQUISITION PROCESS | FUNCTIONS, PORTS, PROTOCOLS, AND SERVICES IN USE

Require the developer of the system, system component, or system service to identify the functions, ports, protocols, and services intended for organizational use.

Supplemental Guidance: The identification of functions, ports, protocols, and services early in the system development life cycle, for example, during the initial requirements definition and design phases, allows organizations to influence the design of the system, system component, or system service. This early involvement in the system life cycle helps organizations to avoid or minimize the use of functions, ports, protocols, or services that pose unnecessarily high risks and understand the trade-offs involved in blocking specific ports, protocols, or services or when requiring system service providers to do so. Early identification of functions, ports, protocols, and services avoids costly retrofitting of controls after the system, component, or system service has been implemented. SA-9 describes the requirements for external system services with organizations identifying which functions, ports, protocols, and services are provided from external sources.

Related Controls: CM-7, SA-9.

(10) ACQUISITION PROCESS | USE OF APPROVED PIV PRODUCTS

Employ only information technology products on the FIPS 201-approved products list for Personal Identity Verification (PIV) capability implemented within organizational systems.

Supplemental Guidance: None.

Related Controls: IA-2, IA-8, PM-9.

References: ISO/IEC 15408; FIPS Publications 140-2, 201; NIST Special Publications 800-23, 800-35, 800-36, 800-37, 800-64, 800-70, 800-73, 800-137, 800-161; NIST Interagency Reports 7539, 7622, 7676, 7870, 8062.

SA-5   SYSTEM DOCUMENTATION

Control:

a. Obtain administrator documentation for the system, system component, or system service that describes:

   1. Secure configuration, installation, and operation of the system, component, or service;

   2. Effective use and maintenance of security and privacy functions and mechanisms; and

   3. Known vulnerabilities regarding configuration and use of administrative or privileged functions;

b. Obtain user documentation for the system, system component, or system service that describes:

   1. User-accessible security and privacy functions and mechanisms and how to effectively use those functions and mechanisms;

   2. Methods for user interaction, which enables individuals to use the system, component, or service in a more secure manner and protect individual privacy; and

   3. User responsibilities in maintaining the security of the system, component, or service and privacy of individuals;

c. Document attempts to obtain system, system component, or system service documentation when such documentation is either unavailable or nonexistent and takes [*Assignment: organization-defined actions*] in response;

d. Protect documentation as required, in accordance with the organizational risk management strategy; and

e. Distribute documentation to [*Assignment: organization-defined personnel or roles*].

Supplemental Guidance: This control helps organizational personnel understand the implementation and operation of security and privacy controls associated with systems, system components, and system services. Organizations consider establishing specific measures to determine the quality and completeness of the content provided. System documentation may be used, for example, to support the management of supply chain risk, incident response, and other functions. Personnel or roles requiring documentation may include, for example, system owners, system security officers, and system administrators. Attempts to obtain documentation may include, for example, directly contacting manufacturers or suppliers and conducting web-based searches. The inability to obtain needed documentation may occur, for example, due to the age of the system or component or lack of support from developers and contractors. In those situations, organizations may need to recreate selected documentation if such documentation is essential to the implementation or operation of the security and privacy controls. The level of protection provided for the system, component, or service documentation is commensurate with the security category or classification of the system. Documentation that addresses system vulnerabilities may require an increased level of protection. Secure operation of the system, includes, for example, initially starting the system and resuming secure system operation after any lapse in system operation.

Related Controls: CM-4, CM-6, CM-7, CM-8, PL-2, PL-4, PL-8, PS-2, SA-3, SA-4, SA-9, SA-10, SA-11, SA-15, SA-16, SA-17, SI-12.

Control Enhancements:

(1) SYSTEM DOCUMENTATION | FUNCTIONAL PROPERTIES OF SECURITY CONTROLS
[Withdrawn: Incorporated into SA-4(1)].

(2) SYSTEM DOCUMENTATION | SECURITY-RELEVANT EXTERNAL SYSTEM INTERFACES
[Withdrawn: Incorporated into SA-4(2)].

(3) SYSTEM DOCUMENTATION | HIGH-LEVEL DESIGN
[Withdrawn: Incorporated into SA-4(2)].

(4) SYSTEM DOCUMENTATION | LOW-LEVEL DESIGN
[Withdrawn: Incorporated into SA-4(2)].

(5) SYSTEM DOCUMENTATION | SOURCE CODE
[Withdrawn: Incorporated into SA-4(2)].

References: None.

SA-6 SOFTWARE USAGE RESTRICTIONS

[Withdrawn: Incorporated into CM-10 and SI-7].

SA-7 USER-INSTALLED SOFTWARE

[Withdrawn: Incorporated into CM-11 and SI-7].

SA-8 SECURITY AND PRIVACY ENGINEERING PRINCIPLES

Control: Apply [*Assignment: organization-defined systems security engineering principles*] in the specification, design, development, implementation, and modification of the system and system components.

Supplemental Guidance: Organizations can apply systems security and privacy engineering principles to new systems under development or to systems undergoing upgrades. For legacy systems, organizations apply systems security and privacy engineering principles to system upgrades and modifications to the extent feasible, given the current state of hardware, software, and firmware components within those systems. The application of systems security and privacy engineering concepts and principles help to develop trustworthy, secure systems and system components and reduce the susceptibility of organizations to disruptions, hazards, threats, and creating privacy-related problems for individuals. Examples of these concepts and principles include, developing layered protections; establishing security and privacy policies, architecture, and controls as the foundation for design and development, incorporating security and privacy requirements into the system development life cycle; delineating physical and logical security boundaries; ensuring that developers are trained on how to build secure software; tailoring security and privacy controls to meet organizational and operational needs; performing threat modeling to identify use cases, threat agents, attack vectors and patterns, design patterns, and compensating controls needed to mitigate risk. Organizations that apply security and privacy engineering concepts and principles can facilitate the development of trustworthy, secure systems, system components, and system services; reduce risk to acceptable levels; and make informed risk management decisions. Security engineering principles can also be used to protect against certain supply chain risks including, for example, incorporating tamper-resistant hardware into a design.

Related Controls: PL-8, PM-7, RA-2, RA-3, RA-9, SA-3, SA-4, SA-12, SA-15, SA-17, SA-20, SC-2, SC-3, SC-32, SC-39.

Control Enhancements: None.

References: FIPS Publications 199, 200; NIST Special Publications 800-53A, 800-60-1, 800-60-2, 800-64, 800-160; NIST Interagency Report 8062.

SA-9   EXTERNAL SYSTEM SERVICES

Control:

a. Require that providers of external system services comply with organizational security and privacy requirements and employ [*Assignment: organization-defined security and privacy controls*];

b. Define and document organizational oversight and user roles and responsibilities with regard to external system services; and

c. Employ [*Assignment: organization-defined processes, methods, and techniques*] to monitor security and privacy control compliance by external service providers on an ongoing basis.

Supplemental Guidance: External system services are those services that are implemented external to authorization boundaries of organizational systems. This includes services that are used by, but not a part of, organizational systems. Organizations establish relationships with external service providers in a variety of ways including, for example, through business partnerships, contracts, interagency agreements, lines of business arrangements, licensing agreements, joint ventures, and supply chain exchanges. The responsibility for managing risks from the use of external system services remains with authorizing officials. For services external to organizations, a chain of trust requires that organizations establish and retain a level of confidence that each provider in the consumer-provider relationship provides adequate protection for the services rendered. The extent and nature of this chain of trust varies based on the relationships between organizations and the external providers. Organizations document the basis for trust relationships so the relationships can be monitored over time. External system services documentation includes government, service providers, end user security roles and responsibilities, and service-level agreements. Service-level agreements define expectations of performance for implemented security and privacy controls; describe measurable outcomes, and identify remedies and response requirements for identified instances of noncompliance.

Related Controls: CA-3, CP-2, IR-4, IR-7, PL-10, PL-11, PS-7, SA-2, SA-4, SA-12.

Control Enhancements:

(1) EXTERNAL SYSTEM SERVICES | RISK ASSESSMENTS AND ORGANIZATIONAL APPROVALS

    (a) Conduct an organizational assessment of risk prior to the acquisition or outsourcing of information security services; and

    (b) Verify that the acquisition or outsourcing of dedicated information security services is approved by [*Assignment: organization-defined personnel or roles*].

    Supplemental Guidance: Examples of information security services include the operation of security devices such as firewalls, or key management services; and incident monitoring, analysis and response. Risks assessed may include, for example, system-related, mission-related, privacy-related, or supply chain-related risks.

Related Controls: CA-6, RA-3.

(2) EXTERNAL SYSTEM SERVICES | IDENTIFICATION OF FUNCTIONS, PORTS, PROTOCOLS, AND SERVICES

Require providers of [*Assignment: organization-defined external system services*] to identify the functions, ports, protocols, and other services required for the use of such services.

Supplemental Guidance: Information from external service providers regarding the specific functions, ports, protocols, and services used in the provision of such services can be useful when the need arises to understand the trade-offs involved in restricting certain functions and services or blocking certain ports and protocols.

Related Controls: CM-6, CM-7.

(3) EXTERNAL SYSTEM SERVICES | ESTABLISH AND MAINTAIN TRUST RELATIONSHIP WITH PROVIDERS

Establish, document, and maintain trust relationships with external service providers based on [*Assignment: organization-defined security and privacy requirements, properties, factors, or conditions defining acceptable trust relationships*].

Supplemental Guidance: The degree of confidence that the risk from using external services is at an acceptable level depends on the trust that organizations place in the external providers, individually or in combination. Trust relationships can help organizations to gain increased levels of confidence that participating service providers are providing adequate protection for the services rendered. They can also be useful when conducting incident response or when planning for upgrades or obsolescence. Trust relationships can be complicated due to the number of potential entities participating in the consumer-provider interactions, subordinate relationships and levels of trust, and types of interactions between the parties. In some cases, the degree of trust is based on the level of control organizations can exert on external service providers regarding the controls necessary for the protection of the service, information, or individual privacy and the evidence brought forth as to the effectiveness of the implemented controls. The level of control is established by the terms and conditions of the contracts or service-level agreements. Extensive control may include negotiating contracts or agreements that specify security and privacy requirements for providers. Limited control may include using contracts or service-level agreements to obtain commodity services such as commercial telecommunications services.

Related Controls: SA-12.

(4) EXTERNAL SYSTEM SERVICES | CONSISTENT INTERESTS OF CONSUMERS AND PROVIDERS

Take [*Assignment: organization-defined actions*] to verify that the interests of [*Assignment: organization-defined external service providers*] are consistent with and reflect organizational interests.

Supplemental Guidance: As organizations increasingly use external service providers, it is possible that the interests of the service providers may diverge from organizational interests. In such situations, simply having the required technical, management, or operational controls in place may not be sufficient if the providers that implement and manage those controls are not operating in a manner consistent with the interests of the consuming organizations. The actions that organizations might take to address such concerns include, for example, requiring background checks for selected service provider personnel; examining ownership records; employing only trustworthy service providers, including providers with which organizations have had successful trust relationships; and conducting routine periodic, unscheduled visits to service provider facilities.

Related Controls: None.

(5) EXTERNAL SYSTEM SERVICES | PROCESSING, STORAGE, AND SERVICE LOCATION

Restrict the location of [*Selection (one or more): information processing; information or data; system services*] to [*Assignment: organization-defined locations*] based on [*Assignment: organization-defined requirements or conditions*].

Supplemental Guidance: The location of information processing, information and data storage, or system services that are critical to organizations can have a direct impact on the ability of than organizations in successfully executing their mission and business functions. This occurs when external providers control the location of processing, storage, or services. The criteria that external providers use for the selection of processing, storage, or service locations may be different from the criteria organizations use. For example, organizations may desire that data or information storage locations are restricted to certain locations to help facilitate incident response activities in case of information security or privacy incidents. Such incident response activities including, for example, forensic analyses and after-the-fact investigations, may be adversely affected by the governing laws or protocols in the locations where processing and storage occur and/or the locations from which system services emanate.

Related Controls: SA-5, SA-12.

(6) EXTERNAL SYSTEM SERVICES | ORGANIZATION-CONTROLLED CRYPTOGRAPHIC KEYS
Maintain exclusive control of cryptographic keys.

Supplemental Guidance: Maintaining exclusive control of cryptographic keys in an external system prevents decryption of organizational data by external system staff. This enhancement can be implemented, for example, by encrypting and decrypting data inside the organization as data is sent to and received from the external system or through use of a component that permits encryption and decryption functions to be local to the external system, but allows the organization exclusive access to encryption keys.

Related Controls: SC-12, SC-13, SI-4.

(7) EXTERNAL SYSTEM SERVICES | ORGANIZATION-CONTROLLED INTEGRITY CHECKING
Provide the capability to check the integrity of organizational information while it resides in the external system.

Supplemental Guidance: Storage of organizational information in an external system could limit organizational visibility into the security status of its data. The ability for the organization to verify and validate the integrity of its stored data without transferring it out of the external system provides such visibility.

Related Controls: SI-7.

References: NIST Special Publications 800-35, 800-161.

SA-10 DEVELOPER CONFIGURATION MANAGEMENT

Control: Require the developer of the system, system component, or system service to:

a. Perform configuration management during system, component, or service [*Selection (one or more): design; development; implementation; operation; disposal*];

b. Document, manage, and control the integrity of changes to [*Assignment: organization-defined configuration items under configuration management*];

c. Implement only organization-approved changes to the system, component, or service;

d. Document approved changes to the system, component, or service and the potential security and privacy impacts of such changes; and

e. Track security flaws and flaw resolution within the system, component, or service and report findings to [*Assignment: organization-defined personnel*].

Supplemental Guidance: Organizations consider the quality and completeness of the configuration management activities conducted by developers as direct evidence of applying effective security controls. Controls include, for example, protecting from unauthorized modification or destruction, the master copies of material used to generate security-relevant portions of the system hardware, software, and firmware. Maintaining the integrity of changes to the system, system component, or system service requires strict configuration control throughout the system development life cycle to track authorized changes and to prevent unauthorized changes. The configuration items that are placed under configuration management include: the formal model; the functional, high-level, and low-level design specifications; other design data; implementation documentation; source code and hardware schematics; the current running version of the object code; tools for comparing new versions of security-relevant hardware descriptions and source code with previous versions; and test fixtures and documentation. Depending on the mission and business needs of organizations and the nature of the contractual relationships in place, developers may provide configuration management support during the operations and maintenance phases of the system life cycle.

Related Controls: CM-2, CM-3, CM-4, CM-7, CM-9, SA-4, SA-5, SA-12, SI-2.

Control Enhancements:

(1) DEVELOPER CONFIGURATION MANAGEMENT | SOFTWARE AND FIRMWARE INTEGRITY VERIFICATION

Require the developer of the system, system component, or system service to enable integrity verification of software and firmware components.

Supplemental Guidance: This control enhancement allows organizations to detect unauthorized changes to software and firmware components using developer-provided tools, techniques, and mechanisms. Integrity checking mechanisms can also address counterfeiting of software and firmware components. Organizations verify the integrity of software and firmware components, for example, through secure one-way hashes provided by developers. Delivered software and firmware components also include any updates to such components.

Related Controls: SI-7.

(2) DEVELOPER CONFIGURATION MANAGEMENT | ALTERNATIVE CONFIGURATION MANAGEMENT PROCESSES

Provide an alternate configuration management process using organizational personnel in the absence of a dedicated developer configuration management team.

Supplemental Guidance: Alternate configuration management processes may be required, for example, when organizations use commercial off-the-shelf information technology products. Alternate configuration management processes include organizational personnel that review and approve proposed changes to systems, system components, and system services; and that conduct security and privacy impact analyses prior to the implementation of changes to systems, components, or services.

Related Controls: None.

(3) DEVELOPER CONFIGURATION MANAGEMENT | HARDWARE INTEGRITY VERIFICATION

Require the developer of the system, system component, or system service to enable integrity verification of hardware components.

Supplemental Guidance: This control enhancement allows organizations to detect unauthorized changes to hardware components using developer-provided tools, techniques, methods, and mechanisms. Organizations verify the integrity of hardware components, for example, with hard-to-copy labels and verifiable serial numbers provided by developers, and by requiring the implementation of anti-tamper technologies. Delivered hardware components also include updates to such components.

Related Controls: SI-7.

(4) DEVELOPER CONFIGURATION MANAGEMENT | TRUSTED GENERATION

Require the developer of the system, system component, or system service to employ tools for comparing newly generated versions of security-relevant hardware descriptions, source code, and object code with previous versions.

Supplemental Guidance: This control enhancement addresses authorized changes to hardware, software, and firmware components between versions during development. The focus is on the efficacy of the configuration management process by the developer to ensure that newly generated versions of security-relevant hardware descriptions, source code, and object code continue to enforce the security policy for the system, system component, or system service. In contrast, SA-10(1) and SA-10(3) allow organizations to detect unauthorized changes to hardware, software, and firmware components using tools, techniques, and/or mechanisms provided by developers.

Related Controls: None.

(5)   DEVELOPER CONFIGURATION MANAGEMENT | MAPPING INTEGRITY FOR VERSION CONTROL

Require the developer of the system, system component, or system service to maintain the integrity of the mapping between the master build data (hardware drawings and software/firmware code) describing the current version of security-relevant hardware, software, and firmware and the on-site master copy of the data for the current version.

Supplemental Guidance: This control enhancement addresses changes to hardware, software, and firmware components during initial development and during system life cycle updates. Maintaining the integrity between the master copies of security-relevant hardware, software, and firmware (including designs and source code) and the equivalent data in master copies on-site in operational environments is essential to ensure the availability of organizational systems supporting critical missions and business functions.

Related Controls: None.

(6)   DEVELOPER CONFIGURATION MANAGEMENT | TRUSTED DISTRIBUTION

Require the developer of the system, system component, or system service to execute procedures for ensuring that security-relevant hardware, software, and firmware updates distributed to the organization are exactly as specified by the master copies.

Supplemental Guidance: The trusted distribution of security-relevant hardware, software, and firmware updates ensure that such updates are correct representations of the master copies maintained by the developer and have not been tampered with during distribution.

Related Controls: None.

References: FIPS Publications 140-2, 180-4, 202; NIST Special Publication 800-128.

SA-11 DEVELOPER TESTING AND EVALUATION

Control: Require the developer of the system, system component, or system service, at all post-design phases of the system development life cycle, to:

a.   Create and implement a security and privacy assessment plan;

b.   Perform [Selection (one or more): unit; integration; system; regression] testing/evaluation [Assignment: organization-defined frequency] at [Assignment: organization-defined depth and coverage];

c.   Produce evidence of the execution of the assessment plan and the results of the testing and evaluation;

d.   Implement a verifiable flaw remediation process; and

e.   Correct flaws identified during testing and evaluation.

Supplemental Guidance: Developmental testing and evaluation confirms that the required security and privacy controls are implemented correctly, operating as intended, enforcing the desired security and privacy policies, and meeting established security and privacy requirements. Security properties of systems and the privacy of individuals may be affected by the interconnection of system components or changes to those components. These interconnections or changes including, for example, upgrading or replacing applications, operating systems, and firmware, may adversely affect previously implemented security and privacy controls. This control provides additional types of testing and evaluation that developers can conduct to reduce or eliminate potential flaws. Testing custom software applications may require approaches such as static analysis, dynamic analysis, binary analysis, or a hybrid of the three approaches. Developers can use these analysis approaches in a variety of tools and in source code reviews. Security and privacy assessment plans provide the specific activities that developers plan to carry out including the types of analyses, testing, evaluation, and reviews of software and firmware components, the degree of rigor to be applied, and the types of artifacts produced during those processes. The depth of testing and evaluation refers to the rigor and level of detail associated with the assessment process. The coverage of testing and evaluation refers to the scope (i.e., number and type) of the artifacts included in the assessment process. Contracts specify the acceptance criteria for security and privacy assessment plans, flaw remediation processes, and the evidence that the plans and processes have been diligently applied. Methods for reviewing and protecting assessment plans, evidence, and documentation are commensurate with the security category or classification level of the system. Contracts may specify documentation protection requirements.

Related Controls: CA-2, CA-7, CM-4, SA-3, SA-4, SA-5, SA-12, SA-15, SA-17, SI-2.

Control Enhancements:

(1) DEVELOPER TESTING AND EVALUATION | STATIC CODE ANALYSIS

Require the developer of the system, system component, or system service to employ static code analysis tools to identify common flaws and document the results of the analysis.

Supplemental Guidance: Static code analysis provides a technology and methodology for security reviews and may include, for example, checking for weaknesses in the code and checking for incorporation of libraries or other included code with known vulnerabilities or that are out-of-date and not supported. Such analysis can be used to identify vulnerabilities and enforce secure coding practices. Static code analysis is most effective when used early in the development process, when each code change can be automatically scanned for potential weaknesses. Static analysis can provide clear remediation guidance along with defects to enable developers to fix such defects. Evidence of correct implementation of static analysis can include, for example, aggregate defect density for critical defect types; evidence that defects were inspected by developers or security professionals; and evidence that defects were remediated. An excessively high density of ignored findings, commonly referred to as false positives, indicates a potential problem with the analysis process or the analysis tool. In such cases, organizations weigh the validity of the evidence against evidence from other sources.

Related Controls: None.

(2) DEVELOPER TESTING AND EVALUATION | THREAT MODELING AND VULNERABILITY ANALYSES

Require the developer of the system, system component, or system service to perform threat modeling and vulnerability analyses at [*Assignment: organization-defined breadth and depth*] during development and during the subsequent testing and evaluation of the system, component, or service that:

(a) Uses [*Assignment: organization-defined information concerning impact, environment of operations, known or assumed threats, and acceptable risk levels*];

(b) Employs [*Assignment: organization-defined tools and methods*]; and

(c) Produces evidence that meets [*Assignment: organization-defined acceptance criteria*].

Supplemental Guidance: Systems, system components, and system services may deviate significantly from the functional and design specifications created during the requirements and design phases of the system development life cycle. Therefore, threat modeling and vulnerability analyses of those systems, system components, and system services prior to delivery are critical to the effective operation of those systems, components, and services. Threat modeling and vulnerability analyses at this phase of the system development life cycle ensure that design and implementation changes have been accounted for and vulnerabilities created because of those changes have been reviewed and mitigated.

Related controls: PM-15, RA-3, RA-5.

(3) DEVELOPER TESTING AND EVALUATION | INDEPENDENT VERIFICATION OF ASSESSMENT PLANS AND EVIDENCE

(a) Require an independent agent satisfying [*Assignment: organization-defined independence criteria*] to verify the correct implementation of the developer security and privacy assessment plans and the evidence produced during testing and evaluation; and

(b) Verify that the independent agent is provided with sufficient information to complete the verification process or granted the authority to obtain such information.

Supplemental Guidance: Independent agents have the necessary qualifications, including the expertise, skills, training, certifications, and experience, to verify the correct implementation of developer security and privacy assessment plans.

Related Controls: AT-3, RA-5.

(4)   DEVELOPER TESTING AND EVALUATION | MANUAL CODE REVIEWS

Require the developer of the system, system component, or system service to perform a manual code review of [Assignment: *organization-defined specific code*] using [Assignment: *organization-defined processes, procedures, and/or techniques*].

Supplemental Guidance: Manual code reviews are usually reserved for the critical software and firmware components of systems. Such code reviews are effective in identifying weaknesses that require knowledge of the application's requirements or context which in most cases, are unavailable to automated analytic tools and techniques including static and dynamic analysis. Components benefiting from manual review include, for example, verifying access control matrices against application controls and reviewing more detailed aspects of cryptographic implementations and controls.

Related Controls: None.

(5)   DEVELOPER TESTING AND EVALUATION | PENETRATION TESTING

Require the developer of the system, system component, or system service to perform penetration testing at [Assignment: *organization-defined breadth and depth*] and with [Assignment: *organization-defined constraints*].

Supplemental Guidance: Penetration testing is an assessment methodology in which assessors, using all available information technology product or system documentation and working under specific constraints, attempt to circumvent implemented security and privacy features of information technology products and systems. Useful information for assessors conducting penetration testing can include, for example, product and system design specifications, source code, and administrator and operator manuals. Penetration testing can include white-box, gray-box, or black box testing with associated analyses performed by skilled professionals simulating adversary actions. The objective of penetration testing is to uncover the potential vulnerabilities in systems, system components and services resulting from implementation errors, configuration faults, or other operational weaknesses or deficiencies. Penetration tests can be performed in conjunction with automated and manual code reviews to provide greater levels of analysis than would ordinarily be possible.

Related Controls: CA-8.

(6)   DEVELOPER TESTING AND EVALUATION | ATTACK SURFACE REVIEWS

Require the developer of the system, system component, or system service to perform attack surface reviews.

Supplemental Guidance: Attack surfaces of systems and system components are exposed areas that make those systems more vulnerable to attacks. This includes any accessible areas where weaknesses or deficiencies in the hardware, software, and firmware components provide opportunities for adversaries to exploit vulnerabilities. Attack surface reviews ensure that developers analyze the design and implementation changes to systems and mitigate attack vectors generated as a result of the changes. Correction of identified flaws includes, for example, deprecation of unsafe functions.

Related Controls: None.

(7)   DEVELOPER TESTING AND EVALUATION | VERIFY SCOPE OF TESTING AND EVALUATION

Require the developer of the system, system component, or system service to verify that the scope of testing and evaluation provides complete coverage of required security and privacy controls at [Assignment: *organization-defined depth of testing and evaluation*].

Supplemental Guidance: Verifying that testing and evaluation provides complete coverage of required security and privacy controls can be accomplished by a variety of analytic techniques ranging from informal to formal. Each of these techniques provides an increasing level of assurance corresponding to the degree of formality of the analysis. Rigorously demonstrating control coverage at the highest levels of assurance can be provided using formal modeling and analysis techniques including correlation between control implementation and corresponding test cases.

Related Controls: None.

(8) DEVELOPER TESTING AND EVALUATION | DYNAMIC CODE ANALYSIS

Require the developer of the system, system component, or system service to employ dynamic code analysis tools to identify common flaws and document the results of the analysis.

Supplemental Guidance: Dynamic code analysis provides run-time verification of software programs, using tools capable of monitoring programs for memory corruption, user privilege issues, and other potential security problems. Dynamic code analysis employs run-time tools to ensure that security functionality performs in the way it was designed. A specialized type of dynamic analysis, known as fuzz testing, induces program failures by deliberately introducing malformed or random data into software programs. Fuzz testing strategies derive from the intended use of applications and the associated functional and design specifications for the applications. To understand the scope of dynamic code analysis and hence the assurance provided, organizations may also consider conducting code coverage analysis (checking the degree to which the code has been tested using metrics such as percent of subroutines tested or percent of program statements called during execution of the test suite) and/or concordance analysis (checking for words that are out of place in software code such as non-English language words or derogatory terms).

Related Controls: None.

References: ISO/IEC 15408; NIST Special Publications 800-30, 800-53A, 800-154.

SA-12 SUPPLY CHAIN RISK MANAGEMENT

Control:

a. Employ [*Assignment: organization-defined supply chain safeguards*] to protect against supply chain risks to the system, system component, or system service and to limit the harm or consequences from supply chain-related events; and

b. Document the selected and implemented supply chain safeguards in [*Selection: security and privacy plans; supply chain risk management plan; [Assignment: organization-defined document]*].

Supplemental Guidance: Supply chain-related events including, for example, disruption, theft, insertion of counterfeits, insertion of malicious code, malicious development practices, improper delivery practices, and use of defective components, can adversely impact the confidentiality, integrity, or availability of information processed, stored, or transmitted by a system. Such events can also adversely impact organizational operations (including mission, functions, image, or reputation), organizational assets, individuals, other organizations, and the Nation. Supply chain-related events may be unintentional or malicious and occur at any point during the system life cycle. Managing supply chain risks involves gaining visibility and understanding of the processes and procedures used to protect the system, system component, or system service throughout the system life cycle. This allows organizations to make appropriate acquisition decisions and to identify appropriate mitigation strategies. A supply chain risk management plan includes, for example, an unambiguous expression of the supply chain risk tolerance for the system, acceptable supply chain risk mitigation strategies or controls, a description of and justification for supply chain protection measures taken, a process for consistently evaluating and monitoring supply chain risk, approaches for implementing and communicating the supply chain risk management plan, and associated roles and responsibilities.

Related Controls: AT-3, CM-8, IR-4, IR-6, MA-2, MA-6, PE-3, PE-16, PL-8, PM-31, RA-3, RA-7, RA-9, SA-2, SA-3, SA-4, SA-5, SA-8, SA-9, SA-10, SA-15, SA-18, SA-19, SC-7, SC-29, SC-30, SC-38, SI-7.

Control Enhancements:

(1) SUPPLY CHAIN RISK MANAGEMENT | ACQUISITION STRATEGIES, TOOLS, AND METHODS

Employ [*Assignment: organization-defined acquisition strategies, contract tools, and procurement methods*] to protect against, identify, and mitigate supply chain risks.

Supplemental Guidance: The use of the acquisition process early in the system development life cycle provides an important vehicle to protect the supply chain. There are many useful tools and techniques available, including, for example, obscuring the end use of a system or system component, using blind or filtered buys, requiring tamper-evident packaging, or using trusted or controlled distribution. The results from a supply chain risk assessment can inform which strategies, tools, and methods are most applicable to the situation. Tools and techniques may provide protections against the insertion of counterfeits, tampering, theft, unauthorized production, insertion of malicious software, as well as poor manufacturing and development practices throughout the system development life cycle. Organizations also consider creating incentives for suppliers who implement security and privacy controls; promote transparency into their organizational processes and security and privacy practices; provide additional vetting of the processes and practices of subordinate suppliers, critical system components, and services; restrict purchases from specific suppliers; and provide contract language that addresses the prohibition of tainted or counterfeit components. Finally, organizations consider providing training, education, and awareness programs for organizational personnel regarding supply chain risk, available mitigation strategies, and when they should be used. Methods for reviewing and protecting development plans, evidence, and documentation are commensurate with the security category or classification level of the information system. Contracts may specify documentation protection requirements.

Related Controls: None.

(2) SUPPLY CHAIN RISK MANAGEMENT | SUPPLIER REVIEWS

Review the supply chain-related risks associated with suppliers or contractors and the system, system component, or system service they provide [*Assignment: organization-defined frequency*].

Supplemental Guidance: A review of supplier risk may include, for example, the ability of the supplier to effectively assess or vet any subordinate second-tier and third-tier suppliers and contractors. These reviews may be conducted by the organization or by an independent third party. The reviews consider documented processes, documented controls, publicly available information related to the supplier or contractor, and all-source intelligence where possible. The organization can use open-source information to monitor for indications of stolen CUI, poor development and quality control practices, information spillage, or counterfeits. In some cases, it may be appropriate to share review results with other organizations in accordance with any applicable inter-organizational agreements or contracts.

Related Controls: None.

(3) SUPPLY CHAIN RISK MANAGEMENT | TRUSTED SHIPPING AND WAREHOUSING
[Withdrawn: Incorporated into SA-12(1)].

(4) SUPPLY CHAIN RISK MANAGEMENT | DIVERSITY OF SUPPLIERS
[Withdrawn: Incorporated into SA-12(13)].

(5) SUPPLY CHAIN RISK MANAGEMENT | LIMITATION OF HARM

Employ [*Assignment: organization-defined safeguards*] to limit harm from potential adversaries identifying and targeting the organizational supply chain.

Supplemental Guidance: Safeguards that can be implemented to reduce the probability of adversaries successfully identifying and targeting the supply chain include, for example, avoiding the purchase of custom or non-standardized configurations; employing a diverse set of suppliers; employing approved vendor lists with standing reputations in industry; using procurement carve outs that provide exclusions to commitments or obligations; and designing the system to include diversity of materials, components, and paths. In addition, organizations consider minimizing the time between purchase decisions and required delivery to limit the opportunities for adversaries to corrupt system components.

Related Controls: None.

(6) SUPPLY CHAIN RISK MANAGEMENT | MINIMIZING PROCUREMENT TIME
[Withdrawn: Incorporated into SA-12(1)].

(7) SUPPLY CHAIN RISK MANAGEMENT | ASSESSMENTS PRIOR TO SELECTION, ACCEPTANCE, AND UPDATE

Assess the system, system component, or system service prior to selection, acceptance, modification, or update.

Supplemental Guidance: Organizational personnel or independent, external entities conduct assessments of systems, components, products, tools, and services to uncover unintentional and intentional vulnerabilities, evidence of tampering, or evidence of non-compliance with supply chain controls. These include, for example, malicious code, malicious processes, defective software, and counterfeits. Assessments can include, for example, visual or physical inspection; evaluations; design proposal reviews; static and dynamic analyses; visual, x-ray, or magnetic particle inspections; simulations; white, gray, and black box testing; fuzz testing; stress testing; and penetration testing. Organizations can also ensure that the components or services are genuine by using, for example, tags, cryptographic hash verifications, or digital signatures. Evidence generated during security assessments is documented for follow-on actions carried out by organizations.

Related Controls: CA-2, CA-8, RA-5, SA-11, SI-7.

(8)   SUPPLY CHAIN RISK MANAGEMENT | USE OF ALL-SOURCE INTELLIGENCE
Use all-source intelligence to assist in the analysis of supply chain risk.

Supplemental Guidance: Organizations employ all-source intelligence to inform engineering, acquisition, and supply chain risk management decisions. All-source intelligence consists of information derived from all available sources, including, for example, publicly available or open-source information; human intelligence; signals intelligence; imagery intelligence; and measurement and signature intelligence. This information is used to analyze the risk of intentional and unintentional vulnerabilities from development, manufacturing, and delivery processes, people, and the environment. This review may be performed on suppliers at multiple tiers in the supply chain sufficient to manage risks. Organizations may develop agreements to share all-source intelligence information or resulting decisions with other organizations, as appropriate.

Related Controls: None.

(9)   SUPPLY CHAIN RISK MANAGEMENT | OPERATIONS SECURITY
Employ [*Assignment: organization-defined Operations Security (OPSEC) safeguards*] to protect supply chain-related information for the system, system component, or system service.

Supplemental Guidance: Supply chain information includes, for example, user identities; uses for systems, system components, and system services; supplier identities; supplier processes; security requirements; design specifications; testing and evaluation results; and system and component configurations. This control enhancement expands the scope of OPSEC to include suppliers and potential suppliers. OPSEC is a process of identifying critical information and subsequently analyzing friendly actions attendant to operations and other activities to identify those actions that can be observed by potential adversaries; determine indicators that potential adversaries might obtain that could be interpreted or pieced together to derive information in sufficient time to cause harm to organizations; implement safeguards or countermeasures to eliminate or reduce to an acceptable level, exploitable vulnerabilities; and finally, consider how aggregated information may compromise the confidentiality of users or the specific uses of the supply chain. OPSEC may require organizations to withhold specific mission/business information from suppliers and may include the use of intermediaries to hide the end use, or users of systems, system components, or system services.

Related Controls: SC-38.

(10)   SUPPLY CHAIN RISK MANAGEMENT | VALIDATE AS GENUINE AND NOT ALTERED
Employ [*Assignment: organization-defined security safeguards*] to validate that the system or system component received is genuine and has not been altered.

Supplemental Guidance: For many systems and system components, especially hardware, there are technical means to determine if the items are genuine or have been altered, including, for example, optical and nanotechnology tagging; physically unclonable functions; side-channel analysis; and visible anti-tamper stickers and labels. Safeguards can also include monitoring for out of specification performance, which can be an indicator of tampering or counterfeits. Suppliers and contractors may have processes for validating that a system or component is genuine and has not been altered, and for replacing a suspect system or component, which the organization may leverage. Some indications of tampering may be visibly and additionally before accepting delivery, including, for example, broken seals, inconsistent packaging, and incorrect labels. The organization may consider providing training to appropriate personnel on how to identify suspicious system or component deliveries. When a system or component is suspected of being altered or counterfeit, the organization considers notifying the supplier, contractor, or original equipment manufacturer who may be able to replace the item or provide a forensic capability to determine the origin of the counterfeit or altered item.

Related Controls: SA-19.

(11) SUPPLY CHAIN RISK MANAGEMENT | PENETRATION TESTING AND ANALYSIS

Employ [*Selection (one or more): organizational analysis, independent third-party analysis, organizational penetration testing, independent third-party penetration testing*] of [*Assignment: organization-defined supply chain elements, processes, and actors*] associated with the *system, system component, or system service*.

Supplemental Guidance: This control enhancement addresses analysis or testing of the supply chain. It also considers the relationships or linkages between entities and procedures within the supply chain including, for example, development and delivery. Supply chain elements include system components that contain programmable logic and that are critically important to system functions. Supply chain processes include, for example, hardware, software, and firmware development processes; shipping and handling procedures; personnel and physical security programs; configuration management tools, techniques, and measures to maintain provenance; and programs, processes, or procedures associated with the production and distribution of supply chain elements. Supply chain actors are individuals with specific roles and responsibilities in the supply chain. The evidence generated and collected during analyses and testing of supply chain elements, processes, and actors is documented and used to inform organizational risk management activities and decisions.

Related Controls: RA-5.

(12) SUPPLY CHAIN RISK MANAGEMENT | NOTIFICATION AGREEMENTS

Establish agreements and procedures with entities involved in the supply chain for the system, system component, or system service for the [*Selection (one or more): notification of supply chain compromises; results of assessments or audits; [*Assignment: organization-defined information*]].

Supplemental Guidance: The establishment of agreements and procedures provides for formal communications among supply chain entities. Early notification of compromises in the supply chain that can potentially adversely affect or have adversely affected organizational systems, including critical system components, is essential for organizations to effectively respond to such incidents. The results of assessments or audits may include open-source information that contributed to a decision or result and could be used to help the supply chain entity resolve a concern or improve its processes.

Related Controls: IR-8.

(13) SUPPLY CHAIN RISK MANAGEMENT | CRITICAL SYSTEM COMPONENTS

[Withdrawn: Incorporated into MA-6 and RA-9].

(14) SUPPLY CHAIN RISK MANAGEMENT | IDENTITY AND TRACEABILITY

Establish and maintain unique identification of [*Assignment: organization-defined supply chain elements, processes, and personnel*] associated with the [*Assignment: organization-defined system, critical system components*].

Supplemental Guidance: Knowing who and what is in the supply chains of organizations is critical to gaining visibility into what is happening within such supply chains. It is also important for monitoring and identifying high-risk events and activities. Without reasonable visibility and traceability into supply chains (i.e., elements, processes, and personnel), it is very difficult for organizations to understand, and therefore manage risk, and ultimately reduce the likelihood of or susceptibility to adverse events. Supply chain elements are systems or system components that contain programmable logic and that are critically important to system functions. Supply chain processes include, for example, hardware, software, and firmware development processes; shipping and handling procedures; personnel and physical security programs; configuration management tools, techniques, and measures to maintain provenance; or other programs, processes, or procedures associated with the production and distribution of supply chain elements. Supply chain personnel are individuals in the supply chain with specific roles and responsibilities related to, for example, the secure development, delivery, maintenance, and disposal of a system or system component. Tracking the unique identifiers of supply chain elements, processes, and personnel establishes a foundational identity structure for assessment of supply chain activities and for the establishment and maintenance of provenance. For example, supply chain elements may be labeled using serial numbers or tagged using radio-frequency identification tags. These labels and tags can help provide the organization better visibility into the provenance of that element. Identification methods are sufficient to support a forensic investigation in the event of a supply chain compromise or event.

Related Controls: CM-8, IA-2, IA-8.

(15) SUPPLY CHAIN RISK MANAGEMENT | PROCESSES TO ADDRESS WEAKNESSES OR DEFICIENCIES

Establish a process or processes to address weaknesses or deficiencies in supply chain elements in coordination with [*Assignment: organization-defined supply chain personnel*].

Supplemental Guidance: Supply chain elements are system or system components that contain programmable logic and that are critically important to system functions. Supply chain processes include, for example, hardware, software, and firmware development processes; shipping and handling procedures; personnel and physical security programs; configuration management tools, techniques, and measures to maintain provenance; or other programs, processes, or procedures associated with the production and distribution of supply chain elements. Supply chain personnel are individuals with specific roles and responsibilities in the supply chain. The evidence generated during the independent or organizational assessments of designated supply chain elements may be used to improve the supply chain processes and inform the organization's supply chain risk management process. The evidence can also be leveraged in follow-on assessments. Evidence and other related documentation may be shared in accordance with organizational agreements.

Related Controls: None.

(16) SUPPLY CHAIN RISK MANAGEMENT | PROVENANCE

Document, monitor, and maintain valid provenance of [*Assignment: organization-defined systems, system components, and associated data*].

Supplemental Guidance: Every system and system component has a point of origin and may be changed throughout its existence. Provenance is the chronology of the origin, development, ownership, location, and changes to a system or system component and associated data. It may also include personnel and processes used to interact with or make modifications to the system, component, or associated data. Organizations consider developing procedures for allocating responsibilities for the creation, maintenance, and monitoring of provenance for systems and components; transferring provenance documentation and responsibility between organizations; and preventing and monitoring for unauthorized changes to the provenance records. Organizations consider developing methods to document, monitor, and maintain valid provenance baselines for systems, system components, and related data. Such actions help track, assess, and document changes to the provenance, including changes in supply chain elements or configuration, and ensure non-repudiation of provenance information and the provenance change records.

Related Controls: RA-9.

References: FIPS Publications 140-2, 180-4, 186-4, 202; NIST Special Publications 800-30, 800-161; NIST Interagency Report 7622.

SA-13 TRUSTWORTHINESS

[Withdrawn: Incorporated into SA-8].

SA-14 CRITICALITY ANALYSIS

[Withdrawn: Incorporated into RA-9].

SA-15 DEVELOPMENT PROCESS, STANDARDS, AND TOOLS

Control:

a. Require the developer of the system, system component, or system service to follow a documented development process that:

1. Explicitly addresses security requirements;

2. Identifies the standards and tools used in the development process;

3. Documents the specific tool options and tool configurations used in the development process; and

4. Documents, manages, and ensures the integrity of changes to the process and/or tools used in development; and

b. Review the development process, standards, tools, tool options, and tool configurations [*Assignment: organization-defined frequency*] to determine if the process, standards, tools, tool options and tool configurations selected and employed can satisfy [*Assignment: organization-defined security and privacy requirements*].

Supplemental Guidance: Development tools include, for example, programming languages and computer-aided design systems. Reviews of development processes can include, for example, the use of maturity models to determine the potential effectiveness of such processes. Maintaining the integrity of changes to tools and processes facilitates effective supply chain risk assessment and mitigation. Such integrity requires configuration control throughout the system development life cycle to track authorized changes and to prevent unauthorized changes.

Related Controls: MA-6, SA-3, SA-4, SA-8, SA-11, SA-12.

Control Enhancements:

(1) DEVELOPMENT PROCESS, STANDARDS, AND TOOLS | QUALITY METRICS

Require the developer of the system, system component, or system service to:

(a) Define quality metrics at the beginning of the development process; and

(b) Provide evidence of meeting the quality metrics [*Selection (one or more): [Assignment: organization-defined frequency]; [Assignment: organization-defined program review milestones]; upon delivery*].

Supplemental Guidance: Organizations use quality metrics to establish acceptable levels of system quality. Metrics may include quality gates which are collections of completion criteria or sufficiency standards representing the satisfactory execution of specific phases of the system development project. A quality gate, for example, may require the elimination of all compiler warnings or a determination that such warnings have no impact on the effectiveness of required security or privacy capabilities. During the execution phases of development projects, quality gates provide clear, unambiguous indications of progress. Other metrics apply to the entire development project. These metrics can include defining the severity thresholds of vulnerabilities, for example, requiring no known vulnerabilities in the delivered system with a Common Vulnerability Scoring System (CVSS) severity of Medium or High.

Related Controls: None.

(2) DEVELOPMENT PROCESS, STANDARDS, AND TOOLS | SECURITY TRACKING TOOLS

Require the developer of the system, system component, or system service to select and employ a security tracking tool for use during the development process.

Supplemental Guidance: System development teams select and deploy security tracking tools, including, for example, vulnerability/work item tracking systems that facilitate assignment, sorting, filtering, and tracking of completed work items or tasks associated with system development processes.

Related Controls: SA-11.

(3) DEVELOPMENT PROCESS, STANDARDS, AND TOOLS | CRITICALITY ANALYSIS

Require the developer of the system, system component, or system service to perform a criticality analysis at [*Assignment: organization-defined breadth/depth*] and at [*Assignment: organization-defined decision points in the system development life cycle*].

Supplemental Guidance: This control enhancement provides developer input to the criticality analysis performed by organizations. Developer input is essential to such analysis because organizations may not have access to detailed design documentation for system components that are developed as commercial off-the-shelf products. Such design documentation includes, for example, functional specifications, high-level designs, low-level designs, and source code and hardware schematics. Criticality analysis is important for organizational systems that are designated as high value assets. Such assets can be moderate- or high-impact systems due to the potential for serious, severe, or catastrophic adverse impacts on organizational missions or business functions.

Related Controls: RA-9.

(4) DEVELOPMENT PROCESS, STANDARDS, AND TOOLS | THREAT MODELING AND VULNERABILITY ANALYSIS

[Withdrawn: Incorporated into SA-11(2)].

(5) DEVELOPMENT PROCESS, STANDARDS, AND TOOLS | ATTACK SURFACE REDUCTION

Require the developer of the system, system component, or system service to reduce attack surfaces to [*Assignment: organization-defined thresholds*].

Supplemental Guidance: Attack surface reduction is closely aligned with developer threat and vulnerability analyses and system architecture and design. Attack surface reduction is a means of reducing risk to organizations by giving attackers less opportunity to exploit weaknesses or deficiencies (i.e., potential vulnerabilities) within systems, system components, and system services. Attack surface reduction includes, for example, employing the concept of layered defenses; applying the principles of least privilege and least functionality; deprecating unsafe functions; applying secure software development practices including, for example, reducing the amount of code executing and reducing entry points available to unauthorized users; and eliminating application programming interfaces (APIs) that are vulnerable to attacks.

Related Controls: AC-6, CM-7, RA-3.

(6) DEVELOPMENT PROCESS, STANDARDS, AND TOOLS | CONTINUOUS IMPROVEMENT

Require the developer of the system, system component, or system service to implement an explicit process to continuously improve the development process.

Supplemental Guidance: Developers of systems, system components, and system services consider the effectiveness and efficiency of their current development processes for meeting quality objectives and for addressing the security and privacy capabilities in current threat environments.

Related Controls: None.

(7) DEVELOPMENT PROCESS, STANDARDS, AND TOOLS | AUTOMATED VULNERABILITY ANALYSIS

Require the developer of the system, system component, or system service to:

(a) Perform an automated vulnerability analysis using [*Assignment: organization-defined tools*];

(b) Determine the exploitation potential for discovered vulnerabilities;

(c) Determine potential risk mitigations for delivered vulnerabilities; and

(d) Deliver the outputs of the tools and results of the analysis to [*Assignment: organization-defined personnel or roles*].

Supplemental Guidance: None.

Related Controls: RA-5, SA-11.

(8) DEVELOPMENT PROCESS, STANDARDS, AND TOOLS | REUSE OF THREAT AND VULNERABILITY INFORMATION

Require the developer of the system, system component, or system service to use threat modeling and vulnerability analyses from similar systems, components, or services to inform the current development process.

Supplemental Guidance: Analysis of similar systems, similar system components, or similar hardware applications can inform potential design and implementation issues for systems under development. Similar systems or system components may exist within developer organizations. Vulnerability information is available from a variety of public and private sector sources including, for example, the NIST National Vulnerability Database.

Related Controls: None.

(9) DEVELOPMENT PROCESS, STANDARDS, AND TOOLS | USE OF LIVE DATA

[Withdrawn: Incorporated into SA-3(2)].

(10) DEVELOPMENT PROCESS, STANDARDS, AND TOOLS | INCIDENT RESPONSE PLAN

Require the developer of the system, system component, or system service to provide, implement, and test an incident response plan.

Supplemental Guidance: The incident response plan provided by developers of systems, system components, and system services may be incorporated into organizational incident response plans. This information provides the type of incident response information that is not readily available to organizations. Such information may be extremely helpful, for example, when organizations respond to vulnerabilities in commercial off-the-shelf products.

Related Controls: IR-8.

(11) DEVELOPMENT PROCESS, STANDARDS, AND TOOLS | ARCHIVE SYSTEM OR COMPONENT

Require the developer of the system or system component to archive the system or component to be released or delivered together with the corresponding evidence supporting the final security and privacy review.

Supplemental Guidance: Archiving system or system components requires the developer to retain key development artifacts including, for example, hardware specifications, source code, object code, and any relevant documentation from the development process that can provide a readily available configuration baseline for system and component upgrades or modifications.

Related Controls: None.

References: None.

SA-16 DEVELOPER-PROVIDED TRAINING

Control: Require the developer of the system, system component, or system service to provide [*Assignment: organization-defined training*] on the correct use and operation of the implemented security and privacy functions, controls, and/or mechanisms.

Supplemental Guidance: This control applies to external and internal (in-house) developers. Training of personnel is an essential element to ensure the effectiveness of the security and privacy controls implemented within organizational systems. Training options include, for example, web-based and computer-based training; classroom-style training; and hands-on training. Organizations can also request training materials from developers to conduct in-house training or offer self-training to organizational personnel. Organizations determine the type of training necessary and may require different types of training for different security and privacy functions, controls, and mechanisms.

Related Controls: AT-2, AT-3, PE-3, SA-4, SA-5.

Control Enhancements: None.

References: None.

SA-17 DEVELOPER SECURITY ARCHITECTURE AND DESIGN

Control: Require the developer of the system, system component, or system service to produce a design specification and security architecture that:

a. Is consistent with and supportive of the organization's security architecture which is established within and is an integrated part of the organization's enterprise architecture;

b. Accurately and completely describes the required security functionality, and the allocation of security controls among physical and logical components; and

c. Expresses how individual security functions, mechanisms, and services work together to provide required security capabilities and a unified approach to protection.

Supplemental Guidance: This control is primarily directed at external developers, although it could also be used for internal (in-house) development. In contrast, PL-8 is primarily directed at internal developers to ensure that organizations develop a security architecture and that the architecture is integrated or tightly coupled to the enterprise architecture. This distinction is important when organizations outsource the development of systems, system components, or system services to external entities, and when there is a requirement to demonstrate consistency with the enterprise architecture and security architecture of the organization. ISO/IEC 15408 provides additional information on security architecture and design including, for example, formal policy models, security-relevant components, formal and informal correspondence, conceptually simple design, and structuring for least privilege and testing.

Related Controls: PL-2, PL-8, PM-7, SA-3, SA-4, SA-8.

Control Enhancements:

(1) DEVELOPER SECURITY ARCHITECTURE AND DESIGN | FORMAL POLICY MODEL

Require the developer of the system, system component, or system service to:

(a) Produce, as an integral part of the development process, a formal policy model describing the [Assignment: organization-defined elements of organizational security policy] to be enforced; and

(b) Prove that the formal policy model is internally consistent and sufficient to enforce the defined elements of the organizational security policy when implemented.

Supplemental Guidance: Formal models describe specific behaviors or security policies using formal languages, thus enabling the correctness of those behaviors and policies to be formally proven. Not all components of systems can be modeled. Generally, formal specifications are scoped to the specific behaviors or policies of interest, for example, nondiscretionary access control policies. Organizations choose the formal modeling language and approach based on the nature of the behaviors and policies to be described and the available tools. Examples of formal modeling tools include Gypsy and Zed.

Related Controls: None.

(2) DEVELOPER SECURITY ARCHITECTURE AND DESIGN | SECURITY-RELEVANT COMPONENTS

Require the developer of the system, system component, or system service to:

(a) Define security-relevant hardware, software, and firmware; and

(b) Provide a rationale that the definition for security-relevant hardware, software, and firmware is complete.

Supplemental Guidance: The security-relevant hardware, software, and firmware represent the portion of the system, component, or service that must be trusted to perform correctly to maintain required security properties.

Related Controls: SA-5.

(3) DEVELOPER SECURITY ARCHITECTURE AND DESIGN | FORMAL CORRESPONDENCE

Require the developer of the system, system component, or system service to:

(a) Produce, as an integral part of the development process, a formal top-level specification that specifies the interfaces to security-relevant hardware, software, and firmware in terms of exceptions, error messages, and effects;

(b) Show via proof to the extent feasible with additional informal demonstration as necessary, that the formal top-level specification is consistent with the formal policy model;

(c) Show via informal demonstration, that the formal top-level specification completely covers the interfaces to security-relevant hardware, software, and firmware;

(d) Show that the formal top-level specification is an accurate description of the implemented security-relevant hardware, software, and firmware; and

(e) Describe the security-relevant hardware, software, and firmware mechanisms not addressed in the formal top-level specification but strictly internal to the security-relevant hardware, software, and firmware.

Supplemental Guidance: Correspondence is an important part of the assurance gained through modeling. It demonstrates that the implementation is an accurate transformation of the model, and that any additional code or implementation details that are present have no impact on the behaviors or policies being modeled. Formal methods can be used to show that the high-level security properties are satisfied by the formal system description, and that the formal system description is correctly implemented by a description of some lower level, for example a hardware description. Consistency between the formal top-level specification and the formal policy models is generally not amenable to being fully proven. Therefore, a combination of formal and informal methods may be needed to show such consistency. Consistency between the formal top-level specification and the actual implementation may require the use of an informal demonstration due to limitations in the applicability of formal methods to prove that the specification accurately reflects the implementation. Hardware, software, and firmware mechanisms strictly internal to security-relevant hardware, software, and firmware include, for example, mapping registers and direct memory input and output.

Related Controls: SA-5.

(4) DEVELOPER SECURITY ARCHITECTURE AND DESIGN | INFORMAL CORRESPONDENCE

Require the developer of the system, system component, or system service to:

(a) Produce, as an integral part of the development process, an informal descriptive top-level specification that specifies the interfaces to security-relevant hardware, software, and firmware in terms of exceptions, error messages, and effects;

(b) Show via [Selection: informal demonstration, convincing argument with formal methods as feasible] that the descriptive top-level specification is consistent with the formal policy model;

(c) Show via informal demonstration, that the descriptive top-level specification completely covers the interfaces to security-relevant hardware, software, and firmware;

(d) Show that the descriptive top-level specification is an accurate description of the interfaces to security-relevant hardware, software, and firmware; and

(e) Describe the security-relevant hardware, software, and firmware mechanisms not addressed in the descriptive top-level specification but strictly internal to the security-relevant hardware, software, and firmware.

Supplemental Guidance: Correspondence is an important part of the assurance gained through modeling. It demonstrates that the implementation is an accurate transformation of the model, and that any additional code or implementation details present has no impact on the behaviors or policies being modeled. Consistency between the descriptive top-level specification (i.e., high-level/low-level design) and the formal policy model is generally not amenable to being fully proven. Therefore, a combination of formal and informal methods may be needed to show such consistency. Hardware, software, and firmware mechanisms strictly internal to security-relevant hardware, software, and firmware include, for example, mapping registers and direct memory input and output.

Related Controls: SA-5.

(5) DEVELOPER SECURITY ARCHITECTURE AND DESIGN | CONCEPTUALLY SIMPLE DESIGN

Require the developer of the system, system component, or system service to:

(a) Design and structure the security-relevant hardware, software, and firmware to use a complete, conceptually simple protection mechanism with precisely defined semantics; and

(b) Internally structure the security-relevant hardware, software, and firmware with specific regard for this mechanism.

Supplemental Guidance: None.

Related Controls: SC-3.

(6) DEVELOPER SECURITY ARCHITECTURE AND DESIGN | STRUCTURE FOR TESTING

Require the developer of the system, system component, or system service to structure security-relevant hardware, software, and firmware to facilitate testing.

Supplemental Guidance: None.

Related Controls: SA-5, SA-11.

(7) DEVELOPER SECURITY ARCHITECTURE AND DESIGN | STRUCTURE FOR LEAST PRIVILEGE

Require the developer of the system, system component, or system service to structure security-relevant hardware, software, and firmware to facilitate controlling access with least privilege.

Supplemental Guidance: None.

Related Controls: AC-5, AC-6.

References: ISO/IEC 15408; NIST Special Publication 800-160.

SA-18   TAMPER RESISTANCE AND DETECTION

Control: Implement a tamper protection program for the system, system component, or system service.

Supplemental Guidance: Anti-tamper technologies, tools, and techniques provide a level of protection for systems and system components against many threats including reverse engineering, modification, and substitution. Strong identification combined with tamper resistance and/or tamper detection is essential to protecting systems and components during distribution and when in use.

Related Controls: PE-3, SA-12, SI-7.

Control Enhancements:

(1) TAMPER RESISTANCE AND DETECTION | MULTIPLE PHASES OF SYSTEM DEVELOPMENT LIFE CYCLE

Employ anti-tamper technologies, tools, and techniques during multiple phases in the system development life cycle including design, development, integration, operations, and maintenance.

Supplemental Guidance: Organizations use a combination of hardware and software techniques for tamper resistance and detection. Organizations employ obfuscation and self-checking, for example, to make reverse engineering and modifications more difficult, time-consuming, and expensive for adversaries. The customization of systems and system components can make substitutions easier to detect and therefore limit damage.

Related Controls: SA-3.

(2) TAMPER RESISTANCE AND DETECTION | INSPECTION OF SYSTEMS OR COMPONENTS

Inspect [*Assignment: organization-defined systems or system components*] [*Selection (one or more): at random; at [Assignment: organization-defined frequency], upon [Assignment: organization-defined indications of need for inspection]*] to detect tampering.

Supplemental Guidance: This control enhancement addresses physical and logical tampering and is typically applied to mobile devices, notebook computers, or other system components taken out of organization-controlled areas. Indications of a need for inspection include, for example, when individuals return from travel to high-risk locations.

Related Controls: SI-4.

References: None.

SA-19   COMPONENT AUTHENTICITY

Control:

a.   Develop and implement anti-counterfeit policy and procedures that include the means to detect and prevent counterfeit components from entering the system; and

b.   Report counterfeit system components to [*Selection (one or more): source of counterfeit component; [Assignment: organization-defined external reporting organizations]; [Assignment: organization-defined personnel or roles]*].

Supplemental Guidance: Sources of counterfeit components include, for example, manufacturers, developers, vendors, and contractors. Anti-counterfeiting policy and procedures support tamper resistance and provide a level of protection against the introduction of malicious code. External reporting organizations include, for example, US-CERT.

Related Controls: PE-3, SA-12, SI-7.

Control Enhancements:

(1) COMPONENT AUTHENTICITY | ANTI-COUNTERFEIT TRAINING

Train [*Assignment: organization-defined personnel or roles*] to detect counterfeit system components (including hardware, software, and firmware).

Supplemental Guidance: None.

Related Controls: AT-3.

(2) COMPONENT AUTHENTICITY | CONFIGURATION CONTROL FOR COMPONENT SERVICE AND REPAIR

Maintain configuration control over [*Assignment: organization-defined system components*] awaiting service or repair and serviced or repaired components awaiting return to service.

Supplemental Guidance: None.

Related Controls: CM-3.

(3) COMPONENT AUTHENTICITY | COMPONENT DISPOSAL

Dispose of system components using [*Assignment: organization-defined techniques and methods*].

Supplemental Guidance: Proper disposal of system components helps to prevent such components from entering the gray market.

Related Controls: MP-6.

(4) COMPONENT AUTHENTICITY | ANTI-COUNTERFEIT SCANNING

Scan for counterfeit system components [*Assignment: organization-defined frequency*].

Supplemental Guidance: None.

Related Controls: RA-5.

References: None.

SA-20 CUSTOMIZED DEVELOPMENT OF CRITICAL COMPONENTS

Control: Re-implement or custom develops [*Assignment: organization-defined critical system components*].

Supplemental Guidance: Organizations determine that certain system components likely cannot be trusted due to specific threats to and vulnerabilities in those components, and for which there are no viable security controls to adequately mitigate the resulting risk. Re-implementation or custom development of such components helps to satisfy requirements for higher assurance. This is accomplished by initiating changes to system components (including hardware, software, and firmware) such that the standard attacks by adversaries are less likely to succeed. In situations where no alternative sourcing is available and organizations choose not to re-implement or custom develop critical system components, additional safeguards can be employed. These include, for example, enhanced auditing; restrictions on source code and system utility access; and protection from deletion of system and application files.

Related Controls: CP-2, RA-9, SA-8.

Control Enhancements: None.

References: None.

SA-21 DEVELOPER SCREENING

Control: Require that the developer of [*Assignment: organization-defined system, system component, or system service*]:

a. Have appropriate access authorizations as determined by assigned [*Assignment: organization-defined official government duties*];

b. Satisfy [*Assignment: organization-defined additional personnel screening criteria*]; and

c. Provide information that the access authorizations and screening criteria specified in a. and b. are satisfied.

Supplemental Guidance: This control is directed at external developers. Because the system, system component, or system service may be employed in critical activities essential to the national or economic security interests of the United States, organizations have a strong interest in ensuring that the developer is trustworthy. The degree of trust required of the developer may need to be consistent with that of the individuals accessing the system/component/service once deployed. Examples of authorization and personnel screening criteria include clearances, background checks, citizenship, and nationality. Trustworthiness of developers may also include a review and analysis of company ownership and any relationships the company has with entities potentially affecting the quality and reliability of the systems, components, or services being developed. Satisfying required access authorizations and personnel screening criteria includes, for example, providing a list of all individuals who are authorized to perform development activities on the selected system, system component, or system service so that organizations can validate that the developer has satisfied the authorization and screening requirements.

Related Controls: PS-2, PS-3, PS-6, PS-7, SA-4.

Control Enhancements:

(1) DEVELOPER SCREENING | VALIDATION OF SCREENING
     [Withdrawn: Incorporated into SA-21].

References: None.

SA-22   UNSUPPORTED SYSTEM COMPONENTS

Control: Replace system components when support for the components is no longer available from the developer, vendor, or manufacturer.

Supplemental Guidance: Support for system components includes, for example, software patches, firmware updates, replacement parts, and maintenance contracts. Unsupported components, for example, when vendors no longer provide critical software patches or product updates, provide an opportunity for adversaries to exploit weaknesses in the installed components. Exceptions to replacing unsupported system components may include, for example, systems that provide critical mission or business capability where newer technologies are not available or where the systems are so isolated that installing replacement components is not an option.

Related Controls: PL-2, SA-3.

Control Enhancements:

(1) UNSUPPORTED SYSTEM COMPONENTS | ALTERNATIVE SOURCES FOR CONTINUED SUPPORT
     Provide [*Selection (one or more): in-house support*; [*Assignment: organization-defined support from external providers*]] for unsupported system components.

     Supplemental Guidance: This control enhancement addresses the need to provide continued support for system components that are no longer supported by the original manufacturers, developers, or vendors when such components remain essential to organizational mission and business operations. Organizations can establish in-house support, for example, by developing customized patches for critical software components or alternatively, obtain the services of external providers who through contractual relationships, provide ongoing support for the designated unsupported components. Such contractual relationships can include, for example, Open Source Software value-added vendors.

     Related Controls: None.

References: None.

DEVELOPMENT OF SYSTEMS, COMPONENTS, AND SERVICES

With a renewed nation-wide emphasis on the use of trustworthy systems and supply chain security, it is essential that organizations can express their security and privacy requirements with clarity and specificity to engage industry and obtain the systems, components, and services necessary for mission/business success. Accordingly, this publication provides a comprehensive set of controls in the System and Services Acquisition (SA) family that address requirements for the development of systems, components, and system services. To that end, many of the controls in the SA family are directed at developers of those systems, components, and services. It is important for organizations to recognize that the scope of the controls in that family includes system, component, and service development and the developers associated with such development whether the development is conducted either internally or externally by industry partners (i.e., manufacturers, vendors, integrators) through the contracting and acquisition processes. The affected controls in the control catalog include SA-8, SA-10, SA-11, SA-15, SA-16, SA-17, SA-20, and SA-21.

3.19 SYSTEM AND COMMUNICATIONS PROTECTION

Quick link to System and Communications Protection summary table

SC-1 SYSTEM AND COMMUNICATIONS PROTECTION POLICY AND PROCEDURES

Control:

a. Develop, document, and disseminate to [*Assignment: organization-defined personnel or roles*]:

 1. A system and communications protection policy that:

 (a) Addresses purpose, scope, roles, responsibilities, management commitment, coordination among organizational entities, and compliance; and

 (b) Is consistent with applicable laws, Executive Orders, directives, regulations, policies, standards, and guidelines; and

 2. Procedures to facilitate the implementation of the system and communications protection policy and the associated system and communications protection controls;

b. Designate an [*Assignment: organization-defined senior management official*] to manage the system and communications protection policy and procedures;

c. Review and update the current system and communications protection:

 1. Policy [*Assignment: organization-defined frequency*]; and

 2. Procedures [*Assignment: organization-defined frequency*];

d. Ensure that the system and communications protection procedures implement the system and communications protection policy and controls; and

e. Develop, document, and implement remediation actions for violations of the system and communications protection policy.

Supplemental Guidance: This control addresses the establishment of policy and procedures for the effective implementation of the controls and control enhancements in the SC family. The risk management strategy is an important factor in establishing policy and procedures. Comprehensive policy and procedures help provide security and privacy assurance. Security and privacy program policies and procedures at the organization level may make the need for system-specific policies and procedures unnecessary. The policy can be included as part of the general security and privacy policy or can be represented by multiple policies reflecting the complex nature of organizations. The procedures can be established for security and privacy programs and for systems, if needed. Procedures describe how policies or controls are implemented and can be directed at the personnel or role that is the object of the procedure. Procedures can be documented in system security and plans or in one or more separate documents. It is important to recognize that restating controls does not constitute an organizational policy or procedure.

Related Controls: PM-9, PS-8, SI-12.

Control Enhancements: None.

References: NIST Special Publications 800-12, 800-100.

SC-2 APPLICATION PARTITIONING

Control: Separate user functionality, including user interface services, from system management functionality.

Supplemental Guidance: System management functionality includes, for example, functions that are necessary to administer databases, network components, workstations, or servers. These functions typically require privileged user access. The separation of user functions from system management functions is either physical or logical. Organizations implement separation of system management functions from user functions, for example, by using different computers, instances of operating systems, central processing units, or network addresses; by employing virtualization techniques; or some combination of these or other methods. This type of separation includes, for example, web administrative interfaces that use separate authentication methods for users of any other system resources. Separation of system and user functions may include isolating administrative interfaces on different domains and with additional access controls.

Related Controls: AC-6, SA-4, SA-8, SC-3, SC-7, SC-22, SC-32, SC-39.

Control Enhancements:

(1) APPLICATION PARTITIONING | INTERFACES FOR NON-PRIVILEGED USERS

Prevent the presentation of system management functionality at an interface for non-privileged users.

Supplemental Guidance: This control enhancement ensures that system administration options including administrator privileges, are not available to general users. This type of restricted access also prohibits the use of the grey-out option commonly used to eliminate accessibility to such information. One potential solution is to withhold administration options until users establish sessions with administrator privileges.

Related Controls: AC-3.

References: None.

SC-3   SECURITY FUNCTION ISOLATION

Control: Isolate security functions from nonsecurity functions.

Supplemental Guidance: The system isolates security functions from nonsecurity functions by means of an isolation boundary implemented via partitions and domains. Such isolation controls access to and protects the integrity of the hardware, software, and firmware that perform those security functions. Systems implement code separation in many ways, for example, through the provision of security kernels via processor rings or processor modes. For non-kernel code, security function isolation is often achieved through file system protections that protect the code on disk and address space protections that protect executing code. Systems can restrict access to security functions using access control mechanisms and by implementing least privilege capabilities. While the ideal is for all code within the defined security function isolation boundary to only contain security-relevant code, it is sometimes necessary to include nonsecurity functions within the isolation boundary as an exception.

Related Controls: AC-3, AC-6, AC-25, CM-2, CM-4, SA-4, SA-5, SA-8, SA-15, SA-17, SC-2, SC-7, SC-32, SC-39, SI-16.

Control Enhancements:

(1) SECURITY FUNCTION ISOLATION | HARDWARE SEPARATION

Use hardware separation mechanisms to implement security function isolation.

Supplemental Guidance: Hardware separation mechanisms include, for example, hardware ring architectures that are commonly implemented within microprocessors, and hardware-enforced address segmentation used to support logically distinct storage objects with separate attributes (i.e., readable, writeable).

Related Controls: None.

(2) SECURITY FUNCTION ISOLATION | ACCESS AND FLOW CONTROL FUNCTIONS

Isolate security functions enforcing access and information flow control from nonsecurity functions and from other security functions.

Supplemental Guidance: Security function isolation occurs because of implementation. The functions can still be scanned and monitored. Security functions that are potentially isolated from access and flow control enforcement functions include, for example, auditing, intrusion detection, and anti-virus functions.

Related Controls: None.

(3) SECURITY FUNCTION ISOLATION | MINIMIZE NONSECURITY FUNCTIONALITY

Minimize the number of nonsecurity functions included within the isolation boundary containing security functions.

Supplemental Guidance: In those instances where it is not feasible to achieve strict isolation of nonsecurity functions from security functions, it is necessary to take actions to minimize the nonsecurity-relevant functions within the security function boundary. Nonsecurity functions contained within the isolation boundary are considered security-relevant because errors or the maliciousness in such software, can directly impact the security functions of systems. The fundamental design objective is that the specific portions of systems providing information security are of minimal size and complexity. Minimizing the number of nonsecurity functions in the security-relevant system components allows designers and implementers to focus only on those functions which are necessary to provide the desired security capability (typically access enforcement). By minimizing nonsecurity functions within the isolation boundaries, the amount of code that must be trusted to enforce security policies is significantly reduced, thus contributing to understandability.

Related Controls: None.

(4) SECURITY FUNCTION ISOLATION | MODULE COUPLING AND COHESIVENESS

Implement security functions as largely independent modules that maximize internal cohesiveness within modules and minimize coupling between modules.

Supplemental Guidance: The reduction in inter-module interactions helps to constrain security functions and to manage complexity. The concepts of coupling and cohesion are important with respect to modularity in software design. Coupling refers to the dependencies that one module has on other modules. Cohesion refers to the relationship between different functions within a module. Best practices in software engineering rely on layering, minimization, and modular decomposition to reduce and manage complexity. This produces software modules that are highly cohesive and loosely coupled.

Related Controls: None.

(5) SECURITY FUNCTION ISOLATION | LAYERED STRUCTURES

Implement security functions as a layered structure minimizing interactions between layers of the design and avoiding any dependence by lower layers on the functionality or correctness of higher layers.

Supplemental Guidance: The implementation of layered structures with minimized interactions among security functions and non-looping layers (i.e., lower-layer functions do not depend on higher-layer functions) further enables the isolation of security functions and management of complexity.

Related Controls: None.

References: None.

SC-4 INFORMATION IN SHARED SYSTEM RESOURCES

Control: Prevent unauthorized and unintended information transfer via shared system resources.

Supplemental Guidance: This control prevents information produced by the actions of prior users or roles (or the actions of processes acting on behalf of prior users or roles) from being available to current users or roles (or current processes acting on behalf of current users or roles) that obtain access to shared system resources after those resources have been released back to the system. This control also applies to encrypted representations of information. The control of information in shared system resources is referred to as object reuse and residual information protection. This control does not address information remanence which refers to the residual representation of data that has been nominally deleted; covert channels (including storage and timing channels) where shared system resources are manipulated to violate information flow restrictions in components or within systems for which there are only single users or roles.

Related Controls: AC-3, AC-4.

Control Enhancements:

(1) INFORMATION IN SHARED SYSTEM RESOURCES | SECURITY LEVELS
[Withdrawn: Incorporated into SC-4].

(2) INFORMATION IN SHARED SYSTEM RESOURCES | MULTILEVEL OR PERIODS PROCESSING
Prevent unauthorized information transfer via shared resources in accordance with [*Assignment: organization-defined procedures*] when system processing explicitly switches between different information classification levels or security categories.

Supplemental Guidance: This control enhancement applies when there are explicit changes in information processing levels during system operations. This situation can occur, for example, during multilevel or periods processing with information at different classification levels or security categories. Organization-defined procedures may include, for example, approved sanitization processes for electronically stored information.

Related Controls: None.

References: None.

SC-5 DENIAL OF SERVICE PROTECTION

Control: Protect against or limit the effects of the following types of denial of service events: [*Assignment: organization-defined types of denial of service events or references to sources for such information*] by employing [*Assignment: organization-defined security safeguards*].

Supplemental Guidance: Denial of service may occur because of an attack by an adversary or a lack of internal planning to support organizational needs with respect to capacity and bandwidth. There are a variety of technologies available to limit or eliminate the effects of denial of service events. For example, boundary protection devices can filter certain types of packets to protect system components on internal networks from being directly affected by denial of service attacks. Employing increased network capacity and bandwidth combined with service redundancy also reduces the susceptibility to denial of service events.

Related Controls: CP-2, IR-4, SC-6, SC-7, SC-40.

Control Enhancements:

(1) DENIAL OF SERVICE PROTECTION | RESTRICT INTERNAL USERS
Restrict the ability of individuals to launch [*Assignment: organization-defined denial of service attacks*] against other systems.

Supplemental Guidance: Restricting the ability of individuals to launch denial of service attacks requires that the mechanisms commonly used for such attacks are unavailable. Individuals of concern can include, for example, hostile insiders or external adversaries that have breached or compromised the system and are subsequently using the system to launch attacks on other individuals or organizations. Organizations can restrict the ability of individuals to connect and transmit arbitrary information on the transport medium (i.e., wired or wireless networks). Organizations can also limit the ability of individuals to use excessive system resources. Protection against individuals having the ability to launch denial of service attacks may be implemented on specific systems or on boundary devices prohibiting egress to potential target systems.

Related Controls: None.

(2) DENIAL OF SERVICE PROTECTION | CAPACITY, BANDWIDTH, AND REDUNDANCY
Manage capacity, bandwidth, or other redundancy to limit the effects of information flooding denial of service attacks.

Supplemental Guidance: Managing capacity ensures that sufficient capacity is available to counter flooding attacks. Managing capacity may include, for example, establishing selected usage priorities, quotas, or partitioning.

Related Controls: None.

(3) DENIAL OF SERVICE PROTECTION | DETECTION AND MONITORING

(a) Employ [*Assignment: organization-defined monitoring tools*] to detect indicators of denial of service attacks against the system; and

(b) Monitor [*Assignment: organization-defined system resources*] to determine if sufficient resources exist to prevent effective denial of service attacks.

Supplemental Guidance: Organizations consider utilization and capacity of system resources when managing risk from denial of service due to malicious attacks. Denial of service attacks can originate from external or internal sources. System resources sensitive to denial of service include, for example, physical disk storage, memory, and CPU cycles. Examples of common safeguards used to prevent denial of service attacks related to storage utilization and capacity include, instituting disk quotas; configuring systems to automatically alert administrators when specific storage capacity thresholds are reached; using file compression technologies to maximize available storage space; and imposing separate partitions for system and user data.

Related Controls: CA-7, SI-4.

References: None.

SC-6 RESOURCE AVAILABILITY

Control: Protect the availability of resources by allocating [*Assignment: organization-defined resources*] by [*Selection (one or more): priority; quota; [Assignment: organization-defined security safeguards*]].

Supplemental Guidance: Priority protection prevents lower-priority processes from delaying or interfering with the system servicing higher-priority processes. Quotas prevent users or processes from obtaining more than predetermined amounts of resources. This control does not apply to system components for which there are only single users or roles.

Related Controls: SC-5.

Control Enhancements: None.

References: None.

SC-7 BOUNDARY PROTECTION

Control:

a. Monitor and control communications at the external boundary of the system and at key internal boundaries within the system;

b. Implement subnetworks for publicly accessible system components that are [*Selection: physically; logically*] separated from internal organizational networks; and

c. Connect to external networks or systems only through managed interfaces consisting of boundary protection devices arranged in accordance with an organizational security and privacy architecture.

Supplemental Guidance: Managed interfaces include, for example, gateways, routers, firewalls, guards, network-based malicious code analysis and virtualization systems, or encrypted tunnels implemented within a security architecture. Subnetworks that are physically or logically separated from internal networks are referred to as demilitarized zones or DMZs. Restricting or prohibiting interfaces within organizational systems includes, for example, restricting external web traffic to designated web servers within managed interfaces and prohibiting external traffic that appears to be spoofing internal addresses. Commercial telecommunications services are typically provided by network components and consolidated management systems shared by customers. These services

may also include third-party provided network lines and other connections. Such provisions may
represent sources of increased risk despite contract security provisions.

Related Controls: AC-4, AC-17, AC-18, AC-19, AC-20, AU-13, CA-3, CM-2, CM-4, CM-7, CM-10, CP-8, CP-10, IR-4, MA-4, PE-3, PM-12, SC-5, SC-19, SC-32, SC-43.

Control Enhancements:

(1) BOUNDARY PROTECTION | PHYSICALLY SEPARATED SUBNETWORKS
[Withdrawn: Incorporated into SC-7].

(2) BOUNDARY PROTECTION | PUBLIC ACCESS
[Withdrawn: Incorporated into SC-7].

(3) BOUNDARY PROTECTION | ACCESS POINTS
Limit the number of external network connections to the system.

Supplemental Guidance: Limiting the number of external network connections facilitates more
comprehensive monitoring of inbound and outbound communications traffic. The Trusted
Internet Connection initiative is an example of limiting the number of external network
connections.

Related Controls: None.

(4) BOUNDARY PROTECTION | EXTERNAL TELECOMMUNICATIONS SERVICES
(a) Implement a managed interface for each external telecommunication service;
(b) Establish a traffic flow policy for each managed interface;
(c) Protect the confidentiality and integrity of the information being transmitted across each interface;
(d) Document each exception to the traffic flow policy with a supporting mission/business need and duration of that need; and
(e) Review exceptions to the traffic flow policy [*Assignment: organization-defined frequency*] and removes exceptions that are no longer supported by an explicit mission/business need.

Supplemental Guidance: None.

Related Controls: AC-3, SC-8.

(5) BOUNDARY PROTECTION | DENY BY DEFAULT — ALLOW BY EXCEPTION
Deny network communications traffic by default and allow network communications traffic by exception at managed interfaces.

Supplemental Guidance: This control enhancement applies to inbound and outbound network
communications traffic. A deny-all, permit-by-exception network communications traffic
policy ensures that only those system connections which are essential and approved are
allowed. This requirement differs from CA-3(5) in that it applies to any type of network
communications while CA-3(5) is applied to a system that is interconnected with another
system.

(6) BOUNDARY PROTECTION | RESPONSE TO RECOGNIZED FAILURES
[Withdrawn: Incorporated into SC-7(18)].

(7) BOUNDARY PROTECTION | PREVENT SPLIT TUNNELING FOR REMOTE DEVICES
Prevent a remote device from simultaneously establishing non-remote connections with the system and communicating via some other connection to resources in external networks.

Supplemental Guidance: This control enhancement is implemented in remote devices including,
for example, notebook computers, through configuration settings to disable split tunneling in
those devices, and by preventing those configuration settings from being readily configurable
by users. This control enhancement is implemented within the system by the detection of split
tunneling (or of configuration settings that allow split tunneling) in the remote device, and by
prohibiting the connection if the remote device is using split tunneling. Split tunneling might
be desirable by remote users to communicate with local system resources such as printers or
file servers. However, split tunneling can allow unauthorized external connections, making
the system more vulnerable to attack and to exfiltration of organizational information. The use
of VPNs for remote connections, when adequately provisioned with the appropriate security

controls, may provide the organization with sufficient assurance that it can effectively treat such connections as non-remote connections with respect to the objectives of confidentiality and integrity. VPNs provide a means for allowing non-remote communications paths from remote devices. The use of an adequately provisioned VPN does not eliminate the need for preventing split tunneling.

Related Controls: None.

(8) BOUNDARY PROTECTION | ROUTE TRAFFIC TO AUTHENTICATED PROXY SERVERS

Route [*Assignment: organization-defined internal communications traffic*] to [*Assignment: organization-defined external networks*] through authenticated proxy servers at managed interfaces.

Supplemental Guidance: External networks are networks outside of organizational control. A proxy server is a server (i.e., system or application) that acts as an intermediary for clients requesting system resources from non-organizational or other organizational servers. These system resources can include, for example, files, connections, web pages, or services. Client requests established through an initial connection to the proxy server are evaluated to manage complexity and to provide additional protection by limiting direct connectivity. Web content filtering devices are one of the most common proxy servers providing access to the Internet. Proxy servers can support logging of individual Transmission Control Protocol sessions and blocking specific Uniform Resource Locators, Internet Protocol addresses, and domain names. Web proxies can be configured with organization-defined lists of authorized and unauthorized websites.

Related Controls: AC-3.

(9) BOUNDARY PROTECTION | RESTRICT THREATENING OUTGOING COMMUNICATIONS TRAFFIC

(a) Detect and deny outgoing communications traffic posing a threat to external systems; and

(b) Audit the identity of internal users associated with denied communications.

Supplemental Guidance: Detecting outgoing communications traffic from internal actions that may pose threats to external systems is known as extrusion detection. Extrusion detection is carried out at system boundaries as part of managed interfaces. This capability includes the analysis of incoming and outgoing communications traffic while searching for indications of internal threats to the security of external systems. Such threats include, for example, traffic indicative of denial of service attacks and traffic containing malicious code.

Related Controls: AU-2, AU-6, SC-5, SC-38, SC-44, SI-3, SI-4.

(10) BOUNDARY PROTECTION | PREVENT EXFILTRATION

(a) Prevent the exfiltration of information; and

(b) Conduct exfiltration tests [*Assignment: organization-defined frequency*].

Supplemental Guidance: This control enhancement applies to intentional and unintentional exfiltration of information. Safeguards to prevent exfiltration of information from systems may be implemented at internal endpoints, external boundaries, and across managed interfaces and include, for example, strict adherence to protocol formats; monitoring for beaconing activity from systems; monitoring for steganography; disconnecting external network interfaces except when explicitly needed; disassembling and reassembling packet headers; employing traffic profile analysis to detect deviations from the volume and types of traffic expected within organizations or call backs to command and control centers; and implementing data loss and data leakage prevention tools. Devices that enforce strict adherence to protocol formats include, for example, deep packet inspection firewalls and XML gateways. These devices verify adherence to protocol formats and specifications at the application layer and identify vulnerabilities that cannot be detected by devices operating at the network or transport layers. This control enhancement is analogous with data loss/data leakage prevention and is closely associated with cross-domain solutions and system guards enforcing information flow requirements.

Related Controls: SI-3.

(11) BOUNDARY PROTECTION | RESTRICT INCOMING COMMUNICATIONS TRAFFIC

Only allow incoming communications from [*Assignment: organization-defined authorized sources*] to be routed to [*Assignment: organization-defined authorized destinations*].

Supplemental Guidance: This control enhancement provides determinations that source and destination address pairs represent authorized/allowed communications. Such determinations can be based on several factors including, for example, the presence of such address pairs in the lists of authorized/allowed communications; the absence of such address pairs in lists of unauthorized/disallowed pairs; or meeting more general rules for authorized/allowed source and destination pairs.

Related Controls: AC-3.

(12) BOUNDARY PROTECTION | HOST-BASED PROTECTION

Implement [*Assignment: organization-defined host-based boundary protection mechanisms*] at [*Assignment: organization-defined system components*].

Supplemental Guidance: Host-based boundary protection mechanisms include, for example, host-based firewalls. Examples of system components employing host-based boundary protection mechanisms include servers, workstations, notebook computers, and mobile devices.

Related Controls: None.

(13) BOUNDARY PROTECTION | ISOLATION OF SECURITY TOOLS, MECHANISMS, AND SUPPORT COMPONENTS

Isolate [*Assignment: organization-defined information security tools, mechanisms, and support components*] from other internal system components by implementing physically separate subnetworks with managed interfaces to other components of the system.

Supplemental Guidance: Physically separate subnetworks with managed interfaces are useful, for example, in isolating computer network defenses from critical operational processing networks to prevent adversaries from discovering the analysis and forensics techniques of organizations.

Related Controls: SC-2, SC-3.

(14) BOUNDARY PROTECTION | PROTECTS AGAINST UNAUTHORIZED PHYSICAL CONNECTIONS

Protect against unauthorized physical connections at [*Assignment: organization-defined managed interfaces*].

Supplemental Guidance: Systems operating at different security categories or classification levels may share common physical and environmental controls, since the systems may share space within the same facilities. In practice, it is possible that these separate systems may share common equipment rooms, wiring closets, and cable distribution paths. Protection against unauthorized physical connections can be achieved, for example, by employing clearly identified and physically separated cable trays, connection frames, and patch panels for each side of managed interfaces with physical access controls enforcing limited authorized access to these items.

Related Controls: PE-4, PE-19.

(15) BOUNDARY PROTECTION | ROUTE PRIVILEGED NETWORK ACCESSES

Route all networked, privileged accesses through a dedicated, managed interface for purposes of access control and auditing.

Supplemental Guidance: None.

Related Controls: AC-2, AC-3, AU-2, SI-4.

(16) BOUNDARY PROTECTION | PREVENT DISCOVERY OF COMPONENTS AND DEVICES

Prevent the discovery of specific system components that represent a managed interface.

Supplemental Guidance: This control enhancement protects network addresses of system components that are part of managed interfaces from discovery through common tools and techniques used to identify devices on networks. Network addresses are not available for discovery, requiring prior knowledge for access. This can be accomplished by not publishing network addresses or entering the addresses in domain name systems. Another obfuscation technique is to periodically change network addresses.

Related Controls: None.

(17) BOUNDARY PROTECTION | AUTOMATED ENFORCEMENT OF PROTOCOL FORMATS

Enforce adherence to protocol formats.

Supplemental Guidance: Examples of system components that enforce protocol formats include deep packet inspection firewalls and XML gateways. Such components verify adherence to protocol formats and specifications at the application layer and identify vulnerabilities that cannot be detected by devices operating at the network or transport layers.

Related Controls: SC-4.

(18) BOUNDARY PROTECTION | FAIL SECURE

Prevent systems from entering unsecure states in the event of an operational failure of a boundary protection device.

Supplemental Guidance: Fail secure is a condition achieved by employing system mechanisms to ensure that in the event of operational failures of boundary protection devices at managed interfaces, systems do not enter into unsecure states where intended security properties no longer hold. Examples of managed interfaces include routers, firewalls, and application gateways residing on protected subnetworks commonly referred to as demilitarized zones. Failures of boundary protection devices cannot lead to, or cause information external to the devices to enter the devices, nor can failures permit unauthorized information releases.

Related Controls: CP-2, CP-12, SC-24.

(19) BOUNDARY PROTECTION | BLOCK COMMUNICATION FROM NON-ORGANIZATIONALLY CONFIGURED HOSTS

Block inbound and outbound communications traffic between [*Assignment: organization-defined communication clients*] that are independently configured by end users and external service providers.

Supplemental Guidance: Communication clients independently configured by end users and external service providers include, for example, instant messaging clients. Traffic blocking does not apply to communication clients that are configured by organizations to perform authorized functions.

Related Controls: None.

(20) BOUNDARY PROTECTION | DYNAMIC ISOLATION AND SEGREGATION

Provide the capability to dynamically isolate or segregate [*Assignment: organization-defined system components*] from other system components.

Supplemental Guidance: The capability to dynamically isolate or segregate certain internal components of organizational systems is useful when it is necessary to partition or separate certain system components of questionable origin from those components possessing greater trustworthiness. Component isolation reduces the attack surface of organizational systems. Isolating selected system components can also limit the damage from successful attacks when such attacks occur.

Related Controls: None.

(21) BOUNDARY PROTECTION | ISOLATION OF SYSTEM COMPONENTS

Employ boundary protection mechanisms to separate [*Assignment: organization-defined system components*] supporting [*Assignment: organization-defined missions and/or business functions*].

Supplemental Guidance: Organizations can isolate system components performing different missions or business functions. Such isolation limits unauthorized information flows among system components and provides the opportunity to deploy greater levels of protection for selected system components. Separating system components with boundary protection mechanisms provides the capability for increased protection of individual components and to more effectively control information flows between those components. This type of enhanced protection limits the potential harm from hostile attacks and errors. The degree of separation provided varies depending upon the mechanisms chosen. Boundary protection mechanisms include, for example, routers, gateways, and firewalls separating system components into physically separate networks or subnetworks; cross-domain devices separating subnetworks;

virtualization techniques; and encrypting information flows across ... system components using distinct encryption keys.

Related Controls: CA-9, SC-3.

(22) BOUNDARY PROTECTION | SEPARATE SUBNETS FOR CONNECTING TO DIFFERENT SECURITY DOMAINS

Implement separate network addresses to connect to systems in different security domains.

Supplemental Guidance: The decomposition of systems into subnetworks (subnets) helps to provide the appropriate level of protection for network connections to different security domains containing information with different security categories or classification levels.

Related Controls: None.

(23) BOUNDARY PROTECTION | DISABLE SENDER FEEDBACK ON PROTOCOL VALIDATION FAILURE

Disable feedback to senders on protocol format validation failure.

Supplemental Guidance: Disabling feedback to senders when there is a failure in protocol validation format prevents adversaries from obtaining information which would otherwise be unavailable.

Related Controls: None.

(24) BOUNDARY PROTECTION | PERSONALLY IDENTIFIABLE INFORMATION

For systems that process, store, or transmit personally identifiable information:

    (a) **Apply [*Assignment: organization-defined processing rules*] to data elements of personally identifiable information;**

    (b) **Monitor for permitted processing at the external boundary of the system and at key internal boundaries within the system;**

    (c) **Document each processing exception; and**

    (d) **Review and remove exceptions that are no longer supported.**

Supplemental Guidance: Managing the transmission of personally identifiable information and how such information is used is an important aspect of safeguarding an individual's privacy. Processing rules that determine how or when personally identifiable information may be used or transmitted ensures that such information is used or transmitted only in accordance with established privacy requirements.

Related Controls: SI-15.

References: FIPS Publication 199; NIST Special Publications 800-41, 800-77.

SC-8   TRANSMISSION CONFIDENTIALITY AND INTEGRITY

Control: Protect the [*Selection (one or more): confidentiality; integrity*] of transmitted information.

Supplemental Guidance: This control applies to internal and external networks and any system components that can transmit information including, for example, servers, notebook computers, desktop computers, mobile devices, printers, copiers, scanners, facsimile machines, and radios. Unprotected communication paths are exposed to the possibility of interception and modification. Protecting the confidentiality and integrity of information can be accomplished by physical means or by logical means. Physical protection can be achieved by employing protected distribution systems. Logical protection can be achieved by employing encryption techniques. Organizations relying on commercial providers offering transmission services as commodity services rather than as fully dedicated services, may find it difficult to obtain the necessary assurances regarding the implementation of needed security controls for transmission confidentiality and integrity. In such situations, organizations determine what types of confidentiality/integrity services are available in standard, commercial telecommunication service packages. If it is infeasible or impractical to obtain the necessary security controls and assurances of control effectiveness through appropriate contracting vehicles, organizations can implement appropriate compensating security controls or explicitly accept the additional risk.

Related Controls: AC-17, AC-18, AU-10, IA-3, IA-8, IA-9, MA-4, PE-4, SA-4, SC-7, SC-16, SC-20, SC-23, SC-28.

Control Enhancements:

(1) TRANSMISSION CONFIDENTIALITY AND INTEGRITY | CRYPTOGRAPHIC PROTECTION

Implement cryptographic mechanisms to [*Selection (one or more): prevent unauthorized disclosure of information; detect changes to information*] during transmission.

Supplemental Guidance: Encrypting information for transmission protects information from unauthorized disclosure and modification. Cryptographic mechanisms implemented to protect information integrity include, for example, cryptographic hash functions which have common application in digital signatures, checksums, and message authentication codes.

Related Controls: SC-13.

(2) TRANSMISSION CONFIDENTIALITY AND INTEGRITY | PRE- AND POST-TRANSMISSION HANDLING

Maintain the [*Selection (one or more): confidentiality; integrity*] of information during preparation for transmission and during reception.

Supplemental Guidance: Information can be either unintentionally or maliciously disclosed or modified during preparation for transmission or during reception including, for example, during aggregation, at protocol transformation points, and during packing and unpacking. These unauthorized disclosures or modifications compromise the confidentiality or integrity of the information.

Related Controls: AU-10.

(3) TRANSMISSION CONFIDENTIALITY AND INTEGRITY | CRYPTOGRAPHIC PROTECTION FOR MESSAGE EXTERNALS

Implement cryptographic mechanisms to protect message externals unless otherwise protected by [*Assignment: organization-defined alternative physical safeguards*].

Supplemental Guidance: This control enhancement addresses protection against unauthorized disclosure of information. Message externals include, for example, message headers and routing information. This control enhancement prevents the exploitation of message externals and applies to internal and external networks or links that may be visible to individuals who are not authorized users. Header and routing information is sometimes transmitted in the clear (i.e., unencrypted) because the information is not properly identified by organizations as having significant value or because encrypting the information can result in lower network performance or higher costs. Alternative physical safeguards include, for example, protected distribution systems.

Related Controls: SC-12, SC-13.

(4) TRANSMISSION CONFIDENTIALITY AND INTEGRITY | CONCEAL OR RANDOMIZE COMMUNICATIONS

Implement cryptographic mechanisms to conceal or randomize communication patterns unless otherwise protected by [*Assignment: organization-defined alternative physical safeguards*].

Supplemental Guidance: This control enhancement addresses protection against unauthorized disclosure of information. Communication patterns include, for example, frequency, periods, amount, and predictability. Changes to communications patterns can reveal information having intelligence value especially when combined with other available information related to the missions and business functions supported by organizational systems. This control enhancement prevents the derivation of intelligence based on communications patterns and applies to internal and external networks or links that may be visible to individuals who are not authorized users. Encrypting the links and transmitting in continuous, fixed or random patterns prevents the derivation of intelligence from the system communications patterns. Alternative physical safeguards include, for example, protected distribution systems.

Related Controls: SC-12, SC-13.

References: FIPS Publications 140-2, 197; NIST Special Publications 800-52, 800-77, 800-81, 800-113, 800-177; NIST Interagency Report 8023.

SC-9   TRANSMISSION CONFIDENTIALITY

[Withdrawn: Incorporated into SC-8].

SC-10   NETWORK DISCONNECT

Control: Terminate the network connection associated with a communications session at the end of the session or after [*Assignment: organization-defined time-period*] of inactivity.

Supplemental Guidance: This control applies to internal and external networks. Terminating network connections associated with specific communications sessions include, for example, de-allocating associated TCP/IP address or port pairs at the operating system level and de-allocating networking assignments at the application level if multiple application sessions are using a single operating system-level network connection. Periods of inactivity may be established by organizations and include, for example, time-periods by type of network access or for specific network accesses.

Related Controls: AC-17, SC-23.

Control Enhancements: None.

References: None.

SC-11   TRUSTED PATH

Control:

a. Provide a [*Selection: physically; logically*] isolated trusted communications path for communications between the user and the trusted components of the system; and

b. Permit users to invoke the trusted communications path for communications between the user and the following security functions of the system, including at a minimum, authentication and re-authentication: [*Assignment: organization-defined security functions*].

Supplemental Guidance: Trusted paths are mechanisms by which users (through input devices) can communicate directly with security functions of systems with the requisite assurance to support security policies. These mechanisms can be activated only by users or the security functions of organizational systems. User responses via trusted paths are protected from modifications by or disclosure to untrusted applications. Organizations employ trusted paths for trustworthy, high-assurance connections between security functions of systems and users including, for example, during system logons. The original implementations of trusted path used an out-of-band signal to initiate the path, for example using the <BREAK> key, which does not transmit characters that can be spoofed. In later implementations, a key combination that could not be hijacked was used, for example, the <CTRL> + <ALT> + <DEL> keys. Note, however, that any such key combinations are platform-specific and may not provide a trusted path implementation in every case. Enforcement of trusted communications paths is typically provided by a specific implementation that meets the reference monitor concept.

Related Controls: AC-16, AC-25, SC-12, SC-23.

Control Enhancements:

(1) TRUSTED PATH | LOGICAL ISOLATION

  (a) Provide a trusted communications path that is irrefutably distinguishable from other communications paths; and

  (b) Initiate the trusted communications path for communications between the following security functions of the system and the user [*Assignment: organization-defined security functions*].

Supplemental Guidance: This enhancement permits the system to initiate a trusted path which necessitates that the user can unmistakably recognize the source of the communication as a trusted system component. For example, the trusted path may appear in an area of the display that other applications cannot access, or be based on the presence of an identifier that cannot be spoofed.

Related Controls: None.

References: None.

SC-12   CRYPTOGRAPHIC KEY ESTABLISHMENT AND MANAGEMENT

Control: Establish and manage cryptographic keys for required cryptography employed within the system in accordance with [*Assignment: organization-defined requirements for key generation, distribution, storage, access, and destruction*].

Supplemental Guidance: Cryptographic key management and establishment can be performed using manual procedures or automated mechanisms with supporting manual procedures. Organizations define their key management requirements in accordance with applicable laws, Executive Orders, directives, regulations, policies, standards, and guidelines, specifying appropriate options, levels, and parameters. Organizations manage trust stores to ensure that only approved trust anchors are in such trust stores. This includes certificates with visibility external to organizational systems and certificates related to the internal operations of systems.

Related Controls: AC-17, AU-9, AU-10, CM-3, IA-3, IA-7, SA-4, SA-9, SC-8, SC-11, SC-13, SC-17, SC-20, SC-37, SC-40, SI-3, SI-7.

Control Enhancements:

(1)   CRYPTOGRAPHIC KEY ESTABLISHMENT AND MANAGEMENT | AVAILABILITY

Maintain availability of information in the event of the loss of cryptographic keys by users.

Supplemental Guidance: Escrowing of encryption keys is a common practice for ensuring availability in the event of loss of keys. A forgotten passphrase is an example of losing a cryptographic key.

Related Controls: None.

(2)   CRYPTOGRAPHIC KEY ESTABLISHMENT AND MANAGEMENT | SYMMETRIC KEYS

Produce, control, and distribute symmetric cryptographic keys using [*Selection: NIST FIPS-compliant; NSA-approved*] key management technology and processes.

Supplemental Guidance: None.

Related Controls: None.

(3)   CRYPTOGRAPHIC KEY ESTABLISHMENT AND MANAGEMENT | ASYMMETRIC KEYS

Produce, control, and distribute asymmetric cryptographic keys using [*Selection: NSA-approved key management technology and processes; approved DoD PKI Class 3 certificates; prepositioned keying material; approved DoD PKI Class 3 or Class 4 certificates and hardware security tokens that protect the user's private key; certificates issued in accordance with organization-defined requirements*].

Supplemental Guidance: None.

Related Controls: None.

(4)   CRYPTOGRAPHIC KEY ESTABLISHMENT AND MANAGEMENT | PKI CERTIFICATES

[Withdrawn: Incorporated into SC-12].

(5)   CRYPTOGRAPHIC KEY ESTABLISHMENT AND MANAGEMENT | PKI CERTIFICATES / HARDWARE TOKENS

[Withdrawn: Incorporated into SC-12].

References: NIST Special Publications 800-56A, 800-56B, 800-56C, 800-57-1, 800-57-2, 800-57-3, 95663; NIST Interagency Reports 7956, 7966.

SC-13   CRYPTOGRAPHIC PROTECTION

Control: Implement the following cryptographic uses and type of cryptography for each use: [*Assignment: organization-defined cryptographic uses and type of cryptography required for each use*].

Supplemental Guidance: Cryptography can be employed to support a variety of security solutions including, for example, the protection of classified information and Controlled Unclassified Information; the provision and implementation of digital signatures; and the enforcement of information separation when authorized individuals have the necessary clearances but lack the necessary formal access approvals. Cryptography can also be used to support random number generation and hash generation. Generally applicable cryptographic standards include FIPS-validated cryptography and NSA-approved cryptography. This control does not impose any requirements on organizations to use cryptography. However, if cryptography is required due to the selection of other security controls, organizations define each type of cryptographic use and the type of cryptography required. For example, organizations that need to protect classified information specify the use of NSA-approved cryptography. Organizations that need to provision and implement digital signatures specify the use of FIPS-validated cryptography. In all instances, cryptography is implemented in accordance with applicable laws, Executive Orders, directives, policies, regulations, standards, and guidelines.

Related Controls: AC-2, AC-3, AC-7, AC-17, AC-18, AC-19, AU-9, AU-10, CM-11, CP-9, IA-3, IA-7, MA-4, MP-2, MP-4, MP-5, SA-4, SA-9, SC-8, SC-12, SC-20, SC-23, SC-28, SC-40, SI-3, SI-7.

Control Enhancements: None.

(1) CRYPTOGRAPHIC PROTECTION | FIPS-VALIDATED CRYPTOGRAPHY
[Withdrawn: Incorporated into SC-13].

(2) CRYPTOGRAPHIC PROTECTION | NSA-APPROVED CRYPTOGRAPHY
[Withdrawn: Incorporated into SC-13].

(3) CRYPTOGRAPHIC PROTECTION | INDIVIDUALS WITHOUT FORMAL ACCESS APPROVALS
[Withdrawn: Incorporated into SC-13].

(4) CRYPTOGRAPHIC PROTECTION | DIGITAL SIGNATURES
[Withdrawn: Incorporated into SC-13].

References: FIPS Publication 140-2.

SC-14 PUBLIC ACCESS PROTECTIONS

[Withdrawn: Incorporated into AC-2, AC-3, AC-5, AC-6, SI-3, SI-4, SI-5, SI-7, SI-10].

SC-15 COLLABORATIVE COMPUTING DEVICES AND APPLICATIONS

Control:

a. Prohibit remote activation of collaborative computing devices and applications with the following exceptions: [*Assignment: organization-defined exceptions where remote activation is to be allowed*]; and

b. Provide an explicit indication of use to users physically present at the devices.

Supplemental Guidance: Collaborative computing devices and applications include, for example, remote meeting devices and applications, networked white boards, cameras, and microphones. Explicit indication of use includes, for example, signals to users when collaborative computing devices and applications are activated.

Related Controls: AC-21.

Control Enhancements:

(1) COLLABORATIVE COMPUTING DEVICES | PHYSICAL DISCONNECT
Provide physical disconnect of collaborative computing devices in a manner that supports ease of use.

Supplemental Guidance: Failing to physically disconnect from collaborative computing devices can result in subsequent compromises of organizational information. Providing easy methods to physically disconnect from such devices after a collaborative computing session ensures that participants carry out the disconnect activity without having to go through complex and tedious procedures.

Related Controls: None.

(2) COLLABORATIVE COMPUTING DEVICES | BLOCKING INBOUND AND OUTBOUND COMMUNICATIONS TRAFFIC

[Withdrawn: Incorporated into SC-7].

(3) COLLABORATIVE COMPUTING DEVICES | DISABLING AND REMOVAL IN SECURE WORK AREAS

Disable or remove collaborative computing devices and applications from [*Assignment: organization-defined systems or system components*] in [*Assignment: organization-defined secure work areas*].

Supplemental Guidance: Failing to disable or remove collaborative computing devices and applications from systems or system components can result in subsequent compromises of organizational information including, for example, eavesdropping on conversations.

Related Controls: None.

(4) COLLABORATIVE COMPUTING DEVICES | EXPLICITLY INDICATE CURRENT PARTICIPANTS

Provide an explicit indication of current participants in [*Assignment: organization-defined online meetings and teleconferences*].

Supplemental Guidance: This control enhancement helps to prevent unauthorized individuals from participating in collaborative computing sessions without the explicit knowledge of other participants.

Related Controls: None.

References: None.

SC-16   TRANSMISSION OF SECURITY AND PRIVACY ATTRIBUTES

Control: Associate [*Assignment: organization-defined security and privacy attributes*] with information exchanged between systems and between system components.

Supplemental Guidance: Security and privacy attributes can be explicitly or implicitly associated with the information contained in systems or system components. Attributes are an abstraction representing the basic properties or characteristics of an entity with respect to safeguarding information or the management of personally identifiable information. Attributes are typically associated with internal data structures including, for example, records, buffers, files within the information system. Security and privacy attributes are used to implement access control and flow control policies; reflect special dissemination, management, or distribution instructions, including permitted uses of personally identifiable information; or support other aspects of the information security and privacy policies. Privacy attributes may be used independently, or in conjunction with security attributes.

Related Controls: AC-3, AC-4, AC-16.

Control Enhancements:

(1) TRANSMISSION OF SECURITY AND PRIVACY ATTRIBUTES | INTEGRITY VALIDATION

Validate the integrity of transmitted security and privacy attributes.

Supplemental Guidance: This control enhancement ensures that the integrity verification of transmitted information includes security and privacy attributes.

Related Controls: AU-10, SC-8.

References: None.

SC-17   PUBLIC KEY INFRASTRUCTURE CERTIFICATES

Control: Issue public key certificates under an [*Assignment: organization-defined certificate policy*] or obtain public key certificates from an approved service provider.

Supplemental Guidance: For all certificates, organizations manage system trust stores to ensure only approved trust anchors are in the trust stores. This control addresses certificates with visibility external to organizational systems and certificates related to the internal operations of systems, for example, application-specific time services.

Related Controls: AU-10, IA-5, SC-12.

Control Enhancements: None.

References: NIST Special Publications 800-32, 800-57-1, 800-57-2, 800-57-3, 800-63.

SC-18 MOBILE CODE

Control:

a. Define acceptable and unacceptable mobile code and mobile code technologies;

b. Establish usage restrictions and implementation guidance for acceptable mobile code and mobile code technologies; and

c. Authorize, monitor, and control the use of mobile code within the system.

Supplemental Guidance: Decisions regarding the use of mobile code within organizational systems are based on the potential for the code to cause damage to the systems if used maliciously. Mobile code technologies include, for example, Java, JavaScript, ActiveX, Postscript, PDF, Shockwave movies, Flash animations, and VBScript. Usage restrictions and implementation guidelines apply to both the selection and use of mobile code installed on servers and mobile code downloaded and executed on individual workstations and devices including, for example, notebook computers and smart phones. Mobile code policy and procedures address the specific actions taken to prevent the development, acquisition, and introduction of unacceptable mobile code within organizational systems.

Related Controls: AU-2, AU-12, CM-2, CM-6, SI-3.

Control Enhancements:

(1) MOBILE CODE | IDENTIFY UNACCEPTABLE CODE AND TAKE CORRECTIVE ACTIONS

Identify [*Assignment: organization-defined unacceptable mobile code*] and take [*Assignment: organization-defined corrective actions*].

Supplemental Guidance: Corrective actions when unacceptable mobile code is detected include, for example, blocking, quarantine, or alerting administrators. Blocking includes, for example, preventing transmission of word processing files with embedded macros when such macros have been defined to be unacceptable mobile code.

Related Controls: None.

(2) MOBILE CODE | ACQUISITION, DEVELOPMENT, AND USE

Verify that the acquisition, development, and use of mobile code to be deployed in the system meets [*Assignment: organization-defined mobile code requirements*].

Supplemental Guidance: None.

Related Controls: None.

(3) MOBILE CODE | PREVENT DOWNLOADING AND EXECUTION

Prevent the download and execution of [*Assignment: organization-defined unacceptable mobile code*].

Supplemental Guidance: None.

Related Controls: None.

(4) MOBILE CODE | PREVENT AUTOMATIC EXECUTION

Prevent the automatic execution of mobile code in [*Assignment: organization-defined software applications*] and enforce [*Assignment: organization-defined actions*] prior to executing the code.

Supplemental Guidance: Actions enforced before executing mobile code, include, for example, prompting users prior to opening electronic mail attachments. Preventing automatic execution of mobile code includes, for example, disabling auto execute features on system components employing portable storage devices such as Compact Disks (CDs), Digital Video Disks (DVDs), and Universal Serial Bus (USB) devices.

Related Controls: None.

(5) MOBILE CODE | ALLOW EXECUTION ONLY IN CONFINED ENVIRONMENTS

Allow execution of permitted mobile code only in confined virtual machine environments.

Supplemental Guidance: None.

Related Controls: SC-44, SI-7.

References: NIST Special Publication 800-28.

SC-19 VOICE OVER INTERNET PROTOCOL

Control:

a. Establish usage restrictions and implementation guidelines for Voice over Internet Protocol (VoIP) technologies; and

b. Authorize, monitor, and control the use of VoIP technologies within the system.

Supplemental Guidance: Usage restrictions and implementation guidelines are based on the potential for the VoIP technology to cause damage to the system if used maliciously.

Related Controls: CM-6, SC-7, SC-15.

Control Enhancements: None.

References: NIST Special Publication 800-58.

SC-20 SECURE NAME/ADDRESS RESOLUTION SERVICE (AUTHORITATIVE SOURCE)

Control:

a. Provide additional data origin authentication and integrity verification artifacts along with the authoritative name resolution data the system returns in response to external name/address resolution queries; and

b. Provide the means to indicate the security status of child zones and (if the child supports secure resolution services) to enable verification of a chain of trust among parent and child domains, when operating as part of a distributed, hierarchical namespace.

Supplemental Guidance: This control enables external clients including, for example, remote Internet clients, to obtain origin authentication and integrity verification assurances for the host/service name to network address resolution information obtained through the service. Systems that provide name and address resolution services include, for example, domain name system (DNS) servers. Additional artifacts include, for example, DNS Security (DNSSEC) digital signatures and cryptographic keys. DNS resource records are examples of authoritative data. The means to indicate the security status of child zones includes, for example, the use of delegation signer resource records in the DNS. Systems that use technologies other than the DNS to map between host and service names and network addresses provide other means to assure the authenticity and integrity of response data.

Related Controls: AU-10, SC-8, SC-12, SC-13, SC-21, SC-22.

Control Enhancements:

(1) SECURE NAME/ADDRESS RESOLUTION SERVICE (AUTHORITATIVE SOURCE) | CHILD SUBSPACES

[Withdrawn: Incorporated into SC-20].

(2) SECURE NAME/ADDRESS RESOLUTION SERVICE (AUTHORITATIVE SOURCE) | DATA ORIGIN AND INTEGRITY

Provide data origin and integrity protection artifacts for internal name/address resolution queries.

Supplemental Guidance: None.

Related Controls: None.

References: FIPS Publications 140-2, 186-4; NIST Special Publication 800-81.

SC-21 SECURE NAME/ADDRESS RESOLUTION SERVICE (RECURSIVE OR CACHING RESOLVER)

Control: Request and perform data origin authentication and data integrity verification on the name/address resolution responses the system receives from authoritative sources.

Supplemental Guidance: Each client of name resolution services either performs this validation on its own, or has authenticated channels to trusted validation providers. Systems that provide name and address resolution services for local clients include, for example, recursive resolving or caching domain name system (DNS) servers. DNS client resolvers either perform validation of DNSSEC signatures, or clients use authenticated channels to recursive resolvers that perform such validations. Systems that use technologies other than the DNS to map between host/service names and network addresses provide some other means to enable clients to verify the authenticity and integrity of response data.

Related Controls: SC-20, SC-22.

Control Enhancements: None.

(1) SECURE NAME/ADDRESS RESOLUTION SERVICE (RECURSIVE OR CACHING RESOLVER) | DATA ORIGIN AND INTEGRITY

[Withdrawn: Incorporated into SC-21].

References: NIST Special Publication 800-81.

SC-22 ARCHITECTURE AND PROVISIONING FOR NAME/ADDRESS RESOLUTION SERVICE

Control: Ensure the systems that collectively provide name/address resolution service for an organization are fault-tolerant and implement internal and external role separation.

Supplemental Guidance: Systems that provide name and address resolution services include, for example, domain name system (DNS) servers. To eliminate single points of failure and to enhance redundancy, organizations employ at least two authoritative domain name system servers; one configured as the primary server and the other configured as the secondary server. Additionally, organizations typically deploy the servers in two geographically separated network subnetworks (i.e., not located in the same physical facility). For role separation, DNS servers with internal roles only process name and address resolution requests from within organizations (i.e., from internal clients). DNS servers with external roles only process name and address resolution information requests from clients external to organizations (i.e., on external networks including the Internet). Organizations specify clients that can access authoritative DNS servers in certain roles, for example, by address ranges and explicit lists.

Related Controls: SC-2, SC-20, SC-21, SC-24.

Control Enhancements: None.

References: NIST Special Publication 800-81.

SC-23 SESSION AUTHENTICITY

Control: Protect the authenticity of communications sessions.

Supplemental Guidance: This control addresses communications protection at the session, versus packet level. Such protection establishes grounds for confidence at both ends of communications sessions in the ongoing identities of other parties and in the validity of information transmitted. Authenticity protection includes, for example, protecting against man-in-the-middle attacks and session hijacking, and the insertion of false information into sessions.

Related Controls: AU-10, SC-8, SC-10, SC-11.

Control Enhancements:

(1) SESSION AUTHENTICITY | INVALIDATE SESSION IDENTIFIERS AT LOGOUT

Invalidate session identifiers upon user logout or other session termination.

Supplemental Guidance: This control enhancement curtails the ability of adversaries from capturing and continuing to employ previously valid session IDs.

Related Controls: None.

(2) SESSION AUTHENTICITY | USER-INITIATED LOGOUTS AND MESSAGE DISPLAYS
[Withdrawn: Incorporated into AC-12(1)].

(3) SESSION AUTHENTICITY | UNIQUE SESSION IDENTIFIERS WITH RANDOMIZATION
Generate a unique session identifier for each session with [*Assignment: organization-defined randomness requirements*] and recognize only session identifiers that are system-generated.

Supplemental Guidance: This control enhancement curtails the ability of adversaries from reusing previously valid session IDs. Employing the concept of randomness in the generation of unique session identifiers protects against brute-force attacks to determine future session identifiers.

Related Controls: AC-10, SC-13.

(4) SESSION AUTHENTICITY | UNIQUE SESSION IDENTIFIERS WITH RANDOMIZATION
[Withdrawn: Incorporated into SC-23(3)].

(5) SESSION AUTHENTICITY | ALLOWED CERTIFICATE AUTHORITIES
Only allow the use of [*Assignment: organization-defined certificate authorities*] for verification of the establishment of protected sessions.

Supplemental Guidance: Reliance on certificate authorities (CAs) for the establishment of secure sessions includes, for example, the use of Transport Layer Security (TLS) certificates. These certificates, after verification by their respective CAs, facilitate the establishment of protected sessions between web clients and web servers.

Related Controls: SC-13.

References: NIST Special Publications 800-52, 800-77, 800-95, 800-113.

SC-24   FAIL IN KNOWN STATE

Control: Fail to a [*Assignment: organization-defined known system state*] for [*Assignment: organization-defined types of system failures*] preserving [*Assignment: organization-defined system state information*] in failure.

Supplemental Guidance: Failure in a known state addresses security concerns in accordance with the mission and business needs of organizations. Failure in a known state helps to prevent the loss of confidentiality, integrity, or availability of information in the event of failures of organizational systems or system components. Failure in a known safe state helps to prevent systems from failing to a state that may cause injury to individuals or destruction to property. Preserving system state information facilitates system restart and return to the operational mode of organizations with less disruption of mission and business processes.

Related Controls: CP-2, CP-4, CP-10, CP-12, SC-7, SC-22, SI-13.

Control Enhancements: None.

References: None.

SC-25   THIN NODES

Control: Employ [*Assignment: organization-defined system components*] with minimal functionality and information storage.

Supplemental Guidance: The deployment of system components with minimal functionality reduces the need to secure every user endpoint, and may reduce the exposure of information, systems, and services to attacks. Examples of reduced or minimal functionality include, for example, diskless nodes and thin client technologies.

Related Controls: SC-30, SC-44.

Control Enhancements: None.

References: None.

SC-26   HONEYPOTS

Control: Include components within organizational systems specifically designed to be the target of malicious attacks for detecting, deflecting, and analyzing such attacks.

Supplemental Guidance: A honeypot is established as a decoy to attract adversaries and to deflect their attacks away from the operational systems supporting organizational missions and business functions. Depending upon the specific usage of the honeypot, consultation with the Office of the General Counsel before deployment may be needed.

Related Controls: SC-30, SC-35, SC-44, SI-3, SI-4.

Control Enhancements: None.

(1)   HONEYPOTS | DETECTION OF MALICIOUS CODE
[Withdrawn: Incorporated into SC-35].

References: None.

SC-27   PLATFORM-INDEPENDENT APPLICATIONS

Control: Include within organizational systems: [Assignment: organization-defined platform-independent applications].

Supplemental Guidance: Platforms are combinations of hardware and software used to run software applications. Platforms include operating systems; the underlying computer architectures; or both. Platform-independent applications are those applications with the capability to execute on multiple platforms. Such applications promote portability and reconstitution on different platforms. This increases the availability of critical or essential functions within organizations in situations where systems with specific operating systems are under attack.

Related Controls: SC-29.

Control Enhancements: None.

References: None.

SC-28   PROTECTION OF INFORMATION AT REST

Control: Protect the [Selection (one or more): confidentiality; integrity] of [Assignment: organization-defined information] at rest.

Supplemental Guidance: This control addresses the confidentiality and integrity of information at rest and covers user information and system information. Information at rest refers to the state of information when it is not in process or in transit and is located on storage devices as specific components of systems. The focus of this control is not on the type of storage device or frequency of access but rather the state of the information. System-related information requiring protection includes, for example, configurations or rule sets for firewalls, gateways, intrusion detection and prevention systems, filtering routers, and authenticator content. Organizations may employ different mechanisms to achieve confidentiality and integrity protections, including the use of cryptographic mechanisms and file share scanning. Integrity protection can be achieved, for example, by implementing Write-Once-Read-Many (WORM) technologies. When adequate protection of information at rest cannot otherwise be achieved, organizations may employ other security controls including, for example, frequent scanning to identify malicious code at rest and secure off-line storage in lieu of online storage.

Related Controls: AC-3, AC-6, AC-19, CA-7, CM-3, CM-5, CM-6, CP-9, MP-4, MP-5, PE-3, SC-8, SC-13, SC-34, SI-3, SI-7, SI-16.

Control Enhancements:

(1) PROTECTION OF INFORMATION AT REST | CRYPTOGRAPHIC PROTECTION

Implement cryptographic mechanisms to prevent unauthorized disclosure and modification of [*Assignment: organization-defined information*] when at rest on [*Assignment: organization-defined system components*].

Supplemental Guidance: This control enhancement applies to significant concentrations of digital media in organizational areas designated for media storage. It also applies to limited quantities of media generally associated with system components in operational environments including, for example, portable storage devices, notebook computers, and mobile devices. Selection of cryptographic mechanisms is based on the need to protect the confidentiality and integrity of organizational information. The strength of mechanism is commensurate with the security category or classification of the information. Organizations have the flexibility to encrypt all information on storage devices or encrypt specific data structures including, for example, files, records, or fields. Organizations employing cryptographic mechanisms to protect information at rest also consider cryptographic key management solutions.

Related Controls: AC-19, SC-12.

(2) PROTECTION OF INFORMATION AT REST | OFF-LINE STORAGE

Remove the following information from online storage and store off-line in a secure location: [*Assignment: organization-defined information*].

Supplemental Guidance: Removing organizational information from online system storage to off-line storage eliminates the possibility of individuals gaining unauthorized access to the information through a network. Therefore, organizations may choose to move information to off-line storage in lieu of protecting such information in online storage.

Related Controls: None.

References: NIST Special Publications 800-56A, 800-56B, 800-56C, 800-57-1, 800-57-2, 800-57-3, 800-111, 800-124.

SC-29 HETEROGENEITY

Control: Employ a diverse set of information technologies for [*Assignment: organization-defined system components*] in the implementation of the system.

Supplemental Guidance: Increasing the diversity of information technologies within organizational systems reduces the impact of potential exploitations or compromises of specific technologies. Such diversity protects against common mode failures, including those failures induced by supply chain attacks. Diversity in information technologies also reduces the likelihood that the means adversaries use to compromise one system component will be equally effective against other system components, thus further increasing the adversary work factor to successfully complete planned attacks. An increase in diversity may add complexity and management overhead which could ultimately lead to mistakes and unauthorized configurations.

Related Controls: AU-9, PL-8, SA-12, SC-27, SC-30.

Control Enhancements:

(1) HETEROGENEITY | VIRTUALIZATION TECHNIQUES

Employ virtualization techniques to support the deployment of a diversity of operating systems and applications that are changed [*Assignment: organization-defined frequency*].

Supplemental Guidance: While frequent changes to operating systems and applications pose configuration management challenges, the changes can result in an increased work factor for adversaries to conduct successful attacks. Changing virtual operating systems or applications, as opposed to changing actual operating systems or applications, provides virtual changes that impede attacker success while reducing configuration management efforts. Virtualization techniques can assist in isolating untrustworthy software or software of dubious provenance into confined execution environments.

Related Controls: None.

References. None.

SC-30 CONCEALMENT AND MISDIRECTION

Control: Employ [Assignment: organization-defined concealment and misdirection techniques] for [Assignment: organization-defined systems] at [Assignment: organization-defined time-periods] to confuse and mislead adversaries.

Supplemental Guidance: Concealment and misdirection techniques can significantly reduce the targeting capability of adversaries (i.e., window of opportunity and available attack surface) to initiate and complete attacks. For example, virtualization techniques provide organizations with the ability to disguise systems, potentially reducing the likelihood of successful attacks without the cost of having multiple platforms. Increased use of concealment and misdirection techniques and methods including, for example, randomness, uncertainty, and virtualization, may sufficiently confuse and mislead adversaries and subsequently increase the risk of discovery and/or exposing tradecraft. Concealment and misdirection techniques may also provide organizations additional time to successfully perform core missions and business functions. Because of the time and effort required to support concealment and misdirection techniques, it is anticipated that such techniques would be used by organizations on a very limited basis.

Related Controls: AC-6, SC-25, SC-26, SC-29, SC-44, SI-14.

Control Enhancements:

(1) CONCEALMENT AND MISDIRECTION | VIRTUALIZATION TECHNIQUES
[Withdrawn: Incorporated into SC-29(1)].

(2) CONCEALMENT AND MISDIRECTION | RANDOMNESS
Employ [Assignment: organization-defined techniques] to introduce randomness into organizational operations and assets.

Supplemental Guidance: Randomness introduces increased levels of uncertainty for adversaries regarding the actions organizations take in defending their systems against attacks. Such actions may impede the ability of adversaries to correctly target information resources of organizations supporting critical missions or business functions. Uncertainty may also cause adversaries to hesitate before initiating or continuing their attacks. Misdirection techniques involving randomness include, for example, performing certain routine actions at different times of day, employing different information technologies, using different suppliers, and rotating roles and responsibilities of organizational personnel.

Related Controls: None.

(3) CONCEALMENT AND MISDIRECTION | CHANGE PROCESSING AND STORAGE LOCATIONS
Change the location of [Assignment: organization-defined processing and/or storage] [Selection: [Assignment: organization-defined time frequency]; at random time intervals]].

Supplemental Guidance: Adversaries target critical missions and business functions and the systems supporting those missions and functions while at the same time, trying to minimize exposure of their existence and tradecraft. The static, homogeneous, and deterministic nature of organizational systems targeted by adversaries, make such systems more susceptible to attacks with less adversary cost and effort to be successful. Changing processing and storage locations (sometimes referred to as moving target defense) addresses the advanced persistent threat (APT) using techniques such as virtualization, distributed processing, and replication. This enables organizations to relocate the system components (i.e., processing and/or storage) supporting critical missions and business functions. Changing the locations of processing activities and/or storage sites introduces a degree of uncertainty into the targeting activities by adversaries. This uncertainty increases the work factor of adversaries making compromises or breaches to organizational systems much more difficult and time-consuming. It also increases the chances that adversaries may inadvertently disclose aspects of tradecraft while attempting to locate critical organizational resources.

Related Controls: None.

(4) CONCEALMENT AND MISDIRECTION | MISLEADING INFORMATION

Employ realistic, but misleading information in [*Assignment: organization-defined system components*] about its security state or posture.

Supplemental Guidance: This control enhancement misleads potential adversaries regarding the nature and extent of security safeguards deployed by organizations. Thus, adversaries may employ incorrect and ineffective, attack techniques. One way of misleading adversaries is for organizations to place misleading information regarding the specific controls deployed in external systems that are known to be targeted by adversaries. Another technique is the use of deception nets that mimic actual aspects of organizational systems but use, for example, out-of-date software configurations.

Related Controls: None.

(5) CONCEALMENT AND MISDIRECTION | CONCEALMENT OF SYSTEM COMPONENTS

Employ [*Assignment: organization-defined techniques*] to hide or conceal [*Assignment: organization-defined system components*].

Supplemental Guidance: By hiding, disguising, or concealing critical system components, organizations may be able to decrease the probability that adversaries target and successfully compromise those assets. Potential means for organizations to hide, disguise, or conceal system components include, for example, configuration of routers or the use of honeynets or virtualization techniques.

Related Controls: None.

References: None.

SC-31 COVERT CHANNEL ANALYSIS

Control:

a. Perform a covert channel analysis to identify those aspects of communications within the system that are potential avenues for covert [*Selection (one or more): storage; timing*] channels; and

b. Estimate the maximum bandwidth of those channels.

Supplemental Guidance: Developers are in the best position to identify potential areas within systems that might lead to covert channels. Covert channel analysis is a meaningful activity when there is the potential for unauthorized information flows across handling caveats, discretionary policies, or security domains, for example, in the case of systems containing export-controlled information and having connections to external networks (i.e., networks that are not controlled by organizations). Covert channel analysis is also useful for multilevel secure systems, multiple security level systems, and cross-domain systems.

Related Controls: AC-3, AC-4, SI-11.

Control Enhancements:

(1) COVERT CHANNEL ANALYSIS | TEST COVERT CHANNELS FOR EXPLOITABILITY

Test a subset of the identified covert channels to determine which channels are exploitable.

Supplemental Guidance: None.

Related Controls: None.

(2) COVERT CHANNEL ANALYSIS | MAXIMUM BANDWIDTH

Reduce the maximum bandwidth for identified covert [*Selection (one or more); storage; timing*] channels to [*Assignment: organization-defined values*].

Supplemental Guidance: None.

Related Controls: None.

(3) COVERT CHANNEL ANALYSIS | MEASURE BANDWIDTH IN OPERATIONAL ENVIRONMENTS

Measure the bandwidth of [*Assignment: organization-defined subset of identified covert channels*] in the operational environment of the system.

operational environments versus developmental environments. Measuring covert channel bandwidth in specified operational environments helps organizations to determine how much information can be covertly leaked before such leakage adversely affects missions or business functions. Covert channel bandwidth may be significantly different when measured in those settings that are independent of the specific environments of operation including, for example, laboratories or development environments.

Related Controls: None.

References: None.

SC-32   SYSTEM PARTITIONING

Control: Partition the system into [*Assignment: organization-defined system components*] residing in separate physical domains or environments based on [*Assignment: organization-defined circumstances for physical separation of components*].

Supplemental Guidance: System partitioning is a part of a defense-in-depth protection strategy. Organizations determine the degree of physical separation of system components from physically distinct components in separate racks in the same room, to components in separate rooms for the more critical components, to significant geographical separation of the most critical components. Security categorization can guide the selection of appropriate candidates for domain partitioning. Managed interfaces restrict or prohibit network access and information flow among partitioned system components.

Related Controls: AC-4, AC-6, SA-8, SC-2, SC-3, SC-7, SC-36.

Control Enhancements: None.

References: FIPS Publication 199.

SC-33   TRANSMISSION PREPARATION INTEGRITY

[Withdrawn: Incorporated into SC-8].

SC-34   NON-MODIFIABLE EXECUTABLE PROGRAMS

Control: At [*Assignment: organization-defined system components*]:

a. Load and execute the operating environment from hardware-enforced, read-only media; and

b. Load and execute [*Assignment: organization-defined applications*] from hardware-enforced, read-only media.

Supplemental Guidance: The operating environment for a system contains the specific code that hosts applications, for example, operating systems, executives, or monitors including virtual machine monitors (i.e., hypervisors). It can also include certain applications running directly on hardware platforms. Hardware-enforced, read-only media include, for example, Compact Disk-Recordable (CD-R) and Digital Video Disk-Recordable (DVD-R) disk drives and one-time programmable read-only memory. The use of non-modifiable storage ensures the integrity of software from the point of creation of the read-only image. The use of reprogrammable read-only memory can be accepted as read-only media provided integrity can be adequately protected from the point of initial writing to the insertion of the memory into the system; and there are reliable hardware protections against reprogramming the memory while installed in organizational systems.

Related Controls: AC-3, SI-7, SI-14.

Control Enhancements:

(1) NON-MODIFIABLE EXECUTABLE PROGRAMS | NO WRITABLE STORAGE

Employ [*Assignment: organization-defined system components*] with no writeable storage that is persistent across component restart or power on/off.

Supplemental Guidance: This control enhancement eliminates the possibility of malicious code insertion via persistent, writeable storage within the designated system components. It applies to fixed and removable storage, with the latter being addressed either directly or as specific restrictions imposed through access controls for mobile devices.

Related Controls: AC-19, MP-7.

(2) NON-MODIFIABLE EXECUTABLE PROGRAMS | INTEGRITY PROTECTION ON READ-ONLY MEDIA

Protect the integrity of information prior to storage on read-only media and control the media after such information has been recorded onto the media.

Supplemental Guidance: Security safeguards prevent the substitution of media into systems or the reprogramming of programmable read-only media prior to installation into the systems. Such safeguards include, for example, a combination of prevention, detection, and response.

Related Controls: CM-3, CM-5, CM-9, MP-2, MP-4, MP-5, SC-28, SI-3.

(3) NON-MODIFIABLE EXECUTABLE PROGRAMS | HARDWARE-BASED PROTECTION

(a) Employ hardware-based, write-protect for [*Assignment: organization-defined system firmware components*]; and

(b) Implement specific procedures for [*Assignment: organization-defined authorized individuals*] to manually disable hardware write-protect for firmware modifications and re-enable the write-protect prior to returning to operational mode.

Supplemental Guidance: None.

Related Controls: None.

References: None.

SC-35   HONEYCLIENTS

Control: Include system components that proactively seek to identify network-based malicious code, malicious websites, or web-based malicious code.

Supplemental Guidance: Honeyclients differ from honeypots in that the components actively probe networks including, the Internet, in search of malicious code contained on external websites. Like honeypots, honeyclients require some supporting isolation measures to ensure that any malicious code discovered during the search and subsequently executed does not infect organizational systems. Virtualization is a common technique for achieving such isolation.

Related Controls: SC-26, SC-44, SI-3, SI-4.

Control Enhancements: None.

References: None.

SC-36   DISTRIBUTED PROCESSING AND STORAGE

Control: Distribute [*Assignment: organization-defined processing and storage components*] across multiple physical locations.

Supplemental Guidance: Distributing processing and storage across multiple physical locations provides some degree of redundancy or overlap for organizations, and therefore increases the work factor of adversaries to adversely impact organizational operations, assets, and individuals. This control does not assume a single primary processing or storage location, and therefore, allows for parallel processing and storage.

Related Controls: CP-6, CP-7, PL-8, SC-32.

Control Enhancements:

(1)   DISTRIBUTED PROCESSING AND STORAGE | POLLING TECHNIQUES

(a)   Employ polling techniques to identify potential faults, errors, or compromises to [*Assignment: organization-defined distributed processing and storage components*]; and

(b)   Take [*Assignment: organization-defined action*] in response to identified faults, errors, or compromises.

Supplemental Guidance: Distributed processing and/or storage may be employed to reduce opportunities for adversaries to successfully compromise the confidentiality, integrity, or availability of information and systems. However, distribution of processing and/or storage components does not prevent adversaries from compromising one (or more) of the distributed components. Polling compares the processing results and/or storage content from the various distributed components and subsequently voting on the outcomes. Polling identifies potential faults, errors, or compromises in distributed processing and storage components. Polling techniques may also be applied to processing and storage components that are not physically distributed.

Related Controls: SI-4.

References: None.

SC-37   OUT-OF-BAND CHANNELS

Control: Employ [*Assignment: organization-defined out-of-band channels*] for the physical delivery or electronic transmission of [*Assignment: organization-defined information, system components, or devices*] to [*Assignment: organization-defined individuals or systems*].

Supplemental Guidance: Out-of-band channels include, for example, local nonnetwork accesses to systems; network paths physically separate from network paths used for operational traffic; or nonelectronic paths such as the US Postal Service. This is in contrast with using the same channels (i.e., in-band channels) that carry routine operational traffic. Out-of-band channels do not have the same vulnerability or exposure as in-band channels, and therefore, the confidentiality, integrity, or availability compromises of in-band channels will not compromise or adversely affect the out-of-band channels. Organizations may employ out-of-band channels in the delivery or transmission of many organizational items including, for example, identifiers and authenticators; cryptographic key management information; configuration management changes for hardware, firmware, or software; security updates; system and data backups; maintenance information; and malicious code protection updates.

Related Controls: AC-2, CM-3, CM-5, CM-7, IA-2, IA-4, IA-5, MA-4, SC-12, SI-3, SI-4, SI-7.

Control Enhancements:

(1)   OUT-OF-BAND CHANNELS | ENSURE DELIVERY AND TRANSMISSION

Employ [*Assignment: organization-defined security safeguards*] to ensure that only [*Assignment: organization-defined individuals or systems*] receive the [*Assignment: organization-defined information, system components, or devices*].

Supplemental Guidance: Techniques employed by organizations to ensure that only designated systems or individuals receive certain information, system components, or devices include, for example, sending authenticators via an approved courier service but requiring recipients to show some form of government-issued photographic identification as a condition of receipt.

Related Controls: None.

References: NIST Special Publication 800-57-1, 800-57-2, 800-57-3.

SC-38   OPERATIONS SECURITY

Control: Employ [*Assignment: organization-defined operations security safeguards*] to protect key organizational information throughout the system development life cycle.

Supplemental Guidance: Operations security (OPSEC) is a systematic process by which potential adversaries can be denied information about the capabilities and intentions of organizations by identifying, controlling, and protecting generally unclassified information that specifically relates to the planning and execution of sensitive organizational activities. The OPSEC process involves five steps: identification of critical information; analysis of threats; analysis of vulnerabilities; assessment of risks; and the application of appropriate countermeasures. OPSEC safeguards are applied to organizational systems and the environments in which those systems operate. OPSEC safeguards protect the confidentiality of key information including, for example, limiting the sharing of information with suppliers and potential suppliers of system components and services, and with other non-organizational elements and individuals. Information critical to organizational mission and business success includes, for example, user identities, element uses, suppliers, supply chain processes, functional and security requirements, system design specifications, testing and evaluation protocols, and security control implementation details.

Related Controls: CA-2, CA-7, PL-1, PM-9, PM-12, RA-2, RA-3, RA-5, SA-12, SC-7.

Control Enhancements: None.

References: None.

SC-39   PROCESS ISOLATION

Control: Maintain a separate execution domain for each executing process with the system.

Supplemental Guidance: Systems can maintain separate execution domains for each executing process by assigning each process a separate address space. Each system process has a distinct address space so that communication between processes is performed in a manner controlled through the security functions, and one process cannot modify the executing code of another process. Maintaining separate execution domains for executing processes can be achieved, for example, by implementing separate address spaces. This capability is readily available in most commercial operating systems that employ multi-state processor technologies.

Related Controls: AC-3, AC-4, AC-6, AC-25, SA-8, SC-2, SC-3.

Control Enhancements:

(1) PROCESS ISOLATION | HARDWARE SEPARATION

Implement hardware separation mechanisms to facilitate process separation.

Supplemental Guidance: Hardware-based separation of system processes is generally less susceptible to compromise than software-based separation, thus providing greater assurance that the separation will be enforced. Hardware separation mechanisms include, for example, hardware memory management.

Related Controls: None.

(2) PROCESS ISOLATION | THREAD ISOLATION

Maintain a separate execution domain for each thread in [*Assignment: organization-defined multi-threaded processing*].

Supplemental Guidance: None.

Related Controls: None.

References: None.

SC-40   WIRELESS LINK PROTECTION

Control: Protect external and internal [*Assignment: organization-defined wireless links*] from [*Assignment: organization-defined types of signal parameter attacks or references to sources for such attacks*].

Supplemental Guidance: This control applies to internal and external wireless communication links that may be visible to individuals who are not authorized system users. Adversaries can exploit the signal parameters of wireless links if such links are not adequately protected. There are many ways to exploit the signal parameters of wireless links to gain intelligence, deny service, or spoof users of organizational systems. This control reduces the impact of attacks that are unique to wireless systems. If organizations rely on commercial service providers for transmission services as commodity items rather than as fully dedicated services, it may not be possible to implement this control.

Related Controls: AC-18, SC-5.

Control Enhancements:

(1) WIRELESS LINK PROTECTION | ELECTROMAGNETIC INTERFERENCE

Implement cryptographic mechanisms that achieve [*Assignment: organization-defined level of protection*] against the effects of intentional electromagnetic interference.

Supplemental Guidance: This control enhancement protects against intentional jamming that might deny or impair communications by ensuring that wireless spread spectrum waveforms used to provide anti-jam protection are not predictable by unauthorized individuals. The control enhancement may also coincidentally help to mitigate the effects of unintentional jamming due to interference from legitimate transmitters sharing the same spectrum. Mission requirements, projected threats, concept of operations, and applicable legislation, directives, regulations, policies, standards, and guidelines determine levels of wireless link availability and performance/cryptography needed.

Related Controls: SC-12, SC-13.

(2) WIRELESS LINK PROTECTION | REDUCE DETECTION POTENTIAL

Implement cryptographic mechanisms to reduce the detection potential of wireless links to [*Assignment: organization-defined level of reduction*].

Supplemental Guidance: This control enhancement is needed for covert communications and protecting wireless transmitters from being geo-located by their transmissions. The control enhancement ensures that spread spectrum waveforms used to achieve low probability of detection are not predictable by unauthorized individuals. Mission requirements, projected threats, concept of operations, and applicable legislation, directives, regulations, policies, standards, and guidelines determine the levels to which wireless links should be undetectable.

Related Controls: SC-12, SC-13.

(3) WIRELESS LINK PROTECTION | IMITATIVE OR MANIPULATIVE COMMUNICATIONS DECEPTION

Implement cryptographic mechanisms to identify and reject wireless transmissions that are deliberate attempts to achieve imitative or manipulative communications deception based on signal parameters.

Supplemental Guidance: This control enhancement ensures that the signal parameters of wireless transmissions are not predictable by unauthorized individuals. Such unpredictability reduces the probability of imitative or manipulative communications deception based upon signal parameters alone.

Related Controls: SC-12, SC-13, SI-4.

(4) WIRELESS LINK PROTECTION | SIGNAL PARAMETER IDENTIFICATION

Implement cryptographic mechanisms to prevent the identification of [*Assignment: organization-defined wireless transmitters*] by using the transmitter signal parameters.

Supplemental Guidance: Radio fingerprinting techniques identify the unique signal parameters of transmitters to fingerprint such transmitters for purposes of tracking and mission/user identification. This control enhancement protects against the unique identification of wireless transmitters for purposes of intelligence exploitation by ensuring that anti-fingerprinting alterations to signal parameters are not predictable by unauthorized individuals. This control enhancement helps assure mission success when anonymity is required.

Related Controls: SC-12, SC-13.

References: None.

SC-41   PORT AND I/O DEVICE ACCESS

Control: [*Selection: Physically or Logically*] disable or remove [*Assignment: organization-defined connection ports or input/output devices*] on [*Assignment: organization-defined systems or system components*].

Supplemental Guidance: Connection ports include, for example, Universal Serial Bus (USB) and Firewire (IEEE 1394). Input/output (I/O) devices include, for example, Compact Disk (CD) and Digital Video Disk (DVD) drives. Disabling or removing such connection ports and I/O devices helps prevent exfiltration of information from systems and the introduction of malicious code into systems from those ports or devices. Physically disabling or removing ports and/or devices is the stronger action.

Related Controls: AC-20, MP-7.

Control Enhancements: None.

References: None.

SC-42   SENSOR CAPABILITY AND DATA

Control:

a.   Prohibit the remote activation of environmental sensing capabilities on organizational systems or system components with the following exceptions: [*Assignment: organization-defined exceptions where remote activation of sensors is allowed*]; and

b.   Provide an explicit indication of sensor use to [*Assignment: organization-defined class of users*].

Supplemental Guidance: This control often applies to types of systems or system components characterized as mobile devices, for example, smart phones, tablets, and E-readers. These systems often include sensors that can collect and record data regarding the environment where the system is in use. Sensors that are embedded within mobile devices include, for example, cameras, microphones, Global Positioning System (GPS) mechanisms, and accelerometers. While the sensors on mobiles devices provide an important function, if activated covertly, such devices can potentially provide a means for adversaries to learn valuable information about individuals and organizations. For example, remotely activating the GPS function on a mobile device could provide an adversary with the ability to track the specific movements of an individual.

Related Controls: None.

Control Enhancements:

(1)   SENSOR CAPABILITY AND DATA | REPORTING TO AUTHORIZED INDIVIDUALS OR ROLES

Verify that the system is configured so that data or information collected by the [*Assignment: organization-defined sensors*] is only reported to authorized individuals or roles.

Supplemental Guidance: In situations where sensors are activated by authorized individuals, it is still possible that the data or information collected by the sensors will be sent to unauthorized entities.

Related Controls: None.

(2)   SENSOR CAPABILITY AND DATA | AUTHORIZED USE

Employ [*Assignment: organization-defined measures*] so that data or information collected by [*Assignment: organization-defined sensors*] is only used for authorized purposes.

Supplemental Guidance: Information collected by sensors for a specific authorized purpose could be misused for some unauthorized purpose. For example, GPS sensors that are used to support traffic navigation could be misused to track movements of individuals. Measures to mitigate such activities include, for example, additional training to ensure that authorized individuals do not abuse their authority; and in the case where sensor data or information is maintained by external parties, contractual restrictions on the use of such data/information.

Related Controls: PA-2.

(3)   SENSOR CAPABILITY AND DATA | PROHIBIT USE OF DEVICES

Prohibit the use of devices possessing [*Assignment: organization-defined environmental sensing capabilities*] in [*Assignment: organization-defined facilities, areas, or systems*].

Supplemental Guidance: For example, organizations may prohibit individuals from bringing cell phones or digital cameras into certain designated facilities or controlled areas within facilities where classified information is stored or sensitive conversations are taking place.

Related Controls: None.

(4)   SENSOR CAPABILITY AND DATA | NOTICE OF COLLECTION

Employ the following measures to facilitate an individual's awareness that personally identifiable information is being collected by [*Assignment: organization-defined sensors*]: [*Assignment: organization-defined measures*].

Supplemental Guidance: Awareness that organizational sensors are collecting data enable individuals to more effectively engage in managing their privacy. Measures can include, for example, conventional written notices and sensor configurations that make individuals aware directly or indirectly through other devices that the sensor is collecting information. Usability and efficacy of the notice are important considerations.

Related Controls: IP-1, IP-2, IP-4.

(5)   SENSOR CAPABILITY AND DATA | COLLECTION MINIMIZATION

Employ [*Assignment: organization-defined sensors*] that are configured to minimize the collection of information about individuals that is not needed.

Supplemental Guidance: Although policies to control for authorized use can be applied to information once it is collected, minimizing the collection of information that is not needed mitigates privacy-related risk at the system entry point and mitigates the risk of policy control failures. Sensor configurations include, for example, the obscuring of human features such as blurring or pixelating flesh tones.

Related Controls: None.

References: NIST Special Publication 800-124.

SC-43   USAGE RESTRICTIONS

Control:

a.   Establish usage restrictions and implementation guidelines for [*Assignment: organization-defined system components*]; and

b.   Authorize, monitor, and control the use of such components within the system.

Supplemental Guidance: This control applies to all system components including wired and wireless peripheral components, for example, copiers, printers, scanners, optical devices, and other similar technologies. Usage restrictions and implementation guidelines are based on the potential for the system components to cause damage to the system if used maliciously. Usage restrictions for other technologies such as VoIP, mobile code, mobile devices, and wireless are addressed in SC-19, SC-18, AC-19, and AC-18.

Related Controls: AC-18, AC-19, CM-6, SC-7, SC-18, SC-19.

Control Enhancements: None.

References: NIST Special Publication 800-124.

SC-44   DETONATION CHAMBERS

Control: Employ a detonation chamber capability within [*Assignment: organization-defined system, system component, or location*].

Supplemental Guidance: Detonation chambers, also known as dynamic execution environments, allow organizations to open email attachments, execute untrusted or suspicious applications, and execute Universal Resource Locator requests in the safety of an isolated environment or a virtualized sandbox. These protected and isolated execution environments provide a means of determining whether the associated attachments or applications contain malicious code. While related to the concept of deception nets, this control is not intended to maintain a long-term environment in which adversaries can operate and their actions can be observed. Rather, it is intended to quickly identify malicious code and reduce the likelihood that the code is propagated to user environments of operation or prevent such propagation completely.

Related Controls: SC-7, SC-25, SC-26, SC-30, SC-35, SI-3, SI-7.

Control Enhancements: None.

References: NIST Special Publication 800-177.

3.20 SYSTEM AND INFORMATION INTEGRITY

Quick link to System and Information Integrity summary table

SI-1 SYSTEM AND INFORMATION INTEGRITY POLICY AND PROCEDURES

Control:

a. Develop, document, and disseminate to [*Assignment: organization-defined personnel or roles*]:

  1. A system and information integrity policy that:

     (a) Addresses purpose, scope, roles, responsibilities, management commitment, coordination among organizational entities, and compliance; and

     (b) Is consistent with applicable laws, Executive Orders, directives, regulations, policies, standards, and guidelines; and

  2. Procedures to facilitate the implementation of the system and information integrity policy and the associated system and information integrity controls;

b. Designate an [*Assignment: organization-defined senior management official*] to manage the system and information integrity policy and procedures;

c. Review and update the current system and information integrity:

  1. Policy [*Assignment: organization-defined frequency*]; and

  2. Procedures [*Assignment: organization-defined frequency*];

d. Ensure that the system and information integrity procedures implement the system and information integrity policy and controls; and

e. Develop, document, and implement remediation actions for violations of the system and information integrity policy.

Supplemental Guidance: This control addresses the establishment of policy and procedures for the effective implementation of the controls and control enhancements in the SI family. The risk management strategy is an important factor in establishing policy and procedures. Comprehensive policy and procedures help provide security and privacy assurance. Security and privacy program policies and procedures at the organization level may make the need for system-specific policies and procedures unnecessary. The policy can be included as part of the general security and privacy policy or can be represented by multiple policies reflecting the complex nature of organizations. The procedures can be established for security and privacy programs and for systems, if needed. Procedures describe how policies or controls are implemented and can be directed at the personnel or role that is the object of the procedure. Procedures can be documented in system security and privacy plans or in one or more separate documents. It is important to recognize that restating controls does not constitute an organizational policy or procedure.

Related Controls: PM-9, PS-8, SI-12.

Control Enhancements: None.

References: NIST Special Publications 800-12, 800-100.

SI-2 FLAW REMEDIATION

Control:

a. Identify, report, and correct system flaws;

b. Test software and firmware updates related to flaw remediation for effectiveness and potential side effects before installation;

c.   Install security-relevant software and firmware updates within [*Assignment: organization-defined time-period*] of the release of the updates; and

d.   Incorporate flaw remediation into the organizational configuration management process.

Supplemental Guidance: Organizations identify systems affected by software flaws including potential vulnerabilities resulting from those flaws, and report this information to designated organizational personnel with information security and privacy responsibilities. Security-relevant software updates include, for example, patches, service packs, hot fixes, and anti-virus signatures. Organizations also address flaws discovered during assessments, continuous monitoring, incident response activities, and system error handling. By incorporating flaw remediation into ongoing configuration management processes, required remediation actions can be tracked and verified. Organization-defined time-periods for updating security-relevant software and firmware may vary based on a variety of factors including, for example, the security category of the system or the criticality of the update (i.e., severity of the vulnerability related to the discovered flaw). Some types of flaw remediation may require more testing than other types. Organizations determine the type of testing needed for the specific type of flaw remediation activity under consideration and the types of changes that are to be configuration-managed. In some situations, organizations may determine that testing of software or firmware updates is not necessary or practical, for example, when implementing simple anti-virus signature updates. Organizations also consider in testing decisions, whether security-relevant software or firmware updates are obtained from authorized sources with appropriate digital signatures.

Related Controls: CA-4, CM-3, CM-4, CM-5, CM-6, CM-8, MA-2, RA-5, SA-10, SA-11, SI-3, SI-5, SI-7, SI-11.

Control Enhancements:

(1)   FLAW REMEDIATION | CENTRAL MANAGEMENT

Centrally manage the flaw remediation process.

Supplemental Guidance: Central management is the organization-wide management and implementation of flaw remediation processes. Central management includes planning, implementing, assessing, authorizing, and monitoring the organization-defined, centrally managed flaw remediation controls.

Related Controls: PL-9.

(2)   FLAW REMEDIATION | AUTOMATED FLAW REMEDIATION STATUS

Employ automated mechanisms [*Assignment: organization-defined frequency*] to determine the state of system components with regard to flaw remediation.

Supplemental Guidance: None.

Related Controls: SI-4.

(3)   FLAW REMEDIATION | TIME TO REMEDIATE FLAWS AND BENCHMARKS FOR CORRECTIVE ACTIONS

(a)   **Measure the time between flaw identification and flaw remediation; and**

(b)   **Establish [*Assignment: organization-defined benchmarks*] for taking corrective actions.**

Supplemental Guidance: This control enhancement requires organizations to determine the time it takes on the average to correct system flaws after such flaws have been identified, and subsequently establish organizational benchmarks (i.e., time frames) for taking corrective actions. Benchmarks can be established by the type of flaw or the severity of the potential vulnerability if the flaw can be exploited.

Related Controls: None.

(4)   FLAW REMEDIATION | AUTOMATED PATCH MANAGEMENT TOOLS

[Withdrawn: Incorporated into SI-2].

(5)   FLAW REMEDIATION | AUTOMATIC SOFTWARE AND FIRMWARE UPDATES

Install [*Assignment: organization-defined security-relevant software and firmware updates*] automatically to [*Assignment: organization-defined system components*].

Supplemental Guidance: Due to system checking policy and technology constraints, organizations consider the methodology used to carry out automatic updates. Organizations balance the need to ensure that the updates are installed as soon as possible with the need to maintain configuration management and control with any mission or operational impacts that automatic updates might impose.

Related Controls: None.

(6) FLAW REMEDIATION | REMOVAL OF PREVIOUS VERSIONS OF SOFTWARE AND FIRMWARE

Remove previous versions of [*Assignment: organization-defined software and firmware components*] after updated versions have been installed.

Supplemental Guidance: Previous versions of software or firmware components that are not removed from the system after updates have been installed may be exploited by adversaries. Some products may remove previous versions of software and firmware automatically from the system.

Related Controls: None.

(7) FLAW REMEDIATION | PERSONALLY IDENTIFIABLE INFORMATION

    (a) **Identify and correct flaws related to the collection, usage, processing, or dissemination of personally identifiable information;**

    (b) **Report flaws related to personally identifiable information to the Senior Agency Official for Privacy;**

    (c) **Receive approval for correction of privacy-related flaws from the Senior Agency Official for Privacy;**

    (d) **Prior to installation, assess software and firmware updates related to flaw remediation for effectiveness and consistency with terms agreed upon in the privacy impact assessment;**

    (e) **Install privacy-relevant software and firmware updates within [*Assignment: organization-defined time-period*] of the release of the updates; and**

    (f) **Incorporate flaw remediation of personally identifiable information into the organizational configuration management process.**

Supplemental Guidance: None.

Related Controls: IR-4, IR-5, PM-23.

References: FIPS Publications 140-2, 186-4; NIST Special Publications 800-40, 800-128; NIST Interagency Report 7788.

SI-3   MALICIOUS CODE PROTECTION

Control:

a.   Implement [*Selection (one or more): signature based; non-signature based*] malicious code protection mechanisms at system entry and exit points to detect and eradicate malicious code;

b.   Automatically update malicious code protection mechanisms whenever new releases are available in accordance with organizational configuration management policy and procedures;

c.   Configure malicious code protection mechanisms to:

    1. Perform periodic scans of the system [*Assignment: organization-defined frequency*] and real-time scans of files from external sources at [*Selection (one or more); endpoint; network entry/exit points*] as the files are downloaded, opened, or executed in accordance with organizational policy; and

    2. [*Selection (one or more): block malicious code; quarantine malicious code; send alert to administrator; [Assignment: organization-defined action]*] in response to malicious code detection; and

d.   Address the receipt of false positives during malicious code detection and eradication and the resulting potential impact on the availability of the system.

Supplemental Guidance: System entry and exit points include, for example, firewalls, remote-access servers, workstations, electronic mail servers, web servers, proxy servers, notebook computers, and mobile devices. Malicious code includes, for example, viruses, worms, Trojan horses, and spyware. Malicious code can also be encoded in various formats contained within compressed or hidden files, or hidden in files using techniques such as steganography. Malicious code can be inserted into systems in a variety of ways including, for example, by electronic mail, the world-wide web, and portable storage devices. Malicious code insertions occur through the exploitation of system vulnerabilities. A variety of technologies and methods exist to limit or eliminate the effects of malicious code. Malicious code protection mechanisms include, for example, signature- and nonsignature-based technologies. Nonsignature-based detection mechanisms include, for example, artificial intelligence techniques that use heuristics to detect, analyze, and describe the characteristics or behavior of malicious code and to provide safeguards against such code for which signatures do not yet exist or for which existing signatures may not be effective. This includes polymorphic malicious code (i.e., code that changes signatures when it replicates). Nonsignature-based mechanisms also include reputation-based technologies. In addition to the above technologies, pervasive configuration management, comprehensive software integrity controls, and anti-exploitation software may be effective in preventing execution of unauthorized code. Malicious code may be present in commercial off-the-shelf software and in custom-built software. This could include, for example, logic bombs, back doors, and other types of attacks that could affect organizational missions and business functions.

In situations where malicious code cannot be detected by detection methods and technologies, organizations rely instead on other types of safeguards including, for example, secure coding practices, configuration management and control, trusted procurement processes, and monitoring practices to help ensure that software does not perform functions other than the functions intended. Organizations may determine that in response to the detection of malicious code, different actions may be warranted. For example, organizations can define actions in response to malicious code detection during periodic scans, actions in response to detection of malicious downloads, or actions in response to detection of maliciousness when attempting to open or execute files. Due to system integrity and availability concerns, organizations consider the specific methodology used to carry out automatic updates.

Related Controls: AC-4, AC-19, CM-3, CM-8, IR-4, MA-3, MA-4, RA-5, SC-7, SC-26, SC-28, SC-23, SC-44, SI-2, SI-4, SI-7, SI-8, SI-15.

Control Enhancements:

(1) MALICIOUS CODE PROTECTION | CENTRAL MANAGEMENT
Centrally manage malicious code protection mechanisms.

Supplemental Guidance: Central management is the organization-wide management and implementation of malicious code protection mechanisms. Central management includes planning, implementing, assessing, authorizing, and monitoring the organization-defined, centrally managed flaw and malicious code protection controls.

Related Controls: PL-9.

(2) MALICIOUS CODE PROTECTION | AUTOMATIC UPDATES
[Withdrawn: Incorporated into SI-3].

(3) MALICIOUS CODE PROTECTION | NON-PRIVILEGED USERS
[Withdrawn: Incorporated into AC-6(10)].

(4) MALICIOUS CODE PROTECTION | UPDATES ONLY BY PRIVILEGED USERS
Update malicious code protection mechanisms only when directed by a privileged user.

Supplemental Guidance: This control enhancement is employed in situations where for reasons of security or operational continuity, updates to malicious code protection mechanisms are only applied when approved by designated organizational personnel.

Related Controls: CM-5.

(5) MALICIOUS CODE PROTECTION | PORTABLE STORAGE DEVICES
[Withdrawn: Incorporated into MP-7].

(6) MALICIOUS CODE PROTECTION | TESTING AND VERIFICATION

   (a) Test malicious code protection mechanisms [*Assignment: organization-defined frequency*] by introducing a known benign, non-spreading test case into the system; and

   (b) Verify that the detection of the test case and the associated incident reporting occur.

Supplemental Guidance: None.

Related Controls: CA-2, CA-7, RA-5.

(7) MALICIOUS CODE PROTECTION | NONSIGNATURE-BASED DETECTION

[Withdrawn: Incorporated into SI-3].

(8) MALICIOUS CODE PROTECTION | DETECT UNAUTHORIZED COMMANDS

Detect [*Assignment: organization-defined unauthorized operating system commands*] through the kernel application programming interface at [*Assignment: organization-defined system hardware components*] and [*Selection (one or more): issue a warning; audit the command execution; prevent the execution of the command*].

Supplemental Guidance: This control enhancement can also be applied to critical interfaces other than kernel-based interfaces, including for example, interfaces with virtual machines and privileged applications. Unauthorized operating system commands include, for example, commands for kernel functions from system processes that are not trusted to initiate such commands, or commands for kernel functions that are suspicious even though commands of that type are reasonable for processes to initiate. Organizations can define the malicious commands to be detected by a combination of command types, command classes, or specific instances of commands. Organizations can define hardware components by component type, component, component location in the network, or combination therein. Organizations may select different actions for different types, classes, or instances of malicious commands.

Related Controls: AU-2, AU-6, AU-12.

(9) MALICIOUS CODE PROTECTION | AUTHENTICATE REMOTE COMMANDS

Implement [*Assignment: organization-defined security safeguards*] to authenticate [*Assignment: organization-defined remote commands*].

Supplemental Guidance: This control enhancement protects against unauthorized commands and replay of authorized commands. This capability is important for those remote systems whose loss, malfunction, misdirection, or exploitation would have immediate and/or serious consequences, including, for example, injury or death, property damage, loss of high-value assets, compromise of classified or controlled unclassified information, or failure of missions or business functions. Authentication safeguards for remote commands ensure that systems accept and execute commands in the order intended, execute only authorized commands, and reject unauthorized commands. Cryptographic mechanisms can be employed, for example, to authenticate remote commands.

Related Controls: SC-12, SC-13, SC-23.

(10) MALICIOUS CODE PROTECTION | MALICIOUS CODE ANALYSIS

   (a) Employ [*Assignment: organization-defined tools and techniques*] to analyze the characteristics and behavior of malicious code; and

   (b) Incorporate the results from malicious code analysis into organizational incident response and flaw remediation processes.

Supplemental Guidance: The use of malicious code analysis tools provides organizations with a more in-depth understanding of adversary tradecraft (i.e., tactics, techniques, and procedures) and the functionality and purpose of specific instances of malicious code. Understanding the characteristics of malicious code facilitates more effective organizational responses to current and future threats. Organizations can also conduct malicious code analyses by using reverse engineering techniques or by monitoring the behavior of executing code.

Related Controls: None.

References: NIST Special Publication 800-83, 800-125B, 800-177.

SI-4 SYSTEM MONITORING

Control:

a. Monitor the system to detect:

    1. Attacks and indicators of potential attacks in accordance with [*Assignment: organization-defined monitoring objectives*]; and

    2. Unauthorized local, network, and remote connections;

b. Identify unauthorized use of the system through [*Assignment: organization-defined techniques and methods*];

c. Invoke internal monitoring capabilities or deploy monitoring devices:

    1. Strategically within the system to collect organization-determined essential information; and

    2. At ad hoc locations within the system to track specific types of transactions of interest to the organization;

d. Protect information obtained from intrusion-monitoring tools from unauthorized access, modification, and deletion;

e. Adjust the level of system monitoring activity when there is a change in risk to organizational operations and assets, individuals, other organizations, or the Nation;

f. Obtain legal opinion regarding system monitoring activities; and

g. Provide [*Assignment: organization-defined system monitoring information*] to [*Assignment: organization-defined personnel or roles*] [*Selection (one or more): as needed; [Assignment: organization-defined frequency*]].

Supplemental Guidance: System monitoring includes external and internal monitoring. External monitoring includes the observation of events occurring at system boundaries. Internal monitoring includes the observation of events occurring within the system. Organizations monitor systems, for example, by observing audit activities in real time or by observing other system aspects such as access patterns, characteristics of access, and other actions. The monitoring objectives guide and inform the determination of the events. System monitoring capability is achieved through a variety of tools and techniques, including, for example, intrusion detection systems, intrusion prevention systems, malicious code protection software, scanning tools, audit record monitoring software, and network monitoring software. The distribution and configuration of monitoring devices can impact throughput at key internal and external boundaries, and at other locations across a network due to the introduction of network throughput latency. Therefore, such devices are strategically located and deployed as part of an established organization-wide security architecture. Strategic locations for monitoring devices include, for example, selected perimeter locations and near key servers and server farms supporting critical applications. Monitoring devices are typically employed at the managed interfaces associated with controls SC-7 and AC-17. The information collected is a function of the organizational monitoring objectives and the capability of systems to support such objectives. Specific types of transactions of interest include, for example, Hyper Text Transfer Protocol (HTTP) traffic that bypasses HTTP proxies. System monitoring is an integral part of organizational continuous monitoring and incident response programs and output from system monitoring serves as input to those programs. Adjustments to levels of system monitoring are based on law enforcement information, intelligence information, or other credible sources of information. The legality of system monitoring activities is based on applicable laws, Executive Orders, directives, regulations, policies, standards, and guidelines.

Related Controls: AC-2, AC-3, AC-4, AC-8, AC-17, AU-2, AU-6, AU-7, AU-9, AU-12, AU-14, CA-7, CM-3, CM-8, CM-11, IA-10, IR-4, PE-3, PM-12, PM-24, RA-5, SA-18, SC-7, SC-26, SC-31, SC-35, SC-36, SC-37, SI-3, SI-6, SI-7.

Control Enhancements:

(1) SYSTEM MONITORING | SYSTEM-WIDE INTRUSION DETECTION SYSTEM

Connect and configure individual intrusion detection tools into a system-wide intrusion detection system.

Supplemental Guidance: CM-6.

Related Controls: None.

(2) SYSTEM MONITORING | AUTOMATED TOOLS AND MECHANISMS FOR REAL-TIME ANALYSIS

Employ automated tools and mechanisms to support near real-time analysis of events.

Supplemental Guidance: Automated tools and mechanisms include, for example, host-based, network-based, transport-based, or storage-based event monitoring tools and mechanisms or Security Information and Event Management technologies that provide real time analysis of alerts and notifications generated by organizational systems.

Related Controls: None.

(3) SYSTEM MONITORING | AUTOMATED TOOL AND MECHANISM INTEGRATION

Employ automated tools and mechanisms to integrate intrusion detection tools and mechanisms into access control and flow control mechanisms.

Supplemental Guidance: Using automated tools and mechanisms to integrate intrusion detection tools and mechanisms into access and flow control mechanisms facilitates a rapid response to attacks by enabling reconfiguration of these mechanisms in support of attack isolation and elimination.

Related Controls: None.

(4) SYSTEM MONITORING | INBOUND AND OUTBOUND COMMUNICATIONS TRAFFIC

Monitor inbound and outbound communications traffic [Assignment: organization-defined frequency] for unusual or unauthorized activities or conditions.

Supplemental Guidance: Unusual or unauthorized activities or conditions related to system inbound and outbound communications traffic include, for example, internal traffic that indicates the presence of malicious code within organizational systems or propagating among system components; the unauthorized exporting of information; or signaling to external systems. Evidence of malicious code is used to identify potentially compromised systems or system components.

Related Controls: None.

(5) SYSTEM MONITORING | SYSTEM-GENERATED ALERTS

Alert [Assignment: organization-defined personnel or roles] when the following system-generated indications of compromise or potential compromise occur: [Assignment: organization-defined compromise indicators].

Supplemental Guidance: Alerts may be generated from a variety of sources, including, for example, audit records or inputs from malicious code protection mechanisms, intrusion detection or prevention mechanisms, or boundary protection devices such as firewalls, gateways, and routers. Alerts can be automated or they may be transmitted, for example, telephonically, by electronic mail messages, or by text messaging. Organizational personnel on the alert notification list can include, for example, system administrators, mission or business owners, system owners, system security officers, or privacy officers. This control enhancement focuses on the security alerts generated by the system. Alternatively, alerts generated by organizations in SI-4(12) focus on information sources external to the system such as suspicious activity reports and reports on potential insider threats.

Related Controls: AU-4, AU-5, PE-6.

(6) SYSTEM MONITORING | RESTRICT NON-PRIVILEGED USERS

[Withdrawn: Incorporated into AC-6(10)].

(7) SYSTEM MONITORING | AUTOMATED RESPONSE TO SUSPICIOUS EVENTS

Notify [*Assignment: organization-defined incident response personnel (identified by name and/or by role)*] of detected suspicious events and take [*Assignment: organization-defined least-disruptive actions to terminate suspicious events*].

Supplemental Guidance: Least-disruptive actions include, for example, initiating requests for human responses.

Related Controls: None.

(8) SYSTEM MONITORING | PROTECTION OF MONITORING INFORMATION

[Withdrawn: Incorporated into SI-4].

(9) SYSTEM MONITORING | TESTING OF MONITORING TOOLS AND MECHANISMS

Test intrusion-monitoring tools and mechanisms [*Assignment: organization-defined frequency*].

Supplemental Guidance: Testing intrusion-monitoring tools and mechanism is necessary to ensure that the tools and mechanisms are operating correctly and continue to satisfy the monitoring objectives of organizations. The frequency of testing depends on the types of tools and mechanisms used by organizations and the methods of deployment.

Related Controls: CP-9.

(10) SYSTEM MONITORING | VISIBILITY OF ENCRYPTED COMMUNICATIONS

Make provisions so that [*Assignment: organization-defined encrypted communications traffic*] is visible to [*Assignment: organization-defined system monitoring tools and mechanisms*].

Supplemental Guidance: Organizations balance the potentially conflicting needs for encrypting communications traffic and having visibility into such traffic from a monitoring perspective. For some organizations, the need to ensure the confidentiality of communications traffic is paramount; for other organizations, mission assurance is of greater concern. Organizations determine whether the visibility requirement applies to internal encrypted traffic, encrypted traffic intended for external destinations, or a subset of the traffic types.

Related Controls: None.

(11) SYSTEM MONITORING | ANALYZE COMMUNICATIONS TRAFFIC ANOMALIES

Analyze outbound communications traffic at the external boundary of the system and selected [*Assignment: organization-defined interior points within the system*] to discover anomalies.

Supplemental Guidance: Examples of organization-defined interior points within the system include subnetworks and subsystems. Anomalies within organizational systems include, for example, large file transfers; long-time persistent connections; unusual protocols and ports in use; and attempted communications with suspected malicious external addresses.

Related Controls: None.

(12) SYSTEM MONITORING | AUTOMATED ORGANIZATION-GENERATED ALERTS

Employ automated mechanisms to alert [*Assignment: organization-defined personnel or roles*] when the following organization-generated indications of inappropriate or unusual activities with security or privacy implications occur: [*Assignment: organization-defined activities that trigger alerts*].

Supplemental Guidance: Organizational personnel on the alert notification list can include, for example, system administrators, mission or business owners, system owners, system security officers, or privacy officers. This control enhancement focuses on the security alerts generated by organizations and transmitted using automated means. In contrast to the alerts generated by systems in SI-4(5) that focus on information sources that are internal to the systems such as audit records, the sources of information for this enhancement focus on other entities such as suspicious activity reports and reports on potential insider threats.

Related Controls: None.

(13) SYSTEM MONITORING | ANALYZE TRAFFIC AND EVENT PATTERNS

(a) Analyze communications traffic and event patterns for the system;

(b) Develop profiles representing common traffic and event patterns; and

(c) Use the traffic and event profiles in tuning system-monitoring devices to reduce the number of false positives and false negatives.

Supplemental Guidance: None.

Related Controls: None.

(14) SYSTEM MONITORING | WIRELESS INTRUSION DETECTION

Employ a wireless intrusion detection system to identify rogue wireless devices and to detect attack attempts and potential compromises or breaches to the system.

Supplemental Guidance: Wireless signals may radiate beyond organization-controlled facilities. Organizations proactively search for unauthorized wireless connections including the conduct of thorough scans for unauthorized wireless access points. Scans are not limited to those areas within facilities containing systems, but also include areas outside of facilities to verify that unauthorized wireless access points are not connected to organizational systems.

Related Controls: AC-18, IA-3.

(15) SYSTEM MONITORING | WIRELESS TO WIRELINE COMMUNICATIONS

Employ an intrusion detection system to monitor wireless communications traffic as the traffic passes from wireless to wireline networks.

Supplemental Guidance: None.

Related Controls: AC-18.

(16) SYSTEM MONITORING | CORRELATE MONITORING INFORMATION

Correlate information from monitoring tools and mechanisms employed throughout the system.

Supplemental Guidance: Correlating information from different system monitoring tools and mechanisms can provide a more comprehensive view of system activity. Correlating system monitoring tools and mechanisms that typically work in isolation including, for example, anti-virus software, host monitoring, and network monitoring, can provide an organization-wide monitoring view and may reveal otherwise unseen attack patterns. Understanding capabilities and limitations of diverse monitoring tools and mechanisms and how to maximize the utility of information generated by those tools and mechanisms can help organizations to develop, operate, and maintain effective monitoring programs.

Related Controls: AU-6.

(17) SYSTEM MONITORING | INTEGRATED SITUATIONAL AWARENESS

Correlate information from monitoring physical, cyber, and supply chain activities to achieve integrated, organization-wide situational awareness.

Supplemental Guidance: This control enhancement correlates monitoring information from a more diverse set of information sources to achieve integrated situational awareness. Integrated situational awareness from a combination of physical, cyber, and supply chain monitoring activities enhances the capability of organizations to more quickly detect sophisticated attacks and investigate the methods and techniques employed to carry out such attacks. In contrast to SI-4(16) which correlates the various cyber monitoring information, this control enhancement correlates monitoring beyond the cyber domain. Such monitoring may help reveal attacks on organizations that are operating across multiple attack vectors.

Related Controls: AU-16, PE-6, SA-12.

(18) SYSTEM MONITORING | ANALYZE TRAFFIC AND COVERT EXFILTRATION

Analyze outbound communications traffic at the external boundary or perimeter of the system and at [Assignment: organization-defined interior points within the system] to detect covert exfiltration of information.

Supplemental Guidance: Examples of organization-defined interior points within the system include subnetworks and subsystems. Covert means that can be used for the exfiltration of information include, for example, steganography.

Related Controls: None.

(19) SYSTEM MONITORING | INDIVIDUALS POSING GREATER RISK

Implement [Assignment: organization-defined additional monitoring] of individuals who have been identified by [Assignment: organization-defined sources] as posing an increased level of risk.

<u>Supplemental Guidance</u>: Indications of increased risk from individuals can be obtained from a variety of sources including, for example, human resource records, intelligence agencies, law enforcement organizations, and other credible sources. The monitoring of specific individuals is closely coordinated with management, legal, security, privacy and human resource officials within organizations conducting such monitoring. Monitoring is conducted in accordance with applicable laws, Executive Orders, directives, regulations, policies, standards, and guidelines.

<u>Related Controls</u>: None.

(20) SYSTEM MONITORING | PRIVILEGED USERS

Implement [*Assignment: organization-defined additional monitoring*] of privileged users.

<u>Supplemental Guidance</u>: None.

<u>Related Controls</u>: AC-18.

(21) SYSTEM MONITORING | PROBATIONARY PERIODS

Implement [*Assignment: organization-defined additional monitoring*] of individuals during [*Assignment: organization-defined probationary period*].

<u>Supplemental Guidance</u>: None.

<u>Related Controls</u>: AC-18.

(22) SYSTEM MONITORING | UNAUTHORIZED NETWORK SERVICES

Detect network services that have not been authorized or approved by [*Assignment: organization-defined authorization or approval processes*] and [*Selection (one or more): audit; alert* [*Assignment: organization-defined personnel or roles*]].

<u>Supplemental Guidance</u>: Unauthorized or unapproved network services include, for example, services in service-oriented architectures that lack organizational verification or validation and therefore may be unreliable or serve as malicious rogues for valid services.

<u>Related Controls</u>: CM-7.

(23) SYSTEM MONITORING | HOST-BASED DEVICES

Implement [*Assignment: organization-defined host-based monitoring mechanisms*] at [*Assignment: organization-defined system components*].

<u>Supplemental Guidance</u>: System components where host-based monitoring can be implemented include, for example, servers, notebook computers, and mobile devices. Organizations may consider employing host-based monitoring mechanisms from multiple product developers or vendors.

<u>Related Controls</u>: AC-18, AC-19.

(24) SYSTEM MONITORING | INDICATORS OF COMPROMISE

Discover, collect, and distribute to [*Assignment: organization-defined personnel or roles*], indicators of compromise.

<u>Supplemental Guidance</u>: Indicators of compromise (IOC) are forensic artifacts from intrusions that are identified on organizational systems at the host or network level. IOCs provide valuable information on systems that have been compromised. IOCs for the discovery of compromised hosts can include, for example, the creation of registry key values. IOCs for network traffic include, for example, Universal Resource Locator or protocol elements that indicate malicious code command and control servers. The rapid distribution and adoption of IOCs can improve information security by reducing the time that systems and organizations are vulnerable to the same exploit or attack.

<u>Related Controls</u>: AC-18.

(25) SYSTEM MONITORING | PERSONALLY IDENTIFIABLE INFORMATION MONITORING

Employ automated mechanisms to monitor:

(a) For unauthorized access or usage of personally identifiable information; and

(b) The collection, creation, accuracy, relevance, timeliness, impact, and completeness of personally identifiable information.

<u>Supplemental Guidance</u>: Monitoring the collection, creation, accuracy, relevance, timeliness, impact, and completeness of personally identifiable information helps improve data quality.

~~A~~ ~~controls may connect~~ to external or otherwise unrelated systems. The matching of records between these systems may create linkages with unintended consequences. Organizations assess and document these risks in their privacy impact assessment and make determinations that are in alignment with their privacy program plan.

Related Controls: PM-24, PM-26, SI-19.

References: NIST Special Publications 800-61, 800-83, 800-92, 800-94, 800-137.

SI-5   SECURITY ALERTS, ADVISORIES, AND DIRECTIVES

Control:

a. Receive system security alerts, advisories, and directives from [*Assignment: organization-defined external organizations*] on an ongoing basis;

b. Generate internal security alerts, advisories, and directives as deemed necessary;

c. Disseminate security alerts, advisories, and directives to: [*Selection (one or more):* [*Assignment: organization-defined personnel or roles*]; [*Assignment: organization-defined elements within the organization*]; [*Assignment: organization-defined external organizations*]]; and

d. Implement security directives in accordance with established time frames, or notify the issuing organization of the degree of noncompliance.

Supplemental Guidance: The United States Computer Emergency Readiness Team (US-CERT) generates security alerts and advisories to maintain situational awareness across the federal government. Security directives are issued by OMB or other designated organizations with the responsibility and authority to issue such directives. Compliance to security directives is essential due to the critical nature of many of these directives and the potential immediate adverse effects on organizational operations and assets, individuals, other organizations, and the Nation should the directives not be implemented in a timely manner. External organizations include, for example, external mission or business partners, supply chain partners, external service providers, and other peer or supporting organizations.

Related Controls: PM-15, RA-5, SI-2.

Control Enhancements:

(1)   SECURITY ALERTS, ADVISORIES, AND DIRECTIVES | AUTOMATED ALERTS AND ADVISORIES

Employ automated mechanisms to make security alert and advisory information available throughout the organization.

Supplemental Guidance: The significant number of changes to organizational systems and the environments in which those systems operate requires the dissemination of security-related information to a variety of organizational entities that have a direct interest in the success of organizational missions and business functions. Based on information provided by security alerts and advisories, changes may be required at one or more of the three tiers related to the management of information security and privacy risk including the governance level, mission and business process level, and the system level.

Related Controls: None.

References: NIST Special Publication 800-40.

SI-6   SECURITY AND PRIVACY FUNCTION VERIFICATION

Control:

a. Verify the correct operation of [*Assignment: organization-defined security and privacy functions*];

b.   Perform this verification [*Selection (one or more): [Assignment: organization-defined system transitional states]; upon command by user with appropriate privilege; [Assignment: organization-defined frequency]]*];

c.   Notify [*Assignment: organization-defined personnel or roles*] of failed security and privacy verification tests; and

d.   [*Selection (one or more): Shut the system down; Restart the system; [Assignment: organization-defined alternative action(s)]]*] when anomalies are discovered.

Supplemental Guidance: Transitional states for systems include, for example, system startup, restart, shutdown, and abort. Notifications by the system include, for example, hardware indicator lights, electronic alerts to system administrators, and messages to local computer consoles. In contrast to security function verification, privacy function verification ensures that privacy functions operate as expected and are approved by the Senior Agency Official for Privacy, or that privacy attributes are applied or used as expected.

Related Controls: CA-7, CM-4, CM-6, SI-7.

Control Enhancements:

(1) SECURITY AND PRIVACY FUNCTION VERIFICATION | NOTIFICATION OF FAILED SECURITY TESTS
[Withdrawn: Incorporated into SI-6].

(2) SECURITY AND PRIVACY FUNCTION VERIFICATION | AUTOMATION SUPPORT FOR DISTRIBUTED TESTING
Implement automated mechanisms to support the management of distributed security and privacy function testing.

Supplemental Guidance: None.

Related Controls: SI-2.

(3) SECURITY AND PRIVACY FUNCTION VERIFICATION | REPORT VERIFICATION RESULTS
Report the results of security and privacy function verification to [*Assignment: organization-defined personnel or roles*].

Supplemental Guidance: Organizational personnel with potential interest in the results of the verification of security and privacy function include, for example, system security managers, systems security officers, Senior Agency Information Security Officers, and Senior Agency Officials for Privacy.

Related Controls: SA-12, SI-4.

References: None.

SI-7   SOFTWARE, FIRMWARE, AND INFORMATION INTEGRITY

Control: Employ integrity verification tools to detect unauthorized changes to [*Assignment: organization-defined software, firmware, and information*].

Supplemental Guidance: Unauthorized changes to software, firmware, and information can occur due to errors or malicious activity. Software includes, for example, operating systems (with key internal components such as kernels, drivers), middleware, and applications. Firmware includes, for example, the Basic Input Output System (BIOS). Information includes personally identifiable information and metadata containing security and privacy attributes associated with information. Integrity-checking mechanisms including, for example, parity checks, cyclical redundancy checks, cryptographic hashes, and associated tools can automatically monitor the integrity of systems and hosted applications.

Related Controls: AC-4, CM-3, CM-7, CM-8, MA-3, MA-4, RA-5, SA-9, SA-10, SA-18, SA-19, CM-7, SA-12, SC-8, SC-13, SC-28, SC-37, SI-3.

Control Enhancements:

(1) SOFTWARE, FIRMWARE, AND INFORMATION INTEGRITY | INTEGRITY CHECKS

Perform an integrity check of [*Assignment: organization-defined software, firmware, and information*] [*Selection (one or more): at startup; at* [*Assignment: organization-defined transitional states or security-relevant events*]; [*Assignment: organization-defined frequency*]].

Supplemental Guidance: Security-relevant events include, for example, the identification of a new threat to which organizational systems are susceptible, and the installation of new hardware, software, or firmware. Transitional states include, for example, system startup, restart, shutdown, and abort.

Related Controls: None.

(2) SOFTWARE, FIRMWARE, AND INFORMATION INTEGRITY | AUTOMATED NOTIFICATIONS OF INTEGRITY VIOLATIONS

Employ automated tools that provide notification to [*Assignment: organization-defined personnel or roles*] upon discovering discrepancies during integrity verification.

Supplemental Guidance: The use of automated tools to report integrity violations and to notify organizational personnel in a timely matter is an essential precursor to effective risk response. Personnel having an interest in integrity violations include, for example, mission and business owners, system owners, systems administrators, software developers, systems integrators, and information security officers, and privacy officers.

Related Controls: None.

(3) SOFTWARE, FIRMWARE, AND INFORMATION INTEGRITY | CENTRALLY-MANAGED INTEGRITY TOOLS

Employ centrally managed integrity verification tools.

Supplemental Guidance: None.

Related Controls: AU-3, SI-2, SI-8.

(4) SOFTWARE, FIRMWARE, AND INFORMATION INTEGRITY | TAMPER-EVIDENT PACKAGING

[Withdrawn: Incorporated into SA-12].

(5) SOFTWARE, FIRMWARE, AND INFORMATION INTEGRITY | AUTOMATED RESPONSE TO INTEGRITY VIOLATIONS

Automatically [*Selection (one or more): shut the system down; restart the system; implement* [*Assignment: organization-defined security safeguards*]] when integrity violations are discovered.

Supplemental Guidance: Organizations may define different integrity checking responses by type of information, by specific information, or a combination of both. Examples of types of information include firmware, software, and user data. Examples of specific information include boot firmware for certain types of machines. The automatic implementation of safeguards within organizational systems includes, for example, reversing the changes, halting the system, or triggering audit alerts when unauthorized modifications to critical security files occur.

Related Controls: None.

(6) SOFTWARE, FIRMWARE, AND INFORMATION INTEGRITY | CRYPTOGRAPHIC PROTECTION

Implement cryptographic mechanisms to detect unauthorized changes to software, firmware, and information.

Supplemental Guidance: Cryptographic mechanisms used for the protection of integrity include, for example, digital signatures and the computation and application of signed hashes using asymmetric cryptography; protecting the confidentiality of the key used to generate the hash; and using the public key to verify the hash information.

Related Controls: SC-12, SC-13.

(7) SOFTWARE, FIRMWARE, AND INFORMATION INTEGRITY | INTEGRATION OF DETECTION AND RESPONSE

Incorporate the detection of the following unauthorized changes into the organizational incident response capability: [*Assignment: organization-defined security-relevant changes to the system*].

Supplemental Guidance: This control enhancement helps to ensure that detected events are tracked, monitored, corrected, and available for historical purposes. Maintaining historical records is important both for being able to identify and discern adversary actions over an extended time-period and for possible legal actions. Security-relevant changes include, for example, unauthorized changes to established configuration settings or unauthorized elevation of system privileges.

Related Controls: AU-2, AU-6, IR-4, IR-5, SI-4.

(8) SOFTWARE, FIRMWARE, AND INFORMATION INTEGRITY | AUDITING CAPABILITY FOR SIGNIFICANT EVENTS

Upon detection of a potential integrity violation, provide the capability to audit the event and initiate the following actions: [*Selection (one or more): generate an audit record; alert current user; alert [Assignment: organization-defined personnel or roles*]; [*Assignment: organization-defined other actions*]].

Supplemental Guidance: Organizations select response actions based on types of software, specific software, or information for which there are potential integrity violations.

Related Controls: AU-2, AU-6, AU-12.

(9) SOFTWARE, FIRMWARE, AND INFORMATION INTEGRITY | VERIFY BOOT PROCESS

Verify the integrity of the boot process of [*Assignment: organization-defined system components*].

Supplemental Guidance: Ensuring the integrity of boot processes is critical to starting system components in known, trustworthy states. Integrity verification mechanisms provide a level of assurance that only trusted code is executed during boot processes.

Related Controls: SI-6.

(10) SOFTWARE, FIRMWARE, AND INFORMATION INTEGRITY | PROTECTION OF BOOT FIRMWARE

Implement [*Assignment: organization-defined security safeguards*] to protect the integrity of boot firmware in [*Assignment: organization-defined system components*].

Supplemental Guidance: Unauthorized modifications to boot firmware may be indicative of a sophisticated, targeted attack. These types of targeted attacks can result in a permanent denial of service or a persistent malicious code presence. These situations can occur, for example, if the firmware is corrupted or if the malicious code is embedded within the firmware. System components can protect the integrity of boot firmware in organizational systems by verifying the integrity and authenticity of all updates to the firmware prior to applying changes to the system component; and preventing unauthorized processes from modifying the boot firmware.

Related Controls: SI-6.

(11) SOFTWARE, FIRMWARE, AND INFORMATION INTEGRITY | CONFINED ENVIRONMENTS WITH LIMITED PRIVILEGES

Require that [*Assignment: organization-defined user-installed software*] execute in a confined physical or virtual machine environment with limited privileges.

Supplemental Guidance: Organizations identify software that may be of concern regarding its origin or potential for containing malicious code. For this type of software, user installations occur in confined environments of operation to limit or contain damage from malicious code that may be executed.

Related Controls: CM-11, SC-44.

(12) SOFTWARE, FIRMWARE, AND INFORMATION INTEGRITY | INTEGRITY VERIFICATION

Require that the integrity of [*Assignment: organization-defined user-installed software*] be verified prior to execution.

Supplemental Guidance: Organizations verify the integrity of user-installed software prior to execution to reduce the likelihood of executing malicious code or code that contains errors from unauthorized modifications. Organizations consider the practicality of approaches to verifying software integrity including, for example, availability of checksums of adequate trustworthiness from software developers or vendors.

Related Controls: CM-11.

(13) SOFTWARE, FIRMWARE, AND INFORMATION INTEGRITY | CODE EXECUTION IN PROTECTED ENVIRONMENTS

Allow execution of binary or machine-executable code only in confined physical or virtual machine environments and with the explicit approval of [*Assignment: organization-defined personnel or roles*] when such code is:

(a) Obtained from sources with limited or no warranty; and/or

(h) Without the installation of source code

Supplemental Guidance: This control enhancement applies to all sources of binary or machine-executable code including, for example, commercial software and firmware and open source software.

Related Controls: CM-10, SC-44.

(14) SOFTWARE, FIRMWARE, AND INFORMATION INTEGRITY | BINARY OR MACHINE EXECUTABLE CODE

(a) **Prohibit the use of binary or machine-executable code from sources with limited or no warranty and without the provision of source code; and**

(b) **Provide exceptions to the source code requirement only for compelling mission or operational requirements and with the approval of the authorizing official.**

Supplemental Guidance: This control enhancement applies to all sources of binary or machine-executable code including, for example, commercial software and firmware and open source software. Organizations assess software products without accompanying source code from sources with limited or no warranty for potential security impacts. The assessments address the fact that these types of software products may be difficult to review, repair, or extend, given that organizations, in most cases, do not have access to the original source code. In addition, there may be no owners who could make such repairs on behalf of organizations.

Related Controls: SA-5.

(15) SOFTWARE, FIRMWARE, AND INFORMATION INTEGRITY | CODE AUTHENTICATION

Implement cryptographic mechanisms to authenticate [*Assignment: organization-defined software or firmware components*] prior to installation.

Supplemental Guidance: Cryptographic authentication includes, for example, verifying that software or firmware components have been digitally signed using certificates recognized and approved by organizations. Code signing is an effective method to protect against malicious code.

Related Controls: CM-5.

(16) SOFTWARE, FIRMWARE, AND INFORMATION INTEGRITY | TIME LIMIT ON PROCESS EXECUTION WITHOUT SUPERVISION

Prohibit processes from executing without supervision for more than [*Assignment: organization-defined time-period*].

Supplemental Guidance: This control enhancement addresses processes for which typical or normal execution periods can be determined and situations in which organizations exceed such periods. Supervision includes, for example, timers on operating systems, automated responses, or manual oversight and response when system process anomalies occur.

Related Controls: None.

References: FIPS Publications 140-2, 180-4, 186-4, 202; NIST Special Publications 800-70, 800-147.

SI-8   SPAM PROTECTION

Control:

a. Employ spam protection mechanisms at system entry and exit points to detect and act on unsolicited messages; and

b. Update spam protection mechanisms when new releases are available in accordance with organizational configuration management policy and procedures.

Supplemental Guidance: System entry and exit points include, for example, firewalls, remote-access servers, electronic mail servers, web servers, proxy servers, workstations, notebook computers, and mobile devices. Spam can be transported by different means including, for example, electronic mail, electronic mail attachments, and web accesses. Spam protection mechanisms include, for example, signature definitions.

Related Controls: SC-5, SC-7, SC-38, SI-3, SI-4.

Control Enhancements:

(1) SPAM PROTECTION | CENTRAL MANAGEMENT

Centrally manage spam protection mechanisms.

Supplemental Guidance: Central management is the organization-wide management and implementation of spam protection mechanisms. Central management includes planning, implementing, assessing, authorizing, and monitoring the organization-defined, centrally managed spam protection controls.

Related Controls: AU-3, CM-6, SI-2, SI-7.

(2) SPAM PROTECTION | AUTOMATIC UPDATES

Automatically update spam protection mechanisms.

Supplemental Guidance: None.

Related Controls: None.

(3) SPAM PROTECTION | CONTINUOUS LEARNING CAPABILITY

Implement spam protection mechanisms with a learning capability to more effectively identify legitimate communications traffic.

Supplemental Guidance: Learning mechanisms include, for example, Bayesian filters that respond to user inputs identifying specific traffic as spam or legitimate by updating algorithm parameters and thereby more accurately separating types of traffic.

Related Controls: None.

References: NIST Special Publications 800-45, 800-177.

SI-9   INFORMATION INPUT RESTRICTIONS

[Withdrawn: Incorporated into AC-2, AC-3, AC-5, AC-6].

SI-10   INFORMATION INPUT VALIDATION

Control: Check the validity of [*Assignment: organization-defined information inputs*].

Supplemental Guidance: Checking the valid syntax and semantics of system inputs including, for example, character set, length, numerical range, and acceptable values, verifies that inputs match specified definitions for format and content. Software applications typically follow well-defined protocols that use structured messages (i.e., commands or queries) to communicate between software modules or system components. Structured messages can contain raw or unstructured data interspersed with metadata or control information. If software applications use attacker-supplied inputs to construct structured messages without properly encoding such messages, then the attacker could insert malicious commands or special characters that can cause the data to be interpreted as control information or metadata. Consequently, the module or component that receives the corrupted output will perform the wrong operations or otherwise interpret the data incorrectly. Prescreening inputs prior to passing to interpreters prevents the content from being unintentionally interpreted as commands. Input validation ensures accurate and correct inputs and prevent attacks such as cross-site scripting and a variety of injection attacks.

Related Controls: None.

Control Enhancements:

(1) INFORMATION INPUT VALIDATION | MANUAL OVERRIDE CAPABILITY

(a) Provide a manual override capability for input validation of [*Assignment: organization-defined inputs*];

(b) Restrict the use of the manual override capability to only [*Assignment: organization-defined authorized individuals*]; and

(c) Audit the use of the manual override capability.

Supplemental Guidance: In certain situations, for example, during events that are defined in organizational contingency plans, a manual override capability for input validation may be

needed. Each command executes an input to some organizational subsystem and with the inputs
defined by the organization.

Related Controls: AC-3, AU-2, AU-12.

(2) INFORMATION INPUT VALIDATION | REVIEW AND RESOLVE ERRORS

Review and resolve input validation errors within [*Assignment: organization-defined time-period*].

Supplemental Guidance: Resolution of input validation errors includes, for example, correcting
systemic causes of errors and resubmitting transactions with corrected input.

Related Controls: None.

(3) INFORMATION INPUT VALIDATION | PREDICTABLE BEHAVIOR

Verify that the system behaves in a predictable and documented manner when invalid inputs are received.

Supplemental Guidance: A common vulnerability in organizational systems is unpredictable
behavior when invalid inputs are received. This control enhancement ensures that there is
predictable behavior in the face of invalid inputs by specifying system responses that facilitate
transitioning the system to known states without adverse, unintended side effects. The invalid
inputs are those inputs related to the information inputs defined by the organization in the
base control.

Related Controls: None.

(4) INFORMATION INPUT VALIDATION | TIMING INTERACTIONS

Account for timing interactions among system components in determining appropriate responses for invalid inputs.

Supplemental Guidance: In addressing invalid system inputs received across protocol interfaces,
timing interactions become relevant, where one protocol needs to consider the impact of the
error response on other protocols within the protocol stack. For example, 802.11 standard
wireless network protocols do not interact well with Transmission Control Protocols (TCP)
when packets are dropped (which could be due to invalid packet input). TCP assumes packet
losses are due to congestion, while packets lost over 802.11 links are typically dropped due to
collisions or noise on the link. If TCP makes a congestion response, it takes the wrong action
in response to a collision event. Adversaries may be able to use what appears to be acceptable
individual behaviors of the protocols in concert to achieve adverse effects through suitable
construction of invalid input.

Related Controls: None.

(5) INFORMATION INPUT VALIDATION | RESTRICT INPUTS TO TRUSTED SOURCES AND APPROVED FORMATS

Restrict the use of information inputs to [*Assignment: organization-defined trusted sources*] and/or [*Assignment: organization-defined formats*].

Supplemental Guidance: This control enhancement applies the concept of whitelisting to
information inputs. Specifying known trusted sources for information inputs and acceptable
formats for such inputs can reduce the probability of malicious activity.

Related Controls: AC-3, AC-6.

References: NIST Special Publication 800-167.

SI-11 ERROR HANDLING

Control:

a. Generate error messages that provide information necessary for corrective actions without
revealing information that could be exploited; and

b. Reveal error messages only to [*Assignment: organization-defined personnel or roles*].

Supplemental Guidance: Organizations consider the structure and the content of error messages. The
extent to which systems can handle error conditions is guided and informed by organizational
policy and operational requirements. Exploitable information includes, for example, erroneous
logon attempts with passwords entered by mistake as the username; mission/business information

that can be derived from, if not stated explicitly by, the information recorded; and personally identifiable information such as account numbers, social security numbers, and credit card numbers. In addition, error messages may provide a covert channel for transmitting information.

Related Controls: AU-2, AU-3, SC-31, SI-2.

Control Enhancements: None.

References: None.

SI-12 INFORMATION MANAGEMENT AND RETENTION

Control: Manage and retain information within the system and information output from the system in accordance with applicable laws, Executive Orders, directives, regulations, policies, standards, guidelines and operational requirements.

Supplemental Guidance: Information management and retention requirements cover the full life cycle of information, in some cases extending beyond system disposal. Information to be retained may also include policies, procedures, plans, and other types of administrative information. The National Archives and Records Administration provides guidance on records retention.

Related Controls: All XX-1 Controls, AC-16, AU-5, AU-11, CA-2, CA-3, CA-5, CA-6, CA-7, CA-9, CM-5, CM-9, CP-2, IR-8, MP-2, MP-3, MP-4, MP-6, PA-1, PA-2, PA-3, PL-2, PL-4, PM-4, PM-8, PM-9, PS-2, PS-6, RA-2, RA-3, SA-5.

Control Enhancements:

(1) INFORMATION MANAGEMENT AND RETENTION | LIMIT PERSONALLY IDENTIFIABLE INFORMATION ELEMENTS

Limit personally identifiable information being processed in the information life cycle to the [*Assignment: organization-defined elements*] identified in the privacy risk assessment.

Supplemental Guidance: Limiting the use of personally identifiable information throughout the information life cycle when such information is not needed for operational purposes helps reduce the level of privacy risk created by a system. The information life cycle includes information creation, collection, use, processing, storage, maintenance, dissemination, disclosure, and disposition.

Related Controls: None.

(2) INFORMATION MANAGEMENT AND RETENTION | MINIMIZE PERSONALLY IDENTIFIABLE INFORMATION IN TESTING, TRAINING, AND RESEARCH

Use [*Assignment: organization-defined techniques*] to minimize the use of personally identifiable information for research, testing, or training, in accordance with the privacy risk assessment.

Supplemental Guidance: Organizations can minimize the risk to an individual's privacy by using techniques such as de-identification or synthetic data. Limiting the use of personally identifiable information throughout the information life cycle when such information is not needed for research, testing, or training helps reduce the level of privacy risk created by a system.

Related Controls: PM-23.

References: NIST SP 800-188.

SI-13 PREDICTABLE FAILURE PREVENTION

Control:

a. Determine mean time to failure (MTTF) for [*Assignment: organization-defined system components*] in specific environments of operation; and

b. Provide substitute system components and a means to exchange active and standby components at [*Assignment: organization-defined MTTF substitution criteria*].

Supplemental Guidance: While MTTF is primarily a reliability issue, this control addresses potential failures of system components that provide security capability. Failure rates reflect installation-specific consideration, not industry-average. Organizations define the criteria for substitution of system components based on the MTTF value with consideration for resulting potential harm from component failures. Transfer of responsibilities between active and standby components does not compromise safety, operational readiness, or security capability. This includes, for example, preservation of system state variables. Standby components remain available at all times except for maintenance issues or recovery failures in progress.

Related Controls: CP-2, CP-10, CP-13, MA-2, MA-6, SC-6.

Control Enhancements:

(1) PREDICTABLE FAILURE PREVENTION | TRANSFERRING COMPONENT RESPONSIBILITIES

Takes system components out of service by transferring component responsibilities to substitute components no later than [*Assignment: organization-defined fraction or percentage*] of mean time to failure.

Supplemental Guidance: None.

Related Controls: None.

(2) PREDICTABLE FAILURE PREVENTION | TIME LIMIT ON PROCESS EXECUTION WITHOUT SUPERVISION

[Withdrawn: Incorporated into SI-7(16)].

(3) PREDICTABLE FAILURE PREVENTION | MANUAL TRANSFER BETWEEN COMPONENTS

Manually initiate transfers between active and standby system components when the use of the active component reaches [*Assignment: organization-defined percentage*] of the mean time to failure.

Supplemental Guidance: For example, if the MTTF for a system component is one hundred days and the organization-defined percentage is ninety percent, the manual transfer would occur after ninety days.

Related Controls: None.

(4) PREDICTABLE FAILURE PREVENTION | STANDBY COMPONENT INSTALLATION AND NOTIFICATION

If system component failures are detected:

(a) Ensure that the standby components are successfully and transparently installed within [*Assignment: organization-defined time-period*]; and

(b) [*Selection (one or more): Activate [Assignment: organization-defined alarm]; Automatically shut down the system; [Assignment: organization-defined action]*]].

Supplemental Guidance: Automatic or manual transfer of components from standby to active mode can occur, for example, upon detection of component failures.

Related Controls: None.

(5) PREDICTABLE FAILURE PREVENTION | FAILOVER CAPABILITY

Provide [*Selection: real-time; near real-time*] [*Assignment: organization-defined failover capability*] for the system.

Supplemental Guidance: Failover refers to the automatic switchover to an alternate system upon the failure of the primary system. Failover capability includes, for example, incorporating mirrored system operations at alternate processing sites or periodic data mirroring at regular intervals defined by recovery time-periods of organizations.

Related Controls: CP-6, CP-7, CP-9.

References: None.

SI-14 NON-PERSISTENCE

Control: Implement non-persistent [*Assignment: organization-defined system components and services*] that are initiated in a known state and terminated [*Selection (one or more): upon end of session of use; periodically at [Assignment: organization-defined frequency]*]].

Supplemental Guidance: This control mitigates risk from advanced persistent threats (APTs) by significantly reducing the targeting capability of adversaries (i.e., window of opportunity and available attack surface) to initiate and complete attacks. By implementing the concept of non-persistence for selected system components, organizations can provide a known state computing resource for a specific time-period that does not give adversaries sufficient time on target to exploit vulnerabilities in organizational systems and the environments in which those systems operate. Since the APT is a high-end, sophisticated threat regarding capability, intent, and targeting, organizations assume that over an extended period, a percentage of attacks will be successful. Non-persistent system components and services are activated as required using protected information and terminated periodically or at the end of sessions. Non-persistence increases the work factor of adversaries in attempting to compromise or breach organizational systems.

Non-persistence can be achieved by refreshing system components, for example, by periodically re-imaging components or by using a variety of common virtualization techniques. Non-persistent services can be implemented using virtualization techniques as part of virtual machines or as new instances of processes on physical machines (either persistent or non-persistent). The benefit of periodic refreshes of system components and services is that it does not require organizations to first determine whether compromises of components or services have occurred (something that may often be difficult to determine). The refresh of selected system components and services occurs with sufficient frequency to prevent the spread or intended impact of attacks, but not with such frequency that it makes the system unstable. Refreshes of critical components and services may be done periodically to hinder the ability of adversaries to exploit optimum windows of vulnerabilities.

Related Controls: SC-30, SC-34.

Control Enhancements:

(1) NON-PERSISTENCE | REFRESH FROM TRUSTED SOURCES

Obtain software and data employed during system component and service refreshes from [*Assignment: organization-defined trusted sources*].

Supplemental Guidance: Trusted sources include, for example, software and data from write-once, read-only media or from selected off-line secure storage facilities.

Related Controls: None.

References: None.

SI-15   INFORMATION OUTPUT FILTERING

Control: Validate information output from [*Assignment: organization-defined software programs and/or applications*] to ensure that the information is consistent with the expected content.

Supplemental Guidance: Certain types of attacks, including for example, SQL injections, produce output results that are unexpected or inconsistent with the output results that would normally be expected from software programs or applications. This control enhancement focuses on detecting extraneous content, preventing such extraneous content from being displayed, and then alerting monitoring tools that anomalous behavior has been discovered.

Related Controls: SI-3, SI-4.

Control Enhancements:

(1) INFORMATION OUTPUT FILTERING | LIMIT PERSONALLY IDENTIFIABLE INFORMATION DISSEMINATION

Limit the dissemination of personally identifiable information to [*Assignment: organization-defined elements*] identified in the privacy risk assessment and consistent with authorized purposes.

Supplemental Guidance: Preventing the sharing of personally identifiable information outside of explicitly determined elements helps mitigate privacy risks that may arise from using such information to detect anomalous system behavior. Organizations weigh the risks created by using personally identifiable information for information output filtering (as either signature or heuristic information) against the security risks they help mitigate and the established privacy posture in the privacy program plan.

Related Controls: PA-2, PA-3, PM-18.

References: None

SI-16 MEMORY PROTECTION

Control: Implement [*Assignment: organization-defined security safeguards*] to protect the system memory from unauthorized code execution.

Supplemental Guidance: Some adversaries launch attacks with the intent of executing code in non-executable regions of memory or in memory locations that are prohibited. Security safeguards employed to protect memory include, for example, data execution prevention and address space layout randomization. Data execution prevention safeguards can either be hardware-enforced or software-enforced with hardware enforcement providing the greater strength of mechanism.

Related Controls: AC-25, SC-3.

Control Enhancements: None.

References: None.

SI-17 FAIL-SAFE PROCEDURES

Control: Implement [*Assignment: organization-defined fail-safe procedures*] when [*Assignment: organization-defined failure conditions occur*].

Supplemental Guidance: Failure conditions include, for example, loss of communications among critical system components or between system components and operational facilities. Fail-safe procedures include, for example, alerting operator personnel and providing specific instructions on subsequent steps to take. These steps include, for example, doing nothing, reestablishing system settings, shutting down processes, restarting the system, or contacting designated organizational personnel.

Related Controls: CP-12, CP-13, SC-24, SI-13.

Control Enhancements: None.

References: None.

SI-18 INFORMATION DISPOSAL

Control: Use [*Assignment: organization-defined techniques or methods*] to dispose of, destroy, or erase information.

Supplemental Guidance: Disposal or destruction of information applies to originals as well as copies and archived records, including system logs that may contain personally identifiable information.

Related Controls: MP-6.

Control Enhancements: None.

References: None.

SI-19 DATA QUALITY OPERATIONS

Control:

a. Upon collection or creation of personally identifiable information, check for the accuracy, relevance, timeliness, impact, completeness, and de-identification of that information across the information life cycle; and

b. Check for and correct as necessary [*Assignment: organization-defined frequency*] and across the information life cycle:

    1. Inaccurate or outdated personally identifiable information;

    2. Personally identifiable information of incorrectly determined impact; or

3. Incorrectly de-identified personally identifiable information.

Supplemental Guidance: The information life cycle includes information creation, collection, use, processing, storage, maintenance, dissemination, disclosure, disposition.

Related Controls: PM-25, SI-4, SI-20.

Control Enhancements:

(1) DATA QUALITY OPERATIONS | UPDATING AND CORRECTING PERSONALLY IDENTIFIABLE INFORMATION

Employ technical controls to correct personally identifiable information used in organizational programs and systems that is inaccurate or outdated, incorrectly determined regarding impact, or incorrectly de-identified.

Supplemental Guidance: Use of controls to improve data quality may inadvertently create privacy risks. Automated controls may connect to external or otherwise unrelated systems, and the matching of records between these systems may create linkages with unintended consequences. Organizations assess and document these risks in their privacy impact assessment and make determinations that are in alignment with their privacy program plan.

Related Controls: PM-18, RA-8.

(2) DATA QUALITY OPERATIONS | DATA TAGS

Employ data tags to automate tracking of personally identifiable information across the information life cycle within organizational systems.

Supplemental Guidance: Data tags that contain information about retention dates, usage or disclosure policies, or other information pertaining to the management of personally identifiable information can support the use of automation tools to enforce relevant data management policies.

Related Controls: None.

(3) DATA QUALITY OPERATIONS | PERSONALLY IDENTIFIABLE INFORMATION COLLECTION

Collect personally identifiable information directly from the individual.

Supplemental Guidance: Organizations take reasonable steps to confirm the accuracy and relevance of personally identifiable information. These steps may include, for example, editing and validating addresses as they are collected or entered into systems using automated address verification look-up application programming interfaces. The types of measures taken to protect data quality are based on the nature and context of the personally identifiable information, how it is to be used, and how it was obtained. Measures taken to validate the accuracy of personally identifiable information used to make determinations about the rights, benefits, or privileges of individuals under federal programs may be more comprehensive than those used to validate less sensitive personally identifiable information. Additional steps may be necessary to validate personally identifiable information that is obtained from sources other than individuals or the authorized representatives of individuals.

Related Controls: None.

References: NIST Special Publication 800-188.

SI-20   DE-IDENTIFICATION

Control: Remove personally identifiable information from datasets.

Supplemental Guidance: Many datasets contain information about individuals that can be used to distinguish or trace an individual's identity, such as name, social security number, date and place of birth, mother's maiden name, or biometric records. Datasets may also contain other information that is linked or linkable to an individual, such as medical, educational, financial, and employment information. Personally identifiable information is removed from datasets by trained individuals when such information is not (or no longer) necessary to satisfy the requirements envisioned for the data. For example, if the dataset is only used to produce aggregate statistics, the identifiers that are not needed for producing those statistics are removed. Removing identifiers improves privacy

production once information that is contained cannot be inadvertently disclosed or improperly
used.

Related Controls: PM-23, PM-24, PM-25, SI-18, SI-19.

Control Enhancements:

(1)   DE-IDENTIFICATION | COLLECTION

De-identify the dataset upon collection by not collecting personally identifiable information.

Supplemental Guidance: If a data source contains personally identifiable information but the
information will not be used, the dataset can be de-identified upon creation by simply not
collecting the data elements containing the personally identifiable information. For example,
if an organization does not intend to use the social security number of an applicant, then
application forms do not ask for a social security number.

Related Controls: None.

(2)   DE-IDENTIFICATION | ARCHIVING

**Refrain from archiving personally identifiable information elements if those elements in a dataset
will not be needed after the dataset is archived.**

Supplemental Guidance: Datasets can be archived for many reasons. The envisioned purposes
for the archived dataset are specified and if personally identifiable information elements are
not required, the elements are not archived. For example, social security numbers may have
been collected for record linkage, but the archived dataset may include the required elements
from the linked records. In this case, it is not necessary to archive the social security numbers.

Related Controls: None.

(3)   DE-IDENTIFICATION | RELEASE

**Remove personally identifiable information elements from a dataset prior to its release if those
elements in the dataset do not need to be part of the data release.**

Supplemental Guidance: Prior to releasing a dataset, a data custodian considers the intended
uses of the released dataset and determines if it is necessary to release personally identifiable
information. If it is not necessary, the personally identifiable information can be removed
using de-identification techniques.

Related Controls: None.

(4)   DE-IDENTIFICATION | REMOVAL, MASKING, ENCRYPTION, HASHING, OR REPLACEMENT OF DIRECT
IDENTIFIERS

Remove, mask, encrypt, hash, or replace direct identifiers in a dataset.

Supplemental Guidance: There are many possible processes for removing direct identifiers from
a dataset. Columns in a dataset that contain a direct identifier can be removed. In masking, the
direct identifier is transformed into a repeating character, for example, XXXXXX or 999999.
Identifiers can be encrypted or hashed, so that the linked records remain linked. In the case of
encryption or hashing, algorithms are employed that require the use of a key, including, for
example, the Advanced Encryption Standard or a Hash-based Message Authentication Code.
Implementations may use the same key for all identifiers or a different key for each identifier.
Using a different key for each identifier provides for a higher degree of security and privacy.
Identifiers can alternatively be replaced with a keyword, including for example, transforming
"George Washington" to "PATIENT," or replaced with a realistic surrogate value, including
for example, transforming "George Washington" to "Abraham Polk."

Related Controls: None.

(5)   DE-IDENTIFICATION | STATISTICAL DISCLOSURE CONTROL

**Manipulate numerical data, contingency tables, and statistical findings so that no person or
organization is identifiable in the results of the analysis.**

Supplemental Guidance: Many types of statistical analyses can result in the disclosure of
information about individuals even if only summary information is provided. For example, if
a school publishes a monthly table with the number of minority students, and in January the

school reports that it has 10-19 such students, but in March it reports that it has 20-29 such students, then it can be inferred that the student who enrolled in February was a minority.

Related Controls: None.

(6) DE-IDENTIFICATION | DIFFERENTIAL PRIVACY

Prevent disclosure of personally identifiable information by adding non-deterministic noise to the results of mathematical operations before the results are reported.

Supplemental Guidance: The mathematical definition for differential privacy holds that the result of a dataset analysis should be approximately the same before and after the addition or removal of a single data record (which is assumed to be the data from a single individual). In its most basic form, differential privacy applies only to online query systems. However, it can also be used to produce machine-learning statistical classifiers and synthetic data. Differential privacy comes at the cost of decreased accuracy of results, forcing organizations to quantify the trade-off between privacy protection and the overall accuracy, usefulness, and utility of the de-identified dataset. Non-deterministic noise can include, for example, adding small random values to the results of mathematical operations in dataset analysis.

Related Controls: None.

(7) DE-IDENTIFICATION | VALIDATED SOFTWARE

Perform de-identification using validated algorithms and software that is validated to implement the algorithms.

Supplemental Guidance: Algorithms that appear to remove personally identifiable information from a dataset may in fact leave information that is personally identifiable or data that are re-identifiable. Software that is claimed to implement a validated algorithm may contain bugs or may implement a different algorithm. Software may de-identify one type of data, for example, integers, but not another type of data, for example, floating point numbers. For these reasons, de-identification is performed using algorithms and software that are validated.

Related Controls: None.

(8) DE-IDENTIFICATION | MOTIVATED INTRUDER

Perform a motivated intruder test on the de-identified dataset to determine if the identified data remains or if the de-identified data can be re-identified.

Supplemental Guidance: A motivated intruder test is a test in which a person or group takes a data release and specified resources and attempts to re-identify one or more individuals in the de-identified dataset. Such tests specify the amount of inside knowledge, financial resources, computational resources, data, and skills that intruders have at their disposal to conduct the tests. A motivated intruder test can identify if de-identification is insufficient. It can also be a useful diagnostic tool to assess if de-identification is likely to be sufficient; however, the test alone cannot prove that de-identification is sufficient.

Related Controls: None.

References: NIST Special Publication 800-188.

APPENDIX A

REFERENCES

LAWS, POLICIES, DIRECTIVES, REGULATIONS, STANDARDS, AND GUIDELINES[34]

LAWS AND EXECUTIVE ORDERS

1. Consolidated Appropriations Act (P.L. 114-92), December 2015.

2. E-Government Act [includes FISMA] (P.L. 107-347), December 2002.

3. Federal Information Security Management Act (P.L. 107-347, Title III), December 2002.

4. Federal Information Security Modernization Act (P.L. 113-283), December 2014.

5. Freedom of Information Act (FOIA), 5 U.S.C. § 552, As Amended By Public Law No. 104-231, 110 Stat. 3048, Electronic Freedom of Information Act Amendments of 1996.

6. Privacy Act (P.L. 93-579), December 1974.

7. USA PATRIOT Act (P.L. 107-56), October 2001.

8. Executive Order 13556, *Controlled Unclassified Information*, November 2010.

9. Executive Order 13587, *Structural Reforms to Improve the Security of Classified Networks and the Responsible Sharing and Safeguarding of Classified Information*, October 2011.

10. Executive Order 13636, *Improving Critical Infrastructure Cybersecurity*, February 2013.

11. Executive Order, *Strengthening the Cybersecurity of Federal Networks and Critical Infrastructure*, May 2017.

POLICIES, MEMORANDA, DIRECTIVES, INSTRUCTIONS, REGULATIONS, AND CIRCULARS

1. Code of Federal Regulations, Title 5, *Administrative Personnel*, Section 731.106, *Designation of Public Trust Positions and Investigative Requirements* (5 C.F.R. 731.106).

2. Committee on National Security Systems Instruction 1253, Security Categorization and Control Selection for National Security Systems, March 2014.

3. Committee on National Security Systems Instruction 4009, *National Information Assurance Glossary*, April 2010.

4. Department of Homeland Security, *National Infrastructure Protection Plan (NIPP)*, 2009.

5. Homeland Security Presidential Directive 7, *Critical Infrastructure Identification, Prioritization, and Protection*, December 2003.

6. Homeland Security Presidential Directive 12, *Policy for a Common Identification Standard for Federal Employees and Contractors*, August 2004.

---

[34] The standards and guidelines cited in this appendix are those that directly support the NIST Risk Management Framework or for which mappings are provided in Appendix I. Additional referential standards, guidelines, and interagency reports are cited with the applicable controls in Chapter Three.

7. Office of Management and Budget Circular A-130, *Managing Information as a Strategic Resource*, July 2016.

8. Office of Management and Budget Memorandum M-17-25, *Reporting Guidance for Executive Order on Strengthening the Cybersecurity of Federal Networks and Critical Infrastructure*, May 2017.

STANDARDS, GUIDELINES, AND INTERAGENCY REPORTS

1. International Organization for Standardization/International Electrotechnical Commission 27001:2013, *Information Technology -- Security techniques -- Information security management systems -- Requirements.*

2. International Organization for Standardization/International Electrotechnical Commission 15408-1:2009, *Information technology -- Security techniques -- Evaluation criteria for IT security -- Part 1: Introduction and general model.*

3. International Organization for Standardization/International Electrotechnical Commission 15408-2:2008, *Information technology -- Security techniques -- Evaluation criteria for IT security -- Part 2: Security functional requirements.*

4. International Organization for Standardization/International Electrotechnical Commission 15408-3:2008, *Information technology -- Security techniques -- Evaluation criteria for IT security -- Part 3: Security assurance requirements.*

5. National Institute of Standards and Technology Federal Information Processing Standards Publication 199, *Standards for Security Categorization of Federal Information and Information Systems*, February 2004.

6. National Institute of Standards and Technology Federal Information Processing Standards Publication 200, *Minimum Security Requirements for Federal Information and Information Systems*, March 2006.

7. National Institute of Standards and Technology Special Publication 800-18, Revision 1, *Guide for Developing Security Plans for Federal Information Systems*, February 2006.

8. National Institute of Standards and Technology Special Publication 800-37, Revision 1, *Guide for Applying the Risk Management Framework to Federal Information Systems: A Security Life Cycle Approach*, February 2010.

9. National Institute of Standards and Technology Special Publication 800-39, *Managing Information Security Risk: Organization, Mission, and Information System View*, March 2011.

10. National Institute of Standards and Technology Special Publication 800-53A, Revision 4, *Assessing Security and Privacy Controls in Federal Information Systems and Organizations: Building Effective Security Assessment Plans*, December 2014.

11. National Institute of Standards and Technology Special Publication 800-59, *Guideline for Identifying an Information System as a National Security System*, August 2003.

12. National Institute of Standards and Technology Special Publication 800-60, Revision 1, *Guide for Mapping Types of Information and Information Systems to Security Categories*, August 2008.

13. National Institute of Standards and Technology Special Publication 800-137, *Information Security Continuous Monitoring for Federal Information Systems and Organizations*, September 2011.

APPENDIX B

GLOSSARY

COMMON TERMS AND DEFINITIONS

Appendix B provides definitions for terminology used within Special Publication 800-53. Sources for terms used in this publication are cited as applicable. Where no citation is noted, the source of the definition is Special Publication 800-53.

adequate security
[OMB Circular A-130, Adapted]

Security commensurate with the risk resulting from the unauthorized access, use, disclosure, disruption, modification, or destruction of information.

advanced persistent threat
[NIST SP 800-39]

An adversary that possesses sophisticated levels of expertise and significant resources which allow it to create opportunities to achieve its objectives by using multiple attack vectors including, for example, cyber, physical, and deception. These objectives typically include establishing and extending footholds within the IT infrastructure of the targeted organizations for purposes of exfiltrating information, undermining or impeding critical aspects of a mission, program, or organization; or positioning itself to carry out these objectives in the future. The advanced persistent threat pursues its objectives repeatedly over an extended period; adapts to defenders' efforts to resist it; and is determined to maintain the level of interaction needed to execute its objectives.

agency
[OMB Circular A-130]

Any executive agency or department, military department, Federal Government corporation, Federal Government-controlled corporation, or other establishment in the Executive Branch of the Federal Government, or any independent regulatory agency. See *executive agency*.

all-source intelligence
[Department of Defense, Joint Publication 1-02]

Intelligence products and/or organizations and activities that incorporate all sources of information, most frequently including human resources intelligence, imagery intelligence, measurement and signature intelligence, signals intelligence, and open source data in the production of finished intelligence.

assessment
[CNSSI 4009, Adapted]

The testing or evaluation of security or privacy controls to determine the extent to which the controls are implemented correctly, operating as intended, and producing the desired outcome with respect to meeting the security requirements for an information system or organization. See *risk assessment*.

assessment plan

The objectives for the security and privacy control assessments and a detailed roadmap of how to conduct such assessments.

assessor

The individual, group, or organization responsible for conducting a security or privacy control assessment.

assurance [ISO/IEC 15026, Adapted]	Grounds for justified confidence that a [security or privacy] claim has been or will be achieved. *Note 1:* Assurance is typically obtained relative to a set of specific claims. The scope and focus of such claims may vary (e.g., security claims, safety claims) and the claims themselves may be interrelated. *Note 2:* Assurance is obtained through techniques and methods that generate credible evidence to substantiate claims.
audit log [CNSSI 4009]	A chronological record of system activities, including records of system accesses and operations performed in a given period.
audit record	An individual entry in an audit log related to an audited event.
audit reduction	A process that manipulates collected audit information and organizes such information in a summary format that is more meaningful to analysts.
audit trail	A chronological record that reconstructs and examines the sequence of activities surrounding or leading to a specific operation, procedure, or event in a security-relevant transaction from inception to result.
authentication [FIPS 200]	Verifying the identity of a user, process, or device, often as a prerequisite to allowing access to resources in a system.
authenticator	Something that the claimant possesses and controls (typically a cryptographic module or password) that is used to authenticate the claimant's identity. This was previously referred to as a token.
authenticity	The property of being genuine and being able to be verified and trusted; confidence in the validity of a transmission, a message, or message originator. See *authentication.*
authorization boundary [OMB Circular A-130]	All components of an information system to be authorized for operation by an authorizing official. This excludes separately authorized systems to which the information system is connected.
authorization to operate [OMB Circular A-130]	The official management decision given by a senior Federal official or officials to authorize operation of an information system and to explicitly accept the risk to agency operations (including mission, functions, image, or reputation), agency assets, individuals, other organizations, and the Nation based on the implementation of an agreed-upon set of security and privacy controls. Authorization also applies to common controls inherited by agency information systems.
authorizing official [OMB Circular A-130]	A senior Federal official or executive with the authority to authorize (i.e., assume responsibility for) the operation of an information system or the use of a designated set of common controls at an acceptable level of risk to agency operations (including mission, functions, image, or reputation), agency assets, individuals, other organizations, and the Nation.
availability [44 U.S.C., Sec. 3542]	Ensuring timely and reliable access to and use of information.

baseline configuration [NIST SP 800-128, adapted]	A documented set of specifications for a system, or a configuration item within a system, that has been formally reviewed and agreed on at a given point in time, and which can be changed only through change control procedures.
blacklisting	The process used to identify software programs that are not authorized to execute on a system or prohibited Universal Resource Locators or websites.
boundary protection	Monitoring and control of communications at the external boundary of a system to prevent and detect malicious and other unauthorized communications, using boundary protection devices, for example, gateways, routers, firewalls, guards, encrypted tunnels.
boundary protection device	A device with appropriate mechanisms that facilitates the adjudication of different interconnected system security policies or provides system boundary protection.
breadth [NIST SP 800-53A]	An attribute associated with an assessment method that addresses the scope or coverage of the assessment objects included with the assessment.
capability	A combination of mutually-reinforcing security and/or privacy controls implemented by technical means, physical means, and procedural means. Such controls are typically selected to achieve a common information security- or privacy-related purpose.
central management	The organization wide management and implementation of selected security and privacy controls and related processes. Central management includes planning, implementing, assessing, authorizing, and monitoring the organization-defined, centrally managed security and privacy controls and processes.
chief information officer [OMB Circular A-130, adapted]	The senior official that provides advice and other assistance to the head of the organization and other senior management personnel of the organization to ensure that IT is acquired and information resources are managed for the organization in a manner that achieves the organization's strategic goals and information resources management goals; and is responsible for ensuring agency compliance with, and prompt, efficient, and effective implementation of, the information policies and information resources management responsibilities, including the reduction of information collection burdens on the public.
chief information security officer	See *Senior Agency Information Security Officer*.
classified information	See classified national security information.
classified national security information [CNSSI 4009]	Information that has been determined pursuant to Executive Order (E.O.) 13526 or any predecessor order to require protection against unauthorized disclosure and is marked to indicate its classified status when in documentary form.

commodity service	A system service provided by a commercial service provider to a large and diverse set of consumers. The organization acquiring or receiving the commodity service possesses limited visibility into the management structure and operations of the provider, and while the organization may be able to negotiate service-level agreements, the organization is typically not able to require that the provider implement specific security or privacy controls.
common carrier	A telecommunications company that holds itself out to the public for hire to provide communications transmission services.
common control [OMB Circular A-130]	A security or privacy control that is inherited by multiple information systems or programs.
common control provider [NIST SP 800-37]	An organizational official responsible for the development, implementation, assessment, and monitoring of common controls (i.e., security or privacy controls inheritable by systems).
common criteria [CNSSI 4009]	Governing document that provides a comprehensive, rigorous method for specifying security function and assurance requirements for products and systems.
common secure configuration [NIST SP 800-128]	A recognized standardized and established benchmark that stipulates specific secure configuration settings for a given information technology platform.
compensating controls	The security and privacy controls employed in lieu of the controls in the baselines described in NIST Special Publication 800-53 that provide equivalent or comparable protection for a system or organization.
component	See *system component*.
confidentiality [44 U.S.C., Sec. 3542]	Preserving authorized restrictions on information access and disclosure, including means for protecting personal privacy and proprietary information.
configuration control [NIST SP 800-128]	Process for controlling modifications to hardware, firmware, software, and documentation to protect the system against improper modifications before, during, and after system implementation.
configuration item [NIST SP 800-128]	An aggregation of system components that is designated for configuration management and treated as a single entity in the configuration management process.
configuration management [NIST SP 800-128]	A collection of activities focused on establishing and maintaining the integrity of information technology products and systems, through control of processes for initializing, changing, and monitoring the configurations of those products and systems throughout the system development life cycle.
configuration settings [NIST SP 800-128]	The set of parameters that can be changed in hardware, software, or firmware that affect the security posture and/or functionality of the system.
control assessment	See *assessment*.

control baseline [FIPS 200, Adapted]	The set of security and privacy controls defined for a low-impact, moderate-impact, or high-impact system or selected based on the privacy selection criteria that provide a starting point for the tailoring process.
control effectiveness	A measure of whether a given security or privacy control is contributing to the reduction of information security or privacy risk.
control enhancement	Augmentation of a security or privacy control to build in additional, but related, functionality to the control; increase the strength of the control; or add assurance to the control.
control inheritance [CNSSI 4009]	A situation in which a system or application receives protection from security or privacy controls (or portions of controls) that are developed, implemented, assessed, authorized, and monitored by entities other than those responsible for the system or application; entities either internal or external to the organization where the system or application resides. See *common control*.
controlled area	Any area or space for which an organization has confidence that the physical and procedural protections provided are sufficient to meet the requirements established for protecting the information and/or information system.
controlled interface [CNSSI 4009]	A boundary with a set of mechanisms that enforces the security policies and controls the flow of information between interconnected systems.
controlled unclassified information [32 CFR part 2002]	Information that the Government creates or possesses, or that an entity creates or possesses for or on behalf of the Government, that a law, regulation, or Government-wide policy requires or permits an agency to handle using safeguarding or dissemination controls. However, CUI does not include classified information or information a non-executive branch entity possesses and maintains in its own systems that did not come from, or was not created or possessed by or for, an executive branch agency or an entity acting for an agency.
countermeasures [FIPS 200]	Actions, devices, procedures, techniques, or other measures that reduce the vulnerability of a system. Synonymous with security controls and safeguards.
covert channel [CNSSI 4009]	An unintended or unauthorized intra-system channel that enables two cooperating entities to transfer information in a way that violates the system's security policy but does not exceed the entities' access authorizations.
covert channel analysis [CNSSI 4009]	Determination of the extent to which the security policy model and subsequent lower-level program descriptions may allow unauthorized access to information.

covert storage channel
[CNSSI 4009]

A system feature that enables one system entity to signal information to another entity by directly or indirectly writing to a storage location that is later directly or indirectly read by the second entity.

covert timing channel
[CNSSI 4009, adapted]

A system feature that enables one system entity to signal information to another by modulating its own use of a system resource in such a way as to affect system response time observed by the second entity.

cross domain solution
[CNSSI 1253]

A form of controlled interface that provides the ability to manually and/or automatically access and/or transfer information between different security domains.

cybersecurity
[OMB Circular A-130]

Prevention of damage to, protection of, and restoration of computers, electronic communications systems, electronic communications services, wire communication, and electronic communication, including information contained therein, to ensure its availability, integrity, authentication, confidentiality, and nonrepudiation.

cyberspace
[CNSSI 4009]

The interdependent network of information technology infrastructures that includes the Internet, telecommunications networks, computer systems, and embedded processors and controllers in critical industries.

data mining

An analytical process that attempts to find correlations or patterns in large data sets for the purpose of data or knowledge discovery.

defense-in-breadth
[CNSSI 4009]

A planned, systematic set of multidisciplinary activities that seek to identify, manage, and reduce risk of exploitable vulnerabilities at every stage of the system, network, or subcomponent life cycle including system, network, or product design and development; manufacturing; packaging; assembly; system integration; distribution; operations; maintenance; and retirement.

defense-in-depth

Information security strategy that integrates people, technology, and operations capabilities to establish variable barriers across multiple layers and missions of the organization.

depth
[NIST SP 800-53A]

An attribute associated with an assessment method that addresses the rigor and level of detail associated with the application of the method.

developer

A general term that includes developers or manufacturers of systems, system components, or system services; systems integrators; vendors; and product resellers. Development of systems, components, or services can occur internally within organizations or through external entities.

digital media

A form of electronic media where data are stored in digital (as opposed to analog) form.

discretionary access control	All access control policy that constrains access of all subjects and objects in a system where the policy specifies that a subject that has been granted access to information can do one or more of the following: pass the information to other subjects or objects; grant its privileges to other subjects; change security attributes on subjects, objects, systems, or system components; choose the security attributes to be associated with newly-created or revised objects; or change the rules governing access control. Mandatory access controls restrict this capability.
domain	An environment or context that includes a set of system resources and a set of system entities that have the right to access the resources as defined by a common security policy, security model, or security architecture. See *security domain*.
enterprise [CNSSI 4009]	An organization with a defined mission/goal and a defined boundary, using systems to execute that mission, and with responsibility for managing its own risks and performance. An enterprise may consist of all or some of the following business aspects: acquisition, program management, human resources, financial management, security, and systems, information and mission management. See *organization*.
enterprise architecture [44 U.S.C. Sec. 3601]	A strategic information asset base, which defines the mission; the information necessary to perform the mission; the technologies necessary to perform the mission; and the transitional processes for implementing new technologies in response to changing mission needs; and includes a baseline architecture; a target architecture; and a sequencing plan.
environment of operation [OMB Circular A-130]	The physical surroundings in which an information system processes, stores, and transmits information.
event [NIST SP 800-61, Adapted]	Any observable occurrence in a system.
executive agency [OMB Circular A-130]	An executive department specified in 5 U.S.C., Sec. 101; a military department specified in 5 U.S.C., Sec. 102; an independent establishment as defined in 5 U.S.C., Sec. 104(1); and a wholly owned Government corporation fully subject to the provisions of 31 U.S.C., Chapter 91.
exfiltration	The unauthorized transfer of information from a system.
external system (or component)	A system or component of a system that is outside of the authorization boundary established by the organization and for which the organization typically has no direct control over the application of required security and privacy controls or the assessment of security and privacy control effectiveness.

external system service	A system service that is implemented outside of the authorization boundary of the organizational system (i.e., a service that is used by, but not a part of, the organizational system) and for which the organization typically has no direct control over the application of required security and privacy controls or the assessment of security and privacy control effectiveness.
external system service provider	A provider of external system services to an organization through a variety of consumer-producer relationships including but not limited to: joint ventures; business partnerships; outsourcing arrangements (i.e., through contracts, interagency agreements, lines of business arrangements); licensing agreements; and/or supply chain exchanges.
external network	A network not controlled by the organization.
failover	The capability to switch over automatically (typically without human intervention or warning) to a redundant or standby system upon the failure or abnormal termination of the previously active system.
federal enterprise architecture [FEA Program Management Office]	A business-based framework for governmentwide improvement developed by the Office of Management and Budget that is intended to facilitate efforts to transform the federal government to one that is citizen-centered, results-oriented, and market-based.
federal information system [40 U.S.C., Sec. 11331]	An information system used or operated by an executive agency, by a contractor of an executive agency, or by another organization on behalf of an executive agency.
FIPS-validated cryptography	A cryptographic module validated by the Cryptographic Module Validation Program (CMVP) to meet requirements specified in FIPS Publication 140-2 (as amended). As a prerequisite to CMVP validation, the cryptographic module is required to employ a cryptographic algorithm implementation that has successfully passed validation testing by the Cryptographic Algorithm Validation Program (CAVP). See *NSA-approved cryptography*.
firmware [CNSSI 4009]	Computer programs and data stored in hardware - typically in read-only memory (ROM) or programmable read-only memory (PROM) - such that the programs and data cannot be dynamically written or modified during execution of the programs. See *hardware* and *software*.
hardware [CNSSI 4009]	The material physical components of a system. See *software* and *firmware*.
high-impact system [FIPS 200]	A system in which at least one security objective (i.e., confidentiality, integrity, or availability) is assigned a FIPS Publication 199 potential impact value of high.
hybrid control [OMB Circular A-130]	A security or privacy control that is implemented for an information system in part as a common control and in part as a system-specific control. See *common control* and *system-specific control*.

identifier [FIPS 201-1]	Unique data used to represent a person's identity and associated attributes. A name or a card number are examples of identifiers. A unique label used by a system to indicate a specific entity, object, or group.
impact	The effect on organizational operations, organizational assets, individuals, other organizations, or the Nation (including the national security interests of the United States) of a loss of confidentiality, integrity, or availability of information or a system.
impact value [FIPS 199]	The assessed worst-case potential impact that could result from a compromise of the confidentiality, integrity, or availability of information expressed as a value of low, moderate or high.
incident [44 U.S.C., Sec. 3552]	An occurrence that actually or imminently jeopardizes, without lawful authority, the confidentiality, integrity, or availability of information or an information system; or constitutes a violation or imminent threat of violation of law, security policies, security procedures, or acceptable use policies.
industrial control system [NIST SP 800-82]	General term that encompasses several types of control systems, including supervisory control and data acquisition (SCADA) systems, distributed control systems (DCS), and other control system configurations such as programmable logic controllers (PLC) often found in the industrial sectors and critical infrastructures. An ICS consists of combinations of control components (e.g., electrical, mechanical, hydraulic, pneumatic) that act together to achieve an industrial objective (e.g., manufacturing, transportation of matter or energy).
information [OMB Circular A-130]	Any communication or representation of knowledge such as facts, data, or opinions in any medium or form, including textual, numerical, graphic, cartographic, narrative, electronic, or audiovisual forms.
information flow control	Safeguards to ensure that information transfers within a system or organization are not made in violation of the security policy.
information leakage	The intentional or unintentional release of information to an untrusted environment.
information owner [NIST SP 800-37]	Official with statutory or operational authority for specified information and responsibility for establishing the controls for its generation, collection, processing, dissemination, and disposal.
information resources [44 U.S.C., Sec. 3502]	Information and related resources, such as personnel, equipment, funds, and information technology.
information security [44 U.S.C., Sec. 3542]	The protection of information and systems from unauthorized access, use, disclosure, disruption, modification, or destruction in order to provide confidentiality, integrity, and availability.

information security architecture [OMB Circular A-130]	An embedded, integral part of the enterprise architecture that describes the structure and behavior of the enterprise security processes, security systems, personnel and organizational subunits, showing their alignment with the enterprise's mission and strategic plans.
information security policy [CNSSI 4009]	Aggregate of directives, regulations, rules, and practices that prescribes how an organization manages, protects, and distributes information.
information security program plan [OMB Circular A-130]	Formal document that provides an overview of the security requirements for an organization-wide information security program and describes the program management controls and common controls in place or planned for meeting those requirements.
information security risk [NIST SP 800-30]	The risk to organizational operations (including mission, functions, image, reputation), organizational assets, individuals, other organizations, and the Nation due to the potential for unauthorized access, use, disclosure, disruption, modification, or destruction of information and/or systems.
information steward [NIST SP 800-37]	An agency official with statutory or operational authority for specified information and responsibility for establishing the controls for its generation, collection, processing, dissemination, and disposal.
information system [44 U.S.C., Sec. 3502]	A discrete set of information resources organized for the collection, processing, maintenance, use, sharing, dissemination, or disposition of information.
information technology [OMB Circular A-130]	Any services, equipment, or interconnected system(s) or subsystem(s) of equipment, that are used in the automatic acquisition, storage, analysis, evaluation, manipulation, management, movement, control, display, switching, interchange, transmission, or reception of data or information by the agency. For purposes of this definition, such services or equipment if used by the agency directly or is used by a contractor under a contract with the agency that requires its use; or to a significant extent, its use in the performance of a service or the furnishing of a product. Information technology includes computers, ancillary equipment (including imaging peripherals, input, output, and storage devices necessary for security and surveillance), peripheral equipment designed to be controlled by the central processing unit of a computer, software, firmware and similar procedures, services (including cloud computing and help-desk services or other professional services which support any point of the life cycle of the equipment or service), and related resources. Information technology does not include any equipment that is acquired by a contractor incidental to a contract which does not require its use.
information technology product	See *system component*.

information type [FIPS 199]	A specific category of information (e.g., privacy, medical, proprietary, financial, investigative, contractor-sensitive, security management) defined by an organization or in some instances, by a specific law, Executive Order, directive, policy, or regulation.
insider [CNSSI 4009, Adapted]	Any person with authorized access to any organizational resource, to include personnel, facilities, information, equipment, networks, or systems.
insider threat [CNSSI 4009, adapted]	The threat that an insider will use her/his authorized access, wittingly or unwittingly, to do harm to the security of organizational operations and assets, individuals, other organizations, and the Nation. This threat can include damage through espionage, terrorism, unauthorized disclosure of national security information, or through the loss or degradation of organizational resources or capabilities.
insider threat program [CNSSI 4009, Adapted]	A coordinated collection of capabilities authorized by the organization and used to deter, detect, and mitigate the unauthorized disclosure of information.
interface [CNSSI 4009]	Common boundary between independent systems or modules where interactions take place.
integrity [44 U.S.C., Sec. 3542]	Guarding against improper information modification or destruction, and includes ensuring information non-repudiation and authenticity.
internal network	A network where the establishment, maintenance, and provisioning of security controls are under the direct control of organizational employees or contractors; or cryptographic encapsulation or similar security technology implemented between organization-controlled endpoints, provides the same effect (at least regarding confidentiality and integrity). An internal network is typically organization-owned, yet may be organization-controlled while not being organization-owned.
label	See *security label*.
least privilege [CNSSI 4009]	The principle that a security architecture is designed so that each entity is granted the minimum system resources and authorizations that the entity needs to perform its function.
line of business	The following OMB-defined process areas common to virtually all federal agencies: Case Management, Financial Management, Grants Management, Human Resources Management, Federal Health Architecture, Systems Security, Budget Formulation and Execution, Geospatial, and IT Infrastructure.
local access	Access to an organizational system by a user (or process acting on behalf of a user) communicating through a direct connection without the use of a network.

logical access control system [FICAM Roadmap and Implementation Guidance]	An automated system that controls an individual's ability to access one or more computer system resources such as a workstation, network, application, or database. A logical access control system requires validation of an individual's identity through some mechanism such as a PIN, card, biometric, or other token. It has the capability to assign different access privileges to different persons depending on their roles and responsibilities in an organization.
low-impact system [FIPS 200]	A system in which all three security objectives (i.e., confidentiality, integrity, and availability) are assigned a FIPS Publication 199 potential impact value of low.
malicious code	Software or firmware intended to perform an unauthorized process that will have adverse impact on the confidentiality, integrity, or availability of a system. A virus, worm, Trojan horse, or other code-based entity that infects a host. Spyware and some forms of adware are also examples of malicious code.
managed interface	An interface within a system that provides boundary protection capability using automated mechanisms or devices.
mandatory access control	An access control policy that is uniformly enforced across all subjects and objects within the boundary of a system. A subject that has been granted access to information is constrained from: passing the information to unauthorized subjects or objects; granting its privileges to other subjects; changing one or more security attributes on subjects, objects, the system, or system components; choosing the security attributes to be associated with newly-created or modified objects; or changing the rules for governing access control. Organization-defined subjects may explicitly be granted organization-defined privileges (i.e., they are trusted subjects) such that they are not limited by some or all the above constraints. Manadory access control is considered a type of nondiscretionary access control.
marking	See *security marking*.
matching agreement [OMB Circular A-108]	A written agreement between a recipient agency and a source agency (or a non-Federal agency) that is required by the Privacy Act for parties engaging in a matching program.
media [FIPS 200]	Physical devices or writing surfaces including, but not limited to, magnetic tapes, optical disks, magnetic disks, Large-Scale Integration memory chips, and printouts (but excluding display media) onto which information is recorded, stored, or printed within a system.
metadata	Information describing the characteristics of data including, for example, structural metadata describing data structures (i.e., data format, syntax, semantics) and descriptive metadata describing data contents (i.e., security labels).

mobile code	Software programs or parts of programs obtained from remote systems, transmitted across a network, and executed on a local system without explicit installation or execution by the recipient.
mobile code technologies	Software technologies that provide the mechanisms for the production and use of mobile code.
moderate-impact system [FIPS 200]	A system in which at least one security objective (i.e., confidentiality, integrity, or availability) is assigned a FIPS Publication 199 potential impact value of moderate and no security objective is assigned a potential impact value of high.
multifactor authentication [NIST SP 800-63]	An authentication system or an authenticator that requires more than one authentication factor for successful authentication. Multifactor authentication can be performed using a single authenticator that provides more than one factor or by a combination of authenticators that provide different factors. The three authentication factors are something you know, something you have, and something you are. See *authenticator*.
multilevel security [CNSSI 4009]	Concept of processing information with different classifications and categories that simultaneously permits access by users with different security clearances and denies access to users who lack authorization.
multiple security levels [CNSSI 4009]	Capability of a system that is trusted to contain, and maintain separation between, resources (particularly stored data) of different security domains.
national security emergency preparedness telecommunications services [47 C.F.R., Part 64, App A]	Telecommunications services that are used to maintain a state of readiness or to respond to and manage any event or crisis (local, national, or international) that causes or could cause injury or harm to the population, damage to or loss of property, or degrade or threaten the national security or emergency preparedness posture of the United States.
national security system [44 U.S.C., Sec. 3542]	Any system (including any telecommunications system) used or operated by an agency or by a contractor of an agency, or other organization on behalf of an agency—(i) the function, operation, or use of which involves intelligence activities; involves cryptologic activities related to national security; involves command and control of military forces; involves equipment that is an integral part of a weapon or weapons system; or is critical to the direct fulfillment of military or intelligence missions (excluding a system that is to be used for routine administrative and business applications, for example, payroll, finance, logistics, and personnel management applications); or (ii) is protected at all times by procedures established for information that have been specifically authorized under criteria established by an Executive Order or an Act of Congress to be kept classified in the interest of national defense or foreign policy.

network	A system implemented with a collection of interconnected components. Such components may include routers, hubs, cabling, telecommunications controllers, key distribution centers, and technical control devices.
network access	Access to a system by a user (or a process acting on behalf of a user) communicating through a network including, for example, a local area network, a wide area network, and Internet.
nonce [NIST SP 800-63]	A value used in security protocols that is never repeated with the same key. For example, nonces used as challenges in challenge-response authentication protocols are not repeated until the authentication keys are changed. Otherwise, there is a possibility of a replay attack.
nondiscretionary access control	See *mandatory access control*.
nonlocal maintenance	Maintenance activities conducted by individuals communicating through a network, either an external network or internal network.
non-organizational user	A user who is not an organizational user (including public users).
non-repudiation	Protection against an individual falsely denying having performed a certain action and provides the capability to determine whether an individual took a certain action such as creating information, sending a message, approving information, and receiving a message.
NSA-approved cryptography	Cryptography that consists of an approved algorithm; an implementation that has been approved for the protection of classified information and/or controlled unclassified information in a specific environment; and a supporting key management infrastructure.
object	Passive system-related entity including, for example, devices, files, records, tables, processes, programs, and domains, that contain or receive information. Access to an object (by a subject) implies access to the information it contains. See *subject*.
operational technology	Programmable systems or devices that interact with the physical environment (or manage devices that interact with the physical environment). These systems/devices detect or cause a direct change through the monitoring and/or control of devices, processes, and events. Examples include industrial control systems, building management systems, fire control systems, and physical access control mechanisms.
operations technology	See *operational technology*.

operations security [CNSSI 4009]	Systematic and proven process by which potential adversaries can be denied information about capabilities and intentions by identifying, controlling, and protecting generally unclassified evidence of the planning and execution of sensitive activities. The process involves five steps: identification of critical information, analysis of threats, analysis of vulnerabilities, assessment of risks, and application of appropriate countermeasures.
organization [FIPS 200, Adapted]	An entity of any size, complexity, or positioning within an organizational structure including, for example, federal agencies, private enterprises, academic institutions, state, local, or tribal governments, or as appropriate, any of their operational elements.
organizational user	An organizational employee or an individual the organization deems to have equivalent status of an employee including, for example, contractor, guest researcher, individual detailed from another organization. Policy and procedures for granting equivalent status of employees to individuals may include need-to-know, relationship to the organization, and citizenship.
overlay [OMB Circular A-130]	A specification of security or privacy controls, control enhancements, supplemental guidance, and other supporting information employed during the tailoring process, that is intended to complement (and further refine) security control baselines. The overlay specification may be more stringent or less stringent than the original security control baseline specification and can be applied to multiple information systems. See *tailoring*.
penetration testing	A test methodology in which assessors, typically working under specific constraints, attempt to circumvent or defeat the security features of a system.
personally identifiable information [OMB Circular A-130]	Information that can be used to distinguish or trace an individual's identity, either alone or when combined with other information that is linked or linkable to a specific individual.
physical access control system [NIST SP 800-116]	An electronic system that controls the ability of people or vehicles to enter a protected area, by means of authentication and authorization at access control points.
plan of action and milestones	A document that identifies tasks needing to be accomplished. It details resources required to accomplish the elements of the plan, any milestones in meeting the tasks, and scheduled completion dates for the milestones.
portable storage device	A system component that can communicate with and be added to or removed from a system or network and that is limited to data storage including, for example, text, video, audio, and/or image data, as its primary function. Examples include, but are not limited to optical discs; external or removable hard drives; external or removable solid state disk drives; magnetic/optical tapes; flash memory devices; flash memory cards; and other external or removable disks.

potential impact [FIPS 199]	The loss of confidentiality, integrity, or availability could be expected to have a limited adverse effect (FIPS Publication 199 low); a serious adverse effect (FIPS Publication 199 moderate); or a severe or catastrophic adverse effect (FIPS Publication 199 high) on organizational operations, organizational assets, or individuals.
privacy control [OMB Circular A-130]	The administrative, technical, and physical safeguards employed within an agency to ensure compliance with applicable privacy requirements and manage privacy risks.
privacy impact assessment [OMB Circular A-130]	An analysis of how information is handled to ensure handling conforms to applicable legal, regulatory, and policy requirements regarding privacy; to determine the risks and effects of creating, collecting, using, processing, storing, maintaining, disseminating, disclosing, and disposing of information in identifiable form in an electronic information system; and to examine and evaluate protections and alternate processes for handling information to mitigate potential privacy concerns. A privacy impact assessment is both an analysis and a formal document detailing the process and the outcome of the analysis.
privacy plan [OMB Circular A-130]	A formal document that details the privacy controls selected for an information system or environment of operation that are in place or planned for meeting applicable privacy requirements and managing privacy risks, details how the controls have been implemented, and describes the methodologies and metrics that will be used to assess the controls.
privacy program plan [OMB Circular A-130]	A formal document that provides an overview of an agency's privacy program, including a description of the structure of the privacy program, the resources dedicated to the privacy program, the role of the Senior Agency Official for Privacy and other privacy officials and staff, the strategic goals and objectives of the privacy program, and the program management controls and common controls in place or planned for meeting applicable privacy requirements and managing privacy risks.
privileged account	A system account with authorizations of a privileged user.
privileged command	A human-initiated command executed on a system involving the control, monitoring, or administration of the system including security functions and associated security-relevant information.
privileged user [CNSSI 4009]	A user that is authorized (and therefore, trusted) to perform security-relevant functions that ordinary users are not authorized to perform.
provenance	The chronology of the origin, development, ownership, location, and changes to a system or system component and associated data. It may also include personnel and processes used to interact with or make modifications to the system, component, or associated data.

public key infrastructure [CNSSI 4009]	The architecture, organization, techniques, practices, and procedures that collectively support the implementation and operation of a certificate-based public key cryptographic system. Framework established to issue, maintain, and revoke public key certificates.
purge [NIST SP 800-88]	A method of sanitization that applies physical or logical techniques that render target data recovery infeasible using state of the art laboratory techniques.
reciprocity [NIST SP 800-37]	Agreement among participating organizations to accept each other's security assessments to reuse system resources and/or to accept each other's assessed security posture to share information.
records [44 U.S.C. §3301]	All recorded information, regardless of form or characteristics, made or received by a Federal agency under Federal law or in connection with the transaction of public business and preserved or appropriate for preservation by that agency or its legitimate successor as evidence of the organization, functions, policies, decisions, procedures, operations, or other activities of the United States Government or because of the informational value of data in them.
red team exercise	An exercise, reflecting real-world conditions, conducted as a simulated adversarial attempt to compromise organizational missions or business processes and to provide a comprehensive assessment of the security capability of an organization and its systems.
reference monitor	A set of design requirements on a reference validation mechanism which as key component of an operating system, enforces an access control policy over all subjects and objects. A reference validation mechanism must be always invoked (i.e., complete mediation); tamperproof; and small enough to be subject to analysis and tests, the completeness of which can be assured (i.e., verifiable).
remote access	Access to an organizational system by a user (or a process acting on behalf of a user) communicating through an external network.
remote maintenance	Maintenance activities conducted by individuals communicating through an external network.
replay resistance	Protection against the capture of transmitted authentication or access control information and its subsequent retransmission with the intent of producing an unauthorized effect or gaining unauthorized access.
resilience [CNSSI 4009]	The ability to prepare for and adapt to changing conditions and withstand and recover rapidly from disruptions. Resilience includes the ability to withstand and recover from deliberate attacks, accidents, or naturally occurring threats or incidents.

restricted data [Atomic Energy Act of 1954]	All data concerning (i) design, manufacture, or utilization of atomic weapons; (ii) the production of special nuclear material; or (iii) the use of special nuclear material in the production of energy, but shall not include data declassified or removed from the Restricted Data category pursuant to Section 142 [of the Atomic Energy Act of 1954].
risk [OMB Circular A-130]	A measure of the extent to which an entity is threatened by a potential circumstance or event, and typically is a function of: (i) the adverse impact, or magnitude of harm, that would arise if the circumstance or event occurs; and (ii) the likelihood of occurrence.
risk assessment [NIST SP 800-39; NISTIR 8062]	The process of identifying risks to organizational operations (including mission, functions, image, reputation), organizational assets, individuals, other organizations, and the Nation, resulting from the operation of a system. Part of risk management, incorporates threat and vulnerability analyses and analyses of privacy-related problems arising from information processing and considers mitigations provided by security and privacy controls planned or in place. Synonymous with *risk analysis*.
risk executive (function) [NIST SP 800-37]	An individual or group within an organization that helps to ensure that security risk-related considerations for individual systems, to include the authorization decisions for those systems, are viewed from an organization-wide perspective with regard to the overall strategic goals and objectives of the organization in carrying out its missions and business functions; and managing risk from individual systems is consistent across the organization, reflects organizational risk tolerance, and is considered along with other organizational risks affecting mission/business success.
risk management [OMB Circular A-130]	The program and supporting processes to manage risk to agency operations (including mission, functions, image, reputation), agency assets, individuals, other organizations, and the Nation, and includes: establishing the context for risk-related activities; assessing risk; responding to risk once determined; and monitoring risk over time.
risk mitigation [CNSSI 4009]	Prioritizing, evaluating, and implementing the appropriate risk-reducing controls/countermeasures recommended from the risk management process.
risk response [OMB Circular A-130]	Accepting, avoiding, mitigating, sharing, or transferring risk to agency operations, agency assets, individuals, other organizations, or the Nation.

role-based access control	(Access control based on user roles (i.e., a collection of access authorizations a user receives based on an explicit or implicit assumption of a given role). Role permissions may be inherited through a role hierarchy and typically reflect the permissions needed to perform defined functions within an organization. A given role may apply to a single individual or to several individuals.
sanitization [NIST SP 800-88]	A process to render access to target data on the media infeasible for a given level of effort. Clear, purge, and destroy are actions that can be taken to sanitize media.
scoping considerations	A part of tailoring guidance providing organizations with specific considerations on the applicability and implementation of security and privacy controls in the control baselines. Considerations include policy/regulatory, technology, physical infrastructure, system component allocation, operational/environmental, public access, scalability, common control, and security objective.
security [CNSSI 4009]	A condition that results from the establishment and maintenance of protective measures that enable an organization to perform its mission or critical functions despite risks posed by threats to its use of systems. Protective measures may involve a combination of deterrence, avoidance, prevention, detection, recovery, and correction that should form part of the organization's risk management approach.
security attribute	An abstraction representing the basic properties or characteristics of an entity with respect to safeguarding information; typically associated with internal data structures including, for example, records, buffers, and files within the system and used to enable the implementation of access control and flow control policies, reflect special dissemination, handling or distribution instructions, or support other aspects of the information security policy.
security categorization	The process of determining the security category for information or a system. Security categorization methodologies are described in CNSS Instruction 1253 for national security systems and in FIPS Publication 199 for other than national security systems. *ee security category*.
security category [OMB Circular A-130]	The characterization of information or an information system based on an assessment of the potential impact that a loss of confidentiality, integrity, or availability of such information or information system would have on agency operations, agency assets, individuals, other organizations, and the Nation.
security control [OMB Circular A-130]	The safeguards or countermeasures prescribed for an information system or an organization to protect the confidentiality, integrity, and availability of the system and its information.
security control baseline [OMB Circular A-130]	The set of minimum security controls defined for a low-impact, moderate-impact, or high-impact information system.

security domain [CNSSI 4009]	A domain that implements a security policy and is administered by a single authority.
security functionality	The security-related features, functions, mechanisms, services, procedures, and architectures implemented within organizational information systems or the environments in which those systems operate.
security functions	The hardware, software, or firmware of the system responsible for enforcing the system security policy and supporting the isolation of code and data on which the protection is based.
security impact analysis [CNSSI 4009]	The analysis conducted by an organizational official to determine the extent to which changes to the system have affected the security state of the system.
security kernel [CNSSI 4009]	Hardware, firmware, and software elements of a trusted computing base implementing the reference monitor concept. Security kernel must mediate all accesses, be protected from modification, and be verifiable as correct.
security label	The means used to associate a set of security attributes with a specific information object as part of the data structure for that object.
security marking	The means used to associate a set of security attributes with objects in a human-readable form, to enable organizational process-based enforcement of information security policies.
security objective [FIPS 199]	Confidentiality, integrity, or availability.
security plan	Formal document that provides an overview of the security requirements for an information system or an information security program and describes the security controls in place or planned for meeting those requirements. The system security plan describes the system boundary; the environment in which the system operates; how the security requirements are implemented; and the relationships with or connections to other systems. See *system security plan*.
security policy [CNSSI 4009]	A set of criteria for the provision of security services.
security policy filter	A hardware and/or software component that performs one or more of the following functions: content verification to ensure the data type of the submitted content; content inspection, analyzing the submitted content to verify it complies with a defined policy; malicious content checker that evaluates the content for malicious code; suspicious activity checker that evaluates or executes the content in a safe manner, such as in a sandbox or detonation chamber and monitors for suspicious activity; or content sanitization, cleansing, and transformation, which modifies the submitted content to comply with a defined policy.

security requirement [FIPS 200, Adapted]	A requirement levied on an information system or an organization that is derived from applicable laws, Executive Orders, directives, policies, standards, instructions, regulations, procedures, and/or mission/business needs to ensure the confidentiality, integrity, and availability of information that is being processed, stored, or transmitted. Note: Security requirements can be used in a variety of contexts from high-level policy-related activities to low-level implementation-related activities in system development and engineering disciplines.
security service [CNSSI 4009]	A capability that supports one or more security requirements (confidentiality, integrity, availability). Examples of security services are key management, access control, and authentication.
security-relevant information	Information within the system that can potentially impact the operation of security functions or the provision of security services in a manner that could result in failure to enforce the system security policy or maintain isolation of code and data.
senior agency information security officer [44 U.S.C., Sec. 3544]	Official responsible for carrying out the Chief Information Officer responsibilities under FISMA and serving as the Chief Information Officer's primary liaison to the agency's authorizing officials, information system owners, and information system security officers. Note: Organizations subordinate to federal agencies may use the term *senior information security officer* or *chief information security officer* to denote individuals filling positions with similar responsibilities to Senior Agency Information Security Officers.
senior agency official for privacy [OMB Circular A-130]	The senior official, designated by the head of each agency, who has agency-wide responsibility for privacy, including implementation of privacy protections; compliance with Federal laws, regulations, and policies relating to privacy; management of privacy risks at the agency; and a central policy-making role in the agency's development and evaluation of legislative, regulatory, and other policy proposals.
senior information security officer	See *Senior Agency Information Security Officer*.
sensitive compartmented information [CNSSI 4009]	Classified information concerning or derived from intelligence sources, methods, or analytical processes, which is required to be handled within formal access control systems established by the Director of National Intelligence.
service-oriented architecture	A set of principles and methodologies for designing and developing software in the form of interoperable services. These services are well-defined business functions that are built as software components (i.e., discrete pieces of code and/or data structures) that can be reused for different purposes.
software [CNSSI 4009]	Computer programs and associated data that may be dynamically written or modified during execution.
spam	The abuse of electronic messaging systems to indiscriminately send unsolicited bulk messages.

special access program [CNSSI 4009]	A program established for a specific class of classified information that imposes safeguarding and access requirements that exceed those normally required for information at the same classification level.
split tunneling	The process of allowing a remote user or device to establish a non-remote connection with a system and simultaneously communicate via some other connection to a resource in an external network. This method of network access enables a user to access remote devices and simultaneously, access uncontrolled networks.
spyware	Software that is secretly or surreptitiously installed into an information system to gather information on individuals or organizations without their knowledge; a type of malicious code.
subject	An individual, process, or device causing information to flow among objects or change to the system state. Also see *object*.
subsystem	A major subdivision or component of an information system consisting of information, information technology, and personnel that performs one or more specific functions.
supplemental guidance	Statements used to provide additional explanatory information for security controls or security control enhancements.
supply chain [ISO 28001, Adapted]	Linked set of resources and processes between multiple tiers of developers that begins with the sourcing of products and services and extends through the design, development, manufacturing, processing, handling, and delivery of products and services to the acquirer.
supply chain element	An information technology product or product component that contains programmable logic and that is critically important to the functioning of a system.
system [CNSSI 4009]	Any organized assembly of resources and procedures united and regulated by interaction or interdependence to accomplish a set of specific functions. Note: Systems also include specialized systems such as industrial/process controls systems, telephone switching and private branch exchange (PBX) systems, and environmental control systems.
[ISO/IEC/IEEE 15288]	Combination of interacting elements organized to achieve one or more stated purposes. Note 1: There are many types of systems. Examples include: general and special-purpose information systems; command, control, and communication systems; crypto modules; central processing unit and graphics processor boards; industrial/process control systems; flight control systems; weapons, targeting, and fire control systems; medical devices and treatment systems; financial, banking, and merchandising transaction systems; and social networking systems. Note 2: The interacting elements in the definition of system include hardware, software, data, humans, processes, facilities, materials, and naturally occurring physical entities. Note 3: System of systems is included in the definition of system.
system boundary	See *authorization boundary*.

system component [NIST SP 800-128]	A discrete, identifiable information technology asset that represents a building block of a system and may include hardware, software, and firmware.
system of records [5 U.S.C. § 552a(a)(5)]	A group of any records under the control of any agency from which information is retrieved by the name of the individual or by some identifying number, symbol, or other identifying particular assigned to the individual.
system of records notice [OMB Circular A-108]	The notice(s) published by an agency in the *Federal Register* upon the establishment and/or modification of a system of records describing the existence and character of the system.
system owner **(or program manager)**	Official responsible for the overall procurement, development, integration, modification, or operation and maintenance of a system.
system **security officer** [NIST SP 800-37]	Individual with assigned responsibility for maintaining the appropriate operational security posture for a system or program.
system security plan	See *security plan*.
system service	A capability provided by a system that facilitates information processing, storage, or transmission.
system-related security risk [NIST SP 800-30]	Risk that arises through the loss of confidentiality, integrity, or availability of information or systems and that considers impacts to the organization (including assets, mission, functions, image, or reputation), individuals, other organizations, and the Nation. See *risk*.
system specific control [OMB Circular A-130]	A security or privacy control for an information system that is implemented at the system level and is not inherited by any other information system.
tailored control baseline	A set of controls resulting from the application of tailoring guidance to a control baseline. See *tailoring*.
tailoring	The process by which security control baselines are modified by: identifying and designating common controls; applying scoping considerations on the applicability and implementation of baseline controls; selecting compensating security controls; assigning specific values to organization-defined security control parameters; supplementing baselines with additional security controls or control enhancements; and providing additional specification information for control implementation.
threat [CNSSI 4009, Adapted]	Any circumstance or event with the potential to adversely impact organizational operations, organizational assets, individuals, other organizations, or the Nation through a system via unauthorized access, destruction, disclosure, modification of information, and/or denial of service.
threat assessment [CNSSI 4009]	Formal description and evaluation of threat to an information system.

threat modeling [NIST SP 800-154]	A form of risk assessment that models aspects of the attack and defense sides of a logical entity, such as a piece of data, an application, a host, a system, or an environment.
threat source [FIPS 200]	The intent and method targeted at the intentional exploitation of a vulnerability or a situation and method that may accidentally trigger a vulnerability. See *threat agent*.
trusted path	A mechanism by which a user (through an input device) can communicate directly with the security functions of the system with the necessary confidence to support the system security policy. This mechanism can only be activated by the user or the security functions of the system and cannot be imitated by untrusted software.
trustworthiness [CNSSI 4009]	The attribute of a person or enterprise that provides confidence to others of the qualifications, capabilities, and reliability of that entity to perform specific tasks and fulfill assigned responsibilities.
trustworthiness (system)	The degree to which an information system (including the information technology components that are used to build the system) can be expected to preserve the confidentiality, integrity, and availability of the information being processed, stored, or transmitted by the system across the full range of threats. A trustworthy information system is a system that is believed to can operate within defined levels of risk despite the environmental disruptions, human errors, structural failures, and purposeful attacks that are expected to occur in its environment of operation.
user [CNSSI 4009, adapted]	Individual, or (system) process acting on behalf of an individual, authorized to access a system. See *organizational user* and *non-organizational user*.
virtual private network [CNSSI 4009]	Protected information system link utilizing tunneling, security controls, and endpoint address translation giving the impression of a dedicated line.
vulnerability [CNSSI 4009]	Weakness in an information system, system security procedures, internal controls, or implementation that could be exploited or triggered by a threat source.
vulnerability analysis	See *vulnerability assessment*.
vulnerability assessment [CNSSI 4009]	Systematic examination of an information system or product to determine the adequacy of security measures, identify security deficiencies, provide data from which to predict the effectiveness of proposed security measures, and confirm the adequacy of such measures after implementation.
whitelisting	The process used to identify software programs that are authorized to execute on an information system; or authorized Universal Resource Locators or websites.

ACRONYMS

COMMON ABBREVIATIONS

ABAC	Attribute Based Access Control
API	Application Programming Interfaces
APT	Advanced Persistent Threat
BIOS	Basic Input Output System
CA	Certificate Authority/Certificate Authorities
CAVP	Cryptographic Algorithm Validation Program
CD	Compact Disk
CD-R	Compact Disk-Recordable
CEE	Common Event Expressions
CMVP	Cryptographic Module Validation Program
CUI	Controlled Unclassified Information
CVE	Common Vulnerabilities and Exposures
CVSS	Common Vulnerability Scoring System
CWE	Common Weakness Enumeration
DHCP	Dynamic Host Configuration Protocol
DMZ	Demilitarized Zone
DNS	Domain Name System
DNSSEC	Domain Name System Security
DoD	Department of Defense
DVD	Digital Video Disk
DVD-R	Digital Video Disk-Recordable
EAP	Extensible Authentication Protocol
EMP	Electromagnetic Pulse
EMSEC	Emissions Security
FBCA	Federal Bridge Certification Authority
FIPPs	Fair Information Practice Principles
FIPS	Federal Information Processing Standards
FISMA	Federal Information Security Modernization Act
FOIA	Freedom of Information Act
FTP	File Transfer Protocol

GMT	Greenwich Mean Time
GPS	Global Positioning System
GSA	General Services Administration
HTTP	Hyper Text Transfer Protocol
ICS	Industrial Control System
I/O	Input/Output
IOC	Indicators of Compromise
IoT	Internet of Things
IP	Internet Protocol
IT	Information Technology
MAC	Media Access Control
MTTF	Mean Time To Failure
NARA	National Archives and Records Administration
NATO	North Atlantic Treaty Organization
NIAP	National Information Assurance Partnership
NIST	National Institute of Standards and Technology
NOFORN	Not Releasable to Foreign Nationals
NSA	National Security Agency
NVD	National Vulnerability Database
OMB	Office of Management and Budget
OPSEC	Operation Security
OVAL	Open Vulnerability Assessment Language
PDF	Portable Document Format
PII	Personally Identifiable Information
PIN	Personal Identification Number
PIV	Personal Identification Verification
PIV-I	Personal Identification Verification Interoperable
PKI	Public Key Infrastructure
RBAC	Role-Based Access Control
RD	Restricted Data
RFID	Radio-Frequency Identification
SAP	Special Access Program
SCAP	Security Content Automation Protocol
SCI	Sensitive Compartmented Information

TCP	Transmission Control Protocol
TCP/IP	Transmission Control Protocol/Internet Protocol
TLS	Transport Layer Security
US-CERT	United States Computer Emergency Readiness Team
USGCB	United States Government Configuration Baseline
USB	Universal Serial Bus
UTC	Coordinated Universal Time
VoIP	Voice Over Internet Protocol
VPN	Virtual Private Network
WORM	Write-Once, Read-Many
XML	Extensible Markup Language

APPENDIX D

CONTROL BASELINES

LOW-IMPACT, MODERATE-IMPACT, AND HIGH-IMPACT SYSTEMS

Table D-1 lists the controls and control enhancements[35] for low-impact, moderate-impact, and high-impact systems to facilitate compliance with applicable laws, Executive Orders, directives, regulations, policies, standards, and guidelines.[36] The controls and control enhancements from the consolidated control catalog in Chapter Three have been allocated to three control baselines. These baselines represent an initial *starting point* in selecting controls for protecting federal systems.[37] The baselines are hierarchical with respect to the controls allocated to those baselines.[38] If a control is allocated to a baseline, the family identifier and control number are listed in the appropriate column. If a control is not allocated to a baseline, the entry is marked with a dash. Control enhancements are indicated by the enhancement number. For example, the AC-11(1) entry in the high baseline indicates that the eleventh control from the Access Control family has been selected along with control enhancement 1. Controls and control enhancements that are not allocated to any baseline can be selected on an optional basis. This can occur, for example, when the results of a risk assessment indicate the need for additional controls or control enhancements to be able to respond to the identified risks. Privacy-related controls are indicated by an "P" in the *privacy-related* column.[39] Control baselines in Table D-1 can be used to address the confidentiality, integrity and availability of personally identifiable information. In addition, the detailed criteria that support federal agency selection of privacy controls to manage the full life cycle processing of personally identifiable information are listed in Appendix F.

---

[35] A complete description of all security and privacy controls is provided in Chapter Three. An online catalog of the security and privacy controls is also available in different formats.

[36] Communities of interest that choose to use the security and privacy controls in this publication, may develop their own control baselines in response to the requirements from the stakeholders in the respective communities. These community-specific baselines may be driven by sector-specific requirements, and/or applicable laws, Executive Orders, directives, policies, regulations, standards. The tailoring guidance described in Appendix G can be effectively applied to community-specific baselines.

[37] For control selection and specification, federal organizations conduct baseline tailoring activities in accordance with OMB policy. In certain situations, OMB may prohibit federal organizations from tailoring out specific security or privacy controls.

[38] This means that the controls in the high baseline are a *superset* of the controls in the moderate baseline and the controls in the moderate baseline are a *superset* of the controls in the low baseline. Conversely, the controls in the low baseline are a *subset* of the controls in the moderate baseline and the controls in the moderate baseline are a *subset* of the controls in the high baseline.

[39] Privacy-related controls and control enhancements are not allocated to baselines in Appendix D. See Appendix F for privacy control selection and implementation guidance.

TABLE D-1: CONTROL BASELINES

CNTL NO.	CONTROL NAME	PRIVACY-RELATED	CONTROL BASELINES		
			LOW	MODERATE	HIGH
Access Control — AC					
AC-1	Access Control Policy and Procedures		AC-1	AC-1	AC-1
AC-2	Account Management		AC-2	AC-2 (1) (2) (3) (4) (5) (10) (13)	AC-2 (1) (2) (3) (4) (5) (10) (11) (12) (13)
AC-3	Access Enforcement		AC-3	AC-3	AC-3
AC-4	Information Flow Enforcement		—	AC-4	AC-4 (4)
AC-5	Separation of Duties		—	AC-5	AC-5
AC-6	Least Privilege		AC-6 (7) (9)	AC-6 (1) (2) (5) (7) (9) (10)	AC-6 (1) (2) (3) (5) (7) (9) (10)
AC-7	Unsuccessful Logon Attempts		AC-7	AC-7	AC-7
AC-8	System Use Notification		AC-8	AC-8	AC-8
AC-9	Previous Logon (Access) Notification		—	—	—
AC-10	Concurrent Session Control		—	—	AC-10
AC-11	Device Lock		—	AC-11 (1)	AC-11 (1)
AC-12	Session Termination		—	AC-12	AC-12
AC-13	Withdrawn				
AC-14	Permitted Actions without Identification or Authentication		AC-14	AC-14	AC-14
AC-15	Withdrawn				
AC-16	Security and Privacy Attributes	P	—	—	—
AC-17	Remote Access		AC-17	AC-17 (1) (2) (3) (4)	AC-17 (1) (2) (3) (4)
AC-18	Wireless Access		AC-18	AC-18 (1) (3)	AC-18 (1) (3) (4) (5)
AC-19	Access Control for Mobile Devices		AC-19	AC-19 (5)	AC-19 (5)
AC-20	Use of External Systems		AC-20	AC-20 (1) (2)	AC-20 (1) (2)
AC-21	Information Sharing	P	—	AC-21	AC-21
AC-22	Publicly Accessible Content		AC-22	AC-22	AC-22
AC-23	Data Mining Protection	P	—	—	—
AC-24	Access Control Decisions		—	—	—
AC-25	Reference Monitor		—	—	—
Awareness and Training — AT					
AT-1	Awareness and Training Policy and Procedures	P	AT-1	AT-1	AT-1
AT-2	Awareness Training	P	AT-2 (2)	AT-2 (2) (3)	AT-2 (2) (3)
AT-3	Role-Based Training	P	AT-3	AT-3	AT-3
AT-4	Training Records	P	AT-4	AT-4	AT-4
AT-5	Withdrawn				

CNTL NO.	CONTROL NAME	PRIVACY-RELATED	CONTROL BASELINES		
			LOW	MODERATE	HIGH
Audit and Accountability – AU					
AU-1	Audit and Accountability Policy and Procedures		AU-1	AU-1	AU-1
AU-2	Audit Events		AU-2	AU-2 (3)	AU-2 (3)
AU-3	Content of Audit Records		AU-3	AU-3 (1)	AU-3 (1) (2)
AU-4	Audit Storage Capacity		AU-4	AU-4	AU-4
AU-5	Response to Audit Processing Failures		AU-5	AU-5	AU-5 (1) (2)
AU-6	Audit Review, Analysis, and Reporting		AU-6	AU-6 (1) (3)	AU-6 (1) (3) (5) (6)
AU-7	Audit Reduction and Report Generation		—	AU-7 (1)	AU-7 (1)
AU-8	Time Stamps		AU-8	AU-8 (1)	AU-8 (1)
AU-9	Protection of Audit Information		AU-9	AU-9 (4)	AU-9 (2) (3) (4)
AU-10	Non-repudiation		—	—	AU-10
AU-11	Audit Record Retention	P	AU-11	AU-11	AU-11
AU-12	Audit Generation		AU-12	AU-12	AU-12 (1) (3)
AU-13	Monitoring for Information Disclosure		—	—	—
AU-14	Session Audit		—	—	—
AU-15	Alternate Audit Capability		—	—	—
AU-16	Cross-Organizational Auditing	P	—	—	—
Assessment, Authorization, and Monitoring – CA					
CA-1	Assessment, Authorization, and Monitoring Policy and Procedures	P	CA-1	CA-1	CA-1
CA-2	Assessments	P	CA-2	CA-2 (1)	CA-2 (1) (2)
CA-3	System Interconnections		CA-3	CA-3 (5)	CA-3 (5) (6)
CA-4	Withdrawn				
CA-5	Plan of Action and Milestones	P	CA-5	CA-5	CA-5
CA-6	Authorization		CA-6	CA-6	CA-6
CA-7	Continuous Monitoring	P	CA-7 (4)	CA-7 (1) (4)	CA-7 (1) (4)
CA-8	Penetration Testing		—	—	CA-8 (1)
CA-9	Internal System Connections		CA-9	CA-9	CA-9
Configuration Management – CM					
CM-1	Configuration Management Policy and Procedures	P	CM-1	CM-1	CM-1
CM-2	Baseline Configuration		CM-2	CM-2 (2) (3) (7)	CM-2 (2) (3) (7)
CM-3	Configuration Change Control		—	CM-3 (2) (4)	CM-3 (1) (2) (4) (6)
CM-4	Security and Privacy Impact Analyses	P	CM-4	CM-4 (2)	CM-4 (1) (2)
CM-5	Access Restrictions for Change		CM-5	CM-5	CM-5 (1) (2) (3)
CM-6	Configuration Settings		CM-6	CM-6	CM-6 (1) (2)
CM-7	Least Functionality		CM-7	CM-7 (1) (2) (5)	CM-7 (1) (2) (5)

CNTL NO.	CONTROL NAME	PRIVACY-RELATED	CONTROL BASELINES		
			LOW	MODERATE	HIGH
CM-8	System Component Inventory		CM-8	CM-8 (1) (3)	CM-8 (1) (2) (3) (4)
CM-9	Configuration Management Plan		—	CM-9	CM-9
CM-10	Software Usage Restrictions		CM-10	CM-10	CM-10
CM-11	User-Installed Software		CM-11	CM-11	CM-11
CM-12	Information Location	P	—	CM-12 (1)	CM-12 (1)
Contingency Planning – CP					
CP-1	Contingency Planning Policy and Procedures	P	CP-1	CP-1	CP-1
CP-2	Contingency Plan	P	CP-2	CP-2 (1) (3) (8)	CP-2 (1) (2) (3) (4) (5) (8)
CP-3	Contingency Training	P	CP-3	CP-3	CP-3 (1)
CP-4	Contingency Plan Testing	P	CP-4	CP-4 (1)	CP-4 (1) (2)
CP-5	Withdrawn				
CP-6	Alternate Storage Site		—	CP-6 (1) (3)	CP-6 (1) (2) (3)
CP-7	Alternate Processing Site		—	CP-7 (1) (2) (3)	CP-7 (1) (2) (3) (4)
CP-8	Telecommunications Services		—	CP-8 (1) (2)	CP-8 (1) (2) (3) (4)
CP-9	System Backup		CP-9	CP-9 (1) (8)	CP-9 (1) (2) (3) (5) (8)
CP-10	System Recovery and Reconstitution		CP-10	CP-10 (2)	CP-10 (2) (4)
CP-11	Alternate Communications Protocols		—	—	—
CP-12	Safe Mode		—	—	—
CP-13	Alternative Security Mechanisms		—	—	—
Identification and Authentication – IA					
IA-1	Identification and Authentication Policy and Procedures	P	IA-1	IA-1	IA-1
IA-2	Identification and Authentication (Organizational Users)		IA-2 (1) (2) (8) (12)	IA-2 (1) (2) (8) (12)	IA-2 (1) (2) (5) (8) (12)
IA-3	Device Identification and Authentication		—	IA-3	IA-3
IA-4	Identifier Management	P	IA-4	IA-4 (4)	IA-4 (4)
IA-5	Authenticator Management		IA-5 (1) (11)	IA-5 (1) (2) (6)	IA-5 (1) (2) (6)
IA-6	Authenticator Feedback		IA-6	IA-6	IA-6
IA-7	Cryptographic Module Authentication		IA-7	IA-7	IA-7
IA-8	Identification and Authentication (Non-Organizational Users)	P	IA-8 (1) (2) (4)	IA-8 (1) (2) (4)	IA-8 (1) (2) (4)
IA-9	Service Identification and Authentication		—	—	—
IA-10	Adaptive Identification and Authentication		—	—	—
IA-11	Re-authentication		IA-11	IA-11	IA-11

CNTL NO.	CONTROL NAME	PRIVACY-RELATED	CONTROL BASELINES		
			LOW	MODERATE	HIGH
IA-12	Identity Proofing		—	IA-12 (2) (3) (5)	IA-12 (2) (3) (4) (5)
Individual Participation – IP					
IP-1	Individual Participation Policy and Procedures	P			
IP-2	Consent	P	Privacy-related controls and enhancements are not allocated to baselines in this table. See **Appendix F** for control selection and implementation guidance.		
IP-3	Redress	P			
IP-4	Privacy Notice	P			
IP-5	Privacy Act Statement	P			
IP-6	Individual Access	P			
Incident Response – IR					
IR-1	Incident Response Policy and Procedures	P	IR-1	IR-1	IR-1
IR-2	Incident Response Training	P	IR-2	IR-2	IR-2 (1) (2)
IR-3	Incident Response Testing	P	—	IR-3 (2)	IR-3 (2)
IR-4	Incident Handling	P	IR-4	IR-4 (1)	IR-4 (1) (4)
IR-5	Incident Monitoring	P	IR-5	IR-5	IR-5 (1)
IR-6	Incident Reporting	P	IR-6	IR-6 (1) (3)	IR-6 (1) (3)
IR-7	Incident Response Assistance	P	IR-7	IR-7 (1)	IR-7 (1)
IR-8	Incident Response Plan	P	IR-8	IR-8	IR-8
IR-9	Information Spillage Response	P	—	—	—
IR-10	Integrated Information Security Analysis Team		—	—	IR-10
Maintenance – MA					
MA-1	System Maintenance Policy and Procedures		MA-1	MA-1	MA-1
MA-2	Controlled Maintenance		MA-2	MA-2	MA-2 (2)
MA-3	Maintenance Tools		—	MA-3 (1) (2) (3)	MA-3 (1) (2) (3)
MA-4	Nonlocal Maintenance		MA-4	MA-4	MA-4 (3)
MA-5	Maintenance Personnel		MA-5	MA-5	MA-5 (1)
MA-6	Timely Maintenance		—	MA-6	MA-6
Media Protection – MP					
MP-1	Media Protection Policy and Procedures		MP-1	MP-1	MP-1
MP-2	Media Access		MP-2	MP-2	MP-2
MP-3	Media Marking		—	MP-3	MP-3
MP-4	Media Storage		—	MP-4	MP-4
MP-5	Media Transport		—	MP-5	MP-5
MP-6	Media Sanitization		MP-6	MP-6	MP-6 (1) (2) (3)
MP-7	Media Use		MP-7	MP-7	MP-7
MP-8	Media Downgrading		—	—	—

CNTL NO.	CONTROL NAME	PRIVACY-RELATED	CONTROL BASELINES		
			LOW	MODERATE	HIGH
Privacy Authorization — PA					
PA-1	Privacy Authorization Policy and Procedures	P	Privacy-related controls and enhancements are not allocated to baselines in this table. See **Appendix F** for control selection and implementation guidance.		
PA-2	Authority to Collect	P			
PA-3	Purpose Specification	P			
PA-4	Information Sharing with External Parties	P			
Physical and Environmental Protection — PE					
PE-1	Physical and Environmental Protection Policy and Procedures		PE-1	PE-1	PE-1
PE-2	Physical Access Authorizations		PE-2	PE-2	PE-2
PE-3	Physical Access Control		PE-3	PE-3	PE-3 (1)
PE-4	Access Control for Transmission		—	PE-4	PE-4
PE-5	Access Control for Output Devices		—	PE-5	PE-5
PE-6	Monitoring Physical Access		PE-6	PE-6 (1)	PE-6 (1) (4)
PE-7	Withdrawn				
PE-8	Visitor Access Records		PE-8	PE-8	PE-8 (1)
PE-9	Power Equipment and Cabling		—	PE-9	PE-9
PE-10	Emergency Shutoff		—	PE-10	PE-10
PE-11	Emergency Power		—	PE-11	PE-11 (1)
PE-12	Emergency Lighting		PE-12	PE-12	PE-12
PE-13	Fire Protection		PE-13	PE-13 (1) (2)	PE-13 (1) (2)
PE-14	Temperature and Humidity Controls		PE-14	PE-14	PE-14
PE-15	Water Damage Protection		PE-15	PE-15	PE-15 (1)
PE-16	Delivery and Removal		PE-16	PE-16	PE-16
PE-17	Alternate Work Site		—	PE-17	PE-17
PE-18	Location of System Components		—	—	PE-18
PE-19	Information Leakage		—	—	—
PE-20	Asset Monitoring and Tracking		—	—	—
PE-21	Electromagnetic Pulse Protection		—	—	—
PE-22	Component Marking		—	—	—
Planning — PL					
PL-1	Planning Policy and Procedures	P	PL-1	PL-1	PL-1
PL-2	System Security and Privacy Plans	P	PL-2	PL-2 (3)	PL-2 (3)
PL-3	Withdrawn				
PL-4	Rules of Behavior	P	PL-4 (1)	PL-4 (1)	PL-4 (1)
PL-5	Withdrawn				
PL-6	Withdrawn				
PL-7	Concept of Operations	P	—	—	—
PL-8	Security and Privacy Architectures	P	—	PL-8	PL-8
PL-9	Central Management	P	—	—	—

CNTL NO.	CONTROL NAME	PRIVACY-RELATED	CONTROL BASELINES		
			LOW	MODERATE	HIGH
PL-10	Baseline Selection		PL-10	PL-10	PL-10
PL-11	Baseline Tailoring		PL-11	PL-11	PL-11
Program Management – PM					
PM-1	Information Security Program Plan				
PM-2	Information Security Program Roles				
PM-3	Information Security and Privacy Resources	P			
PM-4	Plan of Action and Milestones Process	P			
PM-5	System Inventory				
PM-6	Measures of Performance	P			
PM-7	Enterprise Architecture	P			
PM-8	Critical Infrastructure Plan	P			
PM-9	Risk Management Strategy	P			
PM-10	Authorization Process				
PM-11	Mission and Business Process Definition	P			
PM-12	Insider Threat Program				
PM-13	Security and Privacy Workforce	P			
PM-14	Testing, Training, and Monitoring	P			
PM-15	Contacts with Groups and Associations	P			
PM-16	Threat Awareness Program				
PM-17	Protecting Controlled Unclassified Information on External Systems				
PM-18	Privacy Program Plan	P			
PM-19	Privacy Program Roles	P			
PM-20	System of Records Notice	P			
PM-21	Dissemination of Privacy Program Information	P			
PM-22	Accounting of Disclosures	P			
PM-23	Data Quality Management	P			
PM-24	Data Management Board	P			
PM-25	Data Integrity Board	P			
PM-26	Minimization of Personally Identifiable Information	P			
PM-27	Individual Access Control	P			
PM-28	Complaint Management	P			
PM-29	Inventory of Personally Identifiable Information	P			
PM-30	Privacy Reporting	P			
PM-31	Supply Chain Risk Management Plan				
PM-32	Risk Framing				

Security and privacy controls in the **PM family** have been designed to facilitate compliance with laws, Executive Orders, directives, regulations, policies, and standards.

PM controls are independent of any FIPS 200 impact levels and are not directly associated with the control baselines in **Appendix D**. Tailoring guidance can also be applied to the controls. See **Appendix G**.

PM controls focus on the programmatic, organization-wide security and privacy requirements independent of any system and essential for managing security and privacy programs.

Organizations can document the controls in their information security and privacy program plans. These plans, together with the security and privacy plans for the individual systems, cover the totality of security and privacy controls that are employed by the organization.

Privacy-related controls and control enhancements are not allocated to baselines in this table. See **Appendix F** for control selection and implementation guidance.

CNTL NO.	CONTROL NAME	PRIVACY-FELA	CONTROL BASELINES		
			LOW	MODERATE	HIGH
Personnel Security – PS					
PS-1	Personnel Security Policy and Procedures		PS-1	PS-1	PS-1
PS-2	Position Risk Designation		PS-2	PS-2	PS-2
PS-3	Personnel Screening		PS-3	PS-3	PS-3
PS-4	Personnel Termination		PS-4	PS-4	PS-4 (2)
PS-5	Personnel Transfer		PS-5	PS-5	PS-5
PS-6	Access Agreements		PS-6	PS-6	PS-6
PS-7	External Personnel Security		PS-7	PS-7	PS-7
PS-8	Personnel Sanctions		PS-8	PS-8	PS-8
Risk Assessment – RA					
RA-1	Risk Assessment Policy and Procedures	P	RA-1	RA-1	RA-1
RA-2	Security Categorization		RA-2	RA-2	RA-2
RA-3	Risk Assessment	P	RA-3	RA-3 (1)	RA-3 (1)
RA-4	Withdrawn				
RA-5	Vulnerability Scanning		RA-5 (2)	RA-5 (2) (5)	RA-5 (2) (4) (5)
RA-6	Technical Surveillance Countermeasures Survey		—	—	—
RA-7	Risk Response	P	RA-7	RA-7	RA-7
RA-8	Privacy Impact Assessment	P	—	—	—
RA-9	Criticality Analysis		—	RA-9	RA-9
System and Services Acquisition – SA					
SA-1	System and Services Acquisition Policy and Procedures	P	SA-1	SA-1	SA-1
SA-2	Allocation of Resources		SA-2	SA-2	SA-2
SA-3	System Development Life Cycle	P	SA-3	SA-3	SA-3
SA-4	Acquisition Process	P	SA-4 (10)	SA-4 (1) (2) (9) (10)	SA-4 (1) (2) (5) (9) (10)
SA-5	System Documentation		SA-5	SA-5	SA-5
SA-6	Withdrawn				
SA-7	Withdrawn				
SA-8	Security and Privacy Engineering Principles	P	SA-8	SA-8	SA-8
SA-9	External System Services	P	SA-9	SA-9 (2)	SA-9 (2)
SA-10	Developer Configuration Management		—	SA-10	SA-10
SA-11	Developer Security Testing and Evaluation	P	—	SA-11	SA-11
SA-12	Supply Chain Risk Management		—	SA-12	SA-12 (2) (10) (16)
SA-13	Withdrawn				
SA-14	Withdrawn				

CNTL NO.	CONTROL NAME	PRIVACY-RELATED	CONTROL BASELINES		
			LOW	MODERATE	HIGH
SA-15	Development Process, Standards, and Tools		—	SA-15 (3)	SA-15 (3)
SA-16	Developer-Provided Training		—	—	SA-16
SA-17	Developer Security Architecture and Design		—	—	SA-17
SA-18	Tamper Resistance and Detection		—	—	—
SA-19	Component Authenticity		—	—	—
SA-20	Customized Development of Critical Components		—	—	—
SA-21	Developer Screening		—	—	SA-21
SA-22	Unsupported System Components		SA-22	SA-22	SA-22
System and Communications Protection – SC					
SC-1	System and Communications Protection Policy and Procedures	P	SC-1	SC-1	SC-1
SC-2	Application Partitioning		—	SC-2	SC-2
SC-3	Security Function Isolation		—	—	SC-3
SC-4	Information in Shared Systems Resources		—	SC-4	SC-4
SC-5	Denial of Service Protection		SC-5	SC-5	SC-5
SC-6	Resource Availability		—	—	—
SC-7	Boundary Protection		SC-7	SC-7 (3) (4) (5) (7) (8)	SC-7 (3) (4) (5) (7) (8) (18) (21)
SC-8	Transmission Confidentiality and Integrity		—	SC-8 (1)	SC-8 (1)
SC-9	Withdrawn				
SC-10	Network Disconnect		—	SC-10	SC-10
SC-11	Trusted Path		—	—	—
SC-12	Cryptographic Key Establishment and Management		SC-12	SC-12	SC-12 (1)
SC-13	Cryptographic Protection		SC-13	SC-13	SC-13
SC-14	Withdrawn				
SC-15	Collaborative Computing Devices and Applications		SC-15	SC-15	SC-15
SC-16	Transmission of Security and Privacy Attributes	P	—	—	—
SC-17	Public Key Infrastructure Certificates		—	SC-17	SC-17
SC-18	Mobile Code		—	SC-18	SC-18
SC-19	Voice Over Internet Protocol		—	SC-19	SC-19
SC-20	Secure Name /Address Resolution Service (Authoritative Source)		SC-20	SC-20	SC-20
SC-21	Secure Name /Address Resolution Service (Recursive or Caching Resolver)		SC-21	SC-21	SC-21

CNTL NO.	CONTROL NAME	PRIVACY-RELATED	CONTROL BASELINES		
			LOW	MODERATE	HIGH
SC-22	Architecture and Provisioning for Name/Address Resolution Service		SC-22	SC-22	SC-22
SC-23	Session Authenticity		—	SC-23	SC-23
SC-24	Fail in Known State		—	—	SC-24
SC-25	Thin Nodes		—	—	—
SC-26	Honeypots		—	—	—
SC-27	Platform-Independent Applications		—	—	—
SC-28	Protection of Information at Rest		—	SC-28 (1)	SC-28 (1)
SC-29	Heterogeneity		—	—	—
SC-30	Concealment and Misdirection		—	—	—
SC-31	Covert Channel Analysis		—	—	—
SC-32	System Partitioning		—	—	—
SC-33	Withdrawn				
SC-34	Non-Modifiable Executable Programs		—	—	—
SC-35	Honeyclients		—	—	—
SC-36	Distributed Processing and Storage		—	—	—
SC-37	Out-of-Band Channels		—	—	—
SC-38	Operations Security		—	—	—
SC-39	Process Isolation		SC-39	SC-39	SC-39
SC-40	Wireless Link Protection		—	—	—
SC-41	Port and I/O Device Access		—	—	—
SC-42	Sensor Capability and Data	P	—	—	—
SC-43	Usage Restrictions		—	—	—
SC-44	Detonation Chambers		—	—	—
System and Information Integrity – SI					
SI-1	System and Information Integrity Policy and Procedures	P	SI-1	SI-1	SI-1
SI-2	Flaw Remediation		SI-2	SI-2 (2)	SI-2 (1) (2)
SI-3	Malicious Code Protection		SI-3	SI-3 (1)	SI-3 (1)
SI-4	System Monitoring		SI-4	SI-4 (2) (4) (5)	SI-4 (2) (4) (5) (10) (12) (14) (20) (22)
SI-5	Security Alerts, Advisories, and Directives		SI-5	SI-5	SI-5 (1)
SI-6	Security and Privacy Function Verification	P	—	—	SI-6
SI-7	Software, Firmware, and Information Integrity		—	SI-7 (1) (7)	SI-7 (1) (2) (5) (7) (14) (15)
SI-8	Spam Protection		—	SI-8 (1) (2)	SI-8 (1) (2)
SI-9	Withdrawn				
SI-10	Information Input Validation		—	SI-10	SI-10
SI-11	Error Handling		—	SI-11	SI-11
SI-12	Information Management and Retention	P	SI-12	SI-12	SI-12
SI-13	Predictable Failure Prevention		—	—	—

CNTL NO.	CONTROL NAME	PRIVACY-RELATED	CONTROL BASELINES		
			LOW	MODERATE	HIGH
SI-14	Non-Persistence		—	—	—
SI-15	Information Output Filtering		—	—	—
SI-16	Memory Protection		—	SI-16	SI-16
SI-17	Fail-Safe Procedures		—	—	—
SI-18	Information Disposal	P	—	—	—
SI-19	Data Quality Operations	P	—	—	—
SI-20	De-Identification	P	—	—	—

Note: Privacy-related controls and control enhancements are not allocated to baselines in this table. See **Appendix F** for control selection and implementation guidance.

APPENDIX E

CONTROL SUMMARIES

BASELINE, IMPLEMENTATION, WITHDRAWAL, PRIVACY, AND ASSURANCE DESIGNATIONS

Tables E-1 through E-20 provide a summary of the security and privacy controls and control enhancements in Chapter Three. Each table in this appendix focuses on a different control family. A control or control enhancement that has been allocated to a control baseline is indicated by an "X" in the column for that baseline. A control or control enhancement that has not been allocated to a control baseline is indicated by a blank cell. With respect to privacy controls, these control baselines can be used to address the confidentiality, integrity and availability of personally identifiable information. Criteria that support federal agency selection of privacy controls to manage the full life cycle processing of personally identifiable information are listed in Appendix F. A control or control enhancement that has been withdrawn from the control catalog is indicated by an "W" in the *withdrawn* column. Privacy-related controls and control enhancements are indicated by an "P" in the *privacy-related* column.[40] Assurance-related controls and control enhancements are indicated by an "A" in the *assurance* column. Finally, a control or control enhancement that is typically implemented by an organizational system through technical means is indicated by an "S" in the *implemented by* column. A control or control enhancement that is typically implemented by an organization (i.e., by a human through nontechnical means) is indicated by an "O" in the *implemented by* column.[41] A control or control enhancement that can be implemented by an organization or a system or a combination of the two, is indicated by an "O/S". Each control and control enhancement in the following tables is hyperlinked to the text for that control and control enhancement in Chapter Three.

---

[40] Privacy-related controls and control enhancements are not allocated to baselines in Appendix D. See Appendix F for privacy control selection and implementation guidance.

[41] The indication that a certain control or control enhancement is implemented by a *system* or by an *organization* in Tables E-1 through E-20 is notional. Organizations have the flexibility to implement their selected controls and control enhancements in the most cost-effective and efficient manner while simultaneously complying with the basic intent of the control/enhancement. In certain situations, a control or control enhancement may be implemented by the system or by the organization or a combination of the two entities.

TABLE E-1: ACCESS CONTROL FAMILY

CONTROL NUMBER	CONTROL NAME / CONTROL ENHANCEMENT NAME	WITHDRAWN	PRIVACY-RELATED	IMPLEMENTED BY	ASSURANCE	CONTROL BASELINES		
						LOW	MOD	HIGH
AC-1	**Access Control Policy and Procedures**			O	A	X	X	X
AC-2	**Account Management**			O		X	X	X
AC-2(1)	AUTOMATED SYSTEM ACCOUNT MANAGEMENT			O			X	X
AC-2(2)	REMOVAL OF TEMPORARY AND EMERGENCY ACCOUNTS			S			X	X
AC-2(3)	DISABLE ACCOUNTS			S			X	X
AC-2(4)	AUTOMATED AUDIT ACTIONS			S			X	X
AC-2(5)	INACTIVITY LOGOUT			O/S			X	X
AC-2(6)	DYNAMIC PRIVILEGE MANAGEMENT			S				
AC-2(7)	ROLE-BASED SCHEMES			O				
AC-2(8)	DYNAMIC ACCOUNT MANAGEMENT			S				
AC-2(9)	RESTRICTIONS ON USE OF SHARED AND GROUP ACCOUNTS			O				
AC-2(10)	SHARED AND GROUP ACCOUNT CREDENTIAL CHANGE			O			X	X
AC-2(11)	USAGE CONDITIONS			S				X
AC-2(12)	ACCOUNT MONITORING FOR ATYPICAL USAGE			O				X
AC-2(13)	DISABLE ACCOUNTS FOR HIGH-RISK INDIVIDUALS			O			X	X
AC-2(14)	PROHIBIT SPECIFIC ACCOUNT TYPES			O				
AC-2(15)	ATTRIBUTE-BASED SCHEMES			O				
AC-3	**Access Enforcement**			S		X	X	X
AC-3(1)	RESTRICTED ACCESS TO PRIVILEGED FUNCTIONS	W		Incorporated into AC-6.				
AC-3(2)	DUAL AUTHORIZATION			S				
AC-3(3)	MANDATORY ACCESS CONTROL			S				
AC-3(4)	DISCRETIONARY ACCESS CONTROL			S				
AC-3(5)	SECURITY-RELEVANT INFORMATION			S				
AC-3(6)	PROTECTION OF USER AND SYSTEM INFORMATION	W		Incorporated into MP-4, SC-28.				
AC-3(7)	ROLE-BASED ACCESS CONTROL			O/S				
AC-3(8)	REVOCATION OF ACCESS AUTHORIZATIONS			O/S				
AC-3(9)	CONTROLLED RELEASE			O/S				
AC-3(10)	AUDITED OVERRIDE OF ACCESS CONTROL MECHANISMS			O				
AC-3(11)	RESTRICT ACCESS TO SPECIFIC INFORMATION			S				
AC-3(12)	ASSERT AND ENFORCE APPLICATION ACCESS			S				
AC-3(13)	ATTRIBUTE-BASED ACCESS CONTROL			S				
AC-4	**Information Flow Enforcement**			S			X	X
AC-4(1)	OBJECT SECURITY ATTRIBUTES			S				
AC-4(2)	PROCESSING DOMAINS			S				
AC-4(3)	DYNAMIC INFORMATION FLOW CONTROL			S				
AC-4(4)	FLOW CONTROL OF ENCRYPTED INFORMATION			S				X
AC-4(5)	EMBEDDED DATA TYPES			S				
AC-4(6)	METADATA			S				
AC-4(7)	ONE-WAY FLOW MECHANISMS			S				
AC-4(8)	SECURITY POLICY FILTERS			S				
AC-4(9)	HUMAN REVIEWS			O				
AC-4(10)	ENABLE AND DISABLE SECURITY POLICY FILTERS			S				

CONTROL NUMBER	CONTROL NAME / CONTROL ENHANCEMENT NAME	WITHDRAWN	PRIVACY-RELATED	IMPLEMENTED BY	ASSURANCE	CONTROL BASELINES		
						LOW	MOD	HIGH
AC-4(11)	CONFIGURATION OF SECURITY POLICY FILTERS			S				
AC-4(12)	DATA TYPE IDENTIFIERS			S				
AC-4(13)	DECOMPOSITION INTO POLICY-RELEVANT SUBCOMPONENTS			S				
AC-4(14)	SECURITY POLICY FILTER CONSTRAINTS			S				
AC-4(15)	DETECTION OF UNSANCTIONED INFORMATION			S				
AC-4(16)	INFORMATION TRANSFERS ON INTERCONNECTED SYSTEMS	W	Incorporated into AC-4.					
AC-4(17)	DOMAIN AUTHENTICATION			S				
AC-4(18)	SECURITY ATTRIBUTE BINDING	W	Incorporated into AC-16.					
AC-4(19)	VALIDATION OF METADATA			S				
AC-4(20)	APPROVED SOLUTIONS			O				
AC-4(21)	PHYSICAL AND LOGICAL SEPARATION OF INFORMATION FLOWS			S				
AC-4(22)	ACCESS ONLY			S				
AC-5	**Separation of Duties**			O			X	X
AC-6	**Least Privilege**			O			X	X
AC-6(1)	AUTHORIZE ACCESS TO SECURITY FUNCTIONS			O			X	X
AC-6(2)	NON-PRIVILEGED ACCESS FOR NONSECURITY FUNCTIONS			O			X	X
AC-6(3)	NETWORK ACCESS TO PRIVILEGED COMMANDS			O				X
AC-6(4)	SEPARATE PROCESSING DOMAINS			S				
AC-6(5)	PRIVILEGED ACCOUNTS			O			X	X
AC-6(6)	PRIVILEGED ACCESS BY NON-ORGANIZATIONAL USERS			O				
AC-6(7)	REVIEW OF USER PRIVILEGES			O		X	X	X
AC-6(8)	PRIVILEGE LEVELS FOR CODE EXECUTION			S				
AC-6(9)	AUDITING USE OF PRIVILEGED FUNCTIONS			S		X	X	X
AC-6(10)	PROHIBIT NON-PRIVILEGED USERS FROM EXECUTING PRIVILEGED FUNCTIONS			S			X	X
AC-7	**Unsuccessful Logon Attempts**			S		X	X	X
AC-7(1)	AUTOMATIC ACCOUNT LOCK	W	Incorporated into AC-7.					
AC-7(2)	PURGE OR WIPE MOBILE DEVICE			S				
AC-7(3)	BIOMETRIC ATTEMPT LIMITING			O				
AC-7(4)	USE OF ALTERNATE FACTOR			O				
AC-8	**System Use Notification**			O/S		X	X	X
AC-9	**Previous Logon (Access) Notification**			S				
AC-9(1)	UNSUCCESSFUL LOGONS			S				
AC-9(2)	SUCCESSFUL AND UNSUCCESSFUL LOGONS			S				
AC-9(3)	NOTIFICATION OF ACCOUNT CHANGES			S				
AC-9(4)	ADDITIONAL LOGON INFORMATION			S				
AC-10	**Concurrent Session Control**			S				X
AC-11	**Device Lock**			S			X	X
AC-11(1)	PATTERN-HIDING DISPLAYS			S			X	X
AC-11(2)	REQUIRE USER-INITIATED LOCK			O				
AC-12	**Session Termination**			S			X	X

CONTROL NUMBER	CONTROL NAME CONTROL ENHANCEMENT NAME	WITHDRAWN	PRIVACY-RELATED	IMPLEMENTED BY	ASSURANCE	CONTROL BASELINES		
						LOW	MOD	HIGH
AC-12(1)	USER-INITIATED LOGOUTS			O				
AC-12(2)	TERMINATION MESSAGE			S				
AC-12(3)	TIMEOUT WARNING MESSAGE			S				
AC-13	Supervision and Review — Access Control	W	Incorporated into AC-2, AU-6.					
AC-14	**Permitted Actions without Identification or Authentication**			O		X	X	X
AC-14(1)	NECESSARY USES	W	Incorporated into AC-14.					
AC-15	Automated Marking	W	Incorporated into MP-3.					
AC-16	**Security and Privacy Attributes**		P	O				
AC-16(1)	DYNAMIC ATTRIBUTE ASSOCIATION		P	S				
AC-16(2)	ATTRIBUTE VALUE CHANGES BY AUTHORIZED INDIVIDUALS		P	S				
AC-16(3)	MAINTENANCE OF ATTRIBUTE ASSOCIATIONS BY SYSTEM		P	S				
AC-16(4)	ASSOCIATION OF ATTRIBUTES BY AUTHORIZED INDIVIDUALS		P	S				
AC-16(5)	ATTRIBUTE DISPLAYS FOR OUTPUT DEVICES		P	S				
AC-16(6)	MAINTENANCE OF ATTRIBUTE ASSOCIATION BY ORGANIZATION		P	O				
AC-16(7)	CONSISTENT ATTRIBUTE INTERPRETATION		P	O				
AC-16(8)	ASSOCIATION TECHNIQUES AND TECHNOLOGIES		P	S				
AC-16(9)	ATTRIBUTE REASSIGNMENT		P	O				
AC-16(10)	ATTRIBUTE CONFIGURATION BY AUTHORIZED INDIVIDUALS		P	O				
AC-16(11)	AUDIT CHANGES		P	S				
AC-17	**Remote Access**			O		X	X	X
AC-17(1)	AUTOMATED MONITORING AND CONTROL			S			X	X
AC-17(2)	PROTECTION OF CONFIDENTIALITY AND INTEGRITY USING ENCRYPTION			S			X	X
AC-17(3)	MANAGED ACCESS CONTROL POINTS			S			X	X
AC-17(4)	PRIVILEGED COMMANDS AND ACCESS			O			X	X
AC-17(5)	MONITORING FOR UNAUTHORIZED CONNECTIONS	W	Incorporated into SI-4.					
AC-17(6)	PROTECTION OF INFORMATION			O				
AC-17(7)	ADDITIONAL PROTECTION FOR SECURITY FUNCTION ACCESS	W	Incorporated into AC-3(10).					
AC-17(8)	DISABLE NONSECURE NETWORK PROTOCOLS	W	Incorporated into CM-7.					
AC-17(9)	DISCONNECT OR DISABLE ACCESS			O				
AC-18	**Wireless Access**			O		X	X	X
AC-18(1)	AUTHENTICATION AND ENCRYPTION			S			X	X
AC-18(2)	MONITORING UNAUTHORIZED CONNECTIONS	W	Incorporated into SI-4.					
AC-18(3)	DISABLE WIRELESS NETWORKING			O/S			X	X
AC-18(4)	RESTRICT CONFIGURATIONS BY USERS			O				X
AC-18(5)	ANTENNAS AND TRANSMISSION POWER LEVELS			O				X
AC-19	**Access Control for Mobile Devices**			O		X	X	X
AC-19(1)	USE OF WRITABLE AND PORTABLE STORAGE DEVICES	W	Incorporated into MP-7.					
AC-19(2)	USE OF PERSONALLY OWNED PORTABLE STORAGE DEVICES	W	Incorporated into MP-7.					
AC-19(3)	USE OF PORTABLE STORAGE DEVICES WITH NO IDENTIFIABLE OWNER	W	Incorporated into MP-7.					
AC-19(4)	RESTRICTIONS FOR CLASSIFIED INFORMATION			O				

CONTROL NUMBER	CONTROL NAME / CONTROL ENHANCEMENT NAME	WITHDRAWN	PRIVACY-RELATED	IMPLEMENTED	ASSURANCE	CONTROL BASELINE		
						LOW	MOD	HIGH
AC-19(5)	FULL DEVICE AND CONTAINER-BASED ENCRYPTION			O			X	X
AC-20	**Use of External Systems**			O		X	X	X
AC-20(1)	LIMITS ON AUTHORIZED USE			O			X	X
AC-20(2)	PORTABLE STORAGE DEVICES			O			X	X
AC-20(3)	NON-ORGANIZATIONALLY OWNED SYSTEMS AND COMPONENTS			O				
AC-20(4)	NETWORK ACCESSIBLE STORAGE DEVICES			O				
AC-21	**Information Sharing**		P	O			X	X
AC-21(1)	AUTOMATED DECISION SUPPORT			S				
AC-21(2)	INFORMATION SEARCH AND RETRIEVAL			S				
AC-22	**Publicly Accessible Content**			O		X	X	X
AC-23	**Data Mining Protection**		P	O				
AC-24	**Access Control Decisions**			O				
AC-24(1)	TRANSMIT ACCESS AUTHORIZATION INFORMATION			S				
AC-24(2)	NO USER OR PROCESS IDENTITY			S				
AC-25	**Reference Monitor**			S	A			

Note: Privacy-related controls and control enhancements are not allocated to baselines in this table. See **Appendix F** for control selection and implementation guidance.

TABLE E-2: AWARENESS AND TRAINING FAMILY

CONTROL NUMBER	CONTROL NAME CONTROL ENHANCEMENT NAME	WITHDRAWN	PRIVACY-RELATED	IMPLEMENTED BY	ASSURANCE	CONTROL BASELINES		
						LOW	MOD	HIGH
AT-1	**Awareness and Training Policy and Procedures**		P	O	A	X	X	X
AT-2	**Awareness Training**		P	O	A	X	X	X
AT-2(1)	PRACTICAL EXERCISES		P	O	A			
AT-2(2)	INSIDER THREAT			O	A	X	X	X
AT-2(3)	SOCIAL ENGINEERING AND MINING			O	A		X	X
AT-3	**Role-Based Training**		P	O	A	X	X	X
AT-3(1)	ENVIRONMENTAL CONTROLS			O	A			
AT-3(2)	PHYSICAL SECURITY CONTROLS			O	A			
AT-3(3)	PRACTICAL EXERCISES		P	O	A			
AT-3(4)	SUSPICIOUS COMMUNICATIONS AND ANOMALOUS SYSTEM BEHAVIOR			O	A			
AT-3(5)	PERSONALLY IDENTIFIABLE INFORMATION PROCESSING		P	O	A			
AT-4	**Training Records**		P	O	A	X	X	X
AT-5	Contacts with Security Groups and Associations	W	Incorporated into PM-15.					

Note: Privacy-related controls and control enhancements are not allocated to baselines in this table. See **Appendix F** for control selection and implementation guidance.

TABLE E-2: AUDIT AND ACCOUNTABILITY FAMILY

CONTROL NUMBER	CONTROL NAME / CONTROL ENHANCEMENT NAME	WITHDRAWN	PRIVACY-RELATED	IMPLEMENTED BY	ASSURANCE	CONTROL BASELINES		
						LOW	MOD	HIGH
AU-1	**Audit and Accountability Policy and Procedures**			O	A	X	X	X
AU-2	**Audit Events**			O		X	X	X
AU-2(1)	COMPILATION OF AUDIT RECORDS FROM MULTIPLE SOURCES	W	Incorporated into AU-12.					
AU-2(2)	SELECTION OF AUDIT EVENTS BY COMPONENT	W	Incorporated into AU-12.					
AU-2(3)	REVIEWS AND UPDATES			O			X	X
AU-2(4)	PRIVILEGED FUNCTIONS	W	Incorporated into AC-6(9).					
AU-3	**Content of Audit Records**			S		X	X	X
AU-3(1)	ADDITIONAL AUDIT INFORMATION			S			X	X
AU-3(2)	CENTRALIZED MANAGEMENT OF PLANNED AUDIT RECORD CONTENT			S				X
AU-3(3)	LIMIT PERSONALLY IDENTIFIABLE INFORMATION ELEMENTS		P	O				
AU-4	**Audit Storage Capacity**			O/S		X	X	X
AU-4(1)	TRANSFER TO ALTERNATE STORAGE			O				
AU-5	**Response to Audit Processing Failures**			S		X	X	X
AU-5(1)	AUDIT STORAGE CAPACITY			S				X
AU-5(2)	REAL-TIME ALERTS			S				X
AU-5(3)	CONFIGURABLE TRAFFIC VOLUME THRESHOLDS			S				
AU-5(4)	SHUTDOWN ON FAILURE			S				
AU-6	**Audit Review, Analysis, and Reporting**			O	A	X	X	X
AU-6(1)	AUTOMATED PROCESS INTEGRATION			O	A		X	X
AU-6(2)	AUTOMATED SECURITY ALERTS	W	Incorporated into SI-4.					
AU-6(3)	CORRELATE AUDIT REPOSITORIES			O	A		X	X
AU-6(4)	CENTRAL REVIEW AND ANALYSIS			S	A			
AU-6(5)	INTEGRATED ANALYSIS OF AUDIT RECORDS			O	A			X
AU-6(6)	CORRELATION WITH PHYSICAL MONITORING			O	A			X
AU-6(7)	PERMITTED ACTIONS			O	A			
AU-6(8)	FULL TEXT ANALYSIS OF PRIVILEGED COMMANDS			O	A			
AU-6(9)	CORRELATION WITH INFORMATION FROM NONTECHNICAL SOURCES			O	A			
AU-6(10)	AUDIT LEVEL ADJUSTMENT	W	Incorporated into AU-6.					
AU-7	**Audit Reduction and Report Generation**			S	A		X	X
AU-7(1)	AUTOMATIC PROCESSING			S	A		X	X
AU-7(2)	AUTOMATIC SORT AND SEARCH			S				
AU-8	**Time Stamps**			S		X	X	X
AU-8(1)	SYNCHRONIZATION WITH AUTHORITATIVE TIME SOURCE			S			X	X
AU-8(2)	SECONDARY AUTHORITATIVE TIME SOURCE			S				
AU-9	**Protection of Audit Information**			S		X	X	X
AU-9(1)	HARDWARE WRITE-ONCE MEDIA			S				
AU-9(2)	STORE ON SEPARATE PHYSICAL SYSTEMS OR COMPONENTS			S				X
AU-9(3)	CRYPTOGRAPHIC PROTECTION			S				X

CONTROL NUMBER	CONTROL NAME CONTROL ENHANCEMENT NAME	WITHDRAWN	PRIVACY-RELATED	IMPLEMENTED BY	ASSURANCE	CONTROL BASELINES		
						LOW	MOD	HIGH
AU-9(4)	ACCESS BY SUBSET OF PRIVILEGED USERS			O			X	X
AU-9(5)	DUAL AUTHORIZATION			O/S				
AU-9(6)	READ-ONLY ACCESS			O/S				
AU-9(7)	STORE ON COMPONENT WITH DIFFERENT OPERATING SYSTEM			O				
AU-10	**Non-repudiation**			S	A			X
AU-10(1)	ASSOCIATION OF IDENTITIES			S	A			
AU-10(2)	VALIDATE BINDING OF INFORMATION PRODUCER IDENTITY			S	A			
AU-10(3)	CHAIN OF CUSTODY			O/S	A			
AU-10(4)	VALIDATE BINDING OF INFORMATION REVIEWER IDENTITY			S	A			
AU-10(5)	DIGITAL SIGNATURES	W		Incorporated into SI-7.				
AU-11	**Audit Record Retention**		P	O		X	X	X
AU-11(1)	LONG-TERM RETRIEVAL CAPABILITY			O	A			
AU-12	**Audit Generation**			S		X	X	X
AU-12(1)	SYSTEM-WIDE AND TIME-CORRELATED AUDIT TRAIL			S				X
AU-12(2)	STANDARDIZED FORMATS			S				
AU-12(3)	CHANGES BY AUTHORIZED INDIVIDUALS			S				X
AU-12(4)	QUERY PARAMETER AUDITS OF PERSONALLY IDENTIFIABLE INFORMATION		P	S				
AU-13	**Monitoring for Information Disclosure**			O	A			
AU-13(1)	USE OF AUTOMATED TOOLS			O/S	A			
AU-13(2)	REVIEW OF MONITORED SITES			O	A			
AU-14	**Session Audit**			S	A			
AU-14(1)	SYSTEM START-UP			S	A			
AU-14(2)	CAPTURE AND RECORD CONTENT			S	A			
AU-14(3)	REMOTE VIEWING AND LISTENING			S	A			
AU-15	**Alternate Audit Capability**			O				
AU-16	**Cross-Organizational Auditing**		P	O				
AU-16(1)	IDENTITY PRESERVATION			O				
AU-16(2)	SHARING OF AUDIT INFORMATION			O				

Note: Privacy-related controls and control enhancements are not allocated to baselines in this table. See **Appendix F** for control selection and implementation guidance.

TABLE E-4: ASSESSMENT, AUTHORIZATION, AND MONITORING FAMILY

CONTROL NUMBER	CONTROL NAME / CONTROL ENHANCEMENT NAME	WITHDRAWN	PRIVACY-RELATED	IMPLEMENTED BY	ASSURANCE	CONTROL BASELINES		
						LOW	MOD	HIGH
CA-1	Assessment, Authorization, and Monitoring Policies and Procedures		P	O	A	X	X	X
CA-2	Assessments		P	O	A	X	X	X
CA-2(1)	INDEPENDENT ASSESSORS		P	O	A		X	X
CA-2(2)	SPECIALIZED ASSESSMENTS			O	A			X
CA-2(3)	EXTERNAL ORGANIZATIONS		P	O	A			
CA-3	System Interconnections			O	A	X	X	X
CA-3(1)	UNCLASSIFIED NATIONAL SECURITY SYSTEM CONNECTIONS			O				
CA-3(2)	CLASSIFIED NATIONAL SECURITY SYSTEM CONNECTIONS			O				
CA-3(3)	UNCLASSIFIED NON-NATIONAL SECURITY SYSTEM CONNECTIONS			O				
CA-3(4)	CONNECTIONS TO PUBLIC NETWORKS			O				
CA-3(5)	RESTRICTIONS ON EXTERNAL SYSTEM CONNECTIONS			O			X	X
CA-3(6)	SECONDARY AND TERTIARY CONNECTIONS			O				X
CA-4	Security Certification	W	Incorporated into CA-2.					
CA-5	Plan of Action and Milestones		P	O	A	X	X	X
CA-5(1)	AUTOMATION SUPPORT FOR ACCURACY AND CURRENCY			O	A			
CA-6	Authorization			O	A	X	X	X
CA-6(1)	JOINT AUTHORIZATION — SAME ORGANIZATION			O	A			
CA-6(2)	JOINT AUTHORIZATION — DIFFERENT ORGANIZATIONS			O	A			
CA-7	Continuous Monitoring		P	O	A	X	X	X
CA-7(1)	INDEPENDENT ASSESSMENT		P	O	A		X	X
CA-7(2)	TYPES OF ASSESSMENTS	W	Incorporated into CA-2.					
CA-7(3)	TREND ANALYSES			O	A			
CA-7(4)	RISK MONITORING				A	X	X	X
CA-8	Penetration Testing			O	A			X
CA-8(1)	INDEPENDENT PENETRATION AGENT OR TEAM			O	A			X
CA-8(2)	RED TEAM EXERCISES			O	A			
CA-8(3)	FACILITY PENETRATION TESTING			O	A			
CA-9	Internal System Connections			O	X	X	X	X
CA-9(1)	COMPLIANCE CHECKS			S	X			

Note: Privacy-related controls and control enhancements are not allocated to baselines in this table. See Appendix F for control selection and implementation guidance.

TABLE E-5: CONFIGURATION MANAGEMENT FAMILY

CONTROL NUMBER	CONTROL NAME CONTROL ENHANCEMENT NAME	WITHDRAWN	PRIVACY-RELATED	IMPLEMENTED BY	ASSURANCE	CONTROL BASELINES		
						LOW	MOD	HIGH
CM-1	**Configuration Management Policy and Procedures**		P	O	A	X	X	X
CM-2	**Baseline Configuration**			O	A	X	X	X
CM-2(1)	REVIEWS AND UPDATES	W	Incorporated into CM-2.					
CM-2(2)	AUTOMATION SUPPORT FOR ACCURACY AND CURRENCY			O	A		X	X
CM-2(3)	RETENTION OF PREVIOUS CONFIGURATIONS			O	A		X	X
CM-2(4)	UNAUTHORIZED SOFTWARE	W	Incorporated into CM-7.					
CM-2(5)	AUTHORIZED SOFTWARE	W	Incorporated into CM-7.					
CM-2(6)	DEVELOPMENT AND TEST ENVIRONMENTS			O	A			
CM-2(7)	CONFIGURE SYSTEMS AND COMPONENTS FOR HIGH-RISK AREAS			O	A		X	X
CM-3	**Configuration Change Control**			O	A		X	X
CM-3(1)	AUTOMATED DOCUMENTATION, NOTIFICATION, AND PROHIBITION OF CHANGES			O	A			X
CM-3(2)	TESTING, VALIDATION, AND DOCUMENTATION OF CHANGES			O	A		X	X
CM-3(3)	AUTOMATED CHANGE IMPLEMENTATION			O				
CM-3(4)	SECURITY REPRESENTATIVE			O			X	X
CM-3(5)	AUTOMATED SECURITY RESPONSE			S				
CM-3(6)	CRYPTOGRAPHY MANAGEMENT			O				X
CM-4	**Security and Privacy Impact Analyses**		P	O	A	X	X	X
CM-4(1)	SEPARATE TEST ENVIRONMENTS			O	A			X
CM-4(2)	VERIFICATION OF SECURITY AND PRIVACY FUNCTIONS		P	O	A		X	X
CM-5	**Access Restrictions for Change**			O		X	X	X
CM-5(1)	AUTOMATED ACCESS ENFORCEMENT AND AUDITING			S				X
CM-5(2)	REVIEW SYSTEM CHANGES			O				X
CM-5(3)	SIGNED COMPONENTS			O/S				X
CM-5(4)	DUAL AUTHORIZATION			O/S				
CM-5(5)	PRIVILEGE LIMITATION FOR PRODUCTION AND OPERATION			O				
CM-5(6)	LIMIT LIBRARY PRIVILEGES			O				
CM-5(7)	AUTOMATIC IMPLEMENTATION OF SECURITY SAFEGUARDS	W	Incorporated into SI-7.					
CM-6	**Configuration Settings**			O		X	X	X
CM-6(1)	AUTOMATED MANAGEMENT, APPLICATION, AND VERIFICATION			O				X
CM-6(2)	RESPOND TO UNAUTHORIZED CHANGES			O				X
CM-6(3)	UNAUTHORIZED CHANGE DETECTION	W	Incorporated into SI-7.					
CM-6(4)	CONFORMANCE DEMONSTRATION	W	Incorporated into CM-4.					
CM-7	**Least Functionality**			O		X	X	X
CM-7(1)	PERIODIC REVIEW			O			X	X
CM-7(2)	PREVENT PROGRAM EXECUTION			S			X	X
CM-7(3)	REGISTRATION COMPLIANCE			O				
CM-7(4)	UNAUTHORIZED SOFTWARE — BLACKLISTING			O				
CM-7(5)	AUTHORIZED SOFTWARE — WHITELISTING			O			X	X

CONTROL NUMBER	CONTROL NAME CONTROL ENHANCEMENT NAME	WITHDRAWN	PRIVACY-RELATED	IMPLEMENTED BY	ASSURANCE	CONTROL BASELINES		
						LOW	MOD	HIGH
CM-8	**System Component Inventory**			O	A	X	X	X
CM-8(1)	UPDATES DURING INSTALLATION AND REMOVAL			O	A		X	X
CM-8(2)	AUTOMATED MAINTENANCE			O	A			X
CM-8(3)	AUTOMATED UNAUTHORIZED COMPONENT DETECTION			O	A		X	X
CM-8(4)	ACCOUNTABILITY INFORMATION			O	A			X
CM-8(5)	NO DUPLICATE ACCOUNTING OF COMPONENTS			O	A			
CM-8(6)	ASSESSED CONFIGURATIONS AND APPROVED DEVIATIONS			O	A			
CM-8(7)	CENTRALIZED REPOSITORY			O	A			
CM-8(8)	AUTOMATED LOCATION TRACKING			O	A			
CM-8(9)	ASSIGNMENT OF COMPONENTS TO SYSTEMS			O	A			
CM-8(10)	DATA ACTION MAPPING		P	O	A			
CM-9	**Configuration Management Plan**			O			X	X
CM-9(1)	ASSIGNMENT OF RESPONSIBILITY			O				
CM-10	**Software Usage Restrictions**			O		X	X	X
CM-10(1)	OPEN SOURCE SOFTWARE			O				
CM-11	**User-Installed Software**			O		X	X	X
CM-11(1)	ALERTS FOR UNAUTHORIZED INSTALLATIONS	W	Incorporated into CM-8(3).					
CM-11(2)	SOFTWARE INSTALLATION WITH PRIVILEGED STATUS			S				
CM-12	**Information Location**		P	O	A		X	X
CM-12(1)	AUTOMATED TOOLS TO SUPPORT INFORMATION LOCATION		P	O	A		X	X

Note: Privacy-related controls and control enhancements are not allocated to baselines in this table. See Appendix F for control selection and implementation guidance.

TABLE E-6: CONTINGENCY PLANNING FAMILY

CONTROL NUMBER	CONTROL NAME CONTROL ENHANCEMENT NAME	WITHDRAWN	PRIVACY-RELATED	IMPLEMENTED BY	ASSURANCE	CONTROL BASELINES		
						LOW	MOD	HIGH
CP-1	**Contingency Planning Policy and Procedures**		P	O	A	X	X	X
CP-2	**Contingency Plan**		P	O		X	X	X
CP-2(1)	COORDINATE WITH RELATED PLANS		P	O			X	X
CP-2(2)	CAPACITY PLANNING			O				X
CP-2(3)	RESUME ESSENTIAL MISSIONS AND BUSINESS FUNCTIONS		P	O			X	X
CP-2(4)	RESUME ALL MISSIONS AND BUSINESS FUNCTIONS		P	O				X
CP-2(5)	CONTINUE ESSENTIAL MISSIONS AND BUSINESS FUNCTIONS		P	O				X
CP-2(6)	ALTERNATE PROCESSING AND STORAGE SITES			O				
CP-2(7)	COORDINATE WITH EXTERNAL SERVICE PROVIDERS		P	O				
CP-2(8)	IDENTIFY CRITICAL ASSETS		P	O			X	X
CP-3	**Contingency Training**		P	O	A	X	X	X
CP-3(1)	SIMULATED EVENTS		P	O	A			X
CP-3(2)	AUTOMATED TRAINING ENVIRONMENTS		P	O	A			
CP-4	**Contingency Plan Testing**		P	O	A	X	X	X
CP-4(1)	COORDINATE WITH RELATED PLANS		P	O	A		X	X
CP-4(2)	ALTERNATE PROCESSING SITE			O	A			X
CP-4(3)	AUTOMATED TESTING			O	A			
CP-4(4)	FULL RECOVERY AND RECONSTITUTION			O	A			
CP-5	Contingency Plan Update	W	Incorporated into CP-2.					
CP-6	**Alternate Storage Site**			O			X	X
CP-6(1)	SEPARATION FROM PRIMARY SITE			O			X	X
CP-6(2)	RECOVERY TIME AND RECOVERY POINT OBJECTIVES			O				X
CP-6(3)	ACCESSIBILITY			O			X	X
CP-7	**Alternate Processing Site**			O			X	X
CP-7(1)	SEPARATION FROM PRIMARY SITE			O			X	X
CP-7(2)	ACCESSIBILITY			O			X	X
CP-7(3)	PRIORITY OF SERVICE			O			X	X
CP-7(4)	PREPARATION FOR USE			O				X
CP-7(5)	EQUIVALENT INFORMATION SECURITY SAFEGUARDS	W	Incorporated into CP-7.					
CP-7(6)	INABILITY TO RETURN TO PRIMARY SITE			O				
CP-8	**Telecommunications Services**			O			X	X
CP-8(1)	PRIORITY OF SERVICE PROVISIONS			O			X	X
CP-8(2)	SINGLE POINTS OF FAILURE			O			X	X
CP-8(3)	SEPARATION OF PRIMARY AND ALTERNATE PROVIDERS			O				X
CP-8(4)	PROVIDER CONTINGENCY PLAN			O				X
CP-8(5)	ALTERNATE TELECOMMUNICATION SERVICE TESTING			O				
CP-9	**System Backup**			O		X	X	X
CP-9(1)	TESTING FOR RELIABILITY AND INTEGRITY			O			X	X
CP-9(2)	TEST RESTORATION USING SAMPLING			O				X
CP-9(3)	SEPARATE STORAGE FOR CRITICAL INFORMATION			O				X
CP-9(4)	PROTECTION FROM UNAUTHORIZED MODIFICATION	W	Incorporated into CP-9.					
CP-9(5)	TRANSFER TO ALTERNATE STORAGE SITE			O				X

CONTROL NUMBER	CONTROL NAME CONTROL ENHANCEMENT NAME	WITHDRAWN	PRIVACY-RELATED	IMPLEMENTED BY	ASSURANCE	CONTROL BASELINES		
						LOW	MOD	HIGH
CP-9(6)	REDUNDANT SECONDARY SYSTEM			O				
CP-9(7)	DUAL AUTHORIZATION			O				
CP-9(8)	CRYPTOGRAPHIC PROTECTION			O			X	X
CP-10	**System Recovery and Reconstitution**			O		X	X	X
CP-10(1)	CONTINGENCY PLAN TESTING	W	Incorporated into CP-4.					
CP-10(2)	TRANSACTION RECOVERY			O			X	X
CP-10(3)	COMPENSATING SECURITY CONTROLS	W	Incorporated into PL-11.					
CP-10(4)	RESTORE WITHIN TIME-PERIOD			O				X
CP-10(5)	FAILOVER CAPABILITY	W	Incorporated into SI-13.					
CP-10(6)	COMPONENT PROTECTION			O				
CP-11	**Alternate Communications Protocols**			O				
CP-12	**Safe Mode**			S	A			
CP-13	**Alternative Security Mechanisms**			O/S				

Note: Privacy-related controls and control enhancements are not allocated to baselines in this table. See **Appendix F** for control selection and implementation guidance.

TABLE E-7: IDENTIFICATION AND AUTHENTICATION FAMILY

CONTROL NUMBER	CONTROL NAME CONTROL ENHANCEMENT NAME	WITHDRAWN	PRIVACY-RELATED	IMPLEMENTED BY	ASSURANCE	CONTROL BASELINES		
						LOW	MOD	HIGH
IA-1	Identification and Authentication Policy and Procedures		P	O	A	X	X	X
IA-2	Identification and Authentication (Organizational Users)			O/S		X	X	X
IA-2(1)	MULTIFACTOR AUTHENTICATION TO PRIVILEGED ACCOUNTS			S		X	X	X
IA-2(2)	MULTIFACTOR AUTHENTICATION TO NON-PRIVILEGED ACCOUNTS			S		X	X	X
IA-2(3)	LOCAL ACCESS TO PRIVILEGED ACCOUNTS	W	Incorporated into IA-2(1)(2).					
IA-2(4)	LOCAL ACCESS TO NON-PRIVILEGED ACCOUNTS	W	Incorporated into IA-2(1)(2).					
IA-2(5)	INDIVIDUAL AUTHENTICATION WITH GROUP AUTHENTICATION			O				X
IA-2(6)	NETWORK ACCESS TO PRIVILEGED ACCOUNTS — SEPARATE DEVICE	W	Incorporated into IA-2(1)(2).					
IA-2(7)	NETWORK ACCESS TO NON-PRIVILEGED ACCOUNTS — SEPARATE DEVICE	W	Incorporated into IA-2(1)(2).					
IA-2(8)	ACCESS TO ACCOUNTS — REPLAY RESISTANT			S		X	X	X
IA-2(9)	NETWORK ACCESS TO NON-PRIVILEGED ACCOUNTS — REPLAY RESISTANT	W	Incorporated into IA-2(8).					
IA-2(10)	SINGLE SIGN-ON			S				
IA-2(11)	REMOTE ACCESS — SEPARATE DEVICE	W	Incorporated into IA-2(1)(2).					
IA-2(12)	ACCEPTANCE OF PIV CREDENTIALS			S		X	X	X
IA-2(13)	OUT-OF-BAND AUTHENTICATION	W	Incorporated into IA-2(1)(2).					
IA-3	Device Identification and Authentication			S			X	X
IA-3(1)	CRYPTOGRAPHIC BIDIRECTIONAL AUTHENTICATION			S				
IA-3(2)	CRYPTOGRAPHIC BIDIRECTIONAL NETWORK AUTHENTICATION	W	Incorporated into IA-3(1).					
IA-3(3)	DYNAMIC ADDRESS ALLOCATION			O				
IA-3(4)	DEVICE ATTESTATION			O				
IA-4	Identifier Management			O		X	X	X
IA-4(1)	PROHIBIT ACCOUNT IDENTIFIERS AS PUBLIC IDENTIFIERS			O				
IA-4(2)	SUPERVISOR AUTHORIZATION	W	Incorporated into IA-12(1).					
IA-4(3)	MULTIPLE FORMS OF CERTIFICATION	W	Incorporated into IA-12(2).					
IA-4(4)	IDENTIFY USER STATUS		P	O			X	X
IA-4(5)	DYNAMIC MANAGEMENT			S				
IA-4(6)	CROSS-ORGANIZATION MANAGEMENT			O				
IA-4(7)	IN-PERSON REGISTRATION	W	Incorporated into IA-12(4).					
IA-4(8)	PAIRWISE PSEUDONYMOUS IDENTIFIERS		P	O				
IA-5	Authenticator Management			O		X	X	X
IA-5(1)	PASSWORD-BASED AUTHENTICATION			O/S		X	X	X
IA-5(2)	PUBLIC KEY-BASED AUTHENTICATION			S			X	X
IA-5(3)	IN-PERSON OR TRUSTED EXTERNAL PARTY REGISTRATION	W	Incorporated into IA-12(4).					

CONTROL NUMBER	CONTROL NAME / CONTROL ENHANCEMENT NAME	WITHDRAWN	PRIVACY-RELATED	IMPLEMENTED BY	ASSURANCE	CONTROL BASELINES		
						LOW	MOD	HIGH
IA-5(4)	AUTOMATED SUPPORT FOR PASSWORD STRENGTH DETERMINATION	W		Incorporated into IA-5(1).				
IA-5(5)	CHANGE AUTHENTICATORS PRIOR TO DELIVERY			O				
IA-5(6)	PROTECTION OF AUTHENTICATORS			O			X	X
IA-5(7)	NO EMBEDDED UNENCRYPTED STATIC AUTHENTICATORS			O				
IA-5(8)	MULTIPLE SYSTEM ACCOUNTS			O				
IA-5(9)	FEDERATED CREDENTIAL MANAGEMENT			O				
IA-5(10)	DYNAMIC CREDENTIAL BINDING			S				
IA-5(11)	HARDWARE TOKEN-BASED AUTHENTICATION	W		Incorporated into IA-2(1)(2).				
IA-5(12)	BIOMETRIC AUTHENTICATION PERFORMANCE			S				
IA-5(13)	EXPIRATION OF CACHED AUTHENTICATORS			S				
IA-5(14)	MANAGING CONTENT OF PKI TRUST STORES			O				
IA-5(15)	GSA-APPROVED PRODUCTS AND SERVICES			O				
IA-5(16)	IN-PERSON OR TRUSTED EXTERNAL PARTY AUTHENTICATOR ISSUANCE			O				
IA-5(17)	PRESENTATION ATTACK DETECTION FOR BIOMETRIC AUTHENTICATORS			S				
IA-6	**Authenticator Feedback**			S		X	X	X
IA-7	**Cryptographic Module Authentication**			S		X	X	X
IA-8	**Identification and Authentication (Non-Organizational Users)**			S		X	X	X
IA-8(1)	ACCEPTANCE OF PIV CREDENTIALS FROM OTHER AGENCIES			S		X	X	X
IA-8(2)	ACCEPTANCE OF EXTERNAL PARTY CREDENTIALS			S		X	X	X
IA-8(3)	USE OF FICAM-APPROVED PRODUCTS	W		Incorporated into IA-8(2).				
IA-8(4)	USE OF NIST-ISSUED PROFILES			S		X	X	X
IA-8(5)	ACCEPTANCE OF PIV-I CREDENTIALS			S				
IA-8(6)	DISASSOCIABILITY		P	O				
IA-9	**Service Identification and Authentication**			O/S				
IA-9(1)	INFORMATION EXCHANGE			O				
IA-9(2)	TRANSMISSION OF DECISIONS			O				
IA-10	**Adaptive Authentication**			O				
IA-11	**Re-authentication**			O/S		X	X	X
IA-12	**Identity Proofing**			O			X	X
IA-12(1)	SUPERVISOR AUTHORIZATION			O				
IA-12(2)	IDENTITY EVIDENCE			O			X	X
IA-12(3)	IDENTITY EVIDENCE VALIDATION AND VERIFICATION			O			X	X
IA-12(4)	IN-PERSON VALIDATION AND VERIFICATION			O				X
IA-12(5)	ADDRESS CONFIRMATION			O			X	X
IA-12(6)	ACCEPT EXTERNALLY-PROOFED IDENTITIES			O				

Note: Privacy-related controls and control enhancements are not allocated to baselines in this table. See Appendix F for control selection and implementation guidance.

TABLE E-8: INDIVIDUAL PARTICIPATION

CONTROL NUMBER	CONTROL NAME / CONTROL ENHANCEMENT NAME	WITHDRAWN	PRIVACY-RELATED	IMPLEMENTED BY	ASSURANCE	CONTROL BASELINES		
						LOW	MOD	HIGH
IP-1	**Individual Participation Policy and Procedures**		P	O				
IP-2	**Consent**		P	O				
IP-2(1)	ATTRIBUTE MANAGEMENT		P	O				
IP-2(2)	JUST–IN–TIME NOTICE OF CONSENT		P	O				
IP-3	**Redress**		P	O				
IP-3(1)	NOTICE OF CORRECTION OR AMENDMENT		P	O				
IP-3(2)	APPEAL		P	O				
IP-4	**Privacy Notice**		P	O				
IP-4(1)	JUST–IN–TIME NOTICE OF PRIVACY AUTHORIZATION		P	O				
IP-5	**Privacy Act Statements**		P	O				
IP-6	**Individual Access**		P	O				

Note: Privacy-related controls and control enhancements are not allocated to baselines in this table. See **Appendix F** for control selection and implementation guidance.

TABLE E-9: INCIDENT RESPONSE FAMILY

CONTROL NUMBER	CONTROL NAME / CONTROL ENHANCEMENT NAME	WITHDRAWN	PRIVACY-RELATED	IMPLEMENTED BY	ASSURANCE	CONTROL BASELINES		
						LOW	MOD	HIGH
IR-1	Incident Response Policy and Procedures		P	O	A	X	X	X
IR-2	Incident Response Training		P	O	A	X	X	X
IR-2(1)	SIMULATED EVENTS		P	O	A			X
IR-2(2)	AUTOMATED TRAINING ENVIRONMENTS		P	O	A			X
IR-3	Incident Response Testing		P	O	A		X	X
IR-3(1)	AUTOMATED TESTING			O	A			
IR-3(2)	COORDINATION WITH RELATED PLANS		P	O	A		X	X
IR-3(3)	CONTINUOUS IMPROVEMENT			O	A			
IR-4	Incident Handling		P	O		X	X	X
IR-4(1)	AUTOMATED INCIDENT HANDLING PROCESSES			O			X	X
IR-4(2)	DYNAMIC RECONFIGURATION			O				
IR-4(3)	CONTINUITY OF OPERATIONS			O				
IR-4(4)	INFORMATION CORRELATION			O				X
IR-4(5)	AUTOMATIC DISABLING OF SYSTEM			O/S				
IR-4(6)	INSIDER THREATS — SPECIFIC CAPABILITIES			O				
IR-4(7)	INSIDER THREATS — INTRA-ORGANIZATION COORDINATION			O				
IR-4(8)	CORRELATION WITH EXTERNAL ORGANIZATIONS			O				
IR-4(9)	DYNAMIC RESPONSE CAPABILITY			O				
IR-4(10)	SUPPLY CHAIN COORDINATION			O				
IR-5	Incident Monitoring		P	O	A	X	X	X
IR-5(1)	AUTOMATED TRACKING, DATA COLLECTION, AND ANALYSIS		P	O	A			X
IR-6	Incident Reporting		P	O		X	X	X
IR-6(1)	AUTOMATED REPORTING			O			X	X
IR-6(2)	VULNERABILITIES RELATED TO INCIDENTS			O				
IR-6(3)	SUPPLY CHAIN COORDINATION			O			X	X
IR-7	Incident Response Assistance		P	O		X	X	X
IR-7(1)	AUTOMATION SUPPORT FOR AVAILABILITY OF INFORMATION AND SUPPORT			O			X	X
IR-7(2)	COORDINATION WITH EXTERNAL PROVIDERS			O				
IR-8	Incident Response Plan		P	O		X	X	X
IR-8(1)	PERSONALLY IDENTIFIABLE INFORMATION PROCESSES		P	O				
IR-9	Information Spillage Response		P	O				
IR-9(1)	RESPONSIBLE PERSONNEL			O				
IR-9(2)	TRAINING			O				
IR-9(3)	POST-SPILL OPERATIONS			O				
IR-9(4)	EXPOSURE TO UNAUTHORIZED PERSONNEL			O				
IR-10	Integrated Information Security Analysis Team			O				X

Note: Privacy-related controls and control enhancements are not allocated to baselines in this table. See Appendix F for control selection and implementation guidance.

TABLE E-10: MAINTENANCE FAMILY

CONTROL NUMBER	CONTROL NAME CONTROL ENHANCEMENT NAME	WITHDRAWN	PRIVACY-RELATED	IMPLEMENTED BY	ASSURANCE	CONTROL BASELINES		
						LOW	MOD	HIGH
MA-1	**System Maintenance Policy and Procedures**			O	A	X	X	X
MA-2	**Controlled Maintenance**			O		X	X	X
MA-2(1)	RECORD CONTENT	W	Incorporated into MA-2.					
MA-2(2)	AUTOMATED MAINTENANCE ACTIVITIES			O				X
MA-3	**Maintenance Tools**			O			X	X
MA-3(1)	INSPECT TOOLS			O			X	X
MA-3(2)	INSPECT MEDIA			O			X	X
MA-3(3)	PREVENT UNAUTHORIZED REMOVAL			O			X	X
MA-3(4)	RESTRICTED TOOL USE			S				
MA-4	**Nonlocal Maintenance**			O		X	X	X
MA-4(1)	AUDITING AND REVIEW			O				
MA-4(2)	DOCUMENT NONLOCAL MAINTENANCE	W	Incorporated into MA-1, MA-4.					
MA-4(3)	COMPARABLE SECURITY AND SANITIZATION			O				X
MA-4(4)	AUTHENTICATION AND SEPARATION OF MAINTENANCE SESSIONS			O				
MA-4(5)	APPROVALS AND NOTIFICATIONS			O				
MA-4(6)	CRYPTOGRAPHIC PROTECTION			O/S				
MA-4(7)	REMOTE DISCONNECT VERIFICATION			S				
MA-5	**Maintenance Personnel**			O		X	X	X
MA-5(1)	INDIVIDUALS WITHOUT APPROPRIATE ACCESS			O				X
MA-5(2)	SECURITY CLEARANCES FOR CLASSIFIED SYSTEMS			O				
MA-5(3)	CITIZENSHIP REQUIREMENTS FOR CLASSIFIED SYSTEMS			O				
MA-5(4)	FOREIGN NATIONALS			O				
MA-5(5)	NON-SYSTEM MAINTENANCE			O				
MA-6	**Timely Maintenance**			O			X	X
MA-6(1)	PREVENTIVE MAINTENANCE			O				
MA-6(2)	PREDICTIVE MAINTENANCE			O				
MA-6(3)	AUTOMATED SUPPORT FOR PREDICTIVE MAINTENANCE			O				
MA-6(4)	ADEQUATE SUPPLY			O				

Note: Privacy-related controls and control enhancements are not allocated to baselines in this table. See **Appendix F** for control selection and implementation guidance.

TABLE E-11: MEDIA PROTECTION Family

CONTROL NUMBER	CONTROL NAME / CONTROL ENHANCEMENT NAME	WITHDRAWN	PRIVACY-RELATED	IMPLEMENTED BY	ASSURANCE	CONTROL BASELINES		
						LOW	MOD	HIGH
MP-1	**Media Protection Policy and Procedures**			O	A	X	X	X
MP-2	**Media Access**			O		X	X	X
MP-2(1)	AUTOMATED RESTRICTED ACCESS	W	Incorporated into MP-4(2).					
MP-2(2)	CRYPTOGRAPHIC PROTECTION	W	Incorporated into SC-28(1).					
MP-3	**Media Marking**			O			X	X
MP-4	**Media Storage**			O			X	X
MP-4(1)	CRYPTOGRAPHIC PROTECTION	W	Incorporated into SC-28(1).					
MP-4(2)	AUTOMATED RESTRICTED ACCESS			O				
MP-5	**Media Transport**			O			X	X
MP-5(1)	PROTECTION OUTSIDE OF CONTROLLED AREAS	W	Incorporated into MP-5.					
MP-5(2)	DOCUMENTATION OF ACTIVITIES	W	Incorporated into MP-5.					
MP-5(3)	CUSTODIANS			O				
MP-5(4)	CRYPTOGRAPHIC PROTECTION	W	Incorporated into SC-28(1).					
MP-6	**Media Sanitization**			O		X	X	X
MP-6(1)	REVIEW, APPROVE, TRACK, DOCUMENT, VERIFY			O				X
MP-6(2)	EQUIPMENT TESTING			O				X
MP-6(3)	NONDESTRUCTIVE TECHNIQUES			O				X
MP-6(4)	CONTROLLED UNCLASSIFIED INFORMATION	W	Incorporated into MP-6.					
MP-6(5)	CLASSIFIED INFORMATION	W	Incorporated into MP-6.					
MP-6(6)	MEDIA DESTRUCTION	W	Incorporated into MP-6.					
MP-6(7)	DUAL AUTHORIZATION			O				
MP-6(8)	REMOTE PURGING OR WIPING OF INFORMATION			O				
MP-6(9)	DESTRUCTION OF PERSONALLY IDENTIFIABLE INFORMATION			O				
MP-7	**Media Use**			O		X	X	X
MP-7(1)	PROHIBIT USE WITHOUT OWNER	W	Incorporated into MP-7.					
MP-7(2)	PROHIBIT USE OF SANITIZATION-RESISTANT MEDIA			O				
MP-8	**Media Downgrading**			O				
MP-8(1)	DOCUMENTATION OF PROCESS			O				
MP-8(2)	EQUIPMENT TESTING			O				
MP-8(3)	CONTROLLED UNCLASSIFIED INFORMATION			O				
MP-8(4)	CLASSIFIED INFORMATION			O				

Note: Privacy-related controls and control enhancements are not allocated to baselines in this table. See Appendix F for control selection and implementation guidance.

TABLE E-12: PRIVACY AUTHORIZATION

CONTROL NUMBER	CONTROL NAME CONTROL ENHANCEMENT NAME	WITHDRAWN	PRIVACY-RELATED	IMPLEMENTED BY	ASSURANCE	CONTROL BASELINES		
						LOW	MOD	HIGH
PA-1	**Privacy Authorization Policy and Procedures**		P	O				
PA-2	**Authority to Collect**		P	O				
PA-3	**Purpose Specification**		P	O				
PA-3(1)	USAGE RESTRICTIONS OF PERSONALLY IDENTIFIABLE INFORMATION		P	O				
PA-3(2)	AUTOMATION		P	S				
PA-4	**Information Sharing with External Parties**		P	O				

Note: Privacy-related controls and control enhancements are not allocated to baselines in this table. See **Appendix F** for control selection and implementation guidance.

TABLE F-13: PHYSICAL AND ENVIRONMENTAL PROTECTION FAMILY

CONTROL NUMBER	CONTROL NAME CONTROL ENHANCEMENT NAME	WITHDRAWN	PRIVACY-RELATED	IMPLEMENTED BY	ASSURANCE	CONTROL BASELINES		
						LOW	MOD	HIGH
PE-1	Physical and Environmental Protection Policy and Procedures			O	A	X	X	X
PE-2	Physical Access Authorizations			O		X	X	X
PE-2(1)	ACCESS BY POSITION AND ROLE			O				
PE-2(2)	TWO FORMS OF IDENTIFICATION			O				
PE-2(3)	RESTRICT UNESCORTED ACCESS			O				
PE-3	Physical Access Control			O		X	X	X
PE-3(1)	SYSTEM ACCESS			O				X
PE-3(2)	FACILITY AND SYSTEM BOUNDARIES			O				
PE-3(3)	CONTINUOUS GUARDS			O				
PE-3(4)	LOCKABLE CASINGS			O				
PE-3(5)	TAMPER PROTECTION			O				
PE-3(6)	FACILITY PENETRATION TESTING	W	Incorporated into CA-8.					
PE-3(7)	PHYSICAL BARRIERS			O				
PE-4	Access Control for Transmission			O			X	X
PE-5	Access Control for Output Devices			O			X	X
PE-5(1)	ACCESS TO OUTPUT BY AUTHORIZED INDIVIDUALS			O				
PE-5(2)	ACCESS TO OUTPUT BY INDIVIDUAL IDENTITY			S				
PE-5(3)	MARKING OUTPUT DEVICES			O				
PE-6	Monitoring Physical Access			O	A	X	X	X
PE-6(1)	INTRUSION ALARMS AND SURVEILLANCE EQUIPMENT			O	A		X	X
PE-6(2)	AUTOMATED INTRUSION RECOGNITION AND RESPONSES			O	A			
PE-6(3)	VIDEO SURVEILLANCE			O	A			
PE-6(4)	MONITORING PHYSICAL ACCESS TO SYSTEMS			O	A			X
PE-7	Visitor Control	W	Incorporated into PE-2, PE-3.					
PE-8	Visitor Access Records			O	A	X	X	X
PE-8(1)	AUTOMATED RECORDS MAINTENANCE AND REVIEW			O				X
PE-8(2)	PHYSICAL ACCESS RECORDS	W	Incorporated into PE-2.					
PE-9	Power Equipment and Cabling			O			X	X
PE-9(1)	REDUNDANT CABLING			O				
PE-9(2)	AUTOMATIC VOLTAGE CONTROLS			O				
PE-10	Emergency Shutoff			O			X	X
PE-10(1)	ACCIDENTAL AND UNAUTHORIZED ACTIVATION	W	Incorporated into PE-10.					
PE-11	Emergency Power			O			X	X
PE-11(1)	LONG-TERM ALTERNATE POWER SUPPLY — MINIMAL OPERATIONAL CAPABILITY			O				X
PE-11(2)	LONG-TERM ALTERNATE POWER SUPPLY — SELF-CONTAINED			O				
PE-12	Emergency Lighting			O		X	X	X
PE-12(1)	ESSENTIAL MISSIONS AND BUSINESS FUNCTIONS			O				
PE-13	Fire Protection			O		X	X	X
PE-13(1)	DETECTION DEVICES AND SYSTEMS			O			X	X

CONTROL NUMBER	CONTROL NAME / CONTROL ENHANCEMENT NAME	WITHDRAWN	PRIVACY-RELATED	IMPLEMENTED BY	ASSURANCE	CONTROL BASELINES		
						LOW	MOD	HIGH
PE-13(2)	AUTOMATIC SUPPRESSION DEVICES AND SYSTEMS			O				X
PE-13(3)	AUTOMATIC FIRE SUPPRESSION	W	Incorporated into PE-13(2).					
PE-13(4)	INSPECTIONS			O				
PE-14	**Temperature and Humidity Controls**			O		X	X	X
PE-14(1)	AUTOMATIC CONTROLS			O				
PE-14(2)	MONITORING WITH ALARMS AND NOTIFICATIONS			O				
PE-15	**Water Damage Protection**			O		X	X	X
PE-15(1)	AUTOMATION SUPPORT			O				X
PE-16	**Delivery and Removal**			O		X	X	X
PE-17	**Alternate Work Site**			O			X	X
PE-18	**Location of System Components**			O				X
PE-18(1)	FACILITY SITE			O				
PE-19	**Information Leakage**			O				
PE-19(1)	NATIONAL EMISSIONS AND TEMPEST POLICIES AND PROCEDURES			O				
PE-20	**Asset Monitoring and Tracking**			O				
PE-21	**Electromagnetic Pulse Protection**			O				
PE-22	**Component Marking**			O				

Note: Privacy-related controls and control enhancements are not allocated to baselines in this table. See **Appendix F** for control selection and implementation guidance.

TABLE E-10: SUMMARY — PLANNING FAMILY

CONTROL NUMBER	CONTROL NAME CONTROL ENHANCEMENT NAME	WITHDRAWN	PRIVACY-RELATED	IMPLEMENTED BY	ASSURANCE	CONTROL BASELINES		
						LOW	MOD	HIGH
PL-1	**Planning Policy and Procedures**		P	O	A	X	X	X
PL-2	**Security and Privacy Plans**		P	O	A	X	X	X
PL-2(1)	CONCEPT OF OPERATIONS	W	Incorporated into PL-7.					
PL-2(2)	FUNCTIONAL ARCHITECTURE	W	Incorporated into PL-8.					
PL-2(3)	PLAN AND COORDINATE WITH OTHER ORGANIZATIONAL ENTITIES		P	O	A		X	X
PL-3	System Security Plan Update	W	Incorporated into PL-2.					
PL-4	**Rules of Behavior**		P	O	A	X	X	X
PL-4(1)	SOCIAL MEDIA AND NETWORKING RESTRICTIONS			O	A	X	X	X
PL-5	Privacy Impact Assessment	W	Incorporated into RA-8.					
PL-6	Security-Related Activity Planning	W	Incorporated into PL-2.					
PL-7	**Concept of Operations**		P	O				
PL-8	**Security and Privacy Architectures**		P	O	A		X	X
PL-8(1)	DEFENSE-IN-DEPTH			O	A			
PL-8(2)	SUPPLIER DIVERSITY		P	O	A			
PL-9	**Central Management**		P	O	A			
PL-10	**Baseline Selection**			O		X	X	X
PL-11	**Baseline Tailoring**			O		X	X	X

Note: Privacy-related controls and control enhancements are not allocated to baselines in this table. See **Appendix F** for control selection and implementation guidance.

TABLE E-15: PROGRAM MANAGEMENT FAMILY

CONTROL NUMBER	CONTROL NAME CONTROL ENHANCEMENT NAME	WITHDRAWN	PRIVACY-RELATED	IMPLEMENTED BY	ASSURANCE	CONTROL BASELINES		
						LOW	MOD	HIGH
PM-1	Information Security Program Plan			O		Security and privacy controls in the PM family have been designed to facilitate compliance with federal laws, Executive Orders, directives, regulations, policies, and standards. The **PM controls** are independent of any FIPS 200 impact levels and are not directly associated with the control baselines in **Appendix D**. Tailoring guidance can also be applied to the controls. The PM controls focus on the programmatic, organization-wide security and privacy requirements that are independent of any system and essential for managing security and privacy programs. Organizations can document the controls in their information security and privacy program plans. These plans, together with the security and privacy plans for the individual systems, cover the totality of security and privacy controls that are employed by the organization.		
PM-2	Inforamtion Security Program Roles			O				
PM-3	Information Security and Privacy Resources		P	O				
PM-4	Plan of Action and Milestones Process		P	O				
PM-5	System Inventory			O				
PM-6	Measures of Performance		P	O	A			
PM-7	Enterprise Architecture		P	O				
PM-8	Critical Infrastructure Plan		P	O				
PM-9	Risk Management Strategy		P	O	A			
PM-10	Authorization Process			O	A			
PM-11	Mission and Business Process Definition		P	O				
PM-12	Insider Threat Program			O	A			
PM-13	Security and Privacy Workforce		P	O				
PM-14	Testing, Training, and Monitoring		P	O	A			
PM-15	Contacts with Groups and Associations		P	O				
PM-16	Threat Awareness Program			O	A			
PM-16(1)	AUTOMATED MEANS FOR SHARING THREAT INTELLIGENCE			O	A			
PM-17	Protecting CUI on External Systems			O	A			
PM-18	Privacy Program Plan		P	O				
PM-19	Privacy Program Roles		P	O				
PM-20	System of Records Notice		P	O				
PM-21	Dissemination of Privacy Program Information		P	O				
PM-22	Accounting of Disclosures		P	O				
PM-23	Data Quality Management		P	O	A			
PM-23(1)	AUTOMATION		P	O	A			
PM-23(2)	DATA TAGGING		P	O	A			
PM-23(3)	UPDATING PERSONALLY IDENTIFIABLE INFORMATION		P	O	A			
PM-24	Data Management Board		P	O	A			
PM-25	Data Integrity Board		P	O	A			
PM-25(1)	PUBLISH AGREEMENTS ON WEBSITE		P	O				
PM-26	Minimization of PII Used in Testing Training, and Research		P	O				
PM-27	Individual Access Control		P	O				
PM-28	Complaint Management		P	O				
PM-29	Inventory of PII		P	O				
PM-29(1)	AUTOMATION SUPPORT		P	O				
PM-30	Privacy Reporting		P	O				
PM-31	Supply Chain Risk Management Plan			O				
PM-32	Risk Framing		P	O	A			

Note: Privacy-related controls and control enhancements are not allocated to baselines in this table. See **Appendix F** for control selection and implementation guidance.

TABLE E-10. PERSONNEL SECURITY FAMILY

CONTROL NUMBER	CONTROL NAME / CONTROL ENHANCEMENT NAME	WITHDRAWN	PRIVACY-RELATED	IMPLEMENTED BY	ASSURANCE	CONTROL BASELINES		
						LOW	MOD	HIGH
PS-1	Personnel Security Policy and Procedures			O	A	X	X	X
PS-2	Position Risk Designation			O		X	X	X
PS-3	Personnel Screening			O		X	X	X
PS-3(1)	CLASSIFIED INFORMATION			O				
PS-3(2)	FORMAL INDOCTRINATION			O				
PS-3(3)	INFORMATION WITH SPECIAL PROTECTION MEASURES			O				
PS-3(4)	CITIZENSHIP REQUIREMENTS			O				
PS-4	Personnel Termination			O		X	X	X
PS-4(1)	POST-EMPLOYMENT REQUIREMENTS			O				
PS-4(2)	AUTOMATED NOTIFICATION			O				X
PS-5	Personnel Transfer			O		X	X	X
PS-6	Access Agreements			O	A	X	X	X
PS-6(1)	INFORMATION REQUIRING SPECIAL PROTECTION	W	Incorporated into PS-3.					
PS-6(2)	CLASSIFIED INFORMATION REQUIRING SPECIAL PROTECTION			O	A			
PS-6(3)	POST-EMPLOYMENT REQUIREMENTS			O	A			
PS-7	External Personnel Security			O	A	X	X	X
PS-8	Personnel Sanctions			O		X	X	X

Note: Privacy-related controls and control enhancements are not allocated to baselines in this table. See **Appendix F** for control selection and implementation guidance.

TABLE E-17: RISK ASSESSMENT FAMILY

CONTROL NUMBER	CONTROL NAME / CONTROL ENHANCEMENT NAME	WITHDRAWN	PRIVACY-RELATED	IMPLEMENTED BY	ASSURANCE	CONTROL BASELINES		
						LOW	MOD	HIGH
RA-1	**Risk Assessment Policy and Procedures**			O	A	X	X	X
RA-2	**Security Categorization**			O		X	X	X
RA-2(1)	SECOND-LEVEL CATEGORIZATION			O				
RA-3	**Risk Assessment**			O	A	X	X	X
RA-3(1)	SUPPLY CHAIN RISK ASSESSMENT			O			X	X
RA-4	Risk Assessment Update	W	Incorporated into RA-3.					
RA-5	**Vulnerability Scanning**			O	A	X	X	X
RA-5(1)	UPDATE TOOL CAPABILITY	W	Incorporated into RA-5.					
RA-5(2)	UPDATE BY FREQUENCY, PRIOR TO NEW SCAN, OR WHEN IDENTIFIED			O	A	X	X	X
RA-5(3)	BREADTH AND DEPTH OF COVERAGE			O	A			
RA-5(4)	DISCOVERABLE INFORMATION			O	A			X
RA-5(5)	PRIVILEGED ACCESS			O	A		X	X
RA-5(6)	AUTOMATED TREND ANALYSES			O	A			
RA-5(7)	AUTOMATED DETECTION AND NOTIFICATION OF UNAUTHORIZED COMPONENTS	W	Incorporated into CM-8.					
RA-5(8)	REVIEW HISTORIC AUDIT LOGS			O	A			
RA-5(9)	PENETRATION TESTING AND ANALYSES	W	Incorporated into CA-8.					
RA-5(10)	CORRELATE SCANNING INFORMATION			O	A			
RA-6	**Technical Surveillance Countermeasures Survey**			O	A			
RA-7	**Risk Response**			O	A	X	X	X
RA-8	**Privacy Impact Assessments**			O	A			
RA-9	**Criticality Analysis**			O			X	X

Note: Privacy-related controls and control enhancements are not allocated to baselines in this table. See **Appendix F** for control selection and implementation guidance.

TABLE E-18: SYSTEM AND SERVICES ACQUISITION FAMILY

CONTROL NUMBER	CONTROL NAME / CONTROL ENHANCEMENT NAME	WITHDRAWN	PRIVACY-RELATED	IMPLEMENTED BY	ASSURANCE	CONTROL BASELINES		
						LOW	MOD	HIGH
SA-1	System and Services Acquisition Policy and Procedures		P	O	A	X	X	X
SA-2	Allocation of Resources			O	A	X	X	X
SA-3	System Development Life Cycle		P	O	A	X	X	X
SA-3(1)	MANAGE DEVELOPMENT ENVIRONMENT			O	A			
SA-3(2)	USE OF LIVE DATA			O	A			
SA-3(3)	TECHNOLOGY REFRESH			O	A			
SA-4	Acquisition Process		P	O	A	X	X	X
SA-4(1)	FUNCTIONAL PROPERTIES OF CONTROLS			O	A		X	X
SA-4(2)	DESIGN AND IMPLEMENTATION INFORMATION FOR CONTROLS			O	A		X	X
SA-4(3)	DEVELOPMENT METHODS, TECHNIQUES, AND PRACTICES			O	A			
SA-4(4)	ASSIGNMENT OF COMPONENTS TO SYSTEMS	W	Incorporated into CM-8(9).					
SA-4(5)	SYSTEM, COMPONENT, AND SERVICE CONFIGURATIONS			O	A			X
SA-4(6)	USE OF INFORMATION ASSURANCE PRODUCTS			O	A			
SA-4(7)	NIAP-APPROVED PROTECTION PROFILES			O	A			
SA-4(8)	CONTINUOUS MONITORING PLAN FOR CONTROLS			O	A			
SA-4(9)	FUNCTIONS, PORTS, PROTOCOLS, AND SERVICES IN USE			O	A		X	X
SA-4(10)	USE OF APPROVED PIV PRODUCTS			O	A	X	X	X
SA-5	System Documentation			O	A	X	X	X
SA-5(1)	FUNCTIONAL PROPERTIES OF SECURITY CONTROLS	W	Incorporated into SA-4(1).					
SA-5(2)	SECURITY-RELEVANT EXTERNAL SYSTEM INTERFACES	W	Incorporated into SA-4(2)					
SA-5(3)	HIGH-LEVEL DESIGN	W	Incorporated into SA-4(2).					
SA-5(4)	LOW-LEVEL DESIGN	W	Incorporated into SA-4(2).					
SA-5(5)	SOURCE CODE	W	Incorporated into SA-4(2).					
SA-6	Software Usage Restrictions	W	Incorporated into CM-10 and SI-7.					
SA-7	User-Installed Software	W	Incorporated into CM-11 and SI-7.					
SA-8	Security and Privacy Engineering Principles		P	O	A	X	X	X
SA-9	External System Services		P	O	A	X	X	X
SA-9(1)	RISK ASSESSMENTS AND ORGANIZATIONAL APPROVALS			O	A			
SA-9(2)	IDENTIFICATION OF FUNCTIONS, PORTS, PROTOCOLS, AND SERVICES			O	A		X	X
SA-9(3)	ESTABLISH AND MAINTAIN TRUST RELATIONSHIP WITH PROVIDERS		P	O	A			
SA-9(4)	CONSISTENT INTERESTS OF CONSUMERS AND PROVIDERS			O	A			
SA-9(5)	PROCESSING, STORAGE, AND SERVICE LOCATION		P	O	A			
SA-9(6)	ORGANIZATION-CONTROLLED CRYPTOGRAPHIC KEYS			O	A			
SA-9(7)	ORGANIZATION-CONTROLLED INTEGRITY CHECKING			O	A			
SA-10	Developer Configuration Management			O	A		X	X
SA-10(1)	SOFTWARE AND FIRMWARE INTEGRITY VERIFICATION			O	A			
SA-10(2)	ALTERNATIVE CONFIGURATION MANAGEMENT PROCESSES			O	A			
SA-10(3)	HARDWARE INTEGRITY VERIFICATION			O	A			

CONTROL NUMBER	CONTROL NAME CONTROL ENHANCEMENT NAME	WITHDRAWN	PRIVACY-RELATED	IMPLEMENTED BY	ASSURANCE	CONTROL BASELINES		
						LOW	MOD	HIGH
SA-10(4)	TRUSTED GENERATION			O	A			
SA-10(5)	MAPPING INTEGRITY FOR VERSION CONTROL			O	A			
SA-10(6)	TRUSTED DISTRIBUTION			O	A			
SA-11	**Developer Testing and Evaluation**		P	O	A		X	X
SA-11(1)	STATIC CODE ANALYSIS			O	A			
SA-11(2)	THREAT MODELING AND VULNERABILITY ANALYSES			O	A			
SA-11(3)	INDEPENDENT VERIFICATION OF ASSESSMENT PLANS AND EVIDENCE			O	A			
SA-11(4)	MANUAL CODE REVIEWS			O	A			
SA-11(5)	PENETRATION TESTING			O	A			
SA-11(6)	ATTACK SURFACE REVIEWS			O	A			
SA-11(7)	VERIFY SCOPE OF TESTING AND EVALUATION			O	A			
SA-11(8)	DYNAMIC CODE ANALYSIS			O	A			
SA-12	**Supply Chain Risk Management**			O	A		X	X
SA-12(1)	ACQUISITION STRATEGIES, TOOLS, AND METHODS			O	A			
SA-12(2)	SUPPLIER REVIEWS			O	A			
SA-12(3)	TRUSTED SHIPPING AND WAREHOUSING	W	Incorporated into SA-12(1).					
SA-12(4)	DIVERSITY OF SUPPLIERS	W	Incorporated into SA-12(13).					
SA-12(5)	LIMITATION OF HARM			O	A			
SA-12(6)	MINIMIZING PROCUREMENT TIME	W	Incorporated into SA-12(1).					
SA-12(7)	ASSESSMENTS PRIOR TO SELECTION, ACCEPTANCE, AND UPDATE			O	A			
SA-12(8)	USE OF ALL-SOURCE INTELLIGENCE			O	A			
SA-12(9)	OPERATIONS SECURITY			O	A			
SA-12(10)	VALIDATE AS GENUINE AND NOT ALTERED			O	A			
SA-12(11)	PENETRATION TESTING AND ANALYSIS			O	A			
SA-12(12)	NOTIFICATION AGREEMENTS			O	A			
SA-12(13)	CRITICAL SYSTEM COMPONENTS	W	Incorporated into MA-6 and RA-9.					
SA-12(14)	IDENTITY AND TRACEABILITY			O	A			
SA-12(15)	PROCESSES TO ADDRESS WEAKNESSES OR DEFICIENCIES			O	A			
SA-12(16)	PROVENANCE			O	A			
SA-13	Trustworthiness	W	Incorporated into SA-8.					
SA-14	Criticality Analysis	W	Incorporated into RA-9.					
SA-14(1)	CRITICAL COMPONENTS WITH NO VIABLE ALTERNATIVE SOURCING	W	Incorporated into SA-20.					
SA-15	**Development Process, Standards, and Tools**			O	A		X	X
SA-15(1)	QUALITY METRICS			O	A			
SA-15(2)	SECURITY TRACKING TOOLS			O	A			
SA-15(3)	CRITICALITY ANALYSIS			O	A		X	X
SA-15(4)	THREAT MODELING AND VULNERABILITY ANALYSIS	W	Incorporated into SA-11(2).					
SA-15(5)	ATTACK SURFACE REDUCTION			O	A			
SA-15(6)	CONTINUOUS IMPROVEMENT			O	A			
SA-15(7)	AUTOMATED VULNERABILITY ANALYSIS			O	A			

CONTROL NUMBER	CONTROL NAME / CONTROL ENHANCEMENT NAME	WITHDRAWN	PRIVACY-RELATED	IMPLEMENTED BY	ASSURANCE	CONTROL BASELINE		
						LOW	MOD	HIGH
SA-15(8)	REUSE OF THREAT AND VULNERABILITY INFORMATION			O	A			
SA-15(9)	USE OF LIVE DATA	W		Incorporated into SA-3(2).				
SA-15(10)	INCIDENT RESPONSE PLAN			O	A			
SA-15(11)	ARCHIVE SYSTEM OR COMPONENT			O	A			
SA-16	**Developer-Provided Training**			O	A			X
SA-17	**Developer Security Architecture and Design**			O	A			X
SA-17(1)	FORMAL POLICY MODEL			O	A			
SA-17(2)	SECURITY-RELEVANT COMPONENTS			O	A			
SA-17(3)	FORMAL CORRESPONDENCE			O	A			
SA-17(4)	INFORMAL CORRESPONDENCE			O	A			
SA-17(5)	CONCEPTUALLY SIMPLE DESIGN			O	A			
SA-17(6)	STRUCTURE FOR TESTING			O	A			
SA-17(7)	STRUCTURE FOR LEAST PRIVILEGE			O	A			
SA-18	**Tamper Resistance and Detection**			O	A			
SA-18(1)	MULTIPLE PHASES OF SYSTEM DEVELOPMENT LIFE CYCLE			O	A			
SA-18(2)	INSPECTION OF SYSTEMS OR COMPONENTS			O	A			
SA-19	**Component Authenticity**			O	A			
SA-19(1)	ANTI-COUNTERFEIT TRAINING			O	A			
SA-19(2)	CONFIGURATION CONTROL FOR COMPONENT SERVICE AND REPAIR			O	A			
SA-19(3)	COMPONENT DISPOSAL			O	A			
SA-19(4)	ANTI-COUNTERFEIT SCANNING			O	A			
SA-20	**Customized Development of Critical Components**			O	A			
SA-21	**Developer Screening**			O	A			X
SA-21(1)	VALIDATION OF SCREENING	W		Incorporated into SA-21.				
SA-22	**Unsupported System Components**			O	A	X	X	X
SA-22(1)	ALTERNATIVE SOURCES FOR CONTINUED SUPPORT			O	A			

Note: Privacy-related controls and control enhancements are not allocated to baselines in this table. See **Appendix F** for control selection and implementation guidance.

TABLE E-19: SYSTEM AND COMMUNICATIONS PROTECTION FAMILY

CONTROL NUMBER	CONTROL NAME / CONTROL ENHANCEMENT NAME	WITHDRAWN	PRIVACY-RELATED	IMPLEMENTED BY	ASSURANCE	CONTROL BASELINES		
						LOW	MOD	HIGH
SC-1	**System and Communications Protection Policy and Procedures**		P	O	A	X	X	X
SC-2	**Application Partitioning**			S	A		X	X
SC-2(1)	INTERFACES FOR NON-PRIVILEGED USERS			S	A			
SC-3	**Security Function Isolation**			S	A			X
SC-3(1)	HARDWARE SEPARATION			S	A			
SC-3(2)	ACCESS AND FLOW CONTROL FUNCTIONS			S	A			
SC-3(3)	MINIMIZE NONSECURITY FUNCTIONALITY			O/S	A			
SC-3(4)	MODULE COUPLING AND COHESIVENESS			O/S	A			
SC-3(5)	LAYERED STRUCTURES			O/S	A			
SC-4	**Information in Shared System Resources**			S			X	X
SC-4(1)	SECURITY LEVELS	W	Incorporated into SC-4.					
SC-4(2)	MULTILEVEL OR PERIODS PROCESSING			S				
SC-5	**Denial of Service Protection**			S		X	X	X
SC-5(1)	RESTRICT INTERNAL USERS			S				
SC-5(2)	CAPACITY, BANDWIDTH, AND REDUNDANCY			S				
SC-5(3)	DETECTION AND MONITORING			S				
SC-6	**Resource Availability**			S	A			
SC-7	**Boundary Protection**			S		X	X	X
SC-7(1)	PHYSICALLY SEPARATED SUBNETWORKS	W	Incorporated into SC-7.					
SC-7(2)	PUBLIC ACCESS	W	Incorporated into SC-7.					
SC-7(3)	ACCESS POINTS			S			X	X
SC-7(4)	EXTERNAL TELECOMMUNICATIONS SERVICES			O			X	X
SC-7(5)	DENY BY DEFAULT — ALLOW BY EXCEPTION			S			X	X
SC-7(6)	RESPONSE TO RECOGNIZED FAILURES	W	Incorporated into SC-7(18).					
SC-7(7)	PREVENT SPLIT TUNNELING FOR REMOTE DEVICES			S			X	X
SC-7(8)	ROUTE TRAFFIC TO AUTHENTICATED PROXY SERVERS			S			X	X
SC-7(9)	RESTRICT THREATENING OUTGOING COMMUNICATIONS TRAFFIC			S				
SC-7(10)	PREVENT EXFILTRATION			S				
SC-7(11)	RESTRICT INCOMING COMMUNICATIONS TRAFFIC			S				
SC-7(12)	HOST-BASED PROTECTION			S				
SC-7(13)	ISOLATION OF SECURITY TOOLS, MECHANISMS, AND SUPPORT COMPONENTS			S				
SC-7(14)	PROTECTS AGAINST UNAUTHORIZED PHYSICAL CONNECTIONS			S				
SC-7(15)	ROUTE PRIVILEGED NETWORK ACCESSES			S				
SC-7(16)	PREVENT DISCOVERY OF COMPONENTS AND DEVICES			S				
SC-7(17)	AUTOMATED ENFORCEMENT OF PROTOCOL FORMATS			S				
SC-7(18)	FAIL SECURE			S	A			X
SC-7(19)	BLOCK COMMUNICATION FROM NON-ORGANIZATIONALLY CONFIGURED HOSTS			S				
SC-7(20)	DYNAMIC ISOLATION AND SEGREGATION			S				

CONTROL NUMBER	CONTROL NAME / CONTROL ENHANCEMENT NAME	WITHDRAWN	PRIVACY-RELATED	IMPLEMENTED	ASSURANCE	CONTROL BASELINES		
						LOW	MOD	HIGH
SC-7(21)	ISOLATION OF SYSTEM COMPONENTS			O/S	A			X
SC-7(22)	SEPARATE SUBNETS FOR CONNECTING TO DIFFERENT SECURITY DOMAINS			S	A			
SC-7(23)	DISABLE SENDER FEEDBACK ON PROTOCOL VALIDATION FAILURE			S				
SC-7(24)	PERSONALLY IDENTIFIABLE INFORMATION		P	O/S				
SC-8	**Transmission Confidentiality and Integrity**			S			X	X
SC-8(1)	CRYPTOGRAPHIC PROTECTION			S			X	X
SC-8(2)	PRE- AND POST-TRANSMISSION HANDLING			S				
SC-8(3)	CRYPTOGRAPHIC PROTECTION FOR MESSAGE EXTERNALS			S				
SC-8(4)	CONCEAL OR RANDOMIZE COMMUNICATIONS			S				
SC-9	Transmission Confidentiality	W	Incorporated into SC-8.					
SC-10	**Network Disconnect**			S			X	X
SC-11	**Trusted Path**			S	A			
SC-11(1)	LOGICAL ISOLATION			S	A			
SC-12	**Cryptographic Key Establishment and Management**			O/S		X	X	X
SC-12(1)	AVAILABILITY			O/S				X
SC-12(2)	SYMMETRIC KEYS			O/S				
SC-12(3)	ASYMMETRIC KEYS			O/S				
SC-12(4)	PKI CERTIFICATES	W	Incorporated into SC-12.					
SC-12(5)	PKI CERTIFICATES / HARDWARE TOKENS	W	Incorporated into SC-12.					
SC-13	**Cryptographic Protection**			S		X	X	X
SC-13(1)	FIPS-VALIDATED CRYPTOGRAPHY	W	Incorporated into SC-13.					
SC-13(2)	NSA-APPROVED CRYPTOGRAPHY	W	Incorporated into SC-13.					
SC-13(3)	INDIVIDUALS WITHOUT FORMAL ACCESS APPROVALS	W	Incorporated into SC-13.					
SC-13(4)	DIGITAL SIGNATURES	W	Incorporated into SC-13.					
SC-14	Public Access Protections	W	Incorporated into AC-2, AC-3, AC-5, SI-3, SI-4, SI-5, SI-7, SI-10.					
SC-15	**Collaborative Computing Devices and Applications**			S		X	X	X
SC-15(1)	PHYSICAL DISCONNECT			S				
SC-15(2)	BLOCKING INBOUND AND OUTBOUND COMMUNICATIONS TRAFFIC	W	Incorporated into SC-7.					
SC-15(3)	DISABLING AND REMOVAL IN SECURE WORK AREAS			O				
SC-15(4)	EXPLICITLY INDICATE CURRENT PARTICIPANTS			S				
SC-16	**Transmission of Security and Privacy Attributes**		P	S				
SC-16(1)	INTEGRITY VALIDATION			S				
SC-17	**Public Key Infrastructure Certificates**			O/S			X	X
SC-18	**Mobile Code**			O			X	X
SC-18(1)	IDENTIFY UNACCEPTABLE CODE AND TAKE CORRECTIVE ACTIONS			S				
SC-18(2)	ACQUISITION, DEVELOPMENT, AND USE			O				

CONTROL NUMBER	CONTROL NAME CONTROL ENHANCEMENT NAME	WITHDRAWN	PRIVACY-RELATED	IMPLEMENTED BY	ASSURANCE	CONTROL BASELINES		
						LOW	MOD	HIGH
SC-18(3)	PREVENT DOWNLOADING AND EXECUTION			S				
SC-18(4)	PREVENT AUTOMATIC EXECUTION			S				
SC-18(5)	ALLOW EXECUTION ONLY IN CONFINED ENVIRONMENTS			S				
SC-19	**Voice Over Internet Protocol**			O			X	X
SC-20	**Secure Name/Address Resolution Service (Authoritative Source)**			S		X	X	X
SC-20(1)	CHILD SUBSPACES	W	Incorporated into SC-20.					
SC-20(2)	DATA ORIGIN AND INTEGRITY			S				
SC-21	**Secure Name/Address Resolution Service (Recursive or Caching Resolver)**			S		X	X	X
SC-21(1)	DATA ORIGIN AND INTEGRITY	W	Incorporated into SC-21.					
SC-22	**Architecture and Provisioning for Name/Address Resolution Service**			S		X	X	X
SC-23	**Session Authenticity**			S			X	X
SC-23(1)	INVALIDATE SESSION IDENTIFIERS AT LOGOUT			S				
SC-23(2)	USER-INITIATED LOGOUTS AND MESSAGE DISPLAYS	W	Incorporated into AC-12(1).					
SC-23(3)	UNIQUE SESSION IDENTIFIERS WITH RANDOMIZATION			S				
SC-23(4)	UNIQUE SESSION IDENTIFIERS WITH RANDOMIZATION	W	Incorporated into SC-23(3).					
SC-23(5)	ALLOWED CERTIFICATE AUTHORITIES			S				
SC-24	**Fail in Known State**			S	A			X
SC-25	**Thin Nodes**			S				
SC-26	**Honeypots**			S				
SC-26(1)	DETECTION OF MALICIOUS CODE	W	Incorporated into SC-35.					
SC-27	**Platform-Independent Applications**			S				
SC-28	**Protection of Information at Rest**			S			X	X
SC-28(1)	CRYPTOGRAPHIC PROTECTION			S			X	X
SC-28(2)	OFF-LINE STORAGE			O				
SC-29	**Heterogeneity**			O	A			
SC-29(1)	VIRTUALIZATION TECHNIQUES			O	A			
SC-30	**Concealment and Misdirection**			O	A			
SC-30(1)	VIRTUALIZATION TECHNIQUES	W	Incorporated into SC-29(1).					
SC-30(2)	RANDOMNESS			O	A			
SC-30(3)	CHANGE PROCESSING AND STORAGE LOCATIONS			O	A			
SC-30(4)	MISLEADING INFORMATION			O	A			
SC-30(5)	CONCEALMENT OF SYSTEM COMPONENTS			O	A			
SC-31	**Covert Channel Analysis**			O	A			
SC-31(1)	TEST COVERT CHANNELS FOR EXPLOITABILITY			O	A			
SC-31(2)	MAXIMUM BANDWIDTH			O	A			
SC-31(3)	MEASURE BANDWIDTH IN OPERATIONAL ENVIRONMENTS			O	A			
SC-32	**System Partitioning**			O	A			
SC-33	Transmission Preparation Integrity	W	Incorporated into SC-8.					
SC-34	**Non-Modifiable Executable Programs**			S	A			
SC-34(1)	NO WRITABLE STORAGE			O	A			

CONTROL NUMBER	CONTROL NAME / CONTROL ENHANCEMENT NAME	WITHDRAWN	PRIVACY-RELATED	IMPLEMENTED BY	ASSURANCE	CONTROL BASELINES		
						LOW	MOD	HIGH
SC-34(2)	INTEGRITY PROTECTION AND READ-ONLY MEDIA			O	A			
SC-34(3)	HARDWARE-BASED PROTECTION			O	A			
SC-35	**Honeyclients**			S				
SC-36	**Distributed Processing and Storage**			O	A			
SC-36(1)	POLLING TECHNIQUES			O	A			
SC-37	**Out-of-Band Channels**			O	A			
SC-37(1)	ENSURE DELIVERY AND TRANSMISSION			O	A			
SC-38	**Operations Security**			O	A			
SC-39	**Process Isolation**			S	A	X	X	X
SC-39(1)	HARDWARE SEPARATION			S	A			
SC-39(2)	THREAD ISOLATION			S	A			
SC-40	**Wireless Link Protection**			S				
SC-40(1)	ELECTROMAGNETIC INTERFERENCE			S				
SC-40(2)	REDUCE DETECTION POTENTIAL			S				
SC-40(3)	IMITATIVE OR MANIPULATIVE COMMUNICATIONS DECEPTION			S				
SC-40(4)	SIGNAL PARAMETER IDENTIFICATION			S				
SC-41	**Port and I/O Device Access**			O				
SC-42	**Sensor Capability and Data**			S				
SC-42(1)	REPORTING TO AUTHORIZED INDIVIDUALS OR ROLES			O				
SC-42(2)	AUTHORIZED USE		P	O				
SC-42(3)	PROHIBIT USE OF DEVICES			O				
SC-42(4)	NOTICE OF COLLECTION		P	O				
SC-42(5)	COLLECTION MINIMIZATION		P	O				
SC-43	**Usage Restrictions**			O/S				
SC-44	**Detonation Chambers**			O				

Note: Privacy-related controls and control enhancements are not allocated to baselines in this table. See **Appendix F** for control selection and implementation guidance.

TABLE E-20: SYSTEM AND INFORMATION INTEGRITY FAMILY

CONTROL NUMBER	CONTROL NAME CONTROL ENHANCEMENT NAME	WITHDRAWN	PRIVACY-RELATED	IMPLEMENTED BY	ASSURANCE	CONTROL BASELINES		
						LOW	MOD	HIGH
SI-1	System and Information Integrity Policy and Procedures		P	O	A	X	X	X
SI-2	Flaw Remediation			O		X	X	X
SI-2(1)	CENTRAL MANAGEMENT			O				X
SI-2(2)	AUTOMATED FLAW REMEDIATION STATUS			O			X	X
SI-2(3)	TIME TO REMEDIATE FLAWS AND BENCHMARKS FOR CORRECTIVE ACTIONS			O				
SI-2(4)	AUTOMATED PATCH MANAGEMENT TOOLS	W	Incorporated into SI-2.					
SI-2(5)	AUTOMATIC SOFTWARE AND FIRMWARE UPDATES			O				
SI-2(6)	REMOVAL OF PREVIOUS VERSIONS OF SOFTWARE AND FIRMWARE			O				
SI-2(7)	PERSONALLY IDENTIFIABLE INFORMATION		P	O				
SI-3	Malicious Code Protection			O		X	X	X
SI-3(1)	CENTRAL MANAGEMENT			O			X	X
SI-3(2)	AUTOMATIC UPDATES	W	Incorporated into SI-3.					
SI-3(3)	NON-PRIVILEGED USERS	W	Incorporated into AC-6(10).					
SI-3(4)	UPDATES ONLY BY PRIVILEGED USERS			O				
SI-3(5)	PORTABLE STORAGE DEVICES	W	Incorporated into MP-7.					
SI-3(6)	TESTING AND VERIFICATION			O				
SI-3(7)	NONSIGNATURE-BASED DETECTION	W	Incorporated into SI-3.					
SI-3(8)	DETECT UNAUTHORIZED COMMANDS			S				
SI-3(9)	AUTHENTICATE REMOTE COMMANDS			S				
SI-3(10)	MALICIOUS CODE ANALYSIS			O				
SI-4	System Monitoring			O/S	A	X	X	X
SI-4(1)	SYSTEM-WIDE INTRUSION DETECTION SYSTEM			O/S	A			
SI-4(2)	AUTOMATED TOOLS AND MECHANISMS FOR REAL-TIME ANALYSIS			S	A		X	X
SI-4(3)	AUTOMATED TOOL AND MECHANISM INTEGRATION			S	A			
SI-4(4)	INBOUND AND OUTBOUND COMMUNICATIONS TRAFFIC			S	A		X	X
SI-4(5)	SYSTEM-GENERATED ALERTS			S	A		X	X
SI-4(6)	RESTRICT NON-PRIVILEGED USERS	W	Incorporated into AC-6(10).					
SI-4(7)	AUTOMATED RESPONSE TO SUSPICIOUS EVENTS			S	A			
SI-4(8)	PROTECTION OF MONITORING INFORMATION	W	Incorporated into SI-4.					
SI-4(9)	TESTING OF MONITORING TOOLS AND MECHANISMS			O	A			
SI-4(10)	VISIBILITY OF ENCRYPTED COMMUNICATIONS			O	A			X
SI-4(11)	ANALYZE COMMUNICATIONS TRAFFIC ANOMALIES			O/S	A			
SI-4(12)	AUTOMATED ORGANIZATION-GENERATED ALERTS			O/S	A			X
SI-4(13)	ANALYZE TRAFFIC AND EVENT PATTERNS			O/S	A			
SI-4(14)	WIRELESS INTRUSION DETECTION			S	A			X
SI-4(15)	WIRELESS TO WIRELINE COMMUNICATIONS			S	A			
SI-4(16)	CORRELATE MONITORING INFORMATION			O/S	A			
SI-4(17)	INTEGRATED SITUATIONAL AWARENESS			O	A			

CONTROL NUMBER	CONTROL NAME / CONTROL ENHANCEMENT NAME	WITHDRAWN	PRIVACY-RELATED	IMPLEMENTED	ASSURANCE	CONTROL BASELINES		
						LOW	MOD	HIGH
SI-4(18)	ANALYZE TRAFFIC AND COVERT EXFILTRATION			O/S	A			
SI-4(19)	INDIVIDUALS POSING GREATER RISK			O	A			
SI-4(20)	PRIVILEGED USERS			S	A			X
SI-4(21)	PROBATIONARY PERIODS			O	A			
SI-4(22)	UNAUTHORIZED NETWORK SERVICES			S	A			X
SI-4(23)	HOST-BASED DEVICES			O	A			
SI-4(24)	INDICATORS OF COMPROMISE			S	A			
SI-4(25)	PERSONALLY IDENTIFIABLE INFORMATION MONITORING		P	O/S	A			
SI-5	**Security Alerts, Advisories, and Directives**			O	A	X	X	X
SI-5(1)	AUTOMATED ALERTS AND ADVISORIES			O	A			X
SI-6	**Security and Privacy Function Verification**		P	S	A			X
SI-6(1)	NOTIFICATION OF FAILED SECURITY TESTS	W	Incorporated into SI-6.					
SI-6(2)	AUTOMATION SUPPORT FOR DISTRIBUTED TESTING			S				
SI-6(3)	REPORT VERIFICATION RESULTS		P	O				
SI-7	**Software, Firmware, and Information Integrity**			O/S	A		X	X
SI-7(1)	INTEGRITY CHECKS			S	A		X	X
SI-7(2)	AUTOMATED NOTIFICATIONS OF INTEGRITY VIOLATIONS			S	A			X
SI-7(3)	CENTRALLY MANAGED INTEGRITY TOOLS			O	A			
SI-7(4)	TAMPER-EVIDENT PACKAGING	W	Incorporated into SA-12.					
SI-7(5)	AUTOMATED RESPONSE TO INTEGRITY VIOLATIONS			S	A			X
SI-7(6)	CRYPTOGRAPHIC PROTECTION			S	A			
SI-7(7)	INTEGRATION OF DETECTION AND RESPONSE			O	A		X	X
SI-7(8)	AUDITING CAPABILITY FOR SIGNIFICANT EVENTS			S	A			
SI-7(9)	VERIFY BOOT PROCESS			S	A			
SI-7(10)	PROTECTION OF BOOT FIRMWARE			S	A			
SI-7(11)	CONFINED ENVIRONMENTS WITH LIMITED PRIVILEGES			O	A			
SI-7(12)	INTEGRITY VERIFICATION			O/S	A			
SI-7(13)	CODE EXECUTION IN PROTECTED ENVIRONMENTS			O/S	A			
SI-7(14)	BINARY OR MACHINE EXECUTABLE CODE			O/S	A			X
SI-7(15)	CODE AUTHENTICATION			S	A			X
SI-7(16)	TIME LIMIT ON PROCESS EXECUTION WITHOUT SUPERVISION			O	A			
SI-8	**Spam Protection**			O			X	X
SI-8(1)	CENTRAL MANAGEMENT			O			X	X
SI-8(2)	AUTOMATIC UPDATES			S			X	X
SI-8(3)	CONTINUOUS LEARNING CAPABILITY			S				
SI-9	Information Input Restrictions	W	Incorporated into AC-2, AC-3, AC-5, AC-6.					
SI-10	**Information Input Validation**			S	A		X	X
SI-10(1)	MANUAL OVERRIDE CAPABILITY			O/S	A			
SI-10(2)	REVIEW AND RESOLVE OF ERRORS			O	A			
SI-10(3)	PREDICTABLE BEHAVIOR			O	A			
SI-10(4)	TIMING INTERACTIONS			S	A			

CONTROL NUMBER	CONTROL NAME CONTROL ENHANCEMENT NAME	WITHDRAWN	PRIVACY-RELATED	IMPLEMENTED BY	ASSURANCE	CONTROL BASELINES		
						LOW	MOD	HIGH
SI-10(5)	RESTRICT INPUTS TO TRUSTED SOURCES AND APPROVED FORMATS			S	A			
SI-11	**Error Handling**			S			X	X
SI-12	**Information Management and Retention**		P	O		X	X	X
SI-12(1)	LIMIT PERSONALLY IDENTIFIABLE INFORMATION ELEMENTS IN TESTING, TRAINING, AND RESEARCH		P	O				
SI-12(2)	MINIMIZE PERSONALLY IDENTIFIABLE INFORMATION		P	O				
SI-13	**Predictable Failure Prevention**			O	A			
SI-13(1)	TRANSFERRING COMPONENT RESPONSIBILITIES			O	A			
SI-13(2)	TIME LIMIT ON PROCESS EXECUTION WITHOUT SUPERVISION	W	Incorporated into SI-7(16).					
SI-13(3)	MANUAL TRANSFER BETWEEN COMPONENTS			O	A			
SI-13(4)	STANDBY COMPONENT INSTALLATION AND NOTIFICATION			O	A			
SI-13(5)	FAILOVER CAPABILITY			O	A			
SI-14	**Non-Persistence**			O	A			
SI-14(1)	REFRESH FROM TRUSTED SOURCES			O	A			
SI-15	**Information Output Filtering**			S	A			
SI-15(1)	LIMIT PERSONALLY IDENTIFIABLE INFORMATION DISSEMINATION		P	O/S	A			
SI-16	**Memory Protection**			S	A		X	X
SI-17	**Fail-Safe Procedures**			S	A			
SI-18	**Information Disposal**		P	O/S				
SI-19	**Data Quality Operations**		P	O/S				
SI-19(1)	UPDATING AND CORRECTING PERSONALLY IDENTIFIABLE INFORMATION		P	O/S				
SI-19(2)	DATA TAGS		P	O/S				
SI-19(3)	PERSONALLY IDENTIFIABLE INFORMATION COLLECTION		P	O/S				
SI-20	**De-Identification**		P	O/S				
SI-20(1)	COLLECTION		P	O/S				
SI-20(2)	ARCHIVING		P	O/S				
SI-20(3)	RELEASE		P	O/S				
SI-20(4)	REMOVAL, MASKING, ENCRYPTION, HASHING, OR REPLACEMENT OF DIRECT IDENTIFIERS		P	S				
SI-20(5)	STATISTICAL DISCLOSURE CONTROL		P	O/S				
SI-20(6)	DIFFERENTIAL PRIVACY		P	O/S				
SI-20(7)	VALIDATED SOFTWARE		P	O				
SI-20(8)	MOTIVATED INTRUDER		P	O/S				

Note: Privacy-related controls and control enhancements are not allocated to baselines in this table. See **Appendix F** for control selection and implementation guidance.

ATTACHMENT 1

CONSOLIDATED VIEW OF PRIVACY CONTROLS

SUMMARY LISTING OF PRIVACY CONTROLS AND IMPLEMENTATION GUIDANCE

Table F-1 provides a summary view of the base set of controls and enhancements from the control catalog in Chapter Three for which federal privacy programs have authority to select and oversee their implementation. Controls and enhancements are designated as either privacy (**P**) or joint (**J**).[42]

- **Privacy**: For controls and control enhancements that are marked *privacy*, privacy programs have sole authority to select and oversee these controls and enhancements.[43]

- **Joint**: For controls and control enhancements that are marked *joint*, authority and oversight are shared with information security programs. When a control or control enhancement is marked as joint, organizations may opt to do a joint implementation of the control or the privacy program may implement the privacy-relevant aspect of the control separately. For example, for AT-2, a privacy program may develop and conduct separate privacy-related training or it could elect to develop a coordinated privacy and security training with the security program.

Organizations may expand Table F-1 with additional controls from Chapter Three or other sources. Organizations ensure that the responsibility for the implementation, assessment, and monitoring of such controls is clearly defined and delineated between the information security and privacy programs. This includes defining the frequency of the control assessments and responding to any deficiencies in controls when discovered.

Table F-1 also provides guidance to federal privacy programs in the selection of controls through three selection criteria tags: required (**R**); situationally required (**S**); and discretionary (**D**).

- **Required**: Controls or control enhancements that are marked *required* must be selected and implemented based on applicable legal, regulatory, or policy requirements. Nonfederal organizations may use overlays to tailor their control selection to the laws, regulations or policies applicable to their organizations. See Appendix G for guidance on tailoring.

- **Situationally required**: Privacy programs evaluate whether controls or control enhancements that are marked *situationally required* must be selected and implemented based on applicable legal, regulatory, or policy requirements, because these requirements only apply in specific circumstances. In the absence of any such requirements, the organization may treat these controls or enhancements as discretionary.

- **Discretionary**: Controls or control enhancements that are marked *discretionary* can be selected and implemented on an optional basis. Organizations use privacy risk assessments to inform and guide the selection and implementation of these controls or control enhancements to mitigate identified privacy risks. Discretionary controls and control enhancements may not be relevant for all types of systems or in all circumstances. The reason for selecting and implementing discretionary controls may include the technical or resource capabilities of the

---

[42] Privacy-related control enhancements in Table F-1, joint or otherwise, cannot be selected and implemented without the selection and implementation of the associated base control. Such actions may require collaboration with security programs in cases where the security program has responsibility for the base control.

[43] This source of this authority is OMB Circular A-130.

privacy program. Internal organizational policy requirements may require the selection of discretionary controls for individual privacy programs.

Table F-2 provides a mapping between OMB Circular A-130 privacy requirements and relevant controls from the consolidated control catalog in Chapter Three. This mapping supports the implementation of the privacy requirements by federal agencies and nonfederal organizations that are required to meet such requirements based on federal contracts or agreements. However, federal agencies should not assume that the implementation of the controls means that they have met their obligations under OMB Circular A-130. Agencies may need to take additional, separate steps to fully comply with the privacy requirements of OMB Circular A-130.

Some of the controls mapped under Table F-2 may not appear in Table F-1 as privacy or joint controls. To maintain organizational awareness and support collaboration between privacy and security programs, privacy programs may use the keywords in Appendix H to locate privacy references in security controls that are not designated as joint controls.

TABLE F-1: SELECTION CRITERIA FOR PRIVACY-RELATED CONTROLS

CONTROL NUMBER	CONTROL NAME CONTROL ENHANCEMENT NAME	OWNER (PRIVACY [ ] OR JOINT [ ])	SELECTION CRITERIA
Selection Criteria Tags: **R** (Required) – **S** (Situationally-required) – **D** (Discretionary)			
AC-16	**Security and Privacy Attributes**	J	D
AC-16(1)	Security and Privacy Attributes | DYNAMIC ATTRIBUTE ASSOCIATION	J	D
AC-16(2)	Security and Privacy Attributes | ATTRIBUTE VALUE CHANGES BY AUTHORIZED INDIVIDUALS	J	D
AC-16(3)	Security and Privacy Attributes | MAINTENANCE OF ATTRIBUTE ASSOCIATIONS BY SYSTEM	J	D
AC-16(4)	Security and Privacy Attributes | ASSOCIATION OF ATTRIBUTES BY AUTHORIZED INDIVIDUALS	J	D
AC-16(5)	Security and Privacy Attributes | ATTRIBUTE DISPLAYS FOR OUTPUT DEVICES	J	D
AC-16(6)	Security and Privacy Attributes | MAINTENANCE OF ATTRIBUTE ASSOCIATION BY ORGANIZATION	J	D
AC-16(7)	Security and Privacy Attributes | CONSISTENT ATTRIBUTE INTERPRETATION	J	D
AC-16(8)	Security and Privacy Attributes | ASSOCIATION TECHNIQUES AND TECHNOLOGIES	J	D
AC-16(9)	Security and Privacy Attributes | ATTRIBUTE REASSIGNMENT	J	D
AC-16(10)	Security and Privacy Attributes | ATTRIBUTE CONFIGURATION BY AUTHORIZED INDIVIDUALS	J	D
AC-16(11)	Security and Privacy Attributes | AUDIT CHANGES	J	D
AC-21	**Information Sharing**	J	D
AC-23	**Data Mining Protection**	J	D
AT-1	**Security and Privacy Awareness and Training Policy and Procedures**	J	R
AT-2	**Security and Privacy Awareness Training**	J	R
AT-2(1)	Security and Privacy Awareness Training | PRACTICAL EXERCISES	J	D
AT-3	**Role-Based Security and Privacy Training**	J	R
AT-3(3)	Role-Based Security and Privacy Training | PRACTICAL EXERCISES	J	D
AT-3(5)	Role-Based Security and Privacy Training | PERSONALLY IDENTIFIABLE INFORMATION PROCESSING	P	R
AT-4	**Security and Privacy Training Records**	J	R
AU-3(3)	Audit Events | LIMIT PERSONALLY IDENTIFIABLE INFORMATION ELEMENTS	P	D
AU-11	**Audit Record Retention**	J	R
AU-12(4)	Audit Generation | QUERY PARAMETER AUDITS OF PERSONALLY IDENTIFIABLE INFORMATION	P	D
AU-16	**Cross-Organizational Auditing**	J	D
CA-1	**Assessment, Authorization, and Monitoring Policy and Procedures**	J	R
CA-2	**Assessments**	J	R
CA-2(1)	Assessments | INDEPENDENT ASSESSORS	J	D
CA-2(3)	Assessments | EXTERNAL ORGANIZATIONS	J	D
CA-5	**Plan of Action and Milestones**	J	R
CA-7	**Continuous Monitoring**	J	R
CA-7(1)	Continuous Monitoring | INDEPENDENT ASSESSMENT	J	D
CM-1	**Configuration Management Policy and Procedures**	J	R
CM-4	**Security and Privacy Impact Analyses**	J	R
CM-4(2)	Security and Privacy Impact Analyses | VERIFICATION OF SECURITY AND PRIVACY FUNCTIONS	J	D
CM-8(10)	System Component Inventory | DATA ACTION MAPPING	P	D
CM-12	**Information Location**	J	D
CM-12(1)	Information Location | AUTOMATED TOOLS TO SUPPORT INFORMATION LOCATION	J	D
CP-1	**Contingency Planning Policy and Procedures**	J	R

CONTROL NUMBER	CONTROL NAME CONTROL ENHANCEMENT NAME	OWNER (PRIVACY [P] OR JOINT [J])	SELECTION CRITERIA
CP-2	**Contingency Plan**	J	R
CP-2(1)	Contingency Plan | COORDINATE WITH RELATED PLANS	J	D
CP-2(3)	Contingency Plan | RESUME ESSENTIAL MISSIONS AND BUSINESS FUNCTIONS	J	D
CP-2(4)	Contingency Plan | RESUME ALL MISSIONS AND BUSINESS FUNCTIONS	J	D
CP-2(5)	Contingency Plan | CONTINUE ESSENTIAL MISSION AND BUSINESS FUNCTIONS	J	D
CP-2(7)	Contingency Plan | COORDINATE WITH EXTERNAL SERVICE PROVIDERS	J	D
CP-2(8)	Contingency Plan | IDENTIFY CRITICAL ASSETS	J	D
CP-3	**Contingency Training**	J	S
CP-3(1)	Contingency Training | SIMULATED EVENTS	J	D
CP-3(2)	Contingency Training | AUTOMATED TRAINING ENVIRONMENTS	J	D
CP-4	**Contingency Plan Testing**	J	R
CP-4(1)	Contingency Plan Testing | COORDINATE WITH RELATED PLANS	J	D
IA-1	**Identification and Authentication Policies and Procedures**	J	D
IA-4(4)	Identifier Management | IDENTIFY USER STATUS	J	D
IA-4(8)	Identifier Management | PAIRWISE PSEUDONYMOUS IDENTIFIERS	J	D
IA-8(6)	Identification and Authentication (Non-Organizational Users) | DISASSOCIABILITY	P	D
IP-1	**Individual Participation Policies and Procedures**	P	R
IP-2	**Consent**	P	S
IP-2(1)	Consent | ATTRIBUTE MANAGEMENT	P	D
IP-2(2)	Consent | JUST-IN-TIME NOTICE OF CONSENT	P	D
IP-3	**Redress**	P	S
IP-3(1)	Redress | NOTICE OF CORRECTION OR AMENDMENT	P	S
IP-3(2)	Redress | APPEAL	P	S
IP-4	**Privacy Notice**	P	S
IP-4(1)	Privacy Notice | JUST-IN-TIME NOTICE OF PRIVACY AUTHORIZATION	P	D
IP-5	**Privacy Act Statements**	P	S
IP-6	**Individual Access**	P	S
IR-1	**Incident Response Policy and Procedures**	J	R
IR-2	**Incident Response Training**	J	R
IR-2(1)	Incident Response Training | SIMULATED EVENTS	J	D
IR-2(2)	Incident Response Training | AUTOMATED TRAINING ENVIRONMENTS	J	D
IR-3	**Incident Response Testing**	J	D
IR-3(2)	Incident Response Testing | COORDINATION WITH RELATED PLANS	J	D
IR-4	**Incident Handling**	J	R
IR-5	**Incident Monitoring**	J	R
IR-5(1)	Incident Monitoring | AUTOMATED TRACKING, DATA COLLECTION, AND ANALYSIS	J	D
IR-6	**Incident Reporting**	J	R
IR-7	**Incident Response Assistance**	J	R
IR-8	**Incident Response Plan**	J	R
IR-8(1)	Incident Response Plan | PERSONALLY IDENTIFIABLE INFORMATION PROCESSES	P	S
IR-9	**Information Spillage Response**	J	D
MP-6(9)	Media Sanitization | DESTRUCTION OF PERSONALLY IDENTIFIABLE INFORMATION	P	S
PA-1	**Privacy Authorization Policies and Procedures**	P	R

CONTROL NUMBER	CONTROL NAME CONTROL ENHANCEMENT NAME	OWNER (PRIVACY OR JOINT)	SELECTION CRITERIA
PA-2	**Authority to Collect**	P	S
PA-3	**Purpose Specification**	P	S
PA-3(1)	Purpose Specification | USAGE RESTRICTIONS OF PERSONALLY IDENTIFIABLE INFORMATION	P	R
PA-3(2)	Purpose Specification | AUTOMATION	P	D
PA-4	**Information Sharing with Third Parties**	P	S
PL-1	**Policy Planning and Procedures**	J	R
PL-2	**Security and Privacy Plan**	J	R
PL-2(3)	System Security and Privacy Plan | PLAN AND COORDINATE WITH OTHER ORGANIZATIONAL ENTITIES	J	R
PL-4	**Rules of Behavior**	J	R
PL-7	**Concepts of Operation**	J	D
PL-8	**Information Security and Privacy Architecture**	J	R
PL-8(2)	Information Security and Privacy Architecture | SUPPLIER DIVERSITY	J	D
PL-9	**Central Management**	J	R
PM-3	**Information Security and Privacy Resources**	J	R
PM-4	**Plan of Action and Milestones Process**	J	R
PM-6	**Measures of Performance**	J	R
PM-7	**Enterprise Architecture**	J	R
PM-8	**Critical Infrastructure Plan**	J	S
PM-9	**Risk Management Strategy**	J	R
PM-11	**Mission and Business Process Definition**	J	R
PM-13	**Security and Privacy Workforce**	J	R
PM-14	**Testing, Training, And Monitoring**	J	R
PM-15	**Contacts with Security and Privacy Groups and Associations**	J	D
PM-18	**Privacy Program Plan**	P	R
PM-19	**Privacy Program Roles**	P	R
PM-20	**System of Records Notice**	P	S
PM-21	**Dissemination of Privacy Program Information**	P	S
PM-22	**Accounting of Disclosures**	P	S
PM-23	**Data Quality Management**	P	R
PM-23(1)	Data Quality Management | AUTOMATION	P	D
PM-23(2)	Data Quality Management | DATA TAGGING	P	D
PM-23(3)	Data Quality Management | UPDATING PERSONALLY IDENTIFIABLE INFORMATION	P	S
PM-24	**Data Management Board**	P	S
PM-25	**Data Integrity Board**	P	S
PM-26	**Minimization of Personally Identifiable Information Used for Testing, Training, and Research**	P	S
PM-27	**Individual Access Control**	P	S
PM-28	**Complaint Management**	P	S
PM-29	**Inventory of Personally Identifiable Information**	P	R
PM-30	**Privacy Reporting**	P	R
RA-1	**Risk Assessment Policy and Procedures**	J	R
RA-3	**Risk Assessment**	J	S
RA-7	**Risk Response**	J	S

CONTROL NUMBER	CONTROL NAME CONTROL ENHANCEMENT NAME	OWNER (PRIVACY [P] OR JOINT [J])	SELECTION CRITERIA
RA-8	**Privacy Impact Assessments**	P	S
SA-1	**System and Services Acquisition Policy and Procedures**	J	R
SA-3	**System Development Life Cycle**	J	D
SA-4	**Acquisition Process**	J	R
SA-8	**Security and Privacy Engineering Principles**	J	D
SA-9	**External System Services**	J	S
SA-9(3)	External System Services | ESTABLISH AND MAINTAIN TRUST RELATIONSHIP WITH PROVIDERS	J	D
SA-9(5)	External System Services | PROCESSING, STORAGE, AND SERVICE LOCATION	J	D
SA-11	**Developer Testing and Evaluation**	J	S
SC-1	**System and Communications Protections Policy and Procedures**	J	R
SC-7(24)	Boundary Protection | PERSONALLY IDENTIFIABLE INFORMATION	P	D
SC-16	**Transmission of Security and Privacy Attributes**	J	D
SC-42(2)	Sensor Capability and Data | AUTHORIZED USE	J	D
SC-42(4)	Sensor Capability and Data | NOTICE OF COLLECTION	P	D
SC-42(5)	Sensor Capability and Data | COLLECTION MINIMIZATION	P	D
SI-1	**System Information and Integrity Policy and Procedures**	J	D
SI-2(7)	Flaw Remediation | PERSONALLY IDENTIFIABLE INFORMATION	P	D
SI-4(25)	System Monitoring | PERSONALLY IDENTIFIABLE INFORMATION MONITORING	P	D
SI-6	**Security and Privacy Function Verification**	J	D
SI-6(3)	Security and Privacy Function Verification | REPORT VERIFICATION RESULTS	J	D
SI-12	**Information Management and Retention**	J	R
SI-12(1)	Information Management and Retention | LIMIT PERSONALLY IDENTIFIABLE INFORMATION ELEMENTS	J	R
SI-12(2)	Information Management and Retention | MINIMIZE PERSONALLY IDENTIFIABLE INFORMATION IN TESTING, TRAINING, AND RESEARCH	J	R
SI-15(1)	Information Output Filtering | LIMIT PERSONALLY IDENTIFIABLE INFORMATION DISSEMINATION	P	S
SI-18	**Information Disposal**	P	D
SI-19	**Data Quality Operations**	P	D
SI-19(1)	Data Quality Operations | UPDATING AND CORRECTING PERSONALLY IDENTIFIABLE INFORMATION	P	S
SI-19(2)	Data Quality Operations | DATA TAGS	P	D
SI-19(3)	Data Quality Operations | PERSONALLY IDENTIFIABLE INFORMATION COLLECTION	P	S
SI-20	**De-Identification**	P	S
SI-20(1)	De-Identification | COLLECTION	P	D
SI-20(2)	De-Identification | ARCHIVING	P	D
SI-20(3)	De-Identification | RELEASE	P	D
SI-20(4)	De-Identification | REMOVAL, MASKING, ENCRYPTION, HASHING, OR REPLACEMENT OF DIRECT IDENTIFIERS	P	D
SI-20(5)	De-Identification | STATISTICAL DISCLOSURE CONTROL	P	D
SI-20(6)	De-Identification | DIFFERENTIAL PRIVACY	P	D
SI-20(7)	De-Identification | VALIDATED SOFTWARE	P	D
SI-20(8)	De-Identification | MOTIVATED INTRUDER	P	D

TABLE F-2: MAPPING OMB CIRCULAR A-130 REQUIREMENTS TO PRIVACY-RELATED CONTROLS

RESPONSIBILITY	DESCRIPTION	OMB A-130	CONTROLS
General Requirements			
Establish and maintain a comprehensive privacy program.	Agencies shall establish and maintain a comprehensive privacy program that ensures compliance with applicable privacy requirements, develops and evaluates privacy policy, and manages privacy risks.	Main Body § 5(f)(1)(a); Appendix I §§ 3(b), 3(f), 4(e).	PA-1, PM-18
Ensure compliance with privacy requirements and manage privacy risks.	Agencies shall ensure compliance with all applicable statutory, regulatory, and policy requirements and use privacy impact assessments and other tools to manage privacy risks. Agencies shall cost-effectively manage privacy risks and reduce such risks to an acceptable level.	Main Body §§ 4(g), 5(e)(1)(d), 5(f)(1)(a); Appendix I § 3(a), 3(b)(4), 3(f), 3(g).	CA-1, IP-4, PA-1, PM-3, PM-9, PM-19
Monitor Federal law, regulation, and policy for changes.	Agencies shall monitor Federal law, regulation, and policy for changes that affect privacy.	Main Body § 5(f)(1)(c).	IP-4, PM-4, PM-19, SA-1
Develop and maintain a privacy program plan.	Agencies shall develop and maintain a privacy program plan that provides an overview of the agency's privacy program, including a description of the structure of the privacy program, the resources dedicated to the privacy program, the role of the SAOP and other privacy officials and staff, the strategic goals and objectives of the privacy program, the program management controls and common controls in place or planned for meeting applicable privacy requirements and managing privacy risks, and any other information determined necessary by the agency's privacy program.	Appendix I § 4(c)(2), 4(e)(1).	IP-1, IP-2, IP-4, MA-1, MP-1, PA-1, PL-1, PM-4, PM-18, PM-19, PM-20, PM-21, PM-28, SI-1
Designate a Senior Agency Official for Privacy.	The head of each agency shall designate an SAOP who has agency-wide responsibility and accountability for developing, implementing, and maintaining an agency-wide privacy program to ensure compliance with all applicable statues, regulations, and policies regarding the creation, collection, use, processing, storage, maintenance, dissemination, disclosure, and disposal of PII by programs and information systems, developing and evaluating privacy policy, and managing privacy risks at the agency.	Main Body § 5(f)(1)(b); Appendix I § 4(e).	CA-6, PL-9, PM-19
Ensure coordination between privacy and other programs.	Agencies shall ensure that the SAOP and the agency's privacy personnel closely coordinate with the agency CIO, senior agency information security officer, and other agency offices and officials, as appropriate.	Main Body §§ 4(h), 5(f)(1)(k); Appendix I §§ 3(b)(11), 4(e)(10).	PA-4, PL-9, PM-11, PM-15, PM-19, SA-4

RESPONSIBILITY	DESCRIPTION	OMB A-130	CONTROLS
Ensure that privacy is addressed throughout the life cycle of each information system.	Agencies shall ensure that privacy is addressed throughout the life cycle of each agency information system.	Main Body §§ 4(g), 5(a)(1)(c)(i), 5(b)(4); Appendix I § 4(b)(2).	CA-5, PL-7, PL-8, PM-7, PM-23, PM-26, PM-24, SC-1, SC-43, SI-19
Incorporate privacy requirements into enterprise architecture.	Agencies shall incorporate Federal privacy requirements into the agency's enterprise architecture to ensure that risk is addressed and information systems achieve the necessary levels of trustworthiness, protection, and resilience.	Appendix I § 4(b)(5).	AU-2, AU-3, CA-1, CA-3, CA-5, CM-1, MA-1, MA-2, MP-1, PL-2, PL-7, PL-8, PM-7, PM-8, PM-9, SA-3, SA-9, SC-1, SC-7, SI-6
Comply with the Privacy Act.	Agencies shall comply with the requirements of the Privacy Act and ensure that Privacy Act system of records notices are published, revised, and rescinded, as required.	Main Body § 5(f)(1)(g).	IP-1, IP-2, IP-3, IP-4, IP-5, IP-6, PM-20, SC-43
Conduct privacy impact assessments.	Agencies shall conduct privacy impact assessments in accordance with the E-Government Act, absent an applicable exception, and make the privacy impact assessments available to the public in accordance with OMB policy when the agency develops, procures, or uses information technology to create, collect, use, process, store, maintain, disseminate, disclose, or dispose of personally identifiable information (PII).	Main Body § 5(f)(1)(i), Appendix II § 5(e).	CA-1, CA-2, PA-2, PA-3, PL-2, RA-8, SI-10(6), SI-12(1), SI-12(2), SI-15(1)
Balance the need for information collection with the privacy risks.	Agencies shall ensure that the design of information collections is consistent with the intended use of the information, and the need for new information is balanced against any privacy risks.	Main Body § 4(i).	CA-1, CA-2, IP-2, PL-7, PL-9, PM-9, PM-11, SC-1, SC-43
Comply with requirements for disclosure and dissemination.	Agencies shall comply with all applicable privacy statutes and policies governing the disclosure or dissemination of information and comply with any other valid access, use, and dissemination restrictions.	Main Body § 5(e)(1)(b)-(d), 5(e)(7)(h).	AC-21, CA-3, IP-1, IP-2, IP-3, IP-4, IP-5, IP-6, MP-1, PM-22, SA-4, SC-1, SC-7, SI-21
Maintain and post privacy policies on websites, mobile applications, and other digital services.	Agencies shall maintain and post privacy policies on all agency websites, mobile applications, and other digital services, in accordance with the E-Government Act and OMB policy.	Main Body § 5(f)(1)(j).	IP-1, IP-2, IP-3, IP-4, IP-5, IP-6, PM-20, PM-21, PM-22, PM-28, SC-42(4)
Provide performance metrics and reports.	Agencies shall provide performance metrics information and reports in accordance with processes established by OMB and DHS pursuant to FISMA.	Appendix I § 4(1).	AU-2, AU-3, CA-7, IP-4, PM-6, PM-19, SI-20

RESPONSIBILITY	DESCRIPTION	OMB A-130	CONTROLS
Considerations for Managing PII			
Maintain an inventory of agency information systems that involve PII and regularly review and reduce PII to the minimum necessary.	Agencies shall maintain an inventory of the agency's information systems that create, collect, use, process, store, maintain, disseminate, disclose, or dispose of PII to allow the agency to regularly review its PII and ensure, to the extent reasonably practicable, that such PII is accurate, relevant, timely, and complete; and to allow the agency to reduce its PII to the minimum necessary for the proper performance of authorized agency functions.	Main Body § 5(a)(1)(a)(ii), 5(f)(1)(e).	CA-3, CM-8(10), CM-8(11), PL-8, PM-18, PM-29, SC-16, SC-28, SI-20
Eliminate unnecessary collection, maintenance, and use of Social Security numbers.	Agencies shall take steps to eliminate unnecessary collection, maintenance, and use of Social Security numbers, and explore alternatives to the use of Social Security numbers as a personal identifier.	Main Body § 5(f)(1)(f).	CM-8(11), CM-8(12), IA-8(6), IP-2, IP-3, IP-4, IP-5, IP-6, MP-1, MP-6, PL-7, PM-11, PM-26, SC-1, SC-7, SC-28, SC-43, SI-10(6), SI-12(1), SI-12(2), SI-15(1)
Follow approved records retention schedules for records with PII.	Agencies shall ensure that all records with PII are maintained in accordance with applicable records retention or disposition schedules approved by NARA.	Main Body § 5(f)(1)(h).	AU-11, AT-4, MP-6, PL-7, PM-18, PM-26, SC-16, SC-28, SI-7, SI-12(1), SI-12(2)
Limit the creation, collection, use, processing, storage, maintenance, dissemination, and disclosure of PII.	Agencies shall limit the creation, collection, use, processing, storage, maintenance, dissemination, and disclosure of PII to that which is legally authorized, relevant, and reasonably deemed necessary for the proper performance of agency functions.	Main Body § 5(f)(1)(d).	AC-1, MP-1, MP-6, PL-7, PM-11, PM-23, PM-24, PM-26, SA-3, SA-9, SC-1, SC-28, SC-42(5), SC-43, SI-10(6), SI-12(1), SI-12(2), SI-15(1)
Require entities with which PII is shared to maintain the PII in an information system with a particular categorization level.	Agencies that share PII shall require, as appropriate, other agencies and entities with which they share PII to maintain the PII in an information system with a particular NIST FIPS Publication 199 confidentiality impact level, as determined by the agency sharing the PII.	Appendix I § 3(c).	AC-1, AC-21, IA-1, IP-2, MP-1, PA-4, PL-2, PL-7, SC-7, SC-16, SC-28, SI-7, SI-20
Impose conditions on the creation, collection, use, processing, storage, maintenance, dissemination, disclosure, and disposal of shared PII through agreements.	Agencies that share PII with other agencies or entities shall impose, where appropriate, conditions (including the selection and implementation of particular security and privacy controls) that govern the creation, collection, use, processing, storage, maintenance, dissemination, disclosure, and disposal of the PII through written agreements, including contracts, data use agreements, information exchange agreements, and memoranda of understanding.	Appendix I § 3(d).	AC-1, AC-21, CA-3, IA-1, IP-2, IP-3, IP-6, MP-6, PA-4, PL-2, PL-7, PL-8, PM-24, SA-3, SA-9, SC-1, SC-7, SC-16, SC-28, SC-42(5), SC-43, SI-6, SI-7, SI-10(6), SI-12(1), SI-12(2), SI-15(1), SI-19

RESPONSIBILITY	DESCRIPTION	OMB A-130	CONTROLS
Budget and Acquisition			
Identify and plan for resources needed for privacy program.	Agencies shall identify and plan for the resources needed to implement privacy programs.	Appendix I § 4(b)(1).	PM-15, SA-1, SA-4
Include privacy requirements in IT solicitations.	Agencies shall include privacy requirements in solicitations for IT and services.	Main body § 5(d)(1)(j).	CA-3, MA-1, MP-2, MP-6, PL-7, PL-8, SA-1, SA-4,
Establish a process to evaluate privacy risks for IT investments.	Agencies shall consider privacy when analyzing IT investments, and establish a decision-making process that shall cover the life of each information system and include explicit criteria for analyzing the projected and actual costs, benefits, and risks, including privacy risks, associated with the IT investments.	Main Body § 5(d)(3), 5(d)(4)(b).	CA-1, MA-2, PL-1, PL-2, PL-7, PL-8, PM-9, SA-1, SA-4
Ensure that privacy risks are addressed and costs are included in IT capital investment plans and budgetary requests.	The SAOP shall review IT capital investment plans and budgetary requests to ensure that privacy requirements (and associated privacy controls), as well as any associated costs, are explicitly identified and included, with respect to any IT resources that will be used to create, collect, use, process, store, maintain, disseminate, disclose, or dispose of PII. Agencies shall ensure that agency budget justification materials, in their initial budget submission to OMB, include a statement affirming that the SAOP has conducted the necessary review.	Main Body § 5(a)(3)(e)(ii), 5(d)(3)(e); Appendix I § 4(b)(2), 4(e)(6).	PA-1, PL-2, PL-7, PL-8, PM-9, PM-19, SA-4
Ensure that investment plans meet the privacy requirements appropriate for the life cycle stage of the investment.	Agencies shall ensure that investment plans submitted to OMB as part of the budget process meet the privacy requirements appropriate for the life cycle stage of the investment.	Appendix I § 4(b)(4).	MP-1, MP-6, PL-1, PL-2, PL-7, PL-8, SA-4
Upgrade, replace, or retire unprotected information systems.	Agencies shall plan and budget to upgrade, replace, or retire any information systems for which protections commensurate with risk cannot be effectively implemented.	Appendix I § 4(b)(3).	CA-3, CA-5, CM-1, MA-2, MP-1, MP-6, PL-7, PL-8, SC-1, SC-28
Ensure that SAOPs are made aware of information systems and components that cannot be protected.	Agencies shall ensure that, in a timely manner, SAOPs are made aware of information systems and components that cannot be appropriately protected or secured, and that such systems are given a high priority for upgrade, replacement, or retirement.	Main Body § 5(a)(1)(c)(ii); Appendix I § 3(b)(10).	AC-21, CA-5, CA-6, IP-2, IP-4, IP-5, MA-2, MP-1, PA-1, PL-2, PL-7, PL-8, PM-19, SA-4, SC-1, SC-7, SC-28

RESPONSIBILITY	DESCRIPTION	OMB A-130	CONTROLS
Contractors and Third Parties			
Ensure that contracts and other agreements incorporate privacy requirements.	Agencies shall ensure that terms and conditions in contracts, and other agreements involving the creation, collection, use, processing, storage, maintenance, dissemination, disclosure, and disposal of Federal information, incorporate privacy requirements and are sufficient to enable agencies to meet Federal and agency-specific requirements pertaining to the protection of Federal information.	Main Body § 5(a)(1)(b)(ii); Appendix I § 4(j)(1).	AC-21, CA-3, IA-1, IP-2, IP-3, IP-4, IP-5, IP-6, MA-2, MP-1, PA-4, PL-1, PL-2, PL-7, PL-9, PM-18, SA-3, SC-43
Maintain agency-wide privacy training for all employees and contractors.	Agencies shall develop, maintain, and implement mandatory agency-wide privacy awareness and training programs for all employees and contractors.	Appendix I § 4(h)(1)-(2), (4)-(7).	AT-2, AT-3, AT-4, PL-4, PM-14, PM-15, SA-4, SC-43
Ensure that the Privacy Act applies to contractors where required.	Agencies shall, consistent with the agency's authority, ensure that the requirements of the Privacy Act apply to a Privacy Act system of records when a contractor operates the system of records on behalf of the agency to accomplish an agency function.	Appendix I § 4(j)(3).	IP-4, PA-4, PM-20, PM-21, SA-4
Oversee information systems operated by contractors.	Agencies shall provide oversight of information systems used or operated by contractors or other entities on behalf of the Federal Government or that collect or maintain Federal information on behalf of the Federal Government	Appendix I § 4(j)(2).	CA-6, MA-1, MA-2, PA-2, PA-3, PA-4, PL-2, PM-8, SA-9, SC-1, SI-20
Implement policies on privacy oversight of contractors.	Agencies shall document and implement policies and procedures for privacy oversight of contractors and other entities, to include ensuring appropriate vetting and access control processes for contractors and others with access to information systems containing Federal information.	Appendix I § 4(j)(2)(a).	CA-5, IP-1, IP-2, IP-3, IP-4, IP-5, IP-6, PA-4, SA-4, SC-42(4)
Ensure implementation of privacy controls for contractor information systems.	Agencies shall ensure that privacy controls of information systems and services used or operated by contractors or other entities on behalf of the agency are effectively implemented and comply with NIST standards and guidelines and agency requirements.	Appendix I § 4(j)(2)(b).	AC-1, AC-21, IA-1, IA-8, MA-1, MP-1, PA-4, PL-2, SA-4, SA-9, SC-7, SC-28
Maintain an inventory of contractor information systems.	Agencies shall ensure that information systems used or operated by contractors or other entities on behalf of the agency are included in the agency's inventory of information systems.	Appendix I § 4(j)(2)(c).	CM-8(10), CM-8(11), MA-2, PA-4, PL-8, PM-29, SA-4, SA-9, SC-28, SI-20

RESPONSIBILITY	DESCRIPTION	OMB A-130	CONTROLS
Ensure that incident response procedures are in place for contractor information systems.	Agencies shall ensure that procedures are in place for incident response for information systems used or operated by contractors or other entities on behalf of the agency, including timelines for notification of affected individuals and reporting to OMB, DHS, and other entities as required in OMB guidance.	Appendix I § 4(j)(2)(e).	IR-1, IR-7, IR-8, SA-4, SA-9
Privacy Impact Assessments			
See General Requirement: Privacy Impact Assessment	See General Requirement: Conduct Privacy Impact Assessment	Appendix II § 5(e).	Same as General Requirement: Conduct Privacy Impact Assessments
Workforce Management			
Ensure that the SAOP is involved in assessing and addressing privacy hiring, training, and professional development needs.	Agencies shall ensure that the SAOP is involved in assessing and addressing the hiring, training, and professional development needs of the agency with respect to privacy.	Main Body § 5(c)(6).	AT-2, AT-3, PM-13
Maintain a workforce planning process.	Agencies shall ensure that the CHCO, CIO, CAO, and SAOP develop and maintain a current workforce planning process to ensure that the agency can anticipate and respond to changing mission requirements, maintain workforce skills in a rapidly developing IT environment, and recruit and retain the IT talent needed to accomplish the mission.	Main Body § 5(c)(1).	AT-1, PM-11, PM-13, PM-14, PM-19
Develop a set of privacy competency requirements.	Agencies shall ensure that the CHCO, CIO, CAO, and SAOP develop a set of competency requirements for information resources staff, including program managers and information security, privacy, and IT leadership positions.	Main Body § 5(c)(1).	AT-1, AT-2, PM-14, PM-19
Ensure that the workforce has the appropriate knowledge and skill.	Agencies shall ensure that the workforce, which supports the acquisition, management, maintenance, and use of information resources, has the appropriate knowledge and skill.	Main Body § 5(c)(2).	AT-2, AT-3, PM-13, PM-14
Take advantage of flexible hiring authorities for specialized positions.	Agencies shall ensure that the CIO, CHCO, SAOP, and other hiring managers take advantage of flexible hiring authorities for specialized positions, as established by OPM.	Main Body § 5(c)(7).	PM-19, PM-18
Training and Accountability			
Maintain agency-wide privacy training for all employees and contractors.	Agencies shall develop, maintain, and implement mandatory agency-wide privacy awareness and training programs for all employees and contractors.	Appendix I § 4(h)(1).	AT-1, AT-2, AT-3, PM-13

RESPONSIBILITY	DESCRIPTION	OMB A-130	CONTROLS
Ensure that privacy training is consistent with applicable policies.	Agencies shall ensure that the privacy awareness and training programs are consistent with applicable policies, standards, and guidelines issued by OMB, NIST, and OPM.	Appendix I § 4(h)(2).	AT-1, AT-2, AT-3, SC-43
Apprise agency employees about available privacy resources.	Agencies shall apprise agency employees about available privacy resources, such as products, techniques, or expertise.	Appendix I § 4(h)(3).	AT-2, AT-3, PM-15
Provide foundational and advanced privacy training.	Agencies shall provide foundational as well as more advanced levels of privacy training to information system users (including managers, senior executives, and contractors) and ensure that measures are in place to test the knowledge level of information system users.	Appendix I § 4(h)(4).	AT-2, AT-3, PM-13, PM-14, PM-15, SC-43
Provide role-based privacy training to appropriate employees and contractors.	Agencies shall provide role-based privacy training to employees and contractors with assigned privacy roles and responsibilities, including managers, before authorizing access to Federal information or information systems or performing assigned duties.	Appendix I § 4(h)(5).	AT-2, AT-3, PM-13, PM-14
Hold personnel accountable for complying with privacy requirements and policies.	Agencies shall implement policies and procedures to ensure that all personnel are held accountable for complying with agency-wide privacy requirements and policies.	Appendix I § 3(b)(9).	AC-1, AU-2, AT-2, AT-3, AT-4
Establish rules of behavior for employees and contractors with access to PII and consequences for violating the rules.	Agencies shall establish rules of behavior, including consequences for violating rules of behavior, for employees and contractors that have access to Federal information or information systems, including those that create, collect, use, process, store, maintain, disseminate, disclose, or dispose of PII.	Appendix I § 4(h)(6).	AT-1, AT-2, AT-3, PL-4, PM-14, PM-21
Ensure that employees and contractors read and agree to rules of behavior.	Agencies shall ensure that employees and contractors have read and agreed to abide by the rules of behavior for the Federal information and information systems for which they require access prior to being granted access.	Appendix I § 4(h)(7).	AC-1, AT-2, AT-3, AT-4, IA-1, IA-8(6), PL-4
Incident Response			
Maintain formal incident management and response policies and capabilities.	Agencies shall maintain formal incident response capabilities and mechanisms, implement formal incident management policies, and provide adequate training and awareness for employees and contractors on how to report and respond to incidents.	Appendix I § 4(f)(1), (7)-(8).	IR-1, IR-7, IR-8, SI-1, SI-4, SI-19
Establish roles and responsibilities to ensure oversight and coordination of incident response.	Agencies shall establish clear roles and responsibilities to ensure the oversight and coordination of incident response activities and that incidents are documented, reported, investigated, and handled.	Appendix I § 4(f)(3).	IR-1, IR-7, IR-8

RESPONSIBILITY	DESCRIPTION	OMB A-130	CONTROLS
Periodically test incident response procedures.	Agencies shall periodically test incident response procedures to ensure effectiveness of such procedures.	Appendix I § 4(f)(4).	CA-5, IR-1, IR-3, MP-6, SI-2
Document incident response lessons learned and update procedures.	Agencies shall document lessons learned for incident response and update procedures annually or as required by OMB or DHS.	Appendix I § 4(f)(5).	CA-5, IR-1, IR-7, IR-8
Ensure that processes are in place to verify corrective actions.	Agencies shall ensure that processes are in place to verify corrective actions.	Appendix I § 4(f)(6).	CA-5, IR-1, IR-7, IR-8, SI-1, SI-19
Report incidents in accordance with OMB guidance.	Agencies shall report incidents to OMB, DHS, the CIO, the SAOP, their respective inspectors general and general counsel, law enforcement, and Congress in accordance with procedures issued by OMB.	Appendix I § 4(f)(9).	AU-2, AU-11, IR-1, IR-7, IR-8,
Provide reports on incidents as required.	Agencies shall provide reports on incidents as required by FISMA, OMB policy, DHS binding operational directives, Federal information security incident center guidelines, NIST guidelines, and agency procedures.	Appendix I § 4(f)(10).	AU-2, AU-11, CA-5, IR-1, IR-7, IR-8, SI-19
Risk Management Framework			
Implement a risk management framework.	Agencies shall implement a risk management framework to guide and inform the categorization of Federal information and information systems; the selection, implementation, and assessment of privacy controls; the authorization of information systems and common controls; and the continuous monitoring of information systems.	Appendix I § 3(a), 3(b)(5).	CA-1, CA-2, MA-1, PL-1, PL-9, PM-4, PM-9, RA-1, SI-1
Review and approve the categorization of information systems that involve PII.	The SAOP shall review and approve, in accordance with NIST FIPS Publication 199 and NIST Special Publication 800-60, the categorization of information systems that create, collect, use, process, store, maintain, disseminate, disclose, or dispose of PII.	Appendix I § 4(a)(2), 4(e)(7).	CA-2, CM-8(1), CM-8(11), PL-2, PL-8, PM-19, RA-3, RA-8, SA-3, SI-10(6), SI-12(1), SI-12(2), SI-15(1)
Designate program management, common, information system-specific, and hybrid privacy controls.	The SAOP shall designate which privacy controls will be treated as program management, common, information system-specific, and hybrid privacy controls at the agency. Agencies shall designate common controls in order to provide cost-effective privacy capabilities that can be inherited by multiple agency information systems or programs.	Appendix I § 4(c)(12), 4(e)(5).	CA-2, CM-1, MP-1, PL-1, PL-2, PL-9, PM-19, SA-3, SI-1

RESPONSIBILITY	DESCRIPTION	OMB A-130	CONTROLS
Implement a privacy control selection process.	Agencies shall employ a process to select and implement privacy controls for information systems and programs that satisfies applicable privacy requirements in OMB guidance, including, but not limited to, Appendix I to this Circular and OMB Circular A-108, *Federal Agency Responsibilities for Review, Reporting, and Publication under the Privacy Act.*	Appendix I § 4(c)(6).	CA-1, CA-2, CM-1, PL-2, PM-9, SI-1
Develop, approve, and maintain privacy plans for information systems.	The SAOP shall review and approve the privacy plans for agency information systems prior to authorization, reauthorization, or ongoing authorization. Agencies shall develop and maintain a privacy plan that details the privacy controls selected for an information system that are in place or planned for meeting applicable privacy requirements and managing privacy risks, details how the controls have been implemented, and describes the methodologies and metrics that will be used to assess the controls.	Appendix I § 4(c)(9), 4(e)(8).	CA-1, CA-2, CA-3, CA-5, MA-1, MP-1, PA-1, PL-1, PL-2, PL-7, PM-19, SA-3
Identify privacy control assessment methodologies and metrics.	The SAOP shall identify assessment methodologies and metrics to determine whether privacy controls are implemented correctly, operating as intended, and sufficient to ensure compliance with applicable privacy requirements and manage privacy risks.	Appendix I § 4(e)(4).	CA-1, PL-1, PM-6, PM-11, PM-19, RA-3, RA-8
Conduct assessments of privacy controls.	The SAOP shall conduct and document the results of privacy control assessments to verify the continued effectiveness of all privacy controls selected and implemented at the agency across all agency risk management tiers to ensure continued compliance with applicable privacy requirements and manage privacy risks. Agencies shall conduct and document privacy control assessments prior to the operation of an information system, and periodically thereafter, consistent with the frequency defined in the agency privacy continuous monitoring strategy and the agency risk tolerance.	Appendix I §§ 3(b)(6), 4(c)(13) (14), 4(e)(3).	CA-1, CA-2, MA-2, PL-2, PL-7, PM-19, RA-3, RA-8, SI-4
Correct deficiencies that are identified in information systems.	Agencies shall correct deficiencies that are identified through privacy assessments, the privacy continuous monitoring program, or internal or external audits and reviews, to include OMB reviews. Agencies shall use agency plans of action and milestones to record and manage the mitigation and remediation of identified weaknesses and deficiencies, not associated with accepted risks, in agency information systems.	Appendix I § 4(c)(15), 4(k).	CA-3, CA-5, MA-2, MP-6, PL-2, PL-8, PM-9, RA-8, SC-7, SC-16, SI-2, SI-4, SI-7, SI-10(6), SI-12(1), SI-12(2), SI-15, SI-19

RESPONSIBILITY	DESCRIPTION	OMB A-130	CONTROLS
Develop and maintain a privacy continuous monitoring strategy.	The SAOP shall develop and maintain a privacy continuous monitoring strategy, a formal document that catalogs the available privacy controls implemented at the agency across the agency risk management tiers and ensures that the privacy controls are effectively monitored on an ongoing basis by assigning an agency-defined assessment frequency to each control that is sufficient to ensure compliance with applicable privacy requirements and to manage privacy risks.	Appendix I § 4(d)(9), 4(e)(2).	AU-2, AT-4, CA-1, CA-7, MA-1, MA-2, PM-19, SA-3, SI-4, SI-6, SI-20, SI-19
Establish and maintain a privacy continuous monitoring program.	The SAOP shall establish and maintain an agency-wide privacy continuous monitoring program that implements the agency's privacy continuous monitoring strategy and maintains ongoing awareness of threats and vulnerabilities that may pose privacy risks; monitors changes to information systems and environments of operation that create, collect, use, process, store, maintain, disseminate, disclose, or dispose of PII; and conducts privacy control assessments to verify the continued effectiveness of all privacy controls selected and implemented at the agency across the agency risk management tiers to ensure continued compliance with applicable privacy requirements and manage privacy risks. Agencies shall ensure that a robust privacy continuous monitoring program is in place before agency information systems are eligible for ongoing authorization.	Appendix I §§ 3(b)(6), 4(d)(10)-(11), 4(e)(2).	AU-2, AT-4, CA-1, CA-7, MA-2, PL-9, PM-19, SC-43, SI-4, SI-6, SI-20, SI-19
Review authorization packages for information systems that involve PII.	The SAOP shall review authorization packages for information systems that create, collect, use, process, store, maintain, disseminate, disclose, or dispose of PII to ensure compliance with applicable privacy requirements and manage privacy risks, prior to authorizing officials making risk determination and acceptance decisions.	Appendix I § 4(e)(9).	CA-1, CA-2, CA-6, MA-1, MA-2, PA-1, PA-2, PA-3, PL-2, PL-7, PM-11, PM-19, PM-26, SC-43, SI-6, SI-20
Encrypt moderate-impact and high-impact information.	Agencies shall encrypt all NIST FIPS Publication 199 moderate-impact and high-impact information at rest and in transit, unless encrypting such information is technically infeasible or would demonstrably affect the ability of agencies to carry out their respective missions, functions, or operations; and the risk of not encrypting is accepted by the authorizing official and approved by the agency CIO, in consultation with the SAOP (as appropriate).	Appendix I § 4(i)(14).	CA-3, PL-7, PL-8, SA-9, SC-1, SC-16, SC-28 SI-6, SI-7, SI-10(6), SI-12(1), SI-12(2), SI-15(1)

RESPONSIBILITY	DESCRIPTION	OMB A-130	CONTROLS
Managing PII Collected for Statistical Purposes under a Pledge of Confidentiality			
Confidentially manage PII collected for statistical purposes.	Information acquired by an agency or component under a pledge of confidentiality and for exclusively statistical purposes shall be used by officers, employees, or agents of the agency exclusively for statistical purposes. Statistical purpose refers to the description, estimation, or analysis of the characteristics of groups, without identifying the individuals or organizations that comprise such groups. Agencies and components shall protect the integrity and confidentiality of this information against unauthorized access, use, disclosure, modification, or destruction throughout the life cycle of the information. Agencies and components shall also adhere to legal requirements and should follow best practices for protecting the confidentiality of data, including training their employees and agents, and ensuring the physical and information system security of confidential information.	Appendix II § 6.	PL-7, PM-24, PM-25, SC-7, SC-16, SI-7, SI-10(6), SI-12(1), SI-12(2), SI-15(1), SI-19, SI-20

APPENDIX G

TAILORING CONSIDERATIONS
CUSTOMIZING AND SPECIALIZING CONTROL BASELINES

After selecting an appropriate control baseline, organizations initiate a tailoring process to align the controls more closely with the specific protection needs and concerns of their stakeholders.[44] The tailoring process is part of a comprehensive organization-wide risk management process—framing, assessing, responding to, and monitoring information security and privacy risks. Organizational tailoring decisions are not carried out in a vacuum. While such decisions are focused on security and privacy considerations, it is important that the decisions be aligned with other risk factors that organizations must routinely address. Risk factors such as cost, schedule, and performance are considered in the determination of which controls to employ in organizational systems and environments of operation.[45] The tailoring process can include, but is not limited to, the following activities:[46]

- Identifying and designating common controls;

- Applying scoping considerations;

- Selecting compensating controls;

- Assigning values to organization-defined control parameters via explicit assignment and selection statements;

- Supplementing baselines with additional controls and control enhancements; and

- Providing specification information for control implementation.

Organizations use risk management guidance to facilitate risk-based decision making regarding the applicability of the controls in the baselines. Ultimately, organizations employ the tailoring process to achieve cost-effective, risk-based solutions that support organizational missions and business needs. Organizations have the flexibility to tailor at the organization level for systems in support of a line of business or mission/business process, at the individual system level, or by using a combination of the above. However,, organizations should not arbitrarily remove security and privacy controls from baselines. Tailoring decisions should be defensible based on mission and business needs, a sound rationale, and explicit risk-based determinations.[47]

Tailoring decisions, including the justification for those decisions, are documented in the security and privacy plans for organizational systems. Every control from the selected control baseline is

---

[44] It should be noted that some organizations may employ the security and privacy controls in this publication without the use of control baselines. This may occur, for example, when organizations apply the controls as part of a life cycle-based, systems engineering process during the development of systems, system components, system services. In such situations, the security and privacy controls may be selected as part of a well-defined requirements engineering process that is intended to provide a "system capability" provided through technical and non-technical means. See Section 2.1.

[45] It is inappropriate to tailor out security or privacy controls that pertain to specific federal legislative, regulatory, or policy requirements.

[46] See Appendix F for additional guidance on tailoring privacy controls.

[47] Tailoring decisions can be based on timing and applicability of selected controls under certain conditions. That is, security and privacy controls may not apply in every situation or the parameter values for assignment statements may change under certain circumstances. Overlays can define these special situations, conditions, and timing/applicability-related considerations. Federal agencies conduct baseline tailoring activities in accordance with OMB policy. In certain situations, OMB may prohibit agencies from tailoring out specific security or privacy controls.

accounted for by the organization. If certain controls are tailored out, the rationale is recorded in the security and privacy plans and subsequently approved by the responsible officials within the organization as part of the approval process for security and privacy plans. Documenting risk management decisions in the tailoring process is imperative for organizational officials to have the necessary information to make credible, risk-based decisions regarding security and privacy; and to do so in a manner that is transparent and facilitates accountability.

Identifying and Designating Common Controls

Common controls are controls that may be inherited by one or more organizational systems. If a system inherits a common control, there is no need to implement the control within that system. The security or privacy function or capability is being provided by another entity. Organizational decisions on which controls are designated as common controls may affect the responsibilities of individual system owners regarding the implementation of the controls in a baseline. Common control selection can also affect the resource expenditures by organizations—that is, in general, the greater the number of common controls implemented, the greater potential cost savings as the protective measures are amortized over many systems.

Applying Scoping Considerations

Scoping considerations, when applied in conjunction with risk management guidance, provide organizations with a more granular foundation with which to make risk-based decisions.[48] The application of scoping considerations can eliminate unnecessary controls from the initial control baselines and ensure that organizations select *only* those controls that are needed to provide the appropriate level of protection. Organizations may apply the scoping considerations described below to assist with making risk-based decisions regarding control selection and specification.

- *Control Implementation, Applicability, and Placement Considerations*

The growing complexity of systems requires careful analysis in the implementation of security and privacy controls. Controls in the initial baselines may not be applicable to every component in the system. Controls are applicable only to system components that provide or support the security or privacy functions or capabilities addressed by the controls.[49] Organizations make explicit risk-based decisions about where to apply or allocate specific controls in organizational systems to achieve the needed security or privacy function or capability and to satisfy security and privacy requirements.

- *Operational and Environmental Considerations*

Certain controls in the control baselines assume of the existence of operational or environmental factors. Where these factors are absent or significantly diverge from the baseline assumptions, it is justifiable to tailor the baseline. Some of the more common operational/environmental factors include mobile devices and operations; single-user systems and operations; data connectivity and bandwidth; non-networked (i.e., air gapped) systems; systems that have very limited or sporadic bandwidth such as tactical systems that support warfighter or law enforcement missions; cyber-physical systems, sensors, and devices; limited functionality systems or system components such as facsimile machines, printers, scanners, smart phones, tablets, E-readers, and digital cameras;

---

[48] The scoping considerations listed in this section are exemplary and *not* intended to limit organizations in rendering risk-based decisions based on other organization-defined considerations with appropriate justification or rationale. See NIST Special Publication 800-37 for additional information and detailed tailoring guidance on scoping considerations for control baselines required by FISMA, OMB Circular A-130, and Federal Information Processing Standards.

[49] For example, auditing controls are typically applied to components of a system that provide auditing capability and are not necessarily applied to every user-level workstation within the organization.

systems processing, storing, or transmitting non-persistent information or systems that employ virtualization techniques to establish non-persistent instantiations of operating systems and applications; and systems that require public access.

- *Technology Considerations*

Controls that refer to specific technologies including, for example, wireless, cryptography, and public key infrastructure are applicable only if those technologies are employed or are required to be employed within organizational systems. Controls that can be more effectively supported by automated mechanisms do not require the development of such mechanisms if the mechanisms do not already exist or are not readily available in commercial or government off-the-shelf products. If automated mechanisms are not available, cost-effective, or technically feasible, compensating controls, implemented through nonautomated mechanisms or procedures, can be implemented to satisfy specified controls or control enhancements.

- *Mission and Business Considerations*

Certain controls may not be appropriate if implementing those controls in a system or system component has the potential to degrade, debilitate, or otherwise hamper organizational missions or business functions including endangering or harming individuals. However, decsions on the appropriateness of implementing security or privacy controls always consider any legislative, regulatory, or policy requirements.

Selecting Compensating Controls

Compensating controls are employed by organizations in lieu of specific controls in control baselines. This occurs when controls are tailored out by necessity but the protection provided by the controls remains essential to reduce risk to an acceptable level. Compensating controls are chosen most often when implementing a baseline control is technically infeasible, not cost effective, or the implementation negatively affects organizational missions or business functions in an unacceptable manner or to an unsafe extent.[50] For technology-based scoping considerations, compensating controls are often temporary until the system is updated. Compensating controls are intended to provide equivalent or comparable protection[51] for systems, organizations, and individuals.[52] Compensating controls are selected after applying the scoping considerations in the tailoring process. Compensating controls can be used under the following conditions:

- Organizations select compensating controls from the consolidated control catalog in Chapter Three; if appropriate compensating controls are not available, organizations adopt suitable compensating controls from other sources;[53]

- Organizations provide a justification or rationale for how compensating controls provide adequate security or privacy functions or capabilities and why the baseline controls could not be implemented; and

---

[50] For example, additional or stronger physical security controls may be implemented in lieu of a device lock in certain real-time mission applications; in a small organization, more frequent auditing, targeted role-based training, or stronger personnel screening may be implemented in lieu of separation of duties; well-defined procedures, targeted role-based training, and more frequent auditing may be implemented in lieu of automated mechanisms.

[51] Compensating controls are not used to avoid the need to comply with requirements. Rather, the use of such controls provides alternative and suitable security and privacy protections to facilitate risk management.

[52] More than one compensating control may be required to provide the equivalent protection for a control in the catalog.

[53] Organizations should make every attempt to select compensating controls from the consolidated control catalog in Chapter Three. Organization-defined compensating controls are employed *only* when organizations determine that the control catalog does not contain suitable compensating controls.

- Organizations review and accept the security and privacy risk associated with implementing compensating controls.

Assigning Control Parameter Values

Security and privacy controls and control enhancements containing embedded parameters (i.e., *assignment* and *selection* statements) give organizations the flexibility to define certain portions of controls and control enhancements to support specific organizational requirements. After the application of scoping considerations and the selection of compensating controls, organizations review the controls and control enhancements for assignment/selection statements and determine appropriate organization-defined values for the identified parameters. Parameter values may be prescribed by laws, Executive Orders, directives, regulations, policies, standards, guidelines, or industry best practices. Parameter values may also be driven by mission or business requirements. Once organizations define the parameter values for the controls and control enhancements, the assignments and selections become a permanent part of the control and control enhancement and as such, are documented in security and privacy program plans or system security and privacy plans, as appropriate. Organizations can specify the values for parameters before selecting compensating controls since the specification of the parameters completes the control definitions and may affect compensating control requirements. There can also be significant benefits in collaborating on the development of parameter values. For organizations that work together on a frequent basis, it may be useful for those organizations to develop a mutually agreeable set of uniform values for control parameters.

Supplementing Control Baselines

The determination of what controls are needed to provide adequate security for systems and organizations and to protect the privacy of individuals is a function of an organizational risk assessment and what is required to sufficiently mitigate the security and privacy risks. In certain situations, additional controls or control enhancements beyond those controls and enhancements contained in the control baselines in Appendix D and selected based on the guidance in Appendix F, will be required to address specific threats to organizations, mission/business processes, and systems; to address privacy-related issues for individuals; and to satisfy the requirements of applicable laws, Executive Orders, directives, policies, regulations, standards, and guidelines. Organizational assessments of risk provide essential information in determining the necessity and sufficiency of the controls and control enhancements in the control baselines. Organizations are encouraged to make maximum use of the control catalog in Chapter Three to supplement their control baselines with additional controls or control enhancements.

Providing Additional Specification Information for Control Implementation

Since controls and control enhancements are statements of security or privacy functions or capabilities that are conveyed at higher levels of abstraction, the controls may lack sufficient information for implementation. Therefore, additional detail may be necessary to fully define the intent of a given control for implementation purposes and to ensure that the security and privacy requirements related to that control are satisfied. For example, additional information may be provided as part of the process of moving from control to specification requirement, and may involve *refinement* of implementation details, *refinement* of scope, or *iteration* to apply the same control differently to different scopes. This situation occurs routinely when controls are employed in a system engineering process as part of a requirements engineering. Organizations ensure that if existing control information is not sufficient to define the intended application of the control, such information is provided. Organizations have the flexibility to determine whether additional detail is included as a part of the control statement, in supplemental guidance, or in a separate control addendum section. When providing additional detail, organizations are cautioned not to change the intent of the control or modify the original language in the control. The additional implementation information can be documented in security and privacy plans.

Creating Overlays

The previous sections described tailoring control baselines to achieve needed security or privacy functions or capabilities. In certain situations, it may be beneficial for organizations to apply the tailoring guidance to the control baselines to develop a set of controls for particular communities of interest or to address specialized requirements, technologies, or unique missions/environments of operation. An organization may decide to establish a set of controls for specific applications or use cases, for example, cloud-based systems that could be uniformly applied to organizations procuring or implementing such services; industrial control systems generating and transmitting electric power or controlling environmental systems in facilities; systems processing, storing, or transmitting classified information; or systems controlling the safety of transportation systems. In each of the above examples, overlays can be developed for each sector or technology area or for unique circumstances or environments and promulgated to large communities of interest—thus achieving standardized security and privacy capabilities, consistency of implementation, and cost-effective security and privacy solutions.

To address the need for specialized sets of controls for communities of interest, systems, and organizations, the concept of *overlay* is introduced. An overlay is a fully specified set of controls, control enhancements, and supplemental guidance derived from the application of tailoring guidance to control baselines.[54] Overlays complement the initial control baselines by providing the opportunity to add or eliminate controls; providing control applicability and interpretations for specific technologies, computing paradigms, environments of operation, types of systems, types of missions/operations, operating modes, industry sectors, and statutory/regulatory requirements; establishing parameter values for assignment and/or selection statements in controls and control enhancements agreeable to communities of interest; and extending the supplemental guidance for controls, where necessary. Organizations use the overlay concept when there is divergence from the basic assumptions used to create the initial control baselines. In many ways, overlays function like alternative control baselines and may require tailoring like the baselines in Appendix D. That is, using an overlay is not a substitute for the full tailoring process.

The full range of tailoring activities can be employed by organizations to provide a disciplined and structured approach for developing tailored control baselines supporting the areas described above. Overlays provide an opportunity to build consensus across communities of interest and develop security and privacy plans for systems and organizations that have broad-based support for very specific circumstances, situations, and/or conditions. Categories of overlays that may be useful include, for example:

- Communities of interest, industry sectors, or coalitions/partnerships including, for example, healthcare, law enforcement, intelligence, financial, manufacturing, transportation, energy, and allied collaboration/sharing;

- Information technologies and computing paradigms including, for example, cloud, mobile, smart grid, and cross-domain solutions;

- Environments of operation including, for example, space, tactical, or sea;

---

[54] Control baselines can include the federally-mandated baselines in Appendix D; baselines developed by State, local, or tribal governments; or baselines developed by private sector organizations including, for example, manufacturers, consortia, trade associations, industry and critical infrastructure sectors.

- Types of systems and operating modes, including, for example, industrial/process control systems, weapons systems, single-user systems, standalone systems, IoT devices and sensors;

- Types of missions/operations including, for example, counterterrorism, first responders, research, development, test, and evaluation; and

- Statutory/regulatory requirements including, for example, Foreign Intelligence Surveillance Act, Health Insurance Portability and Accountability Act, FISMA, and Privacy Act.

Organizations may use the following outline when developing overlays.[55] The outline is provided as an example only. Organizations may use any format based on organizational needs and the type of overlay being developed. The level of detail included in the overlay is at the discretion of the organization initiating the overlay but should be of sufficient breadth and depth to provide an appropriate justification and rationale for the overlay, including any risk-based decisions made during the overlay development process. The example overlay outline includes the following sections:

- Identification;

- Overlay Characteristics;

- Applicability;

- Overlay Summary;

- Detailed Overlay Control Specifications;

- Tailoring Considerations;

- Definitions; and

- Additional Information or Instructions.

Overlays can be published independently in a variety of venues and publications including, for example, OMB policies, CNSS Instructions, NIST Special Publications, industry standards, and sector-specific guidance.[56]

---

[55] While organizations are encouraged to use the overlay concept to tailor control baselines, the development of widely divergent overlays on the same topic may prove to be counterproductive. The overlay concept is most effective when communities of interest work together to create consensus-based overlays that are not duplicative.

[56] NIST Special Publication 800-82 provides an example of an overlay for industrial/process control system security.

APPENDIX H

CONTROL KEYWORDS

NOTEWORTHY AND RELEVANT TERMS IN CONTROLS AND ENHANCEMENTS

Tables H-1 through H-20 provide a list of *keywords* associated with each control and control enhancement in the twenty families of security and privacy controls. Keywords can be used when searching for controls or control enhancements that may contain similar content or have a similar purpose. Such information may be useful in developing security and privacy plans, conducting tailoring activities, constructing overlays, or using automated tools to support risk management or system life cycle activities.

TABLE H-1: ACCESS CONTROL FAMILY KEYWORDS

CONTROL NUMBER	CONTROL NAME CONTROL ENHANCEMENT NAME	KEYWORDS NOTEWORTHY AND RELEVANT TERMS
AC-1	**Access Control Policy and Procedures**	ASSURANCE; ACCESS CONTROL; POLICY; PROCEDURES; REVIEW; UPDATE
AC-2	**Account Management**	ACCOUNT MANAGEMENT; AUTHORIZED ACCESS; CREDENTIAL MANAGEMENT; GROUP ACCOUNTS; ACCOUNT REVIEW; ACCESS CONTROL; ROLE-BASED ACCESS; SHARED ACCOUNTS; ACCESS PRIVILEGES; TEMPORARY ACCOUNTS; EMERGENCY ACCOUNTS; DISABLING ACCOUNTS; DEACTIVATING ACCOUNTS; SHARED ACCOUNT
AC-2(1)	AUTOMATED SYSTEM ACCOUNT MANAGEMENT	AUTOMATIC NOTIFICATION; MONITOR ACCOUNT USAGE; TELEPHONE NOTIFICATION; EMAIL ALERT AND TEXT ALERT; ATYPICAL SYSTEM ACCOUNT USAGE
AC-2(2)	REMOVAL OF TEMPORARY AND EMERGENCY ACCOUNTS	AUTOMATICALLY REMOVE; AUTOMATICALLY DISABLE; TEMPORARY ACCOUNTS
AC-2(3)	DISABLE ACCOUNTS	AUTOMATICALLY DISABLE; INACTIVE ACCOUNTS
AC-2(4)	AUTOMATED AUDIT ACTIONS	AUTOMATED AUDIT; ACCOUNT CREATION; ACCOUNT MODIFICATION; ACCOUNT ENABLING; ACCOUNT DISABLING; ACCOUNT REMOVAL
AC-2(5)	INACTIVITY LOGOUT	INACTIVITY; LOGOUT
AC-2(6)	DYNAMIC PRIVILEGE MANAGEMENT	DYNAMIC PRIVILEGE MANAGEMENT; DYNAMIC ACCESS CONTROL; RESILIENCY; RESILIENCE
AC-2(7)	ROLE-BASED SCHEMES	PRIVILEGED USER ACCOUNTS; PRIVILEGED ROLE ASSIGNMENTS; ROLE BASED ACCESS
AC-2(8)	DYNAMIC ACCOUNT MANAGEMENT	DYNAMIC ACCOUNT CREATION; TRUST RELATIONSHIPS; RESILIENCY; RESILIENCE
AC-2(9)	RESTRICTIONS ON USE OF SHARED AND GROUP ACCOUNTS	SHARED ACCOUNT RESTRICTIONS; GROUP ACCOUNT RESTRICTIONS
AC-2(10)	SHARED AND GROUP ACCOUNT CREDENTIAL CHANGE	TERMINATION; CREDENTIAL
AC-2(11)	USAGE CONDITIONS	ACCOUNT USAGE CONDITIONS
AC-2(12)	ACCOUNT MONITORING FOR ATYPICAL USAGE	ACCOUNT MONITORING; ATYPICAL USAGE
AC-2(13)	DISABLE ACCOUNTS FOR HIGH-RISK INDIVIDUALS	HIGH RISK USERS; DISABLE ACCOUNT
AC-2(14)	PROHIBIT SPECIFIC ACCOUNT TYPES	PROHIBIT ACCOUNT CREATION; PROHIBIT ACCOUNT USE; GUEST; SHARED; TEMPORARY; EMERGENCY
AC-2(15)	ATTRIBUTE-BASED SCHEMES	ATTRIBUTE-BASED SCHEMES; PRIVILEGED ROLES; PRIVILEGED ACCOUNTS; ATTRIBUTE-BASED ACCESS
AC-3	**Access Enforcement**	ACCESS CONTROL POLICIES; LOGICAL ACCESS; IDENTITY BASED POLICIES; ROLE-BASED POLICIES; CONTROL MATRICES; ACCESS ENFORCEMENT
AC-3(1)	RESTRICTED ACCESS TO PRIVILEGED FUNCTIONS	WITHDRAWN
AC-3(2)	DUAL AUTHORIZATION	DUAL AUTHORIZATION; PRIVILEGED COMMANDS; TWO-PERSON CONTROL; RESILIENCY; RESILIENCE
AC-3(3)	MANDATORY ACCESS CONTROL	MANDATORY ACCESS CONTROL; MAC; MANDATORY ACCESS CONTROL POLICY; LEAST PRIVILEGE; TRUSTED SUBJECTS; SECURITY ATTRIBUTES; ACCESS ENFORCEMENT

CONTROL NUMBER	CONTROL NAME CONTROL ENHANCEMENT NAME	KEYWORDS NOTEWORTHY AND RELEVANT TERMS
AC-3(4)	DISCRETIONARY ACCESS CONTROL	DISCRETIONARY ACCESS CONTROL; DAC; DISCRETIONARY ACCESS CONTROL POLICY; SECURITY ATTRIBUTES
AC-3(5)	SECURITY-RELEVANT INFORMATION	ROUTER FILTERING RULES; FIREWALL FILTERING RULES; CRYPTOGRAPHIC KEY MANAGEMENT; SECURITY SERVICES CONFIGURATION; ACCESS CONTROL LISTS
AC-3(6)	PROTECTION OF USER AND SYSTEM INFORMATION	WITHDRAWN
AC-3(7)	ROLE-BASED ACCESS CONTROL	ROLE-BASED ACCESS CONTROL; RBAC; ROLES; MANDATORY ACCESS CONTROL; MAC; DISCRETIONARY ACCESS CONTROL; DAC; PRIVILEGE ADMINISTRATION
AC-3(8)	REVOCATION OF ACCESS AUTHORIZATIONS	ACCESS REVOCATION
AC-3(9)	CONTROLLED RELEASE	INFORMATION RELEASE VALIDATION; CONTROLLED RELEASE; INFORMATION DISSEMINATION; RESILIENCY; RESILIENCE
AC-3(10)	AUDITED OVERRIDE OF ACCESS CONTROL MECHANISMS	AUDITED OVERRIDE; AUTOMATED ACCESS CONTROL MECHANISMS
AC-3(11)	RESTRICT ACCESS TO SPECIFIC INFORMATION	SPECIFIC INFORMATION; RESTRICT ACCESS
AC-3(12)	ASSERT AND ENFORCE APPLICATION ACCESS	APPLICATION ACCESS
AC-3(13)	ATTRIBUTE-BASED ACCESS CONTROL	ATTRIBUTE-BASED ACCESS; ABAC; ORGANIZATIONAL ATTRIBUTES; ATTRIBUTE RULES; AUTHORIZATIONS; MANDATORY ACCESS CONTROL; MAC; DISCRETIONARY ACCESS CONTROL; DAC
AC-4	**Information Flow Enforcement**	INFORMATION FLOW CONTROL POLICIES; INFORMATION FLOW; FLOW CONTROL RESTRICTIONS; BOUNDARY PROTECTION DEVICES; SECURITY DOMAINS; CROSS-DOMAIN
AC-4(1)	OBJECT SECURITY ATTRIBUTES	SECURITY ATTRIBUTES; INFORMATION FLOW ENFORCEMENT
AC-4(2)	PROCESSING DOMAINS	PROCESSING DOMAINS; DOMAIN ENFORCEMENT; PROTECTED PROCESSING DOMAINS; RESILIENCY; RESILIENCE
AC-4(3)	DYNAMIC INFORMATION FLOW CONTROL	DYNAMIC INFORMATION FLOW CONTROL; RESILIENCY; RESILIENCE
AC-4(4)	FLOW CONTROL OF ENCRYPTED INFORMATION	CHECKING ENCRYPTED INFORMATION CONTENT; DECRYPT INFORMATION; BLOCK FLOW OF ENCRYPTED INFORMATION
AC-4(5)	EMBEDDED DATA TYPES	DATA TYPE EMBEDDING
AC-4(6)	METADATA	METADATA
AC-4(7)	ONE-WAY FLOW MECHANISMS	ONE WAY INFORMATION FLOW ENFORCEMENT; HARDWARE MECHANISMS
AC-4(8)	SECURITY POLICY FILTERS	SECURITY POLICY FILTERS
AC-4(9)	HUMAN REVIEWS	HUMAN REVIEW
AC-4(10)	ENABLE AND DISABLE SECURITY POLICY FILTERS	DISABLE SECURITY POLICY FILTERS; ENABLE SECURITY POLICY FILTERS
AC-4(11)	CONFIGURATION OF SECURITY POLICY FILTERS	CONFIGURE SECURITY POLICY FILTERS; DEFINITIONS
AC-4(12)	DATA TYPE IDENTIFIERS	DATA TYPE IDENTIFIERS; TOKENS; INTERNAL FILE SIGNATURES

CONTROL NUMBER	CONTROL NAME CONTROL ENHANCEMENT NAME	KEYWORDS NOTEWORTHY AND RELEVANT TERMS
AC-4(13)	DECOMPOSITION INTO POLICY-RELEVANT SUBCOMPONENTS	SECURITY DOMAINS; FILTERING RULES; INSPECTION RULES; SANITIZATION RULES
AC-4(14)	SECURITY POLICY FILTER CONSTRAINTS	DATA STRUCTURE RESTRICTIONS; CONTENT RESTRICTIONS
AC-4(15)	DETECTION OF UNSANCTIONED INFORMATION	INAPPROPRIATE CONTENT; UNAUTHORIZED INFORMATION; UNSANCTIONED INFORMATION; MALICIOUS CODE; DIRTY WORDS
AC-4(16)	INFORMATION TRANSFERS ON INTERCONNECTED SYSTEMS	WITHDRAWN
AC-4(17)	DOMAIN AUTHENTICATION	DOMAIN AUTHENTICATION; ATTRIBUTION; SOURCE POINT; DESTINATION POINT; POLICY VIOLATIONS
AC-4(18)	SECURITY ATTRIBUTE BINDING	WITHDRAWN
AC-4(19)	VALIDATION OF METADATA	VALIDATION; METADATA; FILTERING; DATA PAYLOADS
AC-4(20)	APPROVED SOLUTIONS	CROSS-DOMAIN POLICY; UNIFIED CROSS-DOMAIN MANAGEMENT OFFICE; UCDMO
AC-4(21)	PHYSICAL AND LOGICAL SEPARATION OF INFORMATION FLOWS	ENFORCING SEPARATION; LOGICAL; PHYSICAL; RESILIENCY; RESILIENCE
AC-4(22)	ACCESS ONLY	SINGLE DEVICE ACCESS; SECURITY DOMAINS; COMPUTING PLATFORMS
AC-5	**Separation of Duties**	SEPARATION OF DUTIES; ROLES; LEAST PRIVILEGE; ACCESS AUTHORIZATION; MALICIOUS ACTIVITY
AC-6	**Least Privilege**	LEAST PRIVILEGE; AUTHORIZED USER ACCESS RESILIENCY; RESILIENCE;
AC-6(1)	AUTHORIZE ACCESS TO SECURITY FUNCTIONS	EXPLICIT AUTHORIZATION; PERMISSIONS; PRIVILEGES; INTRUSION DETECTION PARAMETERS; RESILIENCY; RESILIENCE
AC-6(2)	NON-PRIVILEGED ACCESS FOR NONSECURITY FUNCTIONS	ROLE-BASED ACCESS CONTROL; RBAC; PRIVILEGED ACCOUNTS; NON-PRIVILEGED ACCOUNTS; RESILIENCY; RESILIENCE
AC-6(3)	NETWORK ACCESS TO PRIVILEGED COMMANDS	PRIVILEGED COMMANDS; USER PRIVILEGES; RESILIENCY; RESILIENCE
AC-6(4)	SEPARATE PROCESSING DOMAINS	DOMAIN SEPARATION; RESILIENCY; RESILIENCE
AC-6(5)	PRIVILEGED ACCOUNTS	RESTRICTS PRIVILEGED ACCOUNTS; RESILIENCY; RESILIENCE
AC-6(6)	PRIVILEGED ACCESS BY NON-ORGANIZATIONAL USERS	NON-ORGANIZATIONAL USER; EXTERNAL USER; RESILIENCY; RESILIENCE
AC-6(7)	REVIEW OF USER PRIVILEGES	USER PRIVILEGE REVIEW; RESILIENCY; RESILIENCE
AC-6(8)	PRIVILEGE LEVELS FOR CODE EXECUTION	PRIVILEGE ESCALATION; CODE EXECUTION; RESILIENCY; RESILIENCE
AC-6(9)	AUDITING USE OF PRIVILEGED FUNCTIONS	AUDITING PRIVILEGED FUNCTIONS
AC-6(10)	PROHIBIT NON-PRIVILEGED USERS FROM EXECUTING PRIVILEGED FUNCTIONS	NON-PRIVILEGED USERS; PRIVILEGED FUNCTIONS; SECURITY SAFEGUARDS; SECURITY COUNTERMEASURES; RESILIENCY; RESILIENCE
AC-7	**Unsuccessful Logon Attempts**	INVALID LOGON; AUTOMATIC LOCKOUT; UNSUCCESSFUL LOGON ATTEMPTS; LIMIT ENFORCEMENT; CONSECUTIVE INVALID LOGO ATTEMPTS
AC-7(1)	AUTOMATIC ACCOUNT LOCK	WITHDRAWN

CONTROL NUMBER	CONTROL NAME CONTROL ENHANCEMENT NAME	KEYWORDS NOTEWORTHY AND RELEVANT TERMS
AC-7(2)	PURGE OR WIPE MOBILE DEVICE	MOBILE DEVICE; WIPING; PURGING; UNSUCCESSFUL LOGON
AC-7(3)	BIOMETRIC ATTEMPT LIMITING	BIOMETRIC; LOGON ATTEMPT LIMIT
AC-7(4)	USE OF ALTERNATE FACTOR	ALTERNATIVE AUTHENTICATION; BYPASS LOCKOUT
AC-8	**System Use Notification**	WARNING BANNER; SYSTEM USE NOTIFICATION; SYSTEM USE INFORMATION; AUTHORIZED USE OF SYSTEM
AC-9	**Previous Logon (Access) Notification**	SUCCESSFUL LOGON; NOTIFICATION; PREVIOUS LOGON
AC-9(1)	UNSUCCESSFUL LOGONS	NOTIFICATION; UNSUCCESSFUL LOGON ATTEMPTS
AC-9(2)	SUCCESSFUL AND UNSUCCESSFUL LOGONS	SUCCESSFUL LOGON; UNSUCCESSFUL LOGON
AC-9(3)	NOTIFICATION OF ACCOUNT CHANGES	ACCOUNT CHANGES
AC-9(4)	ADDITIONAL LOGON INFORMATION	ADDITIONAL LOGON INFORMATION
AC-10	**Concurrent Session Control**	ENFORCE; CONCURRENT SESSION CONTROL
AC-11	**Device Lock**	SESSION LOCK; INACTIVITY; AUTHENTICATION PROCEDURES
AC-11(1)	PATTERN-HIDING DISPLAYS	SCREEN CONCEALMENT; SESSION LOCK
AC-11(2)	REQUIRE USER-INITIATED LOCK	SESSION TERMINATION; NETWORK CONNECTIONS; LOGICAL SESSION
AC-12	**Session Termination**	SESSION TERMINATION; NETWORK CONNECTIONS; LOGICAL SESSION
AC-12(1)	USER-INITIATED LOGOUTS	USER; MESSAGE DISPLAY; LOGOUT
AC-12(2)	TERMINATION MESSAGE	DISPLAY LOGOUT MESSAGE; AUTHENTICATED COMMUNICATION SESSION
AC-12(3)	TIMEOUT WARNING MESSAGE	TIMEOUT WARNING; PENDING SESSION TERMINATION; SESSION ENDING
AC-13	Supervision and Review — Access Control	WITHDRAWN
AC-14	**Permitted Actions without Identification or Authentication**	ACTIONS WITHOUT IDENTIFICATION; WITHOUT AUTHENTICATION; BYPASS; ACTIONS W/O AUTHENTICATION
AC-14(1)	NECESSARY USES	WITHDRAWN
AC-15	Automated Marking	WITHDRAWN
AC-16	**Security and Privacy Attributes**	SECURITY ATTRIBUTES; PRIVACY ATTRIBUTES; ACTIVE ENTITIES; PASSIVE ENTITIES; SUBJECTS; OBJECTS
AC-16(1)	DYNAMIC ATTRIBUTE ASSOCIATION	DYNAMIC; SECURITY ATTRIBUTE ASSOCIATION; PRIVACY ATTRIBUTE ASSOCIATION; RESILIENCY; RESILIENCE
AC-16(2)	ATTRIBUTE VALUE CHANGES BY AUTHORIZED INDIVIDUALS	AUTHORIZED ACCESS; MODIFY SECURITY ATTRIBUTE; VALUE CHANGE; MODIFY PRIVACY ATTRIBUTE
AC-16(3)	MAINTENANCE OF ATTRIBUTE ASSOCIATIONS BY SYSTEM	ATTRIBUTE ASSOCIATION MAINTENANCE; PRIVACY
AC-16(4)	ASSOCIATION OF ATTRIBUTES BY AUTHORIZED INDIVIDUALS	AUTHORIZED ACCESS; MODIFY SECURITY ATTRIBUTE ASSOCIATION; MODIFY PRIVACY ATTRIBUTE ASSOCIATION
AC-16(5)	ATTRIBUTE DISPLAYS FOR OUTPUT DEVICES	SECURITY ATTRIBUTE OUTPUT; OUTPUT DEVICES; PRIVACY ATTRIBUTE OUTPUT
AC-16(6)	MAINTENANCE OF ATTRIBUTE ASSOCIATION BY ORGANIZATION	ASSOCIATE; MAINTAIN ATTRIBUTES; PRIVACY

CONTROL NUMBER	CONTROL NAME CONTROL ENHANCEMENT NAME	KEYWORDS NOTEWORTHY AND RELEVANT TERMS
AC-16(7)	CONSISTENT ATTRIBUTE INTERPRETATION	INTERPRETATION; FLOW ENFORCEMENT; INTERPRETATIONS; PRIVACY
AC-16(8)	ASSOCIATION TECHNIQUES AND TECHNOLOGIES	ASSOCIATION TECHNOLOGY; ASSOCIATION TECHNIQUE; ASSURANCE LEVELS; PRIVACY
AC-16(9)	ATTRIBUTE REASSIGNMENT	REASSIGNMENT; RE-GRADING; PRIVACY
AC-16(10)	ATTRIBUTE CONFIGURATION BY AUTHORIZED INDIVIDUALS	AUTHORIZED ACCESS; ATTRIBUTE CONFIGURATION; INFORMATION ORGANIZATION; PRIVACY
AC-16(11)	AUDIT CHANGES	AUDIT CHANGES; SECURITY ATTRIBUTE; PRIVACY ATTRIBUTE
AC-17	**Remote Access**	ACCESS AUTHORIZATION; REMOTE ACCESS; EXTERNAL NETWORKS; DIAL UP; BROADBAND; WIRELESS; VIRTUAL PRIVATE NETWORK; VPN
AC-17(1)	AUTOMATED MONITORING AND CONTROL	AUTOMATED MONITORING; AUTOMATED CONTROL
AC-17(2)	PROTECTION OF CONFIDENTIALITY AND INTEGRITY USING ENCRYPTION	ENCRYPTION; SESSION CONFIDENTIALITY; SESSION INTEGRITY; SECURITY CATEGORIZATION
AC-17(3)	MANAGED ACCESS CONTROL POINTS	ACCESS CONTROL POINTS; TRUSTED INTERNET CONNECTIONS
AC-17(4)	PRIVILEGED COMMANDS AND ACCESS	PRIVILEGED COMMANDS
AC-17(5)	MONITORING FOR UNAUTHORIZED CONNECTIONS	WITHDRAWN
AC-17(6)	PROTECTION OF INFORMATION	PROTECT INFORMATION; REMOTE-ACCESS MECHANISMS
AC-17(7)	ADDITIONAL PROTECTION FOR SECURITY FUNCTION ACCESS	WITHDRAWN
AC-17(8)	DISABLE NONSECURE NETWORK PROTOCOLS	WITHDRAWN
AC-17(9)	DISCONNECT OR DISABLE ACCESS	DISCONNECT; DISABLE
AC-18	**Wireless Access**	WIRELESS ACCESS; USAGE RESTRICTION; CONFIGURATION REQUIREMENTS; CONNECTION REQUIREMENTS
AC-18(1)	AUTHENTICATION AND ENCRYPTION	WIRELESS AUTHENTICATION; ENCRYPTION
AC-18(2)	MONITORING UNAUTHORIZED CONNECTIONS	WITHDRAWN
AC-18(3)	DISABLE WIRELESS NETWORKING	DISABLE; WIRELESS NETWORKING
AC-18(4)	RESTRICT CONFIGURATIONS BY USERS	AUTHORIZED USER; CONFIGURING WIRELESS NETWORK
AC-18(5)	ANTENNAS AND TRANSMISSION POWER LEVELS	WIRELESS TRANSMISSIONS; REDUCE TRANSMISSION POWER; ANTENNAE
AC-19	**Access Control for Mobile Devices**	MOBILE DEVICE; ACCESS; USAGE RESTRICTION; CONFIGURATION REQUIREMENTS; AUTHORIZED DEVICE ACCESS; LAPTOPS; SMART PHONES; TABLETS; E-READERS
AC-19(1)	USE OF WRITABLE AND PORTABLE STORAGE DEVICES	WITHDRAWN
AC-19(2)	USE OF PERSONALLY OWNED PORTABLE STORAGE DEVICES	WITHDRAWN
AC-19(3)	USE OF PORTABLE STORAGE DEVICES WITH NO IDENTIFIABLE OWNER	WITHDRAWN
AC-19(4)	RESTRICTIONS FOR CLASSIFIED INFORMATION	UNCLASSIFIED MOBILE DEVICES; CLASSIFIED INFORMATION; INFORMATION REVIEW; INFORMATION INSPECTION
AC-19(5)	FULL DEVICE AND CONTAINER-BASED ENCRYPTION	FULL-DEVICE ENCRYPTION; CONTAINER-BASED ENCRYPTION

CONTROL NUMBER	CONTROL NAME CONTROL ENHANCEMENT NAME	KEYWORDS NOTEWORTHY AND RELEVANT TERMS
AC-20	**Use of External Systems**	AUTHORIZED ACCESS; EXTERNAL SYSTEMS; TRUST AGREEMENT; TRUST RELATIONSHIP; SHARED SERVICES
AC-20(1)	LIMITS ON AUTHORIZED USE	CONNECTION AGREEMENT; PROCESSING AGREEMENT; LIMITS; SECURITY ASSESSMENT; EXTERNAL SYSTEM
AC-20(2)	PORTABLE STORAGE DEVICES	PORTABLE STORAGE DEVICES, RESTRICT; PROHIBIT
AC-20(3)	NON-ORGANIZATIONALLY OWNED SYSTEMS AND COMPONENTS	BYOD; EXTERNALLY OWNED; RESTRICTIONS; FORENSIC ANALYSIS; BRING YOUR OWN DEVICE
AC-20(4)	NETWORK ACCESSIBLE STORAGE DEVICES	EXTERNAL SYSTEMS; ONLINE STORAGE; CLOUD BASED SYSTEMS
AC-21	**Information Sharing**	INFORMATION SHARING; ACCESS AUTHORIZATION; COLLABORATION; PRIVACY AUTHORIZATION; PRIVACY IMPACT ASSESSMENTS; PIA
AC-21(1)	AUTOMATED DECISION SUPPORT	SHARING PARTNERS; INFORMATION; SHARED; AUTOMATED
AC-21(2)	INFORMATION SEARCH AND RETRIEVAL	SEARCH; RETRIEVAL
AC-22	**Publicly Accessible Content**	AUTHORIZED INDIVIDUALS; POST INFORMATION; PUBLICLY ACCESSIBLE; REVIEWS; CONTENT
AC-23	**Data Mining Protection**	DATA MINING; PREVENTION; DETECTION; DATA STORAGE OBJECTS; PRIVACY
AC-24	**Access Control Decisions**	ACCESS CONTROL DECISION
AC-24(1)	TRANSMIT ACCESS AUTHORIZATION INFORMATION	ENFORCE SYSTEM TRANSMITS; AUTHORIZATION INFORMATION; TRANSMITTED SECURELY
AC-24(2)	NO USER OR PROCESS IDENTITY	USER IDENTITY; PROCESS IDENTITY
AC-25	**Reference Monitor**	REFERENCE MONITORS; MANDATORY ACCESS CONTROL POLICY; TAMPERPROOF

TABLE H-2: AWARENESS AND TRAINING FAMILY KEYWORDS

CONTROL NUMBER	CONTROL NAME CONTROL ENHANCEMENT NAME	KEYWORDS NOTEWORTHY AND RELEVANT TERMS
AT-1	**Awareness and Training Policy and Procedures**	ASSURANCE; SECURITY AWARENESS TRAINING; PRIVACY AWARENESS TRAINING; SECURITY AWARENESS; PRIVACY AWARENESS; TRAINING POLICY; POLICY; PROCEDURES; REVIEW; UPDATE
AT-2	**Awareness Training**	ASSURANCE; SECURITY AWARENESS TRAINING; PRIVACY AWARENESS TRAINING; RULES OF BEHAVIOR; BASIC SECURITY AWARENESS; BASIC PRIVACY AWARENESS; BASIC SUPPLY CHAIN RISK AWARENESS; TRAINING CONTENT; INITIAL TRAINING
AT-2(1)	PRACTICAL EXERCISES	PHISHING; MALICIOUS LINKS; PRACTICAL EXERCISES; PRIVACY
AT-2(2)	INSIDER THREAT	INSIDER THREAT; INDICATORS; INAPPROPRIATE BEHAVIOR
AT-2(3)	SOCIAL ENGINEERING AND MINING	SOCIAL ENGINEERING; PRIVACY; SOCIAL MINING
AT-3	**Role-Based Training**	ASSURANCE; ROLE-BASED SECURITY TRAINING; ROLE-BASED PRIVACY TRAINING
AT-3(1)	ENVIRONMENTAL CONTROLS	ENVIRONMENTAL CONTROLS
AT-3(2)	PHYSICAL SECURITY CONTROLS	PHYSICAL SECURITY
AT-3(3)	PRACTICAL EXERCISES	PRACTICAL EXERCISES; SOFTWARE VULNERABILITIES; PHISHING; PRIVACY
AT-3(4)	SUSPICIOUS COMMUNICATIONS AND ANOMALOUS SYSTEM BEHAVIOR	UNUSUAL BEHAVIOR; INAPPROPRIATE BEHAVIOR; INSIDER THREAT; MALICIOUS CODE; SUSPICIOUS COMMUNICATIONS; ANOMALOUS SYSTEM BEHAVIOR
AT-3(5)	PERSONALLY IDENTIFIABLE INFORMATION PROCESSING	PRIVACY; PERSONALLY IDENTIFIABLE INFORMATION; PII; SYSTEM OF RECORDS NOTICE; SORN
AT-4	**Training Records**	ASSURANCE; TRAINING RECORD; RECORD RETENTION; PRIVACY
AT-5	Contacts with Security Groups and Associations	WITHDRAWN

TABLE H-3: AUDIT AND ACCOUNTABILITY FAMILY KEYWORDS

CONTROL NUMBER	CONTROL NAME CONTROL ENHANCEMENT NAME	KEYWORDS NOTEWORTHY AND RELEVANT TERMS
AU-1	Audit and Accountability Policy and Procedures	ASSURANCE; AUDIT; ACCOUNTABILITY; POLICY, PROCEDURES; REVIEW; UPDATE
AU-2	Audit Events	AUDITABLE; RATIONALE; SECURITY AUDIT; AUDIT EVENT
AU-2(1)	COMPILATION OF AUDIT RECORDS FROM MULTIPLE SOURCES	WITHDRAWN
AU-2(2)	SELECTION OF AUDIT EVENTS BY COMPONENT	WITHDRAWN
AU-2(3)	REVIEWS AND UPDATES	REVIEW; UPDATE; AUDIT EVENT REVIEW; AUDIT EVENT UPDATE
AU-2(4)	PRIVILEGED FUNCTIONS	WITHDRAWN
AU-3	Content of Audit Records	EVENT OCCURRED; AUDIT RECORD; AUDIT RECORD CONTENT; EVENT SOURCE; EVENT OUTCOME
AU-3(1)	ADDITIONAL AUDIT INFORMATION	ADDITIONAL AUDIT INFORMATION; AUDIT REQUIREMENTS
AU-3(2)	CENTRALIZED MANAGEMENT OF PLANNED AUDIT RECORD CONTENT	CENTRALIZED; MANAGEMENT; CONTENT CONFIGURATION
AU-3(3)	LIMIT PERSONALLY IDENTIFIABLE INFORMATION ELEMENTS	PRIVACY; AUDIT RECORDS; PERSONALLY IDENTIFIABLE INFORMATION; PII; DATA MINIMIZATION
AU-4	Audit Storage Capacity	AUDIT RECORD STORAGE; AUDIT PROCESSING REQUIREMENTS; CAPACITY
AU-4(1)	TRANSFER TO ALTERNATE STORAGE	OFF-LOADING; ALTERNATE STORAGE; TRANSFER AUDIT RECORDS; RESILIENCY; RESILIENCE
AU-5	Response to Audit Processing Failures	AUDIT PROCESSING FAILURE; ALERTS; SHUT DOWN; OVERWRITE; STOP GENERATING; REPOSITORY; STORAGE CAPACITY
AU-5(1)	AUDIT STORAGE CAPACITY	STORAGE CAPACITY; STORAGE VOLUME
AU-5(2)	REAL-TIME ALERTS	REAL-TIME ALERTS; EVENT DETECTION
AU-5(3)	CONFIGURABLE TRAFFIC VOLUME THRESHOLDS	CONFIGURABLE; NETWORK; VOLUME THRESHOLD; TRIGGER
AU-5(4)	SHUTDOWN ON FAILURE	SHUTDOWN; FAILURE
AU-6	Audit Review, Analysis, and Reporting	AUDIT REVIEW; AUDIT ANALYSIS; AUDIT REPORTING; ASSURANCE
AU-6(1)	AUTOMATED PROCESS INTEGRATION	PROCESS INTEGRATION; AUTOMATED PROCESS INTEGRATION
AU-6(2)	AUTOMATED SECURITY ALERTS	WITHDRAWN
AU-6(3)	CORRELATE AUDIT REPOSITORIES	CORRELATE; AUDIT REPOSITORY
AU-6(4)	CENTRAL REVIEW AND ANALYSIS	CENTRAL REVIEW; CENTRAL ANALYSIS
AU-6(5)	INTEGRATED ANALYSIS OF AUDIT RECORDS	SECURITY INFORMATION AND EVENT MANAGEMENT; AGGREGATION; CORRELATION; AUDIT MONITORING CAPABILITIES; INTEGRATE AUDIT RECORDS; RESILIENCY; RESILIENCE
AU-6(6)	CORRELATION WITH PHYSICAL MONITORING	AUDIT INFORMATION CORRELATION; SUSPICIOUS BEHAVIOR; PHYSICAL ACCESS; RESILIENCY; RESILIENCE
AU-6(7)	PERMITTED ACTIONS	PERMITTED ACTION; LEAST PRIVILEGE
AU-6(8)	FULL TEXT ANALYSIS OF PRIVILEGED COMMANDS	PRIVILEGED COMMANDS; FULL TEXT ANALYSIS; RESILIENCY; RESILIENCE

CONTROL NUMBER	CONTROL NAME CONTROL ENHANCEMENT NAME	KEYWORDS NOTEWORTHY AND RELEVANT TERMS
AU-6(9)	CORRELATION WITH INFORMATION FROM NONTECHNICAL SOURCES	CORRELATION; NON-TECHNICAL SOURCES
AU-6(10)	AUDIT LEVEL ADJUSTMENT	WITHDRAWN
AU-7	**Audit Reduction and Report Generation**	AUDIT REDUCTION; REPORT GENERATION
AU-7(1)	AUTOMATIC PROCESSING	AUTOMATIC PROCESSING; EVENTS OF INTEREST
AU-7(2)	AUTOMATIC SORT AND SEARCH	AUTOMATIC SORT; AUTOMATIC SEARCH
AU-8	**Time Stamps**	TIME STAMPS; INTERNAL CLOCKS
AU-8(1)	SYNCHRONIZATION WITH AUTHORITATIVE TIME SOURCE	AUTHORITATIVE TIME SOURCE; SYNCHRONIZATION
AU-8(2)	SECONDARY AUTHORITATIVE TIME SOURCE	SECONDARY AUTHORITATIVE TIME SOURCE; RESILIENCY; RESILIENCE
AU-9	**Protection of Audit Information**	AUDIT INFORMATION PROTECTION; AUDIT TOOLS PROTECTION
AU-9(1)	HARDWARE WRITE-ONCE MEDIA	WRITE-ONCE MEDIA; HARDWARE-ENFORCED; AUDIT TRAILS
AU-9(2)	STORE ON SEPARATE PHYSICAL SYSTEMS OR COMPONENTS	AUDIT RECORD BACKUP; SEPARATE PHYSICAL SYSTEM; RESILIENCY; RESILIENCE
AU-9(3)	CRYPTOGRAPHIC PROTECTION	CRYPTOGRAPHIC PROTECTION; CRYPTOGRAPHIC MECHANISMS; INTEGRITY
AU-9(4)	ACCESS BY SUBSET OF PRIVILEGED USERS	PRIVILEGED ACCESS; PRIVILEGED USER
AU-9(5)	DUAL AUTHORIZATION	DUAL AUTHORIZATION; RESILIENCY; RESILIENCE
AU-9(6)	READ-ONLY ACCESS	READ-ONLY ACCESS
AU-9(7)	STORE ON COMPONENT WITH DIFFERENT OPERATING SYSTEM	AUDIT INFORMATION STORAGE; DIFFERENT OPERATING SYSTEM; DIFFERENT SYSTEM; SEPARATE STORAGE
AU-10	**Non-repudiation**	NON-REPUDIATION; FALSELY DENY
AU-10(1)	ASSOCIATION OF IDENTITIES	IDENTITY ASSOCIATION; IDENTITY BINDING; INFORMATION PRODUCER
AU-10(2)	VALIDATE BINDING OF INFORMATION PRODUCER IDENTITY	VALIDATE BINDING; INFORMATION PRODUCER IDENTITY; INFORMATION MODIFICATION PREVENTION
AU-10(3)	CHAIN OF CUSTODY	CHAIN OF CUSTODY
AU-10(4)	VALIDATE BINDING OF INFORMATION REVIEWER IDENTITY	VALIDATE BINDING; REVIEWER IDENTITY; VALIDATION ERROR; RELEASE POINT; CRYPTOGRAPHIC CHECKSUM
AU-10(5)	DIGITAL SIGNATURES	WITHDRAWN
AU-11	**Audit Record Retention**	AUDIT RECORD RETENTION; RETENTION REQUIREMENTS; NARA; NATIONAL ARCHIVES AND RECORDS ADMINISTRATION; SECURITY INCIDENT INVESTIGATION; PRIVACY INCIDENT INVESTIGATION
AU-11(1)	LONG-TERM RETRIEVAL CAPABILITY	LONG-TERM RETRIEVAL; RETRIEVAL
AU-12	**Audit Generation**	AUDIT RECORD GENERATION; AUDITABLE EVENTS
AU-12(1)	SYSTEM-WIDE AND TIME-CORRELATED AUDIT TRAIL	AUDIT TRAIL; TIME-CORRELATED; TIME STAMPS
AU-12(2)	STANDARDIZED FORMATS	STANDARDIZED FORMAT; COMMON EVENT EXPRESSIONS; CEE
AU-12(3)	CHANGES BY AUTHORIZED INDIVIDUALS	AUTHORIZED CHANGES; AUDIT LIMITING
AU-12(4)	QUERY PARAMETER AUDITS OF PERSONALLY IDENTIFIABLE INFORMATION	PRIVACY; PERSONALLY IDENTIFIABLE INFORMATION; PII; QUERY PARAMETERS; AUTOMATED SYSTEM
AU-13	**Monitoring for Information Disclosure**	UNAUTHORIZED DISCLOSURE; MONITORING

CONTROL NUMBER	CONTROL NAME CONTROL ENHANCEMENT NAME	KEYWORDS NOTEWORTHY AND RELEVANT TERMS
AU-13(1)	USE OF AUTOMATED TOOLS	AUTOMATED MECHANISMS; AUTOMATED SCRIPTS; AUTOMATED TOOLS; ASSURANCE
AU-13(2)	REVIEW OF MONITORED SITES	MONITORING SITES
AU-14	**Session Audit**	AUTHORIZED USER; SESSION AUDIT; ASSURANCE
AU-14(1)	SYSTEM START-UP	SYSTEM START-UP
AU-14(2)	CAPTURE AND RECORD CONTENT	USER SESSION; CAPTURE LOG CONTENT; RECORD LOG CONTENT
AU-14(3)	REMOTE VIEWING AND LISTENING	USER SESSION; REMOTE VIEWING; REMOTE LISTENING
AU-15	**Alternate Audit Capability**	ALTERNATE AUDIT CAPABILITY; RESILIENCY; RESILIENCE
AU-16	**Cross-Organizational Auditing**	CROSS-ORGANIZATIONAL AUDITING; PRIVACY
AU-16(1)	IDENTITY PRESERVATION	IDENTITY PRESERVATION
AU-16(2)	SHARING OF AUDIT INFORMATION	AUDIT INFORMATION SHARING

TABLE H-1: ASSESSMENT, AUTHORIZATION, AND MONITORING KEYWORDS

CONTROL NUMBER	CONTROL NAME CONTROL ENHANCEMENT NAME	KEYWORDS NOTEWORTHY AND RELEVANT TERMS
CA-1	**Assessment, Authorization, and Monitoring Policies and Procedures**	ASSURANCE; SECURITY ASSESSMENT AND AUTHORIZATION; SECURITY ASSESSMENT; SECURITY AUTHORIZATION; POLICY; PROCEDURES; REVIEW; UPDATE; PRIVACY ASSESSMENT AND AUTHORIZATION; PRIVACY ASSESSMENT; PRIVACY AUTHORIZATION; MONITORING
CA-2	**Assessments**	ASSURANCE; SECURITY CONTROL ASSESSMENT; SECURITY ASSESSMENT; SECURITY ASSESSMENT PLAN; SECURITY ASSESSMENT REPORT; SAR; VULNERABILITY SCANNING; SYSTEM MONITORING; ANNUAL ASSESSMENT; PRIVACY CONTROL ASSESSMENT; PRIVACY ASSESSMENT; PRIVACY ASSESSMENT PLAN; PRIVACY ASSESSMENT REPORT
CA-2(1)	INDEPENDENT ASSESSORS	INDEPENDENT ASSESSOR; INDEPENDENT ASSESSMENT TEAM; THIRD-PARTY ASSESSOR; PRIVACY
CA-2(2)	SPECIALIZED ASSESSMENTS	IN DEPTH MONITORING; INSIDER THREAT; MALICIOUS USER TESTING; PERFORMANCE LOAD TESTING; VERIFICATION; VALIDATION; VULNERABILITY SCANNING; SECURITY ASSESSMENT; PRIVACY ASSESSMENT
CA-2(3)	EXTERNAL ORGANIZATIONS	ASSESSMENT; EXTERNAL ASSESSMENTS; PRIVACY
CA-3	**System Interconnections**	ASSURANCE; EXTERNAL SYSTEMS; INTERCONNECTION SECURITY AGREEMENTS; ISA; SYSTEM INTERCONNECTION; INTERFACE REQUIREMENTS; TYPES OF INFORMATION; SECURITY REQUIREMENTS
CA-3(1)	UNCLASSIFIED NATIONAL SECURITY SYSTEM CONNECTIONS	BOUNDARY PROTECTION DEVICES; CONTROLLED UNCLASSIFIED INFORMATION; CONNECTION REQUIREMENTS; DIRECT NETWORK CONNECTION; EXTERNAL NETWORKS; ROUTERS, FIREWALLS; NETWORK CONNECTION; UNCLASSIFIED SYSTEMS; RESILIENCY; RESILIENCE
CA-3(2)	CLASSIFIED NATIONAL SECURITY SYSTEM CONNECTIONS	BOUNDARY PROTECTION DEVICES; CROSS-DOMAIN SYSTEMS; CLASSIFIED INFORMATION; CLASSIFIED SYSTEMS; NATIONAL SECURITY; DIRECT CONNECTION; EXTERNAL NETWORKS; INFORMATION FLOW ENFORCEMENT; RESILIENCY; RESILIENCE
CA-3(3)	UNCLASSIFIED NON-NATIONAL SECURITY SYSTEM CONNECTIONS	BOUNDARY PROTECTION DEVICES; CONTROLLED UNCLASSIFIED INFORMATION; EXTERNAL NETWORKS; ROUTERS; FIREWALLS; UNCLASSIFIED NON-NATIONAL SECURITY SYSTEMS; INFORMATION FLOW ENFORCEMENT; RESILIENCY; RESILIENCE
CA-3(4)	CONNECTIONS TO PUBLIC NETWORKS	DIRECT CONNECTION; EXTERNAL NETWORKS; PUBLIC NETWORKS; RESILIENCY; RESILIENCE
CA-3(5)	RESTRICTIONS ON EXTERNAL SYSTEM CONNECTIONS	BLACKLISTING; DENY-ALL; DENY-BY-EXCEPTION; EXTERNAL SYSTEMS; EXTERNAL DOMAINS; WHITELISTING; ALLOW-ALL; PERMIT-BY-EXCEPTION; RESILIENCY; RESILIENCE

CONTROL NUMBER	CONTROL NAME CONTROL ENHANCEMENT NAME	KEYWORDS NOTEWORTHY AND RELEVANT TERMS
CA-3(6)	SECONDARY AND TERTIARY CONNECTIONS	HIGH-VALUE ASSETS; SECONDARY CONNECTIONS; TERTIARY CONNECTIONS; INTERCONNECTED SYSTEMS; VERIFY CONTROLS; INHERIT RISK
CA-4	Security Certification	WITHDRAWN
CA-5	**Plan of Action and Milestones**	ASSURANCE; PLAN OF ACTIONS AND MILESTONES; POA&M; REMEDIATION ACTIONS; VULNERABILITIES; SECURITY CONTROL ASSESSMENTS; SECURITY IMPACT ANALYSES; CONTINUOUS MONITORING ACTIVITIES; PRIVACY CONTROL ASSESSMENTS; PRIVACY IMPACT ASSESSMENTS; PIA
CA-5(1)	AUTOMATION SUPPORT FOR ACCURACY AND CURRENCY	AUTOMATED MECHANISMS; AUTOMATION SUPPORT
CA-6	**Authorization**	ASSURANCE; AUTHORIZING OFFICIAL; AUTHORIZE; AUTHORIZATION; SECURITY AUTHORIZATION
CA-6(1)	JOINT AUTHORIZATION — SAME ORGANIZATION	JOINT AUTHORIZATION; AUTHORIZING OFFICIAL; SAME ORGANIZATION; CO-AUTHORIZE SYSTEM
CA-6(2)	JOINT AUTHORIZATION — DIFFERENT ORGANIZATIONS	JOINT AUTHORIZATION; AUTHORIZING OFFICIAL; EXTERNAL ORGANIZATION; CO-AUTHORIZE; INTERCONNECTED SYSTEMS; SHARED SYSTEMS; MULTIPLE INFORMATION OWNERS
CA-7	**Continuous Monitoring**	ASSURANCE; CONTINUOUS MONITORING STRATEGY; CONTINUOUS MONITORING; METRICS; FREQUENCY; SECURITY CONTROL ASSESSMENTS; ANALYSIS; REPORTING; PRIVACY CONTROL ASSESSMENTS
CA-7(1)	INDEPENDENT ASSESSMENT	ASSESSORS; ASSESSMENT TEAMS; INDEPENDENT ASSESSMENT; SECURITY CONTROLS; PRIVACY CONTROLS
CA-7(2)	TYPES OF ASSESSMENTS	WITHDRAWN
CA-7(3)	TREND ANALYSES	TREND ANALYSES; SECURITY CONTROL IMPLEMENTATION; CONTINUOUS MONITORING ACTIVITIES; EMPIRICAL DATA
CA-7(4)	RISK MONITORING	CONTINUOUS MONITORING STRATEGY; EFFECTIVENESS MONITORING; COMPLIANCE MONITORING; CHANGE MONITORING; RISK; CONTINUOUS MONITORING
CA-8	**Penetration Testing**	ASSURANCE; PENETRATION TESTING; RESILIENCY; RESILIENCE
CA-8(1)	INDEPENDENT PENETRATION AGENT OR TEAM	INDEPENDENT PENETRATION AGENT; INDEPENDENT PENETRATION TEAM
CA-8(2)	RED TEAM EXERCISES	RED TEAM EXERCISES; ADVERSARIES
CA-8(3)	FACILITY PENETRATION TESTING	FACILITY PENETRATION TESTING; PHYSICAL ACCESS; UNANNOUNCED FACILITY ACCESS ATTEMPTS
CA-9	**Internal System Connections**	ASSURANCE; INTERNAL SYSTEM CONNECTIONS; INTERFACE CHARACTERISTICS; SECURITY REQUIREMENTS; INFORMATION COMMUNICATION
CA-9(1)	COMPLIANCE CHECKS	SECURITY COMPLIANCE CHECKS

TABLE H-1: CONFIGURATION MANAGEMENT FAMILY KEYWORDS

CONTROL NUMBER	CONTROL NAME CONTROL ENHANCEMENT NAME	KEYWORDS NOTEWORTHY AND RELEVANT TERMS
CM-1	**Configuration Management Policy and Procedures**	CONFIGURATION MANAGEMENT POLICY; CONFIGURATION MANAGEMENT PROCEDURES; ASSURANCE; POLICY; PROCEDURES; REVIEW; UPDATE; PRIVACY
CM-2	**Baseline Configuration**	BASELINE CONFIGURATIONS; ASSURANCE; CONFIGURATION SPECIFICATIONS; SYSTEM COMPONENTS; NETWORK TOPOLOGY; LOGICAL PLACEMENT; SYSTEM ARCHITECTURE; ENTERPRISE ARCHITECTURE
CM-2(1)	REVIEWS AND UPDATES	WITHDRAWN
CM-2(2)	AUTOMATION SUPPORT FOR ACCURACY AND CURRENCY	AUTOMATED MECHANISMS; CONFIGURATION MANAGEMENT TOOLS; ACCURACY; CURRENCY
CM-2(3)	RETENTION OF PREVIOUS CONFIGURATIONS	CONFIGURATION RETENTION; ROLLBACK; RESILIENCY; RESILIENCE
CM-2(4)	UNAUTHORIZED SOFTWARE	WITHDRAWN
CM-2(5)	AUTHORIZED SOFTWARE	WITHDRAWN
CM-2(6)	DEVELOPMENT AND TEST ENVIRONMENTS	BASELINE CONFIGURATION FOR TESTING; BASELINE CONFIGURATION FOR DEVELOPMENT; DEVELOPMENT ENVIRONMENT; TEST ENVIRONMENT; SEPARATE TEST ENVIRONMENT; SEPARATE DEVELOPMENT ENVIRONMENT
CM-2(7)	CONFIGURE SYSTEMS AND COMPONENTS FOR HIGH-RISK AREAS	HIGH-RISK AREAS
CM-3	**Configuration Change Control**	CONFIGURATION CHANGE CONTROL; CHANGE CONTROL; CONFIGURATION-CONTROLLED; CONFIGURATION CONTROL BOARD; CCB
CM-3(1)	AUTOMATED DOCUMENTATION, NOTIFICATION, AND PROHIBITION OF CHANGES	AUTOMATED DOCUMENTATION; AUTOMATED NOTIFICATION; PROHIBITION OF CHANGES
CM-3(2)	TESTING, VALIDATION, AND DOCUMENTATION OF CHANGES	HARDWARE MODIFICATION; SOFTWARE MODIFICATION; FIRMWARE MODIFICATION; TEST CHANGES; VALIDATE CHANGES; DOCUMENT CHANGES
CM-3(3)	AUTOMATED CHANGE IMPLEMENTATION	AUTOMATED CHANGE IMPLEMENTATION
CM-3(4)	SECURITY REPRESENTATIVE	SECURITY REPRESENTATIVE
CM-3(5)	AUTOMATED SECURITY RESPONSE	AUTOMATED SECURITY RESPONSE; UNAUTHORIZED CONFIGURATION CHANGE
CM-3(6)	CRYPTOGRAPHY MANAGEMENT	CRYPTOGRAPHY MANAGEMENT; CRYPTOGRAPHIC MECHANISMS
CM-4	**Security and Privacy Impact Analyses**	SECURITY IMPACT ANALYSIS; SECURITY PLAN REVIEW; SYSTEM DESIGN DOCUMENTATION REVIEW; ASSURANCE; PRIVACY IMPACT ASSESSMENTS; PIA; PRIVACY PLAN REVIEW
CM-4(1)	SEPARATE TEST ENVIRONMENTS	SEPARATE TEST ENVIRONMENT
CM-4(2)	VERIFICATION OF SECURITY AND PRIVACY FUNCTIONS	SECURITY FUNCTION VERIFICATION; PRIVACY FUNCTION VERIFICATION
CM-5	**Access Restrictions for Change**	PHYSICAL ACCESS RESTRICTION; LOGICAL ACCESS RESTRICTION
CM-5(1)	AUTOMATED ACCESS ENFORCEMENT AND AUDITING	AUTOMATED ACCESS ENFORCEMENT; AUDITING ACCESS ENFORCEMENT

CONTROL NUMBER	CONTROL NAME CONTROL ENHANCEMENT NAME	KEYWORDS NOTEWORTHY AND RELEVANT TERMS
CM-5(2)	REVIEW SYSTEM CHANGES	CHANGE REVIEW
CM-5(3)	SIGNED COMPONENTS	SIGNED COMPONENTS; DIGITAL SIGNATURES
CM-5(4)	DUAL AUTHORIZATION	DUAL AUTHORIZATION; RESILIENCY; RESILIENCE
CM-5(5)	PRIVILEGE LIMITATION FOR PRODUCTION AND OPERATION	LEAST PRIVILEGE; RESILIENCY; RESILIENCE
CM-5(6)	LIMIT LIBRARY PRIVILEGES	LEAST PRIVILEGE; RESILIENCY; RESILIENCE
CM-5(7)	AUTOMATIC IMPLEMENTATION OF SECURITY SAFEGUARDS	WITHDRAWN
CM-6	**Configuration Settings**	CONFIGURATION SETTINGS; USGCB; UNITED STATES GOVERNMENT CONFIGURATION BASELINE; SECURITY CONTENT AUTOMATION PROTOCOL; SCAP; COMMON CONFIGURATION ENUMERATION; CCE
CM-6(1)	AUTOMATED MANAGEMENT, APPLICATION, AND VERIFICATION	AUTOMATED MANAGEMENT; AUTOMATED APPLICATION; AUTOMATED VERIFICATION
CM-6(2)	RESPOND TO UNAUTHORIZED CHANGES	UNAUTHORIZED CHANGE RESPONSE
CM-6(3)	UNAUTHORIZED CHANGE DETECTION	WITHDRAWN
CM-6(4)	CONFORMANCE DEMONSTRATION	WITHDRAWN
CM-7	**Least Functionality**	LEAST FUNCTIONALITY; ESSENTIAL CAPABILITIES ONLY
CM-7(1)	PERIODIC REVIEW	PERIODIC REVIEW; RESILIENCY; RESILIENCE
CM-7(2)	PREVENT PROGRAM EXECUTION	PROGRAM EXECUTION PREVENTION
CM-7(3)	REGISTRATION COMPLIANCE	REGISTRATION COMPLIANCE
CM-7(4)	UNAUTHORIZED SOFTWARE — BLACKLISTING	UNAUTHORIZED SOFTWARE; BLACKLISTING; DENY-BY-EXCEPTION; ALLOW-ALL
CM-7(5)	AUTHORIZED SOFTWARE — WHITELISTING	AUTHORIZED SOFTWARE; WHITELISTING; PERMIT-BY-EXCEPTION; DENY-ALL
CM-8	**System Component Inventory**	COMPONENT INVENTORY; ASSURANCE; BASELINE CONFIGURATION; CONFIGURATION CHANGE CONTROL; REVIEW; UPDATE; AUTHORIZATION BOUNDARY; HARDWARE; SOFTWARE; FIRMWARE
CM-8(1)	UPDATES DURING INSTALLATION AND REMOVAL	COMPONENT INVENTORY UPDATE; COMPONENT INSTALLATIONS; COMPONENT REMOVAL; SYSTEM UPDATES
CM-8(2)	AUTOMATED MAINTENANCE	AUTOMATED MAINTENANCE; AUTOMATED MECHANISMS
CM-8(3)	AUTOMATED UNAUTHORIZED COMPONENT DETECTION	UNAUTHORIZED COMPONENT DETECTION; AUTOMATED MECHANISMS
CM-8(4)	ACCOUNTABILITY INFORMATION	ACCOUNTABILITY INFORMATION
CM-8(5)	NO DUPLICATE ACCOUNTING OF COMPONENTS	DUPLICATE ACCOUNTING
CM-8(6)	ASSESSED CONFIGURATIONS AND APPROVED DEVIATIONS	ASSESSED CONFIGURATIONS; APPROVED DEVIATIONS
CM-8(7)	CENTRALIZED REPOSITORY	CENTRALIZED REPOSITORY
CM-8(8)	AUTOMATED LOCATION TRACKING	LOCATION TRACKING; SYSTEM COMPONENT TRACKING; AUTOMATED MECHANISM; GEOGRAPHIC LOCATION
CM-8(9)	ASSIGNMENT OF COMPONENTS TO SYSTEMS	COMPONENT ASSIGNMENT
CM-8(10)	DATA ACTION MAPPING	COMPONENT INVENTORY; PRIVACY; DATA ACTION; DATA MAPPING; PERSONALLY IDENTIFIABLE INFORMATION; PII; SYSTEM MAP

CONTROL NUMBER	CONTROL NAME / CONTROL ENHANCEMENT NAME	KEYWORDS / NOTEWORTHY AND RELEVANT TERMS
CM-9	Configuration Management Plan	CONFIGURATION MANAGEMENT PLAN; SYSTEM DEVELOPMENT LIFE CYCLE; SDLC; CONFIGURATION ITEMS; CONFIGURATION MANAGEMENT POLICY; POLICY; CONFIGURATION MANAGEMENT PROCESS; CONFIGURATION MANAGEMENT PROCEDURE; REVIEW; UPDATE
CM-9(1)	ASSIGNMENT OF RESPONSIBILITY	RESPONSIBILITY ASSIGNMENT; SEPARATION OF DUTIES
CM-10	Software Usage Restrictions	SOFTWARE USAGE RESTRICTION; TRACK SOFTWARE USAGE
CM-10(1)	OPEN SOURCE SOFTWARE	OPEN SOURCE SOFTWARE
CM-11	User-Installed Software	USER-INSTALLED SOFTWARE; POLICY, POLICY COMPLIANCE
CM-11(1)	ALERTS FOR UNAUTHORIZED INSTALLATIONS	WITHDRAWN
CM-11(2)	SOFTWARE INSTALLATION WITH PRIVILEGED STATUS	PROHIBIT INSTALLATION; RESILIENCY; RESILIENCE
CM-12	Information Location	INFORMATION LOCATION; SYSTEM COMPONENT LOCATION; PROCESSING; STORAGE; CONTROLLED UNCLASSIFIED INFORMATION; CUI; PRIVACY
CM-12(1)	AUTOMATED TOOLS TO SUPPORT INFORMATION LOCATION	AUTOMATED TOOLS; PRIVACY

TABLE H-6: CONTINGENCY PLANNING FAMILY KEYWORDS

CONTROL NUMBER	CONTROL NAME CONTROL ENHANCEMENT NAME	KEYWORDS NOTEWORTHY AND RELEVANT TERMS
CP-1	**Contingency Planning Policy and Procedures**	CONTINGENCY PLANNING POLICY; CONTINGENCY PLANNING POLICY PROCEDURES; ASSURANCE; REVIEW; UPDATE; POLICY; PROCEDURE; PRIVACY
CP-2	**Contingency Plan**	CONTINGENCY PLAN; ESSENTIAL FUNCTIONS; CONTINGENCY; ROLES; RESPONSIBILITIES; RECOVERY OBJECTIVES; METRICS; ESSENTIAL MISSIONS; BUSINESS FUNCTIONS; UNAUTHORIZED DISCLOSURE; ASSURANCE; PRIVACY; RESILIENCE; RESILIENCY
CP-2(1)	COORDINATE WITH RELATED PLANS	COORDINATE; CONTINGENCY PLAN DEVELOPMENT; ORGANIZATIONAL ELEMENTS; RELATED PLANS; BUSINESS CONTINUITY PLAN; DISASTER RECOVERY PLAN; CONTINUITY OF OPERATIONS PLAN; COOP; CYBER INCIDENT RESPONSE PLAN; SUPPLY CHAIN RISK MANAGEMENT PLAN; PRIVACY
CP-2(2)	CAPACITY PLANNING	CAPACITY PLANNING; THREATS; ORGANIZATIONAL MISSIONS; BUSINESS FUNCTIONS
CP-2(3)	RESUME ESSENTIAL MISSIONS AND BUSINESS FUNCTIONS	ESSENTIAL FUNCTIONS; ESSENTIAL MISSIONS; BUSINESS FUNCTIONS; RESUMPTION; TIME-PERIOD; CONTINGENCY PLAN ACTIVATION; PRIVACY
CP-2(4)	RESUME ALL MISSIONS AND BUSINESS FUNCTIONS	FUNCTIONS; RESUMPTION; TIME-PERIOD; PRIVACY
CP-2(5)	CONTINUE ESSENTIAL MISSIONS AND BUSINESS FUNCTIONS	SUSTAIN; ESSENTIAL FUNCTIONS; PRIMARY; PROCESSING; STORAGE; ESSENTIAL MISSIONS; CONTINUITY; PRIVACY; RESILIENCY; RESILIENCE
CP-2(6)	ALTERNATE PROCESSING AND STORAGE SITES	ALTERNATE; SITE; PROCESSING; STORAGE
CP-2(7)	COORDINATE WITH EXTERNAL SERVICE PROVIDERS	COORDINATE; EXTERNAL SERVICE PROVIDERS; CONTINGENCY REQUIREMENTS; PRIVACY
CP-2(8)	IDENTIFY CRITICAL ASSETS	IDENTIFICATION; CRITICAL ASSETS; CRITICAL SYSTEMS; PRIVACY; RESILIENCY; RESILIENCE
CP-3	**Contingency Training**	CONTINGENCY TRAINING; TIME-PERIOD; FREQUENCY; ASSURANCE; ROLES; RESPONSIBILITIES; PRIVACY
CP-3(1)	SIMULATED EVENTS	SIMULATED EVENTS
CP-3(2)	AUTOMATED TRAINING ENVIRONMENTS	AUTOMATED MECHANISMS; TRAINING ENVIRONMENTS; PRIVACY
CP-4	**Contingency Plan Testing**	CONTINGENCY PLAN TESTING; CORRECTIVE ACTIONS; TEST RESULTS; ASSURANCE; PRIVACY
CP-4(1)	COORDINATE WITH RELATED PLANS	COORDINATION; RELATED PLANS; BUSINESS CONTINUITY PLAN; DISASTER RECOVERY PLAN; CONTINUITY OF OPERATIONS PLAN; COOP; CYBER INCIDENT RESPONSE PLAN; PRIVACY
CP-4(2)	ALTERNATE PROCESSING SITE	ALTERNATE; PROCESSING; ALTERNATE SITE
CP-4(3)	AUTOMATED TESTING	AUTOMATED MECHANISMS; AUTOMATED TESTING
CP-4(4)	FULL RECOVERY AND RECONSTITUTION	FULL RECOVERY; RECONSTITUTION; FULL RECONSTITUTION; KNOWN STATE
CP-5	Contingency Plan Update	WITHDRAWN
CP-6	**Alternate Storage Site**	ALTERNATE STORAGE; GEOGRAPHIC SEPARATION; AGREEMENT; BACKUP INFORMATION; ALTERNATE SITE; RESILIENCY; RESILIENCE

CONTROL NUMBER	CONTROL NAME CONTROL ENHANCEMENT NAME	KEYWORDS NOTEWORTHY AND RELEVANT TERMS
CP-6(1)	SEPARATION FROM PRIMARY SITE	GEOGRAPHIC SEPARATION; ALTERNATE STORAGE SITE; RESILIENCY; RESILIENCE
CP-6(2)	RECOVERY TIME AND RECOVERY POINT OBJECTIVES	RECOVERY TIME OBJECTIVE; RECOVERY POINT OBJECTIVE
CP-6(3)	ACCESSIBILITY	ACCESSIBILITY PROBLEMS; MITIGATION
CP-7	**Alternate Processing Site**	ALTERNATE PROCESSING SITE; GEOGRAPHIC SEPARATION; SECURITY SAFEGUARDS; ALTERNATE SITE; RESILIENCY; RESILIENCE
CP-7(1)	SEPARATION FROM PRIMARY SITE	GEOGRAPHIC SEPARATION; ALTERNATE PROCESSING; THREATS; RESILIENCY; RESILIENCE
CP-7(2)	ACCESSIBILITY	ACCESSIBILITY; ALTERNATE PROCESSING SITE
CP-7(3)	PRIORITY OF SERVICE	PRIORITY OF SERVICE; SERVICE PROVIDERS; AGREEMENTS
CP-7(4)	PREPARATION FOR USE	PREPARATION FOR USE
CP-7(5)	EQUIVALENT INFORMATION SECURITY SAFEGUARDS	WITHDRAWN
CP-7(6)	INABILITY TO RETURN TO PRIMARY SITE	INABILITY TO RETURN TO PRIMARY SITE
CP-8	**Telecommunications Services**	TELECOMMUNICATION; ALTERNATE; RESUMPTION; TIME-PERIOD; AGREEMENTS; AVAILABILITY; QUALITY OF SERVICE; RESILIENCY; RESILIENCE
CP-8(1)	PRIORITY OF SERVICE PROVISIONS	PRIMARY; PRIORITY OF SERVICE
CP-8(2)	SINGLE POINTS OF FAILURE	SINGLE POINT OF FAILURE; TELECOMMUNICATIONS; RESILIENCY; RESILIENCE
CP-8(3)	SEPARATION OF PRIMARY AND ALTERNATE PROVIDERS	SEPARATION; PRIMARY PROVIDERS; ALTERNATE PROVIDERS; RESILIENCY; RESILIENCE
CP 8(4)	PROVIDER CONTINGENCY PLAN	PROVIDERS; PRIMARY; CONTINGENCY PLAN; TESTING; TRAINING
CP-8(5)	ALTERNATE TELECOMMUNICATION SERVICE TESTING	TELECOMMUNICATION; ALTERNATE; TESTING
CP-9	**System Backup**	SYSTEM BACKUP; CONFIDENTIALITY; INTEGRITY; AVAILABILITY; CRYPTOGRAPHY; DIGITAL SIGNATURES; CRYPTOGRAPHIC HASHES; RESILIENCY; RESILIENCE
CP-9(1)	TESTING FOR RELIABILITY AND INTEGRITY	TESTING; RELIABILITY
CP-9(2)	TEST RESTORATION USING SAMPLING	TESTING; RESTORATION
CP-9(3)	SEPARATE STORAGE FOR CRITICAL INFORMATION	SEPARATE STORAGE; INFORMATION; CRITICAL; SECURITY-RELATED; ALTERNATE SITE
CP-9(4)	PROTECTION FROM UNAUTHORIZED MODIFICATION	WITHDRAWN
CP-9(5)	TRANSFER TO ALTERNATE STORAGE SITE	TRANSFER; BACKUP; ALTERNATE SITE; STORAGE; TIME-PERIOD; RECOVERY TIME; RECOVERY POINT
CP-9(6)	REDUNDANT SECONDARY SYSTEM	REDUNDANT; SECONDARY SYSTEM; RESILIENCY; RESILIENCE
CP-9(7)	DUAL AUTHORIZATION	DUAL AUTHORIZATION; BACKUP; DELETION; DESTRUCTION; RESILIENCY; RESILIENCE
CP-9(8)	CRYPTOGRAPHIC PROTECTION	CRYPTOGRAPHY; CRYPTOGRAPHIC MECHANISM; PREVENT DISCLOSURE; PREVENT MODIFICATION
CP-10	**System Recovery and Reconstitution**	SYSTEM; RECOVERY; RECONSTITUTION; KNOWN STATE; AUTOMATED MECHANISMS; MANUAL PROCEDURES; RESILIENCY; RESILIENCE
CP-10(1)	CONTINGENCY PLAN TESTING	WITHDRAWN

CONTROL NUMBER	CONTROL NAME CONTROL ENHANCEMENT NAME	KEYWORDS NOTEWORTHY AND RELEVANT TERMS
CP-10(2)	TRANSACTION RECOVERY	TRANSACTION; RECOVERY; ROLLBACK; JOURNALING
CP-10(3)	COMPENSATING SECURITY CONTROLS	WITHDRAWN
CP-10(4)	RESTORE WITHIN TIME-PERIOD	RESTORE; TIME-PERIOD
CP-10(5)	FAILOVER CAPABILITY	WITHDRAWN
CP-10(6)	COMPONENT PROTECTION	PROTECTION; SAFEGUARDS; PHYSICAL; TECHNICAL; BACKUP HARDWARE; BACKUP SOFTWARE; BACKUP FIRMWARE; RESTORATION HARDWARE; RESTORATION SOFTWARE; RESTORATION FIRMWARE
CP-11	Alternate Communications Protocols	ALTERNATE COMMUNICATION PROTOCOLS; RESILIENCY; RESILIENCE
CP-12	Safe Mode	ASSURANCE; SAFE MODE; RESILIENCY; RESILIENCE
CP-13	Alternative Security Mechanisms	SECURITY MECHANISMS; RESILIENCY; RESILIENCE

TABLE H-7: IDENTIFICATION AND AUTHENTICATION FAMILY KEYWORDS

CONTROL NUMBER	CONTROL NAME CONTROL ENHANCEMENT NAME	KEYWORDS NOTEWORTHY AND RELEVANT TERMS
IA-1	Identification and Authentication Policy and Procedures	IDENTIFICATION AND AUTHENTICATION POLICY; IDENTIFICATION AND AUTHENTICATION PROCEDURE; POLICY; PROCEDURES; REVIEW; UPDATE
IA-2	Identification and Authentication (Organizational Users)	IDENTIFY ORGANIZATIONAL USERS; AUTHENTICATE ORGANIZATIONAL USERS; HOMELAND SECURITY PRESIDENTIAL DIRECTIVE 12; HSPD-12; U.S. GOVERNMENT PERSONAL IDENTITY VERIFICATION; ASSURANCE; PIV
IA-2(1)	MULTIFACTOR AUTHENTICATION TO PRIVILEGED ACCOUNTS	NETWORK ACCESS; PRIVILEGED ACCOUNT; MULTIFACTOR AUTHENTICATION
IA-2(2)	MULTIFACTOR AUTHENTICATION TO NON-PRIVILEGED ACCOUNTS	NETWORK ACCESS; NON-PRIVILEGED ACCOUNT; MULTIFACTOR AUTHENTICATION
IA-2(3)	LOCAL ACCESS TO PRIVILEGED ACCOUNTS	WITHDRAWN
IA-2(4)	LOCAL ACCESS TO NON-PRIVILEGED ACCOUNTS	WITHDRAWN
IA-2(5)	INDIVIDUAL AUTHENTICATION WITH GROUP AUTHENTICATION	GROUP AUTHENTICATION; INDIVIDUAL AUTHENTICATOR
IA-2(6)	NETWORK ACCESS TO PRIVILEGED ACCOUNTS — SEPARATE DEVICE	WITHDRAWN
IA-2(7)	NETWORK ACCESS TO NON-PRIVILEGED ACCOUNTS — SEPARATE DEVICE	WITHDRAWN
IA-2(8)	ACCESS TO ACCOUNTS — REPLAY RESISTANT	NETWORK ACCESS; PRIVILEGED ACCOUNT; REPLAY RESISTANT
IA-2(9)	NETWORK ACCESS TO NON-PRIVILEGED ACCOUNTS — REPLAY RESISTANT	WITHDRAWN
IA-2(10)	SINGLE SIGN-ON	SINGLE SIGN-ON; SSO
IA-2(11)	REMOTE ACCESS — SEPARATE DEVICE	WITHDRAWN
IA-2(12)	ACCEPTANCE OF PIV CREDENTIALS	PERSONAL IDENTITY VERIFICATION; PIV; LOGICAL ACCESS CONTROL SYSTEMS; LOGICAL ACCESS CONTROL; PHYSICAL ACCESS CONTROL SYSTEMS; PHYSICAL ACCESS CONTROL
IA-2(13)	OUT-OF-BAND AUTHENTICATION	WITHDRAWN
IA-3	Device Identification and Authentication	DEVICE IDENTIFICATION; DEVICE AUTHENTICATION; DEVICE-TO-DEVICE IDENTIFICATION
IA-3(1)	CRYPTOGRAPHIC BIDIRECTIONAL AUTHENTICATION	CRYPTOGRAPHIC BIDIRECTIONAL AUTHENTICATION; REMOTE CONNECTIONS
IA-3(2)	CRYPTOGRAPHIC BIDIRECTIONAL NETWORK AUTHENTICATION	WITHDRAWN
IA-3(3)	DYNAMIC ADDRESS ALLOCATION	DYNAMIC ADDRESS ALLOCATION; DHCP
IA-3(4)	DEVICE ATTESTATION	DEVICE ATTESTATION; KNOWN OPERATING STATE; CONFIGURATION
IA-4	Identifier Management	IDENTIFIER MANAGEMENT; SYSTEM IDENTIFIER; MEDIA ACCESS CONTROL; MAC; INTERNET PROTOCOL ADDRESS; IP ADDRESS; UNIQUE TOKEN IDENTIFIERS
IA-4(1)	PROHIBIT ACCOUNT IDENTIFIERS AS PUBLIC IDENTIFIERS	ACCOUNT IDENTIFIERS; PUBLIC IDENTIFIERS; PROHIBITED ACCOUNT IDENTIFIERS
IA-4(2)	SUPERVISOR AUTHORIZATION	WITHDRAWN
IA-4(3)	MULTIPLE FORMS OF CERTIFICATION	WITHDRAWN
IA-4(4)	IDENTIFY USER STATUS	IDENTIFY USER STATUS
IA-4(5)	DYNAMIC MANAGEMENT	DYNAMIC MANAGEMENT; RESILIENCY; RESILIENCE

CONTROL NUMBER	CONTROL NAME CONTROL ENHANCEMENT NAME	KEYWORDS NOTEWORTHY AND RELEVANT TERMS
IA-4(6)	CROSS-ORGANIZATION MANAGEMENT	CROSS-ORGANIZATION MANAGEMENT; CROSS-ORGANIZATION IDENTIFIER
IA-4(7)	IN-PERSON REGISTRATION	WITHDRAWN
IA-4(8)	PAIRWISE PSEUDONYMOUS IDENTIFIERS	PRIVACY; IDENTIFIER MANAGEMENT; PAIRWISE PSEUDONYMOUS IDENTIFIERS; TRACKING; PROFILING; IDENTIFIERS
IA-5	**Authenticator Management**	AUTHENTICATOR MANAGEMENT; AUTHENTICATOR; SYSTEM AUTHENTICATOR; MANAGE AUTHENTICATOR; PASSWORD; TOKENS, BIOMETRICS; PKI CERTIFICATE; KEY CARD
IA-5(1)	PASSWORD-BASED AUTHENTICATION	PASSWORD-BASED AUTHENTICATION; PASSWORD COMPLEXITY; CRYPTOGRAPHICALLY-PROTECTED PASSWORDS
IA-5(2)	PUBLIC KEY-BASED AUTHENTICATION	PUBLIC KEY INFRASTRUCTURE; PKI
IA-5(3)	IN-PERSON OR TRUSTED EXTERNAL PARTY REGISTRATION	WITHDRAWN
IA-5(4)	AUTOMATED SUPPORT FOR PASSWORD STRENGTH DETERMINATION	WITHDRAWN
IA-5(5)	CHANGE AUTHENTICATORS PRIOR TO DELIVERY	UNIQUE AUTHENTICATORS; CHANGE AUTHENTICATORS
IA-5(6)	PROTECTION OF AUTHENTICATORS	PROTECTION OF AUTHENTICATORS; HIGH WATER MARK
IA-5(7)	NO EMBEDDED UNENCRYPTED STATIC AUTHENTICATORS	UNENCRYPTED STATIC AUTHENTICATORS
IA-5(8)	MULTIPLE SYSTEM ACCOUNTS	MULTIPLE SYSTEM ACCOUNTS
IA-5(9)	FEDERATED CREDENTIAL MANAGEMENT	CROSS-ORGANIZATIONAL CREDENTIAL MANAGEMENT
IA-5(10)	DYNAMIC CREDENTIAL BINDING	DYNAMIC CREDENTIAL ASSOCIATION; IDENTITY PROVISIONING; RESILIENCY; RESILIENCE
IA-5(11)	HARDWARE TOKEN-BASED AUTHENTICATION	WITHDRAWN
IA-5(12)	BIOMETRIC AUTHENTICATION PERFORMANCE	BIOMETRIC AUTHENTICATION; PERFORMANCE REQUIREMENT
IA-5(13)	EXPIRATION OF CACHED AUTHENTICATORS	EXPIRED CACHED AUTHENTICATORS
IA-5(14)	MANAGING CONTENT OF PKI TRUST STORES	PKI TRUST STORES; PKI-BASED AUTHENTICATION
IA-5(15)	GSA-APPROVED PRODUCTS AND SERVICES	GENERAL SERVICES ADMINISTRATION; GSA; APPROVED PRODUCTS LIST
IA-5(16)	IN-PERSON OR TRUSTED EXTERNAL PARTY AUTHENTICATOR ISSUANCE	IN-PERSON AUTHENTICATOR ISSUANCE; TRUSTED EXTERNAL PARTY AUTHENTICATOR ISSUANCE
IA-5(17)	PRESENTATION ATTACK DETECTION FOR BIOMETRIC AUTHENTICATORS	PRESENTATION ATTACK DETECTION; LIVENESS DETECTION
IA-6	**Authenticator Feedback**	AUTHENTICATOR FEEDBACK; AUTHENTICATION PROCESS
IA-7	**Cryptographic Module Authentication**	CRYPTOGRAPHIC MODULE AUTHENTICATION; CMVP
IA-8	**Identification and Authentication (Non-Organizational Users)**	IDENTIFY NON-ORGANIZATIONAL USERS; AUTHENTICATE NON-ORGANIZATIONAL USERS
IA-8(1)	ACCEPTANCE OF PIV CREDENTIALS FROM OTHER AGENCIES	PIV ACCEPTANCE; ELECTRONIC PIV VERIFICATION
IA-8(2)	ACCEPTANCE OF EXTERNAL PARTY CREDENTIALS	EXTERNAL PARTY CREDENTIAL ACCEPTANCE; GSA-APPROVED
IA-8(3)	USE OF FICAM-APPROVED PRODUCTS	WITHDRAWN
IA-8(4)	USE OF NIST-ISSUED PROFILES	NIST-ISSUED PROFILES; OPEN IDENTITY MANAGEMENT
IA-8(5)	ACCEPTANCE OF PIV-I CREDENTIALS	PIV-I CREDENTIALS; PERSONAL IDENTITY VERIFICATION INTEROPERABILITY

CONTROL NUMBER	CONTROL NAME / CONTROL ENHANCEMENT NAME	KEYWORDS / NOTEWORTHY AND RELEVANT TERMS
IA-8(6)	DISASSOCIABILITY	PRIVACY; IDENTIFICATION; AUTHENTICATION; DISASSOCIABILITY; FEDERATED IDENTITY; CRYPTOGRAPHIC TECHNIQUES; BLINDING
IA-9	**Service Identification and Authentication**	SERVICE IDENTIFICATION; SERVICE AUTHENTICATION
IA-9(1)	INFORMATION EXCHANGE	INFORMATION EXCHANGE
IA-9(2)	TRANSMISSION OF DECISIONS	TRANSMISSION OF DECISIONS
IA-10	**Adaptive Authentication**	ADAPTIVE IDENTIFICATION; ADAPTIVE AUTHENTICATION; RESILIENCY; RESILIENCE
IA-11	**Re-authentication**	RE-AUTHENTICATION
IA-12	**Identity Proofing**	IDENTITY PROOFING; LOGICAL ACCESS; USER IDENTITY; UNIQUE TO INDIVIDUAL; ACCOUNT ESTABLISHMENT
IA-12(1)	SUPERVISOR AUTHORIZATION	SUPERVISOR AUTHORIZATION; SPONSOR AUTHORIZATION
IA-12(2)	IDENTITY EVIDENCE	IDENTITY EVIDENCE; REGISTRATION AUTHORITY
IA-12(3)	IDENTITY EVIDENCE VALIDATION AND VERIFICATION	IDENTITY EVIDENCE; VALIDATION; VERIFICATION
IA-12(4)	IN-PERSON VALIDATION AND VERIFICATION	IN-PERSON VALIDATION; IN-PERSON VERIFICATION; FRAUDULENT CREDENTIALS
IA-12(5)	ADDRESS CONFIRMATION	ADDRESS CONFIRMATION; OUT-OF-BAND METHOD; TEMPORARY ENROLLMENT CODE; NOTICE OF PROOFING; MAILING ADDRESS; DIGITAL ADDRESS
IA-12(6)	ACCEPT EXTERNALLY-PROOFED IDENTITIES	EXTERNALLY-PROOFED IDENTITIES; FEDERATED IDENTITIES

TABLE H-8: INDIVIDUAL PARTICIPATION FAMILY KEYWORDS

CONTROL NUMBER	CONTROL NAME / CONTROL ENHANCEMENT NAME	KEYWORDS / NOTEWORTHY AND RELEVANT TERMS
IP-1	**Individual Participation Policy and Procedures**	INDIVIDUAL PARTICIPATION POLICY; INDIVIDUAL PARTICIPATION PROCEDURES; POLICY; PROCEDURES; REVIEW; UPDATE; PRIVACY
IP-2	**Consent**	PRIVACY; CONSENT; PERSONALLY IDENTIFIABLE INFORMATION; PII
IP-2(1)	ATTRIBUTE MANAGEMENT	PRIVACY; CONSENT; ATTRIBUTES; ATTRIBUTE MANAGEMENT; DATA ATTRIBUTES
IP-2(2)	JUST-IN-TIME NOTICE OF CONSENT	PRIVACY; CONSENT; JUST-IN-TIME; NOTICE; PERSONALLY IDENTIFIABLE INFORMATION; PII
IP-3	**Redress**	REDRESS; PRIVACY; PERSONALLY IDENTIFIABLE INFORMATION; PII
IP-3(1)	NOTICE OF CORRECTION OR AMENDMENT	PRIVACY; REDRESS; NOTICE; CORRECTION; AMENDMENT; PERSONALLY IDENTIFIABLE INFORMATION; PII
IP-3(2)	APPEAL	REDRESS; APPEAL; SENIOR AGENCY OFFICIAL FOR PRIVACY; SAOP; CORRECTION; AMENDMENT
IP-4	**Privacy Notice**	PRIVACY NOTICE; PERSONALLY IDENTIFIABLE INFORMATION; PII; PLAIN LANGUAGE
IP-4(1)	JUST-IN-TIME NOTICE OF PRIVACY AUTHORIZATION	PRIVACY NOTICE; JUST-IN-TIME; NOTICE; PRIVACY AUTHORIZATION; PERSONALLY IDENTIFIABLE INFORMATION; PII
IP-5	**Privacy Act Statements**	PRIVACY ACT; PERSONALLY IDENTIFIABLE INFORMATION; PII; COLLECT; NOTICE OF AUTHORITY
IP-6	**Individual Access**	PERSONALLY IDENTIFIABLE INFORMATION; PII; INDIVIDUAL ACCESS; PRIVACY ACT; SENIOR AGENCY OFFICIAL FOR PRIVACY; SAOP

TABLE H-9: INCIDENT RESPONSE FAMILY KEYWORDS

CONTROL NUMBER	CONTROL NAME CONTROL ENHANCEMENT NAME	KEYWORDS NOTEWORTHY AND RELEVANT TERMS
IR-1	**Incident Response Policy and Procedures**	INCIDENT RESPONSE POLICY; INCIDENT RESPONSE PROCEDURES; ASSURANCE; POLICY; PROCEDURES; REVIEW; UPDATE; PRIVACY
IR-2	**Incident Response Training**	INCIDENT RESPONSE TRAINING; DEFINED TIME-PERIOD; SYSTEM CHANGES; DEFINED FREQUENCY; ROLES; RESPONSIBILITIES; ASSURANCE; PRIVACY
IR-2(1)	SIMULATED EVENTS	SIMULATED EVENTS; PRIVACY
IR-2(2)	AUTOMATED TRAINING ENVIRONMENTS	AUTOMATED MECHANISMS; TRAINING ENVIRONMENT; PRIVACY
IR-3	**Incident Response Testing**	INCIDENT RESPONSE TESTING; CAPABILITY; ASSURANCE; PRIVACY
IR-3(1)	AUTOMATED TESTING	AUTOMATED TESTING MECHANISMS
IR-3(2)	COORDINATION WITH RELATED PLANS	COORDINATION; ORGANIZATIONAL ELEMENTS; RELATED PLANS; ASSURANCE, BUSINESS CONTINUITY PLANS, CONTINGENCY PLANS, DISASTER RECOVERY PLANS, CONTINUITY OF OPERATIONS PLANS, CRISIS COMMUNICATIONS PLANS, CRITICAL INFRASTRUCTURE PLANS, AND OCCUPANT EMERGENCY PLANS; PRIVACY
IR-3(3)	CONTINUOUS IMPROVEMENT	QUALITATIVE AND QUANTITATIVE DATA; TESTING; INCIDENT RESPONSE PROCESSES; CONTINUOUS IMPROVEMENT; ADVANCED INFORMATION SECURITY PRACTICES; INCIDENT RESPONSE MEASURES AND METRICS
IR-4	**Incident Handling**	INCIDENT HANDLING; PREPARATION; DETECTION; ANALYSIS; CONTAINMENT; ERADICATION; RECOVERY; CONTINGENCY PLAN ACTIVITIES; LESSONS LEARNED; INCIDENT RESPONSE; PROCEDURES; TRAINING; TESTING; IMPLEMENTATION; SUPPLY CHAIN; PRIVACY
IR-4(1)	AUTOMATED INCIDENT HANDLING PROCESSES	AUTOMATED MECHANISMS; INCIDENT HANDLING PROCESSES
IR-4(2)	DYNAMIC RECONFIGURATION	DYNAMIC RECONFIGURATION; TIME FRAMES; RESILIENCY; RESILIENCE
IR-4(3)	CONTINUITY OF OPERATIONS	CONTINUITY OF OPERATIONS; RESILIENCY; RESILIENCE
IR-4(4)	INFORMATION CORRELATION	INFORMATION CORRELATION; INCIDENT INFORMATION; INCIDENT AWARENESS; RESILIENCY; RESILIENCE
IR-4(5)	AUTOMATIC DISABLING OF SYSTEM	SECURITY VIOLATION; AUTOMATICALLY DISABLE SYSTEM
IR-4(6)	INSIDER THREATS — SPECIFIC CAPABILITIES	INSIDER THREATS
IR-4(7)	INSIDER THREATS — INTRA-ORGANIZATION COORDINATION	INSIDER THREATS; INCIDENT HANDLING; PREPARATION; DETECTION; ANALYSIS; CONTAINMENT; ERADICATION; RECOVERY; INTRA-ORGANIZATION COORDINATION
IR-4(8)	CORRELATION WITH EXTERNAL ORGANIZATIONS	COORDINATION WITH EXTERNAL ORGANIZATIONS; INCIDENT INFORMATION
IR-4(9)	DYNAMIC RESPONSE CAPABILITY	DYNAMIC RESPONSE CAPABILITY; SECURITY INCIDENTS; RESILIENCY; RESILIENCE
IR-4(10)	SUPPLY CHAIN COORDINATION	SUPPLY CHAIN; SUPPLY CHAIN INCIDENTS; SUPPLY CHAIN EVENTS; INTERORGANIZATIONAL AGREEMENTS; INCIDENT HANDLING ACTIVITIES; RESILIENCY; RESILIENCE

CONTROL NUMBER	CONTROL NAME CONTROL ENHANCEMENT NAME	KEYWORDS NOTEWORTHY AND RELEVANT TERMS
IR-5	**Incident Monitoring**	INCIDENT MONITORING; DOCUMENTATION; SECURITY INCIDENTS; ASSURANCE; TRACK INCIDENTS; PRIVACY INCIDENTS
IR-5(1)	AUTOMATED TRACKING, DATA COLLECTION, AND ANALYSIS	AUTOMATED TRACKING; SECURITY INCIDENTS; INCIDENT INFORMATION; PRIVACY INCIDENTS
IR-6	**Incident Reporting**	INCIDENT REPORTING; DEFINED TIME=PERIOD; DEFINED AUTHORITIES; UNITED STATES COMPUTER EMERGENCY READINESS TEAM; US-CERT; US-CERT CONCEPT OF OPERATIONS FOR FEDERAL CYBER SECURITY INCIDENT HANDLING; PRIVACY INCIDENT HANDLING
IR-6(1)	AUTOMATED REPORTING	AUTOMATED REPORTING
IR-6(2)	VULNERABILITIES RELATED TO INCIDENTS	INCIDENT VULNERABILITIES; SECURITY INCIDENTS; DEFINED PERSONNEL
IR-6(3)	SUPPLY CHAIN COORDINATION	SECURITY INCIDENT INFORMATION; SUPPLY CHAIN; ORGANIZATIONS; INCIDENTS; SUPPLY CHAIN COORDINATION; INFORMATION SHARING
IR-7	**Incident Response Assistance**	INCIDENT RESPONSE; SUPPORT RESOURCES; ASSISTANCE; PRIVACY
IR-7(1)	AUTOMATION SUPPORT FOR AVAILABILITY OF INFORMATION AND SUPPORT	AUTOMATED SUPPORT MECHANISMS
IR-7(2)	COORDINATION WITH EXTERNAL PROVIDERS	COORDINATION WITH EXTERNAL ORGANIZATIONS; INCIDENT RESPONSE TEAM
IR-8	**Incident Response Plan**	INCIDENT RESPONSE PLAN; DEVELOP; DISTRIBUTE; REVIEW, UPDATE; COMMUNICATE CHANGES; PROTECT; STRUCTURE; REPORTABLE INCIDENTS; PRIVACY
IR-8(1)	PERSONALLY IDENTIFIABLE INFORMATION PROCESSES	INCIDENT RESPONSE PLAN; PERSONALLY IDENTIFIABLE INFORMATION; PII; SENIOR AGENCY OFFICIAL FOR PRIVACY; SAOP; NOTICE
IR-9	**Information Spillage Response**	INFORMATION SPILLAGE; SYSTEM CONTAMINATION; PRIVACY
IR-9(1)	RESPONSIBLE PERSONNEL	RESPONSE; DEFINED PERSONNEL; ROLES
IR-9(2)	TRAINING	ROLE BASED TRAINING
IR-9(3)	POST-SPILL OPERATIONS	POST-SPILL OPERATIONS; CORRECTIVE ACTIONS
IR-9(4)	EXPOSURE TO UNAUTHORIZED PERSONNEL	UNAUTHORIZED PERSONNEL; INFORMATION SPILLS; CONTAMINATED SYSTEMS
IR-10	**Integrated Information Security Analysis Team**	INTEGRATED TEAM; FORENSIC ANALYSTS; MALICIOUS CODE ANALYSTS; TOOL DEVELOPERS; REAL-TIME OPERATORS, RAPID DETECTION; INCIDENT RESPONSE; RESILIENCY; RESILIENCE

TABLE H-10: MAINTENANCE FAMILY KEYWORDS

CONTROL NUMBER	CONTROL NAME CONTROL ENHANCEMENT NAME	KEYWORDS NOTEWORTHY AND RELEVANT TERMS
MA-1	System Maintenance Policy and Procedures	SYSTEM MAINTENANCE POLICY; SYSTEM MAINTENANCE PROCEDURES; ASSURANCE; SCOPE; ROLES; RESPONSIBILITIES; REVIEW; UPDATE; POLICY; PROCEDURE
MA-2	Controlled Maintenance	CONTROLLED MAINTENANCE; EQUIPMENT SANITIZATION; MAINTENANCE RECORDS
MA-2(1)	RECORD CONTENT	WITHDRAWN
MA-2(2)	AUTOMATED MAINTENANCE ACTIVITIES	AUTOMATED MAINTENANCE ACTIVITIES
MA-3	Maintenance Tools	MAINTENANCE TOOLS; DIAGNOSTIC AND REPAIR ACTIONS
MA-3(1)	INSPECT TOOLS	TOOL INSPECTION; UNAUTHORIZED MODIFICATIONS
MA-3(2)	INSPECT MEDIA	DIAGNOSTIC; TEST; INSPECTION; MEDIA; MEDIA PROTECTION
MA-3(3)	PREVENT UNAUTHORIZED REMOVAL	UNAUTHORIZED REMOVAL PREVENTION
MA-3(4)	RESTRICTED TOOL USE	RESTRICTED TOOL USE
MA-4	Nonlocal Maintenance	NONLOCAL MAINTENANCE; DIAGNOSTIC ACTIVITIES
MA-4(1)	AUDITING AND REVIEW	NONLOCAL MAINTENANCE AUDITING; NONLOCAL MAINTENANCE REVIEW
MA-4(2)	DOCUMENT NONLOCAL MAINTENANCE	WITHDRAWN
MA-4(3)	COMPARABLE SECURITY AND SANITIZATION	COMPARABLE SECURITY; COMPARABLE SANITIZATION
MA-4(4)	AUTHENTICATION AND SEPARATION OF MAINTENANCE SESSIONS	DEFINED AUTHENTICATORS; SESSION SEPARATION; MAINTENANCE; NETWORK; RESILIENCY; RESILIENCE
MA-4(5)	APPROVALS AND NOTIFICATIONS	NONLOCAL MAINTENANCE SESSION APPROVAL; NONLOCAL MAINTENANCE SESSION NOTIFICATION; DEFINED PERSONNEL; DEFINED ROLES
MA-4(6)	CRYPTOGRAPHIC PROTECTION	CRYPTOGRAPHIC PROTECTION; CONFIDENTIALITY; INTEGRITY
MA-4(7)	REMOTE DISCONNECT VERIFICATION	REMOTE DISCONNECT VERIFICATION; REMOTE CONNECTION TERMINATION; SESSION TERMINATION; SESSION VERIFICATION
MA-5	Maintenance Personnel	MAINTENANCE PERSONNEL; HARDWARE MAINTENANCE; SOFTWARE MAINTENANCE
MA-5(1)	INDIVIDUALS WITHOUT APPROPRIATE ACCESS	NON U.S. CITIZENS; LACK SECURITY CLEARANCE; ALTERNATE SECURITY SAFEGUARDS; CONTROLLED UNCLASSIFIED INFORMATION; CUI; COMPONENT SANITIZATION; ALTERNATE SECURITY SAFEGUARDS
MA-5(2)	SECURITY CLEARANCES FOR CLASSIFIED SYSTEMS	CLASSIFIED SYSTEMS; SECURITY CLEARANCE; ACCESS APPROVAL; CLASSIFICATION LEVEL
MA-5(3)	CITIZENSHIP REQUIREMENTS FOR CLASSIFIED SYSTEMS	CITIZENSHIP REQUIREMENTS; U.S. CITIZEN; CLASSIFIED SYSTEM; CLASSIFIED INFORMATION
MA-5(4)	FOREIGN NATIONALS	FOREIGN NATIONALS; MEMORANDA OF AGREEMENT
MA-5(5)	NON-SYSTEM MAINTENANCE	NON-SYSTEM MAINTENANCE; NON-ESCORTED PERSONNEL; PHYSICAL PROXIMITY; ACCESS AUTHORIZATIONS
MA-6	Timely Maintenance	TIMELY MAINTENANCE; MAINTENANCE SUPPORT; SPARE PARTS; SPARE COMPONENTS; CONTRACTS
MA-6(1)	PREVENTIVE MAINTENANCE	PREVENTIVE MAINTENANCE; PROACTIVE CARE

CONTROL NUMBER	CONTROL NAME CONTROL ENHANCEMENT NAME	KEYWORDS NOTEWORTHY AND RELEVANT TERMS
MA-6(2)	PREDICTIVE MAINTENANCE	PREDICTIVE MAINTENANCE; CONDITION-BASED MAINTENANCE; EQUIPMENT CONDITION MONITORING
MA-6(3)	AUTOMATED SUPPORT FOR PREDICTIVE MAINTENANCE	AUTOMATED SUPPORT; PREDICTIVE MAINTENANCE; COMPUTERIZED MAINTENANCE MANAGEMENT SYSTEM
MA-6(4)	ADEQUATE SUPPLY	ADEQUATE SUPPLY; SUPPLY CHAIN; CRITICAL SYSTEM COMPONENTS; MULTIPLE SUPPLIERS; STOCKPILE; SIMILAR COMPONENTS; BACKUP COMPONENTS

TABLE H-11: MEDIA PROTECTION FAMILY KEYWORDS

CONTROL NUMBER	CONTROL NAME CONTROL ENHANCEMENT NAME	KEYWORDS NOTEWORTHY AND RELEVANT TERMS
MP-1	Media Protection Policy and Procedures	MEDIA PROTECTION; POLICY; ASSURANCE, PROCESS; PROCEDURE; SCOPE; ROLES; RESPONSIBILITY; REVIEW; UPDATE
MP-2	Media Access	MEDIA ACCESS; RESTRICT ACCESS; DIGITAL; NON-DIGITAL; DEFINED PERSONNEL; ROLES
MP-2(1)	AUTOMATED RESTRICTED ACCESS	WITHDRAWN
MP-2(2)	CRYPTOGRAPHIC PROTECTION	WITHDRAWN
MP-3	Media Marking	MEDIA MARKING; DISTRIBUTION LIMITATIONS; HANDLING CAVEATS; SECURITY MARKING; SECURITY LABELING; DEFINED CONTROLLED AREAS
MP-4	Media Storage	MEDIA STORAGE; PHYSICAL CONTROLS; DIGITAL; NON-DIGITAL; DEFINED CONTROLLED AREAS; MEDIA LIBRARY; SECURITY CATEGORY; CLASSIFICATION
MP-4(1)	CRYPTOGRAPHIC PROTECTION	WITHDRAWN
MP-4(2)	AUTOMATED RESTRICTED ACCESS	AUTOMATED MECHANISMS; RESTRICT ACCESS; AUDIT ACCESS
MP-5	Media Transport	MEDIA TRANSPORT; CONTROLLED AREAS; SECURITY SAFEGUARDS; PHYSICAL; TECHNICAL; MOBILE DEVICES; ACCOUNTABILITY; DOCUMENT ACTIVITIES; AUTHORIZED PERSONNEL; CRYPTOGRAPHY; CRYPTOGRAPHIC MECHANISMS
MP-5(1)	PROTECTION OUTSIDE OF CONTROLLED AREAS	WITHDRAWN
MP-5(2)	DOCUMENTATION OF ACTIVITIES	WITHDRAWN
MP-5(3)	CUSTODIANS	IDENTIFIED CUSTODIAN, POINTS OF CONTACT
MP-5(4)	CRYPTOGRAPHIC PROTECTION	WITHDRAWN
MP-6	Media Sanitization	DIGITAL; NON-DIGITAL; REMOVABLE; SANITIZE SYSTEM MEDIA; DISPOSAL; SANITIZATION TECHNIQUES AND PROCEDURES; CLEARING; PURGING; CRYPTOGRAPHIC ERASE; DESTRUCTION; SANITIZATION MECHANISMS; STRENGTH, INTEGRITY; SECURITY CATEGORY; CLASSIFICATION; NSA STANDARDS; CLASSIFIED INFORMATION
MP-6(1)	REVIEW, APPROVE, TRACK, DOCUMENT, VERIFY	MEDIA SANITIZATION; DISPOSAL; REVIEW; APPROVAL; TRACK; DOCUMENT; VERIFY; RECORDS-RETENTION POLICY
MP-6(2)	EQUIPMENT TESTING	SANITIZATION EQUIPMENT TESTING
MP-6(3)	NONDESTRUCTIVE TECHNIQUES	NONDESTRUCTIVE SANITIZATION TECHNIQUES; PORTABLE STORAGE DEVICES; CONTROLLED UNCLASSIFIED INFORMATION; CUI
MP-6(4)	CONTROLLED UNCLASSIFIED INFORMATION	WITHDRAWN
MP-6(5)	CLASSIFIED INFORMATION	WITHDRAWN
MP-6(6)	MEDIA DESTRUCTION	WITHDRAWN
MP-6(7)	DUAL AUTHORIZATION	DUAL AUTHORIZATION; MEDIA SANITIZATION; TWO-PERSON CONTROL
MP-6(8)	REMOTE PURGING OR WIPING OF INFORMATION	REMOTE PURGE; REMOTE WIPE

CONTROL NUMBER	CONTROL NAME CONTROL ENHANCEMENT NAME	KEYWORDS NOTEWORTHY AND RELEVANT TERMS
MP-6(9)	DESTRUCTION OF PERSONALLY IDENTIFIABLE INFORMATION	MEDIA SANITIZATION; PERSONALLY IDENTIFIABLE INFORMATION; PII; DE-IDENTIFICATION; COPIES; ARCHIVED RECORDS; SYSTEM LOGS; DESTRUCTION; PRIVACY
MP-7	**Media Use**	MEDIA USE; RESTRICT; PROHIBIT; TYPE OF SYSTEM MEDIA; DIGITAL MEDIA; NON-DIGITAL MEDIA; PORTABLE STORAGE; SECURITY SAFEGUARDS
MP-7(1)	PROHIBIT USE WITHOUT OWNER	WITHDRAWN
MP-7(2)	PROHIBIT USE OF SANITIZATION-RESISTANT MEDIA	SANITIZATION-RESISTANT MEDIA
MP-8	**Media Downgrading**	MEDIA; DOWNGRADING PROCESS; DOWNGRADING MECHANISMS; SECURITY CATEGORY; CLASSIFICATION
MP-8(1)	DOCUMENTATION OF PROCESS	EMPLOYED TECHNIQUE; NUMBER OF MEDIA; IDENTITY OF INDIVIDUAL AUTHORIZED/PERFORMED DOWNGRADING
MP-8(2)	EQUIPMENT TESTING	DOWNGRADING EQUIPMENT; EQUIPMENT TESTING; DEFINED FREQUENCY
MP-8(3)	CONTROLLED UNCLASSIFIED INFORMATION	CONTROLLED UNCLASSIFIED INFORMATION; CUI
MP-8(4)	CLASSIFIED INFORMATION	CLASSIFIED INFORMATION; DOWNGRADE; NATIONAL SECURITY AGENCY; NSA STANDARDS AND POLICIES

TABLE H-13: PRIVACY AUTHORIZATION FAMILY KEYWORDS

CONTROL NUMBER	CONTROL NAME CONTROL ENHANCEMENT NAME	KEYWORDS NOTEWORTHY AND RELEVANT TERMS
PA-1	**Privacy Authorization Policy and Procedures**	PRIVACY AUTHORIZATION POLICY; PRIVACY AUTHORIZATION PROCEDURES; POLICY; PROCEDURES; REVIEW; UPDATE; PRIVACY PLANS
PA-2	**Authority to Collect**	SENIOR AGENCY OFFICIAL FOR PRIVACY; SAOP; SYSTEM OF RECORDS NOTICE; SORN; PRIVACY IMPACT ASSESSMENTS; PIA; COMPUTER MATCHING AGREEMENTS; PRIVACY ACT; PERSONALLY IDENTIFIABLE INFORMATION; PII
PA-3	**Purpose Specification**	SENIOR AGENCY OFFICIAL FOR PRIVACY; SAOP; SYSTEM OF RECORDS NOTICE; SORN; PRIVACY IMPACT ASSESSMENTS; PIA; COMPUTER MATCHING AGREEMENTS; PRIVACY ACT; PERSONALLY IDENTIFIABLE INFORMATION; PII
PA-3(1)	USAGE RESTRICTIONS OF PERSONALLY IDENTIFIABLE INFORMATION	PERSONALLY IDENTIFIABLE INFORMATION; PII; SENIOR AGENCY OFFICIAL FOR PRIVACY; SAOP; PRIVACY ACT
PA-3(2)	AUTOMATION	PRIVACY; PERSONALLY IDENTIFIABLE INFORMATION; PII; AUTOMATION
PA-4	**Information Sharing with External Parties**	PERSONALLY IDENTIFIABLE INFORMATION; PII; SENIOR AGENCY OFFICIAL FOR PRIVACY; SAOP, SYSTEM OF RECORDS NOTICE; SORN; PRIVACY IMPACT ASSESSMENTS; PIA; PRIVACY ACT; COMPUTER MATCHING AGREEMENTS; MEMORANDA OF AGREEMENT; MEMORANDA OF UNDERSTANDING; LETTERS OF INTENT

TABLE H-13: PHYSICAL AND ENVIRONMENTAL PROTECTION FAMILY KEYWORDS

CONTROL NUMBER	CONTROL NAME CONTROL ENHANCEMENT NAME	KEYWORDS NOTEWORTHY AND RELEVANT TERMS
PE-1	**Physical and Environmental Protection Policy and Procedures**	PHYSICAL AND ENVIRONMENTAL PROTECTION POLICY; PHYSICAL AND ENVIRONMENTAL PROTECTION PROCEDURE; POLICY; PROCEDURES; REVIEW; UPDATE
PE-2	**Physical Access Authorizations**	PHYSICAL ACCESS AUTHORIZATIONS; AUTHORIZATION CREDENTIALS; ACCESS LIST; EMPLOYEES; CONTRACTORS; VISITORS
PE-2(1)	ACCESS BY POSITION AND ROLE	ACCESS BY POSITION; ACCESS BY ROLE; PHYSICAL ACCESS AUTHORIZATION
PE-2(2)	TWO FORMS OF IDENTIFICATION	TWO FORMS OF IDENTIFICATION; VISITOR ACCESS
PE-2(3)	RESTRICT UNESCORTED ACCESS	RESTRICT UNESCORTED ACCESS; CLASSIFIED INFORMATION; FORMAL ACCESS AUTHORIZATIONS
PE-3	**Physical Access Control**	PHYSICAL ACCESS CONTROL; PHYSICAL ACCESS AUTHORIZATIONS; INDIVIDUAL ACCESS AUTHORIZATIONS; PHYSICAL ACCESS AUDIT LOG; ESCORT VISITORS; MONITOR VISITOR ACTIVITIES; CHANGE COMBINATIONS; CHANGE KEYS; VERIFY ACCESS AUTHORIZATION; INGRESS CONTROL; EGRESS CONTROL; PHYSICAL ACCESS DEVICE
PE-3(1)	SYSTEM ACCESS	SYSTEM ACCESS AUTHORIZATION
PE-3(2)	FACILITY AND SYSTEM BOUNDARIES	FACILITY BOUNDARIES; SYSTEM BOUNDARIES; SECURITY CHECKS; EXFILTRATION; RESILIENCY; RESILIENCE
PE-3(3)	CONTINUOUS GUARDS	CONTINUOUS GUARDS; CONTINUOUS ALARMS; CONTINUOUS MONITORING
PE-3(4)	LOCKABLE CASINGS	LOCKABLE CASINGS; UNAUTHORIZED PHYSICAL ACCESS; RESILIENCY; RESILIENCE
PE-3(5)	TAMPER PROTECTION	TAMPER PROTECTION; PHYSICAL TAMPERING; TAMPER DETECTION; TAMPER PREVENTION; COUNTERFEITING; SUPPLY CHAIN; RESILIENCY; RESILIENCE
PE-3(6)	FACILITY PENETRATION TESTING	WITHDRAWN
PE-3(7)	PHYSICAL BARRIERS	PHYSICAL BARRIERS; LIMIT ACCESS
PE-4	**Access Control for Transmission**	TRANSMISSION MEDIUM; EAVESDROPPING; IN TRANSIT MODIFICATION PREVENTION; ACCESS CONTROL
PE-5	**Access Control for Output Devices**	ACCESS CONTROL; PHYSICAL ACCESS CONTROL; OUTPUT DEVICES
PE-5(1)	ACCESS TO OUTPUT BY AUTHORIZED INDIVIDUALS	PHYSICAL ACCESS CONTROL; AUTHORIZED INDIVIDUALS
PE-5(2)	ACCESS TO OUTPUT BY INDIVIDUAL IDENTITY	ACCESS TO OUTPUT; AUTHORIZED INDIVIDUALS
PE-5(3)	MARKING OUTPUT DEVICES	MARK OUTPUT DEVICES; SECURITY MARKING
PE-6	**Monitoring Physical Access**	MONITOR PHYSICAL ACCESS; PHYSICAL ACCESS LOGS; PHYSICAL SECURITY INCIDENTS; ASSURANCE; COORDINATE; INCIDENT RESPONSE; RESILIENCY; RESILIENCE
PE-6(1)	INTRUSION ALARMS AND SURVEILLANCE EQUIPMENT	INTRUSION ALARMS; SURVEILLANCE EQUIPMENT
PE-6(2)	AUTOMATED INTRUSION RECOGNITION AND RESPONSES	AUTOMATED INTRUSION RECOGNITION; AUTOMATED INTRUSION RESPONSE; RESILIENCY; RESILIENCE
PE-6(3)	VIDEO SURVEILLANCE	VIDEO SURVEILLANCE; SURVEILLANCE VIDEO RETENTION
PE-6(4)	MONITORING PHYSICAL ACCESS TO SYSTEMS	MONITOR PHYSICAL ACCESS TO SYSTEMS; RESILIENCY; RESILIENCE
PE-7	Visitor Control	WITHDRAWN

CONTROL NUMBER	CONTROL NAME CONTROL ENHANCEMENT NAME	KEYWORDS NOTEWORTHY AND RELEVANT TERMS
PE-8	**Visitor Access Records**	MAINTAIN VISITOR ACCESS RECORDS; REVIEW VISITOR ACCESS RECORDS; ASSURANCE; VISITOR ACCESS RECORDS
PE-8(1)	AUTOMATED RECORDS MAINTENANCE AND REVIEW	AUTOMATED RECORDS MAINTENANCE; AUTOMATED RECORDS REVIEW
PE-8(2)	PHYSICAL ACCESS RECORDS	WITHDRAWN
PE-9	**Power Equipment and Cabling**	POWER EQUIPMENT PROTECTION; POWER CABLING PROTECTION
PE-9(1)	REDUNDANT CABLING	REDUNDANT CABLING; RESILIENCY; RESILIENCE
PE-9(2)	AUTOMATIC VOLTAGE CONTROLS	AUTOMATIC VOLTAGE CONTROLS
PE-10	**Emergency Shutoff**	EMERGENCY SHUTOFF; EMERGENCY POWER SHUTOFF PROTECTION
PE-10(1)	ACCIDENTAL AND UNAUTHORIZED ACTIVATION	WITHDRAWN
PE-11	**Emergency Power**	EMERGENCY POWER; UNINTERRUPTIBLE POWER SUPPLY; PRIMARY POWER LOSS
PE-11(1)	LONG-TERM ALTERNATE POWER SUPPLY — MINIMAL OPERATIONAL CAPABILITY	ALTERNATE POWER SUPPLY; MINIMAL OPERATIONAL CAPABILITY; SECONDARY COMMERCIAL POWER SUPPLY; RESILIENCY; RESILIENCE
PE-11(2)	LONG-TERM ALTERNATE POWER SUPPLY — SELF-CONTAINED	ALTERNATE POWER SUPPLY; SELF-CONTAINED; GENERATOR POWER; RESILIENCY; RESILIENCE
PE-12	**Emergency Lighting**	EMERGENCY LIGHTING
PE-12(1)	ESSENTIAL MISSIONS AND BUSINESS FUNCTIONS	ESSENTIAL MISSIONS; BUSINESS FUNCTIONS
PE-13	**Fire Protection**	FIRE PROTECTION; FIRE SUPPRESSION; FIRE DETECTION
PE-13(1)	DETECTION DEVICES AND SYSTEMS	FIRE DETECTION DEVICES; FIRE DETECTION SYSTEMS; AUTOMATIC ACTIVATION AND NOTIFICATION
PE-13(2)	AUTOMATIC SUPPRESSION DEVICES AND SYSTEMS	FIRE SUPPRESSION DEVICES; FIRE SUPPRESSION SYSTEMS; AUTOMATIC ACTIVATION AND NOTIFICATION; AUTOMATIC FIRE SUPPRESSION
PE-13(3)	AUTOMATIC FIRE SUPPRESSION	WITHDRAWN
PE-13(4)	INSPECTIONS	FIRE PROTECTION INSPECTIONS
PE-14	**Temperature and Humidity Controls**	TEMPERATURE CONTROLS; HUMIDITY CONTROLS; MONITOR TEMPERATURE LEVEL; MONITOR HUMIDITY LEVEL
PE-14(1)	AUTOMATIC CONTROLS	AUTOMATIC TEMPERATURE CONTROLS; AUTOMATIC HUMIDITY CONTROLS
PE-14(2)	MONITORING WITH ALARMS AND NOTIFICATIONS	TEMPERATURE MONITORING ALARM; HUMIDITY MONITORING ALARM
PE-15	**Water Damage Protection**	WATER DAMAGE PROTECTION; WATER LEAKAGE
PE-15(1)	AUTOMATION SUPPORT	AUTOMATION SUPPORT; WATER DETECTION SENSORS; WATER DETECTION ALARMS; WATER DETECTION NOTIFICATION SYSTEMS
PE-16	**Delivery and Removal**	ENTRY AUTHORIZATION ENFORCEMENT; EXIT AUTHORIZATION ENFORCEMENT; DELIVERY AREA ACCESS RESTRICTION; AUTHORIZE DELIVERY; AUTHORIZE REMOVAL; MONITOR DELIVERY; MONITOR REMOVAL; MAINTAIN ACCESS RECORDS
PE-17	**Alternate Work Site**	ALTERNATE WORK SITE; ALTERNATE LOCATION; TELEWORK; RESILIENCY; RESILIENCE

CONTROL NUMBER	CONTROL NAME CONTROL ENHANCEMENT NAME	KEYWORDS NOTEWORTHY AND RELEVANT TERMS
PE-18	Location of System Components	SYSTEM COMPONENT LOCATION; PHYSICAL HAZARD PROTECTION; ENVIRONMENTAL HAZARD PROTECTION; PHYSICAL ENTRY POINT PROTECTION
PE-18(1)	FACILITY SITE	FACILITY SITE; SYSTEM LOCATION PLANNING
PE-19	Information Leakage	INFORMATION LEAKAGE; ELECTROMAGNETIC SIGNALS EMANATIONS
PE-19(1)	NATIONAL EMISSIONS AND TEMPEST POLICIES AND PROCEDURES	NATIONAL EMISSIONS; TEMPEST; TEMPEST POLICIES; TEMPEST PROCEDURES
PE-20	Asset Monitoring and Tracking	ASSET MONITORING; ASSET TRACKING; PROVENANCE; ASSET LOCATION TECHNOLOGIES
PE-21	Electromagnetic Pulse Protection	ELECTROMAGNETIC PULSE; EMP; INTERFERENCE; SHIELDING; FARADAY CAGES; SURGE SUPPRESSOR
PE-22	Component Marking	CLASSIFICATION LEVEL; MARKING; SECURITY LABELING; HARDWARE COMPONENTS

TABLE H-14: SUMMARY — PLANNING FAMILY KEYWORDS

CONTROL NUMBER	CONTROL NAME / CONTROL ENHANCEMENT NAME	KEYWORDS / NOTEWORTHY AND RELEVANT TERMS
PL-1	Planning Policy and Procedures	SECURITY PLANNING POLICY; SECURITY PLANNING PROCEDURES; POLICY; PROCEDURES; REVIEW; UPDATE; PRIVACY PLANNING POLICY; PRIVACY PLANNING PROCEDURES
PL-2	Security and Privacy Plans	SYSTEM SECURITY PLAN; SSP; AUTHORIZATION BOUNDARY; SYSTEM REQUIREMENT OVERVIEW; OVERLAY; ASSURANCE; MISSION PROCESS; BUSINESS PROCESS; SECURITY CATEGORIZATION; SECURITY CONTROLS; AUTHORIZING OFFICIAL REVIEW; AUTHORIZING OFFICIAL APPROVE; PERSONNEL ROLES AND RESPONSIBILITIES; REVIEW SSP; UPDATE SSP; SYSTEM PRIVACY PLAN; PRIVACY CONTROLS
PL-2(1)	CONCEPT OF OPERATIONS	WITHDRAWN
PL-2(2)	FUNCTIONAL ARCHITECTURE	WITHDRAWN
PL-2(3)	PLAN AND COORDINATE WITH OTHER ORGANIZATIONAL ENTITIES	SECURITY-RELATED ACTIVITIES; COORDINATE SECURITY ACTIVITIES; PRIVACY-RELATED ACTIVITIES; COORDINATE PRIVACY ACTIVITIES; RESILIENCY; RESILIENCE
PL-3	System Security Plan Update	WITHDRAWN
PL-4	Rules of Behavior	RULES OF BEHAVIOR; ROB; SYSTEM USAGE; REVIEW; UPDATE; USER ACKNOWLEDGE; USER SIGN; PRIVACY
PL-4(1)	SOCIAL MEDIA AND NETWORKING RESTRICTIONS	SOCIAL MEDIA; NETWORK RESTRICTIONS; PUBLIC WEBSITE
PL-5	Privacy Impact Assessment	WITHDRAWN
PL-6	Security-Related Activity Planning	WITHDRAWN
PL-7	Concept of Operations	SECURITY CONCEPT OF OPERATIONS; CONOPS; PRIVACY CONCEPT OF OPERATIONS; PRIVACY
PL-8	Security and Privacy Architectures	SECURITY ARCHITECTURE; ASSURANCE; PRIVACY ARCHITECTURE
PL-8(1)	DEFENSE-IN-DEPTH	DEFENSE-IN-DEPTH; SAFEGUARD ALLOCATION; RESILIENCY; RESILIENCE
PL-8(2)	SUPPLIER DIVERSITY	SUPPLIER DIVERSITY; PRIVACY; RESILIENCY; RESILIENCE
PL-9	Central Management	CENTRAL MANAGEMENT; STANDARDIZED CONTROL IMPLEMENTATION; STANDARDIZED CONTROL MANAGEMENT; ASSURANCE; SECURITY CONTROLS; PRIVACY CONTROLS; PLANNING CONTROLS; IMPLEMENT CONTROLS; ASSESS CONTROLS; MONITOR CONTROLS
PL-10	Baseline Selection	BASELINE SELECTION; STAKEHOLDER NEEDS; MISSION AND BUSINESS REQUIREMENTS
PL-11	Baseline Tailoring	BASELINE TAILORING; TAILORING; CUSTOMIZE BASELINE CONTROLS; TAILORING ACTIONS; SPECIALIZATION; CUSTOMIZATION; MISSION AND BUSINESS FUNCTIONS

TABLE H-15: PROGRAM MANAGEMENT FAMILY KEYWORDS

CONTROL NUMBER	CONTROL NAME CONTROL ENHANCEMENT NAME	KEYWORDS NOTEWORTHY AND RELEVANT TERMS
PM-1	Information Security Program Plan	INFORMATION SECURITY PROGRAM PLAN; MANAGEMENT COMMITMENT; COORDINATION; COMPLIANCE; UNAUTHORIZED DISCLOSURE; MODIFICATION
PM-2	Information Security Program Roles	SENIOR AGENCY INFORMATION SECURITY OFFICER; SISO
PM-3	Information Security and Privacy Resources	INFORMATION SECURITY RESOURCES; CAPITAL PLANNING; INVESTMENT REQUESTS; INFORMATION SECURITY PROGRAM; EXCEPTIONS; EXHIBIT 300; EXHIBIT 53; BUSINESS CASE; PRIVACY RESOURCES; PRIVACY PROGRAM
PM-4	Plan of Action and Milestones Process	PLAN OF ACTION AND MILESTONES; POAM; DEVELOP; MAINTAIN; DOCUMENT; REMEDIAL; ACTIONS; OMB; FISMA; POA&M; REMEDIATION; PRIVACY
PM-5	System Inventory	SYSTEM INVENTORY; DEVELOP; MAINTAIN; OMB; FISMA
PM-6	Measures of Performance	INFORMATION SECURITY MEASURES OF PERFORMANCE; DEVELOP; MONITOR; REPORT; METRICS; OUTCOME-BASED; EFFECTIVENESS; EFFICIENCY; PRIVACY MEASURES OF PERFORMANCE
PM-7	Enterprise Architecture	ENTERPRISE ARCHITECTURE; ALIGNED; PRIVACY
PM-8	Critical Infrastructure Plan	CRITICAL INFRASTRUCTURE PLAN; DEVELOPMENT; DOCUMENTATION; UPDATING; PRIORITIZE CRITICAL ASSETS; PRIORITIZE CRITICAL RESOURCES; PRIVACY
PM-9	Risk Management Strategy	RISK MANAGEMENT STRATEGY; DEVELOP; IMPLEMENT; REVIEW; UPDATE; DEFINED FREQUENCY; ORGANIZATIONAL RISK; OPERATIONAL RISK; ACCEPTABLE RISK; RISK TOLERANCE; RISK MITIGATION STRATEGY; RISK ASSESSMENT STRATEGY; RISK EXECUTIVE; SUPPLY CHAIN; PRIVACY
PM-10	Authorization Process	SECURITY AUTHORIZATION PROCESS; MANAGE; ROLES; RESPONSIBILITIES; INTEGRATE; CONTINUOUS MONITORING PROCESS; PRIVACY
PM-11	Mission and Business Process Definition	MISSION/BUSINESS; PROCESSES; PRIVACY
PM-12	Insider Threat Program	INSIDER THREAT PROGRAM; EXECUTIVE ORDER 13587; NATIONAL POLICY ON INSIDER THREAT; RESILIENCY; RESILIENCE
PM-13	Information Security and Privacy Workforce	INFORMATION SECURITY WORKFORCE; DEVELOPMENT; IMPROVEMENT; CAREER PATHS; PRIVACY WORKFORCE
PM-14	Testing, Training, and Monitoring	SECURITY TESTING; TRAINING; MONITORING; PLANS; DEVELOPED; MAINTAINED; EXECUTED; REVIEW; RISK RESPONSE ACTIONS; PRIVACY
PM-15	Contacts with Groups and Associations	CONTACTS WITH SECURITY GROUPS AND ASSOCIATIONS; EDUCATION; TRAINING; CURRENCY; SHARE; THREATS; VULNERABILITIES; INCIDENTS; CONTACTS WITH PRIVACY GROUPS AND ASSOCIATIONS

CONTROL NUMBER	CONTROL NAME CONTROL ENHANCEMENT NAME	KEYWORDS NOTEWORTHY AND RELEVANT TERMS
PM-16	Threat Awareness Program	THREAT AWARENESS PROGRAM; INFORMATION SHARING; BILATERAL; MULTILATERAL; ADVANCED PERSISTENT THREATS; APT; RESILIENCY; RESILIENCE
PM-17	Protecting Controlled Unclassified Information on External Systems	EXTERNAL AUTHORIZATION; CONTROLLED UNCLASSIFIED INFORMATION; CUI; NONFEDERAL ORGANIZATION; NONFEDERAL SYSTEM; PRIVACY
PM-18	Privacy Program Plan	SENIOR AGENCY OFFICIAL FOR PRIVACY; SAOP; PRIVACY PROGRAM; PRIVACY PLAN
PM-19	Privacy Privacy Program Roles	SENIOR AGENCY OFFICIAL FOR PRIVACY; SAOP
PM-20	System of Records Notice	PRIVACY ACT; SYSTEM OF RECORDS NOTICE; SORN
PM-21	Dissemination of Privacy Program Information	SENIOR AGENCY OFFICIAL FOR PRIVACY; SAOP; PRIVACY IMPACT ASSESSMENTS; PIA, SYSTEM OF RECORDS NOTICE; SORN; DISSEMINATION
PM-22	Accounting of Disclosures	PERSONALLY IDENTIFIABLE INFORMATION; PII; PRIVACY ACT; DISCLOSURE; RECORDS; DISSEMINATION
PM-23	Data Quality Management	DATA QUALITY; PRIVACY; PERSONALLY IDENTIFIABLE INFORMATION; PII; DE-IDENTIFICATION; INTEGRITY
PM-23(1)	AUTOMATION	DATA QUALITY; PRIVACY; PERSONALLY IDENTIFIABLE INFORMATION; PII; AUTOMATION; DATA MINIMIZATION
PM-23(2)	DATA TAGGING	DATA TAGGING; DATA QUALITY; DE-IDENTIFICATION; PRIVACY; PERSONALLY IDENTIFIABLE INFORMATION; PII
PM-23(3)	UPDATING PERSONALLY IDENTIFIABLE INFORMATION	DATA QUALITY; PRIVACY; PERSONALLY IDENTIFIABLE INFORMATION; PII
PM-24	Data Management Board	DATA MANAGEMENT BOARD; SENIOR AGENCY OFFICIAL FOR PRIVACY; SAOP; ARCHIVING; MONITORING
PM-25	Data Integrity Board	DATA INTEGRITY BOARD; DATA MANAGEMENT BOARD; COMPUTER MATCHING AGREEMENTS; SENIOR AGENCY OFFICIAL FOR PRIVACY; SAOP
PM-25(1)	PUBLISH AGREEMENTS ON WEBSITE	PRIVACY; PERSONALLY IDENTIFIABLE INFORMATION; PII; COMPUTER MATCHING AGREEMENTS
PM-26	Minimization of Personally Identifiable Information Used in Testing Training, and Research	PERSONALLY IDENTIFIABLE INFORMATION; PII; SENIOR AGENCY OFFICIAL FOR PRIVACY, SAOP
PM-27	Individual Access Control	PRIVACY ACT; SYSTEM OF RECORDS NOTICE; SORN; SENIOR AGENCY OFFICIAL FOR PRIVACY; SORN; PERSONALLY IDENTIFIABLE INFORMATION; PII
PM-28	Complaint Management	SENIOR AGENCY OFFICIAL FOR PRIVACY; SAOP
PM-29	Inventory of Personally Identifiable Information	PERSONALLY IDENTIFIABLE INFORMATION; PII; SENIOR AGENCY OFFICIAL FOR PRIVACY; SAOP
PM-29(1)	AUTOMATION SUPPORT	AUTOMATION; PRIVACY; PERSONALLY IDENTIFIABLE INFORMATION; PII
PM-30	Privacy Reporting	REPORTING; SENIOR AGENCY OFFICIAL FOR PRIVACY; SAOP
PM-31	Supply Chain Risk Management Plan	SUPPLY CHAIN RISK MANAGEMENT; RISK MANAGEMENT PLAN

CONTROL NUMBER	CONTROL NAME CONTROL ENHANCEMENT NAME	KEYWORDS NOTEWORTHY AND RELEVANT TERMS
PM-32	Risk Framing	ASSUMPTIONS; RISK ASSESSMENTS; RISK RESPONSE; RISK MONITORING; CONSTRAINTS; RISK TOLERANCE; PRIORITIES; TRADE-OFFS

TABLE H-16: PERSONNEL SECURITY FAMILY RELATIONSHIPS

CONTROL NUMBER	CONTROL NAME CONTROL ENHANCEMENT NAME	KEYWORDS NOTEWORTHY AND RELEVANT TERMS
PS-1	Personnel Security Policy and Procedures	PERSONNEL SECURITY POLICY; PERSONNEL SECURITY PROCEDURES; ASSURANCE; POLICY; PROCEDURES; REVIEW; UPDATE; PRIVACY
PS-2	Position Risk Designation	RISK DESIGNATION; SCREENING CRITERIA; POSITION RISK
PS-3	Personnel Screening	PERSONNEL SCREENING; RESCREEN
PS-3(1)	CLASSIFIED INFORMATION	CLASSIFIED INFORMATION; CLEARED; INDOCTRINATED; CLASSIFICATION LEVEL
PS-3(2)	FORMAL INDOCTRINATION	FORMAL INDOCTRINATION; CLASSIFIED INFORMATION
PS-3(3)	INFORMATION WITH SPECIAL PROTECTION MEASURES	SPECIAL PROTECTION; ACCESS AUTHORIZATIONS; ADDITIONAL PERSONNEL SCREENING CRITERIA
PS-3(4)	CITIZENSHIP REQUIREMENTS	CITIZENSHIP REQUIREMENTS
PS-4	Personnel Termination	PERSONNEL TERMINATION; SYSTEM-RELATED PROPERTY; TERMINATE; EXIT INTERVIEW; RETURN PROPERTY; NOTIFICATION
PS-4(1)	POST-EMPLOYMENT REQUIREMENTS	POST-EMPLOYMENT REQUIREMENTS; LEGALLY BINDING; TERMINATION PROCESS
PS-4(2)	AUTOMATED NOTIFICATION	AUTOMATED NOTIFICATION; AUTOMATED MECHANISMS; AUTOMATIC ALERTS; AUTOMATIC NOTIFICATION
PS-5	Personnel Transfer	PERSONNEL TRANSFER; LOGICAL ACCESS AUTHORIZATIONS; PHYSICAL ACCESS AUTHORIZATIONS; TRANSFER ACTIONS, REASSIGNMENT ACTIONS
PS 6	Access Agreements	ACCESS AGREEMENTS; NONDISCLOSURE AGREEMENT; ACCEPTABLE USE AGREEMENT; RULES OF BEHAVIOR; CONFLICT-OF-INTEREST AGREEMENTS; ASSURANCE; REVIEW AGREEMENTS; UPDATE AGREEMENTS
PS-6(1)	INFORMATION REQUIRING SPECIAL PROTECTION	WITHDRAWN
PS-6(2)	CLASSIFIED INFORMATION REQUIRING SPECIAL PROTECTION	CLASSIFIED INFORMATION; SPECIAL PROTECTION; VALID ACCESS AUTHORIZATION; PERSONNEL SECURITY CRITERIA; NONDISCLOSURE AGREEMENT
PS-6(3)	POST-EMPLOYMENT REQUIREMENTS	POST-EMPLOYMENT REQUIREMENTS
PS-7	External Personnel Security	EXTERNAL PARTY PERSONNEL SECURITY; PERSONNEL SECURITY REQUIREMENTS; EXTERNAL PARTY TRANSFER NOTIFICATIONS; EXTERNAL PARTY TERMINATION NOTIFICATIONS; ASSURANCE; MONITOR EXTERNAL PARTY COMPLIANCE
PS-8	Personnel Sanctions	PERSONNEL SANCTIONS; FORMAL SANCTIONS; ORGANIZATIONAL SANCTIONS

TABLE H-17: RISK ASSESSMENT FAMILY KEYWORDS

CONTROL NUMBER	CONTROL NAME CONTROL ENHANCEMENT NAME	KEYWORDS NOTEWORTHY AND RELEVANT TERMS
RA-1	**Risk Assessment Policy and Procedures**	RISK ASSESSMENT; RISK ASSESSMENT POLICY; RISK ASSESSMENT PROCEDURE; ASSURANCE; POLICY; PROCEDURES; REVIEW; UPDATE; PRIVACY
RA-2	**Security Categorization**	SECURITY CATEGORIZATION; INFORMATION CATEGORIZATION; SYSTEM CATEGORIZATION; SECURITY CATEGORIZATION DECISION; USA PATRIOT ACT OF 2001; HOMELAND SECURITY PRESIDENTIAL DIRECTIVE; DOCUMENT CATEGORIZATION; CATEGORIZATION RATIONALE; SSP; SYSTEM SECURITY PLAN; AUTHORIZING OFFICIAL; AUTHORIZING OFFICIAL APPROVE; AUTHORIZATION BOUNDARY
RA-2(1)	SECOND-LEVEL CATEGORIZATION	SECOND-LEVEL CATEGORIZATION; SYSTEM IMPACT LEVEL; SUB-CATEGORIES; PRIORITIZE; HIGH-VALUE ASSET
RA-3	**Risk Assessment**	RISK ASSESSMENT; RISK ASSESSMENT REPORT; ASSURANCE; REVIEW RISK ASSESSMENT; DOCUMENT RISK ASSESSMENT; DISSEMINATE RISK ASSESSMENT RESULTS; UPDATE RISK ASSESSMENT; AUTHORIZATION BOUNDARY; PRIVACY
RA-3(1)	SUPPLY CHAIN RISK ASSESSMENT	SUPPLY CHAIN RISK ASSESSMENT; SUPPLY CHAIN RISK
RA-4	Risk Assessment Update	WITHDRAWN
RA-5	**Vulnerability Scanning**	VULNERABILITY SCANNING; HOSTED APPLICATIONS; VULNERABILITY SCANNING TOOL; VULNERABILITY SCAN REPORT; VULNERABILITY ANALYSES; COMMON WEAKNESS ENUMERATION; CWE; NATIONAL VULNERABILITY DATABASE; NVD; COMMON VULNERABILITY SCORING SYSTEM; CVSS; ASSURANCE; REMEDIATE VULNERABILITIES; CHECKLISTS; TEST PROCEDURES; VULNERABILITY ASSESSMENT; INFORMATION SHARING
RA-5(1)	UPDATE TOOL CAPABILITY	WITHDRAWN
RA-5(2)	UPDATE BY FREQUENCY, PRIOR TO NEW SCAN, OR WHEN IDENTIFIED	UPDATE SCANNED VULNERABILITIES; NEW SCAN; UPDATE BY FREQUENCY
RA-5(3)	BREADTH AND DEPTH OF COVERAGE	BREADTH OF COVERAGE; DEPTH OF COVERAGE
RA-5(4)	DISCOVERABLE INFORMATION	DISCOVERABLE INFORMATION; CORRECTIVE ACTIONS
RA-5(5)	PRIVILEGED ACCESS	PRIVILEGED ACCESS; SCANNING ACTIVITIES; NEED TO KNOW; RESILIENCY; RESILIENCE
RA-5(6)	AUTOMATED TREND ANALYSES	AUTOMATED TREND ANALYSIS; RESILIENCY; RESILIENCE
RA-5(7)	AUTOMATED DETECTION AND NOTIFICATION OF UNAUTHORIZED COMPONENTS	WITHDRAWN
RA-5(8)	REVIEW HISTORIC AUDIT LOGS	REVIEW HISTORIC AUDIT LOGS; RESILIENCY; RESILIENCE
RA-5(9)	PENETRATION TESTING AND ANALYSES	WITHDRAWN
RA-5(10)	CORRELATE SCANNING INFORMATION	CORRELATE SCANNING INFORMATION; MULTI-VULNERABILITY ATTACK VECTORS; MULTI-HOP ATTACK VECTORS; RESILIENCY; RESILIENCE

CONTROL NUMBER	CONTROL NAME CONTROL ENHANCEMENT NAME	KEYWORDS NOTEWORTHY AND RELEVANT TERMS
RA-6	Technical Surveillance Countermeasures Survey	TECHNICAL SURVEILLANCE COUNTERMEASURES SURVEY; TECHNICAL SECURITY WEAKNESS; TECHNICAL PENETRATION; TECHNICAL SECURITY POSTURE; ORGANIZATIONAL EXPOSURE; RISK ASSESSMENTS
RA-7	Risk Response	RISK RESPONSE; RESPOND TO FINDINGS; MITIGATE RISK; ACCEPT RISK; SHARE RISK; TRANSFER RISK; REJECT RISK; RISK TREATMENT; RISK TOLERANCE; PRIVACY
RA-8	Privacy Impact Assessment	PRIVACY IMPACT ASSESSMENTS; PIA
RA-9	Criticality Analysis	CRITICALITY ANALYSIS; SUPPLY CHAIN RISK MANAGEMENT; PROTECTION PRIORITIZATION

TABLE H-18: SYSTEM AND SERVICES ACQUISITION FAMILY KEYWORDS

CONTROL NUMBER	CONTROL NAME CONTROL ENHANCEMENT NAME	KEYWORDS NOTEWORTHY AND RELEVANT TERMS
SA-1	**System and Services Acquisition Policy and Procedures**	SYSTEM AND SERVICES ACQUISITION; POLICY; PROCEDURES; REVIEW; UPDATE; PRIVACY
SA-2	**Allocation of Resources**	SECURITY REQUIREMENTS; ALLOCATION OF RESOURCES; CAPITAL PLANNING; ASSURANCE; BUDGET; FUNDING; PRIVACY
SA-3	**System Development Life Cycle**	SYSTEM DEVELOPMENT LIFE CYCLE; SDLC; ROLES; RESPONSIBILITIES; SECURITY RISK MANAGEMENT; SECURITY RISK MANAGEMENT; SUPPLY CHAIN RISK MANAGEMENT; PRIVACY RISK MANAGEMENT
SA-3(1)	MANAGE DEVELOPMENT ENVIRONMENT	DEVELOPMENT ENVIRONMENT; TEST ENVIRONMENT INTEGRATION ENVIRONMENT
SA-3(2)	USE OF LIVE DATA	LIVE DATA; DEVELOPMENT ENVIRONMENT; TEST ENVIRONMENT INTEGRATION ENVIRONMENT
SA-3(3)	TECHNOLOGY REFRESH	TECHNOLOGY REFRESH SCHEDULE; UPGRADE TECHNOLOGY; UPDATE TECHNOLOGY; PRIVACY
SA-4	**Acquisition Process**	ACQUISITION PROCESS; REQUIREMENTS; SECURITY; FUNCTIONAL REQUIREMENTS; STRENGTH REQUIREMENTS; DOCUMENTATION; ACCEPTANCE CRITERIA; SUPPLY CHAIN RISK; PRIVACY
SA-4(1)	FUNCTIONAL PROPERTIES OF CONTROLS	SECURITY CONTROLS; FUNCTIONAL PROPERTIES; DEVELOPER PROVIDED; DEVELOPER; PRIVACY CONTROLS
SA-4(2)	DESIGN AND IMPLEMENTATION INFORMATION FOR CONTROLS	IMPLEMENTATION INFORMATION; SECURITY-RELEVANT EXTERNAL SYSTEM INTERFACE; HIGH-LEVEL DESIGN; LOW-LEVEL DESIGN; SOURCE CODE; HARDWARE SCHEMATICS; DEVELOPER PROVIDED; DEVELOPER; RESILIENCE; RESILIENCY
SA-4(3)	DEVELOPMENT METHODS, TECHNIQUES, AND PRACTICES	STATE OF THE ART ENGINEERING METHODS; SECURITY; SOFTWARE DEVELOPMENT METHODS; TESTING; EVALUATION; VALIDATION; QUALITY CONTROL PROCESSES; DEVELOPER PROVIDED; DEVELOPER; PRIVACY ENGINEERING
SA-4(4)	ASSIGNMENT OF COMPONENTS TO SYSTEMS	WITHDRAWN
SA-4(5)	SYSTEM, COMPONENT, AND SERVICE CONFIGURATIONS	SECURITY CONFIGURATIONS; U.S. GOVERNMENT CONFIGURATION BASELINE; USGCB; FUNCTIONS; PORTS; PROTOCOLS; SERVICES; SECURITY CHARACTERISTICS; DEVELOPER PROVIDED; DEVELOPER
SA-4(6)	USE OF INFORMATION ASSURANCE PRODUCTS	GOVERNMENT OFF-THE-SHELF; GOTS; COMMERCIAL OFF-THE-SHELF; COTS; INFORMATION ASSURANCE; IA; IA-ENABLED; NATIONAL SECURITY AGENCY; NSA; EVALUATED; VALIDATED; APPROVED; CRYPTOGRAPHY
SA-4(7)	NIAP-APPROVED PROTECTION PROFILES	NATIONAL INFORMATION ASSURANCE PARTNERSHIP; NIAP; PROTECTION PROFILE; CRYPTOGRAPHIC MODULE; FEDERAL INFORMATION SYSTEM PROCESSING STANDARDS; FIPS; VALIDATED
SA-4(8)	CONTINUOUS MONITORING PLAN FOR CONTROLS	CONTINUOUS MONITORING PLAN; SECURITY CONTROLS; DEVELOPER PROVIDED; DEVELOPER; PRIVACY CONTROLS

CONTROL NUMBER	CONTROL NAME / CONTROL ENHANCEMENT NAME	KEYWORDS / NOTEWORTHY AND RELEVANT TERMS
SA-4(9)	FUNCTIONS, PORTS, PROTOCOLS, AND SERVICES IN USE	IDENTIFICATION; FUNCTIONS; PORTS; PROTOCOLS; SERVICES; LIFE CYCLE; DEVELOPER PROVIDED; DEVELOPER
SA-4(10)	USE OF APPROVED PIV PRODUCTS	FEDERAL INFORMATION PROCESSING STANDARDS; FIPS 201; PERSONAL IDENTITY VERIFICATION; PIV
SA-5	**System Documentation**	DOCUMENTATION; ADMINISTRATOR; USER; SECURE CONFIGURATION; INSTALLATION; OPERATION; SECURITY FUNCTIONS; SECURITY MECHANISMS; PRIVILEGED FUNCTIONS; ADMINISTRATIVE FUNCTIONS; RESPONSIBILITIES; RISK MANAGEMENT STRATEGY; ASSURANCE; DEVELOPER PROVIDED; DEVELOPER; PROVENANCE; PRIVACY FUNCTIONS
SA-5(1)	FUNCTIONAL PROPERTIES OF SECURITY CONTROLS	WITHDRAWN
SA-5(2)	SECURITY-RELEVANT EXTERNAL SYSTEM INTERFACES	WITHDRAWN
SA-5(3)	HIGH-LEVEL DESIGN	WITHDRAWN
SA-5(4)	LOW-LEVEL DESIGN	WITHDRAWN
SA-5(5)	SOURCE CODE	WITHDRAWN
SA-6	Software Usage Restrictions	WITHDRAWN
SA-7	User-Installed Software	WITHDRAWN
SA-8	**Security and Privacy Engineering Principles**	ASSURANCE; SYSTEM SECURITY ENGINEERING PRINCIPLES; LEGACY SYSTEMS; RISK MANAGEMENT DECISIONS; THREAT MODELING; TRUSTWORTHY; SYSTEM PRIVACY ENGINEERING PRINCIPLES
SA-9	**External System Services**	ASSURANCE; EXTERNAL SYSTEM SERVICES; REQUIREMENTS; SECURITY CONTROLS; PROVIDERS; USER; ROLES; RESPONSIBILITIES; MONITOR; FEDERAL INFORMATION SECURITY MANAGEMENT ACT; FISMA; OFFICE OF MANAGEMENT AND BUDGET; OMB; CHAIN OF TRUST; SERVICE-LEVEL AGREEMENT; SLA; SERVICE PROVIDERS; SUPPLY CHAIN RISK MANAGEMENT; PRIVACY CONTROLS
SA-9(1)	RISK ASSESSMENTS AND ORGANIZATIONAL APPROVALS	RISK ASSESSMENT; ORGANIZATIONAL APPROVAL; SUPPLY CHAIN; PRIVACY
SA-9(2)	IDENTIFICATION OF FUNCTIONS, PORTS, PROTOCOLS, AND SERVICES	EXTERNAL SYSTEM; FUNCTIONS; PORTS; PROTOCOLS; SERVICES
SA-9(3)	ESTABLISH AND MAINTAIN TRUST RELATIONSHIP WITH PROVIDERS	TRUST RELATIONSHIP; ESTABLISH; DOCUMENT; MAINTAIN; PRIVACY
SA-9(4)	CONSISTENT INTERESTS OF CONSUMERS AND PROVIDERS	INTERESTS; ORGANIZATION; SERVICE PROVIDER; CONSUMER
SA-9(5)	PROCESSING, STORAGE, AND SERVICE LOCATION	RESTRICT; LOCATION; PROCESSING; STORAGE; SERVICE; PRIVACY
SA-9(6)	ORGANIZATION-CONTROLLED CRYPTOGRAPHIC KEYS	CRYPTOGRAPHIC KEYS; EXCLUSIVE CONTROL
SA-9(7)	ORGANIZATION-CONTROLLED INTEGRITY CHECKING	INTEGRITY CHECK; ORGANIZATION CONTROLLED; EXTERNAL SYSTEM; DATA INTEGRITY

CONTROL NUMBER	CONTROL NAME CONTROL ENHANCEMENT NAME	KEYWORDS NOTEWORTHY AND RELEVANT TERMS
SA-10	**Developer Configuration Management**	ASSURANCE; DEVELOPER; CONFIGURATION MANAGEMENT; FORMAL MODEL; FUNCTIONAL HIGH-LEVEL DESIGN; FUNCTIONAL LOW-LEVEL DESIGN; IMPLEMENTATION DOCUMENTATION; SOURCE CODE; HARDWARE SCHEMATICS; DOCUMENT CHANGES; MANAGE CHANGES; APPROVE; TRACK SECURITY FLAWS; FLAW RESOLUTION; REPORTING; PRIVACY
SA-10(1)	SOFTWARE AND FIRMWARE INTEGRITY VERIFICATION	SOFTWARE INTEGRITY VERIFICATION; FIRMWARE INTEGRITY VERIFICATION; UNAUTHORIZED CHANGES; CRYPTOGRAPHY; ONE-WAY HASH
SA-10(2)	ALTERNATIVE CONFIGURATION MANAGEMENT PROCESSES	ALTERNATE CONFIGURATION MANAGEMENT PROCESS; ORGANIZATIONAL PERSONNEL; COMMERCIAL OFF-THE-SHELF; COTS; CONFIGURATION CONTROL BOARD; CCB; DETECT CHANGES; PRIVACY IMPACT ASSESSMENTS; PIA
SA-10(3)	HARDWARE INTEGRITY VERIFICATION	HARDWARE INTEGRITY VERIFICATION
SA-10(4)	TRUSTED GENERATION	COMPARING VERSIONS; PREVIOUS VERSIONS; AUTHORIZED CHANGES
SA-10(5)	MAPPING INTEGRITY FOR VERSION CONTROL	MASTER COPY INTEGRITY; INITIAL DEVELOPMENT; SYSTEM LIFE CYCLE UPDATE; OPERATIONAL ENVIRONMENT; VERSION CONTROL; INTEGRITY
SA-10(6)	TRUSTED DISTRIBUTION	TRUSTED DISTRIBUTION; MASTER COPY
SA-11	**Developer Testing and Evaluation**	SECURITY TESTING/EVALUATION; UNIT; INTEGRATION; SYSTEM; REGRESSION; SECURITY ASSESSMENT PLAN; FLAW REMEDIATION PROCESS; FLAW CORRECTION; INTERCONNECTIONS; SECURITY TESTING AND EVALUATION; ASSURANCE; DEVELOPER; SYSTEM DEVELOPMENT LIFE CYCLE; SDLC; ST&E; PRIVACY ASSESSMENT PLAN; PRIVACY TESTING AND EVALUATION
SA-11(1)	STATIC CODE ANALYSIS	STATIC CODE ANALYSIS; SECURITY VULNERABILITIES; SECURITY CODING PRACTICES
SA-11(2)	THREAT MODELING AND VULNERABILITY ANALYSES	THREAT ANALYSIS; VULNERABILITY ANALYSIS
SA-11(3)	INDEPENDENT VERIFICATION OF ASSESSMENT PLANS AND EVIDENCE	INDEPENDENT AGENT; VERIFICATION; SECURITY ASSESSMENT PLAN; SECURITY TESTING; SECURITY EVALUATION; PRIVACY ASSESSMENT PLAN; PRIVACY TESTING; PRIVACY EVALUATION
SA-11(4)	MANUAL CODE REVIEWS	MANUAL CODE REVIEW
SA-11(5)	PENETRATION TESTING	PENETRATION TESTING; WHITE-BOX; BLACK-BOX; GREY-BOX; PRIVACY
SA-11(6)	ATTACK SURFACE REVIEWS	ATTACK SURFACE REVIEW
SA-11(7)	VERIFY SCOPE OF TESTING AND EVALUATION	SCOPE OF SECURITY TESTING/EVALUATION; SCOPE OF PRIVACY TESTING/EVALUATION
SA-11(8)	DYNAMIC CODE ANALYSIS	DYNAMIC CODE ANALYSIS; FUZZ TESTING; RUN TIME TOOLS; CONCORDANCE ANALYSIS

CONTROL NUMBER	CONTROL NAME CONTROL ENHANCEMENT NAME	KEYWORDS NOTEWORTHY AND RELEVANT TERMS
SA-12	**Supply Chain Risk Management**	SUPPLY CHAIN THREATS; SUPPLY CHAIN RISK MANAGEMENT; SUPPLY CHAIN RISK MANAGEMENT PLAN; ACQUISITION PROCESS; PROCUREMENT PROCESS; SECURITY SAFEGUARDS; DEFENSE-IN-BREATH; PRIVACY SAFEGUARDS; RESILIENCY; RESILIENCE
SA-12(1)	ACQUISITION STRATEGIES, TOOLS, AND METHODS	ACQUISITION STRATEGIES; PURCHASE RESTRICTIONS; CONTRACTS; AGREEMENTS; RESILIENCY; RESILIENCE
SA-12(2)	SUPPLIER REVIEWS	SUPPLIER REVIEW; SUBORDINATE SUPPLIERS; SUBCONTRACTORS; SUPPLIER PROCESSES; PRIVACY
SA-12(3)	TRUSTED SHIPPING AND WAREHOUSING	WITHDRAWN
SA-12(4)	DIVERSITY OF SUPPLIERS	WITHDRAWN
SA-12(5)	LIMITATION OF HARM	ADVANCED PERSISTENT THREAT; APT; APPROVED VENDOR; LIMIT HARM; CUSTOM CONFIGURATION; REMOVE APT; RESILIENCY; RESILIENCE
SA-12(6)	MINIMIZING PROCUREMENT TIME	WITHDRAWN
SA-12(7)	ASSESSMENTS PRIOR TO SELECTION, ACCEPTANCE, AND UPDATE	SECURITY ASSESSMENT; SELECTION; ACCEPTANCE; UPDATE
SA-12(8)	USE OF ALL-SOURCE INTELLIGENCE	ALL-SOURCE INTELLIGENCE ANALYSIS; SUPPLIERS; POTENTIAL SUPPLIERS
SA-12(9)	OPERATIONS SECURITY	OPERATIONS SECURITY; OPSEC; SUPPLIERS; POTENTIAL SUPPLIERS; SUPPLY CHAIN INFORMATION
SA-12(10)	VALIDATE AS GENUINE AND NOT ALTERED	VALIDATION; SYSTEM COMPONENTS; GENUINE; NOT ALTERED; ALTERED; COUNTERFEIT; RESILIENCY; RESILIENCE
SA-12(11)	PENETRATION TESTING AND ANALYSIS	SUPPLY CHAIN ELEMENTS; SUPPLY CHAIN PROCESSES; ORGANIZATIONAL ANALYSIS; INDEPENDENT EXTERNAL ANALYSIS; ORGANIZATIONAL PENETRATION TESTING; INDEPENDENT EXTERNAL PENETRATION TESTING; SUPPLY CHAIN TESTING; SUPPLY CHAIN ANALYSIS; RESILIENCY; RESILIENCE
SA-12(12)	NOTIFICATION AGREEMENTS	SUPPLY CHAIN COMPROMISES; INTER-ORGANIZATIONAL AGREEMENTS; SUPPLY CHAIN COMMUNICATIONS; RESILIENCY; RESILIENCE
SA-12(13)	CRITICAL SYSTEM COMPONENTS	WITHDRAWN
SA-12(14)	IDENTITY AND TRACEABILITY	UNIQUE IDENTIFICATION; SUPPLY CHAIN ELEMENTS; PROCESSES; VISIBILITY; TRACEABILITY; RESILIENCY; RESILIENCE
SA-12(15)	PROCESSES TO ADDRESS WEAKNESSES OR DEFICIENCIES	RISK RESPONSE; WEAKNESSES; DEFICIENCIES
SA-12(16)	PROVENANCE	PROVENANCE; POINT OF ORIGIN; DEVELOPMENT; OWNERSHIP; LOCATION; CHANGES TO COMPONENT OR DATA; PROVENANCE RECORDS
SA-13	Trustworthiness	WITHDRAWN
SA-14	Criticality Analysis	WITHDRAWN
SA-14(1)	CRITICAL COMPONENTS WITH NO VIABLE ALTERNATIVE SOURCING	WITHDRAWN

CONTROL NUMBER	CONTROL NAME CONTROL ENHANCEMENT NAME	KEYWORDS NOTEWORTHY AND RELEVANT TERMS
SA-15	**Development Process, Standards, and Tools**	ASSURANCE; DEVELOPMENT PROCESS; SECURITY REQUIREMENTS; TOOLS; CONFIGURATIONS; CHANGE MANAGEMENT; PROCESS REVIEW; DEVELOPER; SUPPLY CHAIN RISK MANAGEMENT; PRIVACY
SA-15(1)	QUALITY METRICS	QUALITY METRICS; COMPLETION CRITERIA; COMMON VULNERABILITY SCORING SYSTEM; CVSS; QUALITY GATE; PRIVACY
SA-15(2)	SECURITY TRACKING TOOLS	SECURITY TRACKING TOOL
SA-15(3)	CRITICALITY ANALYSIS	CRITICAL ANALYSIS
SA-15(4)	THREAT MODELING AND VULNERABILITY ANALYSIS	WITHDRAWN
SA-15(5)	ATTACK SURFACE REDUCTION	ATTACK SURFACE REDUCTION; RESILIENCY; RESILIENCE
SA-15(6)	CONTINUOUS IMPROVEMENT	DEVELOPMENT PROCESS; CONTINUOUS IMPROVEMENT; PRIVACY
SA-15(7)	AUTOMATED VULNERABILITY ANALYSIS	AUTOMATED VULNERABILITY ANALYSIS; EXPLOITATION POTENTIAL; RISK MITIGATION
SA-15(8)	REUSE OF THREAT AND VULNERABILITY INFORMATION	THREAT MODELING; VULNERABILITY ANALYSIS; AUTHORITATIVE VULNERABILITY INFORMATION; DISCOVERED VULNERABILITIES
SA-15(9)	USE OF LIVE DATA	WITHDRAWN
SA-15(10)	INCIDENT RESPONSE PLAN	INCIDENT RESPONSE PLAN
SA-15(11)	ARCHIVE SYSTEM OR COMPONENT	ARCHIVE SYSTEM; ARCHIVE COMPONENT; PRIVACY
SA-16	**Developer-Provided Training**	TRAINING; DEVELOPERS; INTERNAL; EXTERNAL; SECURITY FUNCTIONS; ASSURANCE; PRIVACY FUNCTIONS
SA-17	**Developer Security Architecture and Design**	EXTERNAL DEVELOPERS; SECURITY ARCHITECTURE; SECURITY DESIGN; SECURITY FUNCTIONALITY; SECURITY CONTROLS; ASSURANCE; DESIGN SPECIFICATION
SA-17(1)	FORMAL POLICY MODEL	FORMAL POLICY MODEL
SA-17(2)	SECURITY-RELEVANT COMPONENTS	SECURITY RELEVANT; HARDWARE; SOFTWARE; FIRMWARE
SA-17(3)	FORMAL CORRESPONDENCE	FORMAL CORRESPONDENCE; TOP-LEVEL SPECIFICATION
SA-17(4)	INFORMAL CORRESPONDENCE	INFORMAL CORRESPONDENCE; TOP-LEVEL SPECIFICATION
SA-17(5)	CONCEPTUALLY SIMPLE DESIGN	CONCEPTUALLY SIMPLE DESIGN; PRECISELY DEFINED SEMANTICS
SA-17(6)	STRUCTURE FOR TESTING	SECURITY TESTING
SA-17(7)	STRUCTURE FOR LEAST PRIVILEGE	LEAST PRIVILEGE; RESILIENCY; RESILIENCE
SA-18	**Tamper Resistance and Detection**	TAMPER PROTECTION; MODIFICATION; REVERSE ENGINEERING; SUBSTITUTION; IDENTIFICATION; TAMPER RESISTANCE; TAMPER DETECTION; ASSURANCE; SUPPLY CHAIN RISK; RESILIENCY; RESILIENCE
SA-18(1)	MULTIPLE PHASES OF SYSTEM DEVELOPMENT LIFE CYCLE	ANTI-TAMPER; TECHNOLOGIES; TECHNIQUES; SYSTEM DEVELOPMENT LIFE CYCLE; SDLC; SELF-CHECKING; RESILIENCY; RESILIENCE

CONTROL NUMBER	CONTROL NAME CONTROL ENHANCEMENT NAME	KEYWORDS NOTEWORTHY AND RELEVANT TERMS
SA-18(2)	INSPECTION OF SYSTEMS OR COMPONENTS	INSPECTION; TAMPERING; PHYSICAL; LOGICAL; MOBILE DEVICES; NOTEBOOK COMPUTERS; HIGH-RISK LOCATIONS; SYSTEM INSPECTION; COMPONENT INSPECTION; RESILIENCY; RESILIENCE
SA-19	**Component Authenticity**	ASSURANCE; ANTI-COUNTERFEIT; POLICY; PROCEDURES; TAMPER RESISTANCE; MALICIOUS CODE; INTEGRITY; SUPPLY CHAIN RISK; RESILIENCY; RESILIENCE
SA-19(1)	ANTI-COUNTERFEIT TRAINING	ANTI-COUNTERFEIT TRAINING; TRAINING
SA-19(2)	CONFIGURATION CONTROL FOR COMPONENT SERVICE AND REPAIR	CONFIGURATION CONTROL; SERVICE/REPAIR
SA-19(3)	COMPONENT DISPOSAL	COMPONENT DISPOSAL
SA-19(4)	ANTI-COUNTERFEIT SCANNING	ANTI-COUNTERFEIT SCANNING
SA-20	**Customized Development of Critical Components**	SYSTEM COMPONENTS; RE-IMPLEMENTATION; CUSTOM DEVELOPMENT; ASSURANCE; CRITICAL COMPONENTS; RESILIENCY; RESILIENCE
SA-21	**Developer Screening**	DEVELOPER SCREENING; ACCESS AUTHORIZATIONS; TRUSTWORTHY; DEGREE OF TRUST; CLEARANCE; BACKGROUND CHECKS; CITIZENSHIP; NATIONALITY; ASSURANCE
SA-21(1)	VALIDATION OF SCREENING	WITHDRAWN
SA-22	**Unsupported System Components**	UNSUPPORTED SYSTEM COMPONENTS; CONTINUED USE; JUSTIFICATION; DOCUMENTED APPROVAL; ASSURANCE; REPLACE
SA-22(1)	ALTERNATIVE SOURCES FOR CONTINUED SUPPORT	IN-HOUSE SUPPORT; CONTRACTUAL RELATIONSHIPS; OPEN SOURCE SOFTWARE; ALTERNATE SOURCE

TABLE H-19: SYSTEM AND COMMUNICATIONS PROTECTION FAMILY KEYWORDS

CONTROL NUMBER	CONTROL NAME CONTROL ENHANCEMENT NAME	KEYWORDS NOTEWORTHY AND RELEVANT TERMS
SC-1	System and Communications Protection Policy and Procedures	SYSTEM AND COMMUNICATION PROTECTION; ASSURANCE; POLICY; PROCEDURES; REVIEW; UPDATE; PRIVACY
SC-2	Application Partitioning	APPLICATION PARTITIONING; USER FUNCTIONALITY; MANAGEMENT FUNCTIONALITY; SEPARATION OF FUNCTIONALITY; ASSURANCE
SC-2(1)	INTERFACES FOR NON-PRIVILEGED USERS	INTERFACE; ADMINISTRATOR PRIVILEGES; NON-PRIVILEGED USER
SC-3	Security Function Isolation	ISOLATION; SEPARATION; SECURITY FUNCTIONS; NON-SECURITY FUNCTIONS; ISOLATION BOUNDARY; ASSURANCE; SECURITY FUNCTION ISOLATION; RESILIENCY; RESILIENCE
SC-3(1)	HARDWARE SEPARATION	HARDWARE SEPARATION
SC-3(2)	ACCESS AND FLOW CONTROL FUNCTIONS	ENFORCE ACCESS; ENFORCE INFORMATION FLOW CONTROL
SC-3(3)	MINIMIZE NONSECURITY FUNCTIONALITY	MINIMIZE NON-SECURITY FUNCTIONS; RESILIENCY; RESILIENCE
SC-3(4)	MODULE COUPLING AND COHESIVENESS	INTER-MODULE INTERACTIONS; COUPLING; COHESION; SOFTWARE ENGINEERING; MODULAR DECOMPOSITION; LAYERING; MINIMIZATION; MODULE COUPLING; MODULE COHESIVENESS; INDEPENDENT MODULES
SC-3(5)	LAYERED STRUCTURES	LAYERED STRUCTURES; MINIMIZED INTERACTIONS; NON-LOOPING LAYERS
SC-4	Information in Shared System Resources	SHARED SYSTEM RESOURCES; INFORMATION TRANSFER; UNAUTHORIZED; UNINTENDED; OBJECT REUSE; RESIDUAL INFORMATION PROTECTION
SC-4(1)	SECURITY LEVELS	WITHDRAWN
SC-4(2)	MULTILEVEL OR PERIODS PROCESSING	MULTILEVEL PROCESSING; PERIODS PROCESSING; CLASSIFICATION LEVELS; SECURITY CATEGORIES
SC-5	Denial of Service Protection	DENIAL-OF-SERVICE; DOS; BOUNDARY PROTECTION DEVICES; BANDWIDTH; CAPACITY; PACKET FILTERING; BOUNDARY PROTECTION; SERVICE REDUNDANCY
SC-5(1)	RESTRICT INTERNAL USERS	RESTRICTION; INTERNAL USERS; SYSTEM ACCESS
SC-5(2)	CAPACITY, BANDWIDTH, AND REDUNDANCY	EXCESS CAPACITY; BANDWIDTH; FLOODING DENIAL-OF-SERVICE ATTACKS; DOS
SC-5(3)	DETECTION AND MONITORING	DETECTION; MONITORING
SC-6	Resource Availability	RESOURCE AVAILABILITY; QUOTAS; LOWER-PRIORITY; HIGHER-PRIORITY; ASSURANCE
SC-7	Boundary Protection	BOUNDARY PROTECTION; COMMUNICATIONS; EXTERNAL BOUNDARY; KEY INTERNAL BOUNDARY; SUBNETWORKS; MANAGED INTERFACES; DEMILITARIZED ZONES; DMZ; COMMERCIAL TELECOMMUNICATIONS; BOUNDARY PROTECTION DEVICES; PRIVACY
SC-7(1)	PHYSICALLY SEPARATED SUBNETWORKS	WITHDRAWN
SC-7(2)	PUBLIC ACCESS	WITHDRAWN

CONTROL NUMBER	CONTROL NAME CONTROL ENHANCEMENT NAME	KEYWORDS NOTEWORTHY AND RELEVANT TERMS
SC-7(3)	ACCESS POINTS	LIMITED EXTERNAL NETWORK CONNECTION; TRUSTED INTERNET CONNECTION; ACCESS POINTS
SC-7(4)	EXTERNAL TELECOMMUNICATIONS SERVICES	EXTERNAL COMMUNICATION SERVICES; MANAGED INTERFACE; TRAFFIC FLOW POLICY; PROTECT; CONFIDENTIALITY; INTEGRITY; TRANSMITTED INFORMATION; EXCEPTION; DOCUMENT; REVIEW; REMOVE
SC-7(5)	DENY BY DEFAULT — ALLOW BY EXCEPTION	NETWORK COMMUNICATIONS TRAFFIC POLICY; DENY BY DEFAULT; DENY ALL; PERMIT BY EXCEPTION
SC-7(6)	RESPONSE TO RECOGNIZED FAILURES	WITHDRAWN
SC-7(7)	PREVENT SPLIT TUNNELING FOR REMOTE DEVICES	REMOTE DEVICES; SPLIT TUNNELING; VIRTUAL PRIVATE NETWORK; VPN
SC-7(8)	ROUTE TRAFFIC TO AUTHENTICATED PROXY SERVERS	EXTERNAL NETWORKS; PROXY SERVERS; MANAGED INTERFACES; WEB CONTENT FILTERING; TRANSMISSION CONTROL PROTOCOL; TCP; UNIFORM RESOURCE LOCATOR; URL; DOMAIN NAME; INTERNET PROTOCOL; IP; ROUTE TRAFFIC
SC-7(9)	RESTRICT THREATENING OUTGOING COMMUNICATIONS TRAFFIC	EXTRUSION DETECTION; ANALYSIS; COMMUNICATION TRAFFIC; INCOMING; OUTBOUND
SC-7(10)	PREVENT EXFILTRATION	EXFILTRATION; MANAGED INTERFACES; RESILIENCY; RESILIENCE
SC-7(11)	RESTRICT INCOMING COMMUNICATIONS TRAFFIC	ADDRESS PAIRS; SOURCE; DESTINATION; AUTHORIZED/ALLOWED COMMUNICATIONS; INCOMING TRAFFIC; RESTRICT; RESILIENCY; RESILIENCE
SC-7(12)	HOST-BASED PROTECTION	HOST BASED BOUNDARY PROTECTION
SC-7(13)	ISOLATION OF SECURITY TOOLS, MECHANISMS, AND SUPPORT COMPONENTS	ISOLATION; INFORMATION SECURITY; TOOLS; MECHANISMS; SUPPORT COMPONENTS; SUBNETWORKS; RESILIENCY; RESILIENCE
SC-7(14)	PROTECTS AGAINST UNAUTHORIZED PHYSICAL CONNECTIONS	UNAUTHORIZED PHYSICAL CONNECTIONS
SC-7(15)	ROUTE PRIVILEGED NETWORK ACCESSES	PRIVILEGED ACCESS; MANAGED INTERFACE; RESILIENCY; RESILIENCE
SC-7(16)	PREVENT DISCOVERY OF COMPONENTS AND DEVICES	PREVENT DISCOVERY; NETWORK ADDRESS
SC-7(17)	AUTOMATED ENFORCEMENT OF PROTOCOL FORMATS	ENFORCE PROTOCOL FORMATS; AUTOMATED
SC-7(18)	FAIL SECURE	FAIL SECURE
SC-7(19)	BLOCK COMMUNICATION FROM NON-ORGANIZATIONALLY CONFIGURED HOSTS	NON-ORGANIZATIONALLY CONFIGURED HOSTS; TRAFFIC BLOCKING; INBOUND; OUTBOUND
SC-7(20)	DYNAMIC ISOLATION AND SEGREGATION	DYNAMIC ISOLATION/SEGREGATION; COMPONENTS; RESILIENCY; RESILIENCE
SC-7(21)	ISOLATION OF SYSTEM COMPONENTS	ISOLATE COMPONENTS; MISSION; BUSINESS FUNCTION; UNAUTHORIZED INFORMATION FLOW; BOUNDARY PROTECTION MECHANISMS; DEGREE OF SEPARATION; RESILIENCY; RESILIENCE
SC-7(22)	SEPARATE SUBNETS FOR CONNECTING TO DIFFERENT SECURITY DOMAINS	SUBNETS; NETWORK CONNECTIONS; DIFFERENT SECURITY DOMAINS; RESILIENCY; RESILIENCE
SC-7(23)	DISABLE SENDER FEEDBACK ON PROTOCOL VALIDATION FAILURE	DISABLE FEEDBACK; PROTOCOL FORMAT VALIDATION FAILURE
SC-7(24)	PERSONALLY IDENTIFIABLE INFORMATION	PRIVACY; PERSONALLY IDENTIFIABLE INFORMATION; PII
SC-8	**Transmission Confidentiality and Integrity**	TRANSMISSION; CONFIDENTIALITY; INTEGRITY

CONTROL NUMBER	CONTROL NAME CONTROL ENHANCEMENT NAME	KEYWORDS NOTEWORTHY AND RELEVANT TERMS
SC-8(1)	CRYPTOGRAPHIC PROTECTION	CRYPTOGRAPHIC MECHANISMS; ENCRYPTING; ALTERNATIVE PHYSICAL SAFEGUARDS; PREVENT UNAUTHORIZED DISCLOSURE OF INFORMATION; DETECT CHANGES TO INFORMATION
SC-8(2)	PRE- AND POST-TRANSMISSION HANDLING	INFORMATION; PREPARATION FOR TRANSMISSION; DURING RECEPTION; UNAUTHORIZED DISCLOSURE; PRE-TRANSMISSION- POST TRANSMISSION
SC-8(3)	CRYPTOGRAPHIC PROTECTION FOR MESSAGE EXTERNALS	CRYPTOGRAPHIC MECHANISMS; MESSAGE EXTERNALS; HEADER/ROUTING
SC-8(4)	CONCEAL OR RANDOMIZE COMMUNICATIONS	CRYPTOGRAPHIC MECHANISMS; COMMUNICATION PATTERNS; CONCEAL; RANDOMIZE; INTERNAL NETWORKS; EXTERNAL NETWORKS; RESILIENCY; RESILIENCE
SC-9	Transmission Confidentiality	WITHDRAWN
SC-10	**Network Disconnect**	NETWORK DISCONNECT; TIME-PERIOD OF INACTIVITY
SC-11	**Trusted Path**	ASSURANCE; TRUSTED COMMUNICATIONS PATH; PREVENT MODIFICATION; PREVENT DISCLOSURE; TRUSTED PATH
SC-11(1)	LOGICAL ISOLATION	LOGICAL ISOLATION
SC-12	**Cryptographic Key Establishment and Management**	CRYPTOGRAPHIC KEY; ESTABLISHMENT; MANAGEMENT; TRUST STORES; TRUST ANCHORS
SC-12(1)	AVAILABILITY	AVAILABILITY; ESCROW
SC-12(2)	SYMMETRIC KEYS	SYMMETRIC KEYS; NIST FIPS; NATIONAL INSTITUTE OF STANDARDS AND TECHNOLOGY; FEDERAL INFORMATION PROCESSING STANDARDS; FIPS; NATIONAL SECURITY AGENCY-APPROVED; NSA-APPROVED; KEY MANAGEMENT TECHNOLOGY AND PROCESSES
SC-12(3)	ASYMMETRIC KEYS	ASYMMETRIC KEYS; NSA-APPROVED; KEY MANAGEMENT TECHNOLOGY AND PROCESSES; PUBLIC KEY INFRASTRUCTURE; PKI; CLASS 3; CLASS 4; PRIVATE KEY; PUBLIC KEY
SC-12(4)	PKI CERTIFICATES	WITHDRAWN
SC-12(5)	PKI CERTIFICATES / HARDWARE TOKENS	WITHDRAWN
SC-13	**Cryptographic Protection**	CRYPTOGRAPHIC PROTECTION; FIPS-VALIDATED CRYPTOGRAPHY; NSA-APPROVED CRYPTOGRAPHY; CLASSIFIED; CONTROLLED UNCLASSIFIED INFORMATION; CUI
SC-13(1)	FIPS-VALIDATED CRYPTOGRAPHY	WITHDRAWN
SC-13(2)	NSA-APPROVED CRYPTOGRAPHY	WITHDRAWN
SC-13(3)	INDIVIDUALS WITHOUT FORMAL ACCESS APPROVALS	WITHDRAWN
SC-13(4)	DIGITAL SIGNATURES	WITHDRAWN
SC-14	Public Access Protections	WITHDRAWN
SC-15	**Collaborative Computing Devices and Applications**	COLLABORATIVE COMPUTING DEVICES
SC-15(1)	PHYSICAL DISCONNECT	PHYSICAL DISCONNECT
SC-15(2)	BLOCKING INBOUND AND OUTBOUND COMMUNICATIONS TRAFFIC	WITHDRAWN
SC-15(3)	DISABLING AND REMOVAL IN SECURE WORK AREAS	DISABLE; REMOVE; SECURE WORK AREAS

CONTROL NUMBER	CONTROL NAME / CONTROL ENHANCEMENT NAME	KEYWORDS / NOTEWORTHY AND RELEVANT TERMS
SC-15(4)	EXPLICITLY INDICATE CURRENT PARTICIPANTS	EXPLICIT INDICATION OF CURRENT PARTICIPANTS; ONLINE MEETINGS; TELECONFERENCES
SC-16	**Transmission of Security and Privacy Attributes**	TRANSMITTED SECURITY ATTRIBUTES; EXPLICITLY; IMPLICITLY; TRANSMITTED PRIVACY ATTRIBUTES
SC-16(1)	INTEGRITY VALIDATION	VALIDATE; INTEGRITY
SC-17	**Public Key Infrastructure Certificates**	PUBLIC KEY CERTIFICATES; TRUST STORE; TRUST ANCHOR
SC-18	**Mobile Code**	MOBILE CODE; USAGE RESTRICTIONS; IMPLEMENTATION GUIDANCE; JAVA; JAVASCRIPT; ACTIVEX; PDF; SHOCKWAVE; FLASH; VBSCRIPT
SC-18(1)	IDENTIFY UNACCEPTABLE CODE AND TAKE CORRECTIVE ACTIONS	UNACCEPTABLE CODE; CORRECTIVE ACTIONS; QUARANTINE CODE; BLOCK CODE
SC-18(2)	ACQUISITION, DEVELOPMENT, AND USE	MOBILE CODE ACQUISITION; MOBILE CODE DEVELOPMENT; MOBILE CODE USE
SC-18(3)	PREVENT DOWNLOADING AND EXECUTION	PREVENT MOBILE CODE DOWNLOADING; PREVENT MOBILE CODE EXECUTION
SC-18(4)	PREVENT AUTOMATIC EXECUTION	PREVENT AUTOMATIC EXECUTION
SC-18(5)	ALLOW EXECUTION ONLY IN CONFINED ENVIRONMENTS	PERMITTED MOBILE CODE EXECUTION; CONFINED ENVIRONMENTS; VIRTUAL MACHINES
SC-19	**Voice Over Internet Protocol**	VOICE OVER INTERNET PROTOCOL; VoIP
SC-20	**Secure Name/Address Resolution Service (Authoritative Source)**	SECURE NAME/ADDRESS RESOLUTION SERVICE; DATA ORIGIN AUTHENTICATION; INTEGRITY VERIFICATION ARTIFACTS; CHILD ZONES; CHAIN OF TRUST; CHILD DOMAINS
SC-20(1)	CHILD SUBSPACES	WITHDRAWN
SC-20(2)	DATA ORIGIN AND INTEGRITY	DATA ORIGIN; DATA INTEGRITY
SC-21	**Secure Name/Address Resolution Service (Recursive or Caching Resolver)**	RECURSIVE RESOLVER; CACHING RESOLVER; DATA ORIGIN AUTHENTICATION; DATA INTEGRITY VERIFICATION
SC-21(1)	DATA ORIGIN AND INTEGRITY	WITHDRAWN
SC-22	**Architecture and Provisioning for Name/Address Resolution Service**	ADDRESS RESOLUTION SERVICE; FAULT-TOLERANT; INTERNAL ROLE SEPARATION; EXTERNAL ROLE SEPARATION; PROVISIONING FOR NAME/ADDRESS RESOLUTION; DNS; DOMAIN NAME SYSTEM SERVERS
SC-23	**Session Authenticity**	SESSION AUTHENTICITY; COMMUNICATION SESSION PROTECTIONS
SC-23(1)	INVALIDATE SESSION IDENTIFIERS AT LOGOUT	INVALIDATE SESSION IDENTIFIERS; USER LOGOUT; SESSION TERMINATION
SC-23(2)	USER-INITIATED LOGOUTS AND MESSAGE DISPLAYS	WITHDRAWN
SC-23(3)	UNIQUE SESSION IDENTIFIERS WITH RANDOMIZATION	UNIQUE SESSION IDENTIFIERS; RANDOMIZATION; RESILIENCY; RESILIENCE
SC-23(4)	UNIQUE SESSION IDENTIFIERS WITH RANDOMIZATION	WITHDRAWN
SC-23(5)	ALLOWED CERTIFICATE AUTHORITIES	CERTIFICATE AUTHORITIES; CA; CERTIFICATES; SECURE SOCKET LAYER; SSL; TRANSPORT LAYER SECURITY; TLS
SC-24	**Fail in Known State**	FAIL IN KNOWN STATE; SECURE STATE

CONTROL NUMBER	CONTROL NAME CONTROL ENHANCEMENT NAME	KEYWORDS NOTEWORTHY AND RELEVANT TERMS
SC-25	Thin Nodes	THIN NODES; REDUCED FUNCTIONALITY; MINIMAL FUNCTIONALITY; ENDPOINT SECURITY; RESILIENCY; RESILIENCE
SC-26	Honeypots	HONEYPOT; MALICIOUS ATTACK TARGET; RESILIENCY; RESILIENCE
SC-26(1)	DETECTION OF MALICIOUS CODE	WITHDRAWN
SC-27	Platform-Independent Applications	PLATFORM-INDEPENDENT APPLICATIONS; PORTABILITY; RESILIENCY; RESILIENCE
SC-28	Protection of Information at Rest	INFORMATION AT REST; CONFIDENTIALITY; INTEGRITY
SC-28(1)	CRYPTOGRAPHIC PROTECTION	CRYPTOGRAPHIC PROTECTION; INFORMATION AT REST
SC-28(2)	OFF-LINE STORAGE	OFF-LINE STORAGE
SC-29	Heterogeneity	HETEROGENEITY; INFORMATION TECHNOLOGY DIVERSITY; SUPPLY CHAIN ATTACKS; ASSURANCE; RESILIENCY; RESILIENCE
SC-29(1)	VIRTUALIZATION TECHNIQUES	VIRTUALIZATION TECHNIQUES; RESILIENCY; RESILIENCE
SC-30	Concealment and Misdirection	CONCEALMENT; MISDIRECTION; ASSURANCE; RESILIENCY; RESILIENCE
SC-30(1)	VIRTUALIZATION TECHNIQUES	WITHDRAWN
SC-30(2)	RANDOMNESS	RANDOMNESS; RESILIENCY; RESILIENCE
SC-30(3)	CHANGE PROCESSING AND STORAGE LOCATIONS	CHANGE PROCESSING LOCATIONS; CHANGE STORAGE LOCATIONS; INFORMATION RESOURCE RELOCATION; RESILIENCY; RESILIENCE
SC-30(4)	MISLEADING INFORMATION	MISLEADING INFORMATION; RESILIENCY; RESILIENCE
SC-30(5)	CONCEALMENT OF SYSTEM COMPONENTS	SYSTEM COMPONENT CONCEALMENT; HIDING CRITICAL INFORMATION; DISGUISING CRITICAL INFORMATION; RESILIENCY; RESILIENCE
SC-31	Covert Channel Analysis	COVERT CHANNEL ANALYSIS; EXPORT-CONTROLLED INFORMATION; ASSURANCE
SC-31(1)	TEST COVERT CHANNELS FOR EXPLOITABILITY	COVERT CHANNEL TESTING; EXPLOITABILITY
SC-31(2)	MAXIMUM BANDWIDTH	MAXIMUM BANDWIDTH; COVERT STORAGE CHANNELS; COVERT TIMING CHANNELS; REDUCE MAXIMUM BANDWIDTH
SC-31(3)	MEASURE BANDWIDTH IN OPERATIONAL ENVIRONMENTS	MEASURE BANDWIDTH; OPERATIONAL ENVIRONMENTS
SC-32	System Partitioning	SYSTEM PARTITIONING; DEFENSE-IN-DEPTH; ASSURANCE; PHYSICAL SEPARATION; RESILIENCY; RESILIENCE
SC-33	Transmission Preparation Integrity	WITHDRAWN
SC-34	Non-Modifiable Executable Programs	NON-MODIFIABLE; EXECUTABLE PROGRAMS; HARDWARE-ENFORCED; READ-ONLY MEMORY; ASSURANCE; NON-MODIFIABLE STORAGE; RESILIENCY; RESILIENCE
SC-34(1)	NO WRITABLE STORAGE	NO WRITABLE STORAGE; RESILIENCY; RESILIENCE
SC-34(2)	INTEGRITY PROTECTION AND READ-ONLY MEDIA	INTEGRITY PROTECTION; READ-ONLY MEDIA; RESILIENCY; RESILIENCE

CONTROL NUMBER	CONTROL NAME / CONTROL ENHANCEMENT NAME	KEYWORDS / NOTEWORTHY AND RELEVANT TERMS
SC-34(3)	HARDWARE-BASED PROTECTION	HARDWARE-BASED PROTECTION; WRITE-PROTECT; MANUALLY DISABLE; RESILIENCY; RESILIENCE
SC-35	**Honeyclients**	HONEYCLIENTS; ACTIVELY PROBE; RESILIENCY; RESILIENCE
SC-36	**Distributed Processing and Storage**	DISTRIBUTED PROCESSING; DISTRIBUTED STORAGE; REDUNDANCY; ASSURANCE; RESILIENCY; RESILIENCE
SC-36(1)	POLLING TECHNIQUES	POLLING TECHNIQUES; POTENTIAL FAULTS; POTENTIAL ERRORS; POTENTIAL COMPROMISES; RESILIENCY; RESILIENCE
SC-37	**Out-of-Band Channels**	OUT-OF-BAND CHANNELS; ELECTRONIC TRANSMISSION DELIVERY; ASSURANCE; RESILIENCY; RESILIENCE
SC-37(1)	ENSURE DELIVERY AND TRANSMISSION	DELIVERY ASSURANCE; TRANSMISSION ASSURANCE
SC-38	**Operations Security**	OPERATIONS SECURITY; OPSEC; ASSURANCE; SYSTEM DEVELOPMENT LIFE CYCLE; SDLC.
SC-39	**Process Isolation**	PROCESS ISOLATION; SEPARATE EXECUTION DOMAINS; ASSURANCE; SEPARATE ADDRESS SPACE; RESILIENCY; RESILIENCE
SC-39(1)	HARDWARE SEPARATION	HARDWARE SEPARATION; PROCESS SEPARATION
SC-39(2)	THREAD ISOLATION	THREAD ISOLATION
SC-40	**Wireless Link Protection**	WIRELESS LINK PROTECTION; VISIBLE WIRELESS COMMUNICATION LINKS; WIRELESS SYSTEMS
SC-40(1)	ELECTROMAGNETIC INTERFERENCE	ELECTROMAGNETIC INTERFERENCE; INTENTIONAL JAMMING; ANTI-JAM PROTECTION
SC-40(2)	REDUCE DETECTION POTENTIAL	REDUCE DETECTION POTENTIAL; TRANSMISSION GEO-LOCATION PROTECTION
SC-40(3)	IMITATIVE OR MANIPULATIVE COMMUNICATIONS DECEPTION	IMITATIVE COMMUNICATIONS DECEPTION; MANIPULATIVE COMMUNICATIONS DECEPTION
SC-40(4)	SIGNAL PARAMETER IDENTIFICATION	SIGNAL PARAMETER IDENTIFICATION; TRANSMITTER SIGNAL PARAMETERS; RADIO FINGERPRINTING
SC-41	**Port and I/O Device Access**	CONNECTION PORT; CONNECTION PORT ACCESS; I/O DEVICE ACCESS; DISABLE PORT
SC-42	**Sensor Capability and Data**	SENSOR CAPABILITY; SENSOR DATA; SENSOR USE; ENVIRONMENTAL SENSING CAPABILITIES
SC-42(1)	REPORTING TO AUTHORIZED INDIVIDUALS OR ROLES	AUTHORIZED SENSOR REPORTING
SC-42(2)	AUTHORIZED USE	AUTHORIZED SENSOR USE; PRIVACY
SC-42(3)	PROHIBIT USE OF DEVICES	PROHIBIT DEVICE USE
SC-42(4)	NOTICE OF COLLECTION	PRIVACY; PERSONALLY IDENTIFIABLE INFORMATION; PII
SC-42(5)	COLLECTION MINIMIZATION	PRIVACY; PERSONALLY IDENTIFIABLE INFORMATION; PII; DATA MINIMIZATION
SC-43	**Usage Restrictions**	USAGE RESTRICTIONS
SC-44	**Detonation Chambers**	DETONATION CHAMBERS; DYNAMIC EXECUTION ENVIRONMENT; PROTECTED EXECUTION ENVIRONMENT; ISOLATED EXECUTION ENVIRONMENT; MALICIOUS CODE; SANDBOX; RESILIENCY; RESILIENCE

TABLE H-20: SYSTEM AND INFORMATION INTEGRITY FAMILY KEYWORDS

CONTROL NUMBER	CONTROL NAME CONTROL ENHANCEMENT NAME	KEYWORDS NOTEWORTHY AND RELEVANT TERMS
SI-1	**System and Information Integrity Policy and Procedures**	SYSTEM AND INFORMATION INTEGRITY; ASSURANCE; POLICY; PROCEDURES; REVIEW; UPDATE; PRIVACY
SI-2	**Flaw Remediation**	FLAW REMEDIATION; IDENTIFY; REPORT; CORRECT; TEST UPDATES; SOFTWARE; FIRMWARE; DEFINED TIME-PERIOD; SECURITY-RELEVANT; SECURITY ASSESSMENT; CONTINUOUS MONITORING; INCIDENT RESPONSE ACTIVITIES; SYSTEM ERROR HANDLING; COMMON WEAKNESS ENUMERATION; CWE; COMMON VULNERABILITIES AND EXPOSURES; CVE; CONFIGURATION MANAGEMENT PROCESS; REMEDIATION ACTIONS; US-CERT; INFORMATION ASSURANCE VULNERABILITY ALERTS
SI-2(1)	CENTRAL MANAGEMENT	CENTRAL MANAGEMENT; FLAW REMEDIATION SECURITY CONTROLS; PLANNING; IMPLEMENTING; ASSESSING; AUTHORIZING; MONITORING
SI-2(2)	AUTOMATED FLAW REMEDIATION STATUS	AUTOMATED FLAW REMEDIATION STATUS; FREQUENCY
SI-2(3)	TIME TO REMEDIATE FLAWS AND BENCHMARKS FOR CORRECTIVE ACTIONS	TIME TO REMEDIATE; FLAWS; BENCHMARKS; TIME FRAMES; CORRECTIVE ACTION
SI-2(4)	AUTOMATED PATCH MANAGEMENT TOOLS	WITHDRAWN
SI-2(5)	AUTOMATIC SOFTWARE AND FIRMWARE UPDATES	AUTOMATIC UPDATES
SI-2(6)	REMOVAL OF PREVIOUS VERSIONS OF SOFTWARE AND FIRMWARE	REMOVAL OF PREVIOUS VERSION; SOFTWARE; FIRMWARE
SI-2(7)	PERSONALLY IDENTIFIABLE INFORMATION	PERSONALLY IDENTIFIABLE INFORMATION; PII; SENIOR AGENCY OFFICIAL FOR PRIVACY; SAOP
SI-3	**Malicious Code Protection**	MALICIOUS CODE PROTECTION MECHANISMS; ENTRY POINT; EXIT POINT; MALICIOUS CODE; DETECT; ERADICATE; MALICIOUS CODE PROTECTION MECHANISMS UPDATE; PERIODIC SCANS; REAL-TIME SCANS; MALICIOUS CODE DETECTION; RESPONSE; MALICIOUS CODE; BLOCK; QUARANTINE; SEND ALERT; FALSE POSITIVES; PERVASIVE CONFIGURATION MANAGEMENT; COMPREHENSIVE SOFTWARE INTEGRITY; NONSIGNATURE-BASED DETECTION; HEURISTICS; POLYMORPHIC MALICIOUS CODE
SI-3(1)	CENTRAL MANAGEMENT	CENTRALIZED MANAGEMENT
SI-3(2)	AUTOMATIC UPDATES	WITHDRAWN
SI-3(3)	NON-PRIVILEGED USERS	WITHDRAWN
SI-3(4)	UPDATES ONLY BY PRIVILEGED USERS	PRIVILEGED USER
SI-3(5)	PORTABLE STORAGE DEVICES	WITHDRAWN
SI-3(6)	TESTING AND VERIFICATION	TEST; VERIFY
SI-3(7)	NONSIGNATURE-BASED DETECTION	WITHDRAWN
SI-3(8)	DETECT UNAUTHORIZED COMMANDS	UNAUTHORIZED OPERATING SYSTEM COMMANDS; KERNEL-BASED INTERFACES; ISSUES A WARNING; AUDITS COMMAND EXECUTION; PREVENTS EXECUTION; KERNEL FUNCTIONS

CONTROL NUMBER	CONTROL NAME CONTROL ENHANCEMENT NAME	KEYWORDS NOTEWORTHY AND RELEVANT TERMS
SI-3(9)	AUTHENTICATE REMOTE COMMANDS	AUTHENTICATE REMOTE COMMANDS; UNAUTHORIZED COMMANDS; REPLAY OF AUTHORIZED COMMANDS
SI-3(10)	MALICIOUS CODE ANALYSIS	MALICIOUS CODE ANALYSIS; TOOLS; TECHNIQUES; RESILIENCY; RESILIENCE
SI-4	**System Monitoring**	ASSURANCE; SYSTEM MONITORING; INTERNAL; EXTERNAL; MONITOR SYSTEM; DETECT POTENTIAL ATTACKS; DETECT CONNECTIONS; UNAUTHORIZED; LOCAL; NETWORK; UNAUTHORIZED USE; DEPLOY MONITORING DEVICES; STRATEGICALLY; AD HOC LOCATIONS; INTRUSION-MONITORING TOOLS; UNAUTHORIZED ACCESS; MODIFICATION; DELETION; EINSTEIN; DEPARTMENT OF HOMELAND SECURITY; DHS; CONTINUOUS MONITORING; INCIDENT RESPONSE PROGRAM; RESILIENCY; RESILIENCE
SI-4(1)	SYSTEM-WIDE INTRUSION DETECTION SYSTEM	SYSTEM-WIDE INTRUSION DETECTION SYSTEM; IDS; RESILIENCY; RESILIENCE
SI-4(2)	AUTOMATED TOOLS AND MECHANISMS FOR REAL-TIME ANALYSIS	REAL-TIME ANALYSIS; AUTOMATED TOOLS; HOST-BASED; NETWORK-BASED; TRANSPORT-BASED; STORAGE-BASED; SECURITY INFORMATION AND EVENT MANAGEMENT; ALERTS; NOTIFICATIONS; RESILIENCY; RESILIENCE
SI-4(3)	AUTOMATED TOOL AND MECHANISM INTEGRATION	INTEGRATE; MECHANISMS; ACCESS CONTROL; FLOW CONTROL; RECONFIGURATION; ATTACK ISOLATION; ELIMINATION; RESILIENCY; RESILIENCE
SI-4(4)	INBOUND AND OUTBOUND COMMUNICATIONS TRAFFIC	COMMUNICATIONS TRAFFIC; MONITORING; INBOUND; OUTBOUND; RESILIENCY; RESILIENCE
SI-4(5)	SYSTEM-GENERATED ALERTS	ALERTS; SYSTEM-GENERATED; PERSONNEL; ROLES; PRIVACY
SI-4(6)	RESTRICT NON-PRIVILEGED USERS	WITHDRAWN
SI-4(7)	AUTOMATED RESPONSE TO SUSPICIOUS EVENTS	SUSPICIOUS EVENTS; SYSTEM NOTIFIES; PERSONNEL; ROLES; AUTOMATED RESPONSE; LEAST-DISRUPTIVE ACTIONS; TERMINATE SUSPICIOUS EVENTS; RESILIENCY; RESILIENCE
SI-4(8)	PROTECTION OF MONITORING INFORMATION	WITHDRAWN
SI-4(9)	TESTING OF MONITORING TOOLS AND MECHANISMS	TEST INTRUSION MONITORING TOOLS
SI-4(10)	VISIBILITY OF ENCRYPTED COMMUNICATIONS	ENCRYPTED COMMUNICATIONS TRAFFIC; VISIBILITY; SYSTEM MONITORING TOOLS; CONFIDENTIALITY; MISSION-ASSURANCE; RESILIENCY; RESILIENCE
SI-4(11)	ANALYZE COMMUNICATIONS TRAFFIC ANOMALIES	OUTBOUND COMMUNICATIONS TRAFFIC; EXTERNAL BOUNDARY; INTERIOR POINTS; ANOMALIES; RESILIENCY; RESILIENCE
SI-4(12)	AUTOMATED ORGANIZATION-GENERATED ALERTS	AUTOMATED ALERTS; SECURITY PERSONNEL; ACTIVITIES; INAPPROPRIATE; UNUSUAL; PRIVACY
SI-4(13)	ANALYZE TRAFFIC AND EVENT PATTERNS	TRAFFIC/EVENT PATTERNS; ANALYZE COMMUNICATIONS; DEVELOP PROFILES; FALSE POSITIVES; FALSE NEGATIVES
SI-4(14)	WIRELESS INTRUSION DETECTION	WIRELESS INTRUSION DETECTION; ROGUE WIRELESS DEVICES; ATTACK ATTEMPTS; COMPROMISES; BREACHES

CONTROL NUMBER	CONTROL NAME CONTROL ENHANCEMENT NAME	KEYWORDS NOTEWORTHY AND RELEVANT TERMS
SI-4(15)	WIRELESS TO WIRELINE COMMUNICATIONS	INTRUSION DETECTION SYSTEM; MONITOR WIRELESS COMMUNICATIONS; WIRELESS TO WIRELINE COMMUNICATIONS
SI-4(16)	CORRELATE MONITORING INFORMATION	CORRELATE MONITORING INFORMATION; RESILIENCY; RESILIENCE
SI-4(17)	INTEGRATED SITUATIONAL AWARENESS	INTEGRATED SITUATIONAL AWARENESS; MONITORING ACTIVITIES; PHYSICAL; CYBER; SUPPLY CHAIN; RESILIENCY; RESILIENCE
SI-4(18)	ANALYZE TRAFFIC AND COVERT EXFILTRATION	ANALYZE OUTBOUND COMMUNICATIONS TRAFFIC; EXTERNAL BOUNDARY; INTERIOR POINTS; COVERT EXFILTRATION; RESILIENCY; RESILIENCE
SI-4(19)	INDIVIDUALS POSING GREATER RISK	MONITORING; INDIVIDUALS; HIGH RISK; PRIVACY
SI-4(20)	PRIVILEGED USERS	ADDITIONAL MONITORING; PRIVILEGED USERS; RESILIENCY; RESILIENCE
SI-4(21)	PROBATIONARY PERIODS	PROBATIONARY PERIODS
SI-4(22)	UNAUTHORIZED NETWORK SERVICES	NETWORK SERVICES; UNAPPROVED; UNAUTHORIZED; AUDIT; ALERT
SI-4(23)	HOST-BASED DEVICES	HOST-BASED MONITORING
SI-4(24)	INDICATORS OF COMPROMISE	INDICATORS OF COMPROMISE; IOC; FORENSIC ARTIFACTS; DISCOVER; COLLECT; DISTRIBUTE; USE; RESILIENCY; RESILIENCE
SI-4(25)	PERSONALLY IDENTIFIABLE INFORMATION MONITORING	PERSONALLY IDENTIFIABLE INFORMATION; PII; PRIVACY IMPACT ASSESSMENTS; PIA
SI-5	**Security Alerts, Advisories, and Directives**	EXTERNAL ORGANIZATION; RECEIVE; SECURITY ALERTS; ADVISORIES; DIRECTIVES; GENERATE INTERNAL; DISSEMINATE; IMPLEMENT; SECURITY DIRECTIVES; TIME FRAMES; NOTIFY; UNITED STATES COMPUTER EMERGENCY READINESS TEAM; US-CERT; OFFICE OF MANAGEMENT AND BUDGET; OMB; ASSURANCE
SI-5(1)	AUTOMATED ALERTS AND ADVISORIES	AUTOMATED SECURITY ALERTS AND ADVISORIES; PRIVACY
SI-6	**Security and Privacy Function Verification**	SECURITY FUNCTION VERIFICATION; APPROPRIATE PRIVILEGE; NOTIFICATION; FAILED SECURITY VERIFICATION; ANOMALIES DISCOVERED; SHUT SYSTEM DOWN; RESTART SYSTEM; TRANSITION STATES; STARTUP; RESTART; SHUTDOWN; ABORT; ASSURANCE; PRIVACY FUNCTION VERIFICATION; FAILED PRIVACY VERIFICATION; RESILIENCY; RESILIENCE
SI-6(1)	NOTIFICATION OF FAILED SECURITY TESTS	WITHDRAWN
SI-6(2)	AUTOMATION SUPPORT FOR DISTRIBUTED TESTING	AUTOMATION SUPPORT; DISTRIBUTED SECURITY TESTING; DISTRIBUTED PRIVACY TESTING
SI-6(3)	REPORT VERIFICATION RESULTS	REPORT RESULTS; PERSONNEL; ROLES; PRIVACY
SI-7	**Software, Firmware, and Information Integrity**	INTEGRITY VERIFICATION TOOLS; UNAUTHORIZED CHANGES; SOFTWARE; FIRMWARE; INFORMATION; INTEGRITY CHECKING MECHANISMS; ASSURANCE; RESILIENCY; RESILIENCE

CONTROL NUMBER	CONTROL NAME / CONTROL ENHANCEMENT NAME	KEYWORDS / NOTEWORTHY AND RELEVANT TERMS
SI-7(1)	INTEGRITY CHECKS	INTEGRITY CHECK; AT STARTUP; SECURITY RELEVANT CONDITION; DEFINED FREQUENCY; TRANSITIONAL STATES; RESILIENCY; RESILIENCE
SI-7(2)	AUTOMATED NOTIFICATIONS OF INTEGRITY VIOLATIONS	AUTOMATED TOOLS; INTEGRITY VIOLATIONS; NOTIFICATIONS; PRIVACY
SI-7(3)	CENTRALLY MANAGED INTEGRITY TOOLS	CENTRALLY MANAGED INTEGRITY TOOLS
SI-7(4)	TAMPER-EVIDENT PACKAGING	WITHDRAWN
SI-7(5)	AUTOMATED RESPONSE TO INTEGRITY VIOLATIONS	AUTOMATED RESPONSE; INTEGRITY CHECKING; ANOMALY RESPONSE; SHUT SYSTEM DOWN; RESTART SYSTEM; TRIGGER AUDIT ALERTS
SI-7(6)	CRYPTOGRAPHIC PROTECTION	CRYPTOGRAPHIC; PROTECTION MECHANISMS; RESILIENCY; RESILIENCE
SI-7(7)	INTEGRATION OF DETECTION AND RESPONSE	DETECTION; SECURITY RELEVANT CHANGES; TRACKED; MONITORED; CORRECTED; AVAILABLE FOR HISTORIC PURPOSES; ARCHIVE; RESILIENCY; RESILIENCE
SI-7(8)	AUDITING CAPABILITY FOR SIGNIFICANT EVENTS	UPON DETECTION; INTEGRITY VIOLATION; AUDIT EVENTS; GENERATE AUDIT RECORD; ALERT CURRENT USERS; ALERT DEFINED PERSONNEL OR ROLES
SI-7(9)	VERIFY BOOT PROCESS	INTEGRITY; VERIFY BOOT PROCESS; KNOWN/TRUSTWORTHY STATES; INTEGRITY VERIFICATION MECHANISMS; RESILIENCY; RESILIENCE
SI-7(10)	PROTECTION OF BOOT FIRMWARE	PROTECTION OF BOOT FIRMWARE; UNAUTHORIZED MODIFICATION; PERMANENT DENIAL OF SERVICE; PERSISTENT MALICIOUS CODE PRESENCE; RESILIENCY; RESILIENCE
SI-7(11)	CONFINED ENVIRONMENTS WITH LIMITED PRIVILEGES	CONFINED ENVIRONMENTS; LIMITED PRIVILEGES; USER INSTALLED SOFTWARE; ENVIRONMENT; CONFINED PHYSICAL; VIRTUAL MACHINE; RESILIENCY; RESILIENCE
SI-7(12)	INTEGRITY VERIFICATION	INTEGRITY VERIFICATION; USER INSTALLED SOFTWARE; RESILIENCY; RESILIENCE
SI-7(13)	CODE EXECUTION IN PROTECTED ENVIRONMENTS	CODE EXECUTION; PROTECTED ENVIRONMENTS; EXPLICIT APPROVAL; PERSONNEL; ROLES
SI-7(14)	BINARY OR MACHINE EXECUTABLE CODE	BINARY CODE; MACHINE EXECUTABLE CODE
SI-7(15)	CODE AUTHENTICATION	CRYPTOGRAPHY, CRYPTOGRAPHIC MECHANISMS; CRYPTOGRAPHIC AUTHENTICATION; DIGITAL SIGNATURES
SI-7(16)	TIME LIMIT ON PROCESS EXECUTION WITHOUT SUPERVISION	PROCESS EXECUTION; TIME LIMIT; SUPERVISION
SI-8	Spam Protection	SPAM PROTECTION MECHANISMS, ENTRY POINTS; EXIT POINTS; UPDATES; UNSOLICITED MESSAGES
SI-8(1)	CENTRAL MANAGEMENT	CENTRALLY MANAGED
SI-8(2)	AUTOMATIC UPDATES	AUTOMATIC UPDATES
SI-8(3)	CONTINUOUS LEARNING CAPABILITY	CONTINUOUS LEARNING CAPABILITY
SI-9	Information Input Restrictions	WITHDRAWN
SI-10	Information Input Validation	INPUT VALIDATION; SYNTAX; SEMANTICS; STRUCTURED MESSAGES; PRESCREENING; ASSURANCE; RESILIENCY; RESILIENCE
SI-10(1)	MANUAL OVERRIDE CAPABILITY	MANUAL OVERRIDE; RESTRICT; AUDIT

CONTROL NUMBER	CONTROL NAME CONTROL ENHANCEMENT NAME	KEYWORDS NOTEWORTHY AND RELEVANT TERMS
SI-10(2)	REVIEW AND RESOLVE OF ERRORS	INPUT VALIDATION ERRORS; RESOLUTION; DEFINED TIME-PERIOD
SI-10(3)	PREDICTABLE BEHAVIOR	PREDICTABLE BEHAVIOR; RESILIENCY; RESILIENCE
SI-10(4)	TIMING INTERACTIONS	TIMING INTERACTIONS; RESPONSE TO INVALID INPUTS; RESILIENCY; RESILIENCE
SI-10(5)	RESTRICT INPUTS TO TRUSTED SOURCES AND APPROVED FORMATS	RESTRICT INPUTS; WHITELISTING; TRUSTED SOURCES; ACCEPTABLE FORMATS; RESILIENCY; RESILIENCE
SI-11	**Error Handling**	SYSTEM GENERATES ERROR MESSAGES; PERSONNEL; ROLES
SI-12	**Information Management and Retention**	INFORMATION MANAGEMENT AND RETENTION; RECORDS RETENTION; NATIONAL ARCHIVES AND RECORDS ADMINISTRATION; NARA; PRIVACY
SI-12(1)	LIMIT PERSONALLY IDENTIFIABLE INFORMATION ELEMENTS IN TESTING, TRAINING, AND RESEARCH	PRIVACY; PERSONALLY IDENTIFIABLE INFORMATION; PII
SI-12(2)	MINIMIZE PERSONALLY IDENTIFIABLE INFORMATION	PRIVACY; PERSONALLY IDENTIFIABLE INFORMATION; PII; DATA MINIMIZATION
SI-13	**Predictable Failure Prevention**	ASSURANCE; MEAN TIME TO FAILURE; MTTF; INSTALLATION-SPECIFIC; COMPONENTS
SI-13(1)	TRANSFERRING COMPONENT RESPONSIBILITIES	TRANSFERRING COMPONENT RESPONSIBILITY; DEFINED FRACTION OR PERCENTAGE
SI-13(2)	TIME LIMIT ON PROCESS EXECUTION WITHOUT SUPERVISION	WITHDRAWN
SI-13(3)	MANUAL TRANSFER BETWEEN COMPONENTS	MANUAL TRANSFER; MEAN TIME TO FAILURE EXCEEDS; DEFINED FREQUENCY
SI-13(4)	STANDBY COMPONENT INSTALLATION AND NOTIFICATION	TRANSFER OF COMPONENTS; AUTOMATIC; MANUAL; STANDBY; ACTIVE; ACTIVATES ALARM; AUTOMATICALLY SHUTS DOWN SYSTEM
SI-13(5)	FAILOVER CAPABILITY	FAILOVER CAPABILITY; REAL-TIME; NEAR REAL-TIME
SI-14	**Non-Persistence**	ADVANCED PERSISTENT THREAT; APT; NON-PERSISTENCE; COMPONENTS; SERVICES; KNOWN STATE; SPECIFIC PERIOD OF TIME; END OF SESSION; DEFINED FREQUENCY; VIRTUALIZATION; VIRTUAL MACHINES; PHYSICAL MACHINES; ASSURANCE; RESILIENCY; RESILIENCE
SI-14(1)	REFRESH FROM TRUSTED SOURCES	REFRESH; COMPONENT; SERVICES; TRUSTED SOURCE
SI-15	**Information Output Filtering**	INFORMATION OUTPUT FILTERING; VALIDATION; EXTRANEOUS CONTENT; ANOMALOUS BEHAVIOR; ALERTING MONITORING TOOLS; ASSURANCE; PRIVACY
SI-15(1)	LIMIT PERSONALLY IDENTIFIABLE INFORMATION DISSEMINATION	INFORMATION OUTPUT FILTERING; PRIVACY; PERSONALLY IDENTIFIABLE INFORMATION; PII
SI-16	**Memory Protection**	MEMORY PROTECTION; UNAUTHORIZED CODE EXECUTION; PREVENTION; HARDWARE-ENFORCED; SOFTWARE-ENFORCED; ASSURANCE
SI-17	**Fail-Safe Procedures**	FAILURE CONDITION; FAIL SAFE PROCEDURE; ASSURANCE
SI-18	**Information Disposal**	DISPOSAL; PRIVACY; PERSONALLY IDENTIFIABLE INFORMATION; PII

IDENTIFIER NUMBER	CONTROL NAME / CONTROL ENHANCEMENT NAME	KEYWORDS / NOTEWORTHY AND RELEVANT TERMS
SI-19	**Data Quality Operations**	PRIVACY; PERSONALLY IDENTIFIABLE INFORMATION; PII; DE-IDENTIFICATION
SI-19(1)	UPDATING AND CORRECTING PERSONALLY IDENTIFIABLE INFORMATION	PRIVACY; PERSONALLY IDENTIFIABLE INFORMATION; PII
SI-19(2)	DATA TAGS	PRIVACY; PERSONALLY IDENTIFIABLE INFORMATION; PII
SI-19(3)	PERSONALLY IDENTIFIABLE INFORMATION COLLECTION	PRIVACY; PERSONALLY IDENTIFIABLE INFORMATION; PII
SI-20	**De-Identification**	PRIVACY; PERSONALLY IDENTIFIABLE INFORMATION; PII; DE-IDENTIFICATION
SI-20(1)	COLLECTION	PERSONALLY IDENTIFIABLE INFORMATION; PII; DE-IDENTIFICATION
SI-20(2)	ARCHIVING	ARCHIVE; PRIVACY; PERSONALLY IDENTIFIABLE INFORMATION; PII; DE-IDENTIFICATION
SI-20(3)	RELEASE	PRIVACY; PERSONALLY IDENTIFIABLE INFORMATION; PII; DE-IDENTIFICATION
SI-20(4)	REMOVAL, MASKING, ENCRYPTION, HASHING, OR REPLACEMENT OF DIRECT IDENTIFIERS	ENCRYPTION; IDENTIFIERS; MASKING; HASHING; PRIVACY; DE-IDENTIFICATION
SI-20(5)	STATISTICAL DISCLOSURE CONTROL	DISCLOSURE; PRIVACY; DE-IDENTIFICATION
SI-20(6)	DIFFERENTIAL PRIVACY	DIFFERENTIAL PRIVACY; PERSONALLY IDENTIFIABLE INFORMATION; PII; DE-IDENTIFICATION
SI-20(7)	VALIDATED SOFTWARE	DE-IDENTIFICATION
SI-20(8)	MOTIVATED INTRUDER	INTRUDER; DE-IDENTIFICATION

APPENDIX I

INTERNATIONAL STANDARDS

CONTROL MAPPINGS FOR ISO/IEC 27001 AND ISO/IEC 15408

The mapping tables in this appendix provide organizations with a *general* indication of security control coverage with respect to ISO/IEC 27001, *Information technology–Security techniques–Information security management systems–Requirements*[57] and ISO/IEC 15408, *Information technology -- Security techniques -- Evaluation criteria for IT security.*[58] ISO/IEC 27001 may be applied to all types of organizations and specifies requirements for establishing, implementing, operating, monitoring, reviewing, maintaining, and improving a documented information security management system (ISMS) within the context of business risks. NIST Special Publication 800-39 includes guidance on managing risk at the organizational level, mission/business process level, and information system level, is consistent with ISO/IEC 27001. ISO/IEC 15408 (Common Criteria) provides functionality and assurance requirements for developers of systems and system components (i.e., information technology products). Since many of the technical security controls defined in Chapter Three are implemented in hardware, software, and firmware components of systems, organizations can obtain significant benefit from the acquisition and employment of components and systems evaluated against the requirements of ISO/IEC 15408. The use of evaluated systems and components can provide evidence that certain security controls are implemented correctly, operating as intended, and producing the desired effect with respect to satisfying stated security requirements.

To successfully meet the mapping criteria (i.e., a control appearing in one of the mapping tables), the implementation of the mapped controls should result in an equivalent information security function or capability. However, this does not mean that security control equivalency based solely on the mapping tables herein should be assumed by organizations. While the control mappings are accurate as possible, there is still some degree of subjectivity in the mapping analysis because the mappings are not always one-to-one and may not be completely equivalent. To help clarify the control mappings, when a control in the right column of Tables I-1 and I-2 does not fully satisfy the intent of the control in the left column of the tables, the control in the right column is designated with an asterisk (*).

Occasionally, an ISO/IEC 27001 control could only be directly mapped to a NIST Special Publication 800-53 control enhancement. In such cases, the relevant enhancement is specified in Table I-2 indicating that the corresponding ISO/IEC 27001 control meets the intent of the NIST Special Publication 800-53 control enhancement only and does not address the associated base control or any other enhancements under that base control. Where no enhancement is specified, the ISO/IEC 27001 control is relevant only to the NIST Special Publication 800-53 base control. Finally, the controls from ISO/IEC 27002 were not considered in the mapping analysis since the standard is informative rather than normative.

Organizations may leverage the control mappings provided in Tables I-1 and I-2 when dealing with external entities, including, for example, in defining security and privacy requirements in contracts and agreements. Organizations are responsible for analyzing the ISO/IEC controls and

---

[57] ISO/IEC 27001 was published in October 2013 by the International Organization for Standardization (ISO) and the International Electrotechnical Commission (IEC).

[58] ISO/IEC 15408 was published in September 2012 by the International Organization for Standardization (ISO) and the International Electrotechnical Commission (IEC).

requirements that conform with the controls in special publication 800-53 and identifying any gaps in coverage and protection. Additionally, because of the control selection process, controls beyond those implemented as part of the ISO/IEC 27001 and ISO/IEC 15408 standards may be selected, implemented, and assessed to ensure protection of information commensurate with risk. Ultimately, the decision to leverage ISO/IEC 27001 and ISO/IEC 15408 assessments remains with the organization's authorizing official. In leveraging such assessments, authorizing officials determine if the work performed in accordance with the ISO/IEC 27001 and ISO/IEC 15408 standards, is acceptable.

Table I-1 provides a mapping from the security controls in NIST Special Publication 800-53 to the security controls in ISO/IEC 27001. Organizations should review the introductory text at the beginning of Appendix I before employing the mappings in Table I-1.

TABLE I-1: MAPPING NIST 800-53 TO ISO/IEC 27001

NIST 800-53 CONTROLS		ISO/IEC 27001 CONTROLS *An asterisk (*) indicates that the ISO/IEC control does not fully satisfy the intent of the NIST control.*
AC-1	Access Control Policy and Procedures	A.5.1.1, A.5.1.2, A.6.1.1, A.9.1.1, A.12.1.1, A.18.1.1, A.18.2.2
AC-2	Account Management	A.9.2.1, A.9.2.2, A.9.2.3, A.9.2.5, A.9.2.6
AC-3	Access Enforcement	A.6.2.2, A.9.1.2, A.9.4.1, A.9.4.4, A.9.4.5, A.13.1.1, A.14.1.2, A.14.1.3, A.18.1.3
AC-4	Information Flow Enforcement	A.13.1.3, A.13.2.1, A.14.1.2, A.14.1.3
AC-5	Separation of Duties	A.6.1.2
AC-6	Least Privilege	A.9.1.2, A.9.2.3, A.9.4.4, A.9.4.5
AC-7	Unsuccessful Logon Attempts	A.9.4.2
AC-8	System Use Notification	A.9.4.2
AC-9	Previous Logon (Access) Notification	A.9.4.2
AC-10	Concurrent Session Control	None
AC-11	Device Lock	A.11.2.8, A.11.2.9
AC-12	Session Termination	None
AC-13	**Withdrawn**	---
AC-14	Permitted Actions without Identification or Authentication	None
AC-15	**Withdrawn**	---
AC-16	Security and Privacy Attributes	A.18.1.4**
AC-17	Remote Access	A.6.2.1, A.6.2.2, A.13.1.1, A.13.2.1, A.14.1.2
AC-18	Wireless Access	A.6.2.1, A.13.1.1, A.13.2.1
AC-19	Access Control for Mobile Devices	A.6.2.1, A.11.2.6, A.13.2.1
AC-20	Use of External Systems	A.11.2.6, A.13.1.1, A.13.2.1
AC-21	Information Sharing	A.13.2.1, A.13.2.2, A.18.1.4**
AC-22	Publicly Accessible Content	None
AC-23	Data Mining Protection	A.18.1.4**
AC-24	Access Control Decisions	A.9.4.1*
AC-25	Reference Monitor	None
AT-1	Awareness and Training Policy and Procedures	A.5.1.1, A.5.1.2, A.6.1.1, A.12.1.1, A.18.1.1, A.18.1.4**, A.18.2.2
AT-2	Awareness Training	A.7.2.2, A.12.2.1, A.18.1.4**
AT-3	Role-Based Training	A.7.2.2*, A.18.1.4**
AT-4	Training Records	A.18.1.4**
AT-5	**Withdrawn**	---
AU-1	Audit and Accountability Policy and Procedures	A.5.1.1, A.5.1.2, A.6.1.1, A.12.1.1, A.18.1.1, A.18.2.2
AU-2	Audit Events	None
AU-3	Content of Audit Records	A.12.4.1*, A.18.1.4**
AU-4	Audit Storage Capacity	A.12.1.3
AU-5	Response to Audit Processing Failures	A.12.1.3*

NIST 800-53 CONTROLS		ISO/IEC 27001 CONTROLS *An asterisk (*) indicates that the ISO/IEC control does not fully satisfy the intent of the NIST control.*
AU-6	Audit Review, Analysis, and Reporting	A.12.4.1, A.12.4.3*, A.16.1.2, A.16.1.4
AU-7	Audit Reduction and Report Generation	None
AU-8	Time Stamps	A.12.4.4
AU-9	Protection of Audit Information	A.12.4.2, A.12.4.3, A.18.1.3
AU-10	Non-repudiation	None
AU-11	Audit Record Retention	A.12.4.1, A.16.1.7, A.18.1.4**
AU-12	Audit Generation	A.12.4.1, A.12.4.3, A.18.1.4**
AU-13	Monitoring for Information Disclosure	None
AU-14	Session Audit	A.12.4.1*
AU-15	Alternate Audit Capability	None
AU-16	Cross-Organizational Auditing	A.18.1.4**
CA-1	Assessment, Authorization, and Monitoring Policy and Procedures	A.5.1.1, A.5.1.2, A.6.1.1, A.12.1.1, A.18.1.1, A.18.1.4**, A.18.2.2
CA-2	Assessments	A.14.2.8, A.18.2.2, A.18.2.3
CA-3	System Interconnections	A.13.1.2, A.13.2.1, A.13.2.2
CA-4	**Withdrawn**	---
CA-5	Plan of Action and Milestones	A.18.1.4**
CA-6	Authorization	None
CA-7	Continuous Monitoring	A.18.1.4**
CA-8	Penetration Testing	None
CA-9	Internal System Connections	None
CM-1	Configuration Management Policy and Procedures	A.5.1.1, A.5.1.2, A.6.1.1, A.12.1.1, A.18.1.1, A.18.1.4**, A.18.2.2
CM-2	Baseline Configuration	None
CM-3	Configuration Change Control	A.12.1.2, A.14.2.2, A.14.2.3, A.14.2.4
CM-4	Security and Privacy Impact Analyses	A.14.2.3, A.18.1.4**
CM-5	Access Restrictions for Change	A.9.2.3, A.9.4.5, A.12.1.2, A.12.1.4, A.12.5.1
CM-6	Configuration Settings	None
CM-7	Least Functionality	A.12.5.1*
CM-8	System Component Inventory	A.8.1.1, A.8.1.2, A.18.1.4**
CM-9	Configuration Management Plan	A.6.1.1*, A.12.1.2*
CM-10	Software Usage Restrictions	A.18.1.2
CM-11	User-Installed Software	A.12.5.1, A.12.6.2
CM-12	Information Location	A.18.1.4**
CP-1	Contingency Planning Policy and Procedures	A.5.1.1, A.5.1.2, A.6.1.1, A.12.1.1, A.18.1.1, A.18.1.4**, A.18.2.2
CP-2	Contingency Plan	A.6.1.1, A.17.1.1, A.17.2.1, A.18.1.4**
CP-3	Contingency Training	A.7.2.2*, A.18.1.4**
CP-4	Contingency Plan Testing	A.17.1.3, A.18.1.4**
CP-5	**Withdrawn**	---
CP-6	Alternate Storage Site	A.11.1.4, A,12.3.1*, A.17.1.2
CP-7	Alternate Processing Site	A.11.1.4, A.17.1.2, A.17.2.1
CP-8	Telecommunications Services	A.11.2.2, A.17.1.2
CP-9	System Backup	A.12.3.1, A.17.1.2, A.18.1.3

NIST 800-53 CONTROLS		ISO/IEC 27001 CONTROLS *An asterisk (*) indicates that the ISO/IEC control does not fully satisfy the intent of the NIST control.*
CP-10	System Recovery and Reconstitution	A.17.1.2
CP-11	Alternate Communications Protocols	A.17.1.2*
CP-12	Safe Mode	None
CP-13	Alternative Security Mechanisms	A.17.1.2*
IA-1	Identification and Authentication Policy and Procedures	A.5.1.1, A.5.1.2, A.6.1.1, A.12.1.1, A.18.1.1, A.18.1.4**, A.18.2.2
IA-2	Identification and Authentication (Organizational Users)	A.9.2.1*, A.9.4.2*
IA-3	Device Identification and Authentication	None
IA-4	Identifier Management	A.9.2.1, A.18.1.4**
IA-5	Authenticator Management	A.9.2.1, A.9.2.4, A.9.3.1, A.9.4.3
IA-6	Authenticator Feedback	A.9.4.2
IA-7	Cryptographic Module Authentication	A.18.1.5
IA-8	Identification and Authentication (Non-Organizational Users)	A.9.2.1, A.18.1.4**
IA-9	Service Identification and Authentication	None
IA-10	Adaptive Authentication	None
IA-11	Re-authentication	None
IA-12	Identity Proofing	None
IP-1	Individual Participation Policy and Procedures	A.18.1.4**
IP-2	Consent	A.18.1.4**
IP-3	Redress	A.18.1.4**
IP-4	Privacy Notice	A.18.1.4**
IP-5	Privacy Act Statement	A.18.1.4**
IP-6	Individual Access	A.18.1.4**
IR-1	Incident Response Policy and Procedures	A.5.1.1, A.5.1.2, A.6.1.1, A.12.1.1 A.18.1.1, A.18.1.4**, A.18.2.2
IR-2	Incident Response Training	A.7.2.2*, A.18.1.4**
IR-3	Incident Response Testing	A.18.1.4**
IR-4	Incident Handling	A.16.1.4, A.16.1.5, A.16.1.6, A.18.1.4**
IR-5	Incident Monitoring	A.18.1.4**
IR-6	Incident Reporting	A.6.1.3, A.16.1.2, A.18.1.4**
IR-7	Incident Response Assistance	A.18.1.4**
IR-8	Incident Response Plan	A.16.1.1, A.18.1.4**
IR-9	Information Spillage Response	A.18.1.4**
IR-10	Integrated Information Security Analysis Team	None
MA-1	System Maintenance Policy and Procedures	A.5.1.1, A.5.1.2, A.6.1.1, A.12.1.1, A.18.1.1, A.18.2.2
MA-2	Controlled Maintenance	A.11.2.4*, A.11.2.5*
MA-3	Maintenance Tools	A.11.2.5*
MA-4	Nonlocal Maintenance	None
MA-5	Maintenance Personnel	None
MA-6	Timely Maintenance	A.11.2.4
MP-1	Media Protection Policy and Procedures	A.5.1.1, A.5.1.2, A.6.1.1, A.12.1.1, A.18.1.1, A.18.2.2
MP-2	Media Access	A.8.2.3, A.8.3.1, A.11.2.9

NIST 800-53 CONTROLS		ISO/IEC 27001 CONTROLS An asterisk (*) indicates that the ISO/IEC control does not fully satisfy the intent of the NIST control.
MP-3	Media Marking	A.8.2.2
MP-4	Media Storage	A.8.2.3, A.8.3.1, A.11.2.9
MP-5	Media Transport	A.8.2.3, A.8.3.1, A.8.3.3, A.11.2.5, A.11.2.6
MP-6	Media Sanitization	A.8.2.3, A.8.3.1, A.8.3.2, A.11.2.7
MP-7	Media Use	A.8.2.3, A.8.3.1
MP-8	Media Downgrading	None
PA-1	Privacy Authorization Policy and Procedures	A.18.1.4**
PA-2	Authority to Collect	A.18.1.4**
PA-3	Purpose Specification	A.18.1.4**
PA-4	Information Sharing with External Parties	A.13.2.1, A.13.2.2, A.18.1.4**
PE-1	Physical and Environmental Protection Policy and Procedures	A.5.1.1, A.5.1.2, A.6.1.1, A.9.1.1, A.12.1.1, A.18.1.1, A.18.2.2
PE-2	Physical Access Authorizations	A.11.1.2*, A.11.1.5*
PE-3	Physical Access Control	A.11.1.1, A.11.1.2, A.11.1.3
PE-4	Access Control for Transmission	A.11.1.2, A.11.2.3
PE-5	Access Control for Output Devices	A.11.1.2, A.11.1.3
PE-6	Monitoring Physical Access	None
PE-7	**Withdrawn**	---
PE-8	Visitor Access Records	None
PE-9	Power Equipment and Cabling	A.11.1.4, A.11.2.1, A.11.2.2, A.11.2.3
PE-10	Emergency Shutoff	A.11.2.2*
PE-11	Emergency Power	A.11.2.2
PE-12	Emergency Lighting	A.11.2.2*
PE-13	Fire Protection	A.11.1.4, A.11.2.1
PE-14	Temperature and Humidity Controls	A.11.1.4, A.11.2.1, A.11.2.2
PE-15	Water Damage Protection	A.11.1.4, A.11.2.1, A.11.2.2
PE-16	Delivery and Removal	A.8.2.3, A.11.1.6, A.11.2.5
PE-17	Alternate Work Site	A.6.2.2, A.11.2.6, A.13.2.1
PE-18	Location of System Components	A.11.1.4, A.11.2.1
PE-19	Information Leakage	A.11.1.4, A.11.2.1
PE-20	Asset Monitoring and Tracking	A.8.2.3*
PE-21	Electromagnetic Pulse Protection	A.11.1.4*
PE-22	Component Marking	None
PL-1	Planning Policy and Procedures	A.5.1.1, A.5.1.2, A.6.1.1, A.12.1.1, A.18.1.1, A.18.1.4**, A.18.2.2
PL-2	Security and Privacy Plans	A.14.1.1, A.18.1.4**
PL-3	**Withdrawn**	---
PL-4	Rules of Behavior	A.7.1.2, A.7.2.1, A.7.2.2, A.8.1.3, A.18.1.4**
PL-5	**Withdrawn**	---
PL-6	**Withdrawn**	---
PL-7	Concept of Operations	A.14.1.1*, A.18.1.4**
PL-8	Security and Privacy Architectures	A.14.1.1*, A.18.1.4**
PL-9	Central Management	A.18.1.4**

NIST 800-53 CONTROLS		ISO/IEC 27001 CONTROLS *An asterisk (*) indicates that the ISO/IEC control does not fully satisfy the intent of the NIST control.*
PL-10	Baseline Selection	None
PL-11	Baseline Tailoring	None
PM-1	Information Security Program Plan	A.5.1.1, A.5.1.2, A.6.1.1, A.18.1.1, A.18.2.2
PM-2	Information Security Program Roles	A.6.1.1*
PM-3	Information Security and Privacy Resources	A.18.1.4**
PM-4	Plan of Action and Milestones Process	A.18.1.4**
PM-5	System Inventory	None
PM-6	Measures of Performance	A.18.1.4**
PM-7	Enterprise Architecture	A.18.1.4**
PM-8	Critical Infrastructure Plan	A.18.1.4**
PM-9	Risk Management Strategy	A.18.1.4**
PM-10	Authorization Process	A.6.1.1*
PM-11	Mission and Business Process Definition	A.18.1.4**
PM-12	Insider Threat Program	None
PM-13	Security and Privacy Workforce	A.7.2.2*, A.18.1.4**
PM-14	Testing, Training, and Monitoring	A.18.1.4**
PM-15	Contacts with Groups and Associations	A.6.1.4, A.18.1.4**
PM-16	Threat Awareness Program	None
PM-17	Protecting Controlled Unclassified Information on External Systems	A.6.1.1*
PM-18	Privacy Program Plan	A.18.1.4**
PM-19	Privacy Program Roles	A.6.1.1*, A.18.1.4**
PM-20	System of Records Notice	A.18.1.4**
PM-21	Dissemination of Privacy Program Information	A.18.1.4**
PM-22	Accounting of Disclosures	A.18.1.4**
PM-23	Data Quality Management	A.18.1.4**
PM-24	Data Management Board	A.6.1.1*, A.18.1.4**
PM-25	Data Integrity Board	A.6.1.1*, A.18.1.4**
PM-26	Minimization of Personally Identifiable Information	A.18.1.4**
PM-27	Individual Access Control	A.18.1.4**
PM-28	Complaint Management	A.18.1.4**
PM-29	Inventory of Personally Identifiable Information	A.8.1.1, A.8.2.3, A.18.1.4**
PM-30	Privacy Reporting	A.18.1.4**
PM-31	Supply Chain Risk Management Plan	None
PM-32	Risk Framing	None
PS-1	Personnel Security Policy and Procedures	A.5.1.1, A.5.1.2, A.6.1.1, A.12.1.1, A.18.1.1, A.18.2.2
PS-2	Position Risk Designation	None
PS-3	Personnel Screening	A.7.1.1
PS-4	Personnel Termination	A.7.3.1, A.8.1.4, A.9.2.6
PS-5	Personnel Transfer	A.7.3.1, A.8.1.4
PS-6	Access Agreements	A.7.1.2, A.7.2.1, A.13.2.4
PS-7	External Personnel Security	A.6.1.1*, A.7.2.1*

NIST 800-53 CONTROLS		ISO/IEC 27001 CONTROLS *An asterisk (*) indicates that the ISO/IEC control does not fully satisfy the intent of the NIST control.*
PS-8	Personnel Sanctions	A.7.2.3
RA-1	Risk Assessment Policy and Procedures	A.5.1.1, A.5.1.2, A.6.1.1, A.12.1.1, A.18.1.1, A.18.1.4**, A.18.2.2
RA-2	Security Categorization	A.8.2.1
RA-3	Risk Assessment	A.12.6.1*, A.18.1.4**
RA-4	**Withdrawn**	---
RA-5	Vulnerability Scanning	A.12.6.1*
RA-6	Technical Surveillance Countermeasures Survey	None
RA-7	Risk Response	A.12.6.1*, A.18.1.4**
RA-8	Privacy Impact Assessments	A.18.1.4**
RA-9	Criticality Analysis	A.8.2.1*
SA-1	System and Services Acquisition Policy and Procedures	A.5.1.1, A.5.1.2, A.6.1.1, A.12.1.1, A.18.1.1, A.18.1.4**, A.18.2.2
SA-2	Allocation of Resources	None
SA-3	System Development Life Cycle	A.6.1.1, A.6.1.5, A.14.1.1, A.14.2.1, A.14.2.6, A.18.1.4**
SA-4	Acquisition Process	A.14.1.1, A.14.2.7, A.14.2.9, A.15.1.1, A.15.1.2, A.18.1.4**
SA-5	System Documentation	A.12.1.1*
SA-6	**Withdrawn**	---
SA-7	**Withdrawn**	---
SA-8	Security and Privacy Engineering Principles	A.14.2.5, A.18.1.4**
SA-9	External System Services	A.6.1.1, A.6.1.5, A.7.2.1, A.13.1.2, A.13.2.2, A.15.2.1, A.15.2.2, A.18.1.4**
SA-10	Developer Configuration Management	A.12.1.2, A.14.2.1, A.14.2.2, A.14.2.4, A.14.2.7
SA-11	Developer Testing and Evaluation	A.12.6.1, A.14.2.7, A.14.2.8, A.18.1.4**
SA-12	Supply Chain Risk Management	A.14.2.7, A.15.1.1, A.15.1.2, A.15.1.3
SA-13	**Withdrawn**	---
SA-14	**Withdrawn**	---
SA-15	Development Process, Standards, and Tools	A.6.1.5*, A.14.2.1*, A.14.2.2*
SA-16	Developer-Provided Training	None
SA-17	Developer Security Architecture and Design	A.14.2.1, A.14.2.5
SA-18	Tamper Resistance and Detection	None
SA-19	Component Authenticity	A.11.2.7*
SA-20	Customized Development of Critical Components	None
SA-21	Developer Screening	A.7.1.1
SA-22	Unsupported System Components	None
SC-1	System and Communications Protection Policy and Procedures	A.5.1.1, A.5.1.2, A.6.1.1, A.12.1.1, A.18.1.1, A.18.1.4**, A.18.2.2
SC-2	Application Partitioning	None
SC-3	Security Function Isolation	None
SC-4	Information In Shared Resources	None
SC-5	Denial of Service Protection	None

NIST 800-53 CONTROLS		ISO/IEC 27001 CONTROLS *An asterisk (*) indicates that the ISO/IEC control does not fully satisfy the intent of the NIST control.*
SC-6	Resource Availability	None
SC-7	Boundary Protection	A.13.1.1, A.13.1.3, A.13.2.1, A.14.1.3, A.18.1.4**
SC-8	Transmission Confidentiality and Integrity	A.8.2.3*, A.13.1.1, A.13.2.1, A.13.2.3, A.14.1.2, A.14.1.3
SC-9	**Withdrawn**	---
SC-10	Network Disconnect	A.13.1.1*
SC-11	Trusted Path	None
SC-12	Cryptographic Key Establishment and Management	A.10.1.2
SC-13	Cryptographic Protection	A.10.1.1, A.14.1.2, A.14.1.3, A.18.1.5
SC-14	**Withdrawn**	---
SC-15	Collaborative Computing Devices and Applications	A.13.2.1*
SC-16	Transmission of Security and Privacy Attributes	None
SC-17	Public Key Infrastructure Certificates	A.10.1.2
SC-18	Mobile Code	None
SC-19	Voice Over Internet Protocol	None
SC-20	Secure Name/Address Resolution Service (Authoritative Source)	None
SC-21	Secure Name/Address Resolution Service (Recursive or Caching Resolver)	None
SC-22	Architecture and Provisioning for Name/Address Resolution Service	None
SC-23	Session Authenticity	None
SC-24	Fail in Known State	None
SC-25	Thin Nodes	None
SC-26	Honeypots	None
SC-27	Platform-Independent Applications	None
SC-28	Protection of Information at Rest	A.8.2.3*, A.18.1.3*
SC-29	Heterogeneity	None
SC-30	Concealment and Misdirection	None
SC-31	Covert Channel Analysis	None
SC-32	System Partitioning	None
SC-33	**Withdrawn**	---
SC-34	Non-Modifiable Executable Programs	None
SC-35	Honeyclients	None
SC-36	Distributed Processing and Storage	None
SC-37	Out-of-Band Channels	None
SC-38	Operations Security	A.12. x
SC-39	Process Isolation	None
SC-40	Wireless Link Protection	None
SC-41	Port and I/O Device Access	None
SC-42	Sensor Capability and Data	None
SC-43	Usage Restrictions	None
SC-44	Detonation Chambers	None

NIST 800-53 CONTROLS		ISO/IEC 27001 CONTROLS *An asterisk (*) indicates that the ISO/IEC control does not fully satisfy the intent of the NIST control.*
SI-1	System and Information Integrity Policy and Procedures	A.5.1.1, A.5.1.2, A.6.1.1, A.12.1.1, A.18.1.1, A.18.1.4**, A.18.2.2
SI-2	Flaw Remediation	A.12.6.1, A.14.2.2, A.14.2.3, A.16.1.3, A.18.1.4**
SI-3	Malicious Code Protection	A.12.2.1
SI-4	System Monitoring	A.18.1.4**
SI-5	Security Alerts, Advisories, and Directives	A.6.1.4*
SI-6	Security and Privacy Function Verification	A.18.1.4**
SI-7	Software, Firmware, and Information Integrity	None
SI-8	Spam Protection	A.12.2.1*
SI-9	**Withdrawn**	---
SI-10	Information Input Validation	None
SI-11	Error Handling	None
SI-12	Information Management and Retention	A.18.1.4**
SI-13	Predictable Failure Prevention	None
SI-14	Non-Persistence	None
SI-15	Information Output Filtering	A.18.1.4**
SI-16	Memory Protection	None
SI-17	Fail-Safe Procedures	None
SI-18	Information Disposal	A.8.2.3, A.11.2.7*, A.18.1.4**
SI-19	Data Quality Operations	A.8.2.3, A.18.1.4**
SI-20	De-Identification	A.8.2.3, A.18.1.4**

A double asterisk (**) indicates that the NIST control can be used to support the requirement for privacy protection in 18.1.4, but given the general and broad-based nature of 18.1.4, the NIST control in isolation does not provide the breadth and depth of coverage needed for adequate protection of privacy.

Table I-2 provides a mapping from the controls in ISO/IEC 27001 to the controls in NIST Special Publication 800-53. Organizations should review the introductory text at the beginning of Appendix I before employing the mappings in Table I-2.

TABLE I-2: MAPPING ISO/IEC 27001 TO NIST 800-53

ISO/IEC 27001 CONTROLS	NIST 800-53 CONTROLS *An asterisk (*) indicates that the NIST control does not fully satisfy the intent of the ISO/IEC control.*
A.5 Information Security Policies	
A.5.1 Management direction for information security	
A.5.1.1 Policies for information security	All XX-1 controls
A.5.1.2 Review of the policies for information security	All XX-1 controls
A.6 Organization of information security	
A.6.1 Internal organization	
A.6.1.1 Information security roles and responsibilities	All XX-1 controls, CM-9, CP-2, PS-7, SA-3, SA-9, PM-2, PM-10
A.6.1.2 Segregation of duties	AC-5
A.6.1.3 Contact with authorities	IR-6
A.6.1.4 Contact with special interest groups	SI-5, PM-15
A.6.1.5 Information security in project management	SA-3, SA-9, SA-15
A.6.2 Mobile devices and teleworking	
A.6.2.1 Mobile device policy	AC-7(2), AC-17, AC-18, AC-19
A.6.2.2 Teleworking	AC-3, AC-17, PE-17
A.7 Human Resources Security	
A.7.1 Prior to Employment	
A.7.1.1 Screening	PS-3, SA-21
A.7.1.2 Terms and conditions of employment	PL-4, PS-6
A.7.2 During employment	
A.7.2.1 Management responsibilities	PL-4, PS-6, PS-7, SA-9
A.7.2.2 Information security awareness, education, and training	AT-2, AT-3, CP-3, IR-2, PM-13
A.7.2.3 Disciplinary process	PS-8
A.7.3 Termination and change of employment	
A.7.3.1 Termination or change of employment responsibilities	PS-4, PS-5
A.8 Asset Management	
A.8.1 Responsibility for assets	
A.8.1.1 Inventory of assets	CM-8
A.8.1.2 Ownership of assets	CM-8
A.8.1.3 Acceptable use of assets	PL-4
A.8.1.4 Return of assets	PS-4, PS-5
A.8.2 Information Classification	
A.8.2.1 Classification of information	PM-29, RA-2
A.8.2.2 Labelling of Information	AC-16, MP-3, PE-22
A.8.2.3 Handling of Assets	MP-2, MP-4, MP-5, MP-6, MP-7, PE-16, PE-18, PE-20, SC-8, SC-28

ISO/IEC 27001 CONTROLS	NIST 800-53 CONTROLS *An asterisk (*) indicates that the NIST control does not fully satisfy the intent of the ISO/IEC control.*
A.8.3 Media Handling	
A.8.3.1 Management of removable media	MP-2, MP-4, MP-5, MP-6, MP-7
A.8.3.2 Disposal of media	MP-6, SA-19(3)
A.8.3.3 Physical media transfer	MP-5
A.9 Access Control	
A.9.1 Business requirement of access control	
A.9.1.1 Access control policy	AC-1
A.9.1.2 Access to networks and network services	AC-2*, AC-3, AC-6
A.9.2 User access management	
A.9.2.1 User registration and de-registration	AC-2, IA-2, IA-4, IA-5, IA-8
A.9.2.2 User access provisioning	AC-2
A.9.2.3 Management of privileged access rights	AC-2, AC-3, AC-6, CM-5
A.9.2.4 Management of secret authentication information of users	IA-5
A.9.2.5 Review of user access rights	AC-2
A.9.2.6 Removal or adjustment of access rights	AC-2, PS-4, PS-5
A.9.3 User responsibilities	
A.9.3.1 Use of secret authentication information	IA-5
A.9.4 System and application access control	
A.9.4.1 Information access restriction	AC-3, AC-24
A.9.4.2 Secure logon procedures	AC-7, AC-8, AC-9, IA-6
A.9.4.3 Password management system	IA-5
A.9.4.4 Use of privileged utility programs	AC-3, AC-6
A.9.4.5 Access control to program source code	AC-3, AC-6, CM-5
A.10 Cryptography	
A.10.1 Cryptographic controls	
A.10.1.1 Policy on the use of cryptographic controls	SC-13
A.10.1.2 Key Management	SC-12, SC-17
A.11 Physical and environmental security	
A.11.1 Secure areas	
A.11.1.1 Physical security perimeter	PE-3*
A.11.1.2 Physical entry controls	PE-2, PE-3, PE-4, PE-5
A.11.1.3 Securing offices, rooms and facilities	PE-3, PE-5
A.11.1.4 Protecting against external and environmental threats	CP-6, CP-7, PE-9, PE-13, PE-14, PE-15, PE-18, PE-19, PE-21
A.11.1.5 Working in secure areas	SC-42(3)*
A.11.1.6 Delivery and loading areas	PE-16
A.11.2 Equipment	
A.11.2.1 Equipment siting and protection	PE-9, PE-10, PE-12, PE-13, PE-14, PE-15, PE-18, PE-19, PE-21
A.11.2.2 Supporting utilities	CP-8, PE-9, PE-10, PE-11, PE-12, PE-14, PE-15
A.11.2.3 Cabling security	PE-4, PE-9
A.11.2.4 Equipment maintenance	MA-2, MA-6
A.11.2.5 Removal of assets	MA-2, MA-3(3), MP-5, PE-16

ISO/IEC 27001 CONTROLS	NIST 800-53 CONTROLS *An asterisk (*) indicates that the NIST control does not fully satisfy the intent of the ISO/IEC control.*
A.11.2.6 Security of equipment and assets off-premises	AC-19, AC-20, MP-5, PE-17
A.11.2.7 Secure disposal or reuse of equipment	MP-6, SA-19(3)
A.11.2.8 Unattended user equipment	AC-11
A.11.2.9 Clear desk and clear screen policy	AC-11, MP-2, MP-4
A.12 Operations security	
A.12.1 Operational procedures and responsibilities	
A.12.1.1 Documented operating procedures	All XX-1 controls, SA-5
A.12.1.2 Change management	CM-3, CM-5, CM-9, SA-10
A.12.1.3 Capacity management	AU-4, AU-5(1), CP-2(2), SC-5(2)
A.12.1.4 Separation of development, testing, and operational environments	CM-4(1)*, CM-5*
A.12.2 Protection from malware	
A.12.2.1 Controls against malware	AT-2, SI-3, SI-4(24)
A.12.3 Backup	
A.12.3.1 Information backup	CP-6, CP-9
A.12.4 Logging and monitoring	
A.12.4.1 Event logging	AU-3, AU-6, AU-11, AU-12, AU-14
A.12.4.2 Protection of log information	AU-9
A.12.4.3 Administrator and operator logs	AU-9, AU-12
A.12.4.4 Clock synchronization	AU-8
A.12.5 Control of operational software	
A.12.5.1 Installation of software on operational systems	CM-3, CM-5, CM-7(4), CM-7(5), CM-11
A.12.6 Technical vulnerability management	
A.12.6.1 Management of technical vulnerabilities	RA-3, RA-5, SI-2, SI-5
A.12.6.2 Restrictions on software installation	CM-5, CM-7(4), CM-7(5), CM-11
A.12.7 Information systems audit considerations	
A.12.7.1 Information systems audit controls	AU-5*
A.13 Communications security	
A.13.1 Network security management	
A.13.1.1 Network controls	AC-3, AC-17, AC-18, AC-20, SC-7, SC-8, SC-10
A.13.1.2 Security of network services	CA-3, SA-9
A.13.1.3 Segregation in networks	AC-4, SC-7
A.13.2 Information transfer	
A.13.2.1 Information transfer policies and procedures	AC-4, AC-20, AC-21, CA-3, PA-4, SC-7, SC-8
A.13.2.2 Agreements on information transfer	AC-21, CA-3, PA-4, PS-6, SA-9
A.13.2.3 Electronic messaging	SC-8
A.13.2.4 Confidentiality or nondisclosure agreements	PS-6
A.14 System acquisition, development and maintenance	
A.14.1 Security requirements of information systems	
A.14.1.1 Information security requirements analysis and specification	PL-2, PL-7, PL-8, SA-3, SA-4
A.14.1.2 Securing application services on public networks	AC-3, AC-4, AC-17, SC-8, SC-13

ISO/IEC 27001 CONTROLS	NIST 800-53 CONTROLS *An asterisk (*) indicates that the NIST control does not fully satisfy the intent of the ISO/IEC control.*
A.14.1.3 Protecting application services transactions	AC-3, AC-4, SC-7, SC-8, SC-13
A.14.2 Security in development and support processes	
A.14.2.1 Secure development policy	SA-3, SA-15, SA-17
A.14.2.2 System change control procedures	CM-3, SA-10, SI-2
A.14.2.3 Technical review of applications after operating platform changes	CM-3, CM-4, SI-2
A.14.2.4 Restrictions on changes to software packages	CM-3, SA-10
A.14.2.5 Secure system engineering principles	SA-8
A.14.2.6 Secure development environment	SA-3(1)
A.14.2.7 Outsourced development	SA-4, SA-10, SA-11, SA-12, SA-15, SA-17
A.14.2.8 System security testing	CA-2, SA-11
A.14.2.9 System acceptance testing	SA-4, SA-12(7)
A.14.3 Test data	
A.14.3.1 Protection of test data	SA-3(2)*
A.15 Supplier Relationships	
A.15.1 Information security in supplier relationships	
A.15.1.1 Information security policy for supplier relationships	SA-12
A.15.1.2 Address security within supplier agreements	SA-4, SA-12
A.15.1.3 Information and communication technology supply chain	SA-12
A.15.2 Supplier service delivery management	
A.15.2.1 Monitoring and review of supplier services	SA-9
A.15.2.2 Managing changes to supplier services	SA-9
A.16 Information security incident management	
A.16.1 Managing of information security incidents and improvements	
A.16.1.1 Responsibilities and procedures	IR-8
A.16.1.2 Reporting information security events	AU-6, IR-6
A.16.1.3 Reporting information security weaknesses	CA-7, SI-2, SI-4
A.16.1.4 Assessment of and decision on information security events	AU-6, IR-4
A.16.1.5 Response to information security incidents	IR-4
A.16.1.6 Learning from information security incidents	IR-4
A.16.1.7 Collection of evidence	AU-4*, AU-9*, AU-10(3)*, AU-11*
A.17 Information security aspects of business continuity management	
A.17.1 Information security continuity	
A.17.1.1 Planning information security continuity	CP-2
A.17.1.2 Implementing information security continuity	CP-2, CP-6, CP-7, CP-8, CP-9, CP-10, CP-11, CP-13
A.17.1.3 Verify, review, and evaluate information security continuity	CP-3, CP-4
A.17.2 Redundancies	
A.17.2.1 Availability of information processing facilities	CP-2, CP-6, CP-7

ISO/IEC 27001 CONTROLS	NIST 800-53 CONTROLS *An asterisk (*) indicates that the NIST control does not fully satisfy the intent of the ISO/IEC control.*
A.18 Compliance	
A.18.1 Compliance with legal and contractual requirements	
A.18.1.1 Identification of applicable legislation and contractual requirements	All XX-1 controls
A.18.1.2 Intellectual property rights	CM-10
A.18.1.3 Protection of records	AC-3, AC-4, AC-6, AC-21, AC-23, AU-9, AU-10, CP-9, SC-4, SC-8, SC-8(1), SC-13, SC-28, SC-28(1)
A.18.1.4 Privacy and protection of personal information	Appendix F, Table F-1
A.18.1.5 Regulation of cryptographic controls	IA-7, SC-12, SC-13, SC-17
A.18.2 **Information security reviews**	
A.18.2.1 Independent review of information security	CA-2(1), CA-7(1), SA-11(3)
A.18.2.2 Compliance with security policies and standards	All XX-1 controls, CA-2, CA-7
A.18.2.3 Technical compliance review	CA-2, CA-7

Table I-3 provides a generalized mapping from the functional and assurance requirements in ISO/IEC 15408 (Common Criteria) to the controls in NIST Special Publication 800-53. The table represents an *informal* correspondence between requirements and controls (i.e., the table is not intended to determine whether the ISO/IEC 15408 requirements are fully satisfied, partially satisfied, or not satisfied by the associated controls. However, the table can serve as a beneficial starting point for further correspondence analysis. Organizations are cautioned that satisfying ISO/IEC 15408 requirements for an evaluated and validated information technology product as represented by the presence of certain controls from Chapter Three, does not imply that such requirements have been satisfied throughout the entire system (which may consist of multiple, integrated individual component products). Additional information explaining the specific mappings that appear in Table I-3 is available at the National Information Assurance Partnership (NIAP) website.

TABLE I-3: MAPPING ISO/IEC 15408 TO NIST 800-53

ISO/IEC 15408 REQUIREMENTS		NIST 800-53 CONTROLS	
Functional Requirements			
FAU_ARP.1	**Security Audit Automatic Response** Security Alarms	AU-5	**Response to Audit Processing Failures**
		AU-5(1)	**Response to Audit Processing Failures** *Audit Storage Capacity*
		AU-5(2)	**Response to Audit Processing Failures** *Real-Time Alerts*
		AU-5(3)	**Response to Audit Processing Failures** *Configurable Traffic Volume Thresholds*
		AU-5(4)	**Response to Audit Processing Failures** *Shutdown on Failure*
		PE-6(2)	**Monitoring Physical Access** *Automated Intrusion Recognition and Responses*
		SI-3	**Malicious Code Protection**
		SI-3(8)	**Malicious Code Protection** *Detect Unauthorized Commands*
		SI-4(5)	**System Monitoring** *System-Generated Alerts*
		SI-4(7)	**Systems Monitoring** *Automated Response to Suspicious Events*
		SI-4(22)	**Systems Monitoring** *Unauthorized Network Services*
		SI-7(2)	**Software, Firmware, and Information Integrity** *Automated Notifications of Integrity Violations*
		SI-7(5)	**Software, Firmware, and Information Integrity** *Automated Response to Integrity Violations*

ISO/IEC 15408 REQUIREMENTS		NIST 800-53 CONTROLS	
		SI-7(8)	**Software, Firmware, and Information Integrity** *Auditing Capability for Significant Events*
FAU_GEN.1	**Security Audit Data Generation** Audit Data Generation	AU-2	**Audit Events**
		AU-3	**Content of Audit Records**
		AU-3(1)	**Content of Audit Records** *Additional Audit Information*
		AU-12	**Audit Generation**
FAU_GEN.2	**Security Audit Data Generation** User Identity Association	AU-3	**Content of Audit Records**
FAU_SAA.1	**Security Audit Analysis** Potential Violation Analysis	SI-4	**System Monitoring**
FAU_SAA.2	**Security Audit Analysis** Profile-Based Anomaly Detection	AC-2(12)	**Account Management** *Account Monitoring for Atypical Usage*
		SI-4	**System Monitoring**
FAU_SAA.3	**Security Audit Analysis** Simple Attack Heuristics	SI-3	**Malicious Code Protection**
		SI-4	**System Monitoring**
FAU_SAA.4	**Security Audit Analysis** Complex Attack Heuristics	SI-3	**Malicious Code Protection**
		SI-4	**System Monitoring**
FAU_SAR.1	**Security Audit Review** Audit Review	AU-7	**Audit Reduction and Report Generation**
FAU_SAR.2	**Security Audit Review** Restricted Audit Review	AU-9(6)	**Protection of Audit Information** *Read Only Access*
FAU_SAR.3	**Security Audit Review** Selectable Audit Review	AU-7	**Audit Reduction and Report Generation**
		AU-7(1)	**Audit Reduction and Report Generation** *Automatic Processing*
		AU-7(2)	**Audit Reduction and Report Generation** *Automatic Sort and Search*
FAU_SEL.1	**Security Audit Event Selection** Selective Audit	AU-12	**Audit Generation**
FAU_STG.1	**Security Audit Event Storage** Protected Audit Trail Storage	AU-9	**Protection of Audit Information**
FAU_STG.2	**Security Audit Event Storage** Guarantees of Audit Data Availability	AU-9	**Protection of Audit Information** *Alternate audit capability*
FAU_STG.3	**Security Audit Event Storage** Action In Case of Possible Audit Data Loss	AU-5	**Response to Audit Processing Failures**
		AU-5(1)	**Response to Audit Processing Failures** *Audit Storage Capacity*
		AU-5(2)	**Response to Audit Processing Failures** *Real-Time Alerts*
		AU-5(4)	**Response to Audit Processing Failures** *Shutdown on Failure*

ISO/IEC 15408 REQUIREMENTS		NIST 800-53 CONTROLS	
FAU_STG.4	**Security Audit Event Storage** Prevention of Audit Data Loss	AU-4	**Audit Storage Capacity**
		AU-5	**Response to Audit Processing Failures**
		AU-5(2)	**Response to Audit Processing Failures** *Real-Time Alerts*
		AU-5(4)	**Response to Audit Processing Failures** *Shutdown on Failure*
FCO_NRO.1	**Non-Repudiation of Origin** Selective Proof of Origin	AU-10	**Non-Repudiation**
		AU-10(1)	**Non-Repudiation** *Association of Identities*
		AU-10(2)	**Non-Repudiation** *Validate Binding of Information Producer Identity*
FCO_NRO.2	**Non-Repudiation of Origin** Enforced Proof of Origin	AU-10	**Non-Repudiation**
		AU-10(1)	**Non-Repudiation** *Association of Identities*
		AU-10(2)	**Non-Repudiation** *Validate Binding of Information Producer Identity*
FCO_NRR.1	**Non-Repudiation of Receipt** Selective Proof of Receipt	AU-10	**Non-Repudiation**
		AU-10(1)	**Non-Repudiation** *Association of Identities*
		AU-10(2)	**Non-Repudiation** *Validate Binding of Information Producer Identity*
FCO_NRR.2	**Non-Repudiation of Receipt** Enforced Proof of Receipt	AU-10	**Non-Repudiation**
		AU-10(1)	**Non-Repudiation** *Association of Identities*
		AU-10(2)	**Non-Repudiation** *Validate Binding of Information Producer Identity*
FCS_CKM.1	**Cryptographic Key Management** Cryptographic Key Generation	SC-12	**Cryptographic Key Establishment and Management**
FCS_CKM.2	**Cryptographic Key Management** Cryptographic Key Distribution	SC-12	**Cryptographic Key Establishment and Management**
FCS_CKM.3	**Cryptographic Key Management** Cryptographic Key Access	SC-12	**Cryptographic Key Establishment and Management**
FCS_CKM.4	**Cryptographic Key Management** Cryptographic Key Destruction	SC-12	**Cryptographic Key Establishment and Management**
FCS_COP.1	**Cryptographic Operation** Cryptographic Operation	SC-13	**Cryptographic Protection**

ISO/IEC 15408 REQUIREMENTS		NIST 800-53 CONTROLS	
FDP_ACC.1	**Access Control Policy** Subset Access Control	AC-3	**Access Enforcement**
		AC-3(3)	**Access Enforcement** *Mandatory Access Control*
		AC-3(4)	**Access Enforcement** *Discretionary Access Control*
		AC-3(7)	**Access Enforcement** *Role-Based Access Control*
FDP_ACC.2	**Access Control Policy** Complete Access Control	AC-3	**Access Enforcement**
		AC-3(3)	**Access Enforcement** *Mandatory Access Control*
		AC-3(4)	**Access Enforcement** *Discretionary Access Control*
		AC-3(7)	**Access Enforcement** *Role-Based Access Control*
FDP_ACF.1	**Access Control Functions** Security Attribute Based Access Control	AC-3	**Access Enforcement**
		AC-3(3)	**Access Enforcement** *Mandatory Access Control*
		AC-3(4)	**Access Enforcement** *Discretionary Access Control*
		AC-3(7)	**Access Enforcement** *Role-Based Access Control*
		AC-16	**Security and Privacy Attributes**
		SC-16	**Transmission of Security and Privacy Attributes**
FDP_DAU.1	**Data Authentication** Basic Data Authentication	SI-7	**Software, Firmware, and Information Integrity**
		SI-7(1)	**Software, Firmware, and Information Integrity** *Integrity Checks*
		SI-7(6)	**Software, Firmware, And Information Integrity** *Cryptographic Protection*
		SI-10	**Information Input Validation**
FDP_DAU.2	**Data Authentication** Data Authentication With Identity of Guarantor	SI-7	**Software, Firmware, and Information Integrity**
		SI-7(1)	**Software, Firmware, and Information Integrity** *Integrity Checks*
		SI-7(6)	**Software, Firmware, And Information Integrity** *Cryptographic Protection*
		SI-10	**Information Input Validation**

ISO/IEC 15408 REQUIREMENTS		NIST 800-53 CONTROLS	
FDP_ETC.1	**Export from the TOE** Export of User Data without Security Attributes	No Mapping.	
FDP_ETC.2	**Export from the TOE** Export of User Data with Security Attributes	AC-16	**Security and Privacy Attributes**
		AC-16(5)	**Security and Privacy Attributes** *Attribute Displays for Output Devices*
		SC-16	**Transmission of Security and Privacy Attributes**
FDP_IFC.1	**Information Flow Control Policy** Subset Information Flow Control	AC-3	**Access Enforcement**
		AC-3(3)	**Access Enforcement** *Mandatory Access Control*
		AC-4	**Information Flow Enforcement**
		AC-4(1)	**Information Flow Enforcement** *Object Security Attributes*
FDP_IFC.2	**Information Flow Control Policy** Complete Information Flow Control	AC-3	**Access Enforcement**
		AC-3(3)	**Access Enforcement** *Mandatory Access Control*
		AC-4	**Information Flow Enforcement**
FDP_IFF.1	**Information Flow Control Functions** Simple Security Attributes	AC-3	**Access Enforcement**
		AC-3(3)	**Access Enforcement** *Mandatory Access Control*
		AC-4	**Information Flow Enforcement**
		AC 4(1)	**Information Flow Enforcement** *Object Security Attributes*
		AC-4(2)	**Information Flow Enforcement** *Processing Domains*
		AC-4(7)	**Information Flow Enforcement** *One-Way Flow Mechanisms*
		AC-16	**Security and Privacy Attributes**
		SC-7	**Boundary Protection**
FDP_IFF.2	**Information Flow Control Functions** Hierarchical Security Attributes	AC-3	**Access Enforcement**
		AC-3(3)	**Access Enforcement** *Mandatory Access Control*
		AC-4(1)	**Information Flow Enforcement** *Object Security Attributes*
		AC-16	**Security and Privacy Attributes**
FDP_IFF.3	**Information Flow Control Functions** Limited Illicit Information Flows	SC-31	**Covert Channel Analysis**
		SC-31(2)	**Covert Channel Analysis** *Maximum Bandwidth*
FDP_IFF.4	**Information Flow Control Functions**	SC-31	**Covert Channel Analysis**

ISO/IEC 15408 REQUIREMENTS		NIST 800-53 CONTROLS	
	Partial Elimination of Illicit Information Flows	SC-31(2)	**Covert Channel Analysis** *Maximum Bandwidth*
FDP_IFF.5	**Information Flow Control Functions** No Illicit Information Flows	SC-31	**Covert Channel Analysis**
		SC-31(2)	**Covert Channel Analysis** *Maximum Bandwidth*
FDP_IFF.6	**Information Flow Control Functions** Illicit Information Flow Monitoring	SC-31	**Covert Channel Analysis**
		SI-4(18)	**System Monitoring** *Analyze Traffic / Covert Exfiltration*
FDP_ITC.1	**Import from Outside of the TOE** Import of User Data without Security Attributes	AC-4(9)	**Information Flow Enforcement** *Human Reviews*
		AC-4(12)	**Information Flow Enforcement** *Data Type Identifiers*
FDP_ITC.2	**Import from Outside of the TOE** Import of User Data with Security Attributes	AC-16	**Security and Privacy Attributes**
		SC-16	**Transmission of Security and Privacy Attributes**
FDP_ITT.1	**Internal TOE Transfer** Basic Internal Transfer Protection	SC-8	**Transmission Confidentiality and Integrity**
		SC-8(1)	**Transmission Confidentiality and Integrity** *Cryptographic Protection*
		SC-5	**Denial of Service Protection**
FDP_ITT.2	**Internal TOE Transfer** Transmission Separation by Attribute	AC-4(21)	**Information Flow Enforcement** *Physical and Logical Separation of Information Flows*
		SC-8	**Transmission Confidentiality and Integrity**
		SC-8(1)	**Transmission Confidentiality and Integrity** *Cryptographic Protection*
		SC-5	**Denial of Service Protection**
FDP_ITT.3	**Internal TOE Transfer** Integrity Monitoring	SC-8(1)	**Transmission Integrity** *Cryptographic Protection*
		SI-7	**Software, Firmware, and Information Integrity**
		SI-7(1)	**Software, Firmware, and Information Integrity** *Integrity Checks*
		SI-7(5)	**Software, Firmware, and Information Integrity** *Automated Response to Integrity Violations*
FDP_ITT.4	**Internal TOE Transfer** Attribute-Based Integrity Monitoring	AC-4(21)	**Information Flow Enforcement** *Physical and Logical Separation of Information Flows*

ISO/IEC 15408 REQUIREMENTS		NIST 800-53 CONTROLS	
		SC-8(1)	**Transmission Integrity** *Cryptographic Protection*
		SI-7	**Software, Firmware, and Information Integrity**
		SI-7(1)	**Software, Firmware, and Information Integrity** *Integrity Checks*
		SI-7(5)	**Software, Firmware, and Information Integrity** *Automated Response to Integrity Violations*
FDP_RIP.1	**Residual Information Protection** Subset Residual Information Protection	SC-4	**Information in Shared Resources**
FDP_RIP.2	**Residual Information Protection** Full Residual Information Protection	SC-4	**Information in Shared Resources**
FDP_ROL.1	**Rollback** Basic Rollback	CP-10(2)	**System Recovery and Reconstitution** *Transaction Recovery*
FDP_ROL.2	**Rollback** Advanced Rollback	CP-10(2)	**System Recovery and Reconstitution** *Transaction Recovery*
FDP_SDI.1	**Stored Data Integrity** Stored Data Integrity Monitoring	SI-7	**Software, Firmware, and Information Integrity**
		SI-7(1)	**Software, Firmware, and Information Integrity** *Integrity Scans*
FDP_SDI.2	**Stored Data Integrity** Stored Data Integrity Monitoring and Action	SI-7	**Software, Firmware, and Information Integrity**
		SI-7(1)	**Software, Firmware, and Information Integrity** *Integrity Scans*
		SI-7(5)	**Software, Firmware, and Information Integrity** *Automated Response to Integrity Violations*
FDP_UCT.1	**Inter-TSF User Data Confidentiality Transfer Protection** Basic Data Exchange Confidentiality	SC-8	**Transmission Confidentiality and Integrity**
		SC-8(1)	**Transmission Confidentiality and Integrity** *Cryptographic Protection*
FDP_UIT.1	**Inter-TSF User Data Integrity Transfer Protection** Data Exchange Integrity	SC-8	**Transmission Confidentiality and Integrity**
		SC-8(1)	**Transmission Confidentiality and Integrity** *Cryptographic Protection*

ISO/IEC 15408 REQUIREMENTS		NIST 800-53 CONTROLS	
		SI-7	**Software, Firmware, and Information Integrity**
		SI-7(6)	**Software, Firmware, and Information Integrity** *Cryptographic Protection*
FDP_UIT.2	**Inter-TSF User Data Integrity Transfer Protection** Source Data Exchange Recovery	No Mapping.	
FDP_UIT.3	**Inter-TSF User Data Integrity Transfer Protection** Destination Data Exchange Recovery	No Mapping.	
FIA_AFL.1	**Authentication Failure** Authentication Failure Handling	AC-7	**Unsuccessful Logon Attempts**
FIA_ATD.1	**User Attribute Definition** User Attribute Definition	AC-2	**Account Management**
		IA-2	**Identification and Authentication (Organizational Users)**
FIA_SOS.1	**Specification of Secrets** Verification of Secrets	IA-5	**Authenticator Management**
		IA-5(1)	**Authenticator Management** Password-Based Authentication
		IA-2(14)	**Identification and Authentication (Organizational Users)** Biometric Authentication
FIA_SOS.2	**Specification of Secrets** TSF Generation of Secrets	IA-5	**Authenticator Management**
		IA-5(1)	**Authenticator Management** Password-Based Authentication
		IA-2(14)	**Identification and Authentication (Organizational Users)** Biometric Authentication
FIA_UAU.1	**User Authentication** Timing of Authentication	AC-14	**Permitted Actions without Identification or Authentication**
		IA-2	**Identification and Authentication (Organizational Users)**
		IA-8	**Identification and Authentication (Non-Organizational Users)**
FIA_UAU.2	**User Authentication** User Authentication Before Any Action	AC-14	**Permitted Actions without Identification or Authentication**
		IA-2	**Identification and Authentication (Organizational Users)**
		IA-8	**Identification and Authentication (Non-Organizational Users)**
FIA_UAU.3	**User Authentication** Unforgeable Authentication	IA-2(8)	**Identification and Authentication (Organizational Users)** *Access to Accounts - Replay Resistant*

ISO/IEC 15408 REQUIREMENTS		NIST 800-53 CONTROLS	
FIA_UAU.4	**User Authentication** Single-Use Authentication Mechanisms	IA-2(8)	**Identification and Authentication (Organizational Users)** *Access to Accounts - Replay Resistant*
FIA_UAU.5	**User Authentication** Multiple Authentication Mechanisms	IA-2(1)	**Identification and Authentication (Organizational Users)** Multifactor Authentication To Privileged Accounts
		IA-2(2)	**Identification and Authentication (Organizational Users)** Multifactor Authentication To Non-Privileged Accounts
FIA_UAU.6	**User Authentication** Re-Authenticating	IA-11	**Re-authentication**
FIA_UAU.7	**User Authentication** Protected Authentication Feedback	IA-6	**Authenticator Feedback**
FIA_UID.1	**User Identification** Timing of Identification	AC-14	**Permitted Actions without Identification or Authentication**
		IA-2	**Identification and Authentication (Organizational Users)**
		IA-8	**Identification and Authentication (Non-Organizational Users)**
FIA_UID.2	**User Identification** User Identification Before Any Action	AC-14	**Permitted Actions without Identification or Authentication**
		IA-2	**Identification and Authentication (Organizational Users)**
		IA-8	**Identification and Authentication (Non-Organizational Users)**
FIA_USB.1	**User-Subject Binding** User-Subject Binding	AC-16(3)	**Security and Privacy Attributes** Maintenance of Attribute Associations by System
FMT_MOF.1	**Management of Functions in TSF** Management of Security Functions Behavior	AC-3(7)	**Access Enforcement** Role-Based Access Control
		AC-6	**Least Privilege**
		AC-6(1)	**Least Privilege** Authorize Access to Security Functions
FMT_MSA.1	**Management of Security Attributes** Management of Security Attributes	AC-6	**Least Privilege**
		AC-6(1)	**Least Privilege** Authorize Access to Security Functions
		AC-16(2)	**Security and Privacy Attributes** Attribute Value Changes by Authorized Individuals
		AC-16(4)	**Security and Privacy Attributes** Association of Attributes by Authorized Individuals

ISO/IEC 15408 REQUIREMENTS		NIST 800-53 CONTROLS	
		AC-16(10)	**Security and Privacy Attributes** Attribute Configuration by Authorized Individuals
FMT_MSA.2	**Management of Security Attributes** Secure Security Attributes	AC-16	**Security and Privacy Attributes**
		CM-6	**Configuration Settings**
		SI-10	**Information Input Validation**
FMT_MSA.3	**Management of Security Attributes** Static Attribute Initialization	No Mapping.	
FMT_MSA.4	**Management of Security Attributes** Security Attribute Value Inheritance	No Mapping.	
FMT_MTD.1	**Management of TSF Data** Management of TSF Data	AC-3(7)	**Access Enforcement** Role-Based Access Control
		AC-6	**Least Privilege**
		AC-6(1)	**Least Privilege** Authorize Access to Security Functions
		AU-6(7)	**Audit Review, Analysis, and Reporting** Permitted Actions
		AU-9(4)	**Protection of Audit Information** Access by Subset of Privileged Users
FMT_MTD.2	**Management of TSF Data** Management of Limits on TSF Data	AC-3(7)	**Access Enforcement** Role-based Access Control
		AC-6	**Least Privilege**
		AC-6(1)	**Least Privilege** Authorize Access to Security Functions
FMT_MTD.3	**Management of TSF Data** Secure TSF Data	SI-10	**Information Input Validation**
FMT_REV.1	**Revocation** Revocation	AC-3(7)	**Access Enforcement** Rose-based Access Control
		AC-3(8)	**Access Enforcement** Revocation of Access Authorizations
		AC-6	**Least Privilege**
		AC-6(1)	**Least Privilege** Authorize Access to Security Functions
FMT_SAE.1	**Security Attribute Expiration** Time-Limited Authorization	AC-3(7)	**Access Enforcement** Role-based Access Control
		AC-6	**Least Privilege**
		AC-6(1)	**Least Privilege** Authorize Access to Security Functions
FMT_SMF.1	**Specification of Management Functions** Specification of Management Functions	No Mapping.	

ISO/IEC 15408 REQUIREMENTS		NIST 800-53 CONTROLS	
FMT_SMR.1	**Security Management Roles** Security Roles	AC-2(7)	**Account Management** Role-based Schemes
		AC-3(7)	**Access Enforcement** Role-Based Access Control
		AC-5	**Separation of Duties**
		AC-6	**Least Privilege**
FMT_SMR.2	**Security Management Roles** Restrictions on Security Roles	AC-2(7)	**Account Management** Role-based Schemes
		AC-3(7)	**Access Enforcement** Role-Based Access Control
		AC-5	**Separation of Duties**
		AC-6	**Least Privilege**
FMT_SMR.3	**Security Management Roles** Assuming Roles	AC-6(1)	**Least Privilege** Authorized Access to Security Functions
		AC-6(2)	**Least Privilege** Non-Privileged Access for Nonsecurity Functions
FPR_ANO.1	**Anonymity** Anonymity	No Mapping.	
FPR_ANO.2	**Anonymity** Anonymity Without Soliciting Information	No Mapping.	
FPR_PSE.1	**Pseudonymity** Pseudonymity	No Mapping.	
FPR_PSE.2	**Pseudonymity** Reversible Pseudonymity	No Mapping.	
FPR_PSE.3	**Pseudonymity** Alias Pseudonymity	No Mapping.	
FPR_UNL.1	**Unlinkability** Unlinkability	No Mapping.	
FPR_UNO.1	**Unobservability** Unobservability	No Mapping.	
FPR_UNO.2	**Unobservability** Allocation of Information Impacting Unobservability	No Mapping.	
FPR_UNO.3	**Unobservability** Unobservability Without Soliciting Information	No Mapping.	
FPR_UNO.4	**Unobservability** Authorized User Observability	No Mapping.	
FPT_FLS.1	**Fail Secure**	SC-7(18)	**Boundary Protection** Fail Secure

ISO/IEC 15408 REQUIREMENTS		NIST 800-53 CONTROLS	
	Failure with Preservation of Secure State	SC-24	**Fail in Known State**
FPT_ITA.1	**Availability of Exported TSF Data** Inter-TSF Availability within a Defined Availability Metric	CP-10(4)	**System Recovery and Reconstitution** Restore Within Time-Period
		SC-5	**Denial of Service Protection**
		SC-5(2)	**Denial of Service Protection** Capacity, Bandwidth, and Redundancy
		SC-5(3)	**Denial of Service Protection** Detection and Monitoring
FPT_ITC.1	**Confidentiality of Exported TSF Data** Inter-TSF Confidentiality During Transmission	SC-8	**Transmission Confidentiality and Integrity**
		SC-8(1)	**Transmission Confidentiality and Integrity** Cryptographic Protection
FPT_ITI.1	**Integrity of Exported TSF Data** Inter-TSF Detection of Modification	SC-8	**Transmission Confidentiality and Integrity**
		SC-8(1)	**Transmission Confidentiality and Integrity** Cryptographic Protection
		SI-7	**Software, Firmware, and Information Integrity**
		SI-7(1)	**Software, Firmware, and Information Integrity** Integrity Checks
		SI-7(5)	**Software, Firmware, and Information Integrity** Automated Response to Integrity Violations
		SI-7(6)	**Software, Firmware, and Information Integrity** Cryptographic Protection
FPT_ITI.2	**Integrity of Exported TSF Data** Inter-TSF Detection and Correction of Modification	SC-8	**Transmission Confidentiality and Integrity**
		SC-8(1)	**Transmission Confidentiality and Integrity** Cryptographic Protection
		SI-7	**Software, Firmware, and Information Integrity**
		SI-7(1)	**Software, Firmware, and Information Integrity** Integrity Checks
		SI-7(5)	**Software, Firmware, and Information Integrity** Automated Response to Integrity Violations

ISO/IEC 15408 REQUIREMENTS		NIST 800-53 CONTROLS	
		SI-7(6)	**Software, Firmware, and Information Integrity** Cryptographic Protection
FPT_ITT.1	**Internal TOE TSF Data Transfer** Basic Internal TSF Data Transfer Protection	SC-8	**Transmission Confidentiality and Integrity**
		SC-8(1)	**Transmission Confidentiality and Integrity** Cryptographic Protection
FPT_ITT.2	**Internal TOE TSF Data Transfer** TSF Data Transfer Separation	AC-4(21)	**Information Flow Enforcement** Physical and Logical Separation of Information Flows
		SC-8	**Transmission Confidentiality and Integrity**
		SC-8(1)	**Transmission Confidentiality and Integrity** Cryptographic or Alternate Physical Protection
FPT_ITT.3	**Internal TOE TSF Data Transfer** TSF Data Integrity Monitoring	SI-7	**Software, Firmware, and Information Integrity**
		SI-7(1)	**Software, Firmware, and Information Integrity** Integrity Checks
		SI-7(5)	**Software, Firmware, and Information Integrity** Automated Response to Integrity Violations
		SI-7(6)	**Software, Firmware, and Information Integrity** Cryptographic Protection
FPT_PHP.1	**TSF Physical Protection** Passive Detection of Physical Attack	PE-3(5)	**Physical Access Control** Tamper Protection
		PE-6(2)	**Monitoring Physical Access** Automated Intrusion Recognition and Responses
		SA-18	**Tamper Resistance and Detection**
FPT_PHP.2	**TSF Physical Protection** Notification of Physical Attack	PE-3(5)	**Physical Access Control** Tamper Protection
		PE-6(2)	**Monitoring Physical Access** Automated Intrusion Recognition and Responses
		SA-18	**Tamper Resistance and Detection**
FPT_PHP.3	**TSF Physical Protection** Resistance to Physical Attack	PE-3(5)	**Physical Access Control** Tamper Protection
		SA-18	**Tamper Resistance and Detection**
FPT_RCV.1	**Trusted Recovery**	CP-10	**System Recovery and Reconstitution**

ISO/IEC 15408 REQUIREMENTS		NIST 800-53 CONTROLS	
	Manual Recovery	CP-12	Safe Mode
FPT_RCV.2	**Trusted Recovery** Automated Recovery	CP-10	**System Recovery and Reconstitution**
		CP-12	**Safe Mode**
FPT_RCV.3	**Trusted Recovery** Automated Recovery Without Undue Loss	CP-10	**System Recovery and Reconstitution**
		CP-12	**Safe Mode**
FPT_RCV.4	**Trusted Recovery** Function Recovery	SC-24	**Fail in Known State**
		SI-6	**Security and Privacy Function Verification**
		SI-10(3)	**Information Input Validation** Predictable Behavior
FPT_RPL.1	**Replay Detection** Replay Detection	IA-2(8)	**Identification and Authentication (Organizational Users)** Access to Accounts - Replay Resistant
		SC-23	**Session Authenticity**
		SI-3(9)	**Malicious Code Protection** Authenticate Remote Commands
FPT_SSP.1	**State Synchrony Protocol** Simple Trusted Acknowledgement	No Mapping.	
FPT_SSP.2	**State Synchrony Protocol** Mutual Trusted Acknowledgement	No Mapping.	
FPT_STM.1	**Time Stamps** Reliable Time Stamps	AU-8	**Time Stamps**
FPT_TDC.1	**Inter-TSF TSF Data Consistency** Inter-TSF Basic Data Consistency	AC-16(7)	**Security and Privacy Attributes** Consistent Attribute Interpretation
		AC-16(8)	**Security and Privacy Attributes** Association Techniques and Technologies
FPT_TEE.1	**Testing of External Entities** Testing of External Entities	SI-6	**Security and Privacy Functionality Verification**
FPT_TRC.1	**Internal TOE TSF Data Replication Consistency** Internal TSF Consistency	SI-7	**Software, Firmware, and Information Integrity**
FPT_TST.1	**TSF Self-Test** TSF Testing	SI-6	**Security and Privacy Functionality Verification**
		SI-7	**Software, Firmware, and Information Integrity**
FRU_FLT.1	**Fault Tolerance** Degraded Fault Tolerance	AU-15	**Alternate Audit Capability**
		CP-11	**Alternate Communications Protocols**
		SC-24	**Fail in Known State**
		SI-13	**Predictable Failure Prevention**
		SI-13(1)	**Predictable Failure Prevention** Transferring Component Responsibilities

ISO/IEC 15408 REQUIREMENTS		NIST 800-53 CONTROLS	
		SI-7(16)	**Software, Firmware, and Information Integrity** Time Limit on Process Execution without Supervision
		SI-13(3)	**Predictable Failure Prevention** Manual Transfer Between Components
		SI-13(4)	**Predictable Failure Prevention** Standby Component Installation and Notification
		SI-13(5)	**Predictable Failure Prevention** Failover Capability
FRU_FLT.2	**Fault Tolerance** Limited Fault Tolerance	AU-15	**Alternate Audit Capability**
		CP-11	**Alternate Communications Protocols**
		SC-24	**Fail in Known State**
		SI-13	**Predictable Failure Prevention**
		SI-13(1)	**Predictable Failure Prevention** Transferring Component Responsibilities
		SI-7(16)	**Software, Firmware, and Information Integrity** Time Limit on Process Execution without Supervision
		SI-13(3)	**Predictable Failure Prevention** Manual Transfer Between Components
		SI-13(4)	**Predictable Failure Prevention** Standby Component Installation and Notification
		SI-13(5)	**Predictable Failure Prevention** Failover Capability
FRU_PRS.1	**Priority of Service** Limited Priority of Service	SC-6	**Resource Availability**
FRU_PRS.2	**Priority of Service** Full Priority of Service	SC-6	**Resource Availability**
FRU_RSA.1	**Resource Allocation** Maximum Quotas	SC-6	**Resource Availability**
FRU_RSA.2	**Resource Allocation** Minimum and Maximum Quotas	SC-6	**Resource Availability**
FTA_LSA.1	**Limitation on Scope of Selectable Attributes** Limitation on Scope of Selectable Attributes	AC-2(6)	**Account Management** Dynamic Privilege Management
		AC-2(11)	**Account Management** Usage Conditions
FTA_MCS.1	**Limitation on Multiple Concurrent Sessions** Basic Limitation on Multiple Concurrent Sessions	AC-10	**Concurrent Session Control**

ISO/IEC 15408 REQUIREMENTS		NIST 800-53 CONTROLS	
FTA_MCS.2	**Limitation on Multiple Concurrent Sessions** Per-User Limitation on Multiple Concurrent Sessions	AC-10	**Concurrent Session Control**
FTA_SSL.1	**Session Locking and Termination** TSF-Initiated Session Locking	AC-11	**Device Lock**
		AC-11(1)	**Device Lock** Pattern-Hiding Displays
FTA_SSL.2	**Session Locking and Termination** User-Initiated Locking	AC-11	**Device Lock**
		AC-11(1)	**Device Lock** Pattern-Hiding Displays
FTA_SSL.3	**Session Locking and Termination** TSF-Initiated Termination	AC-12	**Session Termination**
		SC-10	**Network Disconnect**
FTA_SSL.4	**Session Locking and Termination** User-Initiated Termination	AC-12(1)	**Session Termination** User-Initiated Logouts
FTA_TAB.1	**TOE Access Banners** Default TOE Access Banners	AC-8	**System Use Notification**
FTA_TAH.1	**TOE Access History** TOE Access History	AC-9	**Previous Logon (Access) Notification**
		AC-9(1)	**Previous Logon (Access) Notification** Unsuccessful Logons
FTA_TSE.1	**TOE Session Establishment** TOE Session Establishment	AC-2(11)	**Account Management** Usage Conditions
FTP_ITC.1	**Inter-TSF Trusted Channel** Inter-TSF Trusted Channel	IA-3(1)	**Device Identification and Authentication** Cryptographic Bidirectional Authentication
		SC-8	**Transmission Confidentiality and Integrity**
		SC-8(1)	**Transmission Confidentiality and Integrity** Cryptographic Protection
FTP_TRP.1	**Trusted Path** Trusted Path	SC-11	**Trusted Path**
Assurance Requirements			
ASE_INT.1 EAL1 EAL2 EAL3 EAL4 EAL5 EAL6 EAL7	**ST Introduction** ST Introduction	SA-4	**Acquisition Process**
ASE_CCL.1	**Conformance Claims**	PL-2	**Security and Privacy Plans**

ISO/IEC 15408 REQUIREMENTS		NIST 800-53 CONTROLS	
EAL1 EAL2 EAL3 EAL4 EAL5 EAL6 EAL7	Conformance Claims	SA-4(7)	**Acquisition Process** NIAP-Approved Protection Profiles
ASE_SPD.1	**Security Problem Definition**	PL-2	**Security and Privacy Plans**
EAL1 EAL2 EAL3 EAL4 EAL5 EAL6 EAL7	Security Problem Definition	SA-4	**Acquisition Process**
ASE_OBJ.1	**Security Objectives**	PL-2	**Security and Privacy Plans**
EAL1	Security Objectives for the Operational Environment	SA-4	**Acquisition Process**
ASE_OBJ.2	**Security Objectives**	PL-2	**Security and Privacy Plans**
EAL2 EAL3 EAL4 EAL5 EAL6 EAL7	Security Objectives	SA-4	**Acquisition Process**
ASE_ECD.1	**Extended Components Definition**	No Mapping.	
EAL1 EAL2 EAL3 EAL4 EAL5 EAL6 EAL7	Extended Components Definition		
ASE_REQ.1	**Security Requirements**	PL-2	**Security and Privacy Plans**
EAL1	Stated Security Requirements	SA-4	**Acquisition Process**
ASE_REQ.2	**Security Requirements**	PL-2	**Security and Privacy Plans**
EAL2 EAL3 EAL4 EAL5 EAL6 EAL7	Derived Security Requirements	SA-4	**Acquisition Process**
ASE_TSS.1	**TOE Summary Specification**	PL-2	**Security and Privacy Plans**
EAL1 EAL2 EAL3 EAL4 EAL5 EAL6 EAL7	TOE Summary Specification	SA-4(1)	**Acquisition Process** Functional Properties of Controls

ISO/IEC 15408 REQUIREMENTS		NIST 800-53 CONTROLS	
ASE_TSS.2	**TOE Summary Specification** TOE Summary Specification with Architectural Design Summary	PL-2	**Security and Privacy Plans**
		SA-4(1)	**Acquisition Process** Functional Properties of Controls
		SA-4(2)	**Acquisition Process** Design and Implementation Information for Controls
		SA-17	**Developer Security Architecture and Design**
ADV_ARC.1 EAL2 EAL3 EAL4 EAL5 EAL6 EAL7	**Security Architecture** Security Architecture Description	AC-25	**Reference Monitor**
		SA-17	**Developer Security Architecture and Design**
		SA-18	**Tamper Resistance and Detection**
		SC-3	**Security Function Isolation**
		SC-3(1)	**Security Function Isolation** Hardware Separation
		SC-3(3)	**Security Function Isolation** Minimize Nonsecurity Functionality
		SC-41	**Process Isolation**
ADV_FSP.1 EAL1	**Functional Specification** Basic Functional Specification	SA-4(1)	**Acquisition Process** Functional Properties of Controls
		SA-4(2)	**Acquisition Process** Design and Implementation Information for Controls
ADV_FSP.2 EAL2	**Functional Specification** Security-Enforcing Functional Specification	SA-4(1)	**Acquisition Process** Functional Properties of Controls
		SA-4(2)	**Acquisition Process** Design and Implementation Information for Controls
		SA-17(4)	**Developer Security Architecture and Design** Informal Correspondence
ADV_FSP.3 EAL3	**Functional Specification** Functional Specification With Complete Summary	SA-4(1)	**Acquisition Process** Functional Properties of Controls
		SA-4(2)	**Acquisition Process** Design and Implementation Information for Controls
		SA-17(4)	**Developer Security Architecture and Design** Informal Correspondence
ADV_FSP.4 EAL4	**Functional Specification** Complete Functional Specification	SA-4(1)	**Acquisition Process** Functional Properties of Controls
		SA-4(2)	**Acquisition Process** Design and Implementation Information for Controls

ISO/IEC 15408 REQUIREMENTS			NIST 800-53 CONTROLS	
		SA-17(4)	**Developer Security Architecture and Design** Informal Correspondence	
ADV_FSP.5 EAL5 EAL6	**Functional Specification** Complete Semi-Formal Functional Specification with Additional Error Information	SA-4(1)	**Acquisition Process** Functional Properties of Controls	
		SA-4(2)	**Acquisition Process** Design and Implementation Information for Controls	
		SA-17(4)	**Developer Security Architecture and Design** Informal Correspondence	
ADV_FSP.6 EAL7	**Functional Specification** Complete Semi-Formal Functional Specification with Additional Formal Specification	SA-4(1)	**Acquisition Process** Functional Properties of Controls	
		SA-4(2)	**Acquisition Process** Design and Implementation Information for Controls	
		SA-17(3)	**Developer Security Architecture and Design** Formal Correspondence	
		SA-17(4)	**Developer Security Architecture and Design** Informal Correspondence	
ADV_IMP.1 EAL4 EAL5	**Implementation Representation** Implementation Representation of the TSF	SA-4(2)	**Acquisition Process** Design and Implementation Information for Controls	
ADV_IMP.2 EAL6 EAL7	**Implementation Representation** Complete Mapping of the Implementation Representation of the TSF	SA-4(2)	**Acquisition Process** Design and Implementation Information for Controls	
		SA-17(3)	**Developer Security Architecture and Design** Formal Correspondence	
ADV_INT.1	**TSF Internals** Well-Structured Subset of TSF Internals	SA-8	**Security and Privacy Engineering Principles**	
		SC-3(3)	**Security Function Isolation** Minimize Nonsecurity Functionality	
		SC-3(4)	**Security Function Isolation** Module Coupling and Cohesiveness	
		SC-3(5)	**Security Function Isolation** Layered Structures	
ADV_INT.2 EAL5	**TSF Internals** Well-Structured Internals	SA-8	**Security and Privacy Engineering Principles**	
		SC-3(3)	**Security Function Isolation** Minimize Nonsecurity Functionality	

ISO/IEC 15408 REQUIREMENTS		NIST 800-53 CONTROLS	
		SC-3(4)	**Security Function Isolation** Module Coupling and Cohesiveness
		SC-3(5)	**Security Function Isolation** Layered Structures
ADV_INT.3 EAL6 EAL7	**TSF Internals** Minimally Complex Internals	SA-8	**Security and Privacy Engineering Principles**
		SA-17(5)	**Developer Security Architecture and Design** Conceptually Simple Design
		SC-3(3)	**Security Function Isolation** Minimize Nonsecurity Functionality
		SC-3(4)	**Security Function Isolation** Module Coupling and Cohesiveness
		SC-3(5)	**Security Function Isolation** Layered Structures
		AC-25	**Reference Monitor**
ADV_SPM.1 EAL6 EAL7	**Security Policy Modeling** Formal TOE Security Policy Model	SA-17(1)	**Developer Security Architecture and Design** Formal Policy Model
		SA-17(3)	**Developer Security Architecture and Design** Formal Correspondence
ADV_TDS.1 EAL2	**TOE Design** Basic Design	SA-4(2)	**Acquisition Process** Design and Implementation Information for Controls
		SA-17	**Developer Security Architecture and Design**
ADV_TDS.2 EAL3	**TOE Design** Architectural Design	SA-4(2)	**Acquisition Process** Design and Implementation Information for Controls
		SA-17	**Developer Security Architecture and Design**
ADV_TDS.3 EAL4	**TOE Design** Basic Modular Design	SA-4(2)	**Acquisition Process** Design and Implementation Information for Controls
		SA-17	**Developer Security Architecture and Design**
ADV_TDS.4 EAL5	**TOE Design** Semiformal Modular Design	SA-4(2)	**Acquisition Process** Design and Implementation Information for Controls
		SA-17	**Developer Security Architecture and Design**

ISO/IEC 15408 REQUIREMENTS		NIST 800-53 CONTROLS	
		SA-17(2)	**Developer Security Architecture and Design** Security-Relevant Components
		SA-17(4)	**Developer Security Architecture and Design** Informal Correspondence
ADV_TDS.5 EAL6	**TOE Design** Complete Semiformal Modular Design	SA-4(2)	**Acquisition Process** Design and Implementation Information for Controls
		SA-17	**Developer Security Architecture and Design**
		SA-17(2)	**Developer Security Architecture and Design** Security-Relevant Components
		SA-17(4)	**Developer Security Architecture and Design** Informal Correspondence
ADV_TDS.6 EAL7	**TOE Design** Complete Semiformal Modular Design with Formal High-Level Design Presentation	SA-4(2)	**Acquisition Process** Design and Implementation Information for Controls
		SA-17	**Developer Security Architecture and Design**
		SA-17(2)	**Developer Security Architecture and Design** Security-Relevant Components
		SA-17(3)	**Developer Security Architecture and Design** Formal Correspondence
		SA-17(4)	**Developer Security Architecture and Design** Informal Correspondence
AGD_OPE.1 EAL1 EAL2 EAL3 EAL4 EAL5 EAL6 EAL7	**Operational User Guidance** Operational User Guidance	SA-5	**System Documentation**
AGD_PRE.1 EAL1 EAL2 EAL3 EAL4 EAL5 EAL6 EAL7	**Preparative Procedures** Preparative Procedures	SA-5	**System Documentation**

ISO/IEC 15408 REQUIREMENTS		NIST 800-53 CONTROLS	
ALC_CMC.1 EAL1	**CM Capabilities** Labeling of the TOE	CM-9	**Configuration Management Plan**
		SA-10	**Developer Configuration Management**
ALC_CMC.2 EAL2	**CM Capabilities** Use of a CM System	CM-9	**Configuration Management Plan**
		SA-10	**Developer Configuration Management**
ALC_CMC.3 EAL3	**CM Capabilities** Authorization Controls	CM-3	**Configuration Change Control**
		CM-9	**Configuration Management Plan**
		SA-10	**Developer Configuration Management**
ALC_CMC.4 EAL4 EAL5	**CM Capabilities** Production Support, Acceptance Procedures, and Automation	CM-3	**Configuration Change Control**
		CM-3(1)	**Configuration Change Control** Automated Document, Notification, and Prohibition of Changes
		CM-3(3)	**Configuration Change Control** Automated Change Implementation
		CM-9	**Configuration Management Plan**
		SA-10	**Developer Configuration Management**
ALC_CMC.5 EAL6 EAL7	**CM Capabilities** Advanced Support	CM-3	**Configuration Change Control**
		CM-3(1)	**Configuration Change Control** Automated Document, Notification, and Prohibition of Changes
		CM-3(2)	**Configuration Change Control** Testing, Validation, and Documentation of Changes
		CM-3(3)	**Configuration Change Control** Automated mechanisms to field and deploy
		CM-9	**Configuration Management Plan**
		SA-10	**Developer Configuration Management**
ALC_CMS.1 EAL1	**CM Scope** TOE CM Coverage	CM-9	**Configuration Management Plan**
		SA-10	**Developer Configuration Management**
ALC_CMS.2 EAL2	**CM Scope** Parts of the TOE CM Coverage	CM-9	**Configuration Management Plan**
		SA-10	**Developer Configuration Management**
ALC_CMS.3 EAL3	**CM Scope** Implementation Representation CM Coverage	CM-9	**Configuration Management Plan**
		SA-10	**Developer Configuration Management**
ALC_CMS.4 EAL4	**CM Scope** Problem Tracking CM Coverage	CM-9	**Configuration Management Plan**
		SA-10	**Developer Configuration Management**
ALC_CMS.5 EAL5 EAL6 EAL7	**CM Scope** Development Tools CM Coverage	CM-9	**Configuration Management Plan**
		SA-10	**Developer Configuration Management**
ALC_DEL.1	**Delivery**	MP-5	**Media Transport**

ISO/IEC 15408 REQUIREMENTS		NIST 800-53 CONTROLS	
EAL2 EAL3 EAL4 EAL5 EAL6 EAL7	Delivery Procedures	SA-10(1)	**Developer Configuration Management** Software and Firmware Integrity Verification
		SA-10(6)	**Developer Configuration Management** Trusted Distribution
		SA-18	**Tamper Resistance and Detection**
		SA-19	**Component Authenticity**
ALC_DVS.1 EAL3 EAL4 EAL5	**Development Security** Identification of Security Measures	SA-1	**System and Services Acquisition Policy and Procedures**
		SA-3	**System Development Life Cycle**
		SA-12	**Supply Chain Risk Management**
ALC_DVS.2 EAL6 EAL7	**Development Security** Sufficiency of Security Measures	CM-5	**Access Restrictions for Change**
		SA-3	**System Development Life Cycle**
		SA-12	**Supply Chain Risk Management**
ALC_FLR.1	**Flaw Remediation** Basic Flaw Remediation	SA-10	**Developer Configuration Management**
		SA-11	**Developer Testing and Evaluation**
		SI-2	**Flaw Remediation**
ALC_FLR.2	**Flaw Remediation** Flaw Reporting Procedures	SA-10	**Developer Configuration Management**
		SA-11	**Developer Testing and Evaluation**
		SI-2	**Flaw Remediation**
ALC_FLR.3	**Flaw Remediation** Systematic Flaw Remediation	SA-10	**Developer Configuration Management**
		SA-11	**Developer Testing and Evaluation**
		SI-2	**Flaw Remediation**
ALC_LCD.1 EAL3 EAL4 EAL5 EAL6	**Life-Cycle Definition** Developer Defined Life-Cycle Model	SA-3	**System Development Life Cycle**
		SA-15	**Development Process, Standards, and Tools**
ALC_LCD.2 EAL7	**Life-Cycle Definition** Measurable Life-Cycle Model	SA-3	**System Development Life Cycle**
		SA-15	**Development Process, Standards, and Tools**
ALC_TAT.1 EAL4	**Tools and Techniques** Well-Defined Development Tools	SA-15	**Development Process, Standards, and Tools**
ALC_TAT.2 EAL5	**Tools and Techniques** Compliance with Implementation Standards	SA-15	**Development Process, Standards, and Tools**
ALC_TAT.3 EAL6 EAL7	**Tools and Techniques** Compliance with Implementation Standards – All Parts	SA-15	**Development Process, Standards, and Tools**
ATE_COV.1	**Coverage**	SA-11	**Developer Testing and Evaluation**

ISO/IEC 15408 REQUIREMENTS		NIST 800-53 CONTROLS	
EAL2	Evidence of Coverage	SA-11(7)	**Developer Testing and Evaluation** *Verify Scope of Testing and Evaluation*
ATE_COV.2	**Coverage** Analysis of Coverage	SA-11	**Developer Testing and Evaluation**
EAL3 EAL4 EAL5		SA-11(7)	**Developer Testing and Evaluation** *Verify Scope of Testing and Evaluation*
ATE_COV.3	**Coverage** Rigorous Analysis of Coverage	SA-11	**Developer Testing and Evaluation**
EAL6 EAL7		SA-11(7)	**Developer Testing and Evaluation** *Verify Scope of Testing and Evaluation*
ATE_DPT.1	**Depth** Testing: Basic Design	SA-11	**Developer Testing and Evaluation**
EAL3		SA-11(7)	**Developer Testing and Evaluation** *Verify Scope of Testing and Evaluation*
ATE_DPT.2	**Depth** Testing: Security Enforcing Modules	SA-11	**Developer Testing and Evaluation**
EAL4		SA-11(7)	**Developer Testing and Evaluation** *Verify Scope of Testing and Evaluation*
ATE_DPT.3	**Depth** Testing: Modular Design	SA-11	**Developer Testing and Evaluation**
EAL5 EAL6		SA-11(7)	**Developer Testing and Evaluation** *Verify Scope of Testing and Evaluation*
ATE_DPT.4	**Depth** Testing: Implementation Representation	SA-11	**Developer Testing and Evaluation**
EAL7		SA-11(7)	**Developer Testing and Evaluation** *Verify Scope of Testing and Evaluation*
ATE_FUN.1 EAL2 EAL3 EAL4 EAL5	**Functional Tests** Functional Testing	SA-11	**Developer Testing and Evaluation**
ATE_FUN.2 EAL6 EAL7	**Functional Tests** Ordered Functional Testing	SA-11	**Developer Testing and Evaluation**
ATE_IND.1 EAL1	**Independent Testing** Independent Testing – Conformance	CA-2	**Assessments**
		CA-2(1)	**Assessments** *Independent Assessors*
		SA-11(3)	**Developer Testing and Evaluation** *Independent Verification of Assessment Plans and Evidence*
ATE_IND.2 EAL2 EAL3 EAL4 EAL5 EAL6	**Independent Testing** Independent Testing – Sample	CA-2	**Assessments**
		CA-2(1)	**Assessments** *Independent Assessors*
		SA-11(3)	**Developer Testing and Evaluation** *Independent Verification of Assessment Plans and Evidence*
ATE_IND.3	**Independent Testing**	CA-2	**Assessments**

ISO/IEC 15408 REQUIREMENTS		NIST 800-53 CONTROLS	
EAL7	Independent Testing – Complete	CA-2(1)	**Assessments** *Independent Assessors*
		SA-11(3)	**Developer Security Testing and Evaluation** *Independent Verification of Assessment Plans and Evidence*
AVA_VAN.1 EAL1	**Vulnerability Analysis** Vulnerability Survey	CA-2(2)	**Assessments** *Specialized Assessments*
		CA-8	**Penetration Testing**
		RA-3	**Risk Assessment**
		SA-11(2)	**Developer Testing and Evaluation** *Threat Modeling and Vulnerability Analyses*
		SA-11(5)	**Developer Testing and Evaluation** *Penetration Testing*
AVA_VAN.2 EAL2 EAL3	**Vulnerability Analysis** Vulnerability Analysis	CA-2(2)	**Assessments** *Specialized Assessments*
		CA-8	**Penetration Testing**
		RA-3	**Risk Assessment**
		SA-11(2)	**Developer Testing and Evaluation** *Threat Modeling and Vulnerability Analyses*
		SA-11(5)	**Developer Testing and Evaluation** *Penetration Testing*
AVA_VAN.3 EAL4	**Vulnerability Analysis** Focused Vulnerability Analysis	CA-2(2)	**Assessments** *Specialized Assessments*
		CA-8	**Penetration Testing**
		RA-3	**Risk Assessment**
		SA-11(2)	**Developer Testing and Evaluation** *Threat Modeling and Vulnerability Analyses*
		SA-11(5)	**Developer Testing and Evaluation** *Penetration Testing*
AVA_VAN.4 EAL5	**Vulnerability Analysis** Methodical Vulnerability Analysis	CA-2(2)	**Assessments** *Specialized Assessments*
		CA-8	**Penetration Testing**
		RA-3	**Risk Assessment**
		SA-11(2)	**Developer Testing and Evaluation** *Threat Modeling and Vulnerability Analyses*
		SA-11(5)	**Developer Testing and Evaluation** *Penetration Testing*
AVA_VAN.5	**Vulnerability Analysis**	CA-2(2)	**Assessments** *Specialized Assessments*

ISO/IEC 15408 REQUIREMENTS		NIST 800-53 CONTROLS	
EAL6 EAL7	Advanced Methodical Vulnerability Analysis	CA-8	**Penetration Testing**
		RA-3	**Risk Assessment**
		SA-11(2)	**Developer Testing and Evaluation** *Threat Modeling and Vulnerability Analyses*
		SA-11(5)	**Developer Testing and Evaluation** *Penetration Testing*
ACO_COR.1	**Composition Rationale** Composition Rationale	SA-17	**Developer Security Architecture and Design**
ACO_DEV.1	**Development Evidence** Functional Description	SA-17	**Developer Security Architecture and Design**
ACO_DEV.2	**Development Evidence** Basic Evidence of Design	SA-17	**Developer Security Architecture and Design**
ACO_DEV.3	**Development Evidence** Detailed Evidence of Design	SA-17	**Developer Security Architecture and Design**
ACO_REL.1	**Reliance on Dependent Component** Basic Reliance Information	SA-17	**Developer Security Architecture and Design**
ACO_REL.2	**Reliance on Dependent Component** Reliance Information	SA-17	**Developer Security Architecture and Design**
ACO_CTT.1	**Composed TOE Testing** Interface Testing	SA-11	**Developer Testing and Evaluation**
ACO_CTT.2	**Composed TOE Testing** Rigorous Interface Testing	SA-11	**Developer Testing and Evaluation**
ACO_VUL.1	**Composition Vulnerability Analysis** Composition Vulnerability Review	CA-2	**Assessments**
		CA-8	**Penetration Testing**
		RA-3	**Risk Assessment**
		SA-11	**Developer Testing and Evaluation**
ACO_VUL.2	**Composition Vulnerability Analysis** Composition Vulnerability Analysis	CA-2	**Assessments**
		CA-8	**Penetration Testing**
		RA-3	**Risk Assessment**
		SA-11	**Developer Testing and Evaluation**
ACO_VUL.3	**Composition Vulnerability Analysis** Enhanced-Basic Composition Vulnerability Review	CA-2	**Assessments**
		CA-8	**Penetration Testing**
		RA-3	**Risk Assessment**
		SA-11	**Developer Testing and Evaluation**

CyberSecurity Standards Library™

NIST SP 500-288   Specification for WS-Biometric Devices (WS-BD)
NIST SP 500-291 V2 NIST Cloud Computing Standard Roadmap
NIST SP 500-292   NIST Cloud Computing Reference Architecture
NIST SP 500-293 V1 & V2 US Government Cloud Computing Technology Roadmap
NIST SP 500-293 V3 US Government Cloud Computing Technology Roadmap
NIST SP 500-299   NIST Cloud Computing Security Reference Architecture
NIST SP 500-304   Data Format for the Interchange of Fingerprint, Facial & Other Biometric Information
NIST SP 800-1   Bibliography of Selected Computer Security Publications January 1980-October 1989
NIST SP 800-12 R1 An Introduction to Information Security
NIST SP 800-13   Telecommunications Security Guidelines for Telecommunications Management Network
NIST SP 800-14   Generally Accepted Principles and Practices for Securing Information Technology Systems
NIST SP 800-15 V1 Minimum Interoperability Specification for PKI Components (MISPC)
NIST SP 800-16 R1 A Role-Based Model for Federal Information Technology/Cybersecurity Training
NIST SP 800-17   Modes of Operation Validation System (MOVS): Requirements and Procedures
NIST SP 800-18 R1 Developing Security Plans for Federal Information Systems
NIST SP 800-19   Mobile Agent Security
NIST SP 800-20   Modes of Operation Validation System for the Triple Data Encryption Algorithm
NIST SP 800-22 R1a A Statistical Test Suite for Random and Pseudorandom Number Generators for Cryptographic Applications
NIST SP 800-23   Guidelines to Federal Organizations on Security Assurance and Acquisition/Use of Tested/Evaluated Products
NIST SP 800-24   PBX Vulnerability Analysis - Finding Holes in Your PBX Before Someone Else Does
NIST SP 800-25   Federal Agency Use of Public Key Technology for Digital Signatures and Authentication
NIST SP 800-27 Rev A Engineering Principles for Information Technology Security (A Baseline for Achieving Security)
NIST SP 800-28   Guidelines on Active Content and Mobile Code
NIST SP 800-29   A Comparison of the Security Requirements for Cryptographic Modules in FIPS 140-1 and FIPS 140-2
NIST SP 800-30   Guide for Conducting Risk Assessments
NIST SP 800-31   Intrusion Detection Systems
NIST SP 800-32   Public Key Technology and the Federal PKI Infrastructure
NIST SP 800-33   Underlying Technical Models for Information Technology Security
NIST SP 800-34 R1 Contingency Planning Guide for Federal Information Systems
NIST SP 800-35   Guide to Information Technology Security Services
NIST SP 800-36   Guide to Selecting Information Technology Security Products
NIST SP 800-37 R1 Applying Risk Management Framework to Federal Information
NIST SP 800-38   Recommendation for Block Cipher Modes of Operation
NIST SP 800-38A Addendum Block Cipher Modes of Operation: Three Variants of Ciphertext Stealing for CBC Mode
NIST SP 800-38B   Block Cipher Modes of Operation: The CMAC Mode for Authentication
NIST SP 800-38C   Block Cipher Modes of Operation: The CCM Mode for Authentication and Confidentiality
NIST SP 800-38D   Block Cipher Modes of Operation: Galois/Counter Mode (GCM) and GMAC
NIST SP 800-38E   Block Cipher Modes of Operation: The XTS-AES Mode for Confidentiality on Storage Devices
NIST SP 800-38F   Block Cipher Modes of Operation: Methods for Key Wrapping
NIST SP 800-38G   Block Cipher Modes of Operation: Methods for Format-Preserving Encryption
NIST SP 800-39   Managing Information Security Risk
NIST SP 800-40 R3 Guide to Enterprise Patch Management Technologies
NIST SP 800-41   Guidelines on Firewalls and Firewall Policy
NIST SP 800-43   Systems Administration Guidance for Securing Microsoft Windows 2000 Professional System
NIST SP 800-44 V2 Guidelines on Securing Public Web Servers
NIST SP 800-45 V2 Guidelines on Electronic Mail Security
NIST SP 800-46 R2 Guide to Enterprise Telework, Remote Access, and Bring Your Own Device (BYOD) Security
NIST SP 800-47   Security Guide for Interconnecting Information Technology Systems
NIST SP 800-48   Guide to Securing Legacy IEEE 802.11 Wireless Networks
NIST SP 800-49   Federal S/MIME V3 Client Profile
NIST SP 800-50   Building an Information Technology Security Awareness and Training Program
NIST SP 800-51 R1 Guide to Using Vulnerability Naming Schemes
NIST SP 800-52 R1 Guidelines for the Selection, Configuration, and Use of Transport Layer Security (TLS) Implementations
NIST SP 800-53 R5 Security and Privacy Controls for Information Systems and Organizations
NIST SP 800-53A R4 Assessing Security and Privacy Controls
NIST SP 800-54   Border Gateway Protocol Security
NIST SP 800-55 R1 Performance Measurement Guide for Information Security
NIST SP 800-56A R3 Pair-Wise Key-Establishment Schemes Using Discrete Logarithm Cryptography
NIST SP 56B R 1   Recommendation for Pair-Wise Key-Establishment Schemes Using Integer Factorization Cryptography
NIST SP 800-56C R1 Recommendation for Key-Derivation Methods in Key-Establishment Schemes - Draft
NIST SP 800-57 R4 Recommendation for Key Management
NIST SP 800-58   Security Considerations for Voice Over IP Systems
NIST SP 800-59   Guideline for Identifying an Information System as a National Security System
NIST SP 800-60   Guide for Mapping Types of Information and Information Systems to Security Categories
NIST SP 800-61 R2 Computer Security Incident Handling Guide
NIST SP 800-63-3   Digital Identity Guidelines
NIST SP 800-63a   Digital Identity Guidelines - Enrollment and Identity Proofing
NIST SP 800-63b   Digital Identity Guidelines - Authentication and Lifecycle Management
NIST SP 800-63c   Digital Identity Guidelines- Federation and Assertions
NIST SP 800-64 R2 Security Considerations in the System Development Life Cycle

Click on a title to obtain a printed copy of these standards at Amazon.com
Copyright © 2017 4th Watch Publishing

CyberSecurity Standards Library™

Click on a title to obtain a printed copy of these standards at Amazon.com

CyberSecurity Standards Library™

NIST SP 800-155	BIOS Integrity Measurement Guidelines
NIST SP 800-156	Representation of PIV Chain-of-Trust for Import and Export
NIST SP 800-157	Guidelines for Derived Personal Identity Verification (PIV) Credentials
NIST SP 800-160	Systems Security Engineering
NIST SP 800-161	Supply Chain Risk Management Practices for Federal Information Systems and Organizations
NIST SP 800-162	Guide to Attribute Based Access Control (ABAC) Definition and Considerations
NIST SP 800-163	Vetting the Security of Mobile Applications
NIST SP 800-164	Guidelines on Hardware- Rooted Security in Mobile Devices Draft
NIST SP 800-166	Derived PIV Application and Data Model Test Guidelines
NIST SP 800-167	Guide to Application Whitelisting
NIST SP 800-168	Approximate Matching: Definition and Terminology
NIST SP 800-171 R1	Protecting Controlled Unclassified Information in Nonfederal Systems
NIST SP 800-175 (A & B)	Guideline for Using Cryptographic Standards in the Federal Government
NIST SP 800-177 R1	Trustworthy Email
NIST SP 800-178	Comparison of Attribute Based Access Control (ABAC) Standards for Data Service Applications
NIST SP 800-179	Guide to Securing Apple OS X 10.10 Systems for IT Professional
NIST SP 800-180	NIST Definition of Microservices, Application Containers and System Virtual Machines
NIST SP 800-181	National Initiative for Cybersecurity Education (NICE) Cybersecurity Workforce Framework
NIST SP 800-183	Networks of 'Things'
NIST SP 800-184	Guide for Cybersecurity Event Recovery
NIST SP 800-185	SHA-3 Derived Functions: cSHAKE, KMAC, TupleHash and ParallelHash
NIST SP 800-187	Guide to LTE Security - Draft
NIST SP 800-188	De-Identifying Government Datasets - (2nd Draft)
NIST SP 800-190	Application Container Security Guide
NIST SP 800-191	The NIST Definition of Fog Computing
NIST SP 800-192	Verification and Test Methods for Access Control Policies/Models
NIST SP 800-193	Platform Firmware Resiliency Guidelines
NIST SP 1800-1	Securing Electronic Health Records on Mobile Devices
NIST SP 1800-2	Identity and Access Management for Electric Utilities 1800-2a & 1800-2b
NIST SP 1800-2	Identity and Access Management for Electric Utilities 1800-2c
NIST SP 1800-3	Attribute Based Access Control NIST 1800-3a & 3b
NIST SP 1800-3	Attribute Based Access Control NIST 1800-3c Chapters 1 - 6
NIST SP 1800-3	Attribute Based Access Control NIST1800-3c Chapters 7 - 10
NIST SP 1800-4a & 4b	Mobile Device Security: Cloud and Hybrid Builds
NIST SP 1800-4c	Mobile Device Security: Cloud and Hybrid Builds
NIST SP 1800-5	IT Asset Management: Financial Services
NIST SP 1800-6	Domain Name Systems-Based Electronic Mail Security
NIST SP 1800-7	Situational Awareness for Electric Utilities
NIST SP 1800-8	Securing Wireless Infusion Pumps
NIST SP 1800-9a & 9b	Access Rights Management for the Financial Services Sector
NIST SP 1800-9c	Access Rights Management for the Financial Services Sector - How To Guide
NIST SP 1800-11a & 11b	Data Integrity Recovering from Ransomware and Other Destructive Events
NIST SP 1800-11c	Data Integrity Recovering from Ransomware and Other Destructive Events - How To Guide
NIST SP 1800-12	Derived Personal Identity Verification (PIV) Credentials
NISTIR 7100	PDA Forensic Tools: An Overview and Analysis
NISTIR 7188	Specification for the Extensible Configuration Checklist Description Format (XCCDF)
NISTIR 7200	Proximity Beacons and Mobile Device Authentication: An Overview and Implementation
NISTIR 7206	Smart Cards and Mobile Device Authentication: An Overview and Implementation
NISTIR 7250	Cell Phone Forensic Tools: An Overview and Analysis
NISTIR 7275 V1.1	Specification for the Extensible Configuration Checklist Description Format (XCCDF)
NISTIR 7275 R4 V1.2	Specification for the Extensible Configuration Checklist Description Format (XCCDF)
NISTIR 7284	Personal Identity Verification Card Management Report
NISTIR 7290	Fingerprint Identification and Mobile Handheld Devices: An Overview and Implementation
NISTIR 7298 R2	Glossary of Key Information Security Terms
NISTIR 7316	Assessment of Access Control Systems
NISTIR 7337	Personal Identity Verification Demonstration Summary
NISTIR 7358	Program Review for Information Security Management Assistance (PRISMA)
NISTIR 7359	Information Security Guide for Government Executives
NISTIR 7387	Cell Phone Forensic Tools: An Overview and Analysis Update
NISTIR 7435	The Common Vulnerability Scoring System (CVSS) and Its Applicability to Federal Agency Systems
NISTIR 7452	Secure Biometric Match-on-Card Feasibility Report
NISTIR 7497	Security Architecture Design Process for Health Information Exchanges (HIEs)
NISTIR 7502	The Common Configuration Scoring System (CCSS): Metrics for Software Security Configuration Vulnerabilities
NISTIR 7511 R4 V1.2	Security Content Automation Protocol (SCAP) Version 1.2 Validation Program Test Requirements
NISTIR 7516	Forensic Filtering of Cell Phone Protocols
NISTIR 7539	Symmetric Key Injection onto Smart Cards
NISTIR 7551	A Threat Analysis on UOCAVA Voting Systems
NISTIR 7559	Forensics Web Services (FWS)
NISTIR 7564	Directions in Security Metrics Research
NISTIR 7581	System and Network Security Acronyms and Abbreviations

Click on a title to obtain a printed copy of these standards at Amazon.com

CyberSecurity Standards Library™

NISTIR 7601	Framework for Emergency Response Officials (ERO)
NISTIR 7611	Use of ISO/IEC 24727
NISTIR 7617	Mobile Forensic Reference Materials: A Methodology and Reification
NISTIR 7621 R1	Small Business Information Security: The Fundamentals
NISTIR 7622	Notional Supply Chain Risk Management Practices for Federal Information Systems
NISTIR 7628 R1 Vol 1	Guidelines for Smart Grid Cybersecurity - Architecture, and High-Level Requirements
NISTIR 7628 R1 Vol 2	Guidelines for Smart Grid Cybersecurity - Privacy and the Smart Grid
NISTIR 7628 R1 Vol 3	Guidelines for Smart Grid Cybersecurity - Supportive Analyses and References
NISTIR 7658	Guide to SIMfill Use and Development
NISTIR 7676	Maintaining and Using Key History on Personal Identity Verification (PIV) Cards
NISTIR 7682	Information System Security Best Practices for UOCAVA-Supporting Systems
NISTIR 7692 V2	Specification for the Open Checklist Interactive Language (OCIL)
NISTIR 7693	Specification for Asset Identification 1.1
NISTIR 7694	Specification for the Asset Reporting Format 1.1
NISTIR 7696 V2.3	Common Platform Enumeration: Name Matching Specification
NISTIR 7697 V2.3	Common Platform Enumeration: Dictionary Specification
NISTIR 7698 V2.3	Common Platform Enumeration: Applicability Language Specification
NISTIR 7711	Security Best Practices for the Electronic Transmission of Election Materials for UOCAVA Voters
NISTIR 7756	CAESARS Framework Extension: An Enterprise Continuous Monitoring Technical Refer
NISTIR 7764	Status Report on the Second Round of the SHA-3 Cryptographic Hash Algorithm Competition
NISTIR 7770	Security Considerations for Remote Electronic UOCAVA Voting
NISTIR 7771 V2	Conformance Test Architecture for Biometric Data Interchange Formats - Beta
NISTIR 7773	An Application of Combinatorial Methods to Conformance Testing for Document Object Model Events
NISTIR 7788	Security Risk Analysis of Enterprise Networks Using Probabilistic Attack Graphs
NISTIR 7791	Conformance Test Architecture and Test Suite for ANSI/NIST-ITL 1-2007
NISTIR 7799	Continuous Monitoring Reference Model, Workflow, and Specifications - Draft
NISTIR 7800	Applying the Continuous Monitoring Technical Reference Model to the Asset, Configuration, and Vulnerability Management Domains - Draft
NISTIR 7823	Advanced Metering Infrastructure Smart Meter Upgradeability Test Framework
NISTIR 7874	Guidelines for Access Control System Evaluation Metrics
NISTIR 7904	Trusted Geolocation in the Cloud: Proof of Concept Implementation
NISTIR 7924	Reference Certificate Policy
NISTIR 7987	Policy Machine: Features, Architecture, and Specification
NISTIR 8006	NIST Cloud Computing Forensic Science Challenges
NISTIR 8011 Vol 1	Automation Support for Security Control Assessments
NISTIR 8011 Vol 2	Automation Support for Security Control Assessments
NISTIR 8040	Measuring the Usability and Security of Permuted Passwords on Mobile Platforms
NISTIR 8053	De-Identification of Personal Information
NISTIR 8054	NSTIC Pilots: Catalyzing the Identity Ecosystem
NISTIR 8055	Derived Personal Identity Verification (PIV) Credentials (DPC) Proof of Concept Research
NISTIR 8060	Guidelines for the Creation of Interoperable Software Identification (SWID) Tags
NISTIR 8062	Introduction to Privacy Engineering and Risk Management in Federal Systems
NISTIR 8074 Vol 1 & Vol 2	Strategic U.S. Government Engagement in International Standardization to Achieve U.S. Objectives for Cybersecurity
NISTIR 8080	Usability and Security Considerations for Public Safety Mobile Authentication
NISTIR 8089	An Industrial Control System Cybersecurity Performance Testbed
NISTIR 8112	Attribute Metadata - Draft
NISTIR 8135	Identifying and Categorizing Data Types for Public Safety Mobile Applications
NISTIR 8138	Vulnerability Description Ontology (VDO)
NISTIR 8144	Assessing Threats to Mobile Devices & Infrastructure
NISTIR 8151	Dramatically Reducing Software Vulnerabilities
NISTIR 8170	The Cybersecurity Framework
NISTIR 8176	Security Assurance Requirements for Linux Application Container Deployments
NISTIR 8179	Criticality Analysis Process Model
NISTIR 8183	Cybersecurity Framework Manufacturing Profile
NISTIR 8192	Enhancing Resilience of the Internet and Communications Ecosystem
Whitepaper	Cybersecurity Framework Manufacturing Profile
Whitepaper	NIST Framework for Improving Critical Infrastructure Cybersecurity
Whitepaper	Challenging Security Requirements for US Government Cloud Computing Adoption
FIPS PUBS 140-2	Security Requirements for Cryptographic Modules
FIPS PUBS 140-2 Annex A	Approved Security Functions
FIPS PUBS 140-2 Annex B	Approved Protection Profiles
FIPS PUBS 140-2 Annex C	Approved Random Number Generators
FIPS PUBS 140-2 Annex D	Approved Key Establishment Techniques
FIPS PUBS 180-4	Secure Hash Standard (SHS)
FIPS PUBS 186-4	Digital Signature Standard (DSS)
FIPS PUBS 197	Advanced Encryption Standard (AES)
FIPS PUBS 198-1	The Keyed-Hash Message Authentication Code (HMAC)
FIPS PUBS 199	Standards for Security Categorization of Federal Information and Information Systems
FIPS PUBS 200	Minimum Security Requirements for Federal Information and Information Systems

Click on a title to obtain a printed copy of these standards at Amazon.com

Copyright © 2017 4th Watch Publishing

CyberSecurity Standards Library™

FIPS 201-2   Personal Identity Verification (PIV) of Federal Employees and Contractors
FIPS PUBS 202   SHA-3 Standard: Permutation-Based Hash and Extendable-Output Functions

DHS Study   DHS Study on Mobile Device Security

OMB A-130 / FISMA OMB A-130/Federal Information Security Modernization Act

DoD
UFC 3-430-11   Boiler Control Systems
UFC 4-010-06   Cybersecurity of Facility-Related Control Systems
FC 4-141-05N   Navy and Marine Corps Industrial Control Systems Monitoring Stations
MIL-HDBK-232A   RED/BLACK Engineering-Installation Guidelines
MIL-HDBK 1195   Radio Frequency Shielded Enclosures
TM 5-601   Supervisory Control and Data Acquisition (SCADA) Systems for C4ISR Facilities
ESTCP   Facility-Related Control Systems Cybersecurity Guideline
ESTCP   Facility-Related Control Systems Ver 4.0
DoD   Self-Assessing Security Vulnerabilities & Risks of Industrial Controls
DoD   Program Manager's Guidebook for Integrating the Cybersecurity Risk Management Framework (RMF) into the
System Acquisition Lifecycle
DoD   Advanced Cyber Industrial Control System Tactics, Techniques, and Procedures (ACI TTP)

NERC
NERC CIP 002-5.1 Cyber Security — BES Cyber System Categorization
NERC CIP 003-6   Cyber Security — Security Management Controls
NERC CIP 003-7(i) Cyber Security — Security Management Controls
NERC CIP 004-6   Cyber Security — Personnel & Training
NERC CIP 005-5   Cyber Security — Electronic Security Perimeter(s)
NERC CIP 006-6   Cyber Security — Physical Security of BES Cyber Systems
NERC CIP 007-6   Cyber Security — Systems Security Management
NERC CIP 008-5   Cyber Security — Incident Reporting and Response Planning
NERC CIP 009-6   Cyber Security — Recovery Plans for BES Cyber Systems
NERC CIP 010-2   Cyber Security — Configuration Change Management and Vulnerability
NERC CIP 011-2   Cyber Security — Information Protection
NERC CIP 014-2   Physical Security

Made in the USA
Middletown, DE
04 January 2020

82589692R00278